THE LAW OF REAL PROPERTY

TITLES IN THE DELMAR PARALEGAL SERIES

Ransford C. Pyle, *Foundations of Law for Paralegals: Cases, Commentary, and Ethics,* 1992.

Peggy N. Kerley, Paul A. Sukys, Joanne Banker Hames, *Civil Litigation for the Paralegal,* 1992.

Jonathan Lynton, Donna Masinter, Terri Mick Lyndall, *Law Office Management for Paralegals,* 1992.

Daniel Hall, *Criminal Law and Procedure,* 1992.

Daniel Hall, *Survey of Criminal Law,* 1993.

Jonathan Lynton, Terri Mick Lyndall, *Ethics for Paralegals,* 1993.

Michael Kearns, *The Law of Real Property,* 1993.

Angela Schneeman, *The Law of Corporations, Partnerships, and Sole Proprietorships,* 1993.

William Buckley, *Torts and Personal Injury Law,* 1993.

Gordon Brown, *Administration of Wills, Trusts, and Estates,* 1993.

Richard Stim, *Intellectual Property: Patents, Copyrights, and Trademarks,* 1993.

Jack Handler, *Ballentine's Law Dictionary: Legal Assistant Edition,* 1993.

THE LAW OF REAL PROPERTY

Michael P. Kearns

Lawyers Cooperative Publishing

Delmar
Publishers Inc.

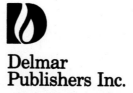

NOTICE TO THE READER

Publisher does not warrant or guarantee any of the products described herein or perform any independent analysis in connection with any of the product information contained herein. Publisher does not assume, and expressly disclaims, any obligation to obtain and include information other than that provided to it by the manufacturer.

The reader is expressly warned to consider and adopt all safety precautions that might be indicated by the activities described herein and to avoid all potential hazards. By following the instructions contained herein, the reader willingly assumes all risks in connection with such instructions.

The publisher makes no representations or warranties of any kind, including but not limited to, the warranties of fitness for particular purpose or merchantability, nor are any such representations implied with respect to the material set forth herein, and the publisher takes no responsibility with respect to such material. The publisher shall not be liable for any special, consequential or exemplary damages resulting, in whole or in part, from the readers' use of, or reliance upon, this material.

Cover design by John Orozco
Cover photo by Mike Gallitelli
Chapter opener illustrations courtesy of Home Planners, Inc.

Delmar staff:
Administrative Editor: Jay Whitney
Developmental Editor: Christopher Anzalone
Project Editor: Judith Boyd Nelson
Production Supervisor: Larry Main
Design Supervisor: Karen Kunz Kemp

For more information, address Delmar Publishers Inc.
3 Columbia Circle, Box 15-015
Albany, New York 12212-5015

Printed in the United States of America
Published simultaneously in Canada
by Nelson Canada,
a division of The Thomson Corporation

2 3 4 5 6 7 8 9 10 XXX 99 98 97 96 95 94

Library of Congress Cataloging-in-Publication Data

Kearns, Michael P.
The law of real property/Michael P. Kearns.
p. cm.
Includes index.
ISBN 0-8273-4878-9
1. Real property—United States. 2. Legal assistants—United States—Handbooks, manuals, etc.
KF570.Z9K4 1993
346.7304'3—dc20
[347.30643]
92-47071
CIP

CONTENTS

APPENDICES

TABLE OF CASES

DELMAR PUBLISHERS INC.

AND

LAWYERS COOPERATIVE PUBLISHING

ARE PLEASED TO ANNOUNCE THEIR PARTNERSHIP
TO CO-PUBLISH COLLEGE TEXTBOOKS FOR
PARALEGAL EDUCATION.

DELMAR, WITH OFFICES AT ALBANY, NEW YORK, IS A PROFESSIONAL EDUCATION PUBLISHER. DELMAR PUBLISHES QUALITY EDUCATIONAL TEXTBOOKS TO PREPARE AND SUPPORT INDIVIDUALS FOR LIFE SKILLS AND SPECIFIC OCCUPATIONS.

LAWYERS COOPERATIVE PUBLISHING (LCP), WITH OFFICES AT ROCHESTER, NEW YORK, HAS BEEN THE LEADING PUBLISHER OF ANALYTICAL LEGAL INFORMATION FOR OVER 100 YEARS. IT IS THE PUBLISHER OF SUCH RENOWNED LEGAL ENCYCLOPEDIAS AS **AMERICAN LAW REPORTS, AMERICAN JURISPRUDENCE, UNITED STATES CODE SERVICE, LAWYERS EDITION,** AS WELL AS OTHER MATERIAL, AND FEDERAL- AND STATE-SPECIFIC PUBLICATIONS. THESE PUBLICATIONS HAVE BEEN DESIGNED TO WORK TOGETHER IN THE DAY-TO-DAY PRACTICE OF LAW AS AN INTEGRATED SYSTEM IN WHAT IS CALLED THE "TOTAL CLIENT-SERVICE LIBRARY®" (TCSL®). EACH LCP PUBLICATION IS COMPLETE WITHIN ITSELF AS TO SUBJECT COVERAGE, YET ALL HAVE COMMON FEATURES AND EXTENSIVE CROSS-REFERENCING TO PROVIDE LINKAGE FOR HIGHLY EFFICIENT LEGAL RESEARCH INTO VIRTUALLY ANY MATTER AN ATTORNEY MIGHT BE CALLED UPON TO HANDLE.

INFORMATION IN ALL PUBLICATIONS IS CAREFULLY AND CONSTANTLY MONITORED TO KEEP PACE WITH AND REFLECT EVENTS IN THE LAW AND IN SOCIETY. UPDATING AND SUPPLEMENTAL INFORMATION IS TIMELY AND PROVIDED CONVENIENTLY.

FOR FURTHER REFERENCE, SEE:

> **AMERICAN JURISPRUDENCE 2D:** AN ENCYCLOPEDIC TEXT COVERAGE OF THE COMPLETE BODY OF STATE AND FEDERAL LAW.
>
> **AM JUR LEGAL FORMS 2D:** A COMPILATION OF BUSINESS AND LEGAL FORMS DEALING WITH A VARIETY OF SUBJECT MATTERS.

AM JUR PLEADING AND PRACTICE FORMS, REV: MODEL PRACTICE FORMS FOR EVERY STAGE OF A LEGAL PROCEEDING.

AM JUR PROOF OF FACTS: A SERIES OF ARTICLES THAT GUIDE THE READER IN DETERMINING WHICH FACTS ARE ESSENTIAL TO A CASE AND HOW TO PROVE THEM.

AM JUR TRIALS: A SERIES OF ARTICLES DISCUSSING EVERY ASPECT OF PARTICULAR SETTLEMENTS AND TRIALS WRITTEN BY 180 CONSULTING SPECIALISTS.

UNITED STATES CODE SERVICE: A COMPLETE AND AUTHORITATIVE ANNOTATED FEDERAL CODE THAT FOLLOWS THE EXACT LANGUAGE OF THE STATUTES AT LARGE AND DIRECTS YOU TO THE COURT AND AGENCY DECISIONS CONSTRUING EACH PROVISION.

ALR AND ALR FEDERAL: SERIES OF ANNOTATIONS PROVIDING IN-DEPTH ANALYSES OF ALL THE CASE LAW ON PARTICULAR LEGAL ISSUES.

U.S. SUPREME COURT REPORTS, L ED 2D: EVERY REPORTED U. S. SUPREME COURT DECISION PLUS IN-DEPTH DISCUSSIONS OF LEADING ISSUES.

FEDERAL PROCEDURE, L ED: A COMPREHENSIVE, A–Z TREATISE ON FEDERAL PROCEDURE—CIVIL, CRIMINAL, AND ADMINISTRATIVE.

FEDERAL PROCEDURAL FORMS, L ED: STEP-BY-STEP GUIDANCE FOR DRAFTING FORMS FOR FEDERAL COURT OR FEDERAL AGENCY PROCEEDINGS.

FEDERAL RULES SERVICE, 2D AND 3D: REPORTS DECISIONS FROM ALL LEVELS OF THE FEDERAL SYSTEM INTERPRETING THE FEDERAL RULES OF CIVIL PROCEDURE AND THE FEDERAL RULES OF APPELLATE PROCEDURE.

FEDERAL RULES DIGEST, 3D: ORGANIZES HEADNOTES FOR THE DECISIONS REPORTED IN FEDERAL RULES SERVICE ACCORDING TO THE NUMBERING SYSTEMS OF THE FEDERAL RULES OF CIVIL PROCEDURE AND THE FEDERAL RULES OF APPELLATE PROCEDURE.

FEDERAL RULES OF EVIDENCE SERVICE: REPORTS DECISIONS FROM ALL LEVELS OF THE FEDERAL SYSTEM INTERPRETING THE FEDERAL RULES OF EVIDENCE.

FEDERAL RULES OF EVIDENCE NEWS

FEDERAL PROCEDURE RULES SERVICE

FEDERAL TRIAL HANDBOOK, 2D

FORM DRAFTING CHECKLISTS: AM JUR PRACTICE GUIDE

GOVERNMENT CONTRACTS: PROCEDURES AND FORMS

HOW TO GO DIRECTLY INTO YOUR OWN COMPUTERIZED SOLO PRACTICE WITHOUT MISSING A MEAL (OR A BYTE)

JONES ON EVIDENCE, CIVIL AND CRIMINAL, 7TH

LITIGATION CHECKISTS: AM JUR PRACTICE GUIDE

MEDICAL LIBRARY, LAWYERS EDITION

MEDICAL MALPRACTICE — ALR CASES AND ANNOTATIONS

MODERN APPELLATE PRACTICE: FEDERAL AND STATE CIVIL APPEALS

MODERN CONSTITUTIONAL LAW

NEGOTIATION AND SETTLEMENT

PATTERN DEPOSITION CHECKLISTS, 2D

QUALITY OF LIFE DAMAGES: CRITICAL ISSUES AND PROOFS

SHEPARD'S CITATIONS FOR ALR

SUCCESSFUL TECHNIQUES FOR CIVIL TRIALS, 2D

STORIES ET CETERA — A COUNTRY LAWYER LOOKS AT LIFE AND THE LAW

SUMMARY OF AMERICAN LAW

THE TRIAL LAWYER'S BOOK: PREPARING AND WINNING CASES

TRIAL PRACTICE CHECKLISTS

2000 CLASSIC LEGAL QUOTATIONS

WILLISTON ON CONTRACTS, 3D AND 4TH

FEDERAL RULES OF EVIDENCE DIGEST: ORGANIZES HEADNOTES FOR THE DECISIONS REPORTED IN FEDERAL RULES OF EVIDENCE SERVICE ACCORDING TO THE NUMBERING SYSTEM OF THE FEDERAL RULES OF EVIDENCE.

ADMINISTRATIVE LAW: PRACTICE AND PROCEDURE

AGE DISCRIMINATION: CRITICAL ISSUES AND PROOFS

ALR CRITICAL ISSUES: DRUNK DRIVING PROSECUTIONS

ALR CRITICAL ISSUES: FREEDOM OF INFORMATION ACTS

ALR CRITICAL ISSUES: TRADEMARKS

ALR CRITICAL ISSUES: WRONGFUL DEATH

AMERICANS WITH DISABILITIES: PRACTICE AND COMPLIANCE MANUAL

ATTORNEYS' FEES

BALLENTINE'S LAW DICTIONARY

CONSTITUTIONAL LAW DESKBOOK

CONSUMER AND BORROWER PROTECTION: AM JUR PRACTICE GUIDE

CONSUMER CREDIT: ALR ANNOTATIONS

DAMAGES: ALR ANNOTATIONS

EMPLOYEE DISMISSAL: CRITICAL ISSUES AND PROOFS

ENVIRONMENTAL LAW: ALR ANNOTATIONS

EXPERT WITNESS CHECKLISTS

EXPERT WITNESSES IN CIVIL TRIALS

FORFEITURES: ALR ANNOTATIONS

FEDERAL LOCAL COURT RULES

FEDERAL LOCAL COURT FORMS

FEDERAL CRIMINAL LAW AND PROCEDURE: ALR ANNOTATIONS

FEDERAL EVIDENCE

FEDERAL LITIGATION DESK SET: FORMS AND ANALYSIS

DEDICATION

For my sons, Steven and Scott:
Amor vincit omnia
(Love conquers all).

PREFACE

This book deals with real property law. It is designed to be as straightforward and clear as possible. Although it was written for paralegal students, it could also be used with equal ease in any undergraduate class about real estate. Nevertheless, there is always the problem of learning a new field; at first, the terms and language of that field are confusing. To alleviate that problem, this book has definitions in the margins next to the text, a glossary at the end of the book, and a textual explanation of each new term where it first appears.

The selection of topics is intended to cover as much as possible, while recognizing that the paralegal's knowledge needs do not compare to those of an attorney. Some topics, however, have been treated with extra depth when they are of particular importance to someone who will be working with real estate transactions. In addition, the financial aspects of the real estate business are covered extensively, because much real estate work is intimately connected with finance. Indeed, much of the actual structuring of the "deal" often reflects the requirements of the financing. It was felt, therefore, that this area needed explanation, because a failure to understand it could lead to difficulties on the job.

This book covers the most important areas of real property. It begins with an overview. Afterwards, the chapters deal with the following material and questions:

Chapter 2—How can this property be located? A chapter on legal descriptions.

Chapter 3—How can one own this property? A chapter on the ownership of real property.

Chapter 4—Who has or had interests in this parcel of property? A chapter on title searches.

Chapter 5—How does one transfer an interest in real property? A chapter on acquiring and transferring real property.

Chapter 6—How can the value of this property be determined? A chapter on appraising real estate.

Chapter 7—How is the buying and selling of real estate financed? A chapter on real estate financing.
Chapter 8—What is involved in a closing? A chapter on closing real estate sales, with emphasis on residential home closings.
Chapter 9—What is involved in renting real property? A chapter on leasing real property.
Chapter 10—What is special about condominiums and cooperatives? A chapter on condominiums and cooperatives.
Chapter 11—What environmental laws and concerns must be addressed? A chapter on environmental laws.
Chapter 12—How is real estate taxed, by whom, and for what purposes? A chapter on real estate taxation.
Chapter 13—What kinds of ethical problems arise in real estate transactions? A chapter on ethics.

Finally, there is an appendix which addresses how a student should approach reading cases; it is entitled "How to Analyze a Case."

A complaint about some texts has been that the text lacks case material. Many teachers believe that cases both illustrate points of law and allow the student to see what actually happened in a real situation. Therefore, a number of case excerpts have been included in this text. These cases range from very recent cases to one more than 50 years old. The older cases were included to indicate the precedent established by common law and passed on from one generation to the next. All were included because they illustrate a particular point of law well. The cases may be used as the instructor desires; they are intended only as illustrations, rather than as the basis for acquiring factual information. The text covers the topics discussed in the cases.

A major and continuing student complaint concerns "legalese" and the difficulty in understanding it. To the greatest extent possible, legalese has been removed and simple direct English has been employed. Nevertheless, there will be a barrier between the material and the student until the student has mastered the terminology of the topic. I have tried to make the student's task less burdensome so that acquiring the knowledge and terms will not overwhelm the student.

Several questions and problems appear at the end of each chapter. After discussion with my editor, we decided to leave both the questions and their answers in the text; the answers are in Appendix B, available but not obtrusive. With a topic as complex as real property, it was thought that these would provide a basis for discussion and learning. Additional materials are provided in the accompanying handbook to assist the instructor in preparing examination questions.

I have also included a number of checklists for various topics in the text. These checklists are not guaranteed to be complete for any particular situation, because local law will, of course, have its own variations that must be reflected in an actual checklist for job use. I have inserted these checklists for three reasons. First, understanding a checklist gives students a sense of control over the material and that leads to self-confidence, a definite aid to learning. Second, this kind of list gives students a start on organizing the work they will be doing in the future. Third, students may want to use the checklists to review and determine what they know and what they are missing. Checklists may serve multiple purposes but, basically, they identify important elements and help students maintain control over the immense amount of material that may be involved in a real estate transaction.

Focusing the text has required careful selection and consideration of what will be useful for the paralegal to know. This focus has been based on the situations and transactions in which the paralegal will most likely be involved. Obviously, the selection of relevant information is personal from my experiences, but the risk is always that too much material will overwhelm the student. I have sought to avoid that result (1) by sticking to the basic patterns of the law of real estate and (2) by trying to provide enough material about the context in which the law operates so that the student can understand and make connections, rather than merely memorize a set of rules. Memorization is often important, but mastery occurs when students understand the context so that the pieces fit together. My students have found that they learn more about the law by learning its context along with its rules.

Another method for helping the student is having more than one discussion of the same topic in the text. Most students do not learn everything the first time through. My experience as an instructor has been that the very best students learn somewhat more than half of the topic the first time through; most students learn considerably less. This learning difficulty is particularly acute when there is a constant need to master a new vocabulary and be certain that the terms are both understood and used properly. Surely, learning real estate law for the first time must be a prime example of this learning problem. Many chapters (compare, for instance, legal title concepts with appraisal concepts) appear with an entirely new vocabulary and approach. Some topics that may be particularly difficult to understand, such as fixtures and financing devices, get repeated coverage in a different way, or with additional material, in different chapters of the book. My purpose is to reinforce and add to what the student has already learned so that the student will learn more.

I must thank Jay Whitney, my Delmar editor, because without his remarkable patience, wise encouragement, and consistent support, I would have been unable to complete this book as I have; I remain truly grateful to him. I also wish to thank Glenna Stanfield for helping me by answering a number of idiot questions that I asked as I was learning to use Word Perfect. Finally, I greatly appreciate the consistent support, encouragement, and tactful nudging of two outstanding personal friends, Teresa Carr King and Ronald Liebman. The persons who spent their time to read, criticize, and edit portions of this book as it emerged from my printer were helpful to me beyond any expression of my gratitude. I have used many of their suggestions and their contributions have significantly improved this text. Any errors or faults, of course, are mine alone. My heartfelt thanks to these professional companions through this journey:

Kathleen Mercer Reed
University of Toledo Community and Technical College
(Ohio)

Paul M. Klein
Duquesne University
(Pennsylvania)

Henry Schildknecht
University of Louisville
(Kentucky)

Jack Owen
West Texas State University
(Texas)

Ray W. Sherman, Jr.
St. Mary's College
(California)

John L. Frank
Chippewa Valley Technical College
(Wisconsin)

Mattha E. Licke
Itasca Community College
(Minnesota).

CHAPTER 1

Introduction to Real Estate

"You want someone who has tasted many different situations, who struggled, who raised a family, who lived in a neighborhood all their lives rather than a penthouse on Sutton Place."

Mario Cuomo, speaking of attorneys

Colonial mansion

OUTLINE

PROLOGUE TO THE PARALEGAL

Real estate is something that we all know about because we live on it, in it, or above it and we use it, in hundreds of ways, directly and indirectly, continuously—from roads to farm products to the paper of this book, which came from a tree that was grown on real property. This chapter introduces you to the ways in which the law understands real estate. As you look at the definitions in this chapter, notice the variety of terms covering many aspects of real property. This text provides you not only with the basics of the legal terminology, but also with a brief introduction to the business of real estate, so that you can see some of the underlying economics (without a lot of technical jargon) and how those economics might affect real estate sales. This text also carefully distinguishes what real property and personal property are, because over the years the law has grown to take significantly different approaches to these two areas. You need to understand this distinction because you will have to deal with both types in the real estate business, although you will deal primarily with real property.

KEY TERMS

air rights
appraisal
appreciation
avulsion
depreciation
easement
erosion
fixture
heterogeneous
immobile
indestructible
improvements
intangible
parcel
personal property
plate tectonics
real estate
severed
subsurface rights
tangible

unimproved land
uniqueness
water rights

1.1 WHAT IS REAL ESTATE?

Real estate has two principal meanings. First, the term **real estate** means a piece of land that can be used for some purpose. It is usually referred to as a **parcel**. Note that when the term is used this way, it means the land. This piece of land can be used for farming, mining, ranching, an industrial plant, a shopping center, a school, a home, an apartment complex, or anything else. This way of referring to real property is the most common—the colloquial—way. However, there is a more technical meaning for the term *real estate*. In this meaning, *real estate* is a bundle of legal rights in relation to a particular parcel of land. Sometimes, though, a distinction is made between the term **real property** and the term *real estate*. When that distinction is being observed, *real estate* means the land and *real property* means the bundle of legal rights. Most often, however, these terms are used interchangeably.

The person who owns real estate or real property has, among other rights:

1. The right to possess the property, such as occupying the property
2. The right to control the property, including determining how others can use it, such as by a lease or an easement
3. The right to enjoy the property (*enjoy* means any legal use of the property, from planting flowers to drilling for oil)
4. The right to dispose of the property, such as giving it away or selling it.

To what does this bundle of legal rights apply? The rights attach to a parcel of land, which has three important areas to understand: surface rights, subsurface rights, and air rights. It is important to make certain that all three of these are available for transfer when a parcel of real property is being sold. Usually, when we think of selling real property, we think of selling the rights to the use and enjoyment of the surface of the land. Generally, therefore, surface rights are what are transferred, but air and subsurface rights may or may not be transferred with the surface rights. Prior owners may have sold or leased those other rights, because each of the three areas may be transferred separately. The separate sale of these areas is a clear demonstration of the landowner's rights to control and dispose of the property as he or she wishes.

In early days, the **air rights** associated with land ownership extended infinitely out into space from the boundaries of the property. But, with the development of air travel and airborne communications, effective limitations have been placed on those rights, so that for all practical purposes the federal government exercises dominion over the extended air space and licenses its use to airlines, radio, television, and other users. Congress has now regulated this area so that persons cannot use their rights in their realty to interfere with air travel and interstate commerce. The remaining interests in air rights are the rights to have air and light come onto one's property for one's benefit.

LEGAL TERMS

real estate
The land.

parcel
Designated piece of real property with its own legal description.

real property
Bundle of legal rights that the owner of real estate has.

air rights
Rights to the area above the surface of the property that the owner of the property has; theoretically extends infinitely into space.

An example of the commercial use of air rights is the construction of a building over an existing surface land use, such as a railroad. Many buildings in large cities are built over old, or still used, railroad sites. The owner of the building must buy the air rights and certain small pieces of property in order to build the support columns (caissons) or foundations upon which the structure will be constructed. In essence, this approach is like putting a building on stilts over a railroad track or any other surface land use.

Subsurface rights are considered as extending to the center of the earth from the surface boundaries of the property. There may be considerable value to these rights when deposits of resources, such as coal, oil, natural gas, copper, gold, iron, or bauxite, are discovered, or when there is a need to use the area beneath the surface, such as to dig a flood control drainage and storage facility or a canal. The owner of the property could sell or lease some or all of his or her interests in any of the underground deposits. This sale or transfer need not include selling any surface rights, but it might imply that the buyer has the right to enter the land on its surface and use the surface so that the minerals or other resources can be extracted. Contracts usually cover these points, but the right to enter and use the property could be considered a license or an **easement** (a right in a nonowner to use the property for a specific purpose).

Deed Reservation—Grant
Easement for light, air, and unobstructed view

Grantor reserves, however, to himself, his heirs, successors and assigns, as and for an appurtenance to the real property described as follows: ________ and for any part thereof, a perpetual easement of right to receive light, air, and unobstructed view over that portion of the real property herein described, to the extent that said light, air, and view will be received and enjoyed by limiting any structure, fence, trees, or shrubs on said property, or any part thereof, to a height not extending above a horizontal plane __________ feet above the level of the sidewalk of ________ *[street]*, as the sidewalk level now exists at the junction of the ________ *[northern]* and ________ *[eastern]* boundary lines of the property herein described. Any obstruction of such view above said horizontal plane, except ________ *[specify existing obstructions and other desired exceptions, including any exceptions to be allowed for radio and television receiving devices, power and telephone poles and lines other than those required to be buried, and required flues or vents, as well as fixtures required under any building regulations]*, shall be considered an unauthorized interference with such right or easement and shall be removed on demand at the expense of ________ *[grantee]*, his heirs, successors and assigns in the ownership of that real property described above or any part thereof.

Surface rights are the principal aspects of land rights. They include not only the land, but also any buildings or additions placed on the land and all other items that are permanently attached to the land. There a number of valuable natural items that are naturally attached to land, such as trees and crops. The principal use and enjoyment of real property comes from the use of surface rights, although great benefit can be derived from subsurface rights or from two of the areas used together, such as placing solar panels on the surface and generating solar power from sunlight (an air right).

There are also **water rights**. Water rights have become increasingly important, because water is a scarce commodity in the western United States, where there is comparatively little rainfall, and it is important everywhere because of increasing consumer and industrial uses. In California, in the early 1990s, restrictions on and selections among different types of water use became necessary during a prolonged drought. Consideration of water rights looks at several factors: first, the ownership of the land over which the water flows; second, the rights to use the water's surface; third, the proportioning of the water among the various potential claimants to the water who would take and use it; and fourth, the landowner's rights in relation to the body of water.

In the first situation, the basic idea is that if the waterway is not navigable, then the owner of the land owns the water. If the waters are navigable, then they are public waters and may be used for commerce, recreation, or other public activities. This use may be controlled by state and local governments, or Congress, under its rights to control interstate commerce, may regulate the waterway.

In regard to surface water rights, landowners generally have the right to use the surface as they see fit. However, the claims to the taking of water fall under two major theories that permit and restrict water use. The first one, riparian rights, generally permits the property owner adjacent to the body of water to take and use the water from the body of water so long as the use is reasonable. The second theory deals with priority in use of the water and recognizes that if two parties are on the body of water and there is an established use of the water, the landowner using the water has first priority. He or she may continue to take for his or her needs as he or she traditionally has, despite any needs of landowners (later in time of use) elsewhere on the stream. This approach amounts to prioritizing on the basis of time of use. Many jurisdictions are now beginning to issue permits to control water usage, particularly in areas where the water is in increasingly short supply.

Fourth, the landowner whose property adjoins the body of water must carefully consider where the property line ends. As a general rule, if the body of water is navigable, the state owns up to the high water mark; if not navigable, the property owner owns halfway, to the middle of the waterway. If the property is adjacent to an ocean, the mean (averaged) high tide mark usually serves as the boundary limit, but some states follow other rules, such as a mean low tide mark.

1.2 THE PHYSICAL ASPECTS OF REAL ESTATE

Real estate has three important physical aspects. First, it does not move, so it is referred to as being **immobile**. Second, it is always there and cannot be destroyed, so it is referred to as **indestructible**. Third, each piece of real

LEGAL TERMS

subsurface rights
Rights to minerals and other items beneath the top of the land; theoretically extends to the center of the earth.

easement
Right of a nonowner to use a piece of property for a specific purpose.

surface rights
Principal rights to real property and includes the land and anything attached to it permanently.

water rights
Comprised of *riparian rights* and *littoral rights*. Riparian rights deal with the rights to water along streams and rivers. If the waterway is nonnavigable, the owner owns to the middle of the body of water; if navigable, the ownership runs to the water's edge, in most cases. Riparian rights differ greatly among states. Littoral rights concern the ownership of property next to large bodies of water such as lakes and oceans. The owner has unrestricted access to use the water, but usually owns only up to the high-tide mark.

immobile
Not moving; incapable of moving.

indestructible
Cannot be destroyed; a characteristic of real estate.

property is different from every other—if only in that it is at a different location than any other piece—so it is referred to as having **uniqueness**. These parcels are said to be **heterogeneous**, that is, they are all different from one another. Although the land cannot be moved, parts of it can be, through the process of mining. But the land on which mining occurs does not go anywhere, even when that mining process produces the world's largest manmade hole, as in a circular strip mine for copper in a western state. Small pieces of land can disappear by gradual wearing away (**erosion**), or by a catastrophic event such as an earthquake or tidal wave (**avulsion**), but these events happen so infrequently that for our purposes land is permanent. Of course, since the 1960s, discoveries in **plate tectonics** have made us all recognize that land is constantly being destroyed by geological processes, but these processes, except when they show up as avulsion, are so long-term that they have little effect on such short-lived creatures as human beings. Further, they not only destroy land, but also create it as well. Some geologists believe that the United States west of the Rocky Mountains is mostly land added by the scraping processes of plate tectonics.

1.3 REAL VERSUS PERSONAL PROPERTY

Property law began as law of real property. Originally, all property was real property. As time passed, however, important distinctions were made between real property and what came to be called **personal property**. Essentially, real property came to be whatever was land and whatever was permanently attached or affixed to the land. Personal property became anything that was not real property. The original concept of personal property was that it was movable. Although that concept remains important in distinguishing **tangible** goods (things that can be touched, moved, and are bought and sold, from computers to cars) from real property, the concept of personal property has gone beyond distinctions based on mere mobility. A newer concept in personal property is **intangible** personal property. This aspect of personal property deals with property that cannot be seen or touched, but the ownership rights in which are represented by pieces of paper such as stock certificates, bonds, or letters patent issued by the U.S. Patent Office. For convenience, we speak as if those pieces of paper were the actual property, but literally they are only the symbols of the property rights and claims to money. One of the earliest examples remains a judgment or, in old language, a *chose in action,* which is still represented by a piece of paper.

Another important concept to recognize is that the nature of property can change in either direction between real property and personal property. If trees or crops are growing on land, they are part of the land—part of the real property. When they are **severed**, or disconnected from the land, they cease to be real property and become personal property. A distinction is made, however, between the plants (*fructus naturales*) growing on the real property over a period of more than a year—trees, bushes, grasses—and vegetation that is planted annually, such as crops (*fructus industriales*). The former are considered so much a part of the real estate that they are owned by the landowner. Plants that are planted by someone's labor, usually annually, though considered part of the real property until their harvest, are the personal property of the planter, because everyone knows they will be severed and removed from the property. If the land is sold, crops may be disposed of separately from the real property, but any trees on the land would pass to the new owner without any question. If crops are not separately disposed of by contract, they are transferred with the real property. Another example of real property becoming personal property is the mineral or resource deposit that is brought to the surface. For instance, a pool of oil underground is real property, but when it comes to the surface and into the pipeline, it becomes personal property (after all, it is moving right along!).

Clearly, the distinction here is between being attached to (being part of) the land and being severed or separate from the land. That change is the point at which an item of real property becomes personal property. This process can occur in the other direction as well. A piece of personal property can come onto the real property and become permanently attached to the land, thereby becoming real property. When a building is constructed, it comes onto the property in its component parts, such as concrete mix for the foundation, water, lumber, nails, electrical wiring, and plumbing pipes, as personal property. When the building is finished, all these elements have become part of the real property. The completed building is permanently attached to the real estate and is a permanent improvement on real estate. But take another example: instead of a house, consider a piece of factory equipment that is added to a building. If it is a permanent addition, and there is no intent to remove it, it becomes real property and is called a **fixture**. If it is not to be permanent, it remains personal property and is called *equipment* (goods used or useful in the conduct of a business). The topic of fixtures is discussed more fully in chapters 2 and 5.

1.4 THE ECONOMIC ASPECTS OF REAL ESTATE

The true importance of real estate lies in its use. That use is an economic aspect of real estate, in the broadest sense of *economics*. To understand real estate—outside of the mere desire to own property or to have a satisfactory place in which to live—one must have some understanding of the economics of real estate. Outside of legal technicalities, most of the excitement and the confusion of dealing with real estate comes from its economics. Although this introductory text cannot impart any expertise, recognition of the economic "ballpark" and of the processes involved in playing the "game" of real estate is important to understanding the real estate business.

Real estate has traditionally been an abundant resource in America. With millions of square miles and billions of acres, the sheer amount of land in the United States is staggering. But it was abundant and cheap when few people wanted it. During the westward expansion (1600–1900), historians have argued that most land was originally taken up for speculative purposes. It was not originally settled by pioneer families. Instead, speculators bought it from the

LEGAL TERMS

uniqueness
Specialness; being one of a kind; an aspect of real estate, as no two parcels have the same area.

heterogeneous
Special, unique, or being separate and different from any thing else.

erosion
Gradual wearing away of the land by means of water or wind action.

avulsion
Ripping away of the land by violent means, such as a tidal wave or an earthquake.

plate tectonics
Geological term referring to the system of slowly moving crustal plates floating on the surface of the earth that interact with one another.

personal property
Any property that is not real property; its most important characteristic is its mobility.

tangible
Capable of being touched; said of a type of personal property which is usually goods.

intangible
Cannot be touched; a type of personal property.

severed
Separated; said of plants that grow on land and are cut or harvested.

fixture
Item of personal property that is affixed to land so permanently as to be part of it and thus part of the real property.

government and resold it to settlers, many of whom were simply smaller scale speculators who resold it to the individuals who actually cleared the land of trees or put up the first buildings. Later, that first settler might have sold out to someone else, who became the first permanent settler. Note that in most of these transactions, the purpose of acquiring the land was to make money on the resale of the land, not to occupy it as a home, a farm, or a business site.

Much of the development of American real estate has been based on turnover and resale for a profit. This use is one of the major economic aspects of the real estate business. Many prominent and great Americans, including George Washington, have been involved in this business. Today, however, land is not readily available for speculative purposes, because the good land has been settled. What remains is mostly desert, mountain, or land far from desirable jobs and cities. Nevertheless, today's land market still has speculators, but most of the speculation is in and around major cities.

This business is founded in certain aspects of the nature of real estate. First, land is a scarce commodity, because it is unique. Second, its value is affected by the use to which it can be put. That use many times is determined by the **improvements** that have been added to the real property. A house, an apartment building, a factory, or a shopping center changes the land's use and thus its value. The term *improvement* has two uses. First, it refers to anything that is a permanent addition to the real property, from a fence to a skyscraper. Second, *improved property* means that the parcel of property has access to utilities and roads; such items as water, electricity, gas, and sewerage are available for the owner or user of that parcel of land. **Unimproved land**, sometimes called *raw land,* lacks access to these elements; its value is generally less than that of improved land.

Another aspect of real property is that it takes a lot of money to buy it and to make improvements on it. Because the land and improvements generally remain unchanged for a long time, a land investment is considered a permanent investment. Even if land is sold, the investment remains, and frequently buyers increase both their investment and the value of the property. The land itself never **depreciates** (declines in value) because it does not change; it is always there. The land is said to be immobile and indestructible. The improvements to the land (usually buildings) do depreciate over a long period of time, usually 10 to 50 years, or even longer. For example, the author had an opportunity in 1983 to visit a home in Connecticut which an ancestor had helped to construct in the 1630s; this building was over 350 years old and fully depreciated! Land can **appreciate** (increase in value), and frequently demand, speculation, scarcity, a growing population, or other economic factors or conditions affect the value of real property so that its current price rises or falls.

A final basic aspect of real estate economics is site preference. The traditional real estate sales rule that expresses the importance of site preference is: "What are the first three rules of selling real estate? Location, location, and location." There are "hot" areas to live in, to build in, and to work in. Since 1950, the industrial heartland of the Northeast and Great Lakes areas has not been hot, but the states of California, Texas, and Florida have been "scorching." These three states now contain close to one-quarter of America's population, its largest cities, its greatest industrial strengths, and some of its worst pollution problems.

This type of population shift because of site preference is on the largest scale, but the purchase of a single home is often determined by the availability of schools, churches, transportation, pollution sources, inexpensive water, and a myriad of other factors. For businesses, site preference can be determined by still other factors, such as taxation, labor force cost and quality, support systems, transportation, and proximity to markets. When multiple uses and factors are involved in the selection process, it is appropriate to refer to the choices as being *interdependent.* In most cases, even though we may not consciously recognize all of the factors involved, there are multiple, interdependent factors involved in the selection of any location for any purpose. Of all the individual factors that influence selection, site preference is considered the single most important one.

There are five basic types of real estate:

1. Residential, ranging from single-family residences to condominium units in a high-rise
2. Business real estate, which can be either (a) commercial (generally for investment purposes) or (b) industrial, ranging from mining to manufacturing to warehousing
3. Rural, for land uses such as farming, grazing, growing forest and lumber products, and sometimes operating recreational facilities
4. Special purpose, for such uses as churches, hospitals, and many educational institutions
5. Public, for uses ranging from water purification plants to courthouses.

Evaluations of real property, called **appraisals**, are based on these different land uses, and each different use requires a different evaluation method because the objectives of the owners differ substantially. For instance, churches are not interested in selling their property; they want to use it for a very long time. Investors in a building, however, want and need to know what return they will receive on their money, because their goal is to receive a financial return. If that return is too low, they will put their money elsewhere; for example, they will want to sell the property and reinvest the proceeds in other land or even in a different type of investment. Differences in appraisal methods, therefore, reflect the different types of interests that real estate owners have in their property.

1.5 REAL ESTATE TRANSACTIONS: SUPPLY AND DEMAND

If you work in real estate, your job will depend on the economics of the real estate business. Although it is technically not a legal matter, economics

LEGAL TERMS

improvements
(1) Additions to real property, usually buildings; or (2) as in "improved real estate," the addition of roads and utilities to a parcel so it is usable for buildings and human occupation.

unimproved land
Land without any additions to its raw state—for example, no sewers, streets, water, or electricity.

depreciation
Decrease in value.

appreciation
Increase in value.

appraisal
Evaluation of the value of real property at a particular point in time.

often determines what can be done and the direction the law will take. Therefore, this section gives a brief overview of the economics of this important American business.

Economics has a number of laws that apply to real estate transactions. Supply and demand laws and pricing rules apply to the real property business; supply and demand always affect one another. For instance, increased demand usually produces a greater supply, and decreased demand causes the supply to go down—in real estate quite slowly, because its properties are relatively inflexible. If a lot of people have a lot of money available and they want to spend it on housing, the supply of housing will expand to meet that demand. Sometimes a greater supply can expand demand. For instance, large amounts of cheap, affordable housing may stimulate the buyers' demand.

Price also often reflects supply. The less there is of an object, the higher the price. That rule explains why gold brings higher prices than silver; there is a great deal less gold than silver in the world. It also explains why homes costing $10 million have fewer buyers than homes that cost $100,000. It should be noted that different price levels may constitute different types of markets. There may be no demand in condominiums, while sales of single-family residences may be booming. In identifying how to sell, it is important to know the exact parameters of your particular market.

Outside factors can control or stimulate the real estate market as well. One of these, the cost of money, has long been a key factor in slowing or encouraging the construction business and the entire real estate industry. When interest rates are low, real estate sales are much better than when the cost of funds is high.

Another factor is speculative buying and selling, which can force the real estate market up. The aftermath of such speculation usually means that the market suffers a severe fall, though, because the prices have risen beyond their economic basis. Those high prices then fall to below what a rational market would support. After the fall, people with cash available can sometimes get good buys.

Other government policies, besides monetary policy affecting the cost of money, can also influence the real estate market. For instance, since the 1930s the federal government has supported home ownership and has encouraged individuals to own their own homes, by insuring bank and savings and loan deposits and, until the 1970s, making certain that cheap funds were available through these financial institutions. These devices encouraged home construction. In the 1990s, however, there is serious question concerning the federal government's level of commitment to home ownership, as the restructuring of the financial services industry may divert funds to other types of investments or higher yielding investments.

Another factor that affects the real estate market is the number of people who can afford to buy the product. High-paying jobs, ample disposable income, and an interest in home ownership all stimulated the home construction and resale markets from 1945 to the 1980s. With many fewer high-paying jobs, and with monthly payments of principal, interest, taxes, and insurance representing an enormous proportion of disposable income, the nature of the business is bound to change significantly over the next decade. Among the factors with potential to counter some of these negative factors may be technological innovations that make housing cheaper and therefore more affordable. One area of potential costcutting is factory-constructed housing modules that are assembled onsite. These modules would replace the onsite construction of buildings from individual components. In this way, much of the labor cost could be reduced and some savings in materials might be possible as well. But how would that affect the high-paying jobs (such as carpentry, plumbing, and others) that make possible the purchase of expensive homes?

Another way of looking at the economics of the real estate business is to understand some of the psychology involved. Many people grew up in homes that their families owned, and thus think of real estate in terms of home ownership, but in most real estate transactions the land is a commodity—just something to be bought and sold for the best price obtainable. This approach is always involved in the real estate "deal," with at least someone (certainly the attorney if no one else) handling the transaction in a hardheaded manner. This unemotional, objective, and realistic approach is the nature of the legal perspective, and there is little romance to real estate when it is bought and sold as a commodity. This approach is necessary because without it there would be no one protecting the interests of the seller or buyer to ensure that the best financial and safest legal arrangement was obtained. Too often, home buyers and investors with little knowledge need someone to be objective to prevent them from making serious mistakes with their money.

1.6 THE USES OF REAL ESTATE IN THE UNITED STATES

The real estate industry has been a very large one and a key component in America's economic prosperity since the end of World War II. It is seen by many economists as a bellwether for the economy in general—what happens in real estate often is a precursor of what will happen in the economy as a whole. America's real estate is primarily held in private ownership (about 60 percent), and various governments, principally the federal government, hold the rest. The large proportion of government land holdings is because much land in the West is desert and has little economic use. Agricultural land use is the largest by far. Crop land, grazing land, and forest account for close to 75 percent of the land usage. Only 2 to 3 percent of our land use goes to cities and urban development.

Consider the variety of uses to which real estate can be put. In the residential housing market, there are multiple arrangements, such as single-family, two-flats, four-flats, apartment complexes, condominiums, cooperatives, shared-wall structures, garages, and vacation homes. There are travelers' housing structures, such as hotels and motels. Industrial real estate includes factories and manufacturing complexes. The products that are produced in these locations can vary from specialized steel and computers to shoes, cloth, and junk food. All require land on which to operate. Commercial uses of land can range from shopping centers and strip malls to warehouses and stores to recreation facilities like Disney World.

There are multiple aspects to the public use of land. Consider the variety of services that government provides to its citizens. Local government is responsible for courts, agencies, roads, sewers, parks, and a multitude of other functions. Most of these require the use of real estate in some way, if for nothing else than housing an agency's recordkeepers and administrators. The major source of income for American local government has been real estate taxes; indeed, there are special real estate officials in local government. There is the official who keeps the records of real estate (often called the *recorder of deeds*) and the official whose office determines the value of each parcel of real estate for taxation in that jurisdiction (often called the *assessor*). State government uses overlap with both local and federal government activities in some areas, but they have interests in real estate such as parks, roads, the state capitol, state universities, and research stations, to mention only a few. The federal government has interests like those of all the other governments, such as parks and roads, plus interests in military bases, national forests, and public dams. The federal government is the residual holder of most of the land in America that has not been purchased or settled.

This vast variety of real estate uses and activities has created a real estate business that is complex and diverse in its activities. Think of the multiple skills required to perform certain needed activities in real estate. First, one must know where the land is. A surveyor meets that need by measuring the boundaries of the parcel of land and recording the results on a piece of paper called a *survey.* Second, someone has to develop the land so that it can be used, or subdivide existing land into smaller units for specialized use. Then, various engineers and architects are needed to design buildings and tie them into the society's social systems and services, which range from water and sewerage to electronic networks and pollution control.

All these elements cost money. Therefore, many different types of financing may be used. The range of financing possibilities runs from banks, savings and loan associations, and secondary mortgage market placements to sophisticated syndications and financings arranged in the bond, stock, and other financial markets. The actual construction work must be done under the guidance of a general contractor, usually with the assistance of a number of specialized subcontractors. The variety of construction workers involved in creating so many types of buildings seems almost endless, but common to most construction projects are carpenters, roofers, electricians, plumbers, glaziers, concrete workers, and general laborers, who do a multitude of tasks from putting up wallboard to cleaning up afterwards. After construction is completed, who manages the property? Not all owners occupy their premises. Many owners are investors who do not want to be bothered running the business. They have agents who collect the rent, sign the leases, and generally do all the things necessary to manage the property. If the owners want to know the value of their property, they hire an appraiser to provide an evaluation of its current worth.

Whenever one is dealing with these various parties in a real estate transaction, it is necessary to identify what each person's interest is in the deal. You must know why those persons are there; what they do; who they deal with; what they want; and how to analyze the risks they and their interests present in comparison to the benefits they and their interests can provide. For instance, two of the parties most frequently involved in real estate transactions are attorneys (maybe the one you work for) and bankers, the people doing the financing.

Lawyers are there to protect their clients, and they can be extremely detailed, fussy, and time-consuming in their requirements. They are said to examine documents so closely that they "fly speck" them; that is, they could pick out the specks the feet of a fly might make on the document if it walked on the paper. Bankers can appear the same way, with their mortgages, notes, title searches, financial statements, and seemingly endless analysis. But all these details are the work of specialists who are trying to ensure that the transaction everyone is working on comes out right, not only in its current documentation, transfer, and other paperwork, but also 3, 5, or 10 years in the future. Despite the sometimes apparent endlessness of the work, if this work were not done, the project could fall apart at any time. Although it is important that the deal not collapse before it is finalized, determination of the future health of the project is also very important. Most of these parties are professionals who try to do their best to contribute to the success of the operation. Besides, all this detailed paperwork provides a great amount of employment!

DISCUSSION AND REVIEW QUESTIONS

1. What is the primary focus of the real estate business?
2. Are there other aspects of the real estate business that must be considered along with the economic ones?
3. What three areas of land does an owner get when he or she purchases property?
4. List the rights that a landowner has in relation to the property and explain each of them briefly.
5. Identify the physical characteristics of real estate.
6. Distinguish between real and personal property.

7. List and explain three of the economic aspects of real estate.
8. What are the five areas or types of real estate?
9. Explain three of the five areas listed in question 8.
10. In a general way, explain the application of supply and demand and pricing rules to the real estate business.

CHAPTER 2
The Legal Definition of Real Property

"It doesn't do good to open doors for someone who doesn't have the price to get in. If he has the price, he may not need the laws."

Ronald Reagan

Georgian-style house

OUTLINE

PROLOGUE TO THE PARALEGAL

The first time you see a legal description in a deed, it appears to be so much gibberish. By the time you have finished studying this chapter, you will understand what those terms mean and be able to explain them to anyone who might want to know. They really are not too difficult, but initially they may seem confusing. To make them less so, this chapter shows you how the system of surveying and describing land came about and how and why it developed. Essentially, this chapter is about surveying tracts of land as large as hundreds of square miles or as small as 2,500 square feet. The crucial point to keep in mind is that precise location is the essence of what the law and the landowner want to achieve. With this precision, the amount of land and the location of land can be determined exactly, so that there should be no need for later dispute of the matter. This permits greater public peace and fewer legal actions to clog the courts. In this chapter, you will learn a new set of terminology. Take time not only to learn what *each term means, but* how *the things it describes operate as well.*

KEY TERMS

acre
actual notice
air rights
benchmark
check
condominium
constructive notice
datum
degree
filing
fixture
government or rectangular survey system
legal description
lis pendens
littoral rights
lot and block method
meridians
metes and bounds
minute
mobile home
monument
parallels
personal property
planned unit development (PUD)
plat of survey

quadrangle
range
real property
recording
riparian rights
search
second
section
subsurface rights
tier
Torrens system
township
trade fixture
Uniform Commercial Code

2.1 INTRODUCTION

The purpose of legal descriptions is to determine, precisely, where one property begins and another property ends. In other words, how do we establish a boundary that all parties can agree upon, that is easily identified, and that is unlikely to create a basis for later dispute? Rival claimants have been fought over real property boundaries from the earliest times. Nations still wage war for real property; wild animals mark their boundaries with scent; and rival gangs "tag" their areas and fight it out for their "turf." These actions are all ways of setting real property boundaries. In communities where people are trying to live together cooperatively, however, a number of ways have evolved to set mutually agreed-upon boundaries.

In medieval England, where the American body of real estate law began, one of the original units was called a *hyde* or a *hide*. Despite several myths about this term's origin (such as the charming story that a hide was the area that could be surrounded by an ox hide cut into one continuous thin strip), a *hyde* was an area adequate to support a minor noble who had a manor house. This area included sufficient people to work the land and do all the things necessary to produce crops and support the noble's fighting men, who were essential to protect the people from domestic gangs, robbers, and foreign invaders such as the Vikings. The actual amount of land varied because of its fertility and productivity. A person could own property described as "1 hide," or "60 hides," or "100 hides." In a society where the settlements were sparse, this type of system worked well.

Another medieval method of land description was to set boundaries by natural objects. This method would use a description from the "large oak tree to the middle of the creek and down to where the creek turns and then to the top of the hill and then back to the oak tree." Although roughly accurate, such descriptions were subject to a number of problems, such as the movement of natural objects. What happens when the oak tree dies or the creek changes direction?

These simple and natural methods were basically adequate, but they were imprecise, and by the eighteenth century, scientific developments had progressed so that various mechanical surveying methods replaced the natural methods. To understand the precision that surveying can provide for legal descriptions, it is necessary to know some basics about the globe and what surveying does.

Our planet is roughly a sphere with a circumference of approximately 25,000 miles at the equator. Although it is a three-dimensional object, we deal with its surface in the measurements at issue here. We think of the surface as circular because, standing on the earth and viewing an unobstructed horizon (as at sea on a calm day), the viewer sees the circular curve of the earth. A circle has 360 degrees (360°). The top of the earth circle is called the North Pole and the bottom, the South Pole. A line going around the exact middle, between the poles, is called the equator. Measuring from either pole to the equator is always 90°. Going around the earth from pole to pole and back again makes a rough circle, or 360°. Each degree going north or south is about 70 miles, and each degree unit is called a **parallel** (see figure 2-1). For example, New York and Chicago are close to 40° north of the equator. With this scheme we can find ourselves anywhere on a north-south line on earth. But how can we find ourselves on an east-west line? Eventually, a fixed point (Greenwich, England, for the English-speaking peoples of the world; Paris, for the French) was agreed upon as 0°, and the lines were drawn from pole to pole across the equator by degrees. One set of lines went west from Greenwich 180° and the other set went east from Greenwich 180°. Thus, the 360 degrees of a circle were achieved, and these lines are called **meridians**. See figure 2-2.

LEGAL TERMS

parallels
Lines running on the globe parallel to the equator; the measurement from the equator to a pole or from a pole to the equator is 90°; continuing to the point of origin covers 360°.

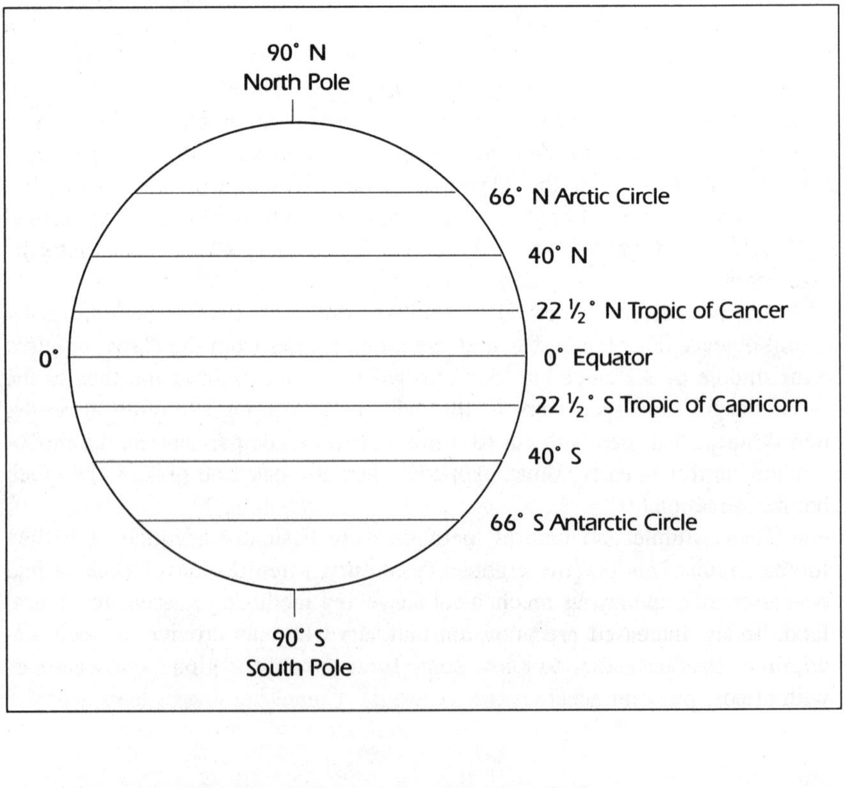

FIGURE 2-1
Examples of parallels: north-south measurements on the globe (360 degrees)

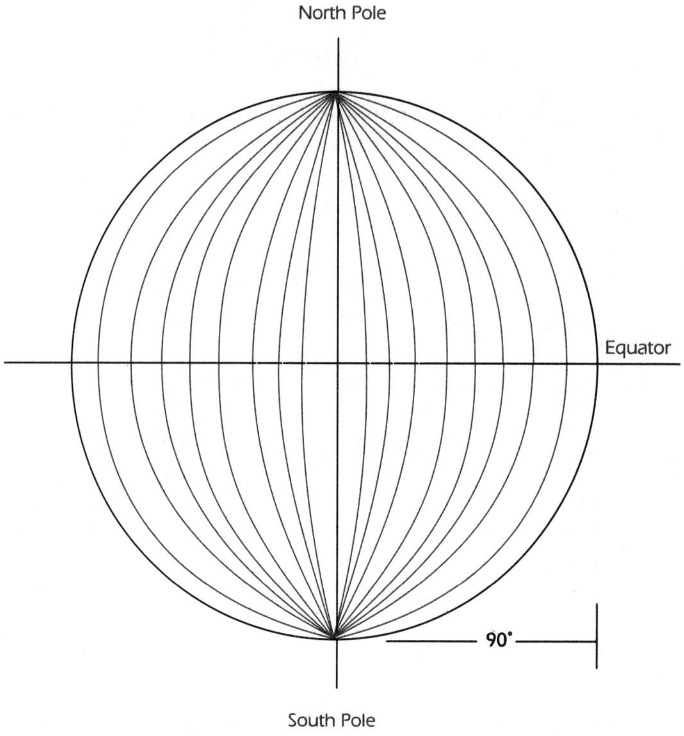

FIGURE 2-2
Examples of meridians

There are four 90-degree units in 360 degrees. On English-language maps the 0 degree location is in Greenwich, England. One counts to 180° east or west from Greenwich to make the complete 360°.

meridians
Lines that run from pole to pole on the globe; the 0-degree line is in Greenwich, England, for the English-speaking world. Measurements are made up to 180 degrees east and 180 degrees west of the 0-degree location to create a vertical aspect of the map grid of the world; together with the parallels, they create the basis for map making.

This pattern of parallels and meridians sets a grid over the face of the earth. But the area included in any rectangle made by one degree of parallels and meridians is thousands of square miles and is not very precise. But each **degree** (the symbol for degree is °) can be broken down into 60 minutes (the symbol for a minute is ′), and each **minute** can be broken down into 60 **seconds** (the symbol for the second is ″). Thus, a minute is about one mile, 293 yards, and a second becomes about 34.22 yards, or a little more than one-third the length of a football field. This precision allows ships to sail and planes to fly across the oceans without worrying about where they are when they are out of sight of land. Today, increased precision allows ships to be pinpointed by satellite to within a few feet and allows intercontinental missiles to arrive at their targets with almost pinpoint accuracy, regardless of whether they were launched from land, air, or beneath the sea. The precision bombing in the 1991 Gulf war was based upon this system—refined and pinpointed.

2.2 COMMONLY USED AMERICAN SURVEYING SYSTEMS

In modern real estate descriptions, three basic methods are used for describing a parcel of land. The first is the *metes and bounds system;* the second is the *government or rectangular survey system;* the third is a subcategory for smaller areas or developments and is called the *plat method.*

Property Lines Fixed by Metes and Bounds

> All of that real property lying in the County of _________, State of _________, bounded as follows: Beginning at a survey monument located at the common corner of government survey sections _________, _________, _________, and _________ *[10, 11, 14 and 15]* of Township _________ *[number]*, Range _________, *[number]* _________ *[West]* of the _________ Principal Meridian; thence _________ *[North]* about _________ feet to a _________ *[describe monument, such as:* bronze nail embedded in a 6-inch clay pipe filled with concrete]; thence _________ *[East]* about _________ feet to a _________ *[describe monument];* thence _________ *[South]* about _________ feet to a _________ *[describe monument];* thence _________ *[West]* about _________ feet to the point of beginning; being an area of _________ square feet, more or less.

LEGAL TERMS

degree
1/360th of a circle; a unit of measurement used in surveying and mathematics; the symbol is °.

minute
Surveying term that describes 1/60th of a degree; the symbol is ′.

second
1/60th of a minute; term describing a distance in surveying terms; the symbol is ″.

metes and bounds
System of surveying different from the rectangular survey method; based upon beginning at a clearly defined point and moving to other such points until a circuit of the property has been described.

The **metes and bounds** method yields a very precise result in the hands of a competent surveyor. The surveyor takes a Point of Beginning (POB) and determines the line of due north-south that runs through the POB. Then, a straight line (called a *bearing*) is determined to the next point. This bearing is a reading from a compass and is called a *compass direction* or *compass bearing* (see figure 2-3). The direction (called an *angle*) of that line is described by the compass direction in which it goes and by its length; thus, a line could go at (have a bearing of) an angle of 36°, 25′, and 15″ west of due south for 275.51 feet. That statement is abbreviated as S. 36°, 25′, and 15″ W. 275.51. This process is repeated from point to point around the perimeters of the property until the point of beginning (POB) is reached again. (Note that the abbreviation for a foot of distance (′) is the same as the abbreviation for a minute of surveying direction (′). Do not confuse them; one has to rely on context to tell the difference.) This technique is somewhat similar to the connect-the-dots game that children play. Originally, the points were set in; these were often natural descriptions such as "the big boulder." But once the surveyor has established that the line is a certain angle and runs a certain distance, the physical points do not have to be maintained, because they can be recreated at any time by any other surveyor. Note that the end of one line is the beginning point for another line. Figure 2-4 is a sample of a simple, basic metes and bounds description. Its written-out format, called a **legal description**, is:

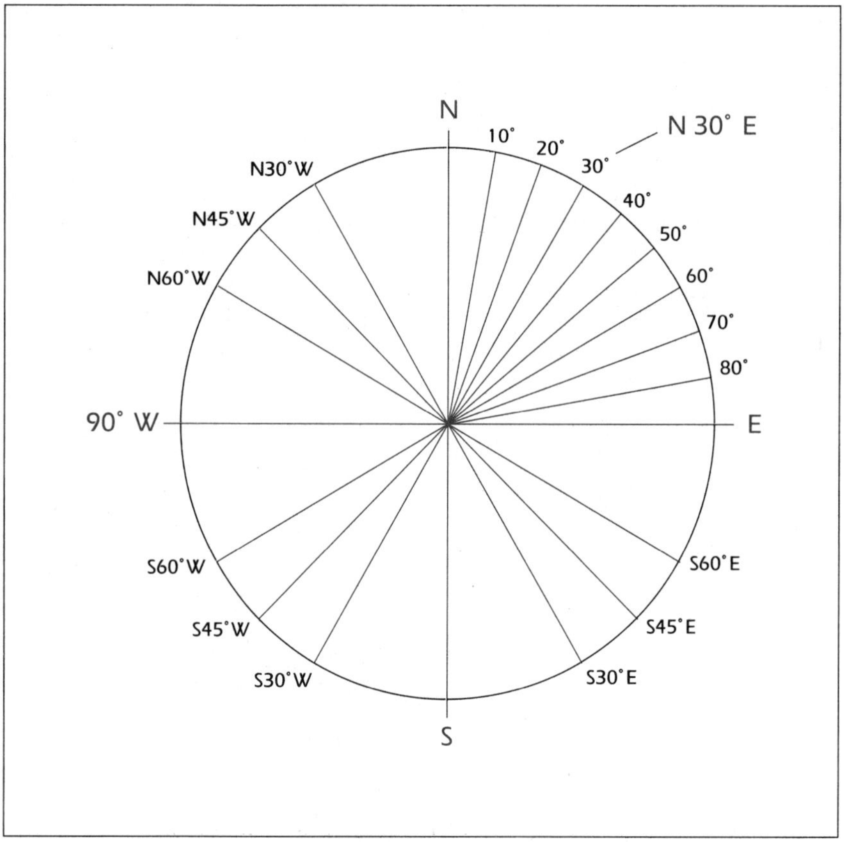

FIGURE 2-3
Compass directions

A circle has 360° (degrees); each degree has 60 minutes ('); each minute has 60 seconds ("). On a map, due N and due S are 0°; for measuring with compass angles, due E and due W are 90°.

This map is facing straight on the middle or 0-degree meridian, which would be Greenwich, England. Although American maps focus squarely on the U.S.A., degree measuring actually begins about 70 degrees west at Cape Cod in Massachusetts (further east for Maine) and about 88 degrees west for Chicago, Illinois.

Note that one measures from due north (N) or south (S) and moves down (or up) to 90 degrees to the east (E) or 90 degrees to the west (W). Consequently, one half of the compass reading is expressed as north, the other as south. The deviations from the original direction are expressed in the direction toward the east or west by degrees, minutes, and seconds.

All that tract or parcel of land situated in the town of East Park, County of York, State of Illinois, bounded and described as follows: Beginning at the junction of the easterly line of Elm Street and the southerly line of Oak Street and running thence north 60 degrees east 535 and 87/100s feet; thence, 90 degrees due east 847 and 79/100s feet along the land of the Town of East Park (common known as Oak Street Park) to the land of Deborah B. Landauer; then, south 30 degrees east 575 and 92/100s feet along the land of the aforesaid Deborah B. Landauer to the land of J. E. Jones; thence south 59 degrees 59 minutes 48 seconds 1023 and 88/100s feet along the land of the aforesaid J. E. Jones to Elm Street; thence north 39 degrees 58 minutes 57 seconds 864 feet along Elm Street to the point or place of beginning.

legal description
Precise description of a parcel of real property so that its location can be accurately determined; generally based upon the government survey system or a metes and bounds system.

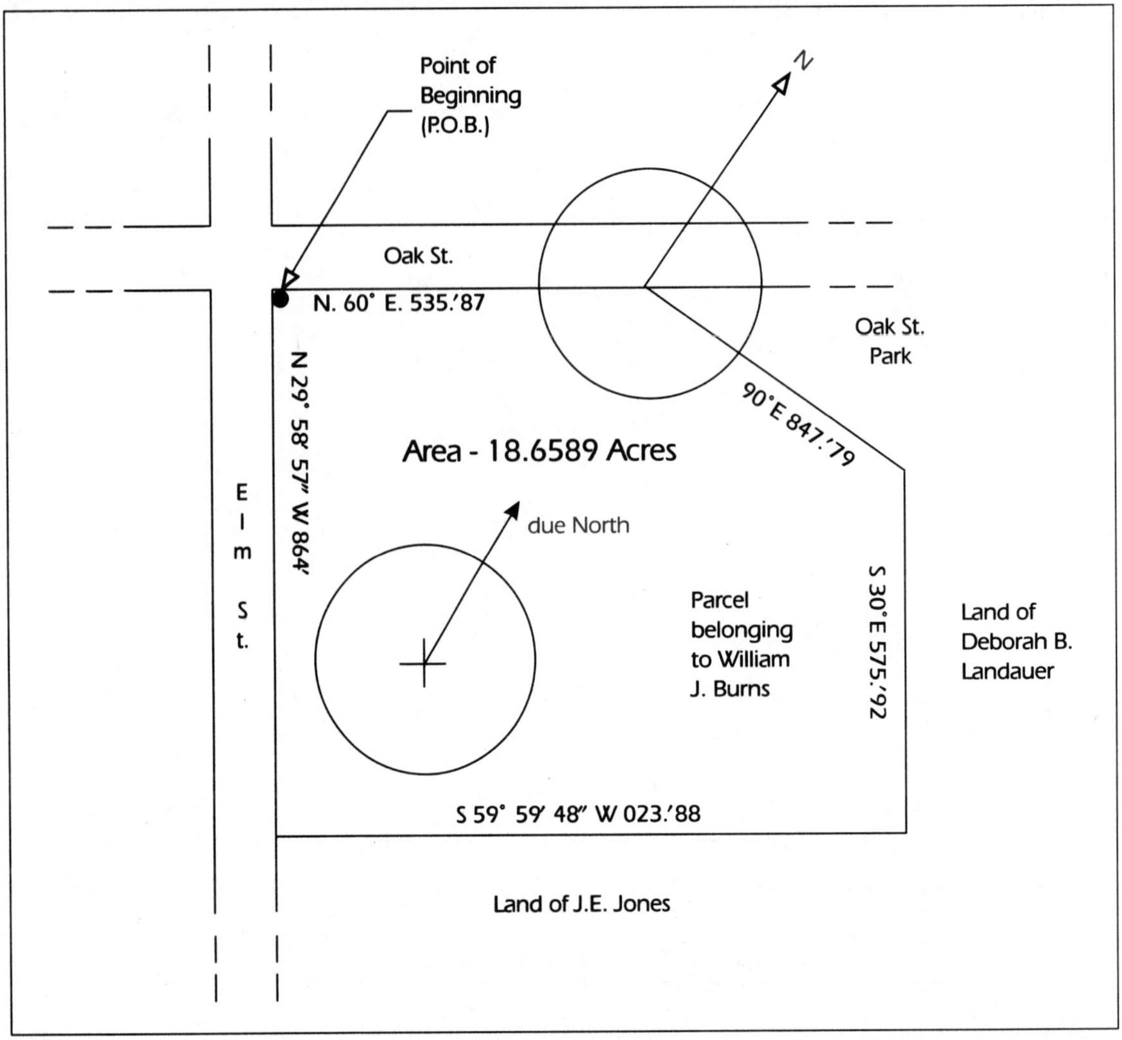

Note: This map is square on the page, for reading ease, but the compass shows the direction of true north. At each point, the compass is laid down and a line is drawn to the next point. The direction of that line is what the reading is—here 90 degrees east—while the following numbers are the distance, 847'79. Do not confuse the marking " "—it means seconds on the compass direction but feet in the distance measurement.

FIGURE 2-4
A metes and bounds parcel description

[Containing an hypothetical measurement per a fictional survey dated August 32, 1908, of David Lloyd George 18.6589 acres. Trail's End, Illinois.]

Today, artificial objects, such as streets, fences, or stakes, have been added to natural objects as points of reference. Both types are referred to as

monuments. This method is not favored because it does not remain precise. Monuments can change. It is not used frequently today and is used primarily when the value of the property is not great. When using a monument, care should be taken to be very specific and detailed so that as much information as possible will remain available for future identification.

The **rectangular or government survey system** covers much of the United States. See figure 2-5.

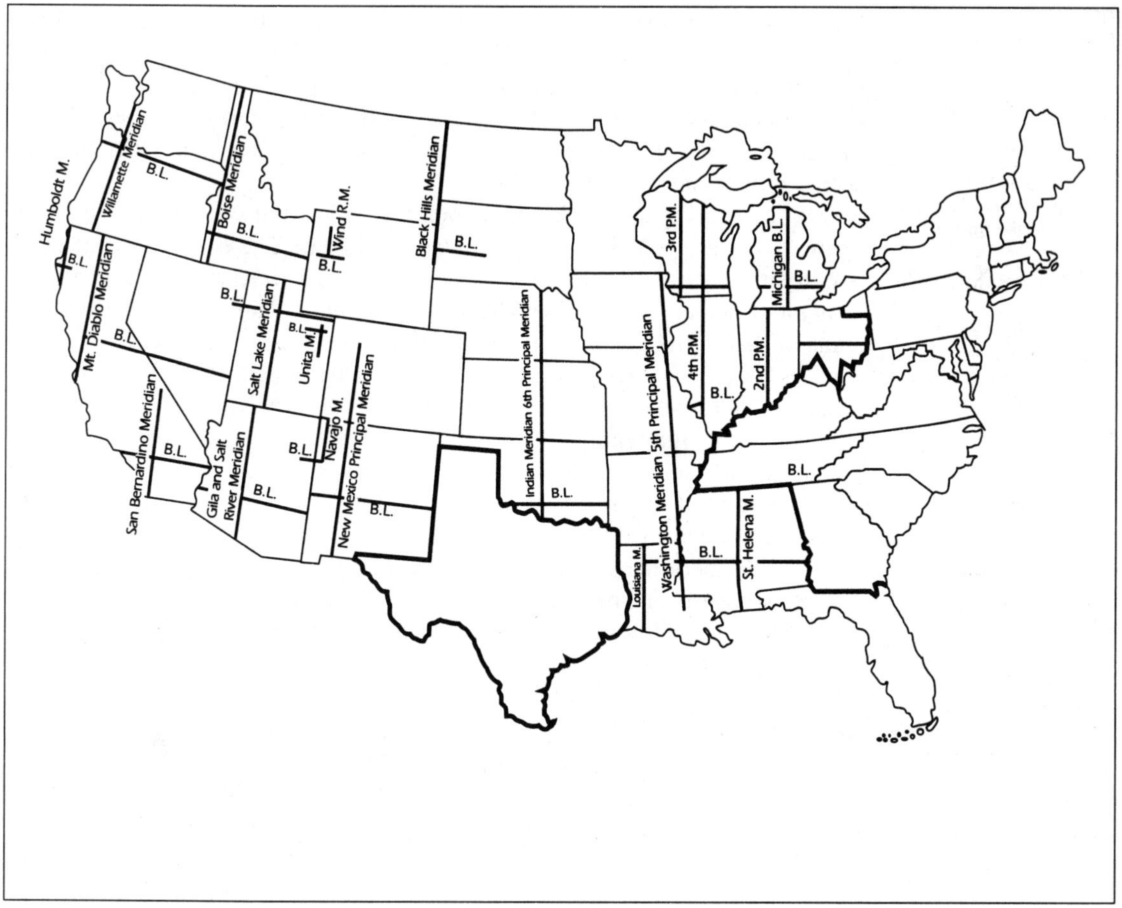

Checks or quadrangles (24 mi. × 24 mi.) = 576 sq. mi.
16 townships = 1 check (6 mi. × 6 mi. = 36 sq. mi.)
36 sections = 1 township
1 section = 640 acres
1 sq. mile = 640 acres

FIGURE 2-5

Map of the United States showing layout of the surveying system called the "government survey" or "rectangular survey" method (not used in all areas). Not all meridians and base lines shown.

Property Described as Numbered Lot in Subdivided Government Survey Section

All that tract or parcel of land known as Lot No. _________, of Section _________, Township _________ *[number],* Range _________ *[number]* _________, *[East]* of the _________ Principal Meridian as the section is subdivided on a plat registered on Page _________ of Book _________ in the recorder's office of County of _________, State of _________.

The federal government created this system to encourage settlement in the old Northwest Territories (parts of Ohio and all of Indiana, Illinois, Michigan, and Wisconsin) in the 1780s. The area was immense, and the settlement was done slowly over the next 50 years. To ensure that the hundreds of thousands of settler landowners (who were voters) had clear title to their property, this system had to be accurate, precise, and verifiable by a surveyor at any time.

The survey system is based upon the standard global grid, shown in figure 2-6, that consists of parallels and meridians. The survey system determines the base lines (parallels) and meridians. The intersection of a base line and a principal meridian is selected. The system is laid out as follows: Starting at that initial intersection point, the surveyors measure 24 miles north, 24 miles west, 24 miles south, and 24 miles east until they have enclosed an area of 576 square miles. This largest of the surveying boxes is called a **check** or a **quadrangle**. It is broken down into sixteen **townships** of 6 miles on a side or 36 square miles each. Each township is broken down into 36 **sections** of one square mile each, and each section is broken down into 640 **acres**. See figure 2-7.

The meridians, as can be seen on the global grid, all converge on the poles so that their lines curve toward each other. To avoid the problem of declining distance toward the poles, guide meridians are set at 24-mile intervals east and west from the principal meridian and are adjusted at every standard parallel north or south of the base line. In this manner, each check is corrected at its boundaries so that it remains close to square. The effect, shown on the map in figure 2-6, is exaggerated so that it can be seen more easily.

Each section is designated by its position in relation to the base line and principal meridian. The designation in north-south terms is by **tiers**, as in Tier 1 North of the base line; the designation in east-west terms is by **ranges**, as in Range 4 West of the Third Principal Meridian. Tier 1 North of the base line simply means that the townships that sit directly north of the base line are in the first tier or layer north of it. Tier 2 North would be the second layer north; Tier 3 South would be the third layer south of the base line. The same process works for the ranges east and west of the Principal Meridian. See figure 2-7.

Each township has 36 sections of one square mile each, and each square mile has 640 acres in it. In figure 2-8, the numbering of those sections is laid out and shown in relation to the adjacent sections in the adjoining

LEGAL TERMS

monument
Object or location that is obvious enough and permanent enough to be used in a metes and bounds description, such as a large rock or mature tree.

government or rectangular survey system
Method the American government began using in the 1780s to survey the American west (at that time, Ohio); used throughout most of the United States.

check or quadrangle
Largest type of measurement in the government survey system; 24 miles on a side or 576 square miles.

township
Chief unit of the rectangular survey system; 36 square miles or 6 miles on a side; the political unit, a township, comes from this surveying unit.

section
Area within a township that is one square mile; there are 36 sections in a township.

acre
Surface land measurement of 43,560 square feet; term *builder's acre* means 40,000 square feet.

tier
Term from the rectangular survey system that refers to the positioning of townships north or south of a principal surveying meridian, called a *base line.*

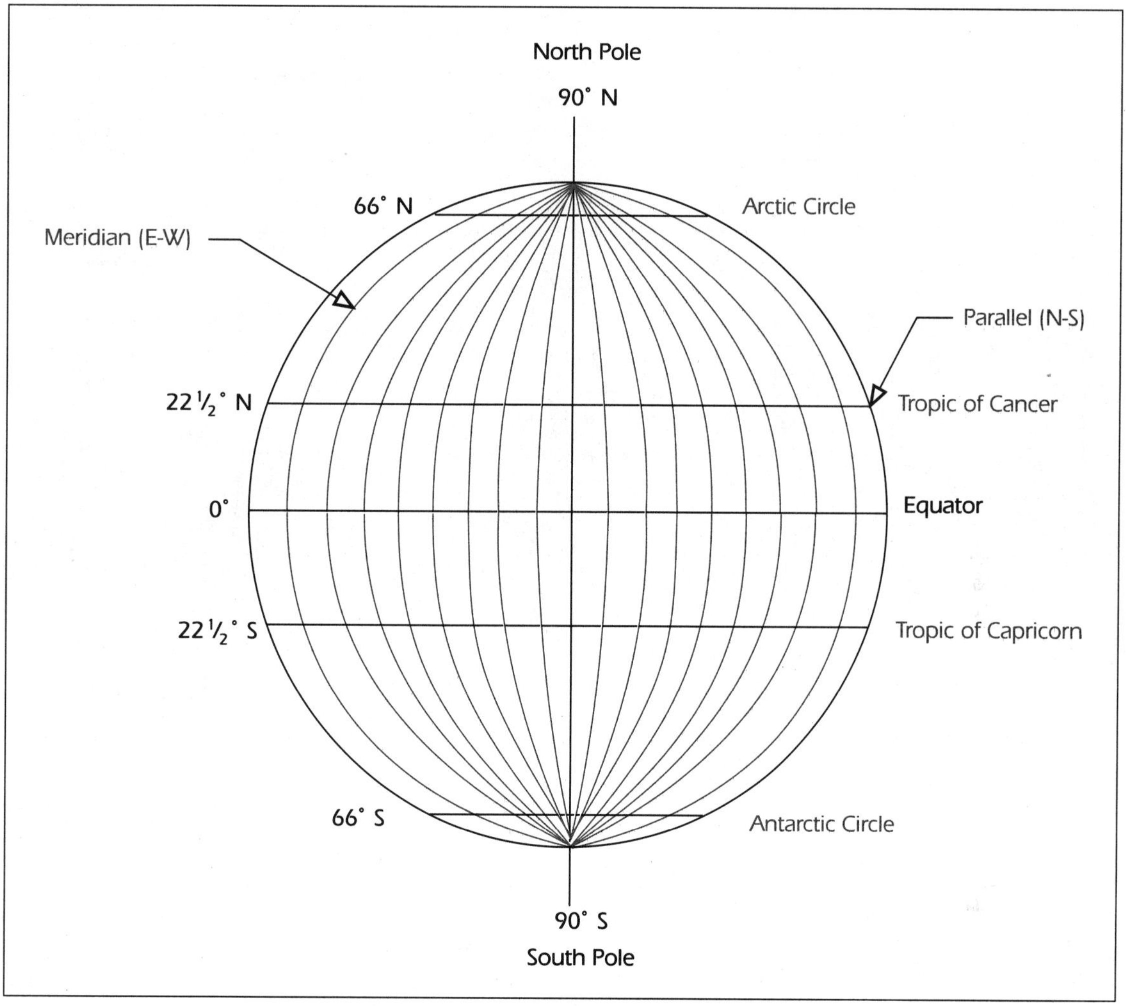

FIGURE 2-6
Global map grid

townships. A legal description begins by identifying the smallest possible area that describes the property and then shows its placement in successively larger patterns. For instance, "the northern one-half of the northeast one-quarter of the northeast one-quarter of Section 3, Tier 3 South, Range 3 East of the Third Principal Meridian, in ________ County, State of . . . ." Note how the section, range, and tier are used to describe the general area. Now that the section can be identified, a different system is used within the section. That system is based on the 640 acres in the section and is described in figure 2-9.

range
Term used in the rectangular survey system to refer to a piece of land that runs parallel to a meridian; it is six miles wide and goes north and south, but is numbered and referred to as being east or west of the meridian.

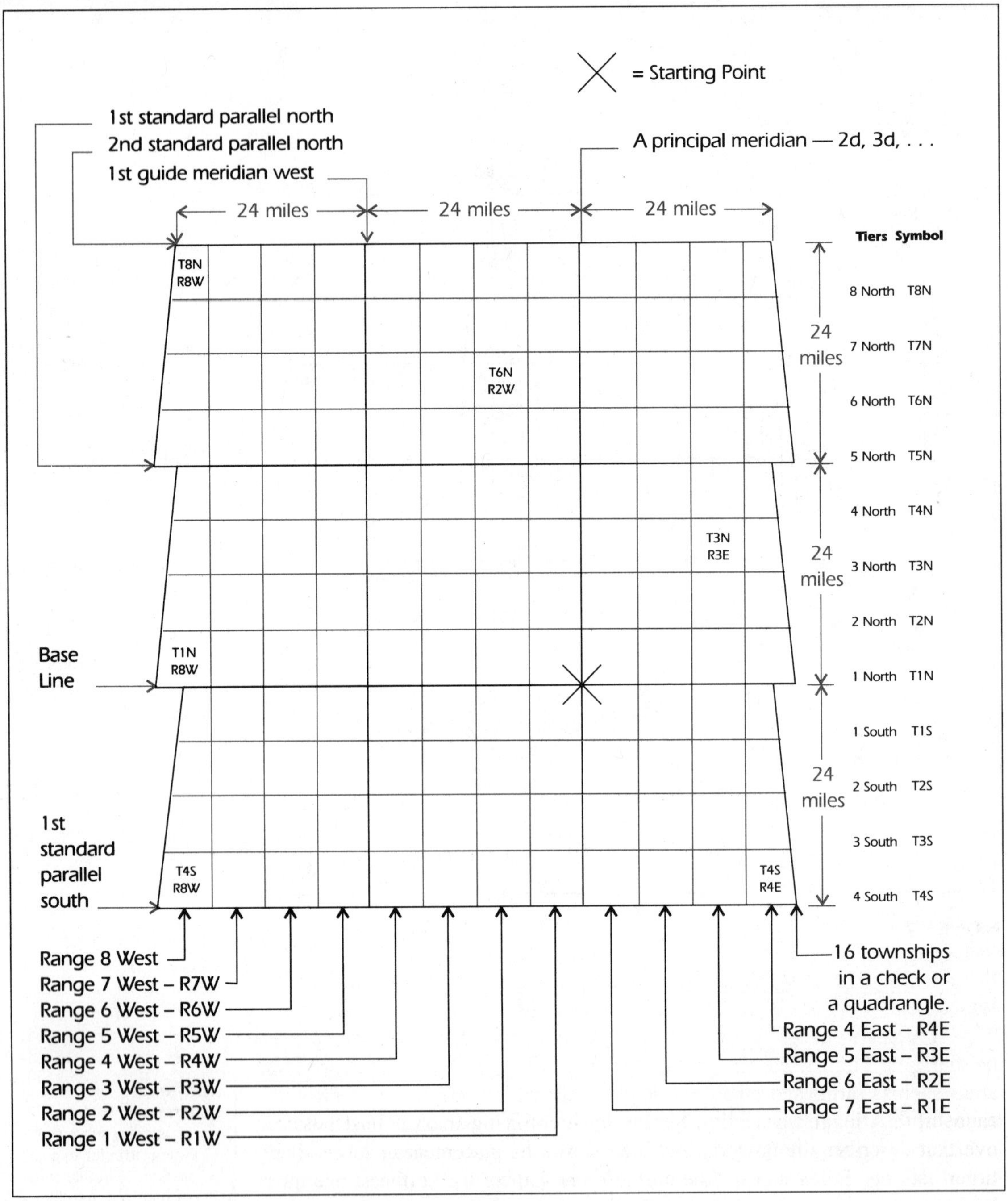

FIGURE 2-7
The large-scale mapping to create quadrangles (checks)

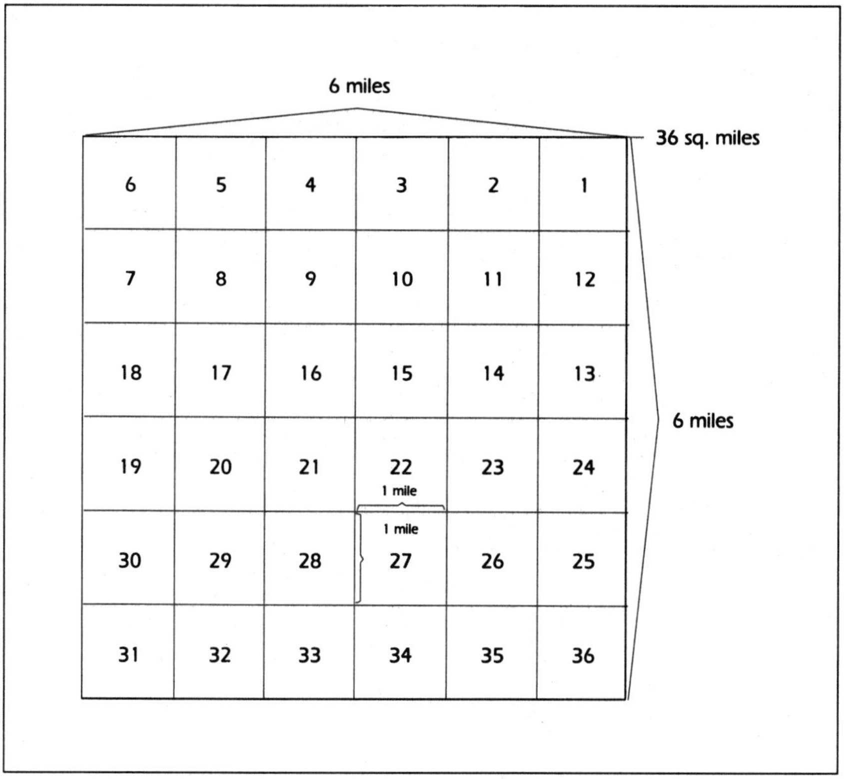

FIGURE 2-8
A township with its 36 numbered sections

The first step is to quarter the 640 acres into 160-acre units. These are simply described as the northwest, northeast, southeast, or southwest quarters of the section. Each quarter section is then again broken down into quarters or halves. A half of a quarter section would have 80 acres in it; a quarter of a quarter section would have 40 acres. Those quarter sections of quarter sections can themselves be divided into quarters, in the same manner, so that there are 10-acre units. One-half of those units would be five acres. Note the logic of the progression to the smaller units. See figure 2-8.

There are several aspects of the government survey system that should be clarified. First, while the government survey system works well for large areas such as farms and ranches, it is very awkward to use in urban areas, because of the tiny portions of real estate owned by one person. This problem is overcome by using both the governmental survey system and another, additional device, called a plat of survey. For example, suppose a large area of land, say 40 acres, that can be identified on the governmental survey system as the SE¼ of the SE¼ of an identified section is going to be developed into homes. The developer buys that parcel of land and hires a surveyor, who lays the 40 acres out into blocks that are bounded by streets. Within each block, lots of the homes are surveyed and their boundaries are established. The surveyor

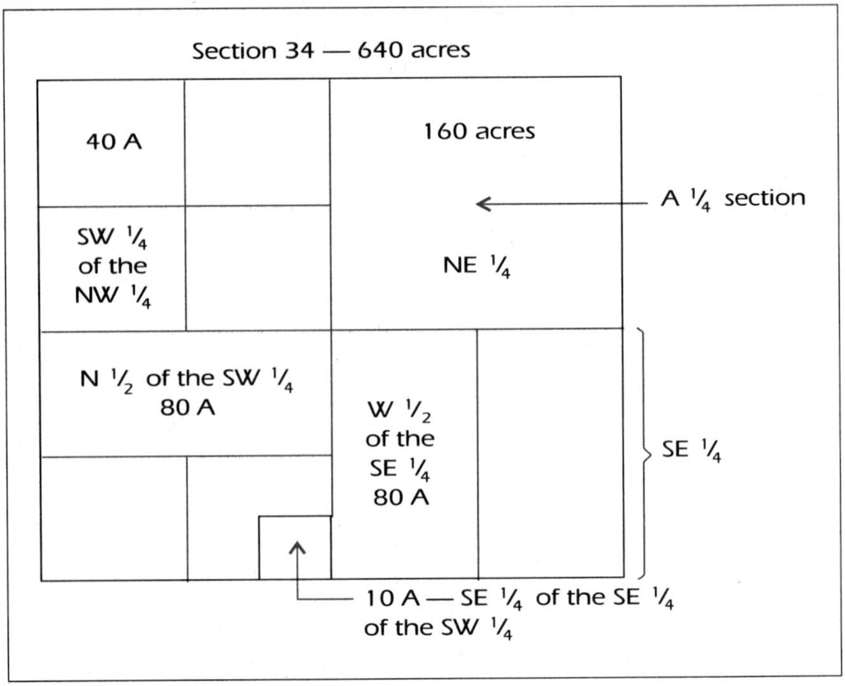

FIGURE 2-9
A section

1 mile × 1 mile = 1 sq. mile
5,280 feet × 5,280 feet = 27,878,400 sq. feet
1,760 yards × 1,760 yards = 3,097,600 sq. yards
27,878,400 sq. feet divided by 640 acres = 43,560
3,097,600 sq. feet divided by 640 acres = 4840
43,650 sq. feet = 1 acre
4840 sq. yards = 1 acre
Notice: Each part is quartered—
640 acres divided by 4 = 160 acres
160 acres divided by 4 = 40 acres
40 acres divided by 4 = 10 acres
Quarters are combined into halves: for example, a ½ section = 320 acres.

identifies the blocks and the lots by a numbering system. The developer might name the area "Buena Vista." The surveyor prepares a map that shows all this information plus where the sewers, power, gas, and other utilities will be placed, and other information that will be needed for this development. This map is called a *plat of survey* and is recorded in the local office where deeds are recorded. The legal description of a particular lot might begin: "Lot 6 in Block 5 in Buena Vista, a subdivision of the SE¼ of the SE¼ of Section 12 of Township 4. . . ."

After the area has been broken down under the government survey method into smaller areas, usually less than 20 acres, surveyors come in, measure each lot, and show its boundaries, as well as identifying the buildings, the locations of utilities and other easements and deed restrictions, and the position of necessary items such as access roads. This **plat of survey** (sometimes also called the **lot and block method**) becomes the final breakdown of area, unless there is vacant land in the plat that can be further subdivided. The plat assigns numbers to lots, a name for the subdivision, and includes the date of the survey, the name of the surveyor, and the name of the subdivider. The plat may also show the date that official approval for the subdivision was received. Finally, it is recorded in the local real estate records (usually at the county level). Thus, having started with an area of thousands of square miles, we have reached a precise and accurate description of lot and house within a city. See figure 2-10.

Property Described by Reference to Recorded Plat

> Lots numbered __________ and __________, Block __________, ________ subdivision, in the City of _______, County of ________, State of _________, a plat of which has been previously filed in the office of the ______ of the County of ________, on _______, 19___ which plat covers a portion of the ________ of Section _________, Township _______ *[number]*, Range _______ *[number]* ________ *[East/West]* of the ________ Principal Meridian.

Second, in addition to this type of subdivision plat, there is also a condominium plat. A **condominium** is an ownership arrangement in a multi-unit building whereby the units are owned individually, rather than the entire building being owned and the units being rented. The condominium ownership arrangement should not be confused with the **planned unit development (PUD)**. In the condominium ownership pattern, the unit owners own their individual units and, as tenants in common, they each have ownership rights in the common areas. Technically, it may be said that the owner owns his or her unit in fee simple and shares ownership as a tenant in common with the other unit owners in the common areas. In the PUD, although the living space unit is owned separately, the common areas are owned by a separate not-for-profit corporation in which each unit owner has a certain number of shares. Either type, condo or PUD, may be a subdivision or a large building and may involve complex surveying descriptions of the vertical and horizontal planes, such as walls, floors, and ceilings. Both types of plats of survey would eventually be recorded and would show the same types of items as previously described, such as the owner's and surveyor's names and any deed restrictions.

Third, the government survey system lacks a capacity to describe odd-shaped or incomplete areas; areas, for example, next to a river or a lake. To describe these irregular-sized areas, a metes and bounds description is added onto the end of the government survey area. Somewhere on that line, a point of beginning is taken and a surveyor describes the area until the line returns to the point of beginning.

Fourth, elevation must also be dealt with. The basic elevation measurement that has been agreed upon is the mean sea level of the harbor of New York City. That element is considered 0° elevation or 0° sea level for the United

LEGAL TERMS

plat of survey
Results of a surveyor's work that shows specifically where a group of properties in a development are on a map. The detailed descriptions of the individual properties are shown and the development is tied into the general surveying system.

lot and block method
Same as plat of survey method.

condominium
Complete, individual ownership of a unit within a multi-unit building, together with common ownership of shared elements such as walkways and laundry rooms. Usually a residential type of ownership; based upon air rights.

planned unit development (PUD)
Real estate development that is planned for multiple types of uses, such as residential, commercial, recreational, or industrial in some combination.

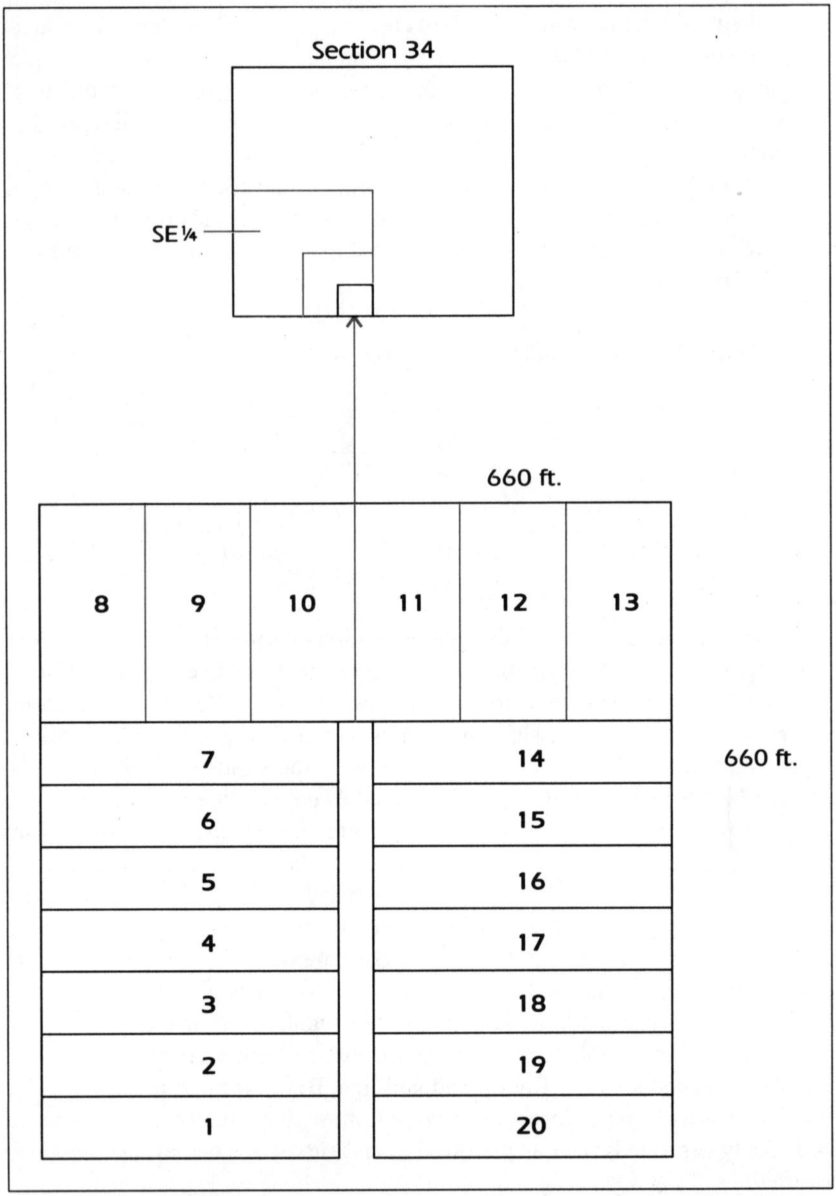

FIGURE 2-10
A subdivision plat of Benson's Acres, Roosevelt County, Ohio

SE ¼ of the SE ¼ of the SW ¼ of Section 34. This unit is 10 acres, 435,600 sq. ft., or 660 feet on both sides. See figure 2-9.

States. To avoid having to return to New York City for each measurement, certain locations in each major city are precisely measured for elevation by a surveyor and an elevation **datum** is established. This **benchmark** shows the elevation at that point and avoids immense amounts of remeasuring. Benchmarks are spread throughout cities to aid surveying and are often embedded in sidewalks on brass plaques. The U.S. Geodetic Survey will provide the locations of benchmarks when requested. Practically, knowing the correct elevation affects setting the height limits of buildings and determines the proper vertical spacing in condominiums.

Fifth, although much more will be said in chapter 3 about patterns of ownership, it must be understood that there are multiple and complex rights concerning the land. Essentially, one owns the land from the center of the earth to the surface boundaries, and vertically from those boundaries upwards. In the Middle Ages and in early modern times, these rights went as far as ad coelum, to the sky, but today there are severe restrictions on the extent and use of these rights. Thus, beneath the soil (**subsurface rights**), there are rights to minerals, water, oil, and other natural resources. On the surface, there are multiple rights. Above the surface (**air rights**), one has rights to air and sunlight, among others. Another area that should be recognized is water rights. These are either **riparian rights** or **littoral rights**. Riparian rights deal with ownership along a river, stream, or lake; littoral rights relate to property adjacent to large and navigable lakes and oceans. With increasing concern about the environment, air, water, and subsurface rights are becoming more important.

Finally, the overall question of what real property is must be addressed. Historically, land was the only source of everything that was good. It provided political power, wealth, food, clothing, and shelter. Even movable things, if they related to the land, were seen as part of that land. Gradually, however, a distinction between real property and personal property developed. **Real property** came to mean anything that is land or permanently attached to the land, such as a building. **Personal property** came to mean anything that was not attached to the land; basically, it became anything that could be moved. An item's capacity to move (such as animals) or to be moved (such as bricks or concrete blocks) became the key element in determining whether it was or was not personal property.

2.3 FIXTURES

One category of property, a *fixture,* remains a difficult category to understand and to handle in the law, because it blurs the distinctions between real and personal property. Technically, a **fixture** is a piece of personal property that is so closely attached to real property that it ceases to be personal property; it becomes so much a part of the real property that it is inseparable from the real property. But, unfortunately, when that happens, how it happens, and why it happens frequently is not clear. A fixture begins its life as a piece of personal property, but through use it becomes a part of the real property. Thus, the law that governs that particular item initially is the law of personal property, but once the item has been attached to or associated with a piece of real estate, it becomes part of the real estate and is subject to the law of real estate. The legal issue usually is whether the item of personal property has become so irremediably attached to the real property that it has become

LEGAL TERMS

datum
Point from which height and depth can be measured; sea level is often used to provide the altitude from which to measure.

benchmark
Surveyor's mark used to determine a basic elevation from which other measurements of height can be made thereafter; often embedded in a brass circle on street corners of major cities.

subsurface rights
Type of rights an owner has in real property; usually refers to such items as water, gas, oil, minerals, and other natural resources; said to continue from the surface boundaries to the center of the earth.

air rights
Landowner's rights that begin above the surface of the land owned and extend, in theory, infinitely; connected with rights to sunlight; limited today by transportation (airplanes), communications (radio and television broadcasts), and adjacent owners' easements and other rights.

riparian rights
Owner's rights to the real property next to a body of water and rights to access to the water.

part of the real property and is now real property itself. It is easy to see that there could be many conflicts in this area.

The parties in conflict are those who claim an interest in the disputed piece of property. These parties are either (1) the financiers-lenders who supplied the money to purchase the fixture (the security interest holder or the secured party) or to purchase the building (the mortgage holder or the mortgagee), or (2) the landlord-building owner, or (3) the tenant. Residential examples of fixtures could be the new wall-to-wall carpeting or the under-the-counter dishwasher that a tenant has installed. But most fixture disputes deal with commercial items, usually equipment, because these items have a higher value. Ultimately, the question is whether the item must be left behind when the tenants leave, because it is a fixture and thus part of the real estate, or whether the tenants may take it with them as an item of personal property.

Consider the following business example. A businessperson leases a building for manufacturing industrial equipment. A tool-stamping machine is brought into the factory dismantled and is assembled in-house. It is bolted to the floor. It cost $575,000 and has a 25-year life span. After five years, the manufacturer finds a better location and plans to remove the machine, but the landlord sues and claims that the machine is a fixture and a permanent part of the building. Who wins? Now, add to the complexity the fact that the manufacturer is financing the machine through a bank or some other long-term commercial financier, and that party has a perfected security interest in the machine. Finally, add the element that the landlord is buying the building on time and that mortgagee-lender regards the machine as an asset that belongs to the building. The mortgagee has a recorded mortgage on the property that covers any additions to the real property as assets included in the mortgage.

It is easy to see that this area of legal conflict between personal property and real property law could lead to confusing and inconsistent decisions. The primary tests of whether a piece of personal property (usually equipment) has become a fixture are (1) how it is attached; (2) the manner of its adaption; and (3) the intent the parties indicated at the time of attachment. The *attachment issue* is whether the item has become so much a part of the building that it is essential to the building's use. Windows and heating ducts are examples of fixtures in buildings; a building cannot be used without them. The *adaption issue* is how specifically tailored the piece of equipment is to the building. Screen and storm windows and curtains cut for that particular window both serve as examples of fixtures. In addition, if a building were constructed around a particular piece of heavy industrial equipment, the equipment would appear to be a fixture. The *intention issue* deals with what the parties thought would be the use of the piece of property, and it is the most important single determinant of whether an item is a fixture. Whatever the parties agreed upon (it is hoped in writing) settles the issue. Risks arise when no one agrees upon what that piece of personal property will be *before* it is installed.

When no prior agreement exists, the other two tests (and a number of others) apply. Recently, to end the confusion over fixtures, some courts have adopted a rule that says an item is not a fixture if it can be removed by "one man in one hour with a simple (appropriate to the job) set of tools." It is important to remember, however, that the courts cannot determine the true intent of the parties in most cases that are litigated. The courts, therefore, use a legal construct called a "reasonable person." The issue frequently is: With these particular facts, what would a reasonable person have intended? The tests of attachment and adaption are used at this point. The newly suggested test might work well with small items, but often large and expensive items of industrial equipment cannot be so removed. Under that test, then, all large, industrial items would automatically be fixtures.

These fixture problems can be resolved prior to installation of the equipment. If there are other claimants to the property, a written agreement should be reached with them wherein their rights are clearly delineated. Many times, a landlord will waive its rights to repossess under a lien for unpaid rent on all the tenant's property. Further, the lessor may agree that any piece of equipment is not a fixture and that it is removable to induce the tenant to use the property. Although the tenant may not be concerned about these waivers, in a commercial transaction, the tenant's banker will want them, because without these waivers, the landlord's lien for unpaid rent and the lender's lien on equipment or inventory may come into conflict if the tenant-borrower does not meet its obligations. If a creditor of the landlord has an interest in the leased building, that mortgagee should waive its rights in any piece of property that could become a fixture. In this way, serious litigation problems can be avoided. Nevertheless, the problem and its risks must be recognized prior to the purchase and installation of the equipment, and the steps necessary to obtain written waivers should be taken at that time.

It is essential, however, not to confuse a true fixture with a **trade fixture**. Trade fixtures are the property of a business tenant who places them in the building, but their method of attachment is so much less permanent that the law does not consider them really to be fixtures. Generally, trade fixtures are items such as shelves, display cases, and counters. Trade fixtures are personal property and remain the tenant's property. A real fixture added or affixed to the building by a tenant, however, would become the property of the landlord and would remain behind when the tenant moved out at the end of the lease. An item that has created a considerable amount of litigation in the last 15 to 20 years is the air-conditioning unit for a computer room. Central air conditioning is clearly a fixture; detachable window air conditioners generally are not fixtures. Where does this one fit? It could go either way, but it might turn on whether the air-conditioning system uses regular building wiring or has special wiring for its electricity. The issue is too complex to discuss in full at this point, but be alert to this type of situation, where such problems can arise, so that they can be prevented before litigation is needed. Being alert to this type of problem can mean that a client's needs are met and conflict or unnecessary litigation are avoided. Use the appropriate drafting when the relationship is created—that is, *before* the new tenant moves in, *before* the borrower gets the loan, and so on.

LEGAL TERMS

littoral rights
Rights along a shoreline: (1) a landowner's claim to use the bodies of water adjacent to his or her property; and (2) the landowner's rights to the land adjacent to such shores up to the high water mark.

real property
Land and that bundle of rights, interests, and responsibilities that comprise an estate holder's ownership.

personal property
Originally, any property that was not real property and, generally, was movable; today, still movable, but divided into tangible and intangible types.

fixture
Personal property that has become so attached to real property that it has become part of the real property and is considered real property itself.

trade fixture
Item of personal property that a business tenant installs in the building space it has leased; not permanently attached to the real property and generally removable by the tenant when the lease ends.

Finally, **mobile homes** must be considered. They should remain personal property so long as they are mobile. Once they are permanently set in place, however, they may cease to be mobile enough to be personal property. The issue could be the extent of their immobility. Attachment to gas and power lines, sewage connections, affixing the unit to blocks and removing the wheels—all of these may happen. Does becoming a fixture require all of them? Does it require only one of them? Or is some combination of them necessary? Could renting versus owning the parking space make any difference? Could the requirement of special hauling equipment for large mobile homes make a difference? The ability to make these distinctions will depend on understanding the cases in your particular jurisdiction. In this area of fixture law, there are frequently differences among the various states, and sometimes even within one state. Finally, the determination of whether the mobile home is real or personal property also makes a difference as to how it is taxed—tax rates may differ substantially on real and personal property.

2.4 RECORDING REAL ESTATE DOCUMENTS IN THE PUBLIC RECORDS

Although a parcel of land may be properly described, it is necessary that no other party interested in that parcel or the owner of any adjacent property be misled. Parties who have a need to know about a parcel include the government authorities for taxing, zoning, and other public purposes, prospective creditors, prospective buyers, utility companies, and a number of others. In order to protect their interests in their property, landowners will want to **record** their interest, that is, to make a public record of their interests, rights, and claims to that particular piece of property by **filing** or recording the appropriate documents with the local public official who keeps real estate records. This action provides others with **constructive notice** of the interests and, when others have claims on the property, their recording of their interests provides landowners with constructive notice of those claims.

What documents are most commonly recorded? The first document would be the one that gives the owner its rights in the property, a *deed.* If there is (2) a plat of survey, that document is also recorded by the developer who had the plat created to define the boundaries of the property being developed. The plat of survey may include (3) a group of restrictions that limit the use of the land in the subdivision. Fourth, the claims of third parties must be recorded. These are usually the claims of creditors, such as persons who do work on the property, who can file notice of (5) mechanic's liens, or the lender who financed the purchase of the home with a (6) note and (7) mortgage. Hereafter, the list of documents that can be filed is endless.

Although one can show **actual notice** to the world that one has an interest in the property by occupying and possessing the property, that activity is not always possible. As a result, a system has been devised whereby recording documents showing interests in a the parcel of real property with the local public official who handles real estate establishes constructive notice.

LEGAL TERMS

mobile home
Truck-like vehicle with facilities that make it into occupiable quarters; originally mobile, but when stationary, its wheels may be removed, it may be placed on blocks, and it becomes immobile—a result that may make it a fixture.

This process has created a system whereby everyone can both have notice from others and provide notice to others. The constructive notice of the real estate recording system is much safer, easier, and more consistent than an actual notice system. The public real estate records are designed to show who has what claims to title in any piece of real property. These records cover transferring, assigning, mortgaging, or any other acts that affect ownership or use of real property. This public notice also prevents any hidden liens or unpleasant surprises.

There are a number of different recording systems that must be checked to determine who has claims on the real property. There is a system called the *grantor-grantee index* (also called a "cross index," because it cross-references various parties with claims to the property). It shows who has had the title to and interests in the searched parcel of real estate up to the present. Thus, a title search can be done from this system. The grantor gives title to the grantee; in the next transfer, that grantee becomes the grantor to a subsequent grantee. This system is indexed alphabetically on the last names of the grantor and the grantee.

The *tract system* is based on the property's legal description. Each transaction is tied to a specific legal description, often under a subdivision that has various numbered lots, each of which has a separate entry. Each successive owner is listed under that entry.

Creditors' mortgages are usually filed in a *mortgagor-mortgagee index,* although sometimes they are filed directly in the grantor-grantee index. The lien document (mortgage or deed of trust) is filed, and when the lien is satisfied, a satisfaction or release is filed. Often, the mortgagee-creditor returns the satisfaction or release to the mortgagor-debtor and lets the former debtor file the document.

Another real estate recordkeeping system in urban areas shows all of the plats of survey and the plans for development in each area. It can be closely tied into a tract system, and has the advantage of allowing one to determine what the boundaries of the property are, what buildings are on it, and what easements affect the property.

Finally, there are *fixture filings* in the real property records. Under Article 9 of the **Uniform Commercial Code** (UCC), the law that governs most personal property transactions, including personal property that may become a fixture, filings for fixtures are to be made in the real estate records where a mortgage would be filed. Special care should be taken at this point, because in many states there is a special form for this filing (a Form UCC-2 financing statement filing form). It has additional requirements beyond the normal financing statement form (UCC-1). Those requirements are that (1) the name of the property owner of record be included, if the owner is not the debtor, and (2) the real property description must be included. That description is the formal legal description, not just a street address. Often the wrong filing form is used and so the proper information is not provided. This is particularly a problem when the omitted information is the legal description, because it is often impossible to complete the filing without that information.

recording
Delivery to a public official of documents relating to real estate for inclusion in the public records; similar to filing on personal property, but recording relates to real property.

filing
Act of placing a document with a public official for inclusion in the public records.

constructive notice
Type of notice based upon recorded information; once information is publicly recorded, it is considered to provide notice to any rational person who, knowing of the system, would use it to determine certain information, such as liens on the property involved in a proposed transaction.

actual notice
Legal requirement that a party really receive the information; contrasted with constructive notice.

Uniform Commercial Code
Important civil code in American law; regulates and makes uniform among the states the law of secured transactions and law concerning the sale of goods and commercial paper. When personal property is involved in a real estate transaction, the UCC may govern it.

The problem is so widespread, however, that some filing officials have begun to maintain a separate record of UCC filings in their real estate recording offices. Nevertheless, that accommodation does not appear to provide a legally correct filing, although it is possible that many parties would be able to obtain constructive notice from the accommodation system. This situation is part of the continuing development of the law and most likely will be resolved through litigation.

In addition to the foregoing title records, there are additional records that relate to real property rights. Various taxing authorities, ranging from the federal and state governments to local authorities (and including a bewildering number of governmental agencies), can impose special assessments for projects that affect the parcel of real property. Suits may be pending in courts that have jurisdiction over the owner or over the property, so one must make a **lis pendens search** (against the court records of lawsuits filed that might affect the specific parcel of land). There can be special property use restrictions from zoning boards, construction and building codes, land use plans, environmental requirements, and subdivision limitations and regulations. Checking these records is referred to as *searching the record.* It is essential to search and to have searches current at the time of any transfer. Most times title is "brought down" one last time on the day of closing to ensure there are no impediments to the closing, such as last-minute surprises occurring after the initial search but before the actual closing and transfer of title.

2.5 THE TORRENS SYSTEM

In the late nineteenth century, an Australian, Sir Robert Torrens, invented a new system of providing public, constructive notice about real estate transactions. That system, named for him, is called the **Torrens System**. It is based on a pattern of ship registration in British maritime law and is used in a few areas of the United States, principally in large metropolitan areas such as New York City, Boston, Chicago, and Minneapolis-St. Paul, but Torrens statutes have been adopted in a number of states. In some urban areas, the Torrens system has proved to be so cumbersome, expensive, and lengthy, because of the required lawsuit, that many property owners dislike it intensely. In those areas, some parcels have been removed from Torrens.

Title to land in the Torrens System is transferred in a court proceeding wherein the landowner applies to the court for title transfer. To obtain the transfer, the landowner must present the court with an application listing all the parties that have interests in the land. A lawsuit is brought against each one of them. Any party to the suit may contest it. If the applicant proves he or she is the owner, the court so finds, lists the encumbrances and restrictions on the title, and orders an official called a *Registrar of Titles* to register the title. A certificate of title is issued and bound as a public record. The registrar gives the owner a duplicate certificate of title. Ownership, therefore, passes when the court orders registration, for the Torrens certificate is the title. No

LEGAL TERMS

lis pendens
"Pending suit"; a lis pendens search reveals lawsuits that have been filed (are pending) that might affect a parcel of land. Notice is filed to stop the landowner from selling the property during the dispute; this notice serves as constructive notice to third-party buyers of a legal claim potentially existing against the property.

search
Check of the public records to determine relevant information about property, who has claims on it, and what those claims are.

Torrens System
Method of registering the land itself; lawsuit establishes title and liens; status of title is shown on a certificate of title; title passes by registration; used in only a few areas of the United States; considered cumbersome by many.

mortgage, judgment, or lien is valid unless it is registered and noted on the certificate of title. This process can take years for each occurrence.

DISCUSSION AND REVIEW QUESTIONS

1. What is a fixture? How does a fixture relate to real property? To personal property? What risks are associated with fixtures? Name three items that would clearly be fixtures. Name three items that, under certain factual situations, could be disputed as to whether they were fixtures or not.
2. Explain how each of the following methods of land description works, in sufficient detail to be clear.
   a. The government survey method.
   b. The metes and bounds method.
   c. The plat of survey method.
3. What problems are there with any of the land description methods?
4. What is the purpose of recording statutes?
5. Describe the various types of recording systems discussed in this chapter.
6. What is the Torrens System and how does it work?
7. Explain how compass readings and map readings differ.
8. Tell the amount of acreage in each of the following legal descriptions:
   a. Southern half of the northwest quarter.
   b. Northwestern quarter of the southwestern quarter of the southwestern quarter.
   c. Eastern half of the northwestern quarter of the northeastern quarter.
   d. Northern half of the southwest quarter of the southeast quarter.
9. Using your understanding of a metes and bounds (surveying) description, create your own drawing, proportionately, with the appropriate directions and distances. Use a compass, maybe a protractor, and a T-square.

CHAPTER 3

The Legal Rules for Owning Real Property

"A lawyer's dream of heaven—every man reclaimed his property at the resurrection, and each tried to recover it from all his forefathers."

Samuel Butler

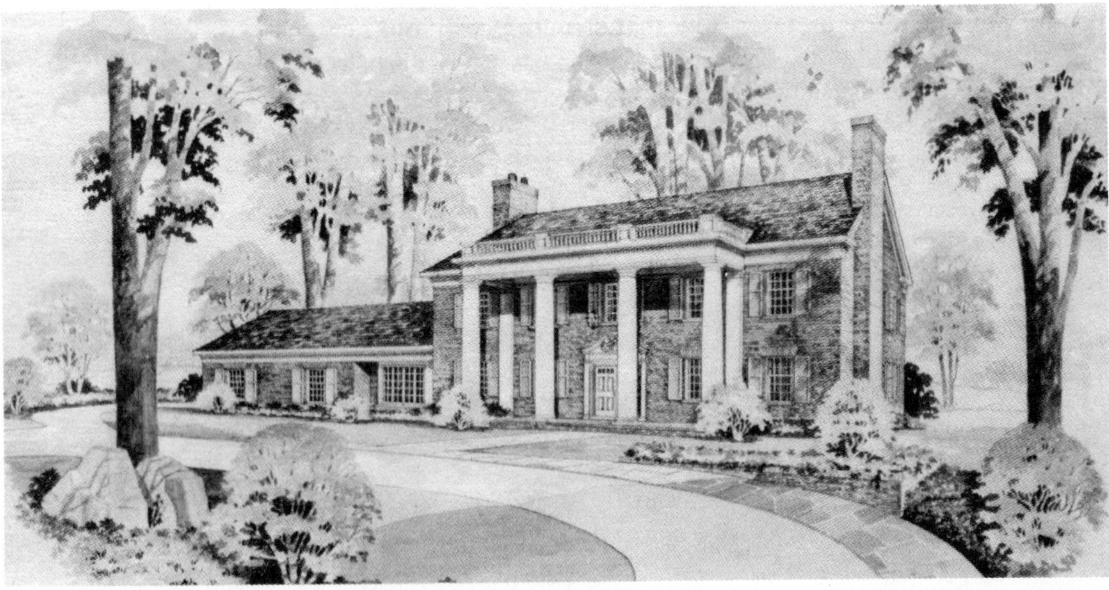

Southern Colonial home

OUTLINE

PROLOGUE TO THE PARALEGAL

Once we know the precise location of a parcel of real property, it is useful to know what rights the owner and others have in that parcel. This chapter will help you understand those rights. A separate chapter deals with the relationship between owners and the tenants to whom they have rented the use of the property for a period of time. This chapter focuses on the rights of owners and some third parties who have rights to use the land. It is important to keep in mind several aspects of these rights as you come to understand this material. The first aspect is: How extensive is my set of rights as owner? Second, how are my ownership rights limited? Third, how long do my rights last? Fourth, how far spatially (up, down, sideways) do my rights extend? Fifth, who else can make claims on my property, and for what purposes or reasons? This question ties into the limitations on ownership rights. Finally, what is the framework within which I must deal with others who have claims on (usually the use of) my property? These topics, plus ownership that involves more than one person and successor interests in the ownership after death or transfer of the property, constitute the core of this chapter. In your work, knowing some of this chapter's terminology, such as "fee simple," will have applications from closing to doing research.

KEY TERMS

assignment
community property
concurrent ownership
conditional fee

condominium
cooperative
constructive eviction
contingent remainder
curtesy
deed
dominant tenement
dower
easement appurtenant
easement in gross
estate
estate for years
fee simple absolute
fee simple on condition subsequent
freehold estate
future interests
joint tenancy with the right of survivorship
landlord
lease
leasehold
leasehold estate
license
life estate
life tenant
partition
periodic tenancy
possibility of reverter
profit à prendre
remainder
remainderman
reversion
right of reverter
right of survivorship
servient tenement
severance
sublease
tenant
tenancy
tenancy at sufferance
tenancy at will
tenancy by the entireties
tenancy in common
vested remainder
waste

3.1 INTRODUCTION

The rules governing the owning (sometimes called "holding") and transferring of real property are centuries old. Some go back to the early days of the Normans in England (shortly after 1066). Because almost a thousand years of legal history are involved, some of the terms have an antique feel to them. Definitions for these terms appear, as needed, in the margins throughout the chapter. Because most people know something about owning a home—or wanting to own a home—this chapter begins with the most common type of real estate ownership, that of one's home.

3.2 FREEHOLD INTERESTS: FEE ESTATES AND LIFE ESTATES

What does it mean to own one's own home? Does one really own it in the same way as a medieval baron did? Will that home really be a castle? The answer is yes—with some qualifications that may appear to imply no. The medieval baron owned his real property in **fee simple absolute** so long as he performed a duty to his overlord: to provide soldiers to fight in his overlord's wars. Later, this duty was changed to providing cash. (Aha! Real estate taxes! They began early and stayed with us.) The baron, the holder of the fee (simple absolute), originally owned everything on the real estate—the cattle, the trees, and the people. Today, movable property, such as cattle, are not real property. (People, of course, are no longer transferrable at all.) Instead, movable property is personal property, and in most situations separate contracts must be made to transfer ownership rights to personal property. (Deciding who gets the curtains and the refrigerator, for instance, in a home sale, can create conflict between the buyer and the seller. Watch for personal property items in real estate sales contracts.)

Today, the greatest interest one can own in real estate is still called a fee simple. The term *fee* comes from the medieval relationship and refers to the land itself; the land is called *the fee.* The rest of the term, *simple absolute,* means that the owner has all the rights belonging to that particular piece of land. The terms *fee simple absolute, fee simple,* and just *fee* mean that the possessor of that set of rights can sell or dispose of the land in any way he or she chooses. The most common ways in which this transfer can be done are:

1. By sale (the owner moves);
2. By gift (to a family member during the owner's lifetime, or after death by the owner's will);
3. By failure to pay an obligation such as a debt (that mortgage payment is monthly and the check had better be in the mail);
4. By government seizure for failure to pay taxes (the government gets its share to support various public purposes); and
5. For public purposes under eminent domain.

In cases three and four, the creditor or the government seizes and sells the property after complying with the appropriate legal procedures. Ownership rights, though apparently absolute, have significant limitations. But that has always been true, as opposed to the myth or romance of ownership, when ownership is examined closely.

Language in the **deed** (the document used to transfer the property) that creates a fee simple might be "I convey Blackacre to Sue Jones in fee simple" or "I give Blackacre to Linda West forever." Traditionally, a grant required language such as "to William J. Smith and his heirs"—the magic words "and his heirs" were necessary. Those words implied that the grant had no limits on the time or duration of the grant; that is, the grant was to last forever rather than for some shorter time such as the life of the grantee. That total grant through time would really happen if the land were transferred to heir after heir. Thus, only William and his heirs could ever claim the property (if the current owner did not transfer it to someone else in fee simple).

One's interest in real property is called an **estate**. The greatest estate—the estate with the most rights, with rights that are not significantly shared with anyone else, and with rights lasting forever—is the fee simple. Another closely related estate is described by a number of terms: a *fee simple defeasible,* a *conditional fee,* a *base fee,* or a *qualified fee.*

LEGAL TERMS

fee simple absolute
Maximum bundle of rights that a person can own in a particular piece of real property.

deed
Written document used to transfer real property.

estate
Generic term for describing the type of interest one has in a parcel of real property; in another context, can also mean a person's entire net worth.

The concept is simple. The property is transferred in fee simple, but the transfer is subject to a condition—thus, a **conditional fee** (the clearest term for this type of holding). If this condition occurs, the transferee will lose the fee (thus, a *fee simple defeasible*). Note that this type of estate involves two parties. The first is the fee holder, who owns the real property until the condition in the granting language is violated. The second (usually the grantor) may get it back, and is said to have a **possibility of reverter**; that is, the property may, if the condition is violated, come back to, or revert to, the grantor. Consider Joe Smith, who owns Blackacre in fee simple. He wants to give it to a charity, such as an art museum, but dislikes what he perceives as the growing commercialism (such as gift shops and art leasing activities) at museums. Smith therefore gives Blackacre to the charity "so long as there shall be no commercial activity conducted on Blackacre." The museum builds a magnificent building to house its art collection on Blackacre. Sometime later (and it could be many years), the museum's management forgets about the restrictions in the deed and moves the gift shop onto Blackacre. Blackacre would now, technically, revert to Smith or his heirs. The term **revert** means "to turn back," and with this type of fee, it is only a possibility that the property will return to Smith or his heirs; the condition must occur first—in this case, putting the gift shop on Blackacre.

The conditional clause can be used in different ways. For example, it may interest you to know that the tradition of passing on first names in colonial Virginia families has been preserved by the devise of land subject to a condition. That condition, in the 1600s, was that the first-born male child be named, say, "Arundel" Jones. In a society like colonial Virginia, which was based on land and family heritages, maintaining family names was important, and this property devise was used to support that system. Today, it is infrequently used, but it remains a potential tool in the grantor's arsenal.

Another type of estate is also closely related to the conditional fee. This estate is called a **fee simple upon condition subsequent**. It is a fee granted with a condition attached to the grant, but instead of having the grantor's interest be a possibility of reverter, the grantor's interest is called a *right of entry* or a *power of termination.* The distinction between the two estates is whether the estate granted terminates *automatically* upon violation of the condition in the granting language. If the estate automatically returns to the grantor, the estate is a conditional or a defeasible fee; if it does not return automatically, but requires the reversionary interest holder (the grantor or a taker from the grantor) to take some action to retrieve the property, it is a fee simple upon condition subsequent with a right of entry (or re-entry) as the reversionary interest.

It is not difficult to distinguish between these two in the language of the document, for the right of entry must be specified clearly. That language would read: "A grants Blackacre to B with the condition that there shall be no production of crops or any food products on Blackacre and if such activity shall occur, A shall have the right to re-enter Blackacre and take possession of it." Note the difference in the language and the resulting difference between the two types of reversionary interests: The first provides for an automatic ending of the granted estate when the condition in the grant is violated; the second requires the grantor (or the subsequent holder of the interest) to take the action of re-entering the land and taking possession. Naturally, these days that action requires a lawsuit to recover the property; people do not yield valuable assets readily. The reader should be aware that this estate, the fee simple upon condition subsequent, is very uncommon; the fee simple conditional is the much more common of the two because it is automatic and does not require any action by the party holding the reversionary interest. In short, the fee simple conditional is a cleaner and clearer legal device for all concerned.

In summary, there are three estates that are complete. They are the fee simple absolute, the fee simple upon condition subsequent, and the fee simple conditional. In these cases, the holder of the rights described by these terms has the greatest possible control over this estate. With the fee simple with condition subsequent and the conditional fee, though, an event may occur that violates the granting condition and, consequently, destroys the holder's interest in that estate and allows his or her interest to be taken away and the fee returned to the original grantor (or the grantor's heirs).

These three estates are called **freehold estates**; there is a fourth as well. It is the rights a person may hold during that person's life or the lifetime of another; it is called a **life estate**. Literally, the life estate exists so long as the named person is alive. After that person dies, the property often reverts, or goes back to, the grantor or his or her heirs. Here again, two parties are involved—the estate holder, called the **life tenant**, and the party to whom the property goes afterwards. After the life estate ceases, the property's owner becomes either the holder of a reversion or a **remainderman**.

The difference between these two is usually simple. The holder of a reversion is the original grantor or that grantor's heirs. In essence, the property goes back to the same party who granted it. But the *remainderman* (a traditional usage that may be changing to *remainder person*) is another party whom the grantor designates to take the property after the life estate ends. For example, Stephanie Boscowicz is concerned that her disabled sister, Susan, may be unable to take care of herself. Stephanie gives Whiteacre "to Susan, for her life." As there is no disposal of Whiteacre after Susan dies, the property goes back or reverts to Stephanie and her heirs, who hold a reversionary interest. But Stephanie could have granted Whiteacre "to Susan, for her life, and then to Elizabeth O'Malley and her heirs." In this case, Susan remains the life tenant, but Elizabeth is the remainderman and would take Whiteacre in fee simple when Susan died.

With all life estates, two parties are involved. There is the current estate holder, called the life tenant, and the future estate holder, who takes the property after the life tenant dies. That future taker is either the holder of the reversion or the remainderman. This situation raises two types of problems: (1) how does the life tenant transfer the property during his or her lifetime, and (2) what rights does the successor in interest have over the uses to which the life tenant puts the property? As to the first problem, the life

LEGAL TERMS

conditional fee
A fee simple with a condition that, if it occurs, will cause the owner to lose the property automatically, without the holder of the reversionary interest having to do anything; also called *fee simple defeasible, base fee*, or *qualified fee*.

possibility of reverter
Interest of the party who would take the property if the condition stated in the grant of a conditional fee occurred.

reversion
Right of the original owner or grantor, her heirs, or her transferees to have the property returned when the user's interest has expired.

fee simple upon condition subsequent
Estate where the reversionary interest holder must re-enter the property to regain ownership of that property; there is no automatic retransfer.

freehold estate
Estate in fee or a life estate.

life estate
Interest in a parcel of real property that a person has for the duration of his or her own life or for the life of another; a freehold estate.

life tenant
Person who has a life estate.

remainderman
Person who has a remainder.

tenant or the successor in interest may sell that interest as it is. However, it is difficult to sell either a life interest or the successor's interest separately, for two reasons: First, the life tenant's interest may cease at any time. Second, for the successor's sale, who would be interested in buying property when it is uncertain when the buyer will be able to begin using the property? Therefore, to transfer the property effectively, both the life tenant and the successor must join in executing the transfer document. It may be difficult to determine the fair value of each party's share, however, and this problem can lead to litigation.

In the second situation—concerning the uses to which the life tenant may put the property—the succeeding interest holder, whether taking by reversion or remainder, has the right to get the property in decent shape so that she can use it in a beneficial way. The life tenant should not have damaged the property in a way that lessens the remainderman's enjoyment of that property. That kind of damage to real property is called **waste**. Committing waste means that the life tenant has changed the property's character in a negative manner or has lessened its value. If the property is a building and the life tenant has not maintained it, its value has lessened. If farm land has been allowed to erode extensively, its character may have changed, since it is no longer usable as farm land or is significantly less productive. At this point, the successor interest holder may sue the life tenant for waste and seek monetary damages. The waste problem usually occurs with a remainderman rather than with the holder of a reversion.

Medieval common law created two other types of life estates, called *dower* and *curtesy.* Many state legislatures have abolished these life estates and have made provision for the surviving spouse in the law governing decedents' estates. Land in the Middle Ages represented not only status and power, but food, shelter, and clothing as well, so the law provided that the surviving spouse had a life estate in a certain amount (often one-third) of the real property of the deceased spouse. **Dower** referred to those rights if the survivor was the wife, **curtesy** if the survivor was the husband. There were differences between them that could be important, but that discussion is best left to learning the details of local law where dower and curtesy exist. Where they have been abolished, the interests of the surviving spouse are usually dealt with in the law of descent and distribution.

3.3 FUTURE INTERESTS

The rights of the persons who take the real property after the earlier property interest holder's interest ceases are called **future interests**. But future interests arise after life estates and other interests. For instance, the conditional fee situation has a possibility of reverter that can be a type of future interest, and landlords almost always retain a reversion after the tenant's lease has expired. Remember, if these rights return to the grantor or his heirs, they are called a *reversion,* and the holder of those rights is said to have a

LEGAL TERMS

waste
Current owner's (usually the life tenant's) use of land in a manner that damages the interests of the future interest holder (usually the remainderman; but if the estate involved had a reversionary interest, it would be the holder of the reversion).

dower
Rights of the wife in the husband's real property; from medieval law.

curtesy
Rights of the husband in the wife's real property; from medieval law.

future interests
Rights of persons to take a parcel of real estate after another person's interest has ceased.

right of reverter
Right to have interests revert to the holder.

right of reverter. If the rights go to someone else (not the grantor or her heir), they are called a **remainder**.

This remainder may be either vested or contingent. The difference between these two types lies in how many contingencies exist before the remainderman can take the property. If taking the property is subject only to the prior estate ending (generally the death of the life tenant), it is a **vested remainder**. If there is an additional event that must occur beyond the ending of the prior estate, the interest is a **contingent remainder**. In the previous example, with Stephanie Boscowicz's grant of a life estate to her sister, Susan, with the remainder to Elizabeth O'Malley, O'Malley has a vested remainder, since the only thing standing in the way of her taking is the life of Susan. If the grant had been "To Susan, for life, and then to Elizabeth O'Malley, if she survives me," O'Malley would have had a contingent remainder, because she must survive both Susan and Stephanie, not just Susan.

In chapter 5, the case of *Brown v. Byrd* contains a will; examine the grant language and determine what the interests of the allegedly taking parties are. For your purpose here, the later failure of the will, due to a prolonged delay in its admission to probate, is not important.

3.4 LEASEHOLD ESTATES

These estates—the fee simple, the conditional estates, and the life estate—are called *freehold estates*. As noted, they represent the greatest set of rights for the longest period of time. There are, obviously, lesser interests in land. Generally, these interests are contrasted with freehold estates and are called **leasehold estates**. Leasehold estates are usually created by a written agreement or a contract, normally called a **lease**, between the **landlord** and the **tenant**. The estate that the landlord grants and the tenant receives is a **leasehold**, and the tenant's interest is called a **tenancy**. The landlord almost always retains a reversion because, in most cases, the property is commercial property, and the landlord's business involves repeated rentals over the years.

It is possible, though, for the other type of succession to occur; there could be a remainderman if the landlord-owner gave the property to someone else at the end of the tenant's lease. Leasing is a generic arrangement—it is a business activity done by the landlord for a profit; the tenant is given certain rights to use the property for a certain time period; in return, the tenant pays rent. That payment may be a fixed amount or a variable payment based on a variety of commercial factors. The lease is usually a *written* contract that specifies all the terms the parties agreed upon. For the transfer of any interest in real estate, the Statute of Frauds—a centuries-old statute designed to protect landowners from harassment and sleazy claimants and to protect the integrity of the courts and the contract-making process—requires that the transfer be evidenced by a writing. Therefore, paperwork abounds with leases, deeds, wills, and all sorts of documents used to transfer real property.

Dealing with leases is not terribly complex in most situations, but one should be aware of the differences between commercial leases, between a business lessor

remainder
Right of another party (not the original fee holder or his or her heirs) to take the land when the current user's interest has expired.

vested remainder
Remainder that has only one contingent event to occur before the remainderman takes the property.

contingent remainder
Potential right to take property; before the holder of this interest can take the property, in addition to the demise of the prior property holder, one or more conditions must be met.

leasehold estate
Interest of the person who uses the property under a lease (contract) with an owner.

lease
Written agreement (contract) between the person who owns the real property and the person who will use the real property.

landlord
Owner of the property that is being leased.

tenant
Person who has the right to use property under a lease; also called *lessee*.

leasehold
Interest in the property that the lessee has under the lease; sometimes used to refer to the actual piece of property. (Note the two slightly different uses of this term.)

tenancy
Rights the owner grants to another so that the other may occupy or use the property.

and a business tenant, and consumer residential leases. Most commercial leases are governed by the law of contracts that relates to real estate. Although residential leases began that way, in many urban areas these leases are now governed by local ordinances and regulations; these require thorough research and understanding before advising the landlord of residential units. Commercial leases can have, among other things, allocations of expenses (such as maintenance), tax benefits, and risks between the parties, as well as standard leasing terms. To handle these commercial clauses, the attorney must know the client's needs (drawn out with interviewing skills), make rational estimates of future developments, and draft carefully clauses for complex situations. A more complete discussion appears in the chapter on leasing.

3.5 TYPES OF TENANCIES

The duration of the tenancy may be for a specified period of time, and a lease for that period creates an **estate for years**. Note, however, that the time period need not be as long as a year. The idea is that the lease is from one specific time (such as June 15, 1994) to another specific time (such as April 15, 1995). It is normal to lease property for different time periods—an overnight hotel leases by the day or the hour; a skyscraper may have a lease for 99 years. It is also possible to lease for 999 years (but many courts would treat that as a transfer of a fee simple). In most leases, the amount of time to be given and the process for notice of termination of the lease are specified in the lease itself.

Another type of duration occurs with a lease that involves a **periodic tenancy**. This arrangement is a tenancy repeated again and again for the same time period. That period could be a week, a month, or a year. This tenancy may be created by a lease or by implication from the actions of the parties. For instance, Joanna moves into an apartment of Leslie's without signing a lease. She pays her rent monthly. Les accepts it monthly, and these actions create a periodic tenancy with a monthly duration. A third type of estate is a **tenancy at will**. Either party may end this tenancy "at will"—at any time, theoretically—but most jurisdictions now require a 30-day notice. Often, there is no indication of the time that the lease will run. Finally, a **tenancy at sufferance** describes the estate that a wrongful occupant of property has. Usually, the tenant has stayed beyond the term of the lease agreement, and now there is no lease. The tenant is said to *hold over.* Common law gave the landlord the right to hold the tenant to a new lease at the same terms or to evict him. Until the landlord makes this decision (called an *election*), a tenancy at sufferance exists between the parties.

Both the landlord and the tenant have rights that can be transferred to third parties. Transfer of the landlord's interest is simpler than transfer of the tenant's interest. Generally, the landlord may transfer its reversionary interest and its contractual rights under the lease without any legal implications beyond that action. However, the landlord may not do so if there are legal prohibitions or there is a nondelegable duty owed the tenant that is expressed in the lease contract.

A word of explanation: in the law, rights are assigned and duties are delegated. *Rights* are something you possess and *duties* are something you owe someone. Both assignment and delegation represent a transfer, but the focus is on what is being transferred and the implications of that transfer for the other party to the contract to whom the transferring party owes a responsibility. Some duties are so personal that only the party who agreed to perform the duty can do it. For example, if you hire the Rolling Stones to do a concert, you do not want anyone else. Only the Rolling Stones will do. The Stones cannot delegate this duty by hiring another band to replace them. This duty is said to be nondelegable. Note that the landlord and the tenant usually have a different situation. The landlord has rights; the tenant has duties. This arrangement has traditionally been the position of the common law, but is gradually changing because the law is very slowly developing duties for the landlord.

Traditionally, the landlord gave up its rights in the land for a period of time, and the tenant agreed to pay rent (a duty). Although most landlords do not care who pays them, so long as they are paid and their property is not damaged, they always want the right to determine if the prospective tenant will be able to pay the rent or whether its use will damage the property. Thus, landlords remain vitally interested in *who* has the duty to pay. This concern makes it more difficult, conceptually, for the tenant to transfer its interest under the lease; its promises include important duties to perform that may be nondelegable. The landlord, on the other hand, has few duties imposed on it, and almost all of them are delegable. Even if the landlord-owner has the duty to repair, for instance, any owner can repair; there is nothing special about one owner or another ensuring that the property was maintained. For the tenant, however, the duty to pay rent could be seen as nondelegable, because the tenant's creditworthiness is a personal matter.

Tenant transfers of their interests are less complicated, however, than this technical discussion suggests. Transfers can be done in one of two ways: by assignment or by sublease. Most contemporary leases, however, prohibit both methods without the prior written consent of the landlord. (In the real world, unfortunately, tenants ignore the lease terms, do not tell the landlord, and transfer their interests anyway.) These two forms of transfer available to the tenant are subtly different. **Assignment** implies a transfer of all the tenant's estate under the lease. The tenant assigns the complete right to possession and the duties to pay rent and not damage the property. No reversionary interest remains with the tenant. In **subleasing**, however, the tenant transfers only a part of what it has; it transfers for a time period less than the time remaining on the lease. Or, to express it differently, the tenant transfers a portion of its time under the lease to a third party by means of a document called a *sublease*.

In the sublease, the tenant retains the right to reoccupy the premises after the sublease has expired. There is an important legal effect to this difference between assignment and subleasing. With the assignment form, the landlord is still a party to the contract. The tenant-assignor has merely transferred its interest to the assignee, who takes the assignor's place—

LEGAL TERMS

estate for years
Estate that is for a specific time period, such as one year, nine months, or twelve years.

periodic tenancy
Holding of a parcel of real property for a (usually short) time period that is repeated again and again.

tenancy at will
Tenancy in which either party is able to terminate the tenancy when he or she chooses ("at will").

tenancy at sufferance
Estate that arises when the tenant was originally in possession legally, usually under a lease, but the lease ended and the tenant remained in possession, without permission. The tenant remains at the "sufferance" of the landlord.

assignment
Transfer of a right under a contract or lease.

sublease
Act by the lessee of real property to set up a new, separate lease for a portion of the lease period with a third party; often done without involvement of the landlord. Also the name for the document transferring the interest.

"stands in its shoes" is the traditional description of this relationship under an assignment—in relation to the landlord. With the sublease, the tenant-sublessor and the sublessee are the only parties. The landlord has no rights against the sublessee because it has no contractual relationship with the sublessee; the landlord only retains its rights against the assignor, that is, the original tenant. If there is an assignment, the practical effect is that the landlord has two parties—the original tenant (who has become the assignor) and the assignee—from whom it can attempt to obtain rental payments or damages. However, only one party, the original tenant, would be liable to the landlord when there is a sublease. An assignment can be voided by the landlord if the lease required its permission and that grant was not obtained. The landlord could also refuse to accept rent from the third party, but once it accepts a rent payment, it waives its right to object to the assignment.

Note the effect on the third party (the assignee or sublessee). In an assignment, the assignee assumes the assignor's obligations under the lease. Thus, the lessor has recourse against the original tenant or that tenant's assignee. Under the sublease, however, it is different. Because the sublease is a separate contract between the tenant (the original lessee) and the party taking over the premises (the sublessee), the landlord is not a party to that second contract. But the landlord retains its rights against the original tenant.

Generally, tenants and landlords have simple and direct obligations to each other. Tenants, however, may owe more exacting obligations to the landlord than the landlord owes to them. This situation is due to the long development of the law, but it is slowly changing, particularly in consumer residential leases. Nevertheless, in some states, even during a legal dispute, the rent must still be paid. When that rent payment requirement exists, the money is frequently paid into an escrow account at a local bank during the legal dispute. This escrow device—in which the funds are held by a third party—is used in real estate in a number of circumstances. Escrow protects both parties—the depositor and the party who will receive the funds—because there is no problem over getting the money if the court should so order at the end of the lawsuit.

3.6 THE LANDLORD'S DUTIES

The landlord, under the common law, has the duty to provide the tenant with the right to possession but not actual possession. To the modern mind, this rule is unfair. (It might be called unconscionable if the transaction concerned the sale of goods under the Uniform Commercial Code.) The rule may disappear within the next generation, but, fortunately, it is rarely a problem. The landlord has the duty to provide quiet enjoyment of the property. Basically, quiet enjoyment means that the landlord has a duty to do nothing that will make the tenant's possession difficult. The landlord may not, for instance, try to evict the tenant wrongfully. Note that it is the actions of the landlord that count, not the actions of third parties. Howling dogs and loud music are not problems of the landlord, because "quiet" does not refer to sound or noise in this context; it means "undisturbed" in the right of possession.

Another changing obligation of the landlord is the obligation to be certain that the premises are fit for use. In early real estate law, what one rented was the land, not the buildings on it. They were incidental. Today, unless the tenant farms, the building, not the land, is valued and is the tenant's primary use of the land. Consequently, modern law often requires that the residential landlord maintain the premises, under the idea of an implied warranty of habitability. Much of this law has arisen from problems with slumlords and their failure to maintain the premises of their buildings. Other government rules, requirements, and regulations may create additional duties for the landlord when there is a consumer residential relationship. These imposed duties may stem from government interests in zoning, health, environmental, or public safety laws.

The landlord's duty to keep the premises in good condition or safe repair depends on the parts of the property under the landlord's control. Common areas, such as halls, steps, and the like, are under the control of the landlord, so they must be maintained. Areas inside leased premises, however, are under the control of the tenant. If the landlord fails to comply with its obligations, and that failure damages the tenant, the tenant has several options. First, the tenant may sue for monetary damages. Second, under some circumstances, the tenant may move out. Moving out may be legitimate if the lease permits it; even if it does not, the legal doctrine of **constructive eviction** may provide the tenant with a basis for moving out. The tenant must claim that the landlord's failure to comply with its obligations was so great that it damaged the tenant's (quiet) enjoyment of the premises. To assert this claim, however, the tenant must move out and end the lease within a reasonable time after the circumstances become intolerable. Rats, falling plaster, lack of functioning sanitary facilities, and similar serious situations have been accepted in some courts.

In the *Gottdiener* case, the tenants moved out because they could not stand their fellow tenants' behavior. Here is a breach of quiet enjoyment that can work for the tenant. Focus on why the court sided with the tenants and what legal reasoning it used to support them. Could the court have decided for the landowner? How?

3.7 THE TENANT'S DUTIES

The tenant's obligations are those specified in the lease and the general obligations imposed by the law. The most important obligations are to pay rent and not to damage the premises in any way beyond normal wear and tear. If the landlord evicts the tenant for noncompliance with a clause in the lease, the tenant may not be liable for any further rent payments. Similarly, after the tenant has moved out and breached the leasing contract without cause, rent payments usually remain an obligation, unless the landlord rents the property to another at a comparable rent. However, in many jurisdictions,

LEGAL TERMS

constructive eviction
Legal doctrine under which the tenant can move out and break the lease when the landlord does not keep the premises in proper condition; usually used in residential situations.

GOTTDIENER v. MAILHOT

179 N.J. Super. 286, 431 A.2d 851 (1981)

KOLE, J. A. D.

The primary question on this appeal is whether defendants, former tenants in plaintiff's apartment complex, may invoke the remedy of constructive eviction by reason of plaintiff's claimed failure to take sufficient measures to protect defendants from excessively noisy and unruly neighboring tenants.

Plaintiffs sought rent (at the rate of $400 a month) for the months of September, October and November 1979, plus late charges and additional sums to repair and restore defendants' apartment. Defendants denied liability for rent for the months in question principally because plaintiffs' breach of the covenant of quiet enjoyment amounted to a constructive eviction. Defendants also counterclaimed for double the amount of their security deposit, pursuant to *N.J.S.A.* 46:8-21.1.

The matter was tried before Judge Gascoyne, sitting without a jury. The proofs showed that defendants originally became tenants in Oakwood Village, a 516-unit apartment complex, in December 1975, and had renewed their tenancy through January 31, 1980. Defendants experienced no problems during their tenancy until the fall of 1978, when new tenants moved into the apartment immediately beneath defendants. On several occasions in December 1978 and January 1979 defendants complained of "intolerable noise" coming from the downstairs apartment, such as slamming doors, yelling and screaming children, and excessive volume from the television and radio after 10 p.m. Plaintiff Alexander Gottdiener, one of the partners who owned Oakwood Village, expressed sympathy with defendants' plight and made some efforts to effect a resolution of the conflict between defendants and their neighbors. These efforts were not successful and, according to Mr. Mailhot, the neighbors began a campaign of harassment and retaliation. He claimed that in late January 1979 someone from the apartment below had maliciously damaged his vehicle, which he kept in a garage available only to defendants, plaintiffs and the downstairs neighbors.

Defendants brought this incident to the attention of Gottdiener and again requested plaintiffs to take some measures to resolve the problem. Gottdiener responded with a suggestion that defendants and their neighbors amicably settle the dispute, but a subsequent meeting proved fruitless. According to Mailhot, one of the downstairs tenants became very angry and threatened defendants.

Defendants began to look for another place to live in early May, and sometime in June entered into a contract to purchase a home. By letter dated June 29, 1979 they notified plaintiffs that they intended to terminate the tenancy as of August 31. The letter of termination stated that defendants had been "continually harassed and intimidated" by the downstairs tenants and that they believed that plaintiffs' failure to correct the situation constituted a "breach of contract." Gottdiener replied that he still hoped that the matter could be amicably solved, and he suggested that defendants move into another building. Defendants declined the offer and vacated their apartment in late August 1979. Plaintiffs procured another tenant effective December and shortly thereafter notified defendants of the disposition of their security deposit. Plaintiffs then brought this action for rent for the months of September, October and November, and the other charges, minus defendants' security deposit, which plaintiffs retained.

Judge Gascoyne found that, while he initially believed that defendants were "hypersensitive" to noise, his analysis of the proofs convinced him that the conduct of the downstairs neighbors constituted a "substantial interference" with defendants' quiet enjoyment of the premises. He found that one of the downstairs neighbors had vandalized Mailhot's automobile. He reasoned that excessive noise, like flooding or roach infestation, can make rented premises unsuitable for the purpose for which the premises were leased. He also found that defendants had vacated their apartment within a reasonable time. Thus, he held that plaintiffs were not entitled to rent for the months of September, October and November. A judgment was entered dismissing the complaint with prejudice and awarding $548.70 to defendants on their counterclaim. Plaintiffs appeal.

Plaintiffs contend that a landlord has no duty to evict one tenant in order to eliminate a "questionable" disturbance by that tenant of another tenant, and that defendants were not constructively evicted, since the landlord diligently tried to alleviate friction between them and their neighboring co-tenants.

The law of landlord and tenant, including that relating to constructive eviction, has undergone considerable change in recent years. In *Reste Realty Corp. v. Cooper,* the court stated that where there is a covenant of quiet enjoyment, whether expressed or implied, which is breached substantially by the landlord, the doctrine of constructive eviction is available as a remedy for the tenant; and that any act or omission of the landlord or anyone acting under his authority which renders the premises substantially unsuitable for the purpose for which they are leased, or which seriously interferes with the beneficial enjoyment of the premises, is a breach of that covenant and constitutes a constructive eviction of the tenant.

In *Millbridge Apartments v. Linden,* the court properly held that the *Reste* principle relating to constructive eviction could be applied to a situation similar to that before us. There defendants-tenants frequently complained to their landlord that their neighbors were extremely loud. When the landlord's efforts to correct the problem were unsuccessful, the tenants began withholding their rent. In the landlord's ensuing action for possession based on nonpayment of rent, the tenants contended that the landlord's failure to correct the problem constituted a breach of the covenant of habitability.

Judge Weinberg stated that "repeated loud noise suffered by a residential tenant, which could have been cured by a landlord, can be a defense to a dispossess action under the rubric of the warranty of habitability."

He said:

> Residential tenants expect to live within reasonable boundaries of quiet. Continual noise of a loud nature infringes upon those expectations and makes one's premises "substantially unsuitable for the purpose for which they are leased," i.e., ordinary residential living. Accordingly, this court holds that noise may constitute a constructive eviction and legally justify a tenant's vacating.

Since noise may constitute a constructive eviction, the court determined that excessive noise could also constitute a breach of the covenant of habitability.

We agree with the reasoning of *Millbridge Apartments v. Linden.* A number of recent cases from other jurisdictions have recognized that a landlord may constructively evict a tenant by failing to prevent other tenants from making excessive amounts of noise.

Furthermore, regulations promulgated pursuant to the Hotel and Multiple Dwelling Law support the reasoning of *Millbridge Apartments v. Linden, supra.* These regulations establish a standard of conduct for landlords and are "available as evidence for determining the duty owed by landlords to tenants." *N.J.A.C.* 5:10-19.4(a)(2) states that the owner of a multiple dwelling "shall be responsible for avoiding, eliminating or abating any noises . . . arising out of the use or occupancy of the premises which shall constitute a nuisance that is harmful or potentially harmful to the health and well-being of persons of ordinary sensitivity occupying or using the premises."

We hold that in order to justify early termination of the lease, or for that matter an abatement of rent, the tenant must show that the noise or conduct of a co-tenant made the premises substantially unsuitable for ordinary residential living and that it was within the landlord's power to abate the nuisance. The test is objective; the noise or disruptive conduct "must be such as truly to render the premises uninhabitable in the eyes of a reasonable person."

Unquestionably plaintiffs had the power to correct the problem. A good cause for evicting a residential tenant is that the "person has continued to be, after written notice to cease, so disorderly as to destroy the peace and quiet of the occupants or other tenants living in said house or neighborhood." The landlord may bring a summary dispossess action against such an unruly tenant by giving only three days' notice prior to the institution of the action. In addition, had the downstairs tenant violated any rules and regulations or lease covenants respecting noise, the landlord had the option of bringing a dispossess action.

There is no merit to plaintiff's argument that the conduct of the downstairs neighbors was not so serious as to constitute a substantial interference with defendants' peaceful enjoyment of the premises, or that plaintiffs did all that reasonably could be expected of them to remedy such conduct. What amounts to a constructive eviction is a question of fact. We find sufficient credible evidence in the record as a whole to support the trial judge's findings and conclusions regarding the nature and extent of the disturbance of defendants' enjoyment of the premises and the constructive eviction of defendants by reason therof.

Plaintiffs further contend that even assuming that they breached the covenant of quiet enjoyment by not abating the noise, defendants waived their right to terminate the lease and abandon the premises because they failed to take such action within a reasonable time after the right to terminate came into existence. As stated in *Reste Realty Corp. v. Cooper, supra:*

> . . . What constitutes a reasonable time depends upon the circumstances of each case. In considering the problem courts must be sympathetic toward the tenant's plight. Vacation of the premises is a drastic course and must be taken at his peril. If he vacates, and it is held at a later time in a suit for rent for the unexpired term that the landlord's course of action did not reach the dimensions of constructive eviction, a substantial liability may be imposed upon him. That risk and the practical inconvenience and difficulties attendant upon finding and moving to suitable quarters counsel caution.

Adequate credible evidence in the record supports the conclusion that defendants waited a reasonable time in order to determine whether plaintiffs would solve the problem, and left only after it was apparent that plaintiffs would not take any further measures. There was thus no waiver of their right to terminate the lease.

We find no merit in plaintiff's contention that the trial judge erred in disallowing certain deductions from defendants' security deposit, such as "assorted cleaning charges," "stain and spot damages," and charges for rerenting and painting. The record supports the judge's findings that the deductions in question were either not authorized by the lease or that the alleged damage represented nothing more than reasonable wear and tear.

Affirmed.

[Some citations omitted.]

when re-renting has occurred, the obligation to pay rent ceases. The lessee may still be liable for the difference between the amount of the new rent and the amount that the defaulting renter paid if the new amount is less. Many leases, however, have clauses setting out the obligations of the parties under most possible circumstances.

3.8 MULTIPLE OWNERS OF A PARCEL OF REAL ESTATE

Although this discussion has covered ownership by one person only, it is clearly possible to have more than one owner of a parcel of real property. Multiple ownership does not alter what has been discussed earlier. For instance, one can have all of the following types of estates with multiple owners—a fee simple, a fee conditional, a life estate, an estate for years, and a periodic estate. Generally, multiple ownership of real estate is called **concurrent ownership**.

In most states, there are two basic forms of concurrent ownership. These are **joint tenancy with the right of survivorship** and **tenancy in common**. The latter is by far the favored form, both in the statutes and in judicial decisions, so that if there is any question as to which form of ownership exists, the courts generally resolve the issue in favor of a tenancy in common. The rationale for favoring the tenancy in common (which goes back centuries) is based in at least two theories. First, the tenancy in common is much simpler and easier to create. Second, the tenancy in common allows property to pass by will, which does not lock it up as tightly as does a joint tenancy. In addition, death duties may apply to the asset of the tenancy in common, but not to property held in joint tenancy.

The **right of survivorship** is the most important aspect of joint tenancy. Essentially, this pattern of ownership allows A, B, and C to own Blackacre together; when one of them dies, the other two share the ownership. Let us say that A dies, and B and C survive him. B and C take his interest in the piece of property. When A was alive, each of them owned a one-third interest as joint tenants, but the instant A dies, B and C each own a one-half interest. A's interest does not go to A's heirs or into his estate, or become available to his creditors. This type of ownership is difficult to create but easy to destroy by conveying (transferring) the interest or mortgaging it. Either of these acts *severs* or breaks the joint tenancy as far as the party acting (let us call her "C") is concerned. **Severance** does not, however, affect the relationship among the other joint tenants. In other words, it affects only C's interest, not the interests of the other joint tenants. With A, B, and C owning Whiteacre in joint tenancy, if C severs her interest by mortgaging her interest, A and B remain joint tenants in two-thirds of Whiteacre, while C becomes a tenant in common with them.

Partition is also a way of ending a joint tenancy or a tenancy in common. This term usually refers to a legal proceeding (although it can be voluntary among the parties) that converts the tenancy's interests into individual

LEGAL TERMS

concurrent ownership
Ownership of real property when there is more than one owner.

joint tenancy with the right of survivorship
Ownership form in which two or more parties own the same property and have (1) the same interests in the entire property and (2) the survivor between/among them takes the entire property.

tenancy in common
Ownership form when two or more parties own the same property and have the same interest in the entire property.

right of survivorship
Rights accruing to a person who outlives his or her fellow owners in a joint tenancy with a right of survivorship.

severance
Act by a joint tenant that destroys the joint tenancy, usually by selling or mortgaging the property.

partition
Legal proceeding to break a joint tenancy so that one party can transfer his or her portion out of it.

interests, usually fee interests, if the property can be divided. If the property cannot be divided, it is sold, and the proceeds are divided proportionately among the parties.

Tenancy in common is the preferred form of concurrent holding. Owners holding under a tenancy in common have a right to possession of the entire property and cannot claim a specific piece of it, although they need not be equal owners of the property. Upon the death of a tenant in common, his or her interest passes in his or her estate. This tenancy has no right of survivorship.

There are two additional forms of concurrent ownership. The first is an old one that existed between husband and wife. While **tenancy by the entireties** may still exist in some states, it has been abolished in many. This tenancy, which exists solely for spouses, allows the husband and wife, in the common law legally one person, to own the property together. It allows the survivor to take the property, and it cannot be broken by partition during the marriage. Thus, one spouse cannot sell off his or her interest. Generally, creditors have difficulty in reaching property held by the entireties for the obligations of either spouse separately.

For spouses to hold real estate in **community property** is common in the western United States (and now Wisconsin as well), as the origins of that law were Spanish. The concept does not apply solely to real estate. It applies to all property acquired during marriage from the efforts of either spouse, including real property. Basically, each spouse is entitled to one-half. Note that community property applies only to property acquired during marriage and from the efforts of either spouse. It excludes property acquired prior to marriage or by gift, as the rationale of the law relates to the spouses' joint effort during marriage. These two types of property are called, respectively, *community property* and *separate property.*

Of course the spouses share the community property in a divorce, but what happens if the husband beats up the wife, is arrested, and to get out of jail, pledges his share of the community property as security for bail? The wife is awarded the property in the divorce settlement. Where does the claim of the bail bondsman fall? Does he have a claim on the property? See the *Head* case.

3.9 CONDOMINIUMS AND COOPERATIVES

Another modern way of holding real property is in a **condominium** or **cooperative** relationship. In the condominium form, each party owns an actual unit in the building. What one actually owns is air space in the building, the boundaries of which are measured from middle of the wall to middle of the wall and from floor to ceiling. The common, shared areas, such as halls, elevators, and parking lots, are owned as tenants in common. This form of ownership is very common in high-rise buildings. Cooperatives, uncommon outside of large urban areas because of the difficulties of transferring ownership, are generally structured as corporations. Each party that owns a unit in

LEGAL TERMS

tenancy by the entireties
A way for husband and wife to hold real property; has survivorship and cannot be broken by partition; abolished in many states.

community property
Device used in the western United States and Wisconsin to share equally property that was acquired during marriage from the work efforts of both partners; excludes gifts, inheritances, and prior owned property.

condominium
Type of ownership that combines fee ownership in the specific unit (usually housing) with a tenancy in common in the building's elements that are used or usable by all owners.

cooperative
Form of building ownership in which a corporation owns the real property and its shareholders are its tenants.

HEAD
v.
CRAWFORD
(156 Cal. App. 3d 11, 202 Cal. Rptr. 534 (1984)

WOOLPERT, J.—Plaintiff wife asks this court to hold that the lis pendens she filed in her dissolution proceeding protected the entire community property from a subsequently recorded bail bond lien incurred without her knowledge by her husband. We agree the lis pendens procedure applies to dissolution actions but find in this case it did not have the effect contemplated by the wife.

THE FACTS

Plaintiff Juda Lee Head (hereafter Juda) and Tracy Lee Head (hereafter Tracy) were married in 1962. In 1963 they purchased real property in Tulare County which we will call the subject property. A copy of the "Agreement of Sale" was recorded the same year. That document describes the buyers as "husband and wife," and as "joint tenants."

In 1980, Juda alleged she was severely beaten after confronting Tracy with accusations that he had abused their foster children. Juda and Tracy separated. Charges were immediately filed and Tracy was arrested the next day.

On the day of his arrest, Tracy signed a "Bail Bond Agreement" and a "Defendant's Financial Declaration" furnished by defendant Crawford, a bail bondsman. The subject property was listed as security in the financial statement. The security agreement was executed without Juda's knowledge or consent. The last sentence of the financial statement provides as follows: "I do hereby agree that *the recording* of this agreement shall constitute a lien on the above property until all monies due hereunder have been paid. . . ." Crawford (hereafter Bondsman) then caused defendant National Automobile and Casualty Insurance Company (hereafter National) to issue a bond for $25,000.

Juda filed an action for dissolution of the marriage. She later filed a "Declaration of Homestead" and recorded a "Lis Pendens" which specifically described the subject property. Tracy was served with the dissolution papers. He has since disappeared. After Tracy failed to appear in the criminal court, bail was forfeited and Bondsman recorded the bond agreement and financial declaration.

In May of 1980, an "Interlocutory Decree for Dissolution of Marriage" was entered. The subject property was confirmed to be community property. However, it was awarded to Juda "to hold forthwith as separate property." A final decree dissolving the marriage followed. Juda then filed this action to cancel the security agreement and to quiet title in her as sole owner of the subject property. Juda and defendants each filed a motion for summary judgment. The court ruled in favor of defendants. She appeals from that judgment.

TRIAL COURT CONCLUSION

The lower court held, in pertinent part, as follows: "The Court is persuaded that Defendant's [*sic*] [Bondsman and National] position is correct. Tracy Lee Head had the power to encumber his half interest in the community realty without the consent of his wife (plaintiff). The encumbrance was not defeated by the subsequent recordation of lis pendens, declaration of homestead, or the judgment of dissolution of marriage of the reasons set forth in Defendant's [*sic*] points and authorities."

PRESENT ISSUES

Juda puts forth three arguments on appeal. First, the doctrine of lis pendens operates in dissolution actions and the protections afforded her by that doctrine require reversal. Second, Tracy did not have the power to encumber the community real property once the couple had separated, reversal therefore being required. Third, even if the lis pendens was without effect and Tracy could encumber one-half the value of the property, that value should be set as closely as possible to the date the security agreement was signed.

STANDARD OF REVIEW

A motion for summary judgment will be granted "if all the papers submitted show that there is no triable issue as to any material fact and that the moving party is entitled to a judgment as a matter of law." The rules relating to such motions are well established and need not be repeated by us.

LIS PENDENS IN DISSOLUTION PROCEEDINGS

Many years ago the Supreme Court seemed to rule out a notice of pendency of action as a viable priority device in a divorce action, concluding: "And the notice of *lis pendens* filed by appellant during the pendency of the divorce suit had no legal significance.

Little attention has been given to the actual holding in *Sun.* Although the court disclaimed any need to consider the effect of a lis pendens in divorce actions, it devoted five pages of the opinion to the use of lis pendens in divorce actions in other states and the reasons why in this California proceeding the pleadings to which the lis pendens referred did not satisfy the specificity requirements which might have placed the creditor on notice. In *Mayberry* the court's pointed conclusion was a product of the times, and perhaps an overstatement. At that time, "[t]he pendency of proceedings for a divorce [did] not, of itself, interrupt the exercise of the husband's powers." With the Family Law Act and its equal treatment of spouses for purposes of marital property rights and obligations came an express approval of the use of lis pendens.

The California Rules of Court provide: "In a proceeding under the Family Law Act, either party may record a notice of pendency of the proceeding under the circumstances and in the manner provided by Section 409 of the Code of Civil Procedure." We find no basis to question the validity of the rule. Instead, we must deal with its effect.

In dictum, in *Kane v. Huntley Financial,* the court suggested a wife could have protected her separate property claim to certain marital property by filing a lis pendens when she commenced action against her husband. However, absent a lis pendens, her claim that joint tenancy residential property had been orally transmuted to her separate property failed against the trust deed lien of a post-separation creditor of her husband. Under these circumstances the creditor could justifiably rely on record title.

In the present case the wife did file a lis pendens; therefore, we must determine what it accomplished. Ordinarily, "[a]nyone with actual notice of the pendency of the proceeding who acquires an interest in the property takes subject to any judgment that may be rendered therein. (Code Civ. Proc., § 1908, subd. 2 . . . .) The lis pendens procedure accomplishes the same result. By its constructive notice it republishes the pleadings, drawing attention to the factual allegations and other facts necessarily arising from those pled.

We agree with the *Kane* observation. A spouse who files a lis pendens to draw attention to the dissolution petition *may* obtain priority over a creditor of the other spouse if the creditor either acts with constructive notice or fails to record a lien document until after the filing of the lis pendens. The priority dates from the filing of the notice, and for those who take subject to the notice the priority depends upon a judgment being reached on the pleadings previously filed.

It is probable the *Sun* court would have prescribed certain requirements if it found the lis pendens procedure applied to the divorce action before it. Citing Freeman's Treatise on Judgments, and out-of-state cases, the court emphasized that the divorce pleadings must designate the specific property to be affected and the nature of the relief sought.

In making use of the lis pendens, the spouse accomplishes positive and negative results. Affirmatively, the spouse's asserted title rights are declared as a warning to the creditor who would rely on record ownership. Negatively, the spouse will be estopped from later challenging the creditor who relies on the spouse's representations in the pleadings.

In filing her petition and lis pendens, Juda publicly acknowledged her position that the subject property belonged to the community and should be distributed as such. She alleged no separate property interest in the property and obtained no court order or judgment which would give her a priority position. Therefore, the lis pendens only fortified the right of the bonding company to rely on the husband's similar statement that the subject property was the residential property of the spouses.

We do not speculate whether a petition alleging an uncertainty as to title would prevail over subsequent creditors of the other spouse. Nor are we presented any question arising from the 1983 enactment of Civil Code section 4800.1 which, according to the legislative committee comment, "has the effect of limiting existing law which permits transmutations of [joint tenancy] property by oral agreements and implications from unilateral statements of a party."

ONE-HALF OF THE PROPERTY
WAS ENCUMBERED

The trial court determined that Tracy had the power, after their separation, to encumber his one-half interest in the community real property without Juda's knowledge. We agree.

In *Mitchell* the court interpreted Civil Code section 5127, which provides, in pertinent part, as follows: "Except as provided in Sections 5113.5 and 5128, either spouse has the management and control of the community real property, whether acquired prior to or on or after January 1, 1975, but both spouses either personally or by duly authorized agent, must join in executing any instrument by which such community real property or any interest therein is leased for a longer period than one year, or is sold, conveyed, or encumbered; . . ."

As the *Mitchell* court phrased it, the rule is as follows: "In the context of a conveyance, the section has been understood to mean that 'a deed to community real property for a valuable consideration, executed without the wife's consent, while ineffective as to her interest, is valid and binding as to the husband's half interest. . . . In such a case the conveyance of the wife's one-half interest without her consent is not void but voidable . . . .' "

"By analogy, where the case involves an encumbrance, the power of the consenting spouse extends in absolute terms no further than to burden his or her own interest, leaving in the nonconsenting spouse the ability to remove the encumbrance insofar as it relates to that spouse's interest." In its holding, *Mitchell* restates a longstanding rule in California.

Juda reminds us that she and Tracy were separated when Tracy encumbered the property. She would have this court read Civil

Code section 5127 as narrowly as possible so as to preclude encumbrances of *any* interest of community real property made without mutual knowledge and consent of the spouses when they are separated at the time the subject property is encumbered. This, however, is not the rule. Final dissolution of the marriage is the relevant date, not the time of separation: A marriage exists until final dissolution.

Since the community is liable for debts arising during the marriage, the community property may still be liable for debts occurring after separation. Although the nonconsenting spouse may clear one-half of the community real property from the lien, the community property of each may still be liable for community debts if the creditor seeks to pursue the usual creditor's remedies. In this case the bonding company has not been afforded personal relief against Juda. The court therefore avoided any need to determine whether the bail bond created a community debt.

VALUATION DATE

Juda requests this court to set a valuation date for the property in question. She suggests a few dates, preferring one as close to the date of separation as possible: We assume the property is increasing in value.

When Juda was awarded the property as her sole and separate property by the dissolution court, she took the property subject to the bond lien. Therefore, when the trial court awarded defendants National and Bondsman a lien against an undivided one-half interest in the real property, it awarded them a security interest in one-half of the property up to the amount of the lien. The value of the property is determined as a consequence of the sale. To the extent the one-half interest does not satisfy the lien, defendants would then have an action against Tracy for an unsecured debt equal to the balance. To the extent that the one-half interest in the real property exceeded the lien, that amount would become Juda's separate property.

We make use of the conclusion reached in *Kane v. Huntley Financial,* . . . substituting our parties: "[Bondsman and National are] entitled to a [lien] encumbering one-half of the property. [They] will be able to cause a . . . sale of that interest only. The buyer at the sale will become a tenant in common with [Juda] and will be able to force partition and sale of the property under Code of Civil Procedure section 872.010 et seq." A similar result was reached in *Kinney v. Vallentyne,* dealing with a judgment lien and subsequent expenditures on the property by the objecting spouse.

The judgment is affirmed.

[Some citations omitted.]

the building owns shares in the corporation, and the corporation may lease to the tenant-shareholder. For instance, four people live in a four-flat building that is a co-op. They each own 25 shares of stock (100 shares outstanding) of the corporation that owns the building, and each occupies one floor of the building. To sell, the agreements usually provide that the corporation has the first right of buy-back. As a result, prior approval of the other shareholders is often necessary to sell the shares (and the unit) back to the corporation. This approach impedes resale, and the condominium device, with few restrictions on resale, is more popular. A more detailed discussion of these matters appears in chapter 10.

3.10 EASEMENTS AND LICENSES

There remain two other ways to have an interest in real estate: an easement and a license. These describe the rights of a third party to use the land of another.

Easements are probably the more important of these forms; they are the right to use another's land for a limited, usually specific, purpose. The most frequent easements are those of utility companies for the lines that go into buildings to provide gas, electricity, telephone, and similar services. Utility companies must use others' property for their business, but since what they provide is something that most people want, this set of easements is more of an enhancement than a restriction on ownership rights.

The more difficult situation is when Betty Jones, who owns property adjacent to the property of Mary Smith, has rights to use Smith's property. The right might have arisen when Smith sold half her property to Jones. Now, to reach her property, Jones must use (that is, she has to cross) Smith's property. This right might also have been reserved in the deed by which the property was transferred to Smith. The easement relationship of these two parcels is described by two technical terms. The piece of property that has attached to it the right of using another piece of property is called the **dominant tenement**; the piece of property that is being used is called the **servient tenement**. This right to use the other piece of property is an easement. Because Betty's property would have no value to her without it, the easement might also be described as a *necessary easement;* it is said to be created by necessity.

Not only may an easement be created by necessity or by legal language in a deed or sales contract, but it may also be created by implication, dedication, or prescription. An easement can be created by implication when Sally Williams, who owns adjacent parcels of property, does two things. First, she adds some improvement, perhaps a sidewalk, that overlaps both parcels. Second, she conveys one of the parcels to someone else, say Stan, and mentions this easement. Both Stan and Sally have an easement. Sally is said to have granted one to Stan and reserved one for herself. These are easements by implication.

Easement by dedication is common for contractors to do. Dedication means committing land to the public use. It occurs often with streets, alleys, and parks.

Easement by prescription is like adverse possession, in which a party uses another's land for a period specified by state law (often 10 to 20 years), the use is hostile to the owner's interest, and the practice is open and notorious. When all of these elements are present, the easement by prescription makes it impossible for the landowner to deny the easement holder the right to continue to use the land.

Almost all easements are divided into two general types. They are either an easement that goes with the land—an **easement appurtenant**—or an easement that is a personal right—an **easement in gross**. The latter is frequently difficult to distinguish from a **license**. A license is a personal right to

LEGAL TERMS

dominant tenement
Piece of property that has a right attached to it which permits its owner to use another's property for a specific purpose.

servient tenement
Parcel of land in which a party other than the owner has rights to use the property for a specific purpose.

easement appurtenant
Easement that runs with the land; stays with the land and is transferred when the land is transferred, usually by deed; not tied to a particular person's right to use the land.

easement in gross
Irrevocable personal right to use the land; does not go with ("run with") the land; tied to the person.

license
Personal right to use real property; difficult to distinguish from an easement in gross.

use the real property. It is most frequently seen in commercial situations. For example, at a concert (or movie theater), the purchase of a ticket gives the holder a license to be on the property during the time of the show, so long as one's behavior is appropriate. An easement appurtenant often is transferred with the land as part of the sale. Common language in the deed, such as transferring land "with all appurtenances," frequently conveys these rights. In the preceding example of Stan and Sally, each of them would have an easement appurtenant.

What happens when a new utility, such as a cable company, wants to use the easements already used by existing utilities such as the gas or electric company? In the *Consolidated Cable* case, note the technicalities involved in the legal proceedings and recall the court's comment about the descriptions of the easements on the plats of survey. What might that comment suggest about preparing proper documentation?

Finally (believe it or not), there is only one other right. It is called a **profit à prendre**; this is a French term for taking a profit from the land. This right permits a person who does not own or lease property belonging to another to remove a part of the land—like coal, gas, the nuts off trees, crops, or lumber—or to use a part of the land for one's own benefit—like grazing cattle on it. Check your local jurisdiction's law to determine the practical applications and uses of this right.

LEGAL TERMS

profit à prendre
Right of a third party (neither an owner nor someone taking from the owner) to use the land to make money.

CONSOLIDATED CABLE UTILITIES INC., an Illinois Corporation, Plaintiff-Appellee, v. AURORA

1082 Ill. App. 3d.1035, 439 N.E.2d 1272 (1982)

HOPF, J.:

Plaintiff, Consolidated Cable Utilities, Inc., brought this action seeking both a declaratory judgment pursuant to section 57.1 of the Civil Practice Act and injunctive relief. The circuit court of Kane County granted the relief sought by Consolidated, giving it access to install cable for television on certain backyard easements. Only defendants Commonwealth Edison Co. (Edison), Northern Illinois Gas Company (NI Gas) and Illinois Bell Telephone Co. (Bell) appeal.

In 1969 Consolidated was granted the franchise to provide cable television service to private customers in both Elgin and Aurora. The franchise ordinances require that Consolidated charge a uniform fee of each user, and in Aurora, provide service where there are at least 50 homes per cable mile; in Elgin, where there are at least 30 homes per cable mile.

Often the cable installation is made by utilizing and leasing poles above ground from public utilities, but certain subdivisions of Aurora and Elgin require, by ordinance, that such services be placed underground. There are 12 such subdivisions involved in this case where Consolidated seeks to install its cable underground on backyard easements.

In late 1979 and early 1980 Consolidated made some effort to obtain homeowner approval for backyard easement access. They hired college students who went door-to-door in an effort to obtain such approval. Eighty to 85% gave their approval for Consolidated's use of the easements. Other than this Consolidated has not involved the homeowners in this suit.

On September 29, 1980, Consolidated filed suit for declaratory judgment and mandatory injunction against the city of Aurora and the city of Elgin, as well as the three utilities. Consolidated's complaint sets forth the Elgin and Aurora grants of authority; the specific subdivisions where the easements are located; and its request for use of the easements.

Edison's motion to strike and dismiss, as well as those filed by NI Gas and Bell, were denied. Edison's motion set forth several contentions; including the contention that Consolidated was improperly trying to expand by implication the easements in question, so as to include unnamed parties; that the owners of the land on which the easements were located should be joined as parties; and that Consolidated was improperly attempting to exercise the power of eminent domain. All three utilities made application to this court for interlocutory appeal pursuant to Supreme Court Rule 308. The applications were denied.

At trial over 90 plats of survey were tendered by Consolidated and admitted as evidence. These consisted of the plats of the subdivisions that Consolidated sought to enter. Unfortunately, the easements are not described on the plats of survey in any uniform manner. The descriptions range from those that list the specific utilities and location of the easements to those that give no indication of an easement interest. Three of the plats named Consolidated as an easement holder. NI Gas concedes that it does not generally have its pipes in the backyard easements that are in issue here.

The trial court found that (1) Consolidated was a public utility within the contemplation of the plats in question; (2) that the enumerated plats reserve to the municipalities the right to license Consolidated, and the landowners are not indispensable parties; (3) that an actual controversy exists, that declaratory relief is appropriate; and (4) Consolidated need not go before the Illinois Commerce Commission. The relief granted gave Consolidated the right to use the majority of the easements, and stated that defendants were enjoined from interfering with the installation of the facilities.

On appeal, NI Gas raises five contentions of error: (1) that necessary or indispensable parties (landowners) were not joined; (2) that Consolidated failed to exhaust alternate remedies, so declaratory judgment is an improper remedy; (3) that Consolidated is not a public utility under the Plat Act that the terms of the easements prohibit utilization of them by consolidated; and (5) that Consolidated must go before the Illinois Commerce Commission before seeking relief in the courts.

Edison makes identical contentions, but adds the argument that there was no actual controversy between the parties, as would be required for declaratory relief.

Bell's contentions on appeal differ because it entered into written stipulation with Consolidated before trial. The agreement recited Bell's disinterest in whether or not Consolidated has a right to use the easements. Because Bell had already agreed not to interfere with Consolidated's installation of facilities, it contends on appeal that the injunction was erroneously entered by the trial court against it. Bell also contends that it has been enjoined from conduct that it never pursued.

First, we address the contention that the trial court erred, as a matter of law, in deciding that the landowners were not indispensable parties. NI Gas contends that the Civil Practice Act requires dismissal of this case because Consolidated had "reasonable opportunity" to join all indispensable parties, yet chose not to do so.

Edison urges that a different provision of the Civil Practice Act requires inclusion of the landowners because, without them, there can be no complete determination of the controversy.

Both Edison and NI Gas urge that case law supports their contentions. In a case not cited by the parties some specific guidelines for what constitutes a necessary party were set forth:

> "A necessary party is one whose presence in the suit is required for any of three reasons: (1) to protect an interest which the absentee has in the subject matter of the controversy which would be materially affected by a judgment entered in his absence; (2) to reach a decision which will protect the interests of those who are before the court; or (3) to enable the court to make a complete determination of the controversy."

The application of these principles to the case before us requires first, consideration of whether the absent parties have an interest which will necessarily be affected by the judgment. If so, they must be joined.

Here the absent parties are the owners of the land encumbered by the easement. The word easement has been defined as a "a right or privilege in the real estate of another." By definition, then, Consolidated's use of the land will affect the landowners' property. Hence, we believe the absent parties do have an interest which will be affected by the judgment.

The second query is whether reaching a decision will protect those who are before the court. Obviously, the orders entered here, which enjoined defendant utilities from interfering with Consolidated's activity, will not protect Consolidated from actions brought by the various homeowners, whether there is merit to the homeowners claims or not. In this sense Consolidated is unprotected. Therefore, the second test also indicates that the homeowners are necessary parties.

For reasons similar to the above, the third test also requires homeowner participation, for without them, complete determination of the controversy is impossible.

All three requirements having been met, we believe the homeowners are necessary and indispensable parties to this cause, and they must be named in the suit.

In *Ragsdale v. Superior Oil Co.,* . . . the failure to join certain leaseholders resulted in the dismissal of a complaint that sought to void a sale of land. Each leaseholder shared an interest in the oil production of the entire tract. Because the effect on the remaining owners, not parties to the suit, would be direct and substantial, the merits could not be reached. The court required all owners and lessees to be made parties because title was in dispute and plaintiff had the burden of proving his title. While the property interest held by the leaseholders differs somewhat from that in the case at bar, the same principles are applicable to the easement claims made by Consolidated: A claim contrary to the record chain of title, or at least a dispute in that regard, requires that all owners of land over which the easement runs, except those few which have granted an easement to Consolidated, be made parties. The question of whether or not Consolidated has a right to use the property should not be decided in a forum that excludes the actual owners of the property. For these reasons we believe that the homeowners are indispensable parties.

It appears the backyard easements in issue here were created when the plats of survey were filed. The exhibits reveal that at least three of the plats specifically name Consolidated. As previously mentioned, the easement terms of the plats vary tremendously. Consolidated did obtain approval from certain of the homeowners. The remaining plats present a different problem. The case law is clear in describing the general rule applicable here. If the easement is limited in scope or purpose, the owner of the property subject to the easement burden is entitled to prevent such burden from being increased.

When, as is the case in certain of the easements here, the easement is reserved for gas, electric and telephone service, the plain meaning of the reservation does not also include other unnamed services. As the *Marlatt* decision noted, easements must be construed according to their terms.

Because some additional issues raised in his appeal are likely to be raised again on remand, we will briefly address them here.

The trial court found that Consolidated was a public utility within the contemplation of the plats in question. Both Edison and NI Gas urge that the trial court erred in this regard.

It has been determined that cable television corporations are not subject to Commerce Commission regulation as public utilities under "An Act concerning Public Utilities." Cable television is not related to phone services under the Act. Therefore, we believe Consolidated need not have sought relief before the Commission. It should be noted that certain aspects of cable television, such as pole attachment agreements, are subject to Commission regulation.

Edison and NI Gas contend that the court erred by expanding the scope of the easements beyond their express terms. We agree. Despite the fact that some of the plats indicate easements with no express terms, it is clear that an additional use of an easement is an additional burden on it. Similarly, it has been held that an easement reserved for "gas, electric and telephone" could not be read to include water service, absent involvement by the property owners. (*Marlatt v. Peoria Water Works Co.* . . . noted that the Plat Act did not necessarily require a limited public utility easement be expanded by implication to include any public utility.

Bell's contentions on appeal differ because of the fact that Consolidated and Bell entered into a written stipulation before trial. The agreement recites Bell's disinterest in whether Consolidated has a right to use the easements or not. Bell contends on appeal that the injunction was erroneously entered by the trial court against them because they had already agreed not to interfere with Consolidated's installation of facilities. Bell contends, therefore, that it has been enjoined from conduct that it never pursued. We believe the injunction was improperly entered against Bell.

Edison and NI Gas also contend that Consolidated is unlawfully exercising powers of eminent domain. While the city, as a municipal corporation, may exercise such powers, we do not believe their franchisees or licensees can. Nor is it clear that Consolidated has tried to exercise such powers. However, Consolidated is a licensee of the city, and may have the right to use whatever easements the city possesses in accordance with their license.

Absent homeowner participation, and evidence from them about the exact nature of the easements through their property, we cannot improve on the trial court's findings, but only remand for a more specific delineation of which easements Consolidated does, or does not, have the right to use. We believe the trial court's findings were too broad in scope to be sustained.

For these reasons the findings of the trial court of Kane County are reversed and remanded for proceedings consistent with this opinion. [Some citations omitted.]

3.11 TITLE HOLDING FOR REAL PROPERTY OWNERSHIP

The following chart summarizes the key aspects of real property ownership in two ways: first, in the rights of the parties, particularly the owner; and second, in the type of control through time that the owner has over the parcel of property. This chart is designed to help you summarize the ideas about title, ownership, and rights to real property that have been discussed in this chapter.

Term	Parties' Rights	Present or Future
Fee simple	Owner has almost all, but can *share with* (1) other owner, (2) government claims, (3) easement holder, or (4) license holder, the maximum rights possible.	Present and future control of land disposition.
Conditional fee	Same as fee simple	Present control—yes. Future control—it can happen, but it is subject to defeat by an act that violates the condition in the deed that granted the land.
Life estate	Same as fee simple	Present—complete during the "life" except for limit of no waste. Future—none in the life tenant. Property disposed of as grantor determined.
Leasehold	Tenant—limited in possession and use as the lease determines. Landlord—limited to lease contract terms; usually holds in fee simple.	Present—for tenant, so long as lease terms complied with; may be held for a variety of periods, such as an estate for years, a periodic tenancy, a tenancy at will, or a tenancy at sufferance. Future—reverts to landlord.

Term	Parties' Rights	Present or Future
Joint tenancy with right of survivorship	Used to describe multiple owners' interest in freehold estate—usually a fee simple; each has rights in entire property.	Present—those living. Future—as owners die, property goes to survivors until last one takes it all.
Tenancy in common	Same as joint tenancy.	Present—those living. Future—each tenant's interest can pass as the tenant-owner determines during life or at death.

(Continued)

3.12 EASEMENT CHECKLIST

From time to time in this book, there will be checklists designed to help you deal with a particular type of problem or situation. Here, the checklist on easements is designed to help you think about the details of real estate law that can be involved in easements; how to structure thinking about them; and how to handle situations involving easements when you are working with documentation (or otherwise). The following checklist is only a start; for your particular situations, you will need to adapt and supplement the items that are in this checklist.

I. What legal entities are involved in the transaction?
   A. Who has title; who is granting the easement? Has a title examination been done to be certain of ownership (see IX)?
   B. Who is the owner of the property that will be benefited?

II. What is the proper legal description of the easement area?
   A. Should this description be a generic description of the entire parcel of grantor's property (without a specialized description of the actual area to be used)?
   B. Should there be a specialized description of the area of the easement? Is there a survey that describes the boundaries of the easement area?
   C. What is the legal description of the property that will receive the benefit of the easement [essential for easements appurtenant, such as a driveway, a sidewalk, or any common usage easement]?

III. Why is the easement being created?
   A. Is it an easement either widely used or often done?

1. A public utility such as water, gas, sewer, electric, or cable television.
2. General access to public streets and highways.
3. Parking facilities.
4. Who, in what document, has given permission for any of these?

B. Is there a clear and accurate description of the use to which the easement will be put? [This description is important because the law interprets the usage of easements against the party that drafted their descriptive language. Further, the language must be adequate to fully describe all the usages that could arise or be needed.]

IV. What is the consideration to make this contract binding?

A. Is there some benefit that both parties get from the easement (for instance, a common usage such as a driveway, where each gets something from the other)?

B. Is it a formal but minimal consideration ("For $10 paid in hand and other good and valuable consideration")?

C. Is there a negotiated price which represents a fair market value?

V. What is the length of time this easement will run?

A. Forever, in perpetuity?

B. An identified time, that is, 6 months, 15 years?

C. Until some subsequent condition or event occurs?

VI. Is the use of the easement to be exclusive to the grantee, for general public, or somewhere in between? In other words, someone has to determine the class of beneficiaries who can use the easement, and that determination must be included in the writing that grants the easement.

VII. Who is responsible for maintaining the easement property?

A. Both parties (the grantor and the grantee of the easement when the easement benefits both of them, such as a sidewalk)? If so, what methods have been set up in the granting document to make sure that both parties will do their share of the work or bear their share of the cost of maintaining the easement?

1. Does enforcement require a lawsuit, or can a lien be filed against the other party's property?
2. Is the easement to be forfeited for nonmaintenance?

B. Is maintenance the responsibility of the grantee?

C. Is maintenance the responsibility of the grantor, but the maintenance costs are reimbursed to the grantor by the grantee?

VIII. Do any outside parties have claims to either parcel of property? Principally, this refers to any mortgage holder on either property, but lien holders should be included as well. Obtain the permission of any lien holder or mortgagee of record so that the easement cannot be terminated if the property is foreclosed upon. Note: Did the title examination to determine who held title also cover who had liens or mortgages on the property?

IX. Who bears the risk of loss for liability for the easement?
   A. Is there cross-indemnification between the parties when the easements are mutually beneficial, as in a joint project?
   B. Does the responsibility lie with the grantee to reimburse the grantor of easement?
   C. Is there liability insurance?
      1. Who are the named insureds? The grantor, the grantee, or both?
      2. Who pays for the insurance? The grantor, the grantee, or both? In what proportions?

X. Are there signature requirements to be concerned about?
   A. The grantor of the easement must sign.
   B. The grantee must sign if there are any contractual provisions for the grantee to be held to, such as insurance or maintenance clauses or any indemnification agreement.
   C. Are the signatures witnessed and notarized in a manner sufficient to permit recording of the document?

XI. Has the easement document been recorded?
   A. The easement must be recorded to protect the easement holder(s) from subsequent purchasers, mortgagees, or lien holders of the easement property.
   B. Date of recording? (This item may seem redundant, but the author has seen people who are *certain* that a document is recorded but are unable to determine the date of recording; of course, it had not been filed. Take the date from the recorded document and be sure!)

DISCUSSION AND REVIEW QUESTIONS

1. How can one distinguish between a freehold and leasehold estate?
2. Identify the differences between the language used to create a fee simple and a conditional fee.
3. Why is waste an issue for future interest holders?
4. Which type of leasehold estate appears to be the most common? Why?
5. What parts of this area of the law cause the greatest problems?
6. Distinguish between the assignment of a lease and a sublease. Be sure to identify the effects of each format on the third party.
7. How do the landlord's and the tenant's duties differ?
8. What changing aspects need a close watch?
9. Distinguish between severance and partition in relation to a joint tenancy.
10. What is the most commonly created type of easement? How is it most frequently created?

11. In 1946, A deeded Blackacre to B, his old and valued friend, for life, and upon B's death to C, his granddaughter, in fee. Valuable mineral rights were discovered on the property in 1964, 12 years after A's death. B proceeds to lease the property to Mineral Development Company. C sues and claims that waste is being committed on the property and seeks monetary damages or an injunction forbidding development. What are the rights of B and C?
12. X owns Whiteacre in fee simple. She has been a teacher for 35 years and is interested in promoting education. When she dies, X wills Whiteacre to Jones County to be used "for educational purposes only. . . . If this land is used for any purpose other than educational, it shall revert to my heirs." As time passes, the county school board builds a school there, but decades later it decides to sell the property because the location is no longer appropriate for a school. When the board sells the property, X's heirs sue and claim that the property should revert to them. Does the board have a right to sell the property? Do X's heirs have a claim against the board for the property?
13. P, the parent of S and D, owns Blackacre, a parcel of land running along the Mississippi River. The family has used the property for 35 years for summer recreation. At P's death, her will divides the property equally between S and D, each taking one-half in fee. The property runs for one-half mile along the river, and next to the property is County Road X. S has the property next to the river, D has the property next to the road. S has no access to his property along the river except by crossing D's property, and D has no access to the river except by crossing S's property. This gift could result in constant family disputes, so what possible legal arrangement could work for this family?
14. A, the landlord, rented an apartment to B for $575 per month for a year beginning on April 1, 1994. The property soon suffered from severe problems, such as leakage from a faulty roof, problems with insects, and plaster falling from the ceilings and walls. By August 15, 1995, B had moved out. Discuss the different ways this situation might be treated under a strict common-law approach and a modern approach.

SAMPLE FORMS

The forms reproduced here may be used as models or guides in appropriate situations. The careful paralegal will, of course, make any necessary adjustments for a particular client, case, and the technical requirements of local law.

SIDEBAR

To avoid endless entanglements when divorce occurs and to protect property. Notice the full disclosure requirements in § 6 and the retention of control in § 2.

Antenuptial Property Agreement

Antenuptial agreement made ________, 19____, between ________ *[prospective husband]*, an adult, of ________ *[address]*, City of________, County of ________, State of ________, and ________ *[prospective wife]*, an adult, of ________ *[address]*, City of ________, County of ________, State of ________, in consideration of the contemplated marriage of the above-named parties __________ *[if additional consideration is given for the agreement, add:* and in further consideration of ________ (cash or bonds or securities *or as the case may be*), in hand paid to _________ *(prospective spouse)* by__________ *(other prospective spouse)].*

RECITALS

The parties stipulate and recite that:

A. A marriage is intended and desired to be solemnized between the parties.

B. Each of the parties is possessed of property, both real and personal, which they separately own or have an interest in their individual right.

C. In anticipation of such marriage, the parties desire to fix and determine the rights of each of them in any and all property of every nature and description and wheresoever located that the other may own or have an interest in at the time of such marriage or may acquire thereafter.

D. Each of the parties desires to retain, manage, or dispose separately by gift, will, or otherwise all of his or her estate to the same extent as if each of such parties remained single.

E. Each of the parties has made a full disclosure to the other party of all of his or her property and assets and of the value thereof, and this agreement is entered into with a full knowledge on the part of each as to the extent and probable value of the estate of the other, and of all the rights conferred by law on each in the estate of the other by virtue of such proposed marriage.

AGREEMENT

In consideration of mutual covenants contained herein, prospective husband and prospective wife agree as follows:

SECTION ONE
MAINTENANCE OF WIFE

Prospective husband, during the continuance of his marriage with the prospective wife, shall provide a home and maintain and support prospective wife.

SECTION TWO
RETENTION OF TITLE, MANAGEMENT, AND
CONTROL OF SEPARATE ESTATE

Each of the parties shall retain the title, management, and control of the estates now owned by each of them, whether real, personal or mixed, and all increase or addition thereto, entirely free and unmolested by the other party and may encumber, sell, dispose, give, or provide by will for the disposition of any or all of such estates so separately owned and possessed.

At the death of either party, no claim by inheritance, descent, surviving spouse award, homestead, dower, or maintenance shall be made by either of the parties against the other or against the estate of the other.

Each of the parties separately waives any and all rights by dower, homestead, surviving spouse award, inheritance, descent, or any other marital right arising by virtue of statute or otherwise in and to any parcel of the estate now owned and possessed by the other, and agrees and consents that each shall have full power and control in all respects to exercise free and undisputed ownership, management, and disposition of each of such estates and increases thereto now owned and possessed by the parties; and each of such parties waives and renounces any legal and statutory rights that might, under any law, be set up against any part of the estate of the other and consents that the estate of each shall descend or be disposed of by will to the heirs or legatees or devisees of each of the parties, free and clear of any claim by inheritance, dower, surviving spouse award, homestead, maintenance, or any claim otherwise given by law to a husband and wife.

SECTION THREE
TRANSFERS, GIFTS; DEVISES AND BEQUESTS

This agrement shall not, in any manner, bar or affect the right of either party to claim and receive any property of any nature or character that the other party, by last will, or by any other instrument, may give, devise, bequeath, transfer, or assign.

SECTION FOUR
JOINDER IN CONVEYANCES

If either party shall mortgage, pledge, or sell and convey, his or her real or personal estate, whether in whole or in part, the other party shall, on demand, join in any and every mortgage, or deed of conveyance, or in any other instrument that may be necessary or desirable to make the instrument effectual.

SECTION FIVE
COMMUNITY PROPERTY

In the event that at any time during the existence of the marital relationship between the parties, they should be or become residents of a state under the laws of which husband and wife acquire property interests commonly known as community property or any other property and interests different from the property interests of husband and wife under the laws of the State of __________, their property interests shall nevertheless remain the same as they would have been under the terms of this agreement construed in accordance with the laws of the State of __________, and the parties will each, at any time during or after the termination of the marital relationship, execute and deliver any and all deeds and other instruments desirable or necessary to transfer any right, title, or interest, in any property or estate of the other which they may acquire by virtue of any so-called community property laws to the persons who would otherwise be entitled thereto by virtue of this agreement.

SECTION SIX
FULL KNOWLEDGE OF BOTH PARTIES

This agreement is entered into by the parties will full knowledge on the part of each of the extent and probable value of all of the property or estate of the other, and of all rights that, but for this agreement, would be conferred by law on each of them, in the property or estate of the other, by virtue of the consummation of the proposed marriage, and the rights of the respective parties in and to each other's property, or estate, of whatsoever character, shall be determined, fixed, and settled by this agreement, and not otherwise.

SECTION SEVEN
ENTIRE AGREEMENT; ALTERATION OR MODIFICATION

This agreement constitutes the entire agreement between the parties relating to their antenuptial property arrangements. There are no oral agreements between the parties respecting such antenuptial property arrangements. Any alteration or modification of this agreement must be in writing, signed and acknowledged by each of the parties.

SECTION EIGHT
BINDING EFFECT

This agreement shall bind the parties and their respective heirs, administrators, and assigns, and shall become effective only on the consummation of the proposed marriage between the parties, and if such marriage does not take place, this agreement shall be null and void.

In witness whereof, the parties have executed this agreement at ______ ______ *[place of execution]* the day and year first above written.

[Signatures]

[Acknowledgment]

Warranty Deed—From Individual to Tenants in Common

SIDEBAR

Notice the different language in the granting section.

WARRANTY DEED

______, of ______ *[address]*, County of ______, State of ________, as grantor, in consideration of the payment to grantor of _______ Dollars ($____), the receipt of which is acknowledged, grants, bargains, sells, and conveys to ________ and ________, as tenants in common, in equal shares, all that real property located in the County of ______, State of _______, described as follows: __________*[legal description]*, together with all improvements on such property and the appurtenances belonging to such property, and warrants the title to such property.

To have and to hold the described premises to ______ and ______, grantees, as tenants in common, forever, free, clear, and discharged of and from all former grants, charges, taxes, judgments, and other liens and encumbrances of any nature.

In witness whereof, the grantor has set grantor's hand _________ [and seal] on _________ *[date]*.

[Signature]
[Seal]

[Attestation]
[Acknowledgment]

Quitclaim Deed

QUITCLAIM DEED

Bargain and sale deed made _________ *[date]*, between _________, transferor, of_________ *[address]*, City of _______, County of _________, State of _______, and ________, transferee, of __________ *[address including post office address]*, City of _______, County of _______, State of _________:

In consideration of __________ *[state consideration]*, transferor remises, releases, and forever quitclaims to transferee all of the following property situated in the County of __________, State of New Jersey: _________ *[legal description of property]*.

In witness whereof, transferor has set transferor's hand and seal on the day and year first written above.

[Signature]

Signed, sealed, and delivered in the presence of _________.
[Acknowledgment]
Prepared by _________ *[name of person drafting deed]*.

Bargain and Sale Deed

BARGAIN AND SALE DEED

This indenture made this __________ day of __________, between _________, of _________ *[address]*, City of __________, County of ________, State of _________, party of the first part, and _________, of _________ *[address]*, City of _________, County of _________, State of _________, party of the second part:

The party of the first part, for and in consideration of the sum of ________ Dollars ($___), to such party in hand paid by the party of the second part, the receipt of which is acknowledged, has granted, bargained, and sold to the party of the second part, and such party's heirs, and assigns forever, the following described land: _________ [legal description of property] in the County of ________, State of ________. And the party of the first part does fully warrant the title to the land conveyed, and will defend the same against the lawful claims of all persons whomsoever.

In witness whereof, the party of the first part has executed this deed on the date first written above.

[Signature]

[Attestation]
[Acknowledgment]
Appraiser's parcel identification number: _________.

CHAPTER 4
Title Determination and Protection

"Law is a bottomless pit."

John Arbuthnot

Spanish-style ranch house

OUTLINE

PROLOGUE TO THE PARALEGAL

Now that the topics of where the property is located and how people have rights in the property have been dealt with, it is possible to take the next step. That step is to understand the public records concerning real estate, which inform interested persons about who has what rights in a piece of property located at a particular spot. One of the jobs that a paralegal may do is to order searches to determine who owns a parcel of property and who has claims against the owner or against the property itself. You will need to understand the different ways of determining who has title, which is preferable, and why. You will also need to get a basic understanding of the process of searching to determine who has claims on the title and the ways in which title insurance is used, generally at minimal cost, to protect the owner's or lender's interests in the parcel of real property. Other types of insurance that can affect real property and the people who have interests in real property are also discussed.

KEY TERMS

abstract company
abstract of title
acknowledgment
ALTA
bona fide purchaser
caveat emptor
chain of title
clean title
co-insurance
constructive notice
deed
delivery
endorsement
extended coverage endorsement
good faith purchaser for value
good title
grantor-grantee index
liability risk

lis pendens
loss payable clause
marketable title
patent
probate court
property risk
title company
title insurance
title search
tract index
witnessing

4.1 INTRODUCTION

Because the price of real estate is high, and becoming proportionately higher in terms of personal disposable income, any buyer of real estate wants to be certain that the title she is receiving is **good title** or **clean title**; in other words, that the title she will possess will be **marketable title**, meaning that the title is readily saleable. The buyer (or the buyer's agent, such as her attorney) must be able to find out if other persons have claims on the property—who has claims, what they claim, when the claim began, and how much money the claim amounts to. If there are no claims affecting the prospective buyer's use of the property or the buyer's ownership rights, the property is said to have clean title.

Clean title, however, need not be perfect title, in which there were no claims of any sort on the property. In a modern, urbanized world, we share our surroundings with many other people, and some of them (or their governmental representatives) may well have claims on the property. For instance, there are always utilities, which make the property more usable, benefit the owner, and increase the uses to which she can put the property. However, the company that provides the gas, the electric power, the cable television, or the telephone must have an easement across the property (and sometimes other properties) to reach the building. The road providing access to the property creates a governmental easement, or right of way, that denies or shares with the owner the use of her property in that area. Overall, this type of outside claim on the property is unobjectionable, because it enables the owner to have access to the property from the outside world.

Another common item that affects the property is local taxes. Because real estate taxes are frequently paid in arrears, unpaid taxes will appear as a claim that the government has against the property. This tax claim must be settled when the closing on the property occurs.

The problems for title determination lie primarily in two areas. First, there may be prior parties in the chain of title. Second, creditors may have filed claims against the seller (or a prior real property title holder) by placing a lien on the property for an unpaid obligation. The first group might be thought of as people who had ownership claims and the second group as people who have been creditors of someone who is or has been in title (usually called an *owner*). The term *creditor* is used here in the broadest sense to imply a person who has provided something for which the owner did not pay (or repay). Such a person can range from a bank that provided a loan and took a mortgage to a roofer who repaired a leak, was not paid, and

LEGAL TERMS

good title (also called clean title and marketable title)
Description of title when the public record contains no apparent impediments to the real property owner's use and transfer of the property as she chooses.

filed a mechanic's lien. Indeed, any creditor who has obtained a judgment and then filed against the property has the rights of a judgment creditor.

Any party making a claim that could affect the real property must make a recording against that parcel in the real property records. That recording provides constructive notice to the world that the claim exists, not only against the person, but against that person's asset, the land. These recorded claims become important when the person tries to sell the property; a buyer will not want to take over any of the seller's financial problems. Consequently, the buyer must determine who has what claims and whether those claims are legitimate. The entire real estate business is based upon this determination and could not exist without it. No individual or legal entity would risk buying a home, leasing long-term commercial space, or investing in an industrial project if they could not determine the quality of the title. No commercial developer would ever construct a project on land where the rights to the title in the land were unclear. Good title is essential.

A two-part system ensures that information about real estate title is available and easily accessible. The first part of the system is a recording system through which all claims to a particular parcel of real property are filed in the public records. The second part is a process of searching those public recordings to determine who has placed claims against the property on record. "To determine title or to search title," as this second part of the system is often referred to, a search of the documents in the public records affecting that particular parcel of real property is done. The search is done at the local government's real estate office (usually at the county level; the office is referred to as the County Recorder of Deeds, the County Recorder, the Register of Deeds, or simply the Recorder's Office). This process is referred to as a **title search**, and it determines the quality of the title that the seller is offering to the buyer. Alas and alack, however, the world is imperfect, and people err. When a mistake occurs, the loss can be substantial, and recovery is time-consuming and difficult, if not impossible. Fortunately, there is a way to protect buyers. They can buy **title insurance** to cover mistakes in the title search.

Today, in most urban areas and the rural areas near them, there are business corporations called **title companies** or **abstract companies**. These businesses have two functions. First, their employees do the actual search and write a report on the status of the title. Second, for what is usually a minimal fee, they provide insurance against any errors in the information provided in that title search. One is said to "order title" or to "bring down title" for the first process and to "buy a title policy" for the second process. The term *title policy* is an abbreviated version of "an insurance policy protecting the title to this parcel of real estate." Much of the preparatory work for the title process is handled by the buyer's attorney or that attorney's paralegal. That person will place the order after acquiring and verifying the proper legal description from the buyer or seller.

These services developed to meet the needs not only of individual buyers and owners, but also of attorneys who wanted to protect their clients.

LEGAL TERMS

title search
Process of investigating and searching the public records concerning real property to determine the status or quality of the title to a parcel of real property; can also mean examination of the abstract of title.

title insurance
Insurance issued to cover potential defects in the title to real property.

title company
Company engaged in the business of searching real estate records, providing reports on the status of real estate title, and, frequently, issuing insurance covering potential title defects.

Most importantly, however, financial institutions (such as banks and insurance companies) that finance the purchase of real estate wanted clear information and protection against mistakes. They needed to be able to rely on the quality of their borrowers' title in the event the borrowers could not or did not pay the loan they had taken out to buy the real estate. In that event, these creditors would have to foreclose on and sell the properties to obtain repayment of the loans. Without clean title, the process would be more expensive and much riskier. If that were normally the case, the costs of lending might be significantly higher, and fewer people would be able to borrow money to purchase homes.

abstract company
Business that prepares a summary of the recorded title documents relating to a parcel of real estate.

good faith purchaser for value
Legal concept that permits a legal entity to take property ahead of others, despite what may appear to be better claims to the property, if this legal entity has satisfied the requirements for good faith (essentially complied with all the steps necessary to determine other claims to the property) and paid roughly the market price for the parcel.

bona fide purchasers
Latin for "good faith" purchasers. A person is, colloquially, said to have, or to have established, his or her "bona fides"; means purchasers who have taken all the steps necessary to inform themselves of the rights of others and how they might affect the purchaser.

constructive notice
Type of notice recognized by law for public real estate records; distinguished from actual notice. To be considered as operating in good faith, one is required to check the public records to determine the claims of others against a particular parcel of real property; these records provide constructive notice to any party having an interest in a parcel of real estate.

4.2 THE LEGAL BASES FOR REAL ESTATE TITLE SEARCHES

The law applies a number of basic principles to different circumstances and areas of the law. Two of these principles underlie the process of searching for real estate title information. The first is the idea of *notice*; the second, the idea of the protections due a **good faith purchaser for value**. (The Latin for the words "good faith" is *bona fide,* and the **bona fide purchaser** is often referred to as a "b.f.p." But don't forget the "value" aspect.) Both of these concepts are deeply rooted in our culture's sense of fair play and, thus, in the equitable side of the law.

First, it is essential to understand the concept of notice. Notice is basically simple. The question is whether the buyer knows or not; if the buyer personally and directly knows something, he or she is said to have *actual notice.* If the buyer can determine it with his or her own senses (vision, hearing, smell), if someone tells the prospective buyer, or if the buyer is held to have a duty to investigate and find out for himself or herself because of some special set of circumstances, then the buyer is involved in an actual notice situation. But actual notice is limited by the running-around, checking-everything-out process that it entails. It is much more useful, efficient, and convenient to have some type of centralized approach for verifying ownership and claims. This verification process is why recording statutes created a land recording system. With recording statutes, the issue is not one of actual notice, but of **constructive notice**—what a reasonable person should know and what the law will require him or her to know.

A situation of constructive notice arises, or constructive notice is imputed to a person, when the person has the right and ability to acquire information from a readily available source. That person is said to have constructive notice of that information regardless of whether she had actually acquired it or not. In relation to real property, constructive notice is the legal rule that a reasonable person should take all the steps necessary to determine any information from the recording process that would affect the person's rights in the parcel of real property. Because any reasonable person would take those steps, the law holds a person responsible for learning that information, because it is readily available in an open and public manner or place—the recording statutes—and would be investigated by any reasonable person who wanted to protect his or her own interests.

Failing to investigate does not change the rule; the buyers could have found out, so they are considered to have constructive notice. In the real estate business, a person can go to the public real estate records and determine (directly, by means of one's attorney, or through a professional title search) all of the other parties who have claims or interests in that parcel of property. All parties are said to have constructive notice of the information in the real estate records. Consequently, ignorance cannot be used as a defense. This idea ties directly into the concept of good faith (in the good faith purchaser for value idea), because no one can be said to be operating in good faith or fairly if they did not do all they reasonably could to determine the information.

Another example of constructive notice is the information obtainable from an actual visit to the premises. If the premises are in possession of someone other than the party trying to sell the property, the prospective buyer is said to have constructive notice of the need for further investigation. Why is this party on the property? Does he or she have a right to be there? Can he or she be removed? Would the buyer have to take the property subject to the rights of the person(s) occupying it? This duty to investigate contains aspects of **caveat emptor**, "buyer beware." The law finds it rational to expect someone to investigate and determine (to the best of her ability) the risks that could be involved in the sale. The law imposes a duty on the purchaser to investigate and protect himself to the best of his ability. Some of the issues that arise regarding the buyer's duty to inspect the premises to be purchased are phrased in terms of the extent of this duty and how well the buyer has fulfilled it. For example, if the buyer is not personally knowledgeable, is it necessary to hire an expert? How can the buyer determine another's expertise? Can the buyer rely on statements made by the seller?

Another type of issue in constructive notice relates to the search of the public records. In searching real estate title records, one could theoretically check title holders back to the original grant from the government. The list of parties in title is called the **chain of title**. If there is any problem with this chain of title, the title search is said to show "a cloud on the title" or an "objection." Clearly, what constitutes the elements of the chain of title is very important. Does one have to pay attention to every document that purports to deal with the parcel of land made by a person who has been in title? Or does one only have to check the documents that purport to affect title made by a person who was, at the time, in title? In essence, one questions either every document that may affect the property executed by a person who has been in title or only those documents that may affect title that were executed when the person held title. The choice between these is important, because it determines the work needed to not be held responsible under the doctrine of constructive notice.

Finally, what if the investigation of the documents in the chain of title uncovers documents that are not recorded? Does the doctrine of constructive notice require that these documents, once discovered, be investigated?

Yes, because discovering them has provided notice; therefore, the documents must be investigated to protect the buyer. Otherwise, the buyer may be liable for whatever obligation that document represents (usually a money payment). Failure to follow through on this matter could greatly increase the price of the property and greatly upset the relationship with the buyer's lender and mortgagee.

The second basic legal principle is that of the good faith purchaser for value. The first idea, that of notice, goes directly to the concept of good faith. If one has not satisfied the requirements of constructive notice, one cannot be said to have acted in good faith. If one does not act in good faith, there is no cut-off of prior claims against the property. The person who buys without acting in good faith becomes responsible to prior claimants against the property. In short, the good faith purchaser for value establishes her good faith (her bona fides) by checking to comply with any items of actual or constructive notice. When the buyer is a good faith purchaser for value, that buyer is protected against unrecorded prior liens and claims, which are said to be "cut off." The purchaser with this legal status takes the property free of them. This concept usually applies to the claims of private parties; it is not as reliable in relation to government claims. Unpaid taxes would still be owed, but a purchaser who recorded the appropriate document would take free and clear of an unrecorded document, such as a private mortgage claim or a deed. The *purchaser* is the party buying the property. The concept of value, while more specific than consideration, causes few problems if the purchase price is arrived at by open negotiation under normal business practices, or is comparable to similar properties.

This concept of the good faith purchaser for value is very important in the law, and it goes back to the very foundations of all law. It exists not only in real estate but also in commercial law. Through its law, society has decided that keeping business transactions flowing easily is more important than protecting parties who are not careful about or do not take the appropriate steps to protect their interests. Note that a system exists to protect the claims and interests of third parties (other than the buyer and seller). They can record documents that will provide public notice of their interests. If these parties make recordings, purchasers cannot become good faith purchasers, and, as a result, remain subject to the claims represented in the recorded documents. This legal rule keeps the arteries of commerce unclogged and money flowing easily. Without this rule, there would be fewer transactions and less business activity. This rule has had an even more powerful impact in other areas of the law, such as commercial law, that deal with the sale of goods and the negotiability of documents and instruments.

Of course, technical legal issues arise in this area. First, what constitutes recording—what does it mean to get your document into the legal record? Second, what is the effect of a clerical error, for example, when a clerk fails to file or misfiles a document? The first issue deals with whether delivery of the document to the clerk constitutes recording, or

LEGAL TERMS

caveat emptor
Latin for "buyer beware"; signifies a legal doctrine whereby the responsibility for the safety and quality of a product lies with the buyer, not with the manufacturer or seller; use of the doctrine has declined substantially in the 20th century.

chain of title
List of the successive owners of a parcel of real property, as shown by the recordation of transfer deeds and other documents in the public real estate records of the county where the real estate is located.

whether the clerk must enter the information in the proper recording book for recording to have occurred. Obviously, courts have gone both ways, and it is necessary to determine what the courts in your jurisdiction have decided on this issue. If the clerk must actually make the proper entry, one must do a search after making the recording to determine if it has been done properly. One should give the recorder a little extra time to complete the task.

The second issue, although it is not always discussed in these terms, is essentially to identify the party responsible for the clerk's error; this issue also has two alternatives. The fault can either be put on the government clerk (that is, the government) or upon the recording party. The recording party usually has the duty to verify that the recording was done properly, as he or she can search a short time after recording. The other approach says that once a document is delivered, whether the clerk has recorded it properly or not, that recording constitutes constructive notice. Clearly, if any risk is involved (and there almost always is), the safe procedure would be to search after recording.

SIDEBAR

Neither approach places the burden of responsibility on the state whose clerk made the error. This approach is from the medieval or Roman view that the sovereign—that is, the government—can do no wrong, and this view remains with us in the legal doctrine of sovereign immunity (the state cannot be sued without its permission). The paralegal will encounter this principle often in the law. Although the doctrine appears to have little rational basis in a democracy that considers government to be the agent of the people, there are practical considerations to support the government's lack of liability. The cost of lawsuits and the price of judgments would have to be borne by general taxation or extremely expensive users' fees, neither of which would be acceptable. In another legal area, where a great many documents are presented for filing—financing statements under Article 9 of the Uniform Commercial Code—the legal rule appears to be heading in the direction of making the party doing the filing responsible. This is a logical position, as those parties are in the best position to help themselves. Parties recording documents would be well advised to check, shortly after the recording has been done, to determine if their recording appears on the search.

4.3 TYPES OF RECORDING STATUTES

There are three types of recording statutes, referred to as notice, race, and notice-race statutes. The differences are how and when the impact of the recording statute comes into play.

Under a *notice statute*, one must give public notice—by recording under the statute the document(s) that reflect the transaction—in order to be protected against a subsequent good faith purchaser for value whose claim to the land would be superior to that of an unrecorded party. In theory, a person who did not record her interest could still win if the other party actually knew of her interest, but proving that the other party had this knowledge is difficult; the fact of recording is public information.

Under a *race statute*, protection is based upon who filed first; first to file wins. There is no issue of good faith or knowledge. There are only a few of these statutes. The notice statute is the most frequently adopted by states, with the notice-race statute close behind.

The *notice-race statute* has elements of both the recording for public notice, so that a good faith checking requirement may be imposed on the subsequent purchaser, but "the race to the courthouse" element is involved as well. Not only must the party concerned record, but he must record prior to other parties to have priority over and protection against a subsequent good faith purchaser for value. The recording serves as constructive notice to all subsequent purchasers; it thus does not allow them to be good faith purchasers, because they could have checked the records.

An example may clarify the differences among the three types of statutes. Consider these facts. Andrew owns Blackacre and sells it to Betty on September 5; Betty records the transfer deed on September 20. Andrew once again sells Blackacre, this time to Carla, on September 15. On

September 16, Carla records her deed. Under the common law, with no recording statute, the first deed in time (Betty's) would prevail, and the second party (Carla) would have to try to find the seller to obtain redress.

Under a notice statute, Carla would prevail, because she had no notice of Betty's deed. Her transaction was completed prior to Betty's recording. Carla would also win under a race statute because she was the first to record. Under a notice-race statute, since Carla was both the first to record and a good faith purchaser, that is, without any notice of Betty's transaction, she would win there as well. Be aware that the subsequent purchaser must be a good faith purchaser to win under notice or notice-race statutes. If Betty had recorded her document prior to Carla's transaction, Betty could have won. Carla would not have been a good faith purchaser because she would have received constructive notice of the transaction from Betty's recording. Only under the race statute does good faith not play a role. It should now be clear why a search is done on the day of closing!

One final item with which the cautious handler of real estate documentation will be concerned is the timing of the recording. Some states require that documents be recorded within a certain time period, such as 90 days, 6 months, or 1 year after their execution or **delivery**. While normal good practice would never permit a document to remain unrecorded that long, accidents do occur. It is useful to know the time limits, if any, that exist for recording. Local statutes should be checked.

4.4 TYPES OF DOCUMENTS TO BE RECORDED

The first category of documents that may be recorded are documents that generally reflect the transfer of real estate or some interest in it. The most common of these are:

1. A **deed**, which is a direct document of transfer of some interest in the real property
2. The will of a decedent, which transfers real property
3. A sales agreement or a memorandum of sale (concerning the real estate).

The transfer of rights can occur in assignments such as:

4. An assignment of a mortgage
5. An assignment of a lease
6. The assignment of any other type of right relating to real estate.

Others that may be recorded are:

7. A lease, particularly a long-term lease
8. A map or plat of a subdivision
9. Condominium documents
10. Homeowners' associations documents
11. Easements, particularly an easement appurtenant

LEGAL TERMS

delivery
Actual passing of a document or instrument from one party to another.

deed
Legal document used to transfer real property.

12. A divorce decree, when the spouses own the property together (in a divorce settlement, two options generally exist—to sell the property and divide the proceeds as the court determines or the parties agree, or to transfer the property into one spouse's exclusive ownership. Both choices involve the use of transfer deeds, and many other options also exist.)
13. Options to purchase (when the option holder has paid a valuable consideration to possess the exclusive right to purchase the particular parcel within a specified period of time)

This list, while long, only begins the enumeration.

The second most common type of documents recorded are those related to credit transactions. The most common of these are:

1. The mortgage on the property
2. A satisfaction of a mortgage
3. A release of mortgage
4. A bankruptcy decree
5. A security agreement
6. A financing statement filed under the Uniform Commercial Code
7. A purchase money mortgage or a second mortgage
8. A mechanic's lien for work done but not paid for.

The documents evidencing legal action are another type often recorded. These include:

1. Judgments
2. Court decrees that directly affect the land
3. Sheriff's deeds reflecting the sheriff's sale of the property
4. **Lis pendens**, that is, a pending lawsuit (recorded to prevent the property owner from transferring the property while the matter is under adjudication)
5. Actions occurring under federal jurisdiction (Federal tax liens and federal court actions must be investigated, but duplication of the effort from the state system to the federal system in all areas is essential for protection. If a corporation is involved, the state authorities to whom the corporation must report should be checked; similarly for any other entity that might come under the control or regulation of the state or be created pursuant to the state's laws.)
6. **Probate court** documents, such as a will or trust documents.

Other types of documents may also be recorded—trust agreements and powers of attorney, which include the power to take actions affecting real estate or transferring an interest in real property. In a trust, a person may put real property into the trust, give up control over the property, transfer that control to the trustee, and keep the benefits as the trust's beneficiary. The trustee has legal title and can transfer the land, borrow money, or otherwise affect the ownership of the land. A power of attorney can give one party the power and authority to act for another, and that power could include power over real estate.

Most recording statutes require that documents presented for recording must be acknowledged. **Acknowledgment** involves the party executing the document going to an impartial official, proving who he or she is, and stating that he or she is aware of the contents of the document and that execution of the document is voluntary. The acknowledging official thereupon states that these events have occurred and so indicates on the document. A notary public usually does acknowledgments, but other public officials, such as a judge, a court clerk, the registrar of deeds, or a justice of the peace, are also permitted. The formalities of all the details, including the imprinting of the notary's seal, should be verified. By and large, this requirement appears to be an antique formality, but it must be observed if the document is to be accepted by the clerk for recording.

Because there are local variations in the requirements for acknowledgment, take care when recording outside your normal jurisdiction. Make certain that the signatures on the document have been witnessed, if this requirement exists in your jurisdiction. A failure to have the document witnessed may destroy the validity of a document even if it has been properly recorded. The failure to witness a document can also present risks. **Witnessing** is simply having someone sign his or her name to the document as a witness of the signing. The signature indicates that the person signing knew that the signor was who she alleged to be—that the person who wrote the name "Jane Doe" actually was Jane Doe. Witnessing avoids having to prove in court that this signature was actually that of the party signing.

Interacting with the government frequently means making a payment of some sort, and there are fees and transfer taxes to pay here as well. There are two basic types of payments. First, there are fees that cover, in whole or part, the costs of providing the recording service. Second, there are taxes. These taxes come in different forms, such as a tax on the document or a tax on the transfer, but they are frequent and cannot be avoided without losing the benefits of recording. The public official cannot accept the document for recording unless there is evidence that the tax has been paid. The tax may be a flat fee or a percentage of the transaction price.

4.5 THE PROCESS OF EXAMINING TITLE

After the recording, a third party may want to check the records, or the recording party may want to verify that the documents actually were recorded. What does one do? First, what is needed to request that a title search be done? The information needed is the legal description of the property, the name of the property owner, and any other information or documents that might affect the search, such as the names of any creditors or the dates of transactions.

LEGAL TERMS

lis pendens
Latin for "pending suit"; when a suit is filed to determine rights in real property, notice is filed to stop the owner from transferring the property and denying the suit's claimant the benefits of a possible win in court. The filing constitutes constructive notice to third-party purchasers.

probate court
Specialized court that deals with wills and the estates of the deceased; actions there can affect title to real property.

acknowledgment
Statement made in front of an authorized official, usually a notary public, that the document was executed freely.

witnessing
Legal formality for documents whereby third parties sign the document to verify that the parties executing the document were actually who they said they were; requirement based in attempts to avoid fraudulent transfers.

There are two basic types of indexes that can be searched. The less common one is a **tract index**, which lists each parcel of land as it was created, described, and recorded. In this index, one can track down through time all the parties who conveyed the parcel, because it shows the successive owners of the property. It is possible to check the chain of title by going down this list. Unfortunately, not all states have had an official survey and created this system.

The more common index that the searcher can use is called the **grantor-grantee index**. This index lists, alphabetically, all the persons by name who have granted (transferred away from themselves—the grantor index) any interest in the property and the persons who have been granted any interest in the property (transferred to themselves—the grantee index). This double index is compiled annually. What one finds is the activities of the party (grantor or grantee) in the appropriate index in the correct year. What exists is a series of annual volumes that list the parties who have granted or been granted any interest in any parcel of real property. One can check back up the chain of title from the party presenting claiming title or any other interest in the real property.

These indexes are not simply lists of the names of the buyers and sellers, but of all the parties who have any interest or claim in real property, such as creditors, like a lender that took a mortgage; transferees, such as a lessee or a life tenant; or any assignor-assignee. The names of the grantor, seller, creditor, and so on are listed alphabetically in one set of books. Names of the other parties to the transaction, such as the grantee, buyer, debtor, and so on, are listed alphabetically in the other set of books. For each transaction, each index also includes the date, name of the other party, location where the document is recorded, and a description of the property, in most cases. For example, if Jane Thomas sold Blackacre to William Peterson, the party checking for Peterson checks the grantee index for the year that Thomas claims to have entered into title. After locating Thomas's name, the searcher goes to the grantor index, checks under Thomas's name, and determines if she granted the property to anyone else while she has been in title. Then, having determined who Thomas's grantor was, the searcher returns to the grantee index, checking that name as grantee. The searcher repeats the process until ultimately the searcher reaches the original grant from the government. This original government grant must be to the original land holder; that grant of title to the property is called a **patent**. The term *patent* comes from English law and is the source of the term *letters patent*. It is not connected with the modern patent given by the government for the invention of a useful device. In many areas, a mortgagor-mortgagee index is also in use. It lists the parties who have filed a lien against real property in that jurisdiction. It works in the same way that the grantor-grantee index does.

Such a complete search, using any or all of these indexes, would be an enormous amount of work in places that have been settled for several hundred years and have rapid turnover in ownership. This situation is particularly acute in urban areas of the eastern United States. To avoid this problem and waste of time, most jurisdictions have time limits on how far back a party must go in searching the chain of title; the most common number of years appears to be 40, but longer times are sometimes required. One should be aware of the details of the local statute regarding what must be checked. After checking these indexes, it is necessary to determine what other indexes or public records are relevant to the search. Some that may be crucial are a separate mortgage index, a judgment index, and a lis pendens index. The best ways to find out what else should be checked are to discuss the matter with an experienced person in the courthouse or to obtain a checklist from a local title company. There are also a number of other authorities who could claim an interest in the land, such as the local taxing authorities, which range from the municipality's claims for water and sewer payments to a list in your jurisdiction of the government liens that are enforceable without being filed.

There are three methods to determine the status of title and protect the prospective transferee—preparing an abstract of title, obtaining title insurance, or having a title registered in the Torrens System. These three are mutually exclusive, and it is highly unlikely that a person would need more than one of them. The most common approach is to obtain title insurance.

First, an attorney may be employed to make an **abstract of title** and prepare a legal opinion evidencing the status and quality of the title to the property. The term *abstract of title* frequently refers to the work of an attorney or an abstract company that examines the documents and makes a list of the documents affecting the chain of title. This abstract lists the documents, explains what has and has not been examined, and provides a synopsis of what the documents mean. But the abstract does not tell the purchaser the status of the title or the risks that she may face. To have that evaluation, an attorney must prepare a legal opinion based on the abstract of title or upon his own evaluation of the documents.

The abstract of title begins with a heading giving a legal description of the parcel of property. After that, the transactions, in chronological order, that have affected the land are listed and each recorded document is briefly explained (the abstract). The list begins with the original taking of title from the government and continues through every deed, will, mortgage, release, judgment, mechanic's lien, tax sale, and so on that has affected the property to the present time. After these documents have been listed and very briefly explained, the abstractor states what documents have and have not been examined. The search and abstract are valid only as of some date prior to the date of the abstractor's work, because the recorder's office has inevitable recording delays.

Still, either the examination or the opinion can leave the prospective purchaser vulnerable because the documents examined are accepted at face value as being correct. No attempt is made to verify the accuracy of the statements in the documents. For example, if a person lacks contractual capacity, such as for having been declared mentally incompetent by a court, the person could execute and deliver as many transfers of the property as

LEGAL TERMS

tract index
Listing in the recorder's office of all the transfers made and claims against a parcel of real property, based on the survey or plat for each particular parcel.

grantor-grantee index
Most common type of listing of records in the real property files of the local real estate recording official; allows ownership of and claims against real property to be searched; based on who transfers an interest (grantor) and who receives an interest (grantee).

patent
The first grant of the land from the original owner—the government—to the first person to hold the property.

abstract of title
Document presenting the summary of the title documents in the public record that affect a parcel of real estate.

can be imagined, but the validity of these transfers would be open to challenge. If the transferor were a minor (another circumstance restricting contractual capacity), most states would allow the minor to recover the property. If the person were under the influence of some drug or alcohol and did not know what she was doing, the transfer could be voided. Most of these contractual aspects of the transfer would not appear in the recorded document. Surely, in the last case, you cannot conceive of the recorded document beginning, "I, Jane Doe, being thoroughly mellow from taking [name of drug] . . ."!

From whom would the purchaser recover? Malpractice suits are difficult to prove, costly, and time-consuming, because the dispute deals not with the facts but with the attorney's interpretation of the facts. The abstractor cannot guarantee title and has only a duty to exercise due care. Further, what is the status of the abstractor's insurance coverage for errors and omissions? There is also a real danger of forgeries and fraudulently executed documents. Anyone could get a release form, execute it, and record it, whereupon it would be in the chain of title. A searcher is unlikely to uncover the work of a careful crook. Nor is a misstatement of marital status, whether deliberate or accidental, detectable on the face of the document, and in most states spouses retain rights to the property which the other spouse cannot transfer away. Consequently, there is no standard protection against the error of the document searcher or the undetectable problem. Purchasers and their financiers wanted more title protection, so a system of title insurance evolved that eventually became a title insurers association (American Land Title Association [**ALTA**]). ALTA established uniform title insurance policies.

Second, one can use a title insurance company. In most parts of the country, this method is the most common. The document search and evaluation are combined with title insurance protecting the policy holder from defects in the title. Essentially, the company has trained staff, many of whom are attorneys, prepare both the abstract and title opinion. When the company is satisfied that the title is in proper order, it issues an insurance policy to protect the title of the buyer. The company's fee is paid once, at the time the policy is issued, and it is usually based on the company's experience with title risks in that area. Since the mid-1970s, title policies have changed by adding inflation protection and by issuing a new form of residential owner's title insurance. This new insurance has a number of benefits for the owner that were not available previously, such as protection against rental expenses incurred because of the loss of a title claim dispute, and others.

There are several types of title insurance policies, but the two most common are for the owner and for the mortgagee (creditor). They are not exactly the same. The lender's policy covers the amount outstanding of the loan. The owner's policy covers the amount of value of the property (with perhaps inflation adjustments and a co-insurance clause [usually 80 percent]). As the years pass and the mortgage is reduced, the amount of title insurance coverage declines and the amount of owner's equity in the property increases. As a result, a landowner would run a severe risk if, late in the period of mortgage payments, a title dispute went against the borrower (mortgagor) and the title company paid off the creditor without there being an owner's policy. The borrower-owner would lose his entire interest unless he had purchased owner's title coverage, as well as paying for the lender's policy, when the loan was made and the title arrangement created. One should make certain that there are two policies covering the two distinct interests, that of the mortgagor and the mortgagee, the debtor and the creditor. Finally, when the title insurance company pays off the creditor, the creditor will assign its interests to the title company. It is usually said that the title company is subrogated to the interests of the bank or that it stands in the shoes of the creditor. As such, the title company may seek to obtain the money it has paid out plus expenses from the debtor.

There are standard forms in the title insurance business. The American Land Title Association (ALTA) is the source of the most important ones. Coverage in the standard residential ALTA policy protects the policy purchaser from someone else owning the title, having a title that is not of sufficient quality to be transferred, being unable to enter or leave the land (lack of access), or having the property be subject to a lien of any sort, or some other title flaw. But title policies do not only provide coverage, they also exclude from coverage. These are called "exclusions and exceptions." Examples of standard ALTA exclusions are items against which the insurer could not protect or know about. Some examples are government regulations, such as zoning or environmental rules; government seizure through eminent domain without fully adequate compensation; actions taken by the owner over which the insurer had no control and probably no knowledge; events that occurred after the policy was issued; and events that did not cause financial injury to the party insured. There are also standard exceptions, both general and specific. The general ones relate to a broad category, such as a defect based on the lack of a current survey or the rights of someone claiming under adverse possession. The specific ones relate to items unique to a particular parcel, for instance, such matters as utility easements. Finally, items that are not covered in the standard policy can be covered through an **endorsement** from the title company, which will provide the additional coverage.

Exceptions to and exclusions from coverage should be examined in detail and explained to the client before deciding what insurance is appropriate to purchase. Title insurance is a comparatively minor expense of making a real estate purchase, and it may be advisable to obtain the most extensive coverage practical in the situation.

The third process of title examination involves going through the Torrens process for parcels of land that have been placed into the Torrens System. This process is not common; Torrens parcels exist side-by-side with the regular recording system, but they do not overlap. As noted earlier, the Torrens System has a number of critics; they see it as time-consuming and expensive and suggest that it be avoided whenever possible. But if the title is in Torrens, following the Torrens process is essential.

LEGAL TERMS

ALTA
Acronym for American Land Title Association, an industry group for the title companies in America.

endorsement
Insurance term that refers to adding insurance coverage to a policy by a special rider.

4.6 OTHER TYPES OF INSURANCE

Besides the risks to the buyer of not having good title, there are other risks in owning real property as well. One is the risk of damage to or total loss of the building due to fire, flood, wind, or other disaster. This risk is called a **property risk**. The basic policy in this area has been the fire insurance policy. A common way of handling property risk is to attach a rider to the fire policy to cover a variety of other risks, such as wind, rain, vehicles, explosions, and civil disturbances. This additional coverage (for an additional premium) added to the fire policy is referred to as an **extended coverage endorsement**, and it is one of the most common endorsements. Another type of risk occurs when the property owner is compelled to pay damages to someone who has been injured on the property, or whose property has been damaged in some way, by the actions (or failure to act) of the landowner. This risk is called a **liability risk**. All real property owners are interested in obtaining insurance coverage in these two areas, so they have become the most common additional insurance coverages. An additional risk to the buyer is the timing that determines when her responsibility begins. The traditional approach in the common law has been that the risk transfers to the buyer, not at the time of closing, but when the sales contract is executed. By agreement, however, the parties can keep the seller responsible until the closing, and in many cases that occurs.

There is yet another insurance problem between the buyer and the seller. Many times the seller's insurance policies covering property and liability risk have unexpired time on them. Why not simply transfer them to the buyer? The answer is simple—it requires the insurance company to approve the new policy holder, the buyer. Until that occurs, there may be no coverage, so the buyer is totally vulnerable to any property or liability risk occurring during the time period between the beginning of the buyer's liability and the insurance company's approval. This should not be permitted to happen.

Different types of coverages in homeowner's insurance relate to a variety of risks. These are specified in the policy, and all the policy types should be reviewed to determine the appropriate cost-benefit relationship. Even when the homeowner purchases the most extensive type of insurance coverage, there will always be exclusions. One of these is flood insurance for real properties that lie in a flood plain, but the homeowner can be advised on whether and how to obtain flood insurance, through the mortgage lender (as required by law) or by the Federal Emergency Management Association (FEMA). Other exclusions from coverage should be carefully considered.

In addition, one must understand the extent of the insurance coverage. There are a number of clauses that may limit the homeowner's or businessperson's recovery. **Co-insurance** can limit the recovery, either because the insured has not maintained sufficient insurance or because the amount of coverage is reduced by the co-insurance provision. A common insurance company requirement is that the building be insured up to 80 percent of its current market value. The other 20 percent is considered essentially indestructible, as in the excavation costs (the hole is already there even if the building is totally destroyed). If a building is insured for less than 80 percent of its current market value, the insurance company will only pay on the basis of the percentage that is insured. For instance, if Sally owns a three-flat with a value of $400,000, she would have to insure it for $320,000 with an 80 percent co-insurance provision. If she allowed the insurance coverage to stay at $320,000 when the building's value rose to $600,000, she would only have 53.33 percent coverage, and the insurance company would only pay that percentage of any loss. If the building were completely destroyed when it was valued at $600,000, she would only recover $319,980. Another limitation is that the insured can only recover for her own interest, so if Sally and Sue owned the property jointly, and Sally were the only insured, she would only recover an amount proportionate to her ownership interest.

Another type of insurance is protection for the creditor-mortgagee against damage to or destruction of the property. This coverage can be obtained in one of three ways. First, the creditor-mortgagee can purchase it in its own name, because it has an insurable interest. Second, the debtor-mortgagor may be required in the loan and collateralization documents to acquire coverage for the benefit of the mortgagee. Finally, the mortgagor may obtain the policy in her own name, but may be required to execute documents assigning any payment under the policy to the mortgagee as the mortgagee's interest may appear at the time of the insurance payment. This last approach is often referred to as having a **loss payable clause** attached to the mortgagor's policy. The assignment must be acknowledged by the insurance company, because it generally requires that the insurer pay the mortgagee regardless of any action by the insured (mortgagee). One example of a protected situation is if the mortgagee failed to pay the premium and damage occurred. Another example: If the insured-mortgagee became a pyromaniac and set fire to the property, and if the insured property were totally consumed, the insurance company would be required to pay the lender-mortgagee the outstanding balance of its loan in this type of insurance arrangement.

Insuring commercial concerns entails many detailed insurance problems beyond the ones discussed here, which apply to all real property. Commercial insurance concerns aspects of business ranging from common real estate business risks, such as having elevators in the building, to any risks unique to the special use of the real property. A common insurance for a commercial lessor covers the loss of rent when fire or disaster damages the building. Another insurance endorsement could cover loss of profits. What endorsements to select should be carefully considered with the help of people who are experienced and knowledgeable in this particular area of insurance coverage.

LEGAL TERMS

property risk
Insurance term describing the area of potential damage where an owner of real property might suffer harm; typical examples would be fire or wind damage.

extended coverage endorsement
Addition of extra insurance coverage for specified perils; added to a standard fire insurance policy.

liability risk
Describes a real estate owner's chance of injury from failure to perform a duty to someone who has come onto the property (someone to whom the owner might be liable); distinguished from *property risk.*

co-insurance
Certain types of real property insurance under which the insured must maintain a certain percentage of replacement value of the property covered by insurance in order to have full coverage; otherwise, the insurance pays only a portion of the loss.

loss payable clause
Agreement that protects the lender-mortgagee so that it receives the benefits of the debtor-mortgagor's insurance even if the debtor has failed to comply with the terms of the insurance agreement; done by agreement among the three parties (debtor, creditor, and insurance company).

Policies for residential tenants may cover their interest in, as well as the contents of, their apartments. Commercial tenants can have much more extensive coverage, specifically related to title, in which the landlord must provide evidence of good title and insurance to protect the tenant's interest. There are now standard ALTA policies to deal with the commercial tenant's situation.

4.7 CHECKLIST: ORDERING OR PERFORMING A TITLE EXAMINATION

The process of title examination requires careful control of its details. This checklist is designed to help you identify and examine those all-important details by which we succeed or fail. Always feel free to make any additions or changes that will help you exercise professional control over your work flow.

I. Why is a title examination being ordered?
   A. Is the property being bought or sold?
   B. Is a new mortgage being placed on the property?
   C. Is this parcel becoming the beneficiary of an easement?
   D. Is a lease to be entered into?

II. What materials are needed for an examination?
   A. Who owns the property?
      1. Is it a seller under a real estate sales contract?
      2. Is it a borrower applying for a loan?
      3. Is it a landlord who wants to lease the property?
   B. What is the parcel's complete and accurate legal description?
   C. Are the plats of survey or a special survey needed?
   D. Have title insurance policies already been issued? Should they be examined to discover possible defects?
   E. Are there any earlier title examinations or abstracts of title on this parcel that can be examined?

III. How extensive a title examination should there be?
   A. A complete examination for the time period in which one can be liable (40 to 60 years)?
   B. A shorter time period?
      1. From the date of issuance of the prior policy?
      2. From the date of execution of the prior mortgage?
      3. From date of the last title examination?

IV. Which indexes should be checked?
   A. Grantee index?
   B. Grantor index?
   C. Mortgagor index?
   D. Mortgagee index?

   E. Plat index?
   F. Tract index?

V. What other records must be consulted for the search to be complete?
   A. Judgment index and records?
   B. Lis pendens?
   C. Uniform Commercial Code (UCC) financing statement filings?
   D. Tax records?
   E. Federal and state tax lien records?
   F. Any special assessments (sanitary and sewer)?
   G. Probate records?
   H. Civil docket?
   I. Local administrative proceedings concerning environmental cleanup proceedings?

VI. Handling the initial title examination
   A. Inform the title company if title insurance is involved.
   B. Obtain statements of all title exceptions.

VII. Identifying any title defects or problems
   A. Breaks in the chain of title?
   B. Any errors from prior recorded deeds?
   C. Any differences in the names involved in the title search?
   D. Is any power of attorney involved?
      1. Is it incomplete?
      2. Is it still valid?
   E. Any pending suits (lis pendens)?
   F. Judgment against the owner?
      1. Federal system?
      2. State system?
   G. Is there any sale contract, any option to purchase, or any recorded lease?
   H. Are there any credit or collateral documents (notes, mortgages, or deeds of trust) that do not show a release or a satisfaction that removes them from possibly causing a risk?
   I. Are there any recorded easements?
      1. What are they?
      2. What effect could they have on your transaction or client's interest?
   J. Are there any restrictions on the land use by means of prior deeds, contracts, developer's grants, etc.?
   K. Are there any mechanic's liens or material supplier's liens?
   L. Taxes, fees, government assessments?

1. Federal?
2. State?
3. County?
4. City?
5. Other local authority?
6. Business taxes unpaid that might have led to a claim against the property?
7. Other—something that might be unique to your situation, here and now?

M. UCC financing statements? Commercial property—any fixtures? Problems?

N. Was the title to the property received from the estate of a decedent? All probate actions completed?

O. Bankruptcy records?

P. Court records of divorce proceedings?

4.8 CHECKLIST: PREPARATION OF A TITLE INSURANCE POLICY

Title insurance often seems pro forma because it is done by another group of professionals. But identifying the needs of the client are crucial to obtaining proper coverage. This checklist is designed to help you consider the needs of your firm's client. If it becomes your job to order title insurance, you will have thought about the process and understand the purpose of title insurance.

I. To whom is the policy being issued?
   A. To the owner?
   B. To the lender?
   C. To another?

II. Have all the elements needed to get a title policy issued been complied with?
   A. Has there been a title examination?
   B. Has the title examiner's certified report gone to the title company?
   C. Is there a commitment to issue a title policy?
   D. Has the survey been received?
   E. Is there a seller's affidavit of title?

III. What information is needed to obtain the owner's policy, Schedule A?
   A. Insured's name.
   B. Effective date of the title policy.
   C. Amount of coverage sought.
   D. An accurate legal description of the parcel of real property.

IV. What information is needed to obtain the lender's policy, Schedule A?
   A. Insured's name—correct corporate name—mortgagor's name.
   B. Effective date of title policy (the date the mortgage was recorded).

C. Name of mortgagee (borrower).
D. Name of the real estate title holder, if other than mortgagee.
E. Amount of coverage sought, which will be the loan amount.
F. An accurate legal description of the parcel of real property.

V. Ways to remove standard Schedule B exceptions
A. Obtain a survey of the parcel according to your title insurance company's rules.
B. Obtain a title affidavit.

VI. How to handle Schedule B, Section 2, exceptions
A. Obtain copies of all exceptions.
B. Review those exceptions to determine whether they can be lived with.
C. Get as many exceptions removed as possible.

VII. The title company may provide special endorsements in the following areas
A. Pending disbursement.
B. Revolving line of credit agreement.
C. Condominium endorsement.
D. Planned unit development (PUD).
E. Adjustable rate on the mortgage note.
F. Zoning.
G. Adjoining parcels.

DISCUSSION AND REVIEW QUESTIONS

1. Identify the following terms and explain the usage of each.
   a. Grantor-grantee index
   b. Constructive notice
   c. Good faith purchaser for value
   d. Title search
   e. Chain of title
   f. Abstract of title
   g. Endorsement
   h. Loss payable clause
2. Explain the rationale for having title insurance companies operate in most urban areas rather than having attorneys provide title searches.
3. How important is the deed in the search? How detailed must the deed be (or how vague can it be) to provide the information essential to the search?
4. Bill and Martha Smith bought their dream home during the summer of 1993. Being somewhat knowledgeable, they hired a good attorney, and he made sure that they got title insurance and received a warranty deed from the seller. Consider the following situations and decide what the effect would be on their title.

a. The seller, Ted Winston, wants the property back three years later. He is now in a drug rehabilitation program and claims that he was addicted to heroin, was high on drugs when he executed the documents, and did not know what he was doing. (Note: This argument is a contract defense.)
b. Sal Maggio, a contractor, has filed a mechanic's lien for repairs he made for Winston 38 days before the closing.
c. The house next door is being sold. In that sale process, a survey is completed, and it reveals that a stone wall, the border between the two properties which has been there for more than 35 years, is two feet onto the next-door neighbor's property. The seller demands that Bill and Martha remove the wall or permit him to take it down.

5. Denise Doe wants to buy a parcel of improved but vacant land from Rita Roe along Route 66 to build a strip mall. Explain the steps Denise would have to take to become a good faith purchaser for value. Obtaining this legal status is important to her. She knows that this area has a family notorious for playing title games with property that their ancestor, Boris Beltsin the First (known locally as "King Boris the Bad"), once owned as the original settler of the area. Boris the Sixth, as the current descendant is known, is married to Natasha Deedovitch, and no one crosses their paths with impunity. Consider what would happen to Doe's purchase from Roe if the following occurred.
   a. Mikhail Minsky obtained a deed from Boris I (for a portion of property now owned by Roe) by getting him drunk and arranging friendly female companionship. Minsky filed the deed, and Boris I was so embarrassed that he swore off "demon vodka." On Minsky's deathbed, years later, he deeply repented his deceptive actions and sent Boris I a long letter apologizing and a deed retransferring the property. When Minsky's letter arrived, however, Boris I had just died, and in the confusion, the letter was put away and never read until recently, when Natasha was investigating the contents of an old trunk.
   b. Two weeks ago, a creditor filed a lawsuit against Roe.
   c. Roe has not paid her portion of the special assessment against the property for repaving the road from the highway into the subdivision behind the property. After three years, Roe is seriously delinquent, and the county may take action to collect the obligation owed it.
6. Discuss the risks involved with real property (except title risks) that can be covered by insurance in real estate transactions. Make a chart showing the risk (in alphabetical order) in one column and the method of insuring against it in another column.
7. On December 23, 1994, G. Davis's warehouse, which stored her own manufactured products, was damaged by fire. At the time of the fire, the warehouse had a value of $650,000 and there was no mortgage. The fire caused $125,000 worth of damage to the structure, which was built in 1974 for $89,000. In 1982, Davis had added another warehouse, attached to and built onto the older structure, for $75,000. In 1974, the

warehouse was insured for the construction cost and the then-current value of $89,000; an additional $125,000 of insurance was obtained at the time of the expansion. The policy contains an 80-percent co-insurance provision. How much can Davis collect and why?

SAMPLE FORMS

Individual Acknowledgment

Commonwealth of Massachusetts
County of ________

On this ________ day of ________, 19___, before me personally appeared ________ *[person or persons acknowledging instrument],* to be known to be the ________ [person *or* persons] described in and who executed the foregoing instrument, and acknowledged that ________ [he *or* she *or* they] executed the same as ________ [his *or* her *or* their] free act and deed.

[Signature]
[Title of officer]

My commission expires on ________, 19___.
[Seal]

Attorney's Opinion of Title

I hereby certify that I have examined the title documents furnished to me by ________ consisting of ________ pages showing title to the premises situated in the City of ________, County of ________, State of ________, and particularly described herein, and certify that in my opinion a marketable and indefeasible fee simple title to the premises is vested in ________ by deed dated ________, 19___, recorded in Deed Book ________, page ___, made by ________ *[grantor],* covering all the lands described herein, subject only to the following estates, liens, defects, and objections:

Preliminary Report on Title Insurance Application

No. ________
Property Address: ________

To: ________ *[name of applicant]*
________ *[address]*

In response to your application for a policy of title insurance, _______ *[insurance company]* hereby reports that it is prepared to issue, or cause to be issued, as of the date hereof, __________ *[describe policy, such as* an American Land Title Association residential form policy of title insurance], describing the land and estate or interest therein herein set forth, insuring against loss which may be sustained by reason of any defect, lien or encumbrance not shown or referred to as an exception

SIDEBAR

Although the acknowledgment is simple, note the title company's disclaimer of liability without the issuance of a commitment in the preliminary report. Why did it do that? Note the different language in the binder.

below, or not excluded from coverage pursuant to the printed schedules, conditions and stipulations of such policy form.

This report (and any supplements or amendments thereto) is issued solely for the purpose of facilitating the issuance of a policy of title insurance and no liability is assumed hereby. If it is desired that liability be assumed prior to the issuance of a policy of title insurance, a binder or commitment should be requested.

The estate or interest in the land herein described or referred to and covered by this report is __________ *[specify, such as,* a fee].

Title to such estate or interest at the date hereof is vested in ___ ________.

The land referred to in this report is situated in the City of __________, County of __________, State of __________, and is described as follows: __________ *[describe property].*

The exceptions to coverage in addition to the printed exceptions and exclusions contained in such policy form are: __________ *[enumerate exceptions].*

Dated ________, 19___, at ________ ____.m.

[Signature]

Title Insurance Binder

Number ________ Property Address: ________
To: ________ *[name of insured]*
________ *[address]*

________ *[Title company]* hereinafter called company hereby insures that the ________ *[describe nature of title, such as* fee simple] title to the property described herein: ________ *[insert description]* was, on the date hereof, vested in ________, subject to the exceptions, defects, liens, encumbrances, and requirements referred to below.

Upon receipt of evidence satisfactory to the company that all exceptions and requirements set forth below have been satisfied, or will be satisfied simultaneously with the transfer of title of the property, and upon payment of the fees and charges incurred, the company shall issue, or cause to be issued, a ________ *[describe policy to be issued, such as* American Land Title Association residential form policy of title insurance], in the amount of $____, insuring against loss which may be sustained by reason of any defect, lien or encumbrance not shown or referred to as an exception below or not excluded from coverage pursuant to the printed conditions, stipulations, and schedules of such policy form, provided that no defects, liens or encumbrances intervene between the above-mentioned date and the date the instrument creating the estate or interest to be insured is filed for record, or that if any defects, liens, or encumbrances intervene, provided they are satisfied or removed to the satisfaction of the company.

This Binder is issued as a commitment prior to the issuance of a policy of title insurance, and shall be null and void unless all the requirements hereof are met, and a policy of title insurance is issued and the premium paid, within ___________ months from the date hereof.

This Binder is issued with the understanding that the insured has, on the date hereof, and at the time of the issuance of the policy of title insurance, no personal knowledge or information of any defect, lien, or encumbrance affecting such property other than those shown below, and that the insured's failure to immediately inform this company of any such personal knowledge or information shall render this Binder, and any policy of title insurance based thereon, null and void with respect to such defect, lien, or encumbrance.

Dated: _________, 19____.

[Signature of authorized officer]
[Title of authorized officer]

CHAPTER 5
Acquisition and Transfer of Real Property

"But many a crime, deem'd innocent on earth, Is registered in Heaven; and these no doubt, Have each their record with a curse annex'd."

William Cowper

Cape Cod house

OUTLINE

PROLOGUE TO THE PARALEGAL

This chapter deals with the intricacies of how title to real property gets transferred. The ways of transfer are many. Some of the most commonly occurring forms are transfer by sale (transfer document, the deed), by gift (the deed), or by death (the will or statutes that operate when there is no will); by natural forces (called avulsion, erosion, accretion, and other terms); and by a legally sanctioned taking by others (called adverse possession), by government seizure for a public purpose (called eminent domain), or by government receipt of land when there is no other party to receive it (called escheat). Other parts of this material introduce you to the intricacies of the financing of real estate. This chapter discusses the legal implications of the type of collateral document a lender uses to place a lien upon the real property to enable the lender to sell the property if the loan is not repaid.

Formalities used in the execution of documentation are also discussed. All these items of information are adding to the knowledge necessary to do a closing and prepare the appropriate documentation (under the supervision of an attorney).

KEY TERMS

accretion
acknowledgment
action to quiet title
adverse possession
attestation
avulsion
bargain and sale deed
beneficiary
chain of title
color of title
covenants
decedent
deed
deed of trust
delivery
devise
devisee
eminent domain
equitable title
escheat
erosion
escrow
escrow agent (escrowee)
execution
foreclosure
grantor
grantee
homestead rights
intestate
legacy
legal description
legatee
lien theory
mechanic's lien
marketable title
mortgage
note
per capita
per stirpes
probate court
quitclaim deed
real estate sales contract
recordation
right of redemption
special warranty deed
Statute of Frauds
tacking
testate
testator (testatrix)
title theory
trust
trustee
unconscionable
warranty deed
warranty of habitability
will

5.1 INTRODUCTION

The law of real estate is one of the oldest areas of Anglo-American jurisprudence. When the Normans conquered England in the 11th century, there was already a Saxon legal system dealing with real estate. The Normans added to it; they increased the formalities because their social system, called *feudalism*, was based on land and its ownership. Almost everything led back to the land, so it was necessary to have accurate records of land ownership and land transfers. The first nationwide land ownership record was created in the Domesday Book in the late 1080s. Land relationships decided whether you were free or a serf; whether you had plenty to eat or starved. They determined almost everything about you. Your identity was tied to your relationship with the land. Consequently, the law has been very conservative about land transfers. There are many formalities to be observed and, although they are similar in all states (except Louisiana, where law is based on French law), there are bound to be differences. It is essential to understand and know these variations to perform properly for your attorney's client. Many times your attorney will handle these local variations or explain them to you, but you must remain alert for them.

Basically, land is acquired or transferred in one of three ways. First, one can transfer it by a *deed*. This document is usually accompanied by a *real estate sales contract*, for most times the real estate will be bought and sold. It is also possible to transfer property by deed as a gift. Second, one can transfer real property at death by will or by intestacy (so that the property passes by the law of descent). A third way to transfer real property is by adverse possession. Finally, one can acquire title to real estate by various legal actions, which frequently involve a creditor foreclosing on the property under court order. An indication of the traditional reluctance to part a person from ownership in real property is the legal axiom that "the law abhors a forfeiture." The phrase arose concerning the courts' reluctance to take a person's real property away. When you study this area, note the many opportunities that a person has to get back the property that is lost or on the verge of being lost. This right is called the *right of redemption* (the right to get it back again), and it can apply at many steps along the way until a person has finally lost the property.

There is always a relationship between at least two parties, such as the seller and the buyer or the decedent and the heirs, but the use of all land also lies in the context of the larger society. This societal context may involve private restrictions or covenants on land use, such as an agreement on lot size, but it is more likely that societal concerns will be expressed through government action, such as laws, regulations, zoning, and eminent domain. Most restrictions relate to the use of land for purposes that benefit the entire community, such as control over landfill and dumps or the density of housing and population. Sometimes, however, the government needs land for its own purposes—to build a post office or a courthouse, or to establish a sewage treatment plant. If a proposed location is privately owned, the government must acquire the land. This acquisition process is called *eminent domain.*

5.2 THE SETTING FOR REAL ESTATE TRANSFERS

It is important to understand what is actually happening when a real estate transaction occurs. The settings of the three areas of transfer—by deed, by death, or by adverse possession—must be understood. A **deed** is the legal document containing the language necessary to transfer a parcel of real property from one person to another. Usually, a sales contract is also involved in this transaction. The setting is a sale, normally for profit.

LEGAL TERMS

deed
Written legal document that transfers real property from one legal entity (individual, corporation, trust, partnership, etc.) to another.

The parties involved are the buyer and seller (with their support teams). Let us look at the seller first. Usually the seller will have an attorney, a banker (who provided the mortgage), and a real estate agent or broker. The buyer may not have a broker, but usually will have an attorney, a financier providing the money to pay off the seller, and possibly an insurance agent who is ready to issue a binder for a new policy to cover the property. This list includes only the bare minimum number. Escrow agents, appraisers, surveyors, taxing authorities, and a number of other parties can also be involved at some point in the transfer process.

Notice that this hypothetical transaction was set up with just one seller and one buyer. Consider multiple owners as buyers and sellers; partnerships, corporations, and trusts can be involved in owning and transferring land as well. In commercial transactions, accountants are essential. Experts in a particular field, such as engineers reporting on oil and gas deposits, may be involved. This list, although actually not endless, certainly appears to be, but the number of persons involved usually reflects of the complexity and importance of the transaction. Still, the basic parties are always the buyer and the seller. The complexities arise when risk has been identified. An accountant wants to determine the capacity of the property to produce a return on the investment or whether its cash flow will cover all the expenses. The lender relies on the information provided by that accountant. An appraiser estimates the current value of the property. What might other experts do in a real estate sales transaction?

The second setting for transfer of real property arises because of death. Because we "can't take it with us," the property has to be transferred to someone else. This transfer is done in one of two ways. First, it can be done voluntarily, through a will. A **will** is a written document, **attested**, that a person creates to dispose of real and personal property after death. Second, some people die without any will. As the maker of a will is called a **testator** or **testatrix**, and is said to die **testate**, so the person dying without a will is said to die **intestate** or in the condition called *intestacy*. Each state has laws governing the distribution of all types of property, and these laws must be consulted when real property is transferred after the owner's death without a will.

If ever there were a case which illustrates the need for complying with all legal formalities to protect the parties involved, *Brown v. Byrd* surely could be it. The facts indicate a will, an attempted deed, and a failure to probate. The top civil court in Texas examined the arguments about admitting the will to probate and dismissed them along with the claim of the plaintiff. Is there anything the plaintiff could have done? Why do you think the plaintiff waited so many years before filing suit? Is the outcome fair? Is it essential to the legal system? If the will does not pass on the property, how is ownership of this property to be determined? By private agreement? Other laws?

The parties that can be involved in transfer by death are the **decedent**, the surviving spouse, children, other family members, friends, charities,

LEGAL TERMS

will
Written document a person uses to dispose of his or her property upon death.

attestation
Person's signature indicating that he or she witnessed the execution or signing of a legal document.

testator (testatrix)
Man (woman) who makes a will.

testate
Person who has died and left a will.

intestate
Person who dies without a will.

decedent
Person who has died.

BROWN v. BYRD
512 S.W.2d 753 (1974)

DUNAGAN, C.J.

This is a contest of an application to probate a will. The appellee, Florrie Gregg Byrd, offered for probate an instrument purporting to be the last will of Elizabeth Francis Gregg, deceased, and from an order of the County Court admitting such will to probate as a muniment of title, appeal has been made to this court. The trial court made and filed, separately, its findings of fact. The court's conclusions of law are found only in the order admitting the will to probate wherein the court found that appellee "was not in default in failing to present the same for probate within the four years aforesaid or prior to the time she so presented same for probate as Muniments of Title * * *."

Elizabeth Francis Gregg died on the 5th day of May, 1940, survived by three children: Eldridge R. Gregg, Florrie Gregg Gee and Nell Gregg Kurth. In April of 1944 the holographic will and first codicil of Elizabeth Francis Gregg were discovered. The will was not offered for probate until December 5, 1973.

At the time of the death of Elizabeth Francis Gregg, her daughter, Nell Gregg Kurth, had four children: Florrie Gregg Byrd, Hattie Kurth Brown, Melvin Kurth and Gregg Kurth. These four children also survived beyond the death of their mother which occurred on October 20, 1952.

The handwritten will in question was dated July 3, 1935, and on the back of it appeared a holographic codicil which was not dated or signed (the trial court refused to permit probate of the codicil, from which no appeal was taken). Elizabeth Francis Gregg willed all her property, both real and personal, as follows:

> "* * * One third each to my son E. R. Gregg, one third to my daughter Florrie Gregg Gee, and one third to my daughter Nellie Gregg Kurth during her lifetime and at her death to my granddaughter Florrie Kurth. I appoint E. R. Gregg and H. W. Gee executors of my will, without bond."

Florrie Kurth, mentioned above, is the same person as Florrie Kurth Byrd and Florrie Gregg Byrd, proponent of the will and appellee before this court.

Hattie Kurth Brown, appellant and sister of appellee, contested the admission of the will to probate in the trial court. Appellant filed five points of error, the essence of which allege the trial court erred in admitting the will to probate as a muniment of title because there is no evidence that Florrie Gregg Byrd, the proponent, was not in default in offering such will for probate prior to four years after the death of Elizabeth Francis Gregg and prior to the day it was presented on December 5, 1973.

The period of time within which a will may be offered for probate is governed by V.A.T.S., Probate Code, Sec. 73(a), which provides, in part, as follows:

> "(a) No will shall be admitted to probate after the lapse of four years from the death of the testator unless it be shown by proof that the party applying for such probate was not in default in failing to present the same for probate within the four years aforesaid; and in no case shall letters testamentary be issued where a will is admitted to probate after the lapse of four years from the death of the testator."

The term "default" means a failure to do the act required; but as used in the statute above quoted, it means a failure due to the absence of reasonable diligence on the part of the party offering the instrument.

In reply to appellant's points of error, the appellee presents a chronological depiction and explanation of the surrounding circumstances to excuse her delay in offering the will for probate at an earlier date. She relies on the fact that she did not learn of the existence of her grandmother's will until April 18, 1944, approximately seventeen days prior to the expiration of four years since the death of Elizabeth Francis Gregg. At the time appellee learned of the will she was living in California with her naval officer husband, Hilton H. Byrd. She testified that arrangements could not have been made to return to Texas in order to probate the will due to the difficulty of travel during the wartime effort.

On April 18th, 1944, appellee received a letter from her aunt, requesting that appellee and her husband sign and acknowledge an agreement already signed and acknowledged by her mother, Nell Gregg Kurth, which agreement appears as follows:

> "THE STATE OF TEXAS
> "COUNTY OF CHEROKEE
>
> "WHEREAS, on July 3, 1935, Mrs. Elizabeth F. Gregg did execute a certain instrument wherein she vested the title to her personal and real property, at her death, as follows:
>
> one-third to E. R. Gregg
> one-third to Florrie Gregg Gee, and
> one-third to Florrie Kurth
>
> Said last mentioned one-third interest subject to a life estate in all the fruits, revenues and income of said property in favor of Nell Gregg Kurth; and
>
> "WHEREAS, the said Mrs. Elizabeth F. Gregg died on May 5, 1940; and
>
> "WHEREAS, it is the desire of each of the hereinafter subscribers that the wishes of the said Mrs. Elizabeth F. Gregg be complied with, and in order to avoid the necessity of any kind of probate proceedings we, the undersigned, do hereby make the following agreement with reference to said property:
>
> "At the death of the said Nell G. Kurth, it is agreed that all the reservations in her favor upon the one-third of the estate of Mrs. Elizabeth F. Gregg will automatically expire so that thereafter title in favor of Florrie Kurth Byrd to said property shall be free of any reservations whatsoever; reserving, however, to Nell Gregg Kurth all of the fruits, income and revenues from said property so long as the said Nell G. Kurth shall live.
>
> "This instrument is executed by the interested parties in recognition of the fact that the title of the said one-third of the Estate of Mrs. Elizabeth F. Gregg is already vested in Florrie Kurth Byrd burdened with a life estate in favor of Nell Gregg Kurth.
>
> "Witness our hands this 15th day of April, A.D. 1944
>
> /s/ Nell Gregg Kurth
> (acknowledgments) /s/ Hilton H. Byrd
> /s/ Florrie Kurth Byrd"

It is appellee's position that even if the will is denied probate, this agreement constitutes a conveyance from Nell Gregg Kurth to her of the same interest she would have received under the will.

In October, 1952, Nell Gregg Kurth died. The following month a family meeting was held at the former residence of Nell Gregg Kurth. The meeting was attended by Hattie Kurth Brown, appellant; John O. Brown, Jr., (husband of appellant); Melvin Kurth; Florrie Gregg Byrd (appellee); Hilton H. Byrd (husband of appellee); and E. R. Gregg. At this meeting the wills of Elizabeth Francis Gregg and her Husband, E. L. Gregg, were discussed. E. L. Gregg had died prior to his wife leaving a holographic will which also had not been probated. E. R. Gregg had managed the estates of both E. L. Gregg and Elizabeth Francis Gregg since their demise. It was agreed among the parties present that E. R. Gregg would continue to manage the combined estates of Mr. & Mrs. Gregg. Further it was agreed that under the terms of the wills of both E. L. Gregg and Elizabeth Francis Gregg their combined estates were owned in the following portions:

> $\frac{1}{3}$ by E. R. Gregg;
> $\frac{1}{3}$ by Florrie Gregg Gee;
> $\frac{5}{24}$ by Florrie Gregg Byrd;
> $\frac{1}{24}$ by Hattie Kurth Brown;
> $\frac{1}{24}$ by Melvin Kurth; and
> $\frac{1}{24}$ by Gregg Gurth.

For twenty-one years following the family meeting, E. R. Gregg administered the combined estates, paying out income, dividing capital distributions and extracting income taxes in the above proportions. Dispute as to the ownership did not arise until suit was filed in the District Court of Cherokee County, attempting to partition the estates of E. L. Gregg and Elizabeth Francis Gregg.

The findings of fact filed by the trial court reveal that Florrie Gregg Byrd has known since April 18, 1944, that E. R. Gregg has had sole possession and custody of the last will and testament and first codicil of Elizabeth Francis Gregg, deceased, until same was produced by him upon trial of this cause; that appellee has known since April 18, 1944, that the will was never offered for probate prior to her application herein; and that appellee at no time from April 18, 1944, up to the filing of her application for probate herein requested the will of Elizabeth Francis Gregg be offered for probate.

Accepting the findings of the trial court as supported by evidence, nevertheless, we do not believe said findings are sufficient as a matter of law to support the court's legal conclusion that appellee was not in default in failing to present the will in question for probate within the four years after the death of Elizabeth Francis Gregg or prior to the time she so presented the will for probate.

Appellee's excuse for not filing her grandmother's will earlier, that she first learned of the will just days prior to the expiration of four years after the death of Elizabeth Francis Gregg while residing in California, we believe is without merit. While this might be an excuse under some circumstances to the extent that it may represent a disability or incapacity excusing delay for a reasonable time, it does not merit a delay of approximately twenty-seven years prior to her filing application. The trial court found that Florrie Gregg Byrd, moved to Lufkin, Texas, in May 1946, and continued to live there until December 31, 1956. So, even after returning to Texas in 1946, at no time prior to December 5, 1973, did she offer the will for probate. Furthermore, there was no showing that the will could not be proved up without her physical presence in the probate court.

Also, to excuse her default, appellee relies heavily upon the verbal family agreement to determine ownership of the estate. Family arrangements are not new to the law and have been dealt with before. We conform to the views of the court in the case of *Armendariz De Acosta v. Cadena.* When confronted with a similar type of agreement to excuse a delay in filing for probate, the Court of Civil Appeals in the Cadena case wrote the following:

> "Proponent seeks by allegations to excuse his default in not making application to probate the will within the time prescribed by the statute. In our opinion, his excuse for not making application within time is insufficient. It appears that he was advised of the contents of the instrument within a month after the death of the testator, and that he

waived the provisions of the will in favor of a verbal agreement which he entered into with the other beneficiaries thereunder. In accordance with the verbal agreement, the estate was administered upon; he being appointed the administrator. Because the other parties to the agreement refused to carry out its terms is not a sufficient excuse under the statute to avoid this delay. We will not attempt to cnumerate reasons why an application for the probate of a will should be made within the time as prescribed by the statute. It is enough to say that sound public policy demands that wills be expeditiously probated. One of the reasons, no doubt, was to prevent the estate from being otherwise administered upon, as was done in the instant case. Besides, title to the estate should be vested in those entitled to receive it, free from the complications which such delays often cause."

For the reasons stated therein, we hold the excuse insufficient to avoid default.

Appellee testified she graduated from high school but had no college, special or legal education. On the other hand, E. R. Gregg was many years her senior, a respected member of the community and President of the Citizens State Bank of Rusk, Texas. Appellee felt he would take any action necessary to protect the estate. However, it was known to appellee that E. R. Gregg was not an attorney and that he had never offered the will for probate. To excuse her failure to take some action herself, appellee testified she had no knowledge of probate proceedings and the term "probate" meant nothing to her. It is a common maxim, familiar to all, that "ignorance of the law" will not excuse any person either civilly or criminally. We deem such maxim applicable under the facts of this case. To hold otherwise would virtually eliminate the element of default from V.A.T.S., Probate Code, Sec. 73(a).

Finally, appellee contends that even if the will of Elizabeth Francis Gregg is ultimately denied probate, that she nevertheless has title to one-third of the estate due to a conveyance from appellee's mother to appellee and her husband. The agreement to which reference is made was set out in toto earlier in this opinion. The agreement was entered into only a short time after the will of Elizabeth Francis Gregg was discovered in 1944. It is appellee's position that although the agreement was not in the usual form of a deed due to the omission of technical words, it is sufficient to pass title to the property.

Admittedly, it is no longer necessary that a deed contain formal paragraphs, nor is it necessary to use technical words. The intention of the parties is determined from the whole of the instrument. If from the whole instrument a grantor and grantee can be ascertained and there are operative words or words of grant showing an intention by the grantor to convey title to land which is sufficiently described to the grantee, and it is signed and acknowledged by the grantor, it is a deed.

The agreement in question does not show an intention on the part of the grantor to convey title to property. Rather, its purpose seems to be to recognize and acquiesce in the terms of the will of Elizabeth Francis Gregg. The last paragraph of the will recognizes the fact that the title of the said one-third of the estate of Mrs. Elizabeth F. Gregg is already vested in Florrie Kurth Byrd burdened with a life estate in favor of Nell Gregg Kurth. If the grantor, Nell Gregg Kurth, expressly recognized that she only had a life estate, then her intent was not to convey a greater interest.

For the reasons stated, the judgment is reversed and rendered for the appellant.

[Some citations omitted.]

attorneys, and the **probate court**. Although the situation can be complex, it is usually simpler than commercial real estate transfers. For those interested in a brief discussion of the formalities of passing title after death, see the end of this chapter.

Finally, transfer by **adverse possession** is yet another type of setting. This process involves one party taking away the real property of another, or a portion of that property. The standard requirements for adverse possession are that the claimant have held the property for a statutorily prescribed length of time and that the claim have been open, notorious, clearly against the other party's interest, and actual. As the phrase *adverse possession* indicates, the activity is against the interests of the other party. It is not a favored situation in the law. It can occur, but it causes a forfeiture of another's interest in the land she owns. On what grounds would the law support this taking? The courts seem to believe that the process is so lengthy that anyone owning real estate who has not noticed that someone is using the property against the owner's interest may not deserve to keep it. There is a strong element of "use it or lose it" in this rationale. It reflects the medieval concept that someone had to use the land effectively if the society's assets were not going to be wasted. The ultimate rationale for adverse possession is that an owner this careless about the property does not deserve to be an owner.

5.3 DOCUMENTS: THE SALES OR PURCHASE CONTRACT

What documents are most frequently used in transferring real property? Although there can be mountains of documents, three of the most important and most common are the sales contract, the deed, and financial documents, such as a note and a mortgage or a deed of trust.

For real estate to be sold—whether the transaction concerns a home, a factory, or a skyscraper—the parties need a document that specifies what they are agreeing to do. This way, no one gets confused, there are fewer misunderstandings, and the path of the true transaction is less litigious. Several aspects of the **real estate sales contract** must be understood. First, what are the most common elements that must be in the contract? Second, what formal legal requirements must be met?

The following elements are usually necessary in a real estate sales contract. First, the parcel of land must be identified. Identification is done by using a formal **legal description** to locate the property precisely; an ordinary street address is completely inadequate because it can change. The legal description does not change. A larger parcel may be divided up, but in the tracking system the land can always be clearly identified.

There are three major systems for describing land, as described in chapter 2. First, and oldest, is the metes and bounds method. It is used east of the Appalachian Mountains and in Texas. The boundaries of the property are

LEGAL TERMS

probate court
Court that deals with decedents' estates and wills.

adverse possession
Possession of real property against the rights of the owner when possession is open, notorious, and hostile for a statutory time; ownership can be transferred at the end of the time period.

real estate sales contract
Agreement between the parties as to what real estate is being sold to whom, by whom, on what terms and conditions, and for what price.

legal description
Words that describe or delineate the boundaries of a parcel of real property.

described in relation to natural objects ("25.4 feet from the large rock to the center of Jones's Creek, then . . . "). There are obvious problems with this method, such as movement of the natural objects. (What happens when a tree dies?) The second method is a surveying process, begun in the 1780s when the frontier area west of the Appalachians, north of the Ohio River, and east of the Mississippi River was surveyed and brought into European settlement. The system is called the rectangular survey or the government (U.S.) survey system and is described more fully in chapter 2. The final descriptive method is a plat of survey in which the lots are laid out. The survey usually locates the lot by beginning, for example, with "lot 52 of Santini's subdivision of . . . "; Santini's subdivision is then tied into a larger described area and then into the larger picture given by the rectangular survey system.

Other items usually specified in the real estate sales contract are:

1. The identities of the buyer and the seller
2. The consideration to be given, that is, the price of the property to be paid at closing
3. The amount of earnest money to be deposited to show good faith interest
4. The time, place, and manner of closing or settlement
5. The date of the sales contract
6. The type of deed the seller will deliver at closing
7. The type of title the parties have agreed to transfer between one another
8. The method of transferring possession from the seller to the buyer
9. The division between buyer and seller of certain overlapping elements such as taxes, utility payments, sewer charges, interest, or special assessments. This splitting between the parties is called *apportionment.* It is negotiable between the parties, but generally follows the customs of a particular area. Details on apportionment are discussed with the materials on closing in chapter 8.

The sales contract may also specify what personal property items will and will not be included in the transfer. These items could be anything from the window coverings—curtains, blinds, shades—in a home to the pieces of equipment in a factory that are fixtures and stay with the building when it is sold. Other items that may be included are who will pay the transfer tax to record the deed of transfer. This responsibility varies from seller, to buyer, to both in equal proportions, depending on local custom, but it may be negotiable.

Remember the purpose of the sales contract. Its job is to specify the agreements that exist between the parties. The legal description only identifies, as precisely as possible, the actual property being discussed. To be absolutely clear and safe, it is essential to identify and cover every area from which a dispute could arise and include whatever the parties agree upon in the sales contract. It is essential, in drafting, to identify everything that could be a risk to the client and to find a way to resolve any conflicts in the contract.

Then there is no question, doubt, or attempts to take advantage at a later date by either party. Nothing is sadder than the party who "thought" something was a certain way, but never got it in writing.

Second, the sales contract has some historical formalities with which it must comply. The sales contract must, under the **Statute of Frauds**, be in writing. No oral real estate sales contracts! This is a formal legal requirement that no sane person would want to avoid. The Statute of Frauds provides that the transfer of any interest—at all—in real estate must be in writing. This writing must have, minimally, (1) the names of the parties, the buyer and the seller; (2) a land description; (3) the signature of the party who will be bound by the contract; (4) the price; and (5) if the sale is not for cash, the terms of the financial arrangements.

This statute applies to legal areas besides interests in real estate. The most important is the requirement that a contract which is not performable within a year be in writing. The Statute of Frauds is intended to protect real property owners from any unwarranted or fraudulent claims. When the Statute of Frauds has been complied with, a person may go into court and seek damages, specific performance of the contract, or both. Specific performance requires the other party to do what was promised in the sales contract. This remedy is important to buyers who want that specific piece of property, particularly if it is to be their new home. Monetary damages are usually sufficient for a seller against a defaulting buyer, but sometimes specific performance is required against a buyer to force the purchase.

When there is no written contract, the Statute of Frauds bars the action, unless an exception to the statute applies in the particular case. One of the most common exceptions is a writing which is not a formal contract but which has sufficient terms to fulfill the requirements of a contract and is signed by the party against whom enforcement is sought. In some states, both parties must sign, and there can be further technical formalities such as witnessing or attesting the signatures of the parties to the contract.

In addition, it is essential to handle the risk of loss once the contract has been signed. Most states follow the common law rule that passes the risk of loss of the real estate to the buyer once the sales contract has been executed. Although this rule may seem irrational (as title remains in the seller until the deed is delivered to the buyer), the risk is easily handled with insurance or by agreement between the parties in the sales contract. The parties must identify the time at which the risk of loss for the property switches from one party to the other and acquire the appropriate insurance. The modern trend, however, is to wait to pass the risk of loss until title has been transferred.

It should be noted that all the parties who own the property (who are in title) must sign the sales agreement. If this simple requirement is not met, there may be problems enforcing the contract later. This problem arises when a home owned by a married couple is being sold and one spouse does not sign. Later, it will probably be impossible to force the sale, because each spouse has certain rights in the property which cannot be taken away; the spouse must consent to sell.

LEGAL TERMS

Statute of Frauds
Statute requiring that any transfer of an interest in real property be made in writing.

If the property is owned by a corporation or a partnership, the appropriate signature requirements should be observed. These may include obtaining a resolution identifying the appropriate corporate officer by title, having the resolution certified by the corporate secretary, having the secretary certify the current office holder by name, and making certain that the form of the corporate signature indicates the agency of the officer signing, by using that person's title and "by:" in front of the signature. Similar requirements exist for partnerships.

Once the contract has been created, the question of title arises. In most states, the seller has an implied obligation to transfer **marketable title** to the buyer, but the actual quality of title to be transferred may be specified between the parties in the sales contract. The contract usually calls for "clean title" (as contrasted to one where there is a "cloud on the title"). Determining the quality of the title is often referred to as "bringing down title." What risks are being considered here? First, are there any liens, judgments, or other encumbrances on this property? Does anyone else have nonownership rights to the property, such as a lessee? Second, is the chain of title good? The **chain of title** is the list of parties who have owned the property—who have been "in title," held title, or recorded an interest in this piece of real property. The issue is whether all the transfers among the prior title holders have been done properly.

This title search, in theory, goes back to the original source of the land, usually a government grant (the patent). In fact, practically no one (or any heir) from that long ago will bring an **action to quiet title**, so the search generally goes back only 30 to 60 years. Otherwise, the time span for these searches would range from slightly over a century in parts of the West to 16th-century Spanish grants in other areas. Another thing that might be noted during a search is whether the property has been conveyed by the same seller more than once. Basically, however, the risk of a competing claimant or potential owner to the property is handled by a title insurance company, which does a title search and insures the title for a minimal fee. Finally, the search looks for any items which in themselves may be minor, but could cause litigation over the title (a suit to quiet title).

Third, are there any mortgages on the property? Fourth, what about other liens, such as mechanic's liens? Fifth, are there any easements on the property? Are these normal ones, such as utility easements, or are they easements that involve the neighbors? Which way do the easements run—on behalf of the property or against the property? Sixth, are there any restrictions on the property from the recorded plat of survey that originally set up the subdivision? Do they restrict the buyer? Seventh, are there any violations of any law governing or affecting the property? Eighth, are there any tenants—even in some homes? This might be a problem; more and more grown children are living at home with aged parents, and the parents might want to sell. Ninth, does the property encroach on any other property, such as a neighbor's property, a street, or an alley, or are there any encroachments onto the land?

If the seller cannot deliver marketable title, what are the effects? Generally, the buyer may legitimately refuse to honor the commitments made in the sales contract, refuse the transfer, and not deliver what was committed to—usually he payment of money. The buyer may also seek damages for any losses, unless the title defects are cleared up rapidly so that the title does become marketable. There are limits to responsibility for title defects, however. The government's activities do not affect marketable title. Zoning, other government regulations, public roads, and sewers are outside the control of the seller. If these aspects create problems for the buyer, the law is unsympathetic. The buyer should have determined what the situation was before signing the sales contract.

A type of seller on whom the courts may impose special standards is the home builder. Under the common law, the doctrine of *caveat emptor* (let the buyer beware) applied. The buyer had to inspect whatever he bought, whether it was a pot or a building. If he missed a defect, it was his fault and his responsibility. In those days, most people were competent to inspect the items they bought, because the items were not made with great skill and were not intended for long use—even many homes. The reverse is true today. As a result, many states have changed that rule for home buyers. When a builder-seller delivers a *new* home to a buyer, it gives an implied **warranty of habitability** that the home is free from hidden defects. Obvious defects that the buyer can see and negotiate about are not covered. Some states have even extended this builder's warranty to later purchasers during what the courts find to be a reasonable time period.

5.4 DOCUMENTS: THE DEED

There are a number of types of deeds, but the four most common are a *warranty deed,* a *special warranty deed,* a *quitclaim deed,* and a *bargain and sale deed.* A warranty deed provides the greatest protection for the buyer, the special warranty substantially less, and the quitclaim virtually no protection. A bargain and sale deed conveys the land without any protective covenants to the buyer from the seller.

In essence, a **warranty deed**, sometimes also called a *general warranty deed,* has the seller (the grantor under the deed) give the buyer (the grantee under the deed) a promise that is very close to a guaranty. Not only does the seller promise that she has valid title to the property, but she also promises to protect the buyer from any harm that may occur from any defect in the title—regardless of when it occurred or who created it. In other words, the seller will defend the buyer in an action to quiet title or to dispossess the buyer from the property when such a suit is brought by a third party. Essentially, the seller insures the title. The most common language creating a warranty deed is "convey and warrant," but other language is also used. If the third party wins the suit and takes the property from the buyer, the seller would be responsible for covering the losses of the buyer.

The promises or covenants that legitimize the seller's promise and the buyer's protection are essentially the following. First, there is a covenant that the seller (under a sales contract) or—grantor (under the deed) has good title to the land being transferred. This is the *seizin* covenant. A second covenant

LEGAL TERMS

marketable title
Chain of title to a parcel of real property that has no defects on it that would harm the buyer; also called *clean title*; contrasted with *cloud on the title*, indicating actual or potential threats to the owner's interests in the real property.

chain of title
List of the parties who have been in title since the government granted the original title, plus any other parties who have had an interest in the property and recorded evidence of their interest in the real property records.

action to quiet title
Lawsuit to remove any matter that would disturb the owner's right to or title in the real property; forces other parties to prove their claim or lose their right to that claim.

warranty of habitability
Warranty given by a builder-seller of a new home (usually) to the buyer that there are no undisclosed defects in the property.

warranty deed
Document transferring real property in which the grantor (seller) guarantees clean title to the grantee (buyer).

provides that the land has no encumbrances against it. This is the *covenant against encumbrances.* Third, the grantor promises that the grantee(s) will not be disturbed in or removed from title by some person who has a better title claim. This is the *covenant of quiet possession* or quiet title.

The second type of deed, a **special warranty deed**, is also a warranty deed, but its promises and buyer protections are not nearly as extensive as those of the warranty deed. This deed, sometimes called a *grant deed,* only promises protection to the buyer (grantee) from anything that the seller (grantor) has done. There is no climbing back up the chain of title if the problem originated before the seller acquired the property. The seller only warrants that he has not done anything that will cause the buyer problems with the title. Further, the special warranty deed does not protect the buyer from the acts of any person other than the seller. The language for this deed is special. The words are "bargain, grant and sell." Be careful in reading the deed; sometimes this language is used and later a separate and different phrase says that the seller will defend the title. When special language is added so that the seller covenants to defend the title, the combination can provide the same result as a warranty deed.

There may be special language in your jurisdiction that creates a special warranty deed. Be certain that you know what the actual words for creation of this type of deed are in your state.

The **quitclaim deed** is literally what its name says. The grantor gives up any claims he or she has to the property, but makes no promise that he or she has any rights in the property at all. It is a simple, bare conveyance of the seller's interest in the property, which provides the buyer with no recourse against the seller under the deed. The language for this deed is usually "quitclaims any and all interest" or "I transfer all my right, title, and interest." Frequently, this deed is used as a transfer release. Buyers love warranty deeds; sellers prefer quitclaim deeds. If there is any doubt about the quality or validity of the title, the seller might insist on the use of a quitclaim deed.

There is one other type of deed, called a **bargain and sale deed**. It simply transfers the land itself, as opposed to the seller's title. It is not frequently used and has no covenants in it.

Elements of a Deed

The deed is the transfer document in a sale of real estate, and there are some formalities that need to be recognized and observed. Consideration is often recited, but it usually is not necessary for the deed itself. For the sales contract, consideration is required. Note that a grantor can give or sell the property. Donation of the property does not require any consideration if the deed is properly executed and delivered. Further, it is necessary to have a proper description of the land. It is best to have a legal description, but the courts have permitted less precise land descriptions when they were clear. In some states, if the grantor referred to the property as "my home," this identification would be clear enough if there were only one home.

LEGAL TERMS

special warranty deed
Document that transfers real property, with guarantees from the grantor that he or she has not done any act that will harm the grantee's title and will be responsible if such an event causes problems with the title.

quitclaim deed
Document that transfers the seller's title and interest in real property, under which the taker gets only the interest of the party transferring; contains no warranties. If the transferor has no interest, that is what the transferee takes.

Another element needed in the deed is the type of estate being granted, whether a fee simple, a fee conditional, or a life estate, for instance. There may also be various promises about the title; these are called **covenants** relating to title, against encumbrances, of quiet enjoyment, and of warranty. These covenants mean, respectively, that the grantor has and will protect good title, will protect the grantee against the claims of others, will not permit others to dispute the ownership of the grantee, and will protect the grantee from others successfully claiming against her. In some states, these rights are implied in the words granting the property, but the term *covenant* has a broader meaning than just these promises. It also refers to any agreements or promises between the parties. For example, the developer of a subdivision often creates restrictive covenants when he files restrictions on the use of the property with his plat of survey at the local recorder's office.

How effective are those restrictions? Notice how long they can last—44 years and counting in the *Chevy Chase Village* case. This case illustrates how courts examine these restrictions and the degree to which they are enforceable. Is practicing medicine out of a home a truly significant violation of the restrictive covenant? Why do you think the court reached the decision it did?

bargain and sale deed
Deed that transfers the real estate itself, without the grantor making any promises.

covenants
Promises made by a party to a contract for the transfer of real estate; among the most common are the covenants of warranty, against encumbrances, for possession, for quiet enjoyment, and for title.

CHEVY CHASE VILLAGE
v.
JAGGERS
261 Md. 309, 275 A.2d 167 (1971)

DIGGES, J.

The beginning of this case, which involves the efficacy of a residential restrictive covenant, can be traced back to 1927 when the Chevy Chase Land Company recorded a plat subdividing a part of what was to become the rather fashionable suburban community of Chevy Chase Village in Montgomery County, Maryland. The subdivision in question, blandly called "Section 1-A Chevy Chase" on the plat, was composed of thirteen blocks, numbered 4 through 16. Blocks 6 and 11 contained 60 lots which, because of their location on the northeast corner of the intersection of Wisconsin and Western Avenues, were set aside for commercial development. Two lots in or near that section were conveyed to public utilities. The other blocks were reserved for exclusively residential purposes. With the exception of six lots conveyed to a church and three lots partially destroyed by later re-subdivision, the 204 remaining lots in the residential blocks were bound by the following series of covenants in each of the original deeds by which they were conveyed:

* * * * * *

It is hereby understood and agreed that no objection will be raised by the said party of

> the second part [grantee], her heirs and assigns, to the rezoning of Lots in Blocks 6 and 11 in said subdivision known as "Section One-A, Chevy Chase," Montgomery County, Maryland, for use for commercial purposes.
>
> * * * * * *
>
> In consideration of the execution of this deed the said party of the second part, for herself her heirs and assigns, hereby covenants and agrees with the party of the first part, its successors and assigns *(such covenants and agreements to run with the land)* as follows, viz:
>
> 1. That all houses upon the premises hereby conveyed shall be built and used for residence purposes exclusively, except stables, carriage houses, sheds or other outbuildings, for use in connection with such residences and that no trade, business, manufacture or sales, or nuisance of any kind shall be carried on or permitted upon said premises. * * * (Covenants 2 through 4 pertaining to location, cost and design of buildings are omitted.)
> 5. That a violation of any of the aforesaid covenants and agreements may be enjoined and the same enforced at the suit of The Chevy Chase Land Company, of Montgomery County, Maryland, its successors and assigns *(assigns including any person deriving title mediately or immediately from said company to any lot or square, or part of a lot or square in the Section of the Subdivision of which the land hereby conveyed forms a part).* [Emphasis added.]

It is these covenants which have spurred the case before us. The plaintiff-appellants, Chevy Chase Village, a landowner and a municipal corporation (having the responsibility by charter to enforce restrictive covenants) and Wales H. Jack and his wife, residents of the subdivision, have appealed from a decision by the Circuit Court for Montgomery County (Shure, J.) denying an injunction against the defendant-appellees, Dr. Frank Y. Jaggers, Jr. and his wife. This action in equity sought to enjoin the doctor from using his property as a principal office for the practice of medicine, alleging that such use was in contravention of the covenants.

In 1947, Dr. Jaggers and his wife purchased a lot in Section 1-A on the corner of Wisconsin Avenue and Grafton Street and lived on the premises until early 1967. During most of those twenty years he maintained his medical office on the property. In 1948 he spent $5,000 converting his garage into office space, and in 1959 an additional $15,000 outlay was made to enlarge this office. During this time he had a very substantial practice, which apparently has tapered off in recent years. In 1954, Dr. Jaggers applied to the Montgomery County Board of Appeals for a special exception to use his property both as his dwelling and for the practice of medicine in association with another doctor. The special exception was granted with no objection being raised by any of the residents of Section 1-A. Although he worked intermittently over the years with other doctors, Dr. Jaggers is at present the sole practitioner in the office. There are also three other doctors in the subdivision who live and maintain principal offices at their home, and have done so for some time. In 1967 the Jaggers moved to Potomac, Maryland, renting their house as a residence, although the doctor continued to maintain the office for his practice. It should be noted that the dwelling is now rented to a physician for residential purposes only.

Chevy Chase Village notified appellees that this action would be in violation of the covenants binding on the property, but the weight of its logic obviously fell on deaf ears, for the doctor was not deterred. We are a more receptive audience, however, and shall reverse the lower court's decision. There are four questions presented for our consideration:

I. Was there sufficient evidence to establish a uniform general scheme or plan of development to entitle the appellants to enforcement of the covenants?

II. Was there an abandonment and failure of the original plan of development and such a change in the general characteristics of the neighborhood as to render the covenants unenforceable?

III. Were the appellants guilty of laches and therefore estopped from the enforcement of the subject covenants?

IV. Under the doctrine of comparative hardship should the court decline to enforce the restrictive covenants?

I

The first contention which the appellees make is that there was insufficient evidence to establish a uniform general plan of development as would entitle appellants to enforce the covenants. However, even if such a plan were absent it would not necessarily defeat their enforcement. The law in Maryland is well settled on this question. In *Rogers v. State Roads Comm.,* we said: "There need not be any general plan of development in order to make a restrictive covenant enforceable if it is imposed by a grantor on a single tract conveyed by him for the benefit of adjacent property retained by him." This view was also expressed by Judge Offutt for the Court in McKenrick v. Savings Bank, 174 Md. 118, 128, 197 A. 580, 584 (1938), where it was said:

> "* * * one owning a tract of land, in granting a part thereof, may validly impose upon the part granted restrictions upon the use thereof for the benefit of the part retained, and upon the part retained for the benefit of the part granted, or upon both for the benefit of both; that, where the covenants in the conveyance are not expressly for or on behalf of the grantor, his heirs and assigns, they are personal and will not run with the land, but that, if in such a case it appears that it was the intention of the grantors that the restrictions were part of a uniform general scheme or plan of development and use which should affect the land granted and the land retained alike, they may be enforced in equity. * * *"

In the present case we need not decide whether there was a uniform general plan of development, though the evidence may well support such a finding. The covenants are enforceable in any event because of the specific language used in the deeds. The applicable law on this point was enunciated years ago and has remained basically unchanged. In *Clem v. Valentine,* our predecessors, quoting form *Halle v. Newbold,* 69 Md. 265, 14 A. 662 (1888), which referred to even earlier decisions, said:

> " 'These cases very conclusively settle the law that the grantor may impose a restriction, in the nature of a servitude or easement, upon the land that he sells or leases, for the benefit of the land he still retains; and if that servitude is imposed upon the heirs and assigns of the grantee, and in favor of the heirs and assigns of the grantor, it may be enforced by the assignee of the grantor against the assignee (with notice) of the grantee.' It is to be noted that that case was one in which the covenant expressly provided that its terms should be binding on the assigns of both the covenantor and the covenantee, and it was there held that his enabled an assignee of the covenantee to enforce the restriction. * * *"

In the case before us, the covenants are clearly binding on the successive owners. Not only is there an express provision that the covenants "run with the land," but it also is explicitly stated that they are binding upon the grantee "her heirs and assigns" and enforceable by the grantor, "its successors and assigns." As if this very lucid language were unclear, the deed defines an assignee as any person who obtains title "mediately or immediately," from the grantor. We need not pursue this question further . . . .

II

The second claim made by the appellees is that there has been an abandonment and failure of the original plan of development and a substantial change in the general characteristics of the neighborhood so as to render the covenants unenforceable. We have no quarrel with the underlying statement of law implicit in this argument, but think it is inapplicable to the facts of this case. Indeed, on many occasions we have held restrictive covenants unenforceable where there has been "* * * deterioration in the residential character of the neighborhood or a failure from the beginning of the restricted development, so that the restrictions no longer served their intended purpose." In that same case we said:

> "Most jurisdictions now recognize a change in the character of a neighborhood as a ground for affirmative relief against restrictive covenants by way of cancellation or modification *where the change has been so radical as to render perpetuation of the restriction of no substantial benefit to the dominant estate, and to defeat the object or purpose of the restriction.*" (Emphasis added.)

The inquiry, therefore, is whether there has been a complete or radical change in the neighborhood causing the restrictions to outlive their usefulness.

The only evidence here in any way tending to support appellees' contention is that a very few of the more than 200 lots have not been utilized for homes. These nonresidential uses are confined to a church, four doctors' offices maintained in their residences, a few feet of several lots located on the outer perimeter utilized for parking, two lots used by public utilities and one full lot with minor parts of two others infringed upon by a building constructed mainly on the commercial blocks. These minimal deviations from the original plan are not sufficient to show a change in the neighborhood that is either complete or radical. In this case, the purpose of the restrictions was to preserve the subdivision predominantly for residential use, and with the few negligible exceptions mentioned this is still being accomplished. On this point we think the following words of Kirkley v. Seipelt are particularly appropriate:

> "The real crux of the inquiry in determining whether there has been such a change in the neighborhood so as to defeat the covenant is to ascertain the purposes to be accomplished by the imposition of the restrictions. * * * [W]e think the reasons for them were to develop an attractive and inviting community. From the evidence, it is apparent the reasons and objects for placing the restrictions on the property are as active and as alive today as they were when first imposed."

The appellees further contend that the trial court was correct in looking beyond Section 1-A to determine if there had been a change in the neighborhood. We agree that this is a proper view of the law, but in applying the law to the facts the appellees are again found wanting. In Texas Co. v. Harker, we permitted an investigation of the broader neighborhood but nevertheless concluded that nearby commercial uses had in no way deteriorated the residential character of the subdivision under fire in that case. From the record before us, which includes aerial photographs and testimony, it is clear that the residential part of Section 1-A has been similarly unaffected. Indeed, it is still a highly desirable place for a home, completely unspoiled by commercialism. The appellees argue that the mere setting aside of Blocks 6 and 11 for commercial purposes was evidence of a failure *ab initio* of the original plan, but we can only comment that this use was exactly what was contemplated in the original plan and was in fact agreed to by nearly all of the lot purchasers. In any event the development of this commercial area has not deteriorated residential development in the remainder of the subdivision. On the contrary, the presence of a tasteful and well planned shopping center, which includes the Washington branch of Saks Fifth Avenue, complements the neighborhood.

III

The Jaggers' third contention is that the appellants have been guilty of laches and should therefore be estopped from seeking enforcement of the covenants. To support this claim they not only rely on the fact that three other doctors in the subdivision are using their homes for their principal offices, but also that Dr. Jaggers had used his property for the practice of medicine for nearly twenty years without objection. We need not decide whether the appellants had waived their rights to enforcement of the restrictions with respect to the other three doctors. It is true that these offices may violate the restrictive covenants, but the appellants, from their testimony, indicate that they have no objections to a combined office-home use. Consistent with this position, they had no objection to Dr. Jaggers' combined use of the property from 1947 on—until the time he moved to Potomac. The real issue then is whether the waiver, if there was one, was broad enough to permit the doctor to move his residence, rent his home, still maintain his office on the premises, and yet not be in violation of the covenant. We hold the possible waiver did not go this far. In February 1967, the appellant, Chevy Chase Village, informed Dr. Jaggers by letter that his property would not be available as an office if he moved his residence elsewhere. Under these new circumstances, precipitated by Dr. Jaggers' own action, this was a timely assertion of their right to enforce the covenants. As the Court said in Schlicht v. Wengert:

> "And toleration of violations, out of friendship or lack of inclination until incidental annoyances grew to make the Schlichts feel a grievance, could not be construed as surrender of those rights. They refrained from a contest until experience with the particular violation stirred them to enforcement; and they might do so without loss of rights from it."

So whether appellants should or should not have been estopped from enforcing the restrictive covenants under the conditions existing prior to 1967 is not relevant to the changed circumstances after 1967. Any waiver that may have existed was limited to the use of the office *incidental* to his living on the property. Once appellees moved, however, such use ceased to be incidental and the appellants could still assert their rights to enforce the restrictions.

Pursuing this same point, the appellees contend that there was great significance in the fact that no one from Section 1-A objected when the Montgomery County Board of Appeals granted the Jaggers' request for a special exception to use their premises for the practice of medicine. In view of our holding in Martin v. Weinberg, that "[c]ontractual restrictions are neither abrogated nor enlarged by zoning restrictions," we do not share their enthusiasm for this evidence of waiver. We point out that even if this silence were relevant on the question, the proceeding before the zoning board would only be indicative of the neighbors' acquiescence in the combined use of the property as a home and as an office, not as an office and rental property without the owner living on the premises.

IV

The final argument the doctor makes is that if he must return to his former home or remove his office to comply with the covenants, he will suffer great hardship and inconvenience when he has only caused negligible harm to his neighbors. He invokes the equitable doctrine of comparative hardship to avoid this result. That doctrine has been explained with forceful clarity by Chief Judge Hammond. . . . It basically provides that a court may decline to issue an injunction where the hardship and inconvenience which would result from the injunction is greatly disproportionate to the harm to be remedied. Innocent mistake on the part of the party to be enjoined is a factor to be considered in applying the doctrine. Overlooking the fact that the doctor, though a mediate purchaser whose deed only made reference to the restrictive covenants in his predecessor's deed, should have been aware of the limits on the use of his property, we do not think he can invoke the doctrine by characterizing the potential harm that might result to his neighbors' homes as comparatively negligible. Their interest in preserving the residential integrity of their community is simply not outweighed by his desire to move to another fashionable and exclusively residential area. With the facts before us in this case, had the trial judge declined to issue the injunction because of comparative hardship, we would not have hesitated to overrule him for a clear abuse of discretion. As he only went so far as to find that there had been a change in the neighborhood capable of vitiating the restrictive covenants, we base our reversal on this fact. On remand we direct that the appellees be enjoined from using their property in Chevy Chase Village for the practice of medicine unless they actually reside on the premises.

Decree reversed and the case remanded for the passage of a decree in conformity with this opinion.

[Citations and footnote omitted.]

Another formal requirement is **execution**. This requirement is met by the grantor signing the document, in some cases sealing it (note the remnants of antique legal formalism here), and often having someone attest her signature. In most jurisdictions, any writing that the party signing intends to be her signature is her signature. It can be "Mom," or "X," or her formal signature, such as "Susan B. Anselme." Attaching a formal seal with wax has gone out of style, but frequently the word "(seal)" appears printed or written after the place for the grantor's signature. That indication is sufficient today in most jurisdictions for individuals; corporate seals are used more frequently. *Attestation* is a formality verifying that the signature is made by the party whose name appears. Although, realistically, attestation is often done by someone simply saying that she is the signer to the notary public, or a third-party witness, without offering any evidence of who she is, attestation often has to be on the deed so that it can be recorded.

LEGAL TERMS

execution
Signing of a contract by the parties to the contract.

Many states have their own prescribed form for the attestation; be sure to check what your state requires.

Sometimes the issue of genuineness of a signature can be established by the signor (in real estate, the grantor of the property) coming forward before some competent authority or court and publicly identifying that signature as his own and affirming that he executed the document voluntarily. This formality is called **acknowledgment**. Failure to comply with this formality may have devastating effects, as illustrated by *Sweeney v. Vasquez*. Could this problem have been avoided, do you think, if someone had just taken a little more care when preparing the documentation?

acknowledgment
Statement by party who is the grantor under a deed, before a competent party, stating that the signature is that of the grantor and that he or she voluntarily executed the deed.

SWEENEY v. VASQUEZ

229 S.W. 2d97 (Tex. Civ. App. 1950)

W.O. MURRAY, C.J.

This suit was instituted by Thomas H. Sweeney, Sr. [and others] against F. W. Balcomb and Francisco P. Vasquez, seeking to recover the title and possession of a tract of land containing thirty-three acres and being out of a larger tract of 250 acres in Partition Share No. 22 of the Espiritu Santo Grant in Cameron County, Texas.

The trial began to a jury but resulted in an instructed verdict in favor of Francisco P. Vasquez for the title and possession of the thirty-three acre tract. From that judgment Thomas H. Sweeney [and others] have prosecuted this appeal.

On the 7the day of January, 1946, F. W. Balcomb, as owner, and the appellants, as purchasers, entered into a contract for the sale and purchase of the above described thirty-three acre tract of land. The contract was signed by Balcomb and appellants on January 7, 1946. It was also acknowledged by Thos. H. Sweeney and Thos. H. Sweeney, Jr., on the same day, and filed for record in Cameron County on January 24, 1946. Thereafter on May 12, 1947, F. W. Balcomb and Francisco P. Vasquez entered into a contract for the purchase and sale of the 250 acre tract above described, which included the thirty-three acre tract here involved. Vasquez testified that he had no actual knowledge of the first contract of sale, and unless the recording of it was constructive knowledge of its contents, he is entitled to prevail in this suit and the trial court's action in instructing a verdict in his favor would be proper.

Art. 1294, Vernon's Ann.Civ.Stat., provides as follows: "Every deed or conveyance of real estate must be signed and acknowledged by the grantor in the presence of at least two credible subscribing witnesses thereto; or must be duly acknowledged before some officer authorized to take acknowledgments, and properly certified to by him for registration."

Art. 6626, Vernon's Ann.Civ.Stats., provides in part as follows: "The following instruments of writing which shall have been acknowledged or proved according to law, are authorized to be recorded, viz: all deeds, mortgages, conveyances, deeds of trust, bonds for title, covenants, defeasances or other instruments of writing concerning any lands or tenements, or goods and chattels, or movable property of any description; * * *."

It will be noted that this article limits its provisions to such instruments which have been "acknowledged or proved according to law."

Art. 6627, Vernon's Ann.Civ.Stats., provides in effect that instruments which are not recorded as required by law are void as to all creditors and subsequent purchasers for valuable consideration without notice.

A contract for the sale and purchase of real estate which is not acknowledged by the grantor is not notice to subsequent purchasers, though it be acknowledged by the purchaser and recorded.

The contract of purchase and sale executed by Balcomb and the Sweeneys passed an equitable title to the thirty-three acres and should have been acknowledged by the vendor and not by the vendees.

Accordingly, the judgment of the trial court is affirmed.

[Citations omitted.]

Delivery

Execution of the deed must be followed by its **delivery** to the grantee. This aspect is rarely a problem in commercial transactions, but when the **grantor** is giving (as opposed to selling) the property to the **grantee**, delivery can be important. Delivery is important because it is the final evidence of the grantor's intent to transfer the property. If Susan B. Anselme completes the deed transferring her property, Blackacre, to her daughter, Hazel A. Parmelee, but leaves the deed in her desk, has a transfer taken place? Probably not. There has been no delivery, so there has been no transfer; the grantor retained control over the property or received its benefits. When that happens, there is no intent on the grantor's part to make what is called a "present conveyance," a transfer at this time.

Generally, the best way to indicate transfer is to hand the deed to the grantee. Sometimes, the deed is given to a third party for delivery upon certain conditions. This type of deed transfer is called an **escrow**. Although it could happen with a gift, the more common occurrence for an escrow is in a sales transaction. In some parts of America, most closings are done by escrow. In these closings, both the buyer and the seller deposit what they have promised in the sales contract to deliver to the **escrow agent (escrowee)**. The most common documents delivered are, for the seller, the deed; for the buyer, the check for the agreed-upon price. The paperwork, final title search, and final transferring and recording are completed by the escrow agent.

The *Griffitts* case poses an interesting question: Is it possible to back out of an escrow after it has been set up? Anything is possible, but for the Griffitts, the attempt was unavailing. Why do you think they wanted out of the escrow? Could Miss Griffitts's illness be a legitimate legal reason to cancel a real estate sale or escrow? What burden on the legal system would allowing reasons like hers to break a contract cause?

LEGAL TERMS

delivery
Actual or constructive passing of a document from one party to another; indicates intent on the part of the grantor to transfer when the document delivered is a deed.

grantor
Person who transfers property to another.

grantee
Person who receives property from another.

escrow
Arrangement whereby both parties to a transaction deposit their required paperwork and/or funds with a third party, who holds everything until all terms of the agreement have been met; often completes final aspects of a real estate transfer or sale.

escrow agent (escrowee)
Third party who does escrow work—holds and transfers paperwork and any monies.

WOOD BUILDING CORP.
v.
GRIFFITTS
330 P.2d 847 (Cal. Ct. App. 1958)

FOURT, J.

This is an appeal from a judgment in an action for specific performance. The defendants were directed to execute and deliver a deed to certain real property to the plaintiff and to perform under an agreement made between the parties.

The following is a summary of the facts of the case. In 1956, the defendants, brother and sister, were the owners of certain real property in Redondo Beach, California, which was located between the United States post office building and a building owned by a telephone company. The telephone company desired to have a building constructed on the lot owned by the defendants according to its plans and specifications and to lease the same under a long-term lease agreement. It engaged Harold Von Rolf, a real estate agent, to work out the transaction. The defendants resided upon the property in question. In February or March of 1956, Von Rolf, the real estate agent, called at the Griffitts' home and asked Miss Griffitts whether they were willing to sell their property. He was told to communicate with Mr. Griffitts, who was not at home at that time.

Later Von Rolf called again and talked over the matter with Mr. Griffitts who stated that he would think about it. Von Rolf did not, at that time, tell the defendants that he was working for any particular company or concern. Some thirty days later Von Rolf called the Griffitts and was told by Mr. Griffitts that he and his sister had talked it over and would sell for $25,000 net to themselves. The real estate agent advised Mr. Griffitts that he would let him know whether a sale could be made at that price. The agent asked Mr. Griffitts if they would pay him a commission for the sale of the real estate and Mr. Griffitts replied that they would not pay any such commission.

Von Rolf obtained the plans and specifications from the telephone company for the construction of a proposed building upon the defendants' property, if the same could be purchased, and also secured construction costs for the building from a contractor. In May or June of 1956, Von Rolf contacted Hugh Darling, the secretary of the plaintiff corporation and told Mr. Darling of the price of defendants' property and the costs for the proposed building. Darling informed Von Rolf that the transaction was satisfactory to him and told Von Rolf to contact William Ehni, the president of the plaintiff corporation and explain the matter to him. The real estate agent did so and Ehni told Von Rolf that the transaction was satisfactory to him. In August of 1956, Darling and Ehni told Von Rolf to consummate the purchase of the defendants' property on behalf of the plaintiff corporation.

On September 12, 1956, Von Rolf telephoned Mr. Griffitts and told him that he was prepared to enter into an escrow and to consummate the sale of the real property. On September 19, 1956, at the Griffitts' suggestion the real estate agent drove defendants to the Bank of America, Redondo Beach branch, to open the escrow. A thirty-day escrow was opened and both defendants signed the escrow instructions on that date, as well as a grant deed with the corporation as the grantee, and placed the deed in the escrow. At the time of the signing of the escrow instructions the defendants were told for the first time that the plaintiff was the purchaser of the property. At this time Von Rolf unconditionally deposited a $1,000 check in the escrow on behalf of the plaintiff, for which he received a receipt from the bank. The check was cashed. The escrow instructions contained the following statements by the buyer: "I will hand you or cause to be handed you the sum of $25,000," and immediately below, "and authorize you to accept for my account from Harold Von Rolf the sum of $1000.00."

Von Rolf had received the $1,000 check from Ehni on September 18, 1956, with instructions to deposit it in the escrow on behalf of the plaintiff. The defendants asked the real estate agent why the selling price was set forth in the escrow at $26,500, instead of $25,000, and further, made inquiries about the real estate agent's fee of $1,500, which was set forth in the escrow instructions. Von Rolf explained that the fee was for services in putting together the entire transaction. The agent had previously secured the approval of Darling and Ehni as to his fee in this particular transaction. On September 20, 1956, the agent mailed to Darling the buyer's instructions. Darling signed the same on September 21, 1956, and on the same mailed them to Ehni. Ehni signed the escrow instructions and on September 26, 1956, mailed them to the Bank of America, which received them on September 27, 1956.

On September 24, 1956, Miss Griffitts telephoned Mrs. Tolley, who was in charge of the escrow for the bank, and asked Mrs. Tolley if the defendants could withdraw from the escrow because of Miss Griffitts' health. Mrs. Tolley told Miss Griffitts to set forth the request in writing, and on the same day Miss Griffitts wrote a letter and personally delivered it to the Bank. The letter in question stated in the first paragraph thereof, "I should like to withdraw from my escrow 221-15022 dated September 19, 1956;" then followed several paragraphs concerning her sick leave from her work and her termination on permanent disability, about her doctor's advice, and her inability to sleep and her inability to move because of her ailment, and concluded, "I certainly hope I can withdraw and quit worrying. Had I known it would have affected me this way I would never have considered a move at this time." Mrs. Tolley forwarded a copy of this letter to Ehni's office on September 24, 1956, and Ehni responded to the letter on September 28, 1956, in which he refused for the corporation to consent to Miss Griffitts' request to withdraw from the escrow. Ehni did not see Miss Griffitts' letter of September 24, 1956, until after he had signed and mailed the buyer's escrow instructions to the bank.

On October 17, 1956, Ehni mailed the plaintiff's check for $25,500, and it was received by the bank the next day. On October 16, 1956, the defendants consulted their attorney who prepared a notice of rescission and a letter which was to the effect that the defendants rescinded the agreement upon the grounds that Von Rolf had made certain misrepresentations to the defendants in connection with the contemplated purchase of an apartment house located in Redondo Beach. This was the first time the defendants had set forth with particularity any such a contention.

Von Rolf testified that he and the defendants had first discussed the purchase of the apartment house on September 19, 1956, after the escrow instructions had been signed. The defendants made no independent inquiry regarding the price of the apartment house until after the instructions had been signed by them and after they had consulted an attorney. It was conceded by both defendants that the health of Miss Griffitts was a factor in their wanting to withdraw from the escrow. Miss Griffitts testified that at the time she wrote the first letter she knew she could not obtain the apartment on the terms purportedly represented to her by the real estate agent, yet she made no reference to that fact in her letter. Another real estate agent testified that about September 19, 1956, Miss Griffitts had indicated she was interested in income property and inquired about properties which the agent had for sale. About one week later she told that same agent that she had changed her mind about buying any income property as she didn't think she would sell her own property.

The Griffitts thereafter refused to close the escrow and an action was filed by the plaintiff in specific performance to compel them to comply with their agreement. The Griffitts answered claiming first that they had cancelled and revoked the instructions prior to the signing of the instructions by the plaintiff, and that the plaintiff had been so advised; secondly that there was no consideration for the signing of the escrow instructions, and thirdly that they had rescinded such instructions upon the grounds that the same had been signed by mistake and because of fraudulent representations. The trial court found against the Griffitts on substantially all of their contentions.

The appellants now contend: (1) that the first letter of Miss Griffitts to the bank constituted a revocation of the escrow agreement; (2) that Miss Griffitts had a right to revoke the contract upon the ground that the plaintiff had not accepted their offer at the time of revocation, and that the contract was not the result of any prior oral agreement with the plaintiff; (3) that the deposit of $1,000 by Von Rolf in the escrow was not the payment of a down payment under the escrow, and (4) that they had a right to rescind, as they did by their letter of October 16, 1956, because of their misunderstanding as to the price of the apartment house in which they had shown some interest as to purchasing.

We believe that there is no merit to any of the contentions of appellants. It is true that there was some testimony which, had it been accepted as true by the trial court, might have sustained some of their assertions; however, there was substantial testimony and evidence adverse to their contentions which the trial court believed and upon which the trial court based its findings, conclusions and judgment.

Considering the contention that appellants could revoke the escrow instructions because no consideration was paid: Von Rolf deposited unconditionally a $1,000 check (which was cashed) on behalf of the plaintiff in connection with the escrow. A reading of the instructions also convinces us that the $1,000 was deposited and under the circumstances of this case made a binding escrow. The instructions provided that the buyer, "will hand you or cause to be handed you the sum of $25,500.00," and below this it is stated, "and authorize you to accept for my account form Harold Von Rolf the sum of $1000.00."

The words "will hand you" refer to the $25,500, and not to the $1,000 check. The check was delivered and cashed and the money therefrom stayed with the bank. We believe that under the circumstances this made a sufficient consideration to make the signing of the escrow instructions by the defendants an irrevocable offer. The bank, at the time of the signing of the escrow instructions, was the agent of the defendants and was authorized to receive payment under the instructions. It was said in Gelber v. Cappeller,

"Under the instructions given by the parties the escrow holder became the common agent of both parties and held all monies and documents deposited with it for the benefit of both until either its powers under their instructions were terminated, or the conditions under which the escrow was to be closed by it had occurred in which latter event it became agent and trustee for the vendors as to the monies and documents deposited by the vendees and agent and trustee for the benefit of the vendees as to the instruments of conveyance of the other documents deposited by the grantor."

As we view it, the vendee made a partial payment, and when accompanied by a writing such as was present in this case, there was then an irrevocable offer for the time set forth in the instruments.

However, as asserted by the respondent, there was evidence to the effect that there was an oral agreement between the plaintiff, as an undisclosed principal, and the defendants with reference to the sale of the property prior to the execution of the instructions. The Griffitts said they would sell their property for $25,000 net to them; the corporation told Von Rolf to go ahead and conclude the purchase at such price; Von Rolf told the Griffitts he was ready to conclude the purchase at the price asked. Arrangements were then made for the escrow with Von Rolf acting for the corporation. An offer and acceptance may be transmitted by an agent between the offeror and offeree and the authority of such agent need not be in writing.

In *Cowan v. Tremble,* it was said:

"It is well settled as a general rule that an undisclosed principal can either sue or be sued on the contract made by his agent, and the fact that plaintiff brought the action thereon was a sufficient ratification of the acts of Jacobson."

The execution of the escrow instructions constituted a sufficient memorandum of the oral agreement for the sale of the property in that it did give the names of the parties, the price, a description of the property, and was subscribed by the owners or parties to be charged. It was appropriately said in Boehle v. Benson,

"We do not agree with appellant's contention that the agreement does not satisfy the Statute of Frauds. In the case of *Cavanaugh v. Casselman,* the court said:

" 'It was not necessary that the plaintiff should himself sign the agreement * * * in order to enable him to enforce it against the defendant. The statute of frauds requires the contract, or some note or memorandum thereof, to be in writing, but it need be subscribed only by the party to be charged [Citation.] * * * The "writing" in question is sufficient to satisfy the statute. It sufficiently names the parties and the price, and gives a complete description of the property. It is also subscribed by the defendant, who is the party to be charged.' "

The monies, in addition to the $1,000 deposited by Von Rolf unconditionally in the escrow were deposited well within the limits provided.

As to fraudulent representations made by Von Rolf, the evidence was contradictory. The judge had a right and a duty to determine the truth as it appeared to him, and apparently he believed Von Rolf. A reading of the transcript of the testimony would indicate that if Von Rolf was believed then there was no fraud or misrepresentation in any respect.

The judgment is affirmed.

[Citations omitted.]

Recording

The final step in making the transfer safe for the grantee is **recording** the deed. Although the recordation is not necessary for the grantee's protection vis-à-vis the grantor, it is almost always necessary to protect against a special type of possible subsequent purchaser. The common law has evolved a number of doctrines based upon general benefit to society and who is best able to protect himself. Consider the following situation. A sells Blackacre to B. B takes delivery of the deed, but never records it. A sells Blackacre to C. A disappears with the double payment. Who has a better claim to Blackacre, B or C? To keep this simple, add that C has no knowledge of B's ownership, and assume that Blackacre is vacant, unimproved land. C looks like a special person in the law—the subsequent good faith purchaser who has no notice. C gets the property. Note that B could have protected himself by recording his deed. Then C would have had constructive notice, because the document would have been in the public records, and he could have checked. When B does not make that possible, the law supports the party who had no way to find out, and it does so partly because it wants the flow of commerce to be unimpeded. Although not as important here, the same result occurs because B had the opportunity to protect himself and did not do it. Always record!

5.5 DOCUMENTS: THE LAND CONTRACT

In contrast to the cash sale, the traditional standard for the home sales industry, there is another device which permits sale of a property over a period of time. There is no reason why this device cannot be used outside the home real estate market. It is an installment sales contract, under which monthly (or periodic) payments are made by the buyer to the seller. This arrangement has several other names as well, such as installment contract and contract for the deed. Note that the buyer does not obtain a formal transfer of the property by deed until the final payment is made. In some jurisdictions, the buyer has **equitable title** because of the payments she has made and her commitment to making all of them. But some states have decided that there is no title in the buyer at all until the final payment is made. The problems that can arise here are complex, and have no really good solution as of this writing, but the usual problem arises when the seller has a lien filed against him. If he is the title holder, his creditor can seize the property. What protection does the buyer have? Even if there is no loss of the property, the eventual title transfer may lack the marketable title the buyer has paid for. The problem can work the other way as well. The buyer may order repairs, not pay for them, default on the contract, and leave the seller with a large obligation of which he knew nothing.

A number of problems can arise in this situation. The seller must be extremely careful, because the seller is not only involved in all of the ordinary concerns of a home sale, but has also become the financier of the buyer as well. In essence, the seller has entered the banking business and is lending to the buyer. This device might be used when the buyer wishes to avoid high interest rates in normal financing channels, thus making it possible for the buyer to handle the payments. It might also be used when the seller wants to defer taxes, or when there is a high prepayment penalty for an early payoff of the seller's loan.

Most buyers lack the skills to understand the lending process, which is an entire business in itself. Outside help should be sought to identify the risks

LEGAL TERMS

recording
Process of filing documents (usually the mortgage, often with the note) in the public records office for real estate; provides notice and is sometimes important to protecting title.

equitable title
Right acquired by the buyer, under a contract for sale, in the property being purchased.

the seller may face. Some of the more important ones follow. The first is that the seller's lender discovers the sale. There is little that can be done about this. Second, what if the buyer wants to assign his contract (technically, delegate his duties)? There should be a clause preventing that, or all the seller's hard work at discovering the buyer's financial solvency will be wasted. Nevertheless, those assignments do happen. Careful thought should be given to the penalties involved, such as making the contract void or making the assignment void. Third, how can the creditworthiness of the buyer be determined? How can the seller know whether it will change over time? Fourth, how are all taxes, assessments, and insurance payments to be made? Will the buyer make deposits into an escrow account, including 8.333% of the estimated annual amount of these payments with each month's contract payment? Fifth, will there be an acceleration clause in the contract for breach of the contract? Last, is there a clause requiring maintenance of the property? Lenders deal with these terms and problems every day. The seller would be well advised to seek legal counsel or, minimally, good bank forms to cover all these contingencies and concerns.

A clause that appears in all land contracts provides that breach of the contract, particularly nonpayment, creates a forfeiture. This seller's remedy permits the seller to end the contract, keep the payments made, and obtain or regain possession of the property. Forfeitures are not favored in the law, and a clause providing for forfeiture must be written into the land contract as an agreed-upon remedy in the parties' bargaining. Otherwise, the law of contracts would ordinarily allow rescission, which means that the parties would be returned to their status at the beginning of the contract; the seller would regain the property and the buyer the payments made (less the value of rent) over the period of occupancy.

Some problems are normal for creditors, but not for land contract sellers. For instance, what if the buyer's payments are late or are less than the amount due? Does the seller notify the buyer every time, stating that he is waiving the default, but will not permit it in the future? What if he does? Does he eventually waive his rights permanently? Should the seller accept the situation for a while, do nothing, and then move to restore his rights by warning the buyer that more failures to comply with the agreement will not be tolerated? Does the seller thereafter begin forfeiture? With what standards must the seller comply?

These are questions that the seller must answer under local law. Generally, the seller must provide proper notice to each buyer, at the right location, prior to forfeiture. Small instances of default are usually not permitted to cause a forfeiture. The seller must declare a forfeiture in writing. However, not all contracts may be forfeited. When the buyer has made most of the payments—that is, has obtained substantial equities in the property—the courts may be reluctant to permit forfeiture. The courts may insist upon the buyer's rights being protected through foreclosure proceedings, which include the right of redemption. In any event, the remedy of foreclosure generally remains available to the seller upon the buyer's default. Some courts that are concerned with the ethics of this situation feel that forfeiture when the buyer has built up substantial equities is **unconscionable**.

5.6 DOCUMENTS: THE FINANCIAL DOCUMENTS

Almost all real estate sales involve some type of financing. Very few persons or businesses have the cash available to purchase outright, and frequently it is not desirable to do so for cash-flow and tax reasons. Consequently, at least one financier is normally involved in the transaction, if not more. The buyer has to have someone put up the money for him. The seller usually financed her purchase of the property, and her financier is at the closing to get the payoff check and deliver releases of any liens. In a construction deal, many financiers may be involved. They could include a party putting up the money on a short-term basis (two to three years) for the actual construction; a party paying off that short-term loan and financing the project over 25 or more years; a party financing the land; a party financing the equipment going into the building; and others. There may also be mechanic's liens by the workers on the construction project to be released. This complexity encourages confusion and mistakes, but learning how financing works will prevent much of it. It often helps to break down each transaction separately and then analyze it to determine how it relates to the other transaction(s).

The Note

The credit transaction involves a series of documents. The first document, technically called an *instrument,* is the **note**. This note is the evidence of the debt owed and the promise to repay the debt. Because the borrower-debtor might be unable to repay the loan on time (or at all), the creditor-lender usually requires another way of getting repaid. The creditor obtains the rights to sell the real property for which she advanced the loan if the borrower does not repay her.

Be aware that there are two types of transactions here. The first is a credit-debt transaction, in which one party borrows and the other lends an agreed-upon amount of money for the purpose of buying a parcel of real property. This transaction is covered by the note. The note may be brief (one page), or much longer, but its length and complexity reflect of what the state's law has determined should or must be in the note and the complexity of the transaction.

The second is a collateral transaction. Although the real property secures the debt, in the technical legal sense the transaction is not a secured transaction. That phrase describes a loan secured by personal property, not by real property. Secured transactions are not governed by real estate law at all; they are governed by Article 9 of the Uniform Commercial Code. Although there is not much difference conceptually, there are significant differences in legal theories between real estate and personal property collateral

LEGAL TERMS

unconscionability
Legal doctrine that allows courts to act on behalf of a disadvantaged party when it appears that the action proposed, though legally proper, is violative of ethical standards, if the result would be entirely one-sided, with one party taking severe advantage and causing great damage to the other party.

note
Instrument that evidences a loan and an obligation to repay it; the written evidence of the signer's financial obligation; accompanies a mortgage.

transactions. The collateral documents in a real estate transaction are usually called a mortgage or a deed of trust.

The Terms of Collateralization

Before we begin this section, a brief word on how to understand some of these new terms is in order. Most people find them confusing, but they are not if the reader knows how to understand them. The party giving the mortgage is the *mortgagor;* the party receiving the mortgage is the *mortgagee.* Generally speaking, when the term ends with "-or" or "-er," like mortgag*or*, credit*or*, or lend*er*, that is the party doing the act. The mortgagor gives the mortgage and the creditor lends the money. The receiving party's name usually ends with "-ee," as in the mortgag*ee* who receives the mortgage from the mortgagor. We do not call the receiver of credit the "creditee," but rather the debtor. Once you understand the endings, these terms make sense. Each term has two parts: the part that tells you what is going on (as in the idea of owing; here, "debt" is the main term), and the suffix, the part that tells you who is doing what.

The Mortgage or the Deed of Trust

In common parlance, we speak of giving or taking a mortgage on real property. The **mortgage** is one of the principal ways of documenting a real estate collateral transaction. The other form is called a **deed of trust**. Both types of documents give the lender the right to take the property when certain events happen. The most common event triggering the retaking (called a **foreclosure**) is the nonpayment, when due, of installments on the loan.

Legal theories and their effects upon foreclosure actions differ significantly. The *mortgage theory* begins with the buyer of the real property taking the title to the land. When she possesses the title, she can give someone a lien on the property—in this case, the lender, in the form of a mortgage. The mortgagor is the title holder.

Under the *deed of trust theory,* the property is transferred into a **trust** and the **trustee** holds the legal title. For many lenders, that trustee is under their direction if it becomes necessary to retake the property. Note that the legal title is not in the hands of the borrower-mortgagor. She is the beneficial interest holder (or the **beneficiary**) of the trust. Theoretically, the mortgage and the deed of trust do the same job of collateralizing the real estate loan, but, practically, the debtor's rights are usually more restricted under the deed of trust because she is not the title holder. Without title, there has traditionally been no right of redemption (a right that permits the "owner" to regain the property by paying off the debt). Therefore, the creditor can gain possession and sell the property much faster. This permits lower costs to both parties (lost interest to the creditor and potential deficiency judgment amounts against the debtor), but it does limit the debtor's chances to recover the property. Some states that permit deeds of trust have recently begun to change

LEGAL TERMS

mortgage
Document pledging real estate as collateral for the repayment of a loan.

deed of trust
Written legal document that transfers real property from the owner to a trust in which the property is controlled by the trustee on behalf of a lender; serves the same purpose as a mortgage, to collateralize a loan usually made to acquire real property.

foreclosure
Court procedure for repossession and sale of property that has been mortgaged or pledged as collateral for a debt that has not been paid.

their laws affecting the debtor's rights of redemption. They have shortened the period in which a debtor can redeem the property with mortgages and required some redemption features under deeds of trust. Clearly, debtors usually favor the mortgage approach, and creditors usually favor the trust deed approach.

The formalities for these collateral documents, because they affect real estate, are the same as for a deed. Both the mortgage and the deed of trust must be in writing, be signed, have a proper legal description of the real property, and be sealed, acknowledged, and delivered. The document is usually a transfer from the debtor to the creditor, and while it appears absolute, it is conditioned upon nonpayment or other serious default. Finally, either form should be recorded as soon as possible.

Another distinction exists between legal theories about collateral transactions. Two separate theories, the *lien theory* and the *title theory*, can have important consequences. The **lien theory** is much more common. It underlies the granting of a mortgage. Here, the owner has title to the property; the only time the mortgagee (lender) has a right to the title is after foreclosure or other court action. Until that time, the mortgagor is entitled to occupy the property. Under the **title theory**, the mortgagee has the title and the right to possession of the property. But, in the real world, the creditor permits the debtor to occupy the premises because the creditor has no use for them until default. The lender is interested in payment of the money—principal and interest—not in possessing real property.

If the debtor occupies the property (is in possession), she has the right to any income from it except when otherwise agreed by contract. Just as there were two parties involved in future interests, so there are here as well. The creditor has an interest that she can protect. The debtor cannot commit waste on the property; that is, she cannot damage the property so that its value is decreased. Failing to maintain a building, not paying the taxes, failing to pay a lien on the land, and destroying the productivity of the land itself are all examples of waste. The lender usually attempts to protect itself by insisting on clauses in its documentation permitting it to make payments to insurance companies or taxing authorities to preserve the property as collateral; the creditor then adds those payments onto the principal of the note.

If the property has been seized by the mortgagee-creditor for nonpayment or any other reason, the mortgagor-debtor has the **right of redemption**. To redeem the property means that the lien of the mortgagee must be fully satisfied, that is, the debt must be fully paid. Remember the preceding comments, however, about the deed of trust format and the right of redemption. There is further discussion of this topic in § 5.10 on foreclosure.

5.7 FIXTURES

Commercial real estate transactions and their mortgages may involve other collateralization problems. Not only may there be real estate mortgages, but there may also be personal property financed by another creditor. Two types of problems can arise. First, when there is a lease, the landlord who has

trust
Legal device for holding property, under which the ownership is divided between a trustee, who has legal title, and a beneficiary, who has equitable title.

trustee
Party who administers the trust for the benefit of another party, the beneficiary.

beneficiary
One of two parties to a trust; the trust party who gets the benefits of a trust; said to hold the "beneficial interest."

lien theory
Legal approach to collateralizing a loan with real property; provides that the debtor-mortgagor keeps title to the property and gives the creditor a lien on the property as collateral for the loan; the mortgagor stays in possession of the property even after default.

title theory
Legal theory that places the real estate title in the mortgagee (lender) when the property is pledged as collateral for a loan; realistically, the lender permits the borrower to occupy the property, although the lender technically owns the property.

right of redemption
Right of the mortgagor who has been foreclosed upon to regain the property upon payment in full of the debt.

a lien for uncollected rent payments may try to seize business property leased from someone else. This action can frequently cause problems between the creditor for the business assets and the landlord. If the lessor is out of the picture, the personal property creditor and the real property creditor may be the parties to the dispute. Second, there could be fixtures. Generally speaking, fixtures are the pieces of equipment (which begin as personal property) that are so closely attached to the real property that they become a part of the real property (and thereafter are treated as real property). A number of rules define whether something is a fixture; the two most important are the intent of the parties and the degree to which the item has been integrated into the real property, usually into the building.

Some technicalities could be useful. Most fixtures begin as equipment. They are financed (often by a bank that takes a security interest in the equipment to collateralize the loan) as part of a business's activities. The business creditor files a public notice, called a *financing statement* (a UCC-1 or a UCC-2, depending on the jurisdiction's statute). If the item is equipment, it belongs to its business creditor if the business goes bankrupt. If the item is a fixture, it belongs to the owner of the real property. Some fixtures can be very valuable when they are large and expensive pieces of industrial equipment.

An aside—note that the catch in fixture notice filing is that the financing statement must be filed in the real estate records—but the filing frequently is not done there. The statement may be filed in the appropriate office, such as the Recorder of Deeds, but often insufficient information is provided to locate the proper real estate record in which to file it. Some real estate records offices have a system of filing for fixtures called a *UCC-1 file*. Such filings are technically incorrect. They are filed in the local real estate records office, but without the real property description, so the filing cannot be tied into the real estate records. Therefore, the filing official maintains a separate UCC-1 file that must also be searched.

Clearly, this area of the law involves some tricky situations, but a new rule to determine whether a piece of personal property has become a fixture may be developing. It is simply this: If one person can remove the disputed property in one hour with an ordinary set of tools, it is not a fixture. It has been referred to as the "one man, one hour, ordinary set of tools" rule. But that rule will not solve all problems, because the question will arise as to what constitutes an ordinary set of tools. It may not be rational to expect it to be the set of tools found around a home. If that were built into the formula, any large piece of equipment would be a fixture. The rule must imply an ordinary set of tools for that particular piece of equipment. Regardless of its problems, this approach attempts to resolve the many conflicts that court decisions about fixtures have created. The legal area of what a fixture is has been chaotic, inconsistent, and often contradictory among jurisdictions. That situation tends to make bad law and gives the law a bad reputation. If the goal of the law is consistency, as Holmes suggested, this approach could promote greater consistency.

But though fixtures are often a problem for commercial transactions, they can also cause trouble in residential situations as well. In many apartment leases, items in the apartment, such as air conditioners, dishwashers, other kitchen utilities, or similar items added or improved upon by the tenant, are considered fixtures. When a tenant installs, upgrades, or replaces the piece of equipment, and that equipment joins the building, it becomes a fixture (in many cases). Many standard leases provide that the item added becomes the property of the lessor. Most tenants are unaware of this. They consider the property theirs, to be reimbursed by the landlord or to take with them. While there is some logic to that position, it is not the law in most jurisdictions. This fact should be explained to tenants who are moving in, entering into a lease, or contemplating installing a new piece of equipment.

5.8 TRANSFERRING COLLATERALIZED INTERESTS

Circumstances frequently make it necessary for one of the parties to a mortgage to transfer her interest in the mortgage. Most frequently, this occurs when the mortgagor (borrower) needs to move, but a mortgage transfer can also happen when the mortgagee (lender) sells the note and mortgage. The latter situation is not difficult, because the mortgagee is merely assigning its right to be paid, but the mortgagor is delegating a duty. Transferring rights is not difficult, but transferring duties can create several problems (the distinction between rights and duties is discussed in chapter 9, on leases). First, does the mortgagee want that subsequent party? The party may not be solvent. Second, what rights does the mortgagee have against the new party? Is it a direct relationship, or must any action be through the original mortgagor?

Consider the differences between *assuming the mortgage* and *taking the property subject to the mortgage.* If the new party becomes obligated on the note and mortgage, he is said to have *assumed* the mortgage. If he does not become obligated on the original note and mortgage, he is said to take the property *subject* to the mortgage. When the property remains subject to the mortgage, the third party will not suffer any loss beyond the loss of the property if the payments are not made. In essence, the subsequent party is personally liable if he assumes the mortgage, but is not personally liable if he takes subject to the mortgage. This difference is important if default, repossession, and a subsequent sale of the land occur. If the amount realized from the sale is greater than the total debt owed, there is never a problem, but when sale of the property does not produce enough money to pay the debt, the mortgagee can go to court and get a deficiency judgment against the debtor-mortgagor. The act of assuming the mortgage creates that obligation, but taking subject to the mortgage does not.

5.9 OTHER TYPES OF TRANSFERS

Transfer of property may occur in several other ways, although such transfers, except for foreclosure, are relatively rare. These methods, including adverse possession, escheat, and eminent domain actions, are outside the mainstream of real estate commerce. Thus, the alert paralegal must know what to look for and what sorts of problems might arise.

Adverse Possession

Adverse possession is a device for involuntarily transferring property against the owner's interest. Another party may occupy the real estate in a manner against the interest of the party then owning the property. Occupation may ripen into possession and ownership. For adverse possession to operate, the party in possession must claim the property openly, notoriously, continuously, hostilely, and adversely to the true owner's interest. *Continuous* means uninterrupted during the statutorily prescribed period, often as long as 20 years, but sometimes as little as 10 years. Property often is transferred during a 20-year period.

Successors to the adverse claim may cumulate their time periods by the process of **tacking**. Mere succession in possession can create tacking in some states, but not in others. Some states require that the party who is trying to benefit from tacking, such as a successor in interest to the prior party who had an adverse claim, take the claim by virtue of a deed transferring the parcel that will benefit from the claim of adverse possession. Since the transferor's developing adverse possession claim cannot mature into clear title before the full time period, any prior transfer would be illegitimate; but if the claim is transferred by a deed transferring the property, the transfer of the claim is said to be done under the **color of title**. This phrase means that an apparently valid deed was used to transfer the property. In states that require the use of a deed to transfer an adverse possession claim, if the subsequent title holder can show such a deed, he can tack his time period in adverse possession onto that of his predecessor and cumulate the time periods. For instance, A owns Blackacre and has a fence that encroaches five feet onto the adjoining property, Whiteacre. The fence has been there 12 years; the statutory time for a claim of adverse possession is 20 years. In year 12, A sells Blackacre to B. In the legal description passing the title in the deed, the extra five feet are included. B may now tack A's time of possession onto his. After eight more years, B may have a complete adverse possession claim, made continuous through tacking via deed transfer under color of title, against the owner of Whiteacre. Although it should not be necessary to explicitly mention the adverse claim in the deed, your jurisdiction may require it.

Escheat

The term **escheat** means that the property owner has no heirs and the property returns to the state. Originally, escheat referred to real property only, but today it is used to describe property lacking anyone to take it. In some states, real property passes to the local government and personal property passes to the state government.

Eminent Domain

Eminent domain is the government's right to take private property for public purposes. The government sometimes permits agencies or

LEGAL TERMS

tacking
Successive series of claims in adverse possession which, taken together, cumulate to the necessary statutory time period; may require transfer of claim by deed from prior to succeeding adverse claimant.

quasi-public organizations to exercise the right of eminent domain. To exercise this right, the state must file a suit of condemnation and establish that the property is needed for public use, the owner will be paid a fair amount for the property, and the rules of due process have been observed. Fair compensation is usually based upon official estimates, which are countered by landowner estimates or appraisals of higher value. These disputes are heard in administrative and subsequent judicial proceedings. The rules of due process focus on two areas—substantive and procedural due process. Substantive due process protects against arbitrary government action. For instance, after the 1992 Los Angeles riots, many residents of the riot-torn area wanted all the liquor stores closed; those that were burned out were to be denied licenses to rebuild. If the Los Angeles city council had done so, its action could have been challenged by liquor store owners as violative of substantive due process. Procedural due process focuses on fairness in governmental procedures. If a fair hearing does not occur, the rights protected by procedural due process could be used as the basis for a challenge. Land taken under eminent domain may be used for a variety of public purposes, such as a highway, a school, or a park, or for semi-public use, such as a utility property like a railroad right of way.

Most people never experience eminent domain proceedings, but it can happen to anyone if the government needs the property for a legitimate public purpose. The *Elmbar* case succinctly illustrates the need to have clear and convincing evidence to establish one's evaluation. It shows the legal process involved in attempting to evaluate the conflicting claims for value that both sides present. Note that the experts cited in the case could well have been appraisers, whose work is discussed in chapter 6.

color of title
Term used in tacking; used when a deed has transferred title to property and purports to transfer an adverse possession claim as part of the deed.

escheat
Transfer of property ownership to the state when no other heir for the property can be located.

eminent domain
Process by which the government seizes land for public use and pays fair compensation; all actions must abide by due process.

ELMBAR ASSOCIATES
v.
STATE
225 N.Y.S.2d 416 (App. Div. 1962)

PER CURIAM.

This is an appeal by the State of New York from a judgment of the Court of Claims entered June 29, 1961 awarding claimant the sum of $88,250 less a partial payment of $12,000 for damages for the appropriation on July 29, 1958 in fee of certain parcels of real property located in the Village of Elmsford, Town of Greenburgh, County of Westchester. The State's appeal alleges that the award is excessive. Claimant cross-appeals on the ground of inadequacy. There were further interests in claimant's property appropriated by temporary easements in parcels 866 and 867 and a permanent easement in parcel 863. The claim arising out of the appropriation of these easements was tried with the claim herein and a separate judgment awarding damages to claimant was entered. No appeal has been taken from that judgment.

Five months prior to the appropriation herein claimant purchased the tract in question for

$25,000 from the New York Central Railroad. The tract was an irregularly shaped piece consisting of 7.781 acres of low-lying marshy ground bounded on the west and north by the Saw Mill River, on the east by tracks of the New York Central Putnam Division and on the south by Route 119, known as the White Plains-Tarrytown Road. The ground level of the tract was some five to six feet on the average below the level of Route 119. The only access to the property was at the southern end onto Route 119. At this point the property was only 43 feet wide and a narrow strip thereof subject to a perpetual easement acquired by the State in 1940 to eliminate the grade crossing where New York Central tracks crossed Route 119.

The instant appropriation was the taking of a 200-foot strip across the parcel and for the purposes of constructing the Cross-Westchester Expressway which divided the tract in two. The northerly portion consisting of approximately 1.756 acres was completely land locked and the southerly portion reduced to approximately 4.429 acres. The testimony of both the State's and claimant's experts was that the property's highest and best use prior to appropriation was for light industry even though at that time all but the frontage on Route 119 was zoned Residence "A". Claimant's evidence was that even considering the irregular shape of the property and the fact that two utility easements prevented placing a building on a portion thereof a 100,000 square foot factory could have been placed on the parcel prior to appropriation but after the taking the size of the building that could be placed in the remaining southerly portion would be so small as to make it economically infeasible. Despite the fact that this tract was purchased only five months previously for $25,000, claimant's real estate expert testified that its *before* value was $220,000 and its *after* value was $20,000. The State's expert testified that its *before* value was $77,500 and its *after* value was $34,500, or total damages exclusive of the easements of $43,000.

On this appeal the State contends that the perpetual easement taken in 1940 by the State on a narrow strip of land on the southerly edge of the parcel adjacent to the northerly edge of Route 119, "for highway purposes for constructing, reconstructing and maintaining thereon a highway and slopes in connection with the proposed grade crossing elimination" might completely bar access to the parcel if the work was ever done, and that since claimant's expert as well as the State's expert gave their testimony on the basis of a right of access, the judgment should be reversed and case remitted for additional testimony as to value based on lack of access. The court below has held that the easement referred to did not bar access. On the record we agree. . . .

After considering all of the testimony and giving it such effect as the record warrants relating to damage, we come to the conclusion that the award of $88,250 is excessive and should be reduced to $43,000.

The judgment should be modified on the law and the facts by reducing the amount thereof to $43,000 less the partial payment of $12,000, with appropriate interest and as so modified affirmed without costs.

Judgment modified, on the law and the facts, by reducing the amount thereof to $43,000 less the partial payment of $12,000 with appropriate interest and as so modified, affirmed, without costs.

[Citations omitted.]

Foreclosure for Nonpayment of Debt

There are other common types of transfers for debt that frequently occur. First, the government may foreclose on the real property if the taxes on it are not paid. Second, persons who have worked on the property and added to its value are entitled to payment. If any of them registers a claim as a publicly recorded **mechanic's lien** within the statutorily set time, they may foreclose the lien and sell the property to be paid for the work. Finally, general creditors who are not paid for a landowner's debt may sue him, win a judgment, and then foreclose on the property and be paid out of the proceeds of the sale. By far the most common foreclosure, however, is by a creditor against property pledged as collateral against the debt.

5.10 FORECLOSURE

All of these actions, regardless of the party doing them, involve foreclosing on the property. Clearly, foreclosure's purpose is to obtain the value of the property for the benefit of the creditor. Note that all the parties foreclosing are creditors of some sort—the lender is a voluntary creditor; the holder of the mechanic's lien is a type of equitable creditor, as she did the work and the landowner received the benefit; and the government has a statutory lien for unpaid taxes and is, through the lien, a creditor.

Although there are several methods of foreclosure, the two most common are the foreclosure suit and sale of the property without court proceedings. In the foreclosure suit, the creditor files suit against the debtor in court and asks the court to order the sale of the property. This sale is usually for nonpayment of the debt when due. When the court issues such an order, it instructs a public official, usually the sheriff, to sell the property at a public sale. Until the sale occurs, anyone may come in and pay off the debt. The right to make this payment is called *equitable redemption.* After the sale, in states having a further redemption period (called s*tatutory redemption*), the purchaser receives a sale certificate indicating that she will have the right to a title if no one redeems the property. In states that lack statutory redemption, the buyer gets a deed giving him title free and clear of the debtor's claims. Statutory redemption can be difficult for creditors, as explained elsewhere. While it was one thing to permit farm owners to redeem their property after a bad crop or a drought made it impossible for them to make payments, in the contemporary urban world the primary effect of the right of redemption has been to raise lenders' costs. Nevertheless, these laws still permit the debtor to repay the debt with a period of up to two years or longer.

In the second method, foreclosure is a private process that does not involve the courts. The mortgage document itself has a power of sale in it. This power of sale permits the mortgagee, or the trustee under a trust deed, to sell the land after the debtor has failed to make timely payments. The mortgage document spells out the terms of this action and usually requires written notice to the debtor. Frequently, the notice must be sent by certified

LEGAL TERMS

mechanic's lien
Claim by a person who has worked on a parcel of real property in some way to improve it; made against the owner of the real property. The claim must be recorded against the property within a short time period, often up to months, to be valid.

mail to establish the time of giving of notice and that the debtor actually received the notice and knew what was happening. The debtor is given a chance to pay off the debt after receiving the notice of default and intended sale. Often, to prevent any unfair actions, the creditor, or any agent of the creditor, is forbidden to buy the property. In some states other methods of foreclosure still exist.

Even in foreclosure, if the property contains a home, the property owner retains certain rights, called **homestead rights**. These rights are defined and limited by statute. They serve as exemptions that put some property beyond creditor's grasp. For instance, in some states, the limit may be in a dollar amount, such as $5,000; in other states, it may be in the amount of land protected, say, one-half acre. These amounts, in dollars or land, cannot be sold to satisfy debts. The homestead statutes were designed to protect the family from outside problems and provide it with a minimum for its survival, but another purpose has been to protect the wife from the husband's unilateral sale of the home. Also, widows' rights under dower were often inadequate; with homestead rights, the widow cannot be forced out of the home. In many states, the documentation of a mortgage or of a deed must deal with this problem directly. The spouse's rights must be waived, or the spouse must join in making the mortgage or deed. Knowledge of local law in this area is essential.

Most private creditors undertake foreclosure only after all other remedies are exhausted. Even the government and the workers operating under a mechanic's lien often take a considerable amount of time to act on these liens. For the lender, foreclosure is the least desirable step. The lender will frequently assign the loan to workout; place the loan on nonaccrual, in which status it generates no interest; reschedule payments; provide time extensions; or help the debtor sell the property to a third party—almost anything to avoid going through foreclosure.

This approach is generally supported by lending practice because it is much easier to get repaid in the regular manner than to go through the lengthy, expensive, and potentially harmful process of foreclosure. How is the creditor harmed? The creditor may suffer in its reputation for fairness or honesty, causing future customers to avoid that lender. Another problem for the lender is that many courts have a strong bias toward borrowers, especially when the loan is for a home. The creditor must take every foreclosure step in the utmost good faith and with full notice, ample opportunity for the borrower to meet with the creditor, discuss, rework, and make the loan viable. Only after those steps and only when the payments are several periods in arrears will many courts permit foreclosure. A negative personal interaction, a mere technical default, or some minor aspect may preclude foreclosure in most courts today.

When mortgages are guaranteed by the Federal Housing Administration or the Veterans Administration, foreclosures entail special procedures. These generally fit within the broad outlines of several months in default and complete fair play to the debtor. There are extensive regulations.

Finally, there are a number of steps after foreclosure that must be identified. The purchaser or new owner must either get an assignment of the existing insurance policies or obtain new policies. If any lessees are on the property, new leases should be obtained as foreclosure often effectively cancels existing contracts. In short, the buyer is now the owner and must treat the property with the same care and concern any owner would. This involves identifying the risks at this time for this piece of property and deciding what one wants to do about them.

5.11 NATURAL TRANSFER OF REAL PROPERTY

Events that occur in nature can transfer real property. One is adding land through the process of **accretion,** the slow accumulation of land through the action of water. **Erosion** is the slow taking away of land by natural processes, such as the action of water or wind. **Avulsion** is the sudden tearing away of land. Earthquakes, tidal waves, and hurricanes can cause avulsion.

5.12 DOCUMENTS: THE WILL

A will is the preferred method of transferring real property after the owner's death. If the decedent leaves a will, he is said to die *testate.* If he lacks a will at death, he dies *intestate.* When the latter occurs, the state's statutes of inheritance determine the takers of the decedent's real and personal property. Some of those rules are discussed later. Under a will, the party taking real property is called the **devisee**, and the gift is called a **devise**. When personal property is transferred by will, it is called a **legacy** or a *bequest,* and the party taking it is called the **legatee**. Not all property passes by means of a will. Life insurance, pension plans, real estate owned in joint tenancy, and other property rights do not come within the will.

A will has certain formal requirements. The maker of the will, the *testator* must be of legal age (usually 18), of sound mind, and under no undue influence. The will must be in the proper format and properly witnessed. Mental capacity requires that the testator know what he is doing sufficiently to intend to dispose of his property. A party declared legally incompetent can have a lucid moment; an old or weak person can make a will. Undue influence, duress, or fraud can invalidate a will. Wills must be in writing, signed by the testator, and attested by witnesses. The rules for signatures are not stringent in many states, and basically any mark intended by the testator as her signature works as the signature. Most wills require two witnesses attesting that the testator executed the will after indicating that the document was her will. The witnesses do not have to know the contents of the will. Some states require three witnesses, and some attorneys prefer to have an extra witness, to avoid problems of proof later. Witnesses usually may not take any interest under the will; that means they can receive nothing from the will.

The law of intestacy, sometimes called the *law of descent,* has two ways of identifying takers. One way is called **per stirpes**; the other, **per capita**. Per capita is simple. The Latin word *capita* means "head"; one takes all the heirs,

LEGAL TERMS

homestead rights
Spousal rights in real property that cannot be reached by creditors; defined by statute.

accretion
Slow deposit of land matter onto property as a result of water movement or a change in the flow of water.

erosion
Gradual wearing away of land by the working of water, wind, or other natural forces.

avulsion
Ripping away of the land by violent means, such as earthquakes or tidal waves.

devisee
Person receiving real property under a will.

devise
Grant of real property to someone under a will.

legacy
Grant of personal property to someone under a will; also called *bequest.*

legatee
Person taking personal property under a will.

per stirpes
Method of taking under a will whereby the taking is through the ancestor; literally through the root or ancestor.

per capita
Method of taking under a will whereby the taking is by the number of persons; literally by a head count.

counts the number of heads, and divides by that number for the number of units into which the estate will be divided. Per stirpes, however, has an additional concept. The term means "by the root." One only takes what one's ancestor (or "root") would take. For instance, take a widower whose property goes to his children and grandchildren per capita. He has two children and three grandchildren. The estate is split by fifths. If the estate went to his children per stirpes, and one of them had died, it would be divided in half (two children). The surviving child would take one half and the children of the deceased child would take the other; if all three grandchildren were children of the deceased child, each would receive one-sixth ($\frac{1}{2}$ divided by 3 = $\frac{1}{6}$). Those grandchildren are said to take per stirpes, through their root, their deceased parent.

Finally, the law of inheritance has in many places replaced the medieval real estate law when it relates to the rights of spouses. In some states, for instance, the surviving spouse may have the right to renounce the will. In medieval law, the husband had the right of curtesy, and the wife had the right of dower. These devices provided rights in the real property of the decedent. In many states these forms have been abolished, but the idea of protecting the spouse of the decedent has not vanished from the law. Instead, the problem is handled through the statutes of inheritance, the law of descent and distribution. Spouses have special rights—either under curtesy and dower or more modern laws—and you should know what those are in relation to real property in your jurisdiction.

5.13 CHECKLIST: EXAMINING A SALES CONTRACT

The real estate sales contract forms the basis for most transactions in real property. Any party involved with buying and selling real property must understand the process and the forms that are used in the process. Checklists remain an essential, though potentially cumbersome, method of controlling the immense amount of material to be dealt with. Feel free to adapt this basic checklist to meet your needs.

I. Who will be the parties to the contract?
   A. Does the seller own the property, i.e., in title?
   B. Have buyers sign the contract as they wish the deed to show their names.
   C. Are there brokers? Brokers are often parties so that they can have legal rights to obtain their commissions.
   D. Other legal entities?
      1. Corporations? Foreign or domestic?
      2. Partnerships?
      3. Trusts?

II. What is the legal description of the premises being sold?
   A. What type of description is being used? Is it correct?
   B. How is the personal property being handled?

1. Is there an itemized list of the items being transferred by a separate bill of sale at the closing?
2. Fixtures: any conflict that needs straightening out now—not later?

C. Have the easements been checked?
1. Do they benefit the property?
2. Do they make the property subservient?
3. Is easement absolutely crucial?
4. Have taxes been paid on the subservient property when the property has a dominant easement?
5. Is the subservient easement in a form that can be insured?

III. Earnest money.
A. Certified check or cashier's check.
B. Amount adequate?

IV. Purchase price.
A. Total amount.
B. Installments?
C. Is there an escrow agent? If so, who?
D. Is there an existing mortgage?
1. To be assumed?
2. To be paid off?

V. Title evidence.
A. What type is to be furnished?
B. Who pays for what?
C. What time is permitted to achieve the agreed-upon performances?
D. What if the seller's title is not clear on closing day?
1. Does the buyer deposit the money in an escrow?
2. Does the buyer not have to deliver any money?

VI. Is the property in compliance with all laws?
A. Are there any special environmental concerns?
B. Are there building restrictions?
C. Are current taxes paid?

VII. Who bears the risk of loss between execution of the sales contract and delivery of the deed?

VIII. When will possession be delivered? How?

IX. Do any incidental documents need to be covered?

X. Have formalities of execution been complied with, so recording can be done?
A. Did parties sign exactly as their names appear?
B. Witnessing?
C. Acknowledgment?

XI. Inspection prior to closing?

XII. How are existing service contracts being handled? Who is responsible for them?

XIII. Are there any special conditions or situations?
   A. Mortgage financing by:
      1. Type—VA, FHA, conventional, etc.
      2. Amount.
      3. Time period.
      4. Interest charged—fixed or variable.
      5. Payment terms.
      6. Fees.
      7. Other.
   B. Personal property to be identified? Separate contract needed?

5.14 CHECKLIST: PREPARING THE DEED

It is almost always exciting to be at a closing when someone is buying something important to them. To ensure that everything is covered and all the paperwork is handled properly, a basic checklist is essential. This checklist introduces you to the process of making a set of controls to handle the deed itself.

I. How do the documents get reviewed?
   A. Review the real estate sales contract or other document that provides for the transfer of ownership.
   B. Obtain and review the title examination.
      1. Correct names of the parties?
      2. Correct spelling of all names?
      3. Real property description correct (identical to one in seller's deed)? Does this description relate to the parcel in the transaction? Any discrepancies?
      4. What exceptions in the title policy should be covered in the deed?
   C. With the buyers or their attorney, determine the type of estate in which they wish to hold the parcel—joint tenancy with right of survivorship or tenancy in common or some other manner.

II. Prepare the deed.
   A. Identify the legal place—county, state, etc.—where the deed will be executed.
   B. Make the date that of actual execution and delivery of the deed. Keep in mind, however, that closings get changed frequently. If you date the deed and the date of closing changes, the deed may have to be changed or redone before execution. Some lawyers prefer to insert the date at closing and have the change initiated by all parties.
   C. Insert the grantor's correct legal name—almost always the name on the prior deed passing the property to the grantor.
   D. Insert the grantee's correct legal name and the type of ownership in which the property will be held (per the information in I.C.).

E. Insert the consideration—usually a nominal amount.

F. Use the proper legal description for the parcel.

   1. Double-check the prior granting deed, any survey, and the description used in the title examination. They should be identical.
   2. If the length of the legal description exceeds the available space, place the description on an exhibit and refer to the exhibit in the space normally used for the legal description. Beware, however! Exhibits can get detached and lost, so either very firmly attach the exhibit (staple, glue, tape) or enlarge the space for the exhibit on the deed (by photocopier or computer) to avoid that problem. Without the legal description, there cannot be a recording, and the results of failure to record properly are horrendous.

G. Include every title exception that shows on the title policy as an item being transferred with the property.

H. Put in the blanks for the signatures.

   1. Only the grantor signs the deed.
   2. Be sure you have the precisely correct grantor's name, that it matches prior usage on this deed, and that it matches the name on the transfer deed to the grantor.
   3. Type the name beneath the signature line.
   4. Have the deed signed and sealed (if necessary).
   5. Be sure the recording requirements of witnessing the signature(s) and attesting are properly complied with.

III. Record the deed with the local recording authority.

DISCUSSION AND REVIEW QUESTIONS

1. Describe the difference between the language used to create a warranty deed, a special warranty deed, and a quitclaim deed.
2. What types of deeds are used in your state? Are there any unique to your state's laws?
3. What techniques can a grantor use in the deed to limit his liability under the covenants?
4. Do deeds have to be witnessed?
5. What is the purpose of a note? Of a mortgage? Of a deed of trust?
6. Identify the proper way to describe real property.
7. Distinguish between the uses of a real estate sales contract and a deed.
8. Discuss why recordation is important.
9. Describe various covenants associated with title transfer. With which type of deed are they usually associated?
10. Allen owned three parcels of real estate in fee simple and wanted to give them to his son, Bill, and Bill's adult children, Kathleen and Matthew. Allen

gave the first parcel to Bill with the following words in the deed: "The gift of this parcel shall only vest in Bill at the time I die." This deed was found in Allen's safe deposit box at his death. Allen gave the second parcel to Kathleen with similar language in the deed, but he gave her the deed, which she promptly recorded after his funeral. Allen gave the third parcel to Matthew by means of a direct transfer of the deed without any limitations. Allen, however, gave the deed to his attorney, with instructions to deliver it to Matthew at the time of Allen's death. His attorney did so. Identify the rights of Bill, Kathleen, and Matthew in the property that Allen has purported to give them.

11. Sally owned Blackacre, which was 10 acres in size. She decided to sell off the front five acres (Whiteacre) to Bill. In the deed transferring the property to him, she reserved an easement so that she could have access to her property. Two years later, Bill fenced in his five acres, but inadvertently put his fence five feet over the boundary on Sally's property. For the next 15 years he maintained the fence, and then he sold the property to Grace. The transfer deed referred to the estate as extending "up to and including the area bounded by the fence" plus the normal legal description. Grace maintained the fence for seven more years. When Sally tried to sell Blackacre, the prospective purchaser had a surveyor measure the estate. The fence problem was discovered.
    a. Describe the type of easement that Sally has reserved.
    b. Who gets that five-foot strip of property across the boundary between the two estates, Sally or Grace?

SAMPLE FORMS

Warranty Deed—Joint Tenancy—Waiver of Homestead Exemption

SIDEBAR

Deeds and sale agreements (contracts) are very frequently used. Their language and the effects of that language should become second nature to you so that you can recognize any omissions or additions. Local law and usage will vary. Consider why this particular wording is here; what should it do? Does it create another risk? How can that risk be dealt with?

WARRANTY DEED—JOINT TENANCY

The grantor, _________ of _________ *[address]*, City of _________, County of ________, State of ________, for and in consideration of ________ Dollars ($____) and other good and valuable consideration, the receipt of which is acknowledged, conveys and warrants to _________, of _________ *[address]*, City of _________, County of _________, State of _________, and to ________, of ________ *[address]*, City of ________, County of ________, State of _________, not as tenants in common, but as joint tenants with full right of survivorship, the following described estate _________ *[set forth legal description of property]*, situated in the _________ [City *or* Town] of ________, County of _________, in the State of _________, releasing and waiving all rights under and by virtue of the homestead exemption laws of the State of _________.

Dated _________.

[Acknowledgment]

[Signature]
[Seal]

Claim for Compensation—Condemnation Creating Easement

SIDEBAR

Read this simple form and track its straightforward approach to making its claim in the eminent domain process.

CLAIM FOR COMPENSATION

Claim for compensation for the permanent appropriation of an easement in land owned by _________, of __________ *[address]*, City of _________, County of _________, State of _________, herein referred to as claimant.

SECTION ONE
BASIS OF CLAIM

A. This claim is for payment for the permanent appropriation of an easement in the property described below, by _________ *[public agency]*, for the public purpose of _________, pursuant to the provisions of _________ *[cite statute]*.

B. The notice of such appropriation, dated _________, was served upon claimant on or about _________ *[date]*, together with a copy of the map attached to this claim, containing a description and diagram of the land involved.

C. Entry was made on such land on or about _________ *[date]*, by the employees and agents of _________ *[public agency]*.

SECTION TWO
CLAIMANT'S INTEREST

Claimant was at the time of the appropriation, and now is, the sole owner in fee of the premises appropriated.

SECTION THREE
DESCRIPTION OF LAND AND
INTEREST APPROPRIATED

The premises appropriated and the interest in land taken by ______ *[public agency]* are described as follows: _________ *[describe premises appropriated and interest taken]*, as shown on the official appropriation map served upon claimant, a copy of which is attached to and incorporated in this claim.

SECTION FOUR
AMOUNT OF DAMAGES

In particular, claimant's damages are as follows:

A. Value of entire tract and buildings before appropriation by _________ *[public agency]:* _________ Dollars ($____).

B. Value of remaining property after the above-described appropriation by _________ *[public agency]:* _________ Dollars ($____).

C. Difference in value before taking and after taking: _________ Dollars ($____).

Claimant therefore claims payment of the sum of _________ Dollars ($____).

Dated: _________ *[month, day and year].*

[Signature]

Agreement for Sale of Real Property—Between Buyer, Seller, and Escrow Agent

REAL PROPERTY SALES AGREEMENT

Agreement made, effective as of _________ *[date],* by, between, and among seller, ________, of ________ *[address],* City of ________, County of ________, State of ________, referred to as seller, ________, of ________ *[address],* City of ________, County of ________, State of __________, referred to as buyer, and ________, of ________ *[address], City of ________, County of ________, County of ________, referred to as escrow agent.*

Seller has agreed to sell and convey, and buyer has agreed to purchase and pay for the following described property located in the County of _________, State of _________: _________ *[describe property],* free of encumbrances except as set out in the escrow instructions attached to and made a part of this agreement, called the instructions.

The sale of the above-described property shall be made on the terms and conditions set out in the instructions and buyer and seller employ escrow agent to effect the closing of the sale. Buyer and seller each agrees to deliver to escrow agent all instruments and forms necessary to comply with this agreement within ________ (___) days after ________ [issuance of preliminary report for title insurance *or* execution of this agreement].

Seller shall, on request of escrow agent, deliver to escrow agent a _________ *[describe deed]* as well as all other documents necessary on _________ [his *or* her] part to convey to buyer the title set forth in the instructions.

Buyer shall, on the request of escrow agent, deliver to escrow agent the amount necessary to complete the purchase of the above-described property, including prorated adjustments, and all documents necessary on _________ [his *or* her] part to complete this agreement.

Buyer and seller agree that escrow agent assumes no liability for and is expressly released from any claim or claims in connection with the reception, retention, and delivery of any papers or documents delivered to escrow agent under and pursuant to this agreement except to account for payments made on such papers and documents, from which escrow agent is authorized to deduct _________ [his *or* her *or* its] customary collection charges and expenses together with any amount that may be required to pay for legal expenses due to any litigation or controversy that may arise in connection with this agreement.

Each party has executed this agreement at __________ *[place of execution]* on the date indicated below.

[Signatures of buyer and seller and date(s) of signing]

Accepted: __________ *[escrow agent]*

Claim or Notice of Lien—Lien Against Single Site—By General Contractor

Notice is given by _________, as general contractor, referred to as lien claimant, as follows:

1. Lien claimant is licensed under the laws of _________ *[state]* as a general contractor.

2. On _________ *[date]*, lien claimant entered into a contract with _________, under the terms of which lien claimant agreed to _________ [furnish all labor and materials for and generally supervise construction of a house] on property described below. A copy of the contract is attached and made a part of this notice.

3. The property on which _________ [the house was constructed] is described as follows: _________ *[insert legal description]*. __________ [The legal] owner of the property is _________.

4. Performance of labor and delivery of materials under the contract commenced on _________ *[date]*. All work under the contract was completed on _________ *[date]*, and _________ days have not elapsed since completion. In the course of performing the contract, lien claimant furnished labor and materials as follows:

Date(s)	Description	Price or Value
__________	__________	$__________
__________	__________	$__________
__________	__________	$__________
		Total $__________

All materials listed above were delivered to __________ [the building site] and were used in performance of the contract.

5. _________ *[If appropriate, list payments and other credits.]*

6. The agreed price and the reasonable value of services rendered by lien claimant is _________ Dollars ($___). Full payment was due on _________ *[date]*, but has not been received by lien claimant despite repeated demand. _________ [After deduction of _________ Dollars ($___) for all just credits and offsets], the sum of _________ Dollars ($___) remains owing to lien claimant.

SIDEBAR

One of the most difficult and potentially irritating problems is the lien of a contractor working on the property. Special controls may be necessary to prevent problems. Notice the claim statement in §§ 4 and 6.

7. Pursuant to __________ *[statute]*, lien claimant claims a lien against the described property for __________ Dollars ($____).

Dated: __________

[Signature]

[Verification]

SIDEBAR

Consider when such a time payment might be used in a sales contract rather than a financing arrangement. Check who is being protected from what—especially in §§ 2 and 3.

Contract of Sale of Residential Property—Time Payments

This contract is entered into at ___________ *[place of execution]*, on ___________, 19___, between ___________, hereinafter called seller, and ___________, hereinafter called purchaser.

RECITALS

1. Seller is the owner of the real property situated in the City of ________, County of ________, State of ________, at ________ *[street address]*, consisting of a residential lot with dwelling ___________ [and detached garage and other outbuildings] thereon, described as follows: __________ *[set forth legal description]*.

2. Seller is also the owner of the following fixtures, equipment and personal property located on and used in connection with the real property described above: __________ *[describe or refer to attached schedule]*. The real and personal property together are the subject of this contract and are hereinafter referred to as property.

3. Seller desires to sell and purchaser desires to purchase property for the purchase price and on the terms and conditions herein set forth.

In consideration of the mutual and reciprocal promises and in furtherance of their objective, seller agrees to sell to purchaser, and purchaser agrees to purchase from seller property above described, and all rights and appurtenances incident thereto, subject only to the mattes hereinafter set forth. The parties further agree:

SECTION ONE
PURCHASE PRICE AND TERMS OF PAYMENT

(1) The entire purchase price for property is ___________ Dollars ($____), including the encumbrance hereinafter referred to. The purchase price shall be paid as follows:

(a) The sum of __________ Dollars ($____) as down payment shall be paid on the execution of this instrument. The receipt of such sum is hereby acknowledged by seller.

(b) Purchaser shall assume the balance due on that certain first ______ [mortgage *or* deed of trust], dated __________, 19____, and recorded in Book _________ of __________, records of ___________ County, State of _________. The present holder of the encumbrance is _________ *[name]*, whose address is ___________. Purchaser shall execute an assumption agreement in form satisfactory to the holder forthwith on the execution of this instrument.

(c) The balance of the purchase price, or ________ Dollars ($____), shall be paid by purchaser to seller, or his order, in ________ [monthly *or as the case may be*] installments of __________ Dollars ($____) each, including interest, commencing __________, 19____, and continuing on the same date of each successive __________ [month *or as the case may be*] until fully paid. The balance shall bear interest at _________ percent (____%) per year, payable with and included in periodic installments.

(2) In addition to the periodic payments to seller hereinabove provided for, purchaser shall pay, before delinquency, all payments due on and after _________, 19____, under the encumbrance which is assumed by purchaser, in accordance with the terms of the _________ [note *or* bond] secured by the encumbrance, and shall hold seller free and harmless therefrom.

SECTION TWO
POSSESSION OF PROPERTY AND RESPONSIBILITIES

Purchaser shall be let into full possession of property _________ [forthwith *or* within _________ days]. Purchaser has inspected property, including the improvements and real property above described, and accepts property in its present condition.

During the life of this contract purchaser shall maintain property, including the improvements and personal property, in a state of good repair and condition. Purchaser shall not sell or otherwise dispose of any article of personal property herein described except for necessary replacements. Seller shall have the right to inspect property at reasonable times, until final performance by purchaser.

Purchaser shall pay before delinquency all taxes and assessments coming due on and after _________, 19____, levied on property _________ [including that portion levied separately against the interest of the mortgagee above referred to, or the vendor's interest of seller hereunder].

During the life of this contract, seller shall insure and keep insured against fire or other casualty, all improvements now on property and improvements that may hereafter be built thereon. Such insurance shall be in the face amount of not less than the balance remaining due from time to time under the encumbrance assumed by purchaser, and the balance remaining due to seller hereunder. All such insurance shall insure the holder of the encumbrance, seller, and purchaser as their interests may appear. All premiums on such policies shall be paid by purchaser.

If purchaser fails or neglects to pay any installment of taxes or any assessment, or any insurance premium, when due, seller shall have the right to make such payment and to add the amount thereof, together with interest at __________ percent (____%) per year, to the obligation of purchaser hereunder. Such right shall be deemed to be an option and shall impose no obligation on seller, and seller may elect to treat such neglect or failure on the part of purchaser as a breach of this contract.

SECTION THREE
TITLE

Seller has obtained, or shall within _________ days from the date hereof obtain, from _________ *[corporate name]*, a qualified title insurer, a standard form policy of title insurance in the face amount of the purchase price, and shall pay the premium therefor. Such policy shall insure purchaser of seller's good and merchantable title in the real property above described, subject to the encumbrance herein assumed by purchaser, this contract, taxes and assessments not yet due or payable, and _________ *[set forth other acceptable defects and burdens, if any]*. The policy shall be delivered to purchaser on its issuance, and shall be accepted by him as evidence of seller's title in the real property above described.

Seller has executed a deed and bill of sale running to purchaser, and purchaser has executed a quitclaim deed to seller. The instruments are satisfactory to each party in form and content, and have been deposited with _________ *[name of depository]* with written instructions to deliver ll instruments to purchaser forthwith upon his full performance hereunder and completion of all payments due from him as hereinabove provided, or to deliver all instruments to seller if purchaser defaults hereunder and seller elects to declare a forfeiture of this contract and rescind the same.

Seller shall not cause or permit any act to be done during the life of this contract that would burden or cloud title to property or interfere with purchaser's full use and enjoyment thereof.

Title in property shall be and is reserved to seller, his heirs, representatives, and assigns, until full performance by purchaser hereunder _________ [*add, if appropriate under local statute:* and seller shall retain a vendor's lien on property until this contract is fully performed].

SECTION FOUR
BREACH BY PURCHASER; REMEDIES OF SELLER

Time is of the essence of this contract. In the event purchaser fails to make any payment required by the terms of this contract, at the time the same falls due and prior to delinquency thereof, including installment payments to seller, payments on the encumbrance assumed by purchaser, taxes, assessments, and insurance premiums, _________ [and if such default continues for _________ days after written notice thereof] seller at his option may:

(1) Declare a forfeiture of purchaser's rights hereunder and cancellation of this contract _________ *[add, if appropriate:* subject to purchaser's rights of reinstatement and redemption under the laws of this state]. On such election all right, title and interest of purchaser hereunder shall cease and determine, and all payments theretofore made by purchaser shall be retained by seller as liquidated damages and as rental for the use and occupation of property _________ [subject to statutory rights of reinstatement and redemption].

(2) In lieu of declaring a forfeiture, accelerate and bring an action for the balance of the purchase price remaining due, or for any other relief available in law or equity, including suit to recover any payment or payments made by seller and repayable by purchaser hereunder, it being stipulated and agreed that such obligation to repay is a separate and independent covenant of purchaser hereunder. No action to recover any payment or payments so made by seller shall constitute waiver by seller of his right to proceed otherwise with respect to any subsequent default. No waiver by seller of any default of purchaser shall be construed as a waiver of any subsequent default.

SECTION FIVE
NOTICES

The addresses of the respective parties are as follows:

Seller: ___________ *[street or other post office address, city and state]*

Purchaser: ___________ *[street or other post office address, city and state]*

Any notice or demand on either party hereunder may be mailed or personally delivered to such party at the address given above or such subsequent address as he may hereafter furnish in writing to the other party. Notice or demand so given shall be sufficient for any purpose under this contract.

In witness whereof, the parties have executed this instrument in _________ *[desired number of original counterparts]* on the day and year first above written. Each counterpart hereof shall be deemed an original of the contract for all purposes.

[Signatures]

[Acknowledgment]

CHAPTER 6
Real Estate Appraisal

"The minute you read something you can't understand, you can almost be sure it was drawn up by a lawyer."

Will Rogers

Modified French provincial house

OUTLINE

PROLOGUE TO THE PARALEGAL

Although it is impossible to provide a complete and detailed discussion of all of the aspects of appraising, the paralegal needs to understand the basics of this topic because appraisal determines the value of a parcel of real estate. Determination of the value of a parcel is often subject to much conflicting expert opinion, and in a lawsuit, the award in a case may turn on the expert testimony of whichever side's appraiser is better prepared and can present more rational and persuasive evidence that his or her evaluation of a parcel of real estate is correct in the current market. For a paralegal, a knowledge of the basic mechanics of appraisal are valuable because the verification of figures, the appropriateness of appraisal technique to the situation, and the reliability of the entire appraisal process may aid the paralegal either in researching an area or in reviewing of the work of others. One of the key aspects of legal work is the mastery of detail and being able to use that detail appropriately in examination—both direct and cross-examination. Knowledge of appraising could be a crucial area of detailed information in your career.

KEY TERMS

accumulated depreciation
adjusted gross income
adjustments
anticipation
capitalization rate
conformity
contribution
cost analysis
depreciation
direct market comparison
economic obsolescence
elements used on site method
functional obsolescence
gross income
highest and best use
net income
obsolescence
rate of return
replacement cost
reproduction cost
site
square foot method
straight line depreciation
substitution
supply and demand
useful life

6.1 INTRODUCTION

What is the job of the professional real estate appraiser? It is the determination of the current value of a parcel of land. In other words, appraisal is the job of determining what a parcel of real property is worth at the present time. The land may be unimproved or it may be improved with utilities and other types of services, such as sewers or roads (if it is, the land is often called a **site**). A key idea for understanding the basis for evaluating the price of a parcel of property is the concept of land use. Appraisers frequently discuss the **highest and best use** of a parcel. This simply means that the property is being used in the manner that will, at this time, produce the most profitable result in the circumstances. This concept is an economic idea; it means that the land is being utilized to produce the maximum yield at present. Various circumstances affect the maximization of the land's use. These circumstances range from the laws and regulations affecting the real estate to the physical limitations the parcel may have (is it in a desert, on a mountain, in a slum, in a wealthy suburb?). As a result, the appraiser looks to the whole set of circumstances in making the evaluation.

Other aspects an appraiser might consider could include the site itself, the building on it, the improvements (other than the building) made to the property, and the community where it is located, together with a host of other elements. Although this concept of the highest and best use provides the base of the appraiser's art, it is not always possible or profitable to subject each parcel to that type of exhaustive scrutiny. For instance, in a locale with mixed zoning of commercial shops and four-flat apartment buildings, the cost of converting a four-flat to an entirely commercial operation on that particular site might be too expensive, even though, ideally, the commercial usage might well be the highest and best use of the property. The additional cost, however, makes it very difficult to justify the conversion so that it is not, realistically, under these circumstances, the highest and best use of the parcel at this time.

Another basic idea in appraisal is that of **substitution**. This means that the appraiser must look at what it would cost to replace or substitute a comparable piece of real property. The appraiser checks comparable locations and comparable parcels of property to determine whether Parcel B can serve as a substitute for Parcel A (the parcel being appraised). If Parcel B is comparable (and whether that parcel is in fact comparable is often a key factual arguing point), then its price or value could be an indication of the price of Parcel A. The problem with substitution is that all real estate is unique, so that no exact comparison is ever possible; there are always differences that may affect the price. It is crucial, therefore, to understand how and why the differences between two parcels affect their respective values.

A third important idea concerning the value of real property comes from the realm of economics: the law of **supply and demand**. Basically, this law states that as demand of an item (our Parcel A) increases, other things being equal, the price will increase as well. The inverse is true as well: the price will decline when the demand declines. Supply will rise as long as there is sufficient demand, until the supply and the demand equal one another. Then, supply and demand are said to be "in equilibrium." Supply will also begin to decline after demand declines. The impact in real estate is often seen in areas that are "hot" at one time, suffer from overproduction, and then fall into a period of severely diminished demand. One example of this is central city office space in many major cities in the early 1990s—Los Angeles, for instance. Another instance is the flurry of condominium developments that occurred in the 1970s and 1980s, which are not as popular in the 1990s as they once were; thus, the demand and the prices for condominiums are down and the supply is stagnant.

Some other basic concepts relate to how well the parcel and its improvements fit into the area where it is located. Is it the same in appearance, value, and improvements? Was it built at the same time as the other buildings? If it does fit, it is said to *conform,* and the principle of **conformity** applies. Conformity is used to describe buildings (usually) or parcels of property that deviate from the norm. If the parcel and its improvements are not in conformity, then they are either below the standard or norm for the neighborhood or above it. If they are below it, the value of the parcel being appraised can be reduced, but if they are above it, no one may want to pay the extra price, so the owner may never recover the investment for the nonconforming improvement. For instance, in a neighborhood that lacks swimming pools, a swimming pool at a home may not be a recoverable investment expense, because most persons buying in that area will not want it or will not be able to afford it. And persons who want a pool may want to live in a much different neighborhood. In that case, this improvement—the swimming pool—may not make a real

LEGAL TERMS

site
Location of the parcel of real property.

highest and best use
Optimal use, in terms of economics, to which the parcel of land could be put at present.

substitution
Basic principle in determining real estate values; states that one equivalent property can replace another, and therefore they can be compared (with adjustments).

supply and demand
Law of economics which states that supply rises to meet demand or the inverse (falling demand will be followed by falling supply).

conformity
Degree to which a building or site fits in or is identical to the other buildings and sites in the area.

contribution to increasing the value of a home, whereas a remodeled kitchen or bathroom may make a positive contribution that raises the price of the parcel and allows the owners to recover their investment.

Another factor for consideration is the effect of *change* on an area. Time changes locations. The quality of the property, the type of occupants of the property, the amount of money spent on maintenance, the extent of ordinary wear and tear, and natural disasters are among the events that can make a profound impact on the value and usage of the property. For example, many large single-family homes in some urban areas were subdivided into rental units and then later "gentrified" back into single-family units. The term, *gentrification*, generally is used to mean that the upper middle class (or the "gentry") has returned to the area. The term is an historical reference which compares some of today's upwardly mobile urban groups with an upwardly mobile rural group in 17th-century England. Both were involved in making major changes in their communities. Changes in the use of a neighborhood affect the value of the building and the highest and best use to which it can put.

Long-term cycles or patterns of use develop in some areas. First, in the 1910s and 1920s, when property was first taken out of farming use and made into housing developments, the property was developed as a neighborhood of single-family residences or small apartment buildings. During the 1930s, when there was little money to pay rent and less for rehabilitating or repairing property, the old couple whose children had moved away may have taken in renters. Then, when their parents died, the children sold the property, and it may have been converted into a rooming house with a sign out front, "Transients Welcome." Gradually, over a generation or two, the property went through an entire cycle of growth and development, through equilibrium into decline. Later, because the area was close to the central business district and had parks, transportation, and other amenities, the building became a "handyman's delight" and a young family moved in and assisted in gentrifying the neighborhood. Values then began to increase. As you can see, it is essential for an appraiser, then, to identify where a community or neighborhood is in this *cycle of growth to decline* as part of the appraisal process.

Another appraisal aspect, which looks to the future, is called **anticipation**. What will the parcel be worth in the future? Consider our home/rooming house example. When and under what circumstances would someone move into an area and build a new building on a vacant lot where a fire had gutted the premises? When would someone be willing to remodel or repair an old building? Potential owners take these positive steps when it appears that the neighborhood is changing in a positive direction and they reasonably anticipate that the change will be sufficient to support their investment. The opposite type of anticipation is often seen in abrupt departures or "flight" from an area. In some cases, this is the product of economic decline (when a major industrial plant closes and the jobs that have supported the community disappear), although it can also be caused by changes in population. If the original inhabitants are uncomfortable with the people or group(s) moving in, they move elsewhere, whether slowly or abruptly. Many of these events can be anticipated in a city by an understanding of group demography, economics, and other factors. In most big cities, most neighborhoods do not remain the same more than 30 or 40 years. Anticipation is closely related to change and is a function of identifying how and when change will occur and what its effects will be.

Some of the most bitter and divisive conflicts between groups in America have occurred in areas where neighborhoods are in the process of changing—principally from one ethnic group to another. The law is clear that no discrimination may be shown in real estate transactions, and great care should be taken to avoid any involvement, through the activities of appraising, either in actual discrimination or in any appearance of discrimination. Either one could generate very bad publicity, and actual discrimination violates the law and the ethical standards which the law attempts to maintain.

6.2 THE THREE BASIC APPRAISAL METHODS

Section 6.3 through 6.5 discuss three different but basic methods of appraisal. Each is commonly used, but each is appropriate for different parcels, properties, and circumstances.

6.3 APPRAISAL BASED ON DIRECT MARKET COMPARISON ANALYSIS

Appraisers use the **direct market comparison** approach primarily for placing a market value on homes and residential properties. The technique is also used in other ways and in other types of appraisals as well. It is the most widely used appraisal concept and method because it is used with some of the other methods, as well as independently for home appraisals. It is also referred to as the *sales comparison* approach, and its essence is to take a series of residential properties—homes, condominiums (whatever the type of legal entity)—and make price comparisons with similar properties. The key to this evaluation process is to determine how similar those properties really are, and that determination is based on a number of factors called **adjustments**. Clearly, no two properties are exactly alike—if for no other reason, because they are on different parcels of land and each parcel of land is unique. But the ways in which one property could differ from another are almost uncountable. On the other hand, one must be cautious about the extent of the adjustments, because if the difference is too great, then the properties are no longer comparable. It is easy to see, at this point, why appraising is an art and why detailed knowledge is crucial.

First, consider the size of the parcel. There are at least two aspects to size: (1) the square footage of the building, and (2) the square footage of the lot. Second, how old is the building? Third, how do the locations of the compared buildings differ from the parcel being appraised? Is there a noise factor? An access factor? Are there other possible buildings (based on permitted zoning)? Fourth, what differences are there between the compared buildings?

LEGAL TERMS

contribution
Expression of the market value of an improvement to real property; not every improvement makes a contribution.

anticipation
Technique appraisers use to identify the value of the property in the future.

direct market comparison
A method of establishing residential values by examining similar residences to determine how closely they resemble the subject (appraised) property.

adjustments
Changes in the value of a property (in comparison to another) due to one property having or lacking certain feature(s).

Some of those differences might be the following. What size is the garage? Is the garage attached to the building or free-standing? What is the number of baths? What size is the kitchen? How recently has the kitchen or bath been remodeled—what is its "modernity"? How well was the remodeling done? What is the exterior finish of the building—brick, siding, wood? What is the description of the basement—full, partial, crawlspace, a mixture? Is the basement finished? How does the square footage of the rooms compare? How does the number of rooms compare? What is the most recent sales price of the property? What is the landscaping like? What style is the building—Tudor, French Provincial, ranch, New England salt box, or whatever? How similar is this style and size to the other buildings in the area—in other words, how well does it conform? What is the condition of the building on the inside? On the outside? What is the current status of the building's financing? What financing might be available for the sale of the property?

All these factors have to be considered, plus any others unique to the particular situation of the lot and building under consideration. Clearly, this whole process can be boiled down to a general approach. The appraiser takes the sale price of a parcel of comparable property as the basis. Then the appraiser makes adjustments upward or downward based on the differences between the comparable property and the property being appraised. When this process is complete, the result is an appraised value for the property in question. Generally, the appraiser attempts to have at least three to five comparable properties, but frequently several more may be used as well. In short, a formula for this process would be as follows:

> Comparable property's price + or – adjustments
> = appraised value of property under consideration.

Be alert to an important element in this formula: *the adjustments apply only to the comparison property,* not the property being appraised. The adjustment makes the comparable property the equivalent of the appraised property, not the reverse.

When one is dealing with an item on the comparable property that does not exist on the appraised property (that is, the comparable property is better), the value of the comparable feature is *subtracted* from the comparable property so that the comparable property matches the property being appraised. However, in dealing with an additional feature on the appraised property (that is, when the appraised property is better), one *adds* the value of the feature to the comparable property's price to bring the comparable property into conformity with the property being appraised. For example, suppose that homes A and B are being compared to appraise home B. Home A sold for $135,000 within the last month and is essentially comparable in all ways to home B, except that home A has an extra bathroom, which has a current market value of $7,000. Home B would then be appraised at $128,000. Note that the amount was subtracted from the comparable home to reach the price for the appraised home. If home A had sold for $128,000 and home B had the extra bathroom worth $7,000, then $7,000 would be added to the value of home B to make the total of $135,000.

In dealing with land that has no buildings on it (vacant land), essentially the same process is used, but there is no reference to buildings. Instead, the appraiser considers a number of factors that may affect vacant land, such as location, access, desirability, installed utilities, zoning, type of soil, shape of the property, and type of terrain (rolling hills, flat, mountainous, desert, etc.). These factors are subject to adjustment between the appraised property and the comparison property.

Consider a more complicated home appraisal situation (table 6-1). For the purposes of this illustration, only one house is used to compare with the appraised property. Normally, there would be a series of properties, with a minimum of three. First, a format must be established showing the categories for comparison and adjustment. The areas of difference, and therefore adjustment, are the amount of living space, the age of the buildings, the number of baths, the difference between the garages, the difference between the basements, the interior condition of the homes, and the landscaping. The difference in square footage for living space, which is only 25 square feet, appears to be minimal and may be dismissed, as may the one-year difference in age.

	App'd Prop.	Comp'n Prop.	Adjust
Sales price		$165,000	
Location	quiet resid.	quiet resid.	
Lot dimensions	60 × 150	60 × 150	
Number of rooms	8	8	—
Number of bedrooms	4	4	—
Number of baths	3	2½	+4,500
Living space (sq. ft.)	1500	1475	—
-Basement	Full	Crawlspace	+12,500
Age (years)	6	7	—
-Landscaping	Normal	Good	–3,000
Type of const.	Brick	Brick	—
Style of bldg.	Colo.	Colo.	—
Bldg. condition—ext.	Good	Good	—
Bldg. condition—int.	Unsatis.	Good	–5,000
Garage	2-car att.	2-car free-standing	+1,000
Financial arrangements	N/A	N/A	—
Sale date	—	2 mos. ago	—
Other	N/A	N/A	—
Total adjustments, net (+ & –)			+$ 10,000
Appraised value			$175,000

TABLE 6-1
Home comparison chart

The interior condition of the homes is important and may make a major difference. If it would require a decorator-painter-carpenter to spend X hours (performing these particular tasks) at $Y, then the price difference would reflect that amount. It is more likely that a contract for bringing the property up to the "good" standard would be the estimated adjustment amount. Let us say that there is a lot of work to do and the price for it in this community is $5,000. There is a difference of a half-bath (toilet and wash basin); the price for this difference in this community is $4,500. The garages are the same size and differ only in their convenience. This item is difficult to determine, and the appraiser's decision could turn on whether the rest of this comparable community has attached or free-standing garages. If the standard is attached, there would be a deduction from the comparison property for having the both inconvenient and nonconforming garage. In this community, that amount is $1,000.

The construction difference between having a full basement and merely having a crawlspace can be significant. This difference cannot be easily changed, as can landscaping or the interior condition of the house. In this community, the difference in value for the extra space is $12,500. Landscaping is largely a matter of taste, but it would appear that the appraised home has less than the community standard for landscaping, or perhaps only minimal landscaping. For these differences the amount is $3,000. Once the amounts of the adjustments are determined, they must be applied properly (see table 6-1). Additional properties with other types of adjustments would be handled in the same way.

The market comparison approach has definite problems, but it is widely used because it is the most accurate method available for dealing with residential properties. The market comparison approach has two major problems. First, there may be no other unit available for comparison, if there just has not been a sale of a comparable unit or there are no really comparable units. Second, the adjustments have little realistic basis for the final evaluation; they have to be done by a "gut" response rather than a rational or objective evaluation. Determination of the price of the half-bath and landscaping differences in the table's example clearly points out this difficulty. The basic problem is that no one places quite the same monetary valuation on the omission or addition of a particular feature.

There are also problems of objectivity in the work of appraisers. It has been widely alleged that appraisers seem to arrive at a value that the party paying for the appraisal wants and that the relevance of the appraisal is questionable. Many banks and savings and loan institutions have found in the past few years that the appraisals they have in their files for their real property loans do not reflect current market values. Although falling market prices contributed to these discrepancies, there were apparently inflated appraisals as well. Real estate lenders and purchasers accepted dubious appraisals when anyone with a child's rationality could have discerned that they were inaccurate. This approach creates the kind of inflationary madness where upward property valuation is perceived as going on forever. The impact on the national economy and the federal government's budget, to begin cleaning up the resulting mess, has been staggering. Accurate, realistic appraising is clearly important for all of us. Regardless of the real estate appraisal problems in the 1980s, the direct market comparison approach has validity if there is good, accurate market data for comparison, if that information (and its adjustments) can be related to the appraised property accurately, and if the whole appraisal process is done on an arm's-length basis. Consider the following ethical question: Should an appraiser note in his or her presentation that there could be problems with the cycle of growth and decline, and that anticipation may have exceeded realistic expectations?

6.4 APPRAISAL BASED ON COST ANALYSIS

The **cost analysis** approach to appraising real property, although used with some residences, is used principally to appraise commercial and industrial properties. The concept underlying the method is simple: The appraiser identifies the cost of constructing the building today, less whatever depreciation has occurred to the structure; total these two items and add the current value of the land itself. This result provides the cost approach's valuation of the property. The formula is:

> Current construction cost of the building (replacement or reproduction) + current land value – accumulated depreciation on the existing building = present value of the parcel with its improvements.

Note that this approach is the most widely used in sheer volume of appraisal cases. This method is also used for valuing buildings and their land when the property is used for public or charitable purposes, such as a school or a church.

What is **depreciation?** Depreciation as a concept does not apply to the land itself, but only to the land's improvements, such as buildings. This concept reflects the changes in value of such an improvement when that improvement has aged, deteriorated, or suffered a physical or other source of value decline such as obsolescence. Depreciation reflects the negative changes through time on the value of the property's improvement. Even though the overall value of the property may increase because of inflation or market demand, the process of deterioration continues to feed the depreciation process. Physical depreciation occurs when use of the improvement (in most cases, a building) has caused wear and tear such as cracked concrete, rotted wood, warped stairs, or the effects of the elements. The building is subject to **obsolescence** either (1) functionally, through outmoded appearance or design, or (2) through its usability. An example of functional obsolescence would be a building whose style or capacities no longer fit current needs, such as a single-car garage when the standard for a home is a two-car garage, or a kitchen that has not been remodeled since the 1950s and has no modern equipment. Its design and function are wrong for modern families and their way of life.

LEGAL TERMS

cost analysis
A major method of appraising property, based on replacement cost of the building, less depreciation, plus site cost.

depreciation
Way of recognizing the decline in value of an asset due to any cause, over a period of time; refers to the improvement, not the land.

obsolescence
Form of depreciation represented by the improvements' no longer meeting individual or sociolegal standards of the present time.

The other major type of obsolescence, often called **economic obsolescence**, lies in the overall ability to use the property itself. Has the usage of the property been changed because the zoning laws have changed? Is there a different—a higher and better—usage of the property now, in contrast to how it was used before, when the building was first constructed? If a higher and better use exists, then the property's current use (and its building) has become obsolete and its value is not being maximized.

What is the effect on an appraisal if the building is evaluated at the current cost of reproducing it, but the building itself is obsolete? In other words, the building itself is perfectly good and sturdy, but it cannot be put to the current highest and best use. If the Egyptian pyramids were returned to their uses as tombs, that would not be the highest and best use; their highest and best use is as an historical and tourist attraction. Would an appraisal be valid if it ignored obsolescence? Clearly not; therefore, the appraiser must be alert to the implications for the value of the property that obsolescence can cause.

Another problem with the cost approach is that the costs of building vary widely among different regions of the country. There may be significant variations in the amount of current demand for this type of construction, the use of prefabricated elements, the number of buildings involved (mass production may lower costs), and the amount of profit that is built into the cost structure. In many situations, it is both difficult and inaccurate to use the simple method of totaling up all the costs to make an appraisal. Some comparative costing may be necessary.

Site Analysis

How will the appraiser arrive at a value for the land itself, the site? Because the land itself is rarely considered as having a declining value, unless it has been subject to waste, it will probably be necessary to make a comparative lot price analysis to arrive at the value of the land. This comparative lot pricing is only the first example of the widespread use of the comparison device in the other appraisal methods, as well as in establishing the price for residences.

There are a number of reasons for determining the current land value, that is, for making a site evaluation. Conceptually, determination of the land value by itself must be done, regardless of whether the location has any improvements on it, because one needs to determine the inherent value of the land itself. There are also a number of other reasons for having the land valued on its own. First, in the cost and income bases for appraisal, the land is valued separately from the improvements. Second, there could be tax reasons for knowing the value of the land. In income taxation, for instance, the depreciation is only on the buildings or other improvements to the land, so the value of the land itself must be subtracted from the total property value to find the basis for tax depreciation. Third, an appraiser may be asked to determine the best use of the land. In this case the appraiser would be required to analyze an entire range of possible uses, which might or might not include improvements to the land. The actual land itself, therefore, must be evaluated separate from any improvements. Finally, if the government is seizing the property for public use under the doctrine of eminent domain, it is frequently required that the land and its improvements be valued separately.

The process of appraisal begins by identifying the location or site with a legal description that is sufficiently detailed to describe the property itself and identify its relation to any neighboring parcels of property. A description of the highest and best use to which the property can be put is also included. Note that for most properties this highest and best use description is limited because of the restrictions that zoning laws place upon the uses to which that property can be put. At this point, the appraiser also notes any restrictions or easements that exist in favor of or lie against the property. Next, the appraiser determines the method to be used for evaluating the land itself.

There are a number of ways in which the land by itself can be appraised. First, there is the market comparison approach. In this method, other properties that have sold recently are compared to the site under consideration. This method is used primarily for sites without any buildings. Second, there is the percentage (sometimes called the allocation) method. This process is similar to the first in that it involves comparison with other sites. The comparison is somewhat different, however, in that it is a generic rather than a specific comparison. The appraiser determines the historic relationship of value between the site and its improvements. If, throughout a long period of time in this area, the site value has generally been 15% (or 20%, or 25%) of the total price, then that percentage is assigned as the value for the site being appraised. Thus, if the property is worth $198,000 and the historic land value is 15%, the land would be considered to be worth about $30,000 and the improvements, $168,000. This approach, however, is only very general and does not consider individual variations. It is a "rule-of-thumb" approach.

A third method for site value determination focuses on how a developer would value the land when creating a new project from existing land. For example, when a developer has purchased 150 acres to put in single-family homes, a strip mall, and the necessary roads and other amenities, she will want to determine how much she can pay for each lot, based upon her expected sales price. This method is also a generic (or "ballpark") method because it uses large estimates instead of specific costs. Here, the developer is interested in knowing how much she can pay for the land and still come in at the estimated profit margin. Therefore, the approach is as follows. First, the appraiser determines the sales price of each lot, after it has been prepared for construction, and multiplies that amount by the number of lots being developed to reach a total sales price of the lots (before home construction) in the development (such as 100 lots at $37,500 each for a grand total [gross sales figure] of $3,750,000). Then, the appraiser estimates the costs, on a percentage of the sales price or dollar basis, for (1) preparing the land, with such items as demolition of existing structures or creation of streets and sewers; (2) the amount of the developer's desired profit; and (3) the overhead costs such as taxes or administrator's and office salaries.

LEGAL TERMS

economic obsolescence
Type of depreciation characterized by changes in the sociolegal situation of the property.

Any of these costs may be determined by a dollar amount (such as $1.5 million for land preparation) or by a percentage of what the total sales of the lots will bring (such as 12% of the sales price or $450,000) for the developer's profit. After the amounts for the estimated sales price and all the costs are identified, the remaining amount is the amount that the site itself is worth to the developer. Dividing that amount by the number of lots in the development shows the developer how much can be paid per lot. As an example, let us fill in the numbers for the preceding scenario:

Total sales price = $3,750,000
Site preparation = $1,450,000
Developer's profit = 12% or $450,000
Overhead costs = 21% or $787,500
Total costs = $2,687,500
The amount available for the lots (total sales price minus total costs) = $1,062,500 or $10,625 per lot.

Finally, the value of money must be included, because the developer will not sell all the lots immediately upon completion of the preparation. In essence, this time value of money has to be considered so that the developer's return (12%) is not reduced by holding the developed land and absorbing the unrecompensed costs during the time between completion of the project and payment. If the developer estimates that she can sell 25 of the lots in the first year (the discounting factor on 11% for one year being .90), their value to the developer would be 25 × $11,000 × .90 = $247,500 for lots with a market value of $275,000. Similar calculations can be done for the remaining periods. The calculations can be done by hand, with the formula of

$$\text{Present value} = 1 / (1 + i)^n$$

or by using a present value table, where *n* is the number of years and *i* is the interest rate. This method is often refined with more specific cost estimates to provide greater accuracy.

The fourth technique to evaluate the land's worth is tied into the income received from the whole property. In general, this approach determines the total annual net income for the property and then breaks out the annual net income received from the improvements, so that the income remaining may be attributed to the land itself. This amount of annual income is then divided by the **capitalization rate** to determine the current market value of the land. This capitalization rate is derived from the current market forces and is determined by comparison with equivalent rentals and sales. There is further discussion of this matter in § 6.5, dealing with the income approach. For clarity now, however, consider the following example:

A piece of property receives $250,000 in net income; the income attributable to the building itself appears to be $225,000. That leaves the income attributable to the land at $25,000. That $25,000 is divided by the capitalization rate, let us assume, at .1375, for a resulting value of the land of $181,818.18. On the same basis, the total property value would be $250,000 ÷ .1375 = $1,818,181.81 with the amount attributable to the building being $1,636,363.63.

Evaluation of Site Improvements

After having determined the value of the land, we must turn to the valuation of the improvements to the land. There are two important, but different, ways of using the cost approach for appraisal of land improvements. The first of these is the **replacement cost** approach. This method is used when the purpose of the appraisal is to determine the current cost of a building that would perform the same tasks or functions of the building under consideration. The second method is the **reproduction cost** approach. This method literally uses exactly the same materials, style, and so forth, with no variations, and estimates the cost of reproducing an exact duplicate of the building in question. For instance, one of the great monuments created by Western man is the Gothic cathedral. Many people consider the finest example of this architectural style to be the Chartres Cathedral in France. Recently, estimates have been made of the cost to *reproduce* that cathedral; the estimates run from the hundreds of millions to billions of dollars. To *replace* that cathedral with a place of worship holding the same number of people would not cost anywhere near the same amount.

A replacement may not provide all the same features, such as the effects on the worshipper of light and space, but the replacement building provides the same function, in this case, a place for religious worship. This contrast is the most basic way of identifying the differences between these two appraisal approaches. Note that the unique features that made the original building special might not reappear at all, even though the replacement building serves the same functional purpose. In the cathedral example, the aesthetic effects that would be preserved by the exact reproduction may actually have a powerful impact on the religious use of the building, but they cannot be attained without an actual reproduction. Nevertheless, in a replacement, the basic activity of religious worship could still be carried on in the replacement building, albeit without the other effects. But in either case, the cost will be for a new building, built today, at today's current costs. This example, of course, is somewhat silly, because the Chartres cathedral is considered unique and irreplaceable; therefore, no adequate value could realistically be placed upon it. It is clear that reproduction is highly unlikely, and one could not replace it with a similarly functional building. Nevertheless, the cathedral example dramatically demonstrates this difference and its associated problem of uniqueness.

Area or Square Foot Method

An appraiser may use one of several methods to determine the cost of a replacement building. One method is based upon the total space within a building. That area is usually measured in square feet, so the method is called the **square foot method**. In this method, a comparison is made to recently constructed buildings of the same type and function or to some standard of comparison such as a

LEGAL TERMS

capitalization rate
Rate of return that can be obtained from investing in a piece of property.

replacement cost
Analysis of what the current costs would be to build a structure that would perform the same function as the building being appraised.

reproduction cost
Analysis of what the current costs would be to recreate precisely the building under appraisal.

square foot method
Comparative method of establishing reproduction costs; the price per square foot of a recently completed and comparable building is multiplied by the number of square feet in the building being appraised.

contractor's construction cost manual (which is frequently updated). The purpose of either approach is to obtain a price per square foot, which is then multiplied by the number of square feet. For instance, in the same area and zoning code, an office building was recently constructed for $1,250,000. It has 3 floors with 7,500 (75 × 100) square feet on the first floor and 5,000 (50 ×100) square feet per floor on floors two and three, for a total of 17,500 square feet. That would result in a price of $71.43 per square foot. If the appraiser could establish that the building for which we were preparing an estimate was sufficiently similar, the appraiser could take that dollar-per-square-foot amount ($71.43) and multiply it times our total number of square feet planned (say, 22,500) and arrive at a cost of approximately $1,607,175—rounded off as $1,607,000.

Of course, there can be differences that require adjustments. For instance, if the construction cost manual were not current, a factor would have to be introduced to adjust for the time difference. If the exact heights of the floors were not the same, so that there was additional expense for additional materials, there might have to be an adjustment. This square foot cost appraisal method is widely used, because the method was nationally standardized in the requirements of the Federal Home Loan Mortgage Corporation (FHLMC [Freddie Mac]) and the Federal National Mortgage Association (FNMA [Fannie Mae]), each of which provides forms for doing cost appraisals.

Elements of Construction Method

The second method could be described as estimating the costs of the structural elements of the building. It is sometimes called the **elements used on site method**. This method estimates the cost of each structural element or unit that will go into the construction—items such as walls, doors, floors, roofs, and windows—and then totals all the units. For example, the amount of each unit is individually estimated, and that amount is multiplied by the number of elements or units used. When each of these individual elements' total cost is identified, then all the elements or units are totalled. This method is laborious and time-consuming, but much more accurate than the square footage method. This method also uses construction cost manuals to obtain industry standard costs for units such as windows, doors, walls, floors, roofs, or framing. For instance, if there were to be 10 windows in the building, and each window would cost $150, then the amount could be priced per window and multiplied by 10 for a total of $1,500. This is the amount it would cost to have the windows placed in the structure. Or the amount might be determined for a floor, wall, window, or roof by an amount per square foot. Other measuring units that might be used could be linear feet for poured concrete, or square feet (a surface measurement) or cubic yards (a volume amount-to-be-purchased measurement) for concrete, asphalt, rock, sand, fill, or the like.

Unit Costs Method

In contrast to the method that uses whole units or elements of construction, the next method approaches the evaluation task from a different basis.

In this approach, all the costs for creating the building are estimated. These costs include direct costs, which now include items such as carpentry, utilities, etc., rather than the categories used in the basic units or elements method. In addition, land preparation costs are included in this type of estimate. Finally, indirect and overhead costs, such as office salaries, profit, and permits, are included in the cost as well. For example, consider the costs of doing an entire construction project. There will be numerous individual costs ranging from plumbing and carpentry to landscaping, insurance, and profits. Each of these costs is totalled and then the list is totalled. The elements of construction method appears to be used more often as a device to estimate building costs, while the unit cost method appears to be used more often to do the costing on an entire project. Unit cost is also sometimes referred to as the quantity survey method. Remember, this process involves identifying each cost and then totalling all the costs to determine the final cost for the entire project.

Other Methods

Finally, there are other methods that can be used in a broad, generic approach to estimating. An index can be used to make comparisons. This index could be as specific as a local construction cost index or as broad as the Consumer Price Index. In either case, the key idea is to determine the amount of change in the index since the time the original cost was determined. This increase is added to the original cost to arrive at a current estimated cost. For instance, if the building had a price of $132,500 on December 31, 1987, and the index amount had increased by 27%, then the $132,500 would be multiplied by 1.27 (the 1 representing the $132,500 and the .27 representing the increase) for an estimated cost of $168,275. This method remains an estimate rather than a measurement and is the most general of this group of methods of estimating replacement costs.

The estimating formula using the cost approach is clear. It involves making estimates regarding the amount of the three elements that make up the property value: (1) the value of the site; (2) the value of the improvements to the site; and (3) the loss or decline of value of those improvements, called depreciation. Therefore, site value + improvements value − depreciation of the improvements = appraised (or estimated or property) value. Since we have discussed the methods of estimating the improvements' value and determining the site value, it is appropriate to determine the methods whereby we estimate the depreciation or decline in value of those improvements.

Depreciation

A brief review of what *depreciation* is and how it works follows. *Depreciation,* a term most widely used in accounting, is the lessening of the value of the product or item due to its being used through time. The term **useful life** is often applied in discussing depreciation because the owner or buyer needs to understand how long an improvement, such as a building, will last. Useful

LEGAL TERMS

elements used on site method
Appraisal method in which each element (or ingredient) used for construction is priced individually; the total of all the various components provides the complete estimate.

useful life
Amount of estimated time remaining during which a building can be functional; a depreciation term.

life refers to the amount of time that will pass before the improvement is worn out or has exhausted its life. Another important term is **accumulated depreciation**; it refers to the total amount of depreciation that has occurred since the depreciation first started. For instance, if a fresh, spanking-new building had a value of $150,000 and a useful life of 50 years, the amount of depreciation would be $3,000 per year (if the depreciation were done on the straight line method, which takes an equal amount of depreciation each year). After the 38th year, the amount of accumulated depreciation would be $114,000. That amount is subtracted from the original value to give the remaining value, which would be shown as $36,000. Sometimes, the term *accrued depreciation* is used for accumulated depreciation, but accumulated depreciation appears to be the better usage. Most property improvements last between 40 and 100 years, but some last centuries (like the cathedral at Chartres) and a few, like the Pyramids in Egypt, have lasted millennia.

Types of Depreciation

Remember that there are several sources of depreciation. Property may be depreciated by the physical item wearing out. The concrete may break, the foundation may sag, the insulation may compact. These are all examples of physical impairment or deterioration in an actual, tangible item. Second, the building may become obsolete because of changes in usage. Small rooms, a lack of closets, and tiny windows may make a house appear to be unacceptable because it does not meet the standards, tastes, and requirements of the present time. This type of depreciation is often called **functional obsolescence** because, despite the building remaining usable, it will not bring as high a price as it once might have, because of its lack of attractiveness to the buyer. The final type is the result of changes in permitted usage of the area, because of local zoning laws, or proximity to some situation that ruins the original tenor of the neighborhood. Examples of this problem include discovery of a carcinogenic source in the land (if the property was built on a landfill or if the source was affecting the water supply) or if a common nuisance (such as a highway with its noise and pollution) had been built. These changes are referred to as *economic obsolescence*. For simplicity's sake, these three situations—which cause the property to be less attractive, and therefore less valuable, than it was originally—can be categorized as (1) physical deterioration; (2) changes in personal taste and usage (sometimes called functional obsolescence); and (3) changes in social rules (sometimes called economic or environmental obsolescence).

The term *depreciation* comes from accounting, because the people who keep the financial records for a business need to show the effects of depreciation on the value of an asset such as the building. The accountant's concern, however, is primarily with physical deterioration rather than obsolescence. Land itself is said never to depreciate; only the improvements depreciate. The land, however, can be damaged or its value destroyed through waste, as discussed in chapter 1.

Another participant besides accountants is vitally important—the Internal Revenue Service (IRS). The IRS has a number of rules concerning the amount of depreciation that a business or any real estate owner may use as a legitimate expense in reducing taxes even though there is no cash or out-of-pocket cost in that year. The ways in which the government has allowed depreciation as an expense and the types of other government tax benefits to real estate owners have played an extremely important role in the vitality of real estate markets and in real estate investment.

One other factor should be recognized. Despite any possible set depreciation schedule, the appraiser must check the property to determine if that schedule is still accurate; remember that the depreciation schedule (the rate of negative change or depreciation) began as an estimate, and estimates may have to be adjusted to match the real rate of change. The rate and amount of deterioration could have occurred either much slower or much faster. If the property has been maintained and cared for properly, it may last much longer than the originally anticipated life span. Although homes generally have a life span of less than a century, there are homes in New England and Virginia that go back to the mid-17th century and are still occupied as homes, not merely as museums or historical points of interest. Clearly, they have been well maintained. On the other hand, minimal—or no—maintenance can increase the effects of deterioration and the rate of depreciation. The effective age of a well-maintained property may be much less than its actual age, while the effective age of a rapidly deteriorating property will probably be much greater.

SIDEBAR

Consider that the pyramids were designed to be the eternal resting places of rulers of Egypt (the Great Pyramid for the Pharaoh Khufu, for instance). Because the graves were robbed within a couple of generations or less, one might say that they were fully depreciated within 20 to 50 years after their completion, despite the amount of time they have lasted, because they lost the purpose for which they were constructed. Since then, they have become the only surviving wonder of the ancient world and a major tourist attraction. Then consider whether they have served a higher and better use after they became functionally obsolete, that is, after they were no longer used as tombs.

Depreciation Methods—Straight Line

There are a number of methods for estimating the rate, and therefore the amount, of annual depreciation. The most common method is the **straight line** method, mentioned previously, which divides the original cost of the improvement by the number of years in the improvement's useful life to obtain an average amount per year that will be expensed on the owner's income statement as a noncash cost for the owner. This idea of depreciation spreads the cost out over the useful life rather than permitting the whole cost to be taken in the year during which the actual cash, out-of-pocket expense occurred. Note that in this example, the building (not the entire package) was worth the $150,000; the site is not depreciated. It would require special accounting procedures to recognize any effects of waste on the value of the site, and this is rarely done. The straight line depreciation method is very commonly used because of its simplicity, but many other methods are used also, particularly for tax deduction purposes.

LEGAL TERMS

accumulated depreciation
Total amount of depreciation taken to the present time.

functional obsolescence
Type of depreciation characterized by changes in individual needs, tastes, and styles.

straight line depreciation
Depreciation method that divides the number of years remaining in the useful life of a building into 100% (e.g., 25 years into 100% = 4%); that resulting percentage is the amount of depreciation taken annually.

Investigated Depreciation

A second method of estimating depreciation is to investigate the building itself and determine the areas in which the building has deteriorated. Recall the three basic aspects of depreciation—commonly called physical, functional, and economic. Some of these can be corrected or cured. Others cannot be. Consequently, all depreciation is categorized as either curable or incurable. Most physical deterioration and depreciation can be corrected when it is possible—based on costs (and return on the money spent), time, and circumstances to make the needed repairs. But not all physical deterioration will be corrected, principally because it is not economically feasible to do so. Much of that type of depreciation is just the long-term, inevitable results of gradual deterioration. For instance, a roof may last anywhere from 20 to 40 years. A five-year-old roof would not be "corrected" because the cost-benefit result is far too expensive. No one would want to replace a roof that had anywhere from 15 to 35 years of life left in it. But that roof no longer has a full value, because it has been used for five years and has deteriorated toward its inevitable replacement. Its depreciation must, therefore, be measured and recognized.

The effect of functional change on the process of depreciation may or may not be corrected. It is possible to get around many such problems, which are essentially cosmetic, with appropriate remodeling. For instance, old, outmoded appliances can be replaced with current models. Within a house, if structural elements are carefully avoided, the walls can be moved to accommodate modern preferences, if this change will produce a net positive benefit in relation to the costs expended. Many times, though, taste and style requirements are too expensive to accommodate in relation to the amount recoverable from the sale of the building. This sort of depreciation cannot be corrected. For instance, the 10- to 12-foot high ceilings in older buildings (versus 8 feet or less in modern buildings) may be a handicap to many, but some may even prefer it as an item of Victorian charm (until their utility bills arrive).

Finally, it seems logical that there is no way to change economic obsolescence or correct its effects, because it is the result of a continuing impact from the outside—often, but not always, some legal requirement—over which the property owner has no control. One can measure the impact of these sociolegal requirements by comparing similar properties, which do not have the problem that affects the subject property, to other properties that do have it. Then observe the difference and how much impact in value (dollar terms) this difference has made. For instance, if a property were subject to the discomforts of a new major highway, which affected it with noise and pollution, one would check to see if any comparable building had been sold in the area affected. Then, after locating a comparable building in an unaffected area, a comparison between the value of the two buildings could be made. The difference between the price estimates would represent the cost to the owner of having the highway nearby. It might also be possible to make a comparison with a building in the same area that was sold before the effects of the highway were known, and then adjust the price for economic changes. The difference between these two sets of prices should indicate the dollar impact of the highway on the price of the building.

6.5 APPRAISAL BASED ON INCOME ANALYSIS

The value of commercial property is usually based upon the return available on the investment of the owner. That return is called income and the determination and analysis of that income is the function of this type of appraisal. The value of the property to the prospective buyer-owner is determined by answering the question, "How much money can I make on this piece of property?" Remember that any investment will be determined by how high the **rate of return**, (the *yield*) is and how safe the investment is—rate of return and risk. Because the market place provides a number of alternative places for putting one's money, the rate on the prospective investment must be competitive with other market rates of similar risk. Further, it is not so much a specific cash amount that is considered in these circumstances as the rate of return on the investment, which is expressed as a percentage yield (e.g., "She made 12.5% on that investment").

To do this type of appraisal, certain types of information are needed:

1. The total annual income produced by the property from all sources, known as the **gross income**
2. The estimated subtractions or adjustments from gross income, such as vacancies and inability to collect from certain tenants, to arrive at the **adjusted gross income**
3. The **net income**, which is calculated by deducting all expenses, such as maintenance and other operating expenses
4. The *capitalization rate,* which is the rate of return (expressed as a decimal or a percentage) that the property will have to produce to get investors to put in their money.

Thus, when the net income is divided by the capitalization rate (rate of return), the value of the property is established.

This approach makes sense because the three elements involved—the investment, the income, and the rate of return—all tie together in an algebraic formula. The investment in or value of the property is divided into the income to obtain the rate of return; or the income is divided by the rate of return to obtain the value of the property. It is a simple mathematical switch to solve for different parts of the equation, and this basic algebra is not difficult to do. As a formula, it looks like this:

$$I \div R = V,$$

where I is the income, R is the rate of return desired, and V is the value of the property expressed in dollars. This formula is used repeatedly in the evaluation of income property. Let us now turn to developing an understanding of the four factors mentioned the paragraph before this one.

Determination of Gross Annual Income

First, there is a simple, but approximate, method to use to determine the property value by gross income. It is based on the idea that a multiplier effect is involved between the annual income and the value of the property. Thus, if the sales price is $100,000 and the gross income is $10,000, one could reach

LEGAL TERMS

rate of return
Amount of money that is earned annually on the investment in the real estate parcel; stated as a percentage (12%) or as a decimal (.12).

gross income
Total amount of income received for a building from all sources.

adjusted gross income
Total income receivable less the unrentable or uncollectible amounts.

net income
Income that remains after the operating expenses have been deducted.

the value of the property by describing it as 10 times the gross income. Thus, the number 10 is described as a gross income multiplier. If a property sold for $300,000 within the last 3 months and had a gross income of $37,500, the multiplier would be 8. This technique is used in conjunction with comparisons to similar buildings. For buildings that are being compared to the building being appraised, one must know their market value and their annual gross income. There may also need to be adjustments in special circumstances. The gross income multiplier rates of the comparable buildings may be determined by dividing the sales price or market value by the gross income for each building; these results would be tabulated and may either be averaged or the most common one may be selected as the standard, appropriate multiplier. That multiplier is then applied to the building being appraised to determine its value. Thus, if the comparable multiplier were determined to be 8.75 and the gross annual income were $17,500, the value of the building (and its estimated market price) would be $153,125. The formula is

gross income × gross income multiplier = estimated market value.

In determining the basis for gross income, some other factors must also be considered. The most important item is rent, the amount that the lessee pays the lessor for the use of the premises. Rent may be determined from the owner, the agent, or the lessee and may be verified by seeing the rental contract. The second item needed is the number of square feet in the building, so that the number of square feet can be divided into the annual rent to give the annual rent per square foot. Thus, if the property were leased for $1,000 a month and 1,500 square feet were leased, the annual rental per square foot would be $1,000 × 12 ÷ 1,500 = $8 per square foot.

Determination of Adjustments to Gross Income

One must recognize in any appraisal that outside factors may be involved as well, such as the supply of that particular type of building, the demand for that type of building, its location, and its access to various services, such as transportation. Further, it is necessary to recognize that a number of buildings may have income other than rental income. These income items could range from washing machines and dryers to vending machines to a newspaper stand in the lobby. There are also sometimes omissions from gross income because some leases, particularly the leases of commercial enterprises, provide that the landlord will receive a percentage of the sales after a certain amount of sales. Another problem can arise when the rent potential for the owner-occupier's or custodian's apartment is ignored. Finally, if there are charges for parking, storage, or other services, these should be included in gross income as well.

Determination of Net Income

In determining net income, the concern is with (1) the identification of all costs, (2) the appropriate handling and recognition of those costs, and

(3) the distinction between costs recognized for appraising and costs recognized for accounting. First, it is essential to identify all the costs that occur. None should be omitted. Many times businesses recognize the distinction between fixed and variable costs, because that distinction can provide a better understanding of opportunities for control over costs. Fixed costs are tied to the building and occur regardless of whether there are any occupants. They do not vary with occupancy, as do variable costs. For instance, the building will need maintenance regardless of whether it is fully occupied or only partially occupied; a custodian will be required. But the amount of insurance coverage required or the rate charged may vary based on the number of occupants in the building or the number of apartments occupied. Another common expense in building operation is a reserve for replacement of items that would usually be depreciated. Such items that wear out could be refrigerators, stoves, hot water heaters, carpeting, and other items whose life expectancy is less than that of the building. The reserve should be funded by the amount that matches the annual depreciation, so that money will be available to replace such items when they cease to work.

Certain expenses are recognized in accounting but not in appraising. These expenses include financing costs (such as mortgage principal and interest payments), income taxes, depreciation on the building and its improvements, and capital improvements. Although capital improvements are recognized in establishing the reserves mentioned earlier, the money for those improvements is not treated as an operating expense but as a reduction of the reserve. Consequently, these items are not included in expenses. A real estate business can, therefore, maintain a higher amount of net income than would be recognized under standard accounting procedures. That result could lead to higher rates of return and higher sales prices.

Determination of the Capitalization Rate

The term *capitalization rate* refers in its broadest usage to the return that the investor-funds supplier will receive on his money (his capital) after his funds have been put into the project. This money may be invested in the project in a number of ways. The funds supplier may lend money, as a bank, savings and loan association, or insurance company might do; the investor may purchase some type of investment certificate, such as a participation, a share, or otherwise; or the investor may outright purchase the property, in the simplest and most direct form of investment. Sometimes the capitalization rate (or "cap rate") is thought of as the rate of return on the invested money, but other times it becomes a more sophisticated analytical term (as discussed more fully later). This rate is expressed as a percentage (say, 10%) or a decimal (say, .10), and it is determined by the amount of income after all expenses (net income) being divided by the amount of money that has been invested or put into the project. In formula form, it looks like this:

Net Income ÷ Investment = Capitalization Rate.

The formula can be solved for any of the three elements by simple algebraic manipulation.

Investment = Capitalization Rate ÷ Net Income
Net Income = Capitalization Rate ÷ Investment.

Often, symbols are used for these terms, so that the first formula becomes NI ÷ I = CR. The other ones would be adjusted accordingly. Suppose, for example, that one wishes to find the capitalization rate (CR); if $5,000,000 were invested and the net income were $600,000, what would the capitalization rate be? Answer—12 percent. In a similar manner, the other aspects of the formula can be solved for either net income or investment. If one knows two of the three, the third can always be determined by making the proper insertions into the formula.

If one had a building for which the net income was known (say $12,500), plus a series of comparable buildings, with their sales prices or some other way of determining their value, and one knew how much these buildings had as net income, one could determine each building's rate of return or capitalization rate. As in other comparisons, any rate of return that greatly exceeded the standard grouping of rates would be discarded and a range of value could be estimated. For instance, if there were six buildings with capitalization rates of .085, .083, .091, .078, .087, and .123, the last rate would be thrown out as being out of the pattern, as it is at least 33 percent more than the other highest rate. The range in the others is from .078 to .091; either an average could be taken, .0845, or the range between the two could be shown. Using the formula discussed earlier, by dividing the rate into the income ($12,500), a price for the property could be determined. If the average rate were used, the value of the property would be $148,000; if the rate were expressed as a range, that range would be from $162,250 (.078) to $137,360 (.091).

When these elements are known, it is relatively simple to run the figures, as shown here. But what if a more sophisticated analysis were needed to reflect the realities of the investment situation? Sometimes that reality requires taking into account two factors in the capitalization rate. The first factor is the repayment (or *recapture*) of the money invested in the building or project (this process might be described as getting one's money back or getting one's capital out of the investment). The second factor is the rate of return on the money itself (this describes how much one is making on the investment). When the capitalization rate deals with this process, both elements must be recognized in the calculation of the rate.

The repayment of the invested capital (the return of the capital that was used to buy the building) is usually tied to the estimated remaining useful life of the subject building or improvement. If the building is 15 years old, and it has a remaining useful life of 50 years, the repayment of invested capital would have to be at a rate of 2% a year for the 50 years to get all (100%) of the investment repaid. This repayment analysis extends only to improvements such as buildings, not to the land itself, because land so rarely declines in value that such an approach is unnecessary. The amount of money invested that is attributable to the land is considered to be recovered from the sale price of the property as a whole. Note that this approach to building investment recapture is almost identical to handling the recovery as a function of straight line depreciation.

In approaching the calculation of the return *on* the investor's money as opposed to the return *of* that money, two important devices are generally used. The first one is a generic, market-based approach; the second is based upon financing and market rates for money. In the first method, a site's income, the sales price, the remaining useful life, and the net operating income need to be known. The amount attributable to the site's contribution to the income would be deducted from the net income. This amount represents the recapture of capital. For instance, if the site has a net income of $60,000, with a sales (market) price of $350,000 and a site value of $65,000 with a remaining life of 25 years, the building value is $285,000 ($350,000 – $65,000). The building recapture rate is .04 (1.00 ÷ 25); therefore, each year, the total income must have within it 4 percent of the $285,000 that will be attributable to the recapture; that amount would be $11,400. [Note: This 4 percent is not of the net income, $60,000, for $2,400.] That $11,400 would be subtracted from the net income ($60,000 – $11,400) for a result of $48,600 of net income that is attributable to the building. This income, divided by the sales price, yields the rate of return—$48,600 ÷ $350,000 = 13.89%.

The second method estimates the rate of return by analyzing the rate of return investors insist upon before they can be induced to put their money into the project. Generally, this approach involves estimating the lender's mortgage rate and the owner's needed rate of return. For instance, a property has a first mortgage that is 60% of the property's price (value), while the owner has put up 40%. The mortgage bears a rate of 12.5%, and the owner—whose position is secondary to the lender and therefore needs a higher rate of return because of a higher risk—wants 15%. The compound rate of return for both parties is calculated by multiplying the rate by the percentage of the value; thus the lender's contribution, .60 × .125 = .075 (7.5%) plus the owner's contribution, .15 × .40 = .06 (6%). These two combined make 13.5% the interest rate.

Other valuation techniques exist as well, but this overview is merely intended to introduce you to the appraiser's way of thinking and some of the basic techniques and procedures used in appraising. This material should adequately demonstrate the most common approaches and a framework for analysis.

DISCUSSION AND REVIEW QUESTIONS

1. In determining a site value, explain how to use the allocation method from these facts. The building-to-land value ratio in this area is 4:1. The price of the parcel (land and building) is $210,000.

2. Name and explain three basic principles of appraising.
3. Name and explain the three basic methods of appraisal.
4. Consider the following facts about a residence: It is 15 years old, has 9 rooms, 2½ baths, good quality construction, comparable landscaping, and is in a neighborhood where the average annual family income exceeds $75,000. Explain which of the following properties might not be comparable based on the variable item given. You may assume that all the properties being compared have been sold within an appropriate time span before this time of appraisal.
   a. 1½ baths.
   b. 40 years old.
   c. no landscaping.
   d. 6 rooms.
   e. in a somewhat less desirable neighborhood.
5. You are appraising an office building that has two stories, with a square footage on the first floor of 6,000 square feet and on the second floor of 5,000 square feet. Recently, a building of 10,000 square feet, of a similar purpose and age, at a nearby location sold for $319,000. What would be a reasonable estimate of the potential sales price for the building you are appraising?
6. Suppose that the net income for a parcel is $50,000 per year and the land value is $75,000. A lender that will loan 70% of the value wants 10.5% interest, while the investor wants 12% as a rate of return. The remaining useful life of the building is 50 years. Calculate the property's value by means of the building residual technique and the land residual technique.
7. Using the direct market comparison approach, consider these facts.
   The property being appraised has moderate traffic, standard landscaping, a lot with the dimensions of 25′ × 125′, is 15 years old, and is of frame construction. It has gables, 8 rooms with 4 bedrooms, 3 baths, and 2,300 sq. ft. There is a full basement. The condition of the exterior is good, but the interior condition is poor. There is a two-car attached garage. There is an additional improvement of an enclosed porch of 12′ × 20′.
   The first comparison property was sold for $287,500 within 2 months of our appraisal. It is on a quiet street. Its landscaping is standard. Its lot size is 30′ × 110′. It is 17 years old and is frame construction. It has gables, 9 rooms, 5 bedrooms, 3 baths, and 2,500 sq. ft. total space. It has a full basement. It has a good exterior and interior condition. It also has a two-car attached garage.
   The second comparison property was sold for $292,500. It is on a quiet street, has standard landscaping and a lot 25′ × 125′. It is 20 years old, made of brick, has gables, 8 rooms, 4 bedrooms, 3 baths, and 2,275 sq. ft. It has a full basement, good condition for both the interior and the

exterior, a two-car attached garage, and was sold within the last three months.

The third comparison house sold for $295,000. It is on a quiet street, has standard landscaping, a 25′ × 125′ lot, is 18 years old, has frame construction, a gabled roof, 7 rooms, 3 bedrooms, and 2½ baths. It has 2,100 sq. ft. It has a full basement and is in good condition both on the exterior and the interior. It has a two-car attached garage and was sold four months ago.

Calculate the adjustments for each significant difference between the property being appraised and the properties being compared to the property being appraised. Total those differences (the pluses and the minuses) and estimate which property would provide the most accurate comparative estimate of the value of the property being appraised. Indicate what you think that price should be.

CHAPTER 7
Real Estate Financing

"Our Laws make law impossible; our liberties destroy all freedom; our property is organized robbery."

George Bernard Shaw

Salt-box house

OUTLINE

PROLOGUE TO THE PARALEGAL

This chapter discusses two important businesses that work together, but sometimes have conflicting interests. These are (1) the financial industry, upon which all turns in (2) the real estate business. When the financial industry is unhealthy, real estate sales are poor. When interest rates are too high, people cannot afford to buy, builders cannot afford to build, and the real estate business languishes. Financial services are one of the most highly regulated industries in the world—perhaps for good reason, because the power over money is very important to the whole society. Our financial industry has been "de-regulated" since the 1970s, but that term does not mean no regulation; it simply means "re-regulation"—different regulations in a different manner. This business is as likely to be unregulated as a living dinosaur is to be discovered. The financial industry is complex because of regulations and because of the number of packages and alternatives the industry offers its customers. As a result, there is a great deal of intricate and complex material for you to master in this chapter. It is essential that you understand the terms and what the documents do in these financial situations, because the financial arrangements are the very core of the contract of sale and the closing. Without satisfactory financing arrangements for the buyer, the sale can fail. This material is essential to you, as a legal assistant, so that you will know what is going on and why it happens on the financing side of the real estate business.

KEY TERMS

acceleration clause
adjustable rate mortgage (ARM)
adjustment period
amortization
annual percentage rate (APR)
appraisal
assumption of the mortgage
balloon mortgage
block busting
cash flow
collateralized mortgage obligation
contract for deed
convertible mortgage
credit life insurance
cure
deed of reconveyance
deed of trust
default
defeasance clause
deficiency judgment
discharge
due on sale clause
equity
equitable mortgage
Federal Home Loan Mortgage Corporation (Freddie Mac; now called the "Mortgage Corporation")
Federal Housing Administration (FHA)
Federal National Mortgage Association (Fannie Mae)
floating interest rate
foreclosure
good faith purchaser for value
Government National Mortgage Association (Ginnie Mae)
graduated payment mortgage (GPM)
holder in due course
home equity loan
interim lender
land sales contract
leverage ration
loaned up
margin
mortgage
negative amortization
note
pass through
pool
real estate installment sales contract
Real Estate Settlement Procedures Act (RESPA)
redlining
release
renegotiable rate mortgage (RRM)
reverse annuity mortgage
right of redemption
right of rescission
rollover mortgage
satisfaction
second mortgage
shared appreciation mortgage (SAM)
steering
subject to the mortgage
subrogation
take-back mortgage
Truth in Lending (TIL)
usury
variable rate mortgage (VRM)
Veterans Administration (VA)
wraparound mortgage

7.1 INTRODUCTION

The financing of real estate transactions lies at the very core of the real estate business. The most important real estate activity is acquiring real estate, and the process of financing real estate—finding the money to buy and sell real estate—is the most difficult part of the acquisition process. When real estate is sold, there is a transfer from one party to another. But a property transfer is not always involved when there is real estate financing; property might simply be refinanced with some type of security instrument when its owner needs cash. An example is the current device called a *home equity loan,* where the home owner borrows money based on the accumulated **equity** in the property. This real estate financing process is both detailed and complex—detailed to assert control over all the myriad aspects involved, to protect the interests of the parties to the transaction, and complex because of the sheer number of factors in any transaction.

There will be extensive documentation and paperwork for the closing documents. There may be an appraisal. There are taxes to consider. More than one lender may be involved. If the property is purchased from a trust or an estate, court approval may be needed. The number and variety of aspects that may be involved when a parcel of real estate is being financed can be bewildering and apparently endless. Nevertheless, it is possible to understand all these factors, control them, and use them effectively.

Financing is complex for a number of reasons. First, money is a scarce commodity; this means that money is frequently difficult or expensive to obtain. This scarcity may be based on a variety of factors, but a primary one is that a high degree of risk is involved in investing money without any certainty that it will be repaid. This risk of repayment factor should remain fresh in real estate lenders' minds for a number of years following the savings and loan debacle, which was heavily based in unrepayable real estate loans.

Second, the real estate business, particularly on its construction side, is highly vulnerable to the cost of money, and this vulnerability means that the business is subject to the up-and-down cycles of the economy. For instance, when money is scarce, one of the first businesses to be affected is real estate. As a consequence, much real estate financing (and therefore the real estate industry itself) is cyclical, because real estate trends traditionally lead the national economy in and out of recessions.

Third, there may be several lenders, each increasing the complexity of the transaction. Depending on the type of transaction, one, two, or even more lenders may be involved. Typically, the home mortgage transaction has two lenders, both of which are usually local banks or savings and loan institutions. In the typical transaction, A sells to B. A has a mortgage that must be paid off. B has a lender that will advance the money to purchase the home. Thus, there are two lenders—A's lender and B's lender. Of course, it is possible for A to introduce B to A's bank, and have B assume or refinance A's loan, but that is not the most common pattern.

Fourth, there is another pattern that was frequent when interest rates were high: B assuming A's mortgage, with A's bank knowing, and A financing the difference between the sales price and the outstanding amount of the mortgage. But there may also be more than one lender if the purchased property is new construction. With home mortgages, the contractor's bank may or may not want to take the individual home, but if it does, it would be the only bank; if not, another bank would finance the purchaser. In commercial

LEGAL TERMS

equity
The amount of funds the owner has invested in the property; if the property were sold and the debt associated with that property paid off, the remaining amount would be referred to as the "owner's equity."

building construction, there is a different process, whereby an **interim** or short-term **lender** finances the builder's land acquisition and construction costs. That lender will be paid off *(taken out)* by a long-term financier, the permanent lender. This pattern of a short-term loan (up to 3 years) to the party that does the land development and building construction—to finance the land acquisition, make the necessary improvements, and do the construction—is usually followed by a long-term loan (20 to 40 years or more) that pays off the construction loan. When the take-out loan (that pays off the short-term lender) is large, it may be that no single lender wants to risk the entire dollar amount for the entire time period. Consequently, there may be multiple take-out lenders to spread the risk.

Fifth, there are many parts of the real estate business, and some of these arrange their financing from different sources than others. For instance, small, community-based, commercial banks rarely make long-term (take-out) real estate loans, but large commercial banks may have an entire department for that type of financing. Financial institutions that have long-term cash surpluses need to put those funds in a long-term secure investment. Traditionally, one such institution has been the life insurance company; the pension fund is another. This part of the insurance industry has frequently provided the long-term financing for commercial real estate construction.

Sixth, real estate financing may involve government agencies such as the **Federal Housing Administration (FHA)** or the **Veterans Administration (VA)**. Each of these agencies may become involved in the lending process by insuring or guaranteeing the private lender's real estate home loan. Although neither agency directly sets standards for lending, their underwriting and construction standards affect certain aspects of the home lending process to individuals.

Seventh, the paper of real estate financing (particularly the borrower's note) may be the subject of resale to or investment by third parties. Some banks have found it profitable to assemble groups (called *packages*) of mortgages and resell those note packages to investors, groups of investors, or a **pool** (a large and usually diverse set of mortgages held together) in which individual investors may invest. Prospective investors can evaluate the risk involved and purchase a portion with a participation certificate or a share.

Another arrangement is a **pass-through**, whereby the loan originator, usually a bank or savings and loan, sells off to investors most of its interest in the note and mortgage (that is, the right to be repaid and the right to seize and sell the collateral upon default), but retains the servicing process, collects the payments, and passes payments received, proportionately, through to the purchasers. Pass throughs usually are done for pools of at least $1 million and are often guaranteed by the Federal Housing Authority (FHA) or the Veterans Administration.

These bundles of instruments are guaranteed as to prompt payment of principal and interest, by the **Government National Mortgage Association (Ginnie Mae)**. Because investors have certain requirements that affect the lending process, and to help meet one of the problems that investors have

LEGAL TERMS

interim lender
Party that makes loans to do the project in the short term and is taken out by a long-term financier.

Federal Housing Administration (FHA)
Federal agency involved in making guarantees of home loans.

had with mortgages, a new financing device has been created, called a **collateralized mortgage obligation** (CMO). It allows an investor to deal with the risk that the homeowner who has to pay the mortgage may refinance his mortgage at a lower rate and thus lower the interest yield on the mortgage pool. When a pooled mortgage is repaid, the mortgage pool becomes unstable, with changing dollar amounts. To reduce that risk, the mortgage term is broken up into time periods, such as five-year units (years 1–5, 6–10, etc.), and the investor can choose which period she wishes to buy into. In that manner, the time risk may be reduced and the burden of choosing the appropriate time period falls on the investor. Finally, it is important to remember that these new financing techniques have made mortgages more liquid and helped to keep interest rates down.

Eighth, as most people lack the cash to purchase real estate outright, not only must they finance the transaction, but they must also use the purchased property as collateral for the transaction. The law relating to the offering and taking of collateral is detailed and the paperwork is often complicated.

Ninth, there are a myriad of government regulations that must be complied with in different aspects of the lending process. These include regulations relating to the lender's selection of prospective borrowers, at the beginning of the lending process. For instance, *redlining*—drawing a line around an area and refusing to lend there for racist reasons—is prohibited, as is *block busting*, that is, trying to force out an entire neighborhood or block by spreading rumors of falling property values because of new types of people moving into the community. Government regulation permeates the entire lending process, extending even to the form of the closing statement and the information it contains, at the end of the process.

Tenth, lenders often need to enhance the products they sell, so they provide additional services to their borrowers. One of these areas, which has added profitability to bank operations, has been the sale of various types of insurance. One of the most important forms of insurance remains the sale of **credit life insurance**, which basically provides that, for the payment of a premium, the borrower may have the balance of the loan paid off if the borrower dies. This arrangement is a term (a covenant) of the lending agreement for which the borrower pays a premium, usually as part of the monthly payment. The cost is disclosed as part of the cost of the loan and its financing arrangements.

What if a bank took the insurance payments, promised to get the insurance but never did so, and then, after the death of the party who thought he was insured, foreclosed on the property? The *Parnell* court dealt with just such a situation.

These ten aspects are only some of the more important reasons for real estate financing transactions being complicated and time-consuming. To understand the process of real estate financing, be sure that you organize all your thoughts about the process and make a checklist. You may even want to make sub-checklists to control some of the steps in the process. Two checklists, one for the note and one for the mortgage, are provided at the end of this chapter to get you started. Breaking the process down into smaller steps can enhance

Veterans Administration (VA)
Federal agency that assists veterans; guarantees repayment of bank or savings and loan home loans to veterans.

pool
Grouping of a number of mortgages so that portions or participations may be sold off to investors.

pass-through
Way of handling home mortgages so that they can be pooled and resold to investors; the bank is said to pass through the principal and interest payments to the pool interest holders.

Government National Mortgage Association (Ginnie Mae)
Federally sponsored corporation involved in real estate transactions, which guarantees the prompt payment of the interest and principal on pooled, pass-through loans.

collateralized mortgage obligation
Recently created pooled mortgage device to allow the buyer of the pooled mortgage interest to select the time period of the mortgage; device to limit risk of the underlying mortgage being repaid early.

credit life insurance
Type of insurance providing that if the borrower dies, the insurance will pay off the outstanding amount of the loan; often offered by lender to borrowers.

PARNELL
v.
FIRST SAVINGS AND LOAN ASSOCIATION OF LEAKESVILLE
336 So. 2d 764 (Miss. 1976)

LEE, J.

Catherine Parnell appeals from a decree of the Chancery Court of Greene County dismissing her bill of complaint against First Savings and Loan Association of Leakesville. We reverse.

Appellant assigns as error:

(1) The judgment of the trial court is contrary to the law and the evidence, and

(2) The trial court erred in admitting certain evidence incompetent under Mississippi Code Annotated § 13-1-7 (1972) [Dead Man's Statute].

On October 31, 1972, Catherine Parnell and Walter Parnell, her husband, obtained a loan from appellee in the sum of thirteen thousand dollars ($13,000.00) for the purpose of buying a home, and they secured the loan by deed of trust on the property. At the time of loan closing, appellee inquired whether they desired credit life insurance, and the Parnells answered in the affirmative. Accordingly, the sum of one hundred twenty-three dollars and three cents ($123.03) was paid to appellee by the Parnells (financed in the loan at the interest rate of 7¾%) for the first year's premium, and the sum of ten dollars and twenty-six cents ($10.26) was added to the monthly loan installments for the purposes of paying the second year's premium.

After closing the loan, appellee's manager discovered that he had failed to secure Parnell's signature on a credit life insurance application, and on November 6, 1972, he wrote Parnell:

> "Today I received your loan file and it was determined that the life insurance application was not filled out.
>
> I urge you to come to this office immediately after receiving this letter."

He also testified he saw Parnell at the Lodge that night and:

> "I mentioned in person to Hank Parnell, which was our way of referring to him in the lodge, I remembered the case and I was excited because it had not been done [application signed] and urged him to come to the office immediately."

He later testified he explained to Parnell that no insurance would be issued until the application was completed and signed.

Suffice it to say, Parnell never signed the application and four (4) consecutive monthly installments, each including $10.26 for credit life premiums, had been paid on the loan when Parnell died March 10, 1973. The sums collected by appellee for the credit life insurance premiums were deposited and retained by it in the Parnell loan escrow account, and the money was still in that account at the time of the trial.

After her husband's death, appellant carried his death certificate to appellee's manager, who received it and placed it in the Parnell file. Appellant denied she and her husband had received a letter from appellee that the application for insurance had not been signed, and she testified she and her husband thought the insurance was in effect. Appellee's manager consulted its attorney and then advised appellant that no policy had been issued and that she had no credit life insurance.

The first step in applying for the loan was the execution of a disclosure statement pursuant to the Federal Truth in Lending Act, which instrument was signed by appellant and appellee, and set forth the terms of the loan, the amount, the due dates and the amount of the insurance, taxes and closing costs. The procedure for obtaining credit life insurance was for the borrower to sign an application for the insurance and the appellee forwarded that application to the representative of the insurance company. If the application were approved and the policy issued, it was sent to appellee, who retained the policy in its file, and notified the borrower that the insurance was in effect.

The appellant contends that appellee, through its manager, was an agent for an insurance company [appellee used Republic National Life Insurance Company], and that by accepting the premiums a contract of insurance was in effect. The cases, relied upon in support of that contention, relate to the powers of insurance agents to bind their principals in their dealing with others, are not in point with the real question here and offer little help. The question is one of first impression in this state, and there is little authority in other jurisdictions that shed light upon it.

In *Burgess v. Charlottesville Savings & Loan Association,* Burgess obtained a loan from appellee and signed a Truth-in-Lending statement which contained a request for credit life insurance. No application for such insurance was ever signed by Burgess, and no premiums were collected or received by appellee. The court held that it was impossible for appellee to form a contract of insurance, that there was no evidence that a contract to procure insurance was formed, and that there was no merit in appellant's claim under Virginia law.

The only question in *Peer v. First Federal Savings & Loan Association of Cumberland* was whether a contract to provide credit life insurance existed between the parties. The following occurred in connection with the fifteen thousand dollar ($15,000.00) loan:

(1) Peer signed a statement in the truth-in-lending notice that "I desire credit life insurance only."

(2) A space provided therein for cost of life and/or health insurance premiums was left blank.

(3) In the payment coupon book and in the annual statement of Peer's loan account listing payments on principal, interest, escrow and late charges, no charge was shown for life insurance.

(4) A letter was given to the Peers at the time of their loan commitment recommending credit life insurance and advising that a life insurance representative would call upon them to explain the program.

(5) No insurance representative ever appeared.

(6) No charge was ever made for credit life insurance.

(7) The Peers never paid any premiums for life insurance.

In emphasizing that no premiums for credit life insurance were ever charged or paid, the court said: "It is manifest on the record before us that First Federal did not contract to provide Mr. Peer with credit life insurance and pay the premiums out of the monthly mortgage payments."

In contrast:

(1) Parnell executed a disclosure statement setting out the escrow account, including the first year's premium and two monthly payments for credit life insurance, which were financed by appellee.

(2) A closing statement in the handwriting of appellee's manager with the title "Walter Parnell and Catherine K. Parnell" itemized the closing costs and reflected therein the sum of one hundred twenty-three dollars and three cents ($123.03), first year's credit life insurance premium, and ten dollars and twenty-six cents ($10.26) separate items for two months' premiums on said insurance.

(3) Parnell's loan account book reflected four monthly payments on the credit life insurance premium for the second year.

(4) Appellee admitted that the Parnells paid the first year's premium on credit life insurance, paid four monthly installments on the second year's premium and that it received and retained those payments in the Parnell escrow account.

We adopt the view expressed in *Watkins v. Valley Fidelity and Trust Company.* Morris Williams financed the purchase of an automobile for twenty-four hundred ninety-seven dollars and fifty cents ($2,497.50) balance, plus two hundred fifty-one dollars ($251.00) insurance, plus eighty-one dollars and thirty-seven cents ($81.37) credit life premiums, aggregating the sum of twenty-eight hundred twenty-nine dollars and eighty-seven cents ($2,829.87) to be financed. A finance charge of five hundred fourteen dollars and sixty-three cents ($514.63) was added, resulting in a loan contract of thirty-three hundred forty-four dollars and fifty cents ($3,344.50) signed by Williams. The amount of $81.37 was held by the bank, through error, in its fees account, whereas it should have been deposited in the account of the automobile dealer designated as credit life insurance for the purchase of the insurance. Upon the death of Williams, payment of the contract amount was declined since no credit life insurance had been purchased to secure the loan. The court said:

> "The bank argues there was no contact between it and the decedent whereby the bank was to purchase credit life insurance, and if a contract be claimed it fails for lack of consideration to the bank. The bank argues it merely contracted to lend money. We hold this contention is not sound under the record.
>
> The contract was proved as Exhibit 2 in the record, designated as Loan No. 0185 made by the bank to Morris Williams. This contract as herein noted included a charge of $81.37 for credit life insurance. That figure was included in the 'Amount to be Financed' upon which a finance charge of $514.63 was figured and added thereto with the resulting $3,344.50 shown as 'The Amount of Contract.' We hold this instrument was the contract, and the $514.63 finance charge was the consideration flowing to the Bank.
>
> When a bank makes a charge against a borrower for credit life insurance premiums, includes that amount in the loan, and retains the money so charged, we hold that bank not only assumes the contractual obligation to properly apply the amount to credit life insurance, but also stands in a fiduciary capacity toward the borrower to see that the amount so charged and withheld is actually applied to the purchase of such insurance.
>
> The inclusion of credit life insurance in a lender-borrower transaction is not for the sole benefit of, nor at the option of the lender. Credit life insurance is also a very important and vital part of the transaction to the borrower because it offers absolute protection to his estate for the unpaid balance of the debt in the event of his death before payment in full.
>
> The bank failed to apply the $81.37 to the purchase of credit life insurance on the life of Morris Williams, and offered no reason therefor except error on the part of an employee. We hold the bank thereby breached its contract with Morris Williams, and breached its fiduciary duty to purchase the insurance, with a resulting loss to the estate of Morris Williams in the sum of $2,262.99, that being the unpaid balance of the debt."

We hold that when the appellee, First Savings and Loan Association of Leakesville, financed, collected and retained the sum of $123.03 for one year's premium on credit life insurance for Parnell, and collected and retained the sum of $10.26 monthly for a period of four months with which to provide credit life insurance for the second year, it assumed a contractual obligation to obtain credit life insurance for Parnell and to apply the amounts so received to credit life insurance, and that it stood in a fiduciary capacity towards the Parnells to see that the amounts so charged, collected and withheld were actually applied to obtaining and purchasing such insurance. . . .

The bill of complaint prayed for cancellation of the deed of trust and for general relief.

We reverse and hold that appellant is entitled to such amount as may be equal to the sum now required to satisfy and discharge the obligation to appellee, and remand the case to the trial court for the purpose of making that determination.

[Some citations omitted.]

control over the entire set of operations. Each checklist or sub-checklist should include the following topics, at a minimum:

1. What is happening?
2. Who are the parties involved?
3. What is each party's function? That is, what does each party do, and when will she be involved?
4. What is the time frame for (a) completing the entire project and (b) for completing each step of the project?
5. What instruments, documents, and other paperwork must be generated by or for each participant at each step along the way?
6. Which parties in this process must be reminded to do something or complete some step so that it is done by the appropriate time deadline? How can this prodding be done both tactfully and effectively? Should a special calendar be created for this process?
7. Do you have follow-up controls (often called *ticklers* because they should "tickle" your memory to do something by providing a reminder) for each action that must be taken at a later date?

This chapter has basic checklists for you to start with, but you will need to adapt them to your situation.

In addition to these participants in the real estate business, there are a number of others to be aware of as well. Some of them are regional institutions, such as mutual savings banks (which are located primarily in the Northeast), but there are also insurance companies whose lending focuses on long-term payouts on construction loans or on purchasing home mortgages that have been guaranteed by federal government programs. In addition, pension funds are also involved in real estate as long-term lenders. Credit unions have likewise begun to diversify their holdings from home improvement loans to long-term lending.

Beyond these direct lenders, there are also entities that guarantee the repayment of real estate loans. Some of the most important of these are the VA and the FHA, as previously mentioned, and private insurance companies that underwrite the borrower's repayment ability (these are usually designed to repay the loan if the borrower fails to pay). Although not guarantors, three institutions are intimately involved with the resale of mortgages. These are called by nicknames from their acronyms:

Ginnie Mae, from GNMA, for Government National Mortgage Association (a part of the federal government's Housing Department, which works with special government housing programs and with Fannie Mae);

Fannie Mae, from FNMA, for Federal National Mortgage Association (a privately owned corporation that has established a secondary market for mortgages); and

Freddie Mac, from its prior title of Federal Home Loan Mortgage Corporation (FHLMC), but now called the Mortgage Corporation; its function is to create and maintain a secondary market for conventional home mortgages.

The term *secondary market* refers to the lender's sale of its loans in a package to investors rather than keeping the loans for itself. The pools mentioned earlier are an example of the process of the lender's transfer of its mortgage loan interests into the secondary market.

In the following sections, various aspects of real estate financing are discussed. First, we investigate the factual and legal setting for real estate financing. Second, we look at the lending process and what happens in it, using the bank's perspective as well as the borrower's. Third, we discuss the role of the government, particularly the United States government, and government regulations in the financing and lending process. Finally, we examine alternative types of financing and some of the instruments and documents used in that process.

7.2 THE FACTUAL SETTING FOR A REAL ESTATE FINANCING TRANSACTION

The most common real estate transaction, for most people, is the purchase of a residence, a place called "home." The actual parcel may be a traditional home, but it may be a condominium in a high-rise or a townhouse. Another set of variables concerns existing financing of this parcel of real property: (1) Is there a debt owed to some financier that must be paid off? or (2) is the property debt-free? These variables affect the amount of searching and paperwork to be done, and they apply whether the home is new construction or an existing building. Typically, A owns a piece of property, owes a debt on it, and wants to sell the property. B wants to buy it. B needs to borrow the money to meet the purchase price. What types of financing arrangements can be set up for these two parties?

The typical arrangement, historically, is for B to go to a community bank or to a savings and loan association (at some point after he has arrived at an approximate or definite price with the seller), make an application for the home loan, and go through the lending process. The basic loan process requires a credit check, an evaluation of the quality and resale value of the property called an **appraisal**, and an estimate of the effects of the loan payments on the cash flow of B, the borrower. This last step involves identifying the sources of B's income and determining whether he is likely to maintain that level of income for the foreseeable future. (Note that these investigations all relate to the risk of repayment—the borrower's history and patterns of repayment and the lender's risk of putting its money in that location.)

The essence of the last step is simple: Will B have enough money to pay the debt as well as meet his other needs? If the investigations concerning these aspects all come up with positive answers, then the home loan will probably be made. The terms of the loan are generally set forth in a **note**, an instrument in which the borrower promises the lender to repay the loan at a certain rate of interest over a certain time period. The legal requirements for a note to be negotiable are that it be in writing, signed by the maker, for a sum certain, with an unconditional promise to pay on demand or at a specified time. Notes on home loans generally provide for a term of between 15 and 30 years, at a fixed rate of interest between 4.5 percent and 8 percent, with a separate (but tied-in) mortgage document giving the lender the right to foreclose and sell the property if the borrower cannot repay the loan. The loan is amortized over a set period of years (see figure 7-1). The appropriate documents are recorded in the local office that handles real estate records, such as a county recorder of deeds.

Collateralizing Documents

These two documents, the note and the collateralizing document (either a mortgage or a trust deed), embody the two essential elements in all real estate financing transactions. First, there is a loan from the lender to the borrower, and the proceeds of that loan are used to pay the seller so that the seller will transfer the property to the buyer. But the note may not remain with the lender; it may be transferred to another investor in a pool or other secondary market device. The transfer is by *indorsement,* which is the noteholder's signature transferring the note to someone else. (There are other technical aspects, based in the law of commercial paper, that relate to transfer by indorsement, but they are beyond the scope of this text.)

Second, there is documentation to protect the lender's interest in the property. In most traditional home transactions, that document is a **mortgage**. The borrower giving the mortgage is called the *mortgagor,* while the lender taking the mortgage is called the *mortgagee.* Mortgages are used because the money is being lent over a relatively long period of time—15 years or longer. The longer the money is outstanding, the greater the risk of something going wrong, so that it becomes difficult or impossible for the debtor to repay the note. Thus, the mortgage protects the lender against being negatively affected by the financial problems of the borrower. The legal

LEGAL TERMS

appraisal
Evaluation of the current market worth of a piece of real property; usually made by a professional appraiser.

note
Instrument in which the borrower promises to repay the loan at an agreed-upon interest rate and by a certain time.

mortgage
Document pledging land as collateral for the repayment of a loan.

MONTHLY PRINCIPAL AND INTEREST PAYMENTS OVER 30 YEARS* ANNUAL PERCENTAGE RATE														
	8.0	8.5	9.0	9.5	10.0	10.5	11.0	11.5	12.0	12.5	13.0	13.5	14.0	14.5
50**	366	384	402	420	439	457	476	495	514	534	553	573	592	612
60	439	460	483	505	527	549	571	594	617	640	664	687	711	735
70	513	538	564	589	614	640	667	693	720	747	774	802	829	857
80	586	615	644	673	701	732	762	792	823	854	885	916	948	980
90	659	692	724	757	790	823	857	891	926	961	996	1031	1066	1102
100	733	769	805	841	878	915	952	990	1029	1067	1106	1145	1185	1225
110	806	846	885	925	965	1006	1048	1089	1131	1174	1217	1260	1303	1347
120	880	923	966	1009	1053	1098	1143	1188	1234	1281	1327	1375	1422	1469
130	953	1000	1046	1093	1141	1189	1238	1287	1337	1387	1438	1489	1540	1592
140	1027	1076	1126	1177	1229	1281	1335	1386	1440	1494	1549	1604	1659	1714
150	1100	1153	1207	1261	1316	1372	1429	1485	1543	1601	1659	1718	1777	1837
160	1173	1230	1287	1345	1404	1464	1524	1584	1646	1708	1770	1833	1896	1959
170	1246	1307	1368	1428	1492	1555	1619	1684	1749	1814	1881	1947	2014	2082
180	1320	1384	1448	1514	1580	1647	1714	1783	1852	1921	1991	2062	2133	2204
190	1393	1461	1529	1598	1667	1738	1809	1882	1954	2028	2102	2176	2251	2327
200	1466	1538	1609	1682	1755	1830	1905	1981	2057	2135	2212	2291	2370	2449
210	1540	1615	1690	1766	1843	1921	2000	2080	2160	2241	2323	2405	2488	2572
220	1612	1692	1770	1850	1931	2012	2095	2179	2263	2348	2434	2520	2607	2694
230	1687	1769	1851	1934	2018	2104	2190	2278	2366	2455	2544	2634	2725	2816
240	1760	1845	1931	2018	2106	2195	2286	2377	2469	2561	2655	2749	2844	2939
5,000 ***	37	38	40	43	44	46	48	50	51	53	55	57	59	61

Note: The monthly principal and interest payments are approximate and do not include property ownership-related taxes, nor do they represent miscellaneous fees.

**Note: This vertical column is the mortgaged amount in thousands of dollars (for example, the 100 represents $100,000).*

***Note: This row represents the increase in monthly payments by annual percentage rates for each increase of $5,000 in mortgaged amount (for example a mortgage of $205,000 at 9.0 percent annual rate would require a monthly payment of approximately $1,649).*

FIGURE 7-1
Amortization schedule

requirements for the mortgage document are similar to those for a deed, because a mortgage can force a transfer of the property. The mortgage must be in writing, contain the names of the parties, have a correct (legal) description of the real property, contain words of conveyance or grant of the property, have the appropriate attestation and execution formalities, and be delivered. In addition, the mortgage must describe the debt that it is securing. When the note is indorsed over to a purchaser, the mortgage goes along with it, and is said to be assigned to the note purchaser.

Another form of real estate collateralization document exists as well—the **deed of trust**. Its purpose is to make it simpler for the mortgagee to obtain the property if it must be seized and sold for repayment of the debt. A trust is created whereby the real property title goes to a trustee, who acts on behalf of the lender if a foreclosure occurs and exercises the power of sale without court proceedings. This format permits much more rapid sale and lower costs for the lender.

Market Changes and New Loan Devices

Home mortgages or trust deeds collateralized most of the large numbers of home sales after World War II. They continued to be the principal documentation in the home lending field until changes began to occur in the 1970s and 1980s. At that point, several problems arose in the traditional home lending business, which caused transactions to become more complicated.

First, lenders began to suffer severe losses, because their costs (particularly of the money they lent) rose to levels that exceeded the fixed rates they had been receiving on their real estate loans. In an attempt to avoid getting caught in this bind again, lenders began using a new type of interest rate in their home loan notes, called a **floating interest rate**. Prior to this time, a floating rate was not possible, because in many states old laws forbade using such a rate. But with the laws changed—as they had to be or there would have been no home lending—these rates worked as follows. The rate of interest was no longer a flat, fixed rate of, say, 6 percent. Instead, it was set to move as the bank's cost of money moved, thus transferring the risk of change in the bank's money cost to the borrower. Generally, the floating rate was pegged to a national standard of some sort, such as the prime rate; it would be stated, for example, as "prime plus 1 percent." That phrase means that the borrower would pay 1 percent more than the prime rate in effect at the lending institution (or some national prime rate, such as listed in *The Wall Street Journal*). When the prime rate (or whatever basis was used) changed, the rate changed, either upward or downward.

Normally, bases such as the prime rate change frequently, but adjustments of the real estate rates are done more slowly, on a semiannual or yearly basis. The floating rate concept had long been used in commercial lending, and its purpose was to transfer the risk of any rapid change in interest costs to the borrower from the lender. The idea was adopted for the home loan market partly because of deregulation and increased competition in the financing

LEGAL TERMS

deed of trust
Device to collateralize a real estate loan, whereby a trust is established and the trustee holds title to the property and is at the lender's direction if there is a default.

floating interest rate
Interest rate that varies from time to time.

industry. These changes removed cheap or free funds (which had existed since the 1930s) from the banks and savings and loans (S&Ls). Because these lenders now had to compete for their funds, their prices (interest charged) had to reflect market pricing.

The change in rates brought about changes in collateral documentation as well. In a period of rising interest rates, it is to the advantage of both buyer and seller to keep the lower interest rate, but if the lender learns of a transfer, it will demand a higher rate to cover its costs. When the rates were stable, and there was a rising and expanding economy, lenders financed straight real estate sales from A to B. A slight increase in interest rates (less than 1 percent), would not severely affect the buyer. But consider the effects of the following. A buys a home when the rates are fixed at 6 percent. She holds it for 15 years. Now, the rates are 11.5 percent, or a floating rate, and during that period the price of the home has risen from $35,000 to $125,000. The cost for a year's interest on $35,000 at 6 percent is $2,100, or $175 per month. The cost of a year's interest on $125,000 at 11.5 percent is $14,375, or almost $1,200 per month. That additional $1,000 per month is an enormous amount of money for most borrowers. (Do not be too concerned about the actual calculation of these note rates; they are provided in preprinted tables that are readily available from banks, local real estate associations, and title companies.)

Technically, this situation would not be a problem if the buyers' disposable income rose as rapidly as the interest rates, or exceeded that rate of increase, but that did not happen after the 1960s. Consequently, buyers had less money to pay more expensive rates. As a result, sellers could not sell and buyers could not afford to buy. The market was drying up from high costs. One partial solution, however, was to change the loan's amortization rate and stretch out the payments over a longer time span. Thus, mortgage time spans went from 20 to 25 years to as long as 40 years. This process reduced the amount of principal paid in each installment so that the payment could be smaller and more manageable. However, the monthly rate remained very high, even without other expenses, such as insurance and taxes (generally included in home loan payments), factored in. When these factors are included, the total monthly payment might reach $1,600 per month or more. Who could afford to buy a home under these financial conditions? Most people could not. What possible remedy could be found?

A number of remedies emerged, but a common one was to make the seller a type of go-between or middleman between the lender and the buyer, so that the seller became involved in the financing and collateralization aspects of the home sale. For instance, the buyer and seller would agree on a price. The buyer would make a down payment and the seller would take a note back for the remainder. There would be three parts of this transaction. First, the agreed-upon price—$125,000. Second, the down payment—$20,000. That leaves a balance of $105,000 for financing. Third, the existing debt at 7.15 percent (with A's bank; it was originally for $35,000 but has been paid down to $25,000). When the $25,000 is removed by the buyer's taking over that obligation, the balance is for $80,000. The seller takes back a note for this amount, usually at a lower rate than the then-current rate of the institutional lender. The buyer has two obligations: the $80,000 note to the seller at 7 percent ($5,600 annual interest payments) and the $25,000 owed to the bank at 7.15 percent ($1,788 annual interest). Suppose the bank had done the financing, with the annual interest cost at 9.5 percent, on the $105,000. The raw, interest-only calculation shows an annual cost of $9,975 with a monthly interest payment of about $831. In contrast, the seller as financier made the interest cost only $7,388—a difference of $2,587 or about $216 per month in interest payments. This difference provided the means for a number of Americans to acquire homes during the 1970s and 1980s.

The documentation is worked out so that there is no public record, because title will not change hands from A to B until the $80,000 note is paid off. B pays A a monthly amount that is substantially less than B could have obtained in the financial marketplace. A pays her loan down at the bank and collects her portion of the principal and interest on the $80,000 note. Neither party is completely happy with this arrangement, however, for this situation, called a **take-back mortgage**, can be abused by both the buyer and the seller—the buyer by not paying and the seller by retaining possession of the title until the final payment is made. What if the bank ever found out? It might well have reserved the right, through its documentation of A's loan, to call the loan or force refinancing of the transaction. Actually, banks got caught by this process at first, but they revised their documentation to prohibit assignment or other transfer of loans to third parties without the banks' prior written permission. They also changed how they checked on who lived in the house and other items. There is a certain logic in the banks' position, because a take-back uses the bank's funds without the bank's permission; outside parties should not have the right to put the money of the bank and its depositors at risk without the bank having a say in the matter.

Another device that is used when standard institutional lenders are unwilling to advance funds is the **real estate installment sales contract**. This contract, like many land sales contracts, can occur with or without a financial institution being in the picture, as there are basically two possibilities. In the first situation, the seller has a mortgage, but the buyer cannot afford to pay the rates for a new mortgage through a bank. In the second situation, the seller has no mortgage, and the buyer and seller, for a variety of possible reasons, strike a deal between themselves. This financing device has much the same effect as a take-back mortgage, but it represents an installment sale of the real property and does not permit title to be transferred until after the final payment under the installment contract.

This device is a combination of a cash sale and a mortgage and is subject to a number of peculiar problems. First, because the process of buying the property may take many years, and the deed technically transferring the property will not be given until the last payment is made, the buyers may put off deciding how they want to hold the property. This issue should be decided up front because, with the length of time involved, there is an increased likelihood of one of the parties dying. The buyer also has the risk that the seller

LEGAL TERMS

take-back mortgage
Collateral document used when a seller finances the sale of the home to a buyer without a bank being involved.

real estate installment sales contract
Agreement to purchase real estate under which the payments for the purchase price, referred to as "installments," are spread over a period of time.

will sell the property a second time, fraudulently and without notice to the buyer, to an innocent third party—our bona fide purchaser for value. The land sales contract can be recorded to avoid any future purchaser from the seller being an innocent party, but what if there were an original lender who searched? This analysis involves a balancing of risks between the original creditor discovering the sale and the seller entering into a fraudulent sale with a third party. This long-term installment repayment (frequently 15 or more years) causes uncertainty and leaves the parties open to risk on both sides. At the time of this writing (1993), interest rates have dropped sufficiently that this type of financing is not as widely used today as it was when interest rates were high.

Another paperwork aspect that can have significant implications is whether the buyer has taken **subject to the mortgage** or has **assumed the mortgage**. In the former case, the sales contract with the buyer will state that the property is taken "subject to" a mortgage, meaning that the borrower is not *personally* liable to the mortgagee. The effect is that, although the mortgagee may be able to reclaim the property for nonpayment, the buyer will not be liable for any deficiency if the sale price does not match or exceed the amount of the outstanding obligation. In the latter case, the buyer executes a sales contract stating that she assumes the mortgage. In that case, she would be personally liable, because the buyer assumes or takes over the seller's contract with the lender. Tied into the lender's contract, the buyer becomes liable to the lender. In both cases, A remains responsible to the original lender.

In summary, the debt obligation expressed by the note may be new and part of the current transaction, or it may a carryover from the prior debt transaction; the funds may come directly from the seller, a bank, an S&L, or yet another financial institution. But common to all of them are (1) the note that indicates the obligation to repay the borrowing, and (2) some type of document (usually a mortgage or deed of trust) that pledges the real property as collateral for the loan in the unhappy event that the borrower cannot repay the loan within the appropriate time frame.

Mortgageable Interests

What ownership interests in real property can be mortgaged? Certainly any property that is a freehold interest, such as any property held in fee simple (including a fee interest in a condominium). But leasehold interests can also be mortgaged; though these are of little use when the real property is residential property, long-term commercial leases (that may last for decades) are often mortgaged, particularly when the value of the use of the building is substantial. The formal requirements for a leasehold mortgage document are similar to those for a deed transferring the property. In many states, the following would be minimally satisfactory: the name of the parties (the mortgagor-borrower and the mortgagee-lender); words conveying the property; identification of the debt by a specific amount; a legal description of the real property being conveyed; signature by the mortgagor; in some states, sealing and witnessing by the appropriate number of witnesses (one to three); and, in all states, acknowledgment before a notary or other appropriate public official prior to recording. In addition, if the land is within a state that uses the title theory of mortgages, the document must state the condition(s) under which the title will be lost or defeated (called a **defeasance clause**).

A problem that can exist when real estate has been transferred is the problem of the **good faith** (or *bona fide*) **purchaser for value**. This problem was discussed in chapter 4, but to review the concept, a good faith purchaser almost always takes precedence over any other party. Thus, if A sells Blackacre to B on October 1 and in consideration receives Whiteacre from B, and if B again conveys her interest in both Whiteacre and Blackacre to C for cash on October 2, and if A records on October 3, A could not recover the property from C if C had no knowledge (actual or constructive) of the fraudulent situation; if, that is, C had purchased the property in good faith. One can hope that A will find B, but, in this situation, often neither B nor C's money in B's possession can be located.

In all note assignments by a mortgagee-lender to a third party, the mortgage follows the note and is conceptually attached to the note, because the mortgage merely represents collateralization of the debt that the note represents. Once the note is negotiated, the mortgage follows the note, so that the party buying the note receives the mortgage as well. A few states still appear to use nonnegotiable notes—which does not allow transfer with the powerful protections of a holder in due course—but the modern tendency is against nonnegotiable notes. The problem that arises is the extent to which the party acquiring the note and mortgage takes subject to the mortgagor's defenses.

With note negotiability and the **holder in due course** doctrine, the party acquiring the note and mortgage generally does not take subject to the borrower's defenses. Once the mortgagee-lender has assigned the documents, it is best to notify the mortgagor-borrower of the assignment so that payments may flow easily. It should be noted that, although the Federal Trade Commission has abolished the holder in due course doctrine as it relates to the sale of consumer goods, it specifically did not abolish it in relation to the purchase and sale of real property. As a result, the consumer can assert his or her defenses against the purchaser of the paper (the holder in due course) when the property purchased is an automobile or a television set, but not if the buyers are "scammed" in a real estate sale. The rationale for this apparent disparity is that the sale of a parcel of real estate is checked out so closely (and almost always with an attorney) that a buyer is adequately protected in most cases. Frequently, however, the original mortgagee—assignor will retain a portion of the loan and do the paperwork, so that the payment continues go to the same party.

Another fair play concept with a document used to collateralize a real property loan is the **equitable mortgage**. It arises when the borrower (A) makes a loan and agrees to give a mortgage on certain real property that A owns, but after receiving the funds, A refuses to execute the mortgage and give it to the lender (B). In this case, courts would hold that B has an

LEGAL TERMS

subject to the mortgage
Phrase relating to collateral documents; refers to a third party's taking over a borrower's obligation to the lender without becoming contractually obligated to the lender.

assumption of the mortgage
When a third party takes over the obligations of the borrower to repay the loan; party assuming the debt is personally liable; compare with *subject to the mortgage.*

defeasance clause
Required clause in mortgages in title theory states that explains the conditions under which the title may be lost.

good faith purchaser for value
Legal concept to determine who, among parties with conflicting interests, has a better claim to a piece of property; a party who gives value and has no knowledge of any improprieties in a transaction has a better claim than other claiming parties.

holder in due course
Party who has special rights to be paid when in possession of an instrument (term from the law of negotiable instruments); similar to a *good faith purchaser for value.*

equitable mortgage
Court-created mortgage when a borrower, having received the funds and having agreed to give a mortgage, refuses to do so.

equitable mortgage on the property that can be enforced against A. If, however, a good faith purchaser (C) had acquired the property from A without any knowledge of the transactions between A and B, B would not be able to enforce the equitable mortgage against C's ownership of the property.

Are there any requirements that the mortgagor (who is in possession of the land) must follow? The general idea is that the mortgagor cannot do acts or omit to take actions that impair the value of the land as collateral for the debt. This approach seems very similar to the reversionary or remainder interest after a life estate, and the lender's interest in the property is conceptually similar. In that situation, a life tenant may not commit waste to the property and damage the interest of the party who will succeed to the land when the life estate ends. Thus, the mortgagor may repair the property, but is not required to do so unless the failure to repair would affect the collateral value of the property. There is nevertheless a duty to pay taxes, assessments, and other governmental obligations that would, if not paid, reduce the value of the land by the amount of the government's lien for the unpaid obligation. In most mortgage documents, these obligations are clearly stated as being the mortgagor's. If the mortgagor fails to pay these obligations, the mortgage gives the mortgagee the right to pay them and add the amount paid to the outstanding debt. Another standard mortgage clause provides that the mortgagor must insure the property to protect against losses from fire, damage from the elements, accidents, and similar risks. Like taxes and assessments, these insurance obligations may also be paid by the mortgagee, and the amounts paid may be added to the existing debt.

In most cases, the interest of the mortgagee is terminated when the debt is paid. If land is used in a cross-collateralization arrangement (an arrangement in which the property secures another debt as well as the original one for the purchase of the land), however, that piece of real property is not released as collateral; only one of the debt obligations for which the real property was pledged is removed. Once all debts for which the property has been pledged as collateral are paid, the appropriate procedure is to have the mortgagee execute the appropriate release or satisfaction forms for recording in the local real estate office.

Without recording, there would be a defect in the title (debt paid but no public record of the release form), so it is essential to make certain that the recording is done. That document may be as simple as having the lender's original of the note stamped "PAID" and its original of the mortgage stamped "SATISFIED," with the appropriate signatures on each document from the lender's officers. But it may be necessary to obtain new, formal documentation, such as a **release** (which "releases" all of the lender's claims against the property) or a **satisfaction** (which indicates that the debt owing the lender has been "satisfied" or paid) to record; other, similar documents are a **deed of reconveyance** or a **discharge**. The best way to decide which format to follow is to determine the practice your local courts approve as valid. Nevertheless, the land owner should always obtain all the documents he or she executed when incurring the debt and delivering the mortgage. Nothing should remain in the hands of the lender.

Third parties can sometimes complicate the situation. First, a third party may claim that she is an agent who represents the lender and that she is authorized to accept the payment on the lender's behalf. The risks of paying the wrong person are obvious, and anyone making such a claim should be thoroughly investigated before any money is delivered to her. It may be legitimate, but concern for one's money should make one especially cautious. Second, a third party may have been a guarantor of or surety for the loan. If the borrower became unable to pay, the lender may have called upon that party to pay the outstanding obligation. If this third party did so, she would stand in the same position as the original lender under the legal doctrine of **subrogation**. She would be entitled to an assignment transferring all of the lender's documents to her; in essence, by paying the debt, she has purchased them. Should this surety choose to do so, she may now begin enforcement proceedings to acquire the land by means of a suit in foreclosure, or take any other actions the documentation permits.

Foreclosure

Foreclosure is an action that most lenders at most times would prefer not to have to do. The court proceeding or contractually authorized process is established by the law of each state, and the statute's requirements should be noted and closely followed. The objective of foreclosure is to extinguish the rights of the debtor-mortgagor in that particular parcel of real property. The most common event of **default** that triggers foreclosure is the borrower not making the payments on the debt. The technical term for this failure to perform as agreed is a *default;* a default usually breaches both the note and mortgage contracts. Other events or failure to perform may also create a default, such as failure to pay the taxes, but courts frequently permit borrowers to **cure** their default, with the consequence that acceleration and foreclosure are stopped. By the time events require the drastic remedy of foreclosure, there is usually serious human tragedy unfolding, such as the loss of property or perhaps the loss of employment, or the breakup of a family. As a result, it may be personally difficult for the lender's officer to take the actions necessary to start the procedures for foreclosure. Many lending institutions transfer such accounts to a special operating area (often called *workouts*) that specializes in foreclosure actions to avoid this type of problem.

Suppose that a borrower, who was in default, tried to cure the default by paying the next default a month late, but then kept falling into default monthly and trying to cure it monthly for several months. Finally, the lender would begin foreclosure proceedings. The *Bryant* case discusses these real-world problems.

Clearly, most lenders would prefer to be paid on time, each and every time a payment comes due. Foreclosures are messy, costly, time-consuming, and sometimes create losses that are greater than the amount for which the property can be sold. Costs arise from the legal expenses and the amount of time that this process can require to be completed. One of the principal elements

LEGAL TERMS

release
Document given by the lender to the borrower when the loan has been fully repaid; usually recorded.

satisfaction
Document given to a borrower by a lender to indicate that the debt has been paid in full.

deed of reconveyance
Document used to release the lender's interest in the real property after the loan has been fully paid.

discharge
Document given to a borrower, after the loan has been paid in full, to show that the lender has no more interest in the property.

subrogation
Legal doctrine that permits a person to take over the rights of another; for example, to have the rights of the creditor after paying the creditor, when the debtor has not done so.

foreclosure
Court procedure for possession and sale of property that has been mortgaged or pledged for a debt that has not been paid.

default
Event that occurs when a borrower fails to live up to a promise made in the mortgage or note contract.

cure
Right to make good and repair any harm done from a borrower's default.

FEDERAL NATIONAL MORTGAGE ASSOCIATION v. BRYANT

62 Ill. App. 3d 25, 378 N.E. 2d 333, 18 Ill. Dec. 869 (1978)

MORAN, J.

Defendants Bobby Bryant and Mary Bryant appeal from an order of the circuit court of St. Clair County entering a decree of foreclosure and directing the sale of the mortgaged property. They contend that there was no showing of default in the payments under the terms of the agreement.

In October of 1968, the appellants executed a mortgage and mortgage note relating to the property in question in the amount of $6000. The Modern American Mortgage Corporation was the mortgagee under the agreement. Its interest was later assigned to the plaintiff-appellee, the Federal National Mortgage Association. The mortgage was insured under the provisions of the National Housing Act (12 U.S.C.A. 1701 et seq.). Under the terms of the agreement, payment was due on the first day of each successive month. Payments were made during the period from 1968-1975.

A total of $72 was due on January 1, 1976. The amount payable in February, due on February 1, 1976, was $94. No payment was sent during the month of January. On February 1, 1976, the appellants sent payment in the amount of $94. The check was returned on February 12 with a letter indicating that the January payment, plus a $1.44 late charge, remained due and that the February payment, plus another late charge, was also due. Similar $94 payments were made in March and April of 1976 and were returned by the Federal National Mortgage Association. In May of 1976, the foreclosure suit leading to this appeal was filed.

The parties agree that the propriety of the foreclosure decree is dependent upon a finding of default in January of 1976. Payments for the preceding eight years were timely made by the appellants. It appears from the evidence that each payment was accompanied by a payment card supplied by the mortgagee. The payments cards were designed to insure a proper crediting of the account, and were required by the mortgagee with each monthly payment. The appellant testified that he received no payment cards for January of 1976 until the 25th day of January. After receipt of the cards, payment for February was sent. The mortgagee's representative testified that the cards were issued in January for each successive February-January period. According to the appellee, the proper card for January 1976 was in the possession of the appellant from January of 1975.

The appellants' basic contention is that no default in payment occurred in January of 1976 because of the subsequent payment of an amount sufficient to cover the deficit. According to the appellant, the February payment was wrongfully rejected since it cured any default arising from the failure to pay promptly in January. Appellant contends that the contract itself requires the acceptance of the late payment. In addition, the appellant contends that a court of equity must not countenance such overreaching by a mortgagee creditor. We agree with this latter contention and reverse the trial court's order.

In support of his interpretation of the contract, the appellant notes that the agreement requires the payment of a predetermined amount of principal and interest each month. In addition to this amount, subsection (b) of the mortgage agreement requires variable payments to the mortgagee in an amount sufficient to cover the installments due for mortgage insurance premium, ground rents, fire and other hazard insurance premiums, taxes and assessments. A late charge is authorized for each payment unpaid 15 days after its due date. The failure to make a sufficient monthly payment constitutes an event of default under the mortgage. The agreement also provides:

> "If the total of the payments made by the Mortgagor under subsection (b) of the preceding paragraph shall exceed the amount of payments actually made by the Mortgagee for ground rents, taxes, and assessments, or insurance premiums, as the case may be, such excess shall be credited by the Mortgagee on subsequent payments to be made by the Mortgagor. * * *"

The appellants contend that this provision requires the acceptance of the late payment and application of the excess to the February payment. We do not agree. The provision refers only to the variable costs of insurance, taxes, and the like. It does not refer to the payment of principal and interest. Because the payments are variable, and the mortgagee may not be required to pay the entire amount collected from the mortgagor, the provision allows the mortgagee to credit the mortgagor's account instead of returning the excess. The provision is not intended to require the acceptance of late payments or to negate any of the mortgagee's rights upon default. The contract itself does not require the acceptance of late payments.

A proceeding to foreclose a mortgage is a proceeding in equity. Under long-standing equitable principles, a party seeking to invoke the aid of a court of equity must do equity. In this case, the Federal National Mortgage Association received a $94 payment on February 1, 1976. This payment was sufficient to cover the entire amount owing from January 1, 1976, including the late charge. Rather than accepting the tender of payment and crediting the excess to the amount due for February, the appellee rejected payment and demanded prompt payment for January and February. In addition, this demand included a late charge for February even though the 15-day period during which the mortgagor could pay without incurring a charge had not elapsed. We hold that the failure to accept the payment and to apply it to the amount due in January, thereby curing the default, is in violation of the principle that one who seeks equity must do equity.

This result is buttressed by those cases which hold the acceptance of partial payments by the mortgagee does not prevent the subsequent enforcement of the terms of the mortgage, including any right to foreclose upon the failure to pay the balance. Had the appellant offered to pay less than the required amount due in January, acceptance of the monies by the mortgagee would not have deprived them of the right to institute foreclosure proceedings for default. But where, as here, the late payments are sufficient to cure the default, the refusal to accept is inequitable.

Then too, under the provisions of [the Illinois statute], a defaulting mortgagor has the right to cure a default in payment by tendering the principal then due, excluding acceleration, plus costs, expenses, and reasonable attorney fees within 90 days after service of summons or prior to the entry of the foreclosure decree, whichever first occurs. Under the statute, the appellants' tender of $94 on February 1, 1976 would have cured the January default had the foreclosure suit been instituted before payment. No costs or attorney fees were incurred prior to February 1. Since the law allows a defaulting mortgagor to cure his default by payment of the principal due plus attorney fees, it is equitable that a defaulting mortgagor be permitted to cure his default by tender of the principal and interest due before suit has been filed. Since no attorney fees prior to the filing of the foreclosure suit have been claimed here, the tender need not include a reasonable amount for attorney fees. The Federal National Mortgage Association had no right to reject the February payment of $94 since this amount was sufficient to cure the January default of $73.44. Where there is no default, there is no right to institute a foreclosure proceeding.

Although neither party has directed our attention to the rules promulgated by the Department of Housing and Urban Development under the authority granted in the National Housing Act (12 U.S.C.A. 1701 *et seq.*) and subsequent amendments, an independent examination establishes a result consistent with our decision on equitable principles. Title 24 C.F.R. 203.31 provides:

> "For the purpose of this subpart, the date of default shall be considered as 30 days after—
>
> (a) The first uncorrected failure to perform any obligation under the mortgage; or
>
> (b) The first failure to make a monthly payment which subsequent payments by the mortgagor are insufficient to cover when applied to the overdue monthly payments in the order in which they became due."

Under this rule, the mortgagee has the right to correct a default in monthly payments through subsequent payments. Where subsequent payments are sufficient to cover the amount outstanding, the date of default is extended. Since the February 1 payment was sufficient to cover the amount due in January, the date of default would be extended. The same result would be reached under the HUD rules as achieved by the application of equitable principles.

Since the appellant's tender of payment on February 1 cured the January default, the plaintiff-appellee had no right to reject payment and institute foreclosure proceedings. Accordingly, the judgment of the circuit court of St. Clair County is reversed and this cause is remanded for further proceedings consistent with this opinion.

Reversed and remanded.

[Some citations omitted.]

that adds time to the process is the right of the mortgagor to have one or several opportunities to get the property back. That right is called the **right of redemption**, and it requires that the mortgagor pay off the lender for the mortgage debt and any expenses that have arisen. It does not frequently happen, but the law provides the person who is losing the property with statutory time periods during which redemption can occur. These times must elapse before the lender can obtain the clean title necessary to sell the property.

Sometimes, borrowers are willing to cooperate in the foreclosure process and thereby reduce the time period. A cooperative solution, in which the borrower sells the property on the market, is much preferable to a foreclosure action. If the procedure is hostile, however, the amount of time involved can be measured in years, not months, and over that time, only expenses are rising; no income is being realized from the funds that have been loaned. Despite the problems and drawbacks, foreclosing on the property, selling it, and applying the proceeds to the debt owed may be the only means the lender has of getting back the money that it has lent out. Any surplus received from the foreclosure sale—after the principal, interest, and expenses have been paid—would be returned to the borrower. If the funds realized from the sale of the collateral are insufficient to repay the obligation, the lender will still have an unsecured claim against the borrower. Sometimes banks will pursue this debt and levy on wages and take other actions, but many times, the amount is written off or sent to a collection agency, as the collection costs are likely to exceed the recovery.

In many states, the following foreclosure proceedings are followed. First, the debtor, by failure to pay, creates a default. The documentation always provides that default accelerates the payment of the obligations; acceleration means that, upon any default, all obligations become due and payable immediately. If this language were not in the documentation (the note and the mortgage), the lender would have to sue each time a payment was not made. An **acceleration clause** can be optional, so that the lender has the right to accelerate but is not required to, or it can be automatic. Even with automatic acceleration, however, the lender can waive the acceleration, although any waiver should be in writing. Nonpayment is the most common default that accelerates the payments, but other defaults can also bring that result. Courts, however, watch carefully for any abuse of defaults not based in the borrower's failure to pay on time.

After acceleration, the creditor-mortgagee declares the debt due and payable and notifies the borrower of that action. If the borrower fails to pay off the debt, the lender brings suit requesting the right to foreclose on and sell the specific parcel of property. Foreclosure is handled as is any other lawsuit: the defendant-borrower is given notice, there is a hearing, and a judgment is rendered. If the defendant does not respond, a default judgment may be entered against him. In either case, if a judgment is entered against the defendant, the court will order that the property be sold. If the proceeds received from this sale of the property do not cover all of the obligations involved, the lender may seek and obtain a **deficiency judgment** against the borrower to make up the difference from other funds or assets of the borrower.

The courts generally abide by the maxim that "equity abhors a forfeiture." The foreclosure process can be extremely cumbersome when there is more than one mortgagee or when more than one parcel of land is involved in the proceedings. The courts will give every borrower as much opportunity as possible to prevent the final loss of the property. For instance, there may be several types or stages of notices that must be sent out to the mortgagor or published in local papers. The court can limit the property to be sold to a single parcel among several, if the amount realized from that single parcel is adequate to repay the outstanding obligation of the mortgagee. Further, courts can review the whole process and void the sale if they find there has been a procedural mistake that may have harmed the mortgagee. Finally, the court must confirm the foreclosure sale unless there are legitimate reasons for refusing its approval.

Although the procedure described here is the most common for foreclosure, others are used in some states. Some of these are called (1) entry and

LEGAL TERMS

right of redemption
Ancient right in the law to regain property seized in satisfaction of a debt when the debt is fully paid.

acceleration clause
Provision giving the lender the right to make all payments immediately due and payable on a defaulted note.

deficiency judgment
Judgment against the borrower for any amount remaining to be paid after the collateral has been sold.

possession, whereby the mortgagee retakes possession of the property peaceably; (2) strict foreclosure, which is a limited court procedure that vests title of the property in the mortgagee; and (3) a writ of entry, which allows the mortgagee to get a court order after a hearing to permit it to retake possession.

One of the formalities of real estate lending requires that the note and the mortgage be tied together. In the *Watson* case, there was a disparity concerning the amount of interest and how it was to be paid. In addition, the borrower transferred its interest and reacquired it. Will a foreclosure be permitted, or will the note's correct statement about interest payments be accepted by the court?

WATSON v. COLLINS

21 Cal. Rptr. 832 (Ct. App. 1962)

TOBRINER, J.

In this action to foreclose a deed of trust . . ., [w]e have concluded [that as] to the substantive issue, we believe that respondents may raise the defense that their promissory note did not conform to the deed and failed to express the true nature of the obligation. Respondents' transfer of their interest in the property and subsequent re-acquisition of it did not strip them of their right to disclose the actual obligation.

On January 19, 1954, appellant and her husband, who is now deceased, entered into an agreement with Elmer and Stella Collins, intervenors and respondents (hereinafter called respondents), whereby the respondents agreed to purchase certain real and personal property owned by appellant and her husband for the total amount of $19,000. The agreement provided for a down payment of $500 and $6,000 upon delivery of the deed; the "[b]alance of $12,500.00 to be paid at $1,000.00 per year or more, *including 6% interest.*" (Emphasis added.) The terms of the promissory note for $12,500 dated January 28, 1954, which was secured by a deed of trust and a chattel mortgage, differed from the agreement, in that it stipulated "that the interest is to be paid separately and in addition to the $1,000.00 per annum." The note provided for payment of interest "at the rate of six per cent per annum, payable monthly" and payment of the principal "in annual Installments of One Thousand Dollars ($1,000.00) or more each, on the 28th day of each and every January, beginning on the 28th day of January, 1955 * * *."

Pursuant to the agreement respondents paid $1,000 per annum, including interest. In September 1957, respondents transferred their interest in the property to Guy T. and Viola Bruno (hereinafter called the Brunos), who continued to make payments in the same manner. Appellant accepted without objection these amounts, giving receipts for such payments and recording them on the back of the original note. The payments amounted to $1,000 for each year from 1954 through 1957.

Appellant first registered her discontent with the payments on March 20, 1958; her attorney sent the respondents a letter, with a copy to the Brunos, declaring the respondents "delinquent upon your note in the sum of $2,975.00." On May 26, 1958, appellant brought this action against the Brunos and four fictitious defendants to foreclose the deed of trust as a mortgage and for $11,455, the unpaid balance of the note, with accrued interest, upon the theory that, since the payments were in default, an acceleration clause became effective and the entire amount of the loan fell due. Appellant sought an adjudication that such sums become a lien on the property and that a sale be ordered.

"Subsequent to the filing of this suit," the court found, "the Brunos transferred their interest in said real property back to the intervenors" (the respondents). On October 2, 1958, appellant accepted from the respondents, who had not been included in the action as defendants, the interest payment for the period Sept 28 to Oct 28 1958.

The sheriff served Viola Bruno in Lake County on June 26, 1958, and Guy T. Bruno in Alameda County on September 3, 1958. Then, on October 8, 1958, after the Brunos had failed to answer appellant's complaint, the clerk of the court at appellant's request entered their default. At no time did appellant apply to the court for entry of default judgment against the defendant Brunos; the court entered no judgment.

On October 24, 1958, respondents noticed their motion for leave to intervene in the action upon the grounds that they owned the property as a result of its retransfer to them by the Brunos. Appellant did not oppose the motion; on November 3, 1958, the court granted it. Subsequently, respondents filed their "Answer and Complaint in Intervention" in which they claimed that the agreement of sale, executed by appellant and themselves, expressed the parties' true agreement that the total payments on the note, including interest at six per cent, were to be $1,000 per annum, but that the note executed pursuant to that contract erroneously provided for separate and additional interest payments. Respondents denied any default in payments and cross-complained for a declaration of the invalidity of the note or for its reformation to conform with the agreement of sale and for damages due to the loss of the profits of their sale to the Brunos.

Appellant did not demur to, or move to strike, respondents' pleading, but answered, denying their right to file a cross-complaint and stating that respondents "stand in the shoes of their predecessors, Guy T. Bruno and Viola Bruno, and must therefore restrict their defenses to those defenses" available to their predecessors.

After a trial on the merits the superior court rendered judgment for respondents. The court found that the parties had intended that the trustors pay $1,000 per annum including interest, that the terms of the note erroneously required interest payments separate and additional to the $1,000, that "as the parties acted upon the original agreement * * * for the five-year period, they cannot rely upon the note as evidence of the transaction," that "as the defendants, the Brunos, have transferred their interest in said real property back to the intervenors * * * the intervenors are real parties in interest and necessary parties to this suit." Appellant brings this appeal on the judgment roll; we must therefore accept as true the trial court's findings as to the parties' agreement.

Turning to the substantive issue, we do not believe that respondents' transfer of their interest in the property, followed by the Brunos' transfer of the property back to the respondents, stripped respondents of their defense to the foreclosure of the deed of trust, that is, their right to disclose the true nature of the transaction.

Appellant cannot successfully contend that "the Brunos did not have any right to raise the defense of mistake since they were not original parties to the execution of the note, and now that the Collinses [respondents] have re-purchased the property, they stand in the shoes of the Brunos and may not raise the defense of mistake." The Brunos, however, as grantees of respondents, "stood in the shoes" of respondents and could raise the defense of mistake. As the early case of Goodenow v. Ewer states, "If he [the mortgagor] has parted with the estate, his grantee stands in his shoes, and possesses the same right to contest the lien and to object to the sale." The right to reformation of an instrument is not restricted to the original parties to the transaction; for example, a purchaser from the original grantee of real property may seek reformation of the original deed because of a mistake resulting in a misdescription of the property. Section 3399 of the Civil Code provides that a contract may be reformed for various reasons "on the application of *a party aggrieved* * * *." (Emphasis added.) An aggrieved party need not be an original party to the transaction; it clearly includes one who has suffered prejudice or pecuniary loss.

Respondents acquired the interest of the Brunos, including, of course, the "right to contest the lien and to object to the sale." Indeed, respondents as the primary parties to the transaction did no more than reassume those rights and duties which they had in fact and in truth originally undertaken. Just as the transfer of the property to the Brunos did not strip the Brunos of the right to disclose the true transaction, so the retransfer of the property by the Brunos to the respondents did not strip respondents of their right to disclose the true transaction. The transfers did not diminish or destroy the transferees' right to defend against, and contest, the lien, particularly as respondents were the parties to the original transaction.

The terms of the original bargain did not change by reason of the transfers. Appellant did not acquire a new and different bargain because of the successive delegations of the rights and duties under it. To contend that appellant gained a more advantageous contract against the respondents, the very parties to the agreement, because respondents transferred and reacquired their rights and duties pursuant to it would be to ignore the principle of the decisions and to violate the basic equities.

While appellant also contends that there is not sufficient evidence to sustain the judgment, her claim fails to surmount three hurdles. First, appellant may not attack the sufficiency of the evidence in the absence of a reporter's transcript. Second, the exhibits before this court show that appellant and her husband accepted payments, without objection, in accordance with the terms of the note. Their conduct may be used to aid in the interpretation of the contract between the parties. Finally, "[s]everal contracts relating to the same matters, between the same parties, and made as parts of substantially one transaction, are to be taken together."

In essence appellant asks us here to accord to her some rather unique advantages which are supposed to fall into her lap by legal legerdemain. Although she did not object to respondents' motion to intervene, and although a full trial, in which she participated, has been concluded, she now claims upon appeal that the intervention should not have been permitted and she should now acquire a second chance to prevail at a second trial. Her inaction at the trial level is to endow her through the appellate process with the bonus of a second chance. In like manner the actual transaction into which she entered is to expand to her advantage because the other parties transferred their rights and duties pursuant to it and later re-acquired them. We know of no theory or reason why appellant should acquire these strange profits.

We affirm the judgment.

[Some citations omitted.]

7.3 THE REAL ESTATE LENDING PROCESS

To understand the process of lending, one must know something about that mysterious entity the *lender,* usually a bank or a savings and loan. As a society, we use banks continually, for a variety of services, from checking and savings accounts and getting cash to car loans and foreign currency exchange. But very few people ever understand what a bank really does. Although it has a number of functions, a bank's first job is to serve as a transferor of funds from its depositors to its borrowers. The lending institution, therefore, is an intermediary between depositors and borrowers. Depositors provide the money, and borrowers use that money for a fee called *interest.* The funds that depositors put into a bank may take a variety of forms, ranging from checking accounts to savings accounts to certificates of deposit.

The vast majority of a bank's available money is from its depositors, not its owners. Banks have had about 6 percent capital and 94 percent depositors' or borrowed funds that they owe to someone else. This is a **leverage ratio** of 12.5:1 from the debt to the worth of the business. Almost no prudent or rational bank would lend to a business with a leverage ratio of that size! Federal regulators are now insisting that the banks become less leveraged and raise their equity to 8 percent. These requirements mean that banks have to try to make more money to put into their capital accounts or have to sell more shares of the banking corporation to raise capital. This need for capital affects their lending policies, because capital is usually a more expensive form of money than borrowed money. For instance, most banks feel that they need to make at least 10 to 15 percent as a return on their equity investment; savings accounts have paid a maximum of about 6 percent to depositors. As a result, the interest rates charged the borrowers will be affected and will rise.

The lending function of banking is constantly in a dilemma. It wants to make loans—as many as it can at as high a rate as it can. Combining those two would increase the bank's profitability. The fly in the ointment, however, is when the rate is high, the risk is usually also high. When the risk is high, it means the loan may not be repaid; if the money is lost, that loss impinges directly on profitability and perhaps even on the capital of the bank itself. Consequently, banks try to make loans that can be repaid, but also try to get a high enough rate to make a good return for the bank.

The horns of the dilemma are safety versus profitability. Many of the banks and savings and loan failures in the 1980s and early 1990s occurred because the desire for high returns outweighed the sense of vulnerability to risk. With such a small amount of capital, banks have very little cushion for mistakes in lending. Their capital can be destroyed quickly if a significant number of their customers are unable to repay, for whatever reason. It need not be the borrower's fault or any malfeasance; it can simply be the problems of the economy. Thus, a bank that wants to survive must very carefully evaluate not only its individual loans, but also the balance of types of loans in its overall portfolio. This loan-type imbalance, when heavily weighted in real

LEGAL TERMS

leverage ratio
Ratio between debt and net worth (term from financing); the higher the proportion of debt, the greater the leverage.

estate or energy loans, for instance, caused immense banking problems for the Texas banks in the 1980s, when those two lending areas collapsed. Consequently, the highly leveraged position of banks leaves them in a position similar to a tightrope walker with a very small safety net beneath him. These twin elements of high return and safety are in the mind of every banker—particularly these days—whenever someone comes into the bank to apply for a loan.

This applicant, to be successful, needs to bring into the bank a number of information items. First, there should be a completed (and accurate) loan application—on the bank's own form, not that of a competitor's. This application usually consists of a financial history, if it is in the form of a personal financial statement. If the property to be purchased is to be used as a residence, the purpose of the loan is clear, but if the land is for a business or commercial purpose, the land's use and economic benefit should be clearly and fully explained, with projections and supporting financial documents.

Second, there should be information about the parcel of real estate that the applicant wants to buy. Where is it? Is there an appraisal? If so, how old, by whom, and what qualifications does the appraiser have? Is that appraised value realistic? Is there a survey? Has a recent title search determined outside claims, such as other creditor's liens or any delinquent taxes? Starting with this information, and other information about the business or individual uses that the lender may develop, the lending process begins, so that the lender may determine the potential risk and profitability of this lending opportunity. Various analysis tools are used to determine the prospects for the continuing availability of funds to repay the loan (often called availability of **cash flow**). The bank also identifies any government regulations covering this type of real estate loan and gives the applicant any required notices or statements. (More on this topic later.)

The availability of bank funds to make this loan is considered. At this point, it is necessary to understand that banks can be **loaned up**, that is, they can lack funds to make loans. Or, there may be other, different funding reasons to reject a loan application.

Perhaps the bank currently has a sufficient number of loans of this type in its loan portfolio, and to make more loans of this kind would be imprudent because it would cause an overly risky loan concentration. The thinking is that the more diversified a loan portfolio is, generally, the more likely it is that the lender's risk will be lessened. This prudent approach identifies risks and avoids imbalances such as the Texas banks had (discussed earlier). Exceeding reasonable proportions for various types of loans, such as commercial real estate, home loans, auto loans, commercial loans, or credit card loans, makes the lender very vulnerable if that particular area is suddenly hit with a downturn. Because real estate is particularly subject to downturns in the overall economy, many lenders are especially careful about making commercial real estate loans.

In addition, there is the problem of industries with local plants. What happens to the home loans that the bank has made to MegaCorp employees when MegaCorp closes its local plant? If the bank made a lot of those loans, or concentrated on them to make money, the risk to its portfolio and its overall security would rise significantly when that plant closed. (Bank examiners, boards of directors, and federal regulators particularly—and vocally—dislike such risks.) An inappropriate concentration is always a concern to lenders, as most financial institutions operate with very thin margins of equity, as previously discussed. As a result, if the type of loan being requested would push the bank into too high a concentration of funds in that area, the lender may reject the loan.

Another reason, aside from the inherent creditworthiness of the borrower, that could lead to rejection of the application is the loan's encountering some legal impediment. For example, in the past, usury limits were a concern, but since the early 1980s, the limits have either been lifted in most states; been irrelevant, because interest rates were low; or been avoidable in other ways. As a result, **usury** (the charging of an illegally high rate of interest) is not generally a problem in lending today.

There is also an attempt to force banks to lend within their communities to support those communities and prevent their deterioration. These rules are generally expressed in the Federal Reserve Board's Regulation C (deriving from the Community Reinvestment Act). During the 1980s, Regulation C was not enforced very strongly, but in the early 1990s, Congress began pushing for increased implementation.

Government Regulations

The most important government regulation of real estate lending occurs in the area of consumer real estate lending. These regulations come from several different government sources, but their general purposes are (1) to promote competition among lenders by making information, particularly information about interest rates, available to the prospective borrower; and (2) to prevent any kind of fraudulent activity or misstatement concerning any of the financial arrangements. The two most famous and important of these regulations are the Consumer Credit Protection Act, commonly known as **Truth in Lending** and often abbreviated as TIL, which is enforced as the Federal Reserve Board's Regulation Z, and the Real Estate Settlement Procedures Act, commonly known by its acronym, RESPA, enforced as Regulation K. The former regulates accuracy of lender information provided to the borrower, while the latter covers the information format of real estate closings. Nevertheless, many other federal regulations also apply to bank real estate lending. A partial list includes the Fair Housing Act, the Home Mortgage Disclosure Act, the Flood Disaster and Insurance Acts, Equal Credit Opportunity Act (Regulation B), and the Community Reinvestment Act. The Fair Housing, Equal Credit Opportunity, Home Mortgage Disclosure, and Community Reinvestment (Regulation C) Acts are in the nature of civil rights acts, to protect special groups against discrimination in lending practices; the others are in the nature of consumer protection acts including RESPA and Truth in Lending.

LEGAL TERMS

cash flow
Process of obtaining and using cash so that there is a sufficient amount to meet current obligations as they come due; usually used to refer to a business.

loaned up
Banking phrase referring to the bank's inability to lend more money because it lacks funds or is unable, by policy, to make more loans of a particular type.

usury
Originally referred to charging interest in any amount, which was forbidden; later, prohibition related to how high a rate a lender could charge— in short, a legal interest rate cap; now limited in its effects, but still applicable in many consumer transactions.

Truth in Lending (TIL)
Federal act requiring various disclosures by lenders to borrowers, so that borrowers will understand the terms of their agreements and can do competitive price shopping.

Congress passed Truth in Lending during the 1960s to ensure that there were competitive rates between various lenders and to be certain that consumer borrowers were aware of alternative financing possibilities in clear, unambiguous terms that they could understand. Truth-in-Lending does not control interest rates. Rather, it controls the provision of information about bank interest rates, programs, and services. Congress intended that consumers be given information so that they could shop for the best interest rates and overall fee costs. Because banks had developed practices over the centuries which were clear to them, but unclear to the general public or the consumer (an early example of a bureaucracy talking to itself instead of those to whom it relates and serves), much of what banks told consumers before Truth in Lending was accurate but not communicative. For instance, banks would quote an interest rate, say 8 percent, and would say that that rate was on a 360-day basis. What did that mean? Is that 8 percent or not? Not quite. The regular, straight, 8-percent interest rate would be on a 365-day basis. Thus, on every $1,000 borrowed, a 360-day year would cost the borrower $81.11, as opposed to the $80 it would regularly cost on a 365-day basis. (Incidentally, the reason for the 360-day rate was that most clerks in 19-century banks were not too good at calculating interest; they made a lot more mistakes when they had to do three transactions (dividing by a 3, a 6, and a 5) instead of two (a 3 and a 6). For example, $5,475 is lent at 6.75% interest for 247 days. The calculation formula is $\$5{,}475 \times .0675 \times 247 \div 365 = \$250.09$, but a lot of mistakes can be avoided if the clerk does not have to divide by the 5 in 365.)

Consumers were not being cheated, but the appearances were not positive for the industry. Truth in Lending did not forbid calculation of interest on a 360-day basis; it simply said that the calculation had to be disclosed to the prospective borrower in terms the borrower could understand. The law requires that all the financing terms of the contract be disclosed in language that the borrower can understand and in type the size and darkness of which makes clear the importance of its contents. In essence, the law requires that the finance charges and interest rates be calculated on the basis of an **annual percentage rate (APR)** and disclosed uniformly. Despite the fact that the price of most real estate exceeds $25,000 (the TIL cut-off amount), to avoid clerical errors in judgment (to decide when the law applies is not a clerical function), most banks comply with TIL's disclosure requirements in *all* cases involving consumers.

The importance of this regulation is (1) to understand the rights of the borrower that your law firm may be representing, and (2) to make sure, if you are working for a real estate business, that the realtor is not within the definition of the term *creditor* under the Act. Generally, realtors are not covered because they are not direct lenders, but those who arrange for credit are also included in the definition of *creditor.* Usually, however, the broker, realtor, or real estate operative must meet two tests before coming within the scope of the TIL Act: the broker (1) must have knowledge of the credit terms and (2) must prepare or help to prepare the loan documents. Requirement number two is usually not met and must be guarded against. For the lender, however, disclosure of rate, time, amount of interest charged, options, and other items is essential. Truth in Lending (Federal Reserve Board Regulation Z) also requires that a lender give the borrower notice of her **right of rescission**. This right permits the borrower to cancel the loan transaction within three business days when the borrower's home is used as collateral for the loan and the loan is a refinancing or a second mortgage. Exemptions from Regulation Z's coverage include business, commercial, agricultural, or organizational credits, credit exceeding $25,000 and not secured by real estate or a dwelling, credit to a public utility, or a security or commodities account, or a home fuel budget plan.

A 1987 revision to Truth in Lending provided new rules about disclosure in relation to variable or adjustable rate mortgages (ARMs). These were a new lending device (on which more in § 7.4) through which banks could adjust the interest rate that they charged on loans which had mortgages collateralizing repayment of the note. The old common law had required "a sum certain" in the mortgage note for the note to be a negotiable instrument. Until the legislatures changed that provision, adjustable rates were illegal in some states, and would create nonnegotiable instruments in others—or both. With legislative change, however, a whole new set of devices and required disclosures occurred. The ARM disclosure rules require that all the disclosures be made when the first of two events occurred: (1) when the creditor received a nonrefundable fee, or (2) when the creditor gave the prospective borrower an application. This disclosure package requires that the creditor tell the consumer the terms of each ARM that it offers to prospective customers and that the creditor give the consumer a handbook explaining what ARMs are and how they work.

The **Real Estate Settlement Procedures Act (RESPA)** has a complementary purpose to Truth in Lending. Its goals were originally to reduce the cost of borrowing for the purchase of real estate, by preventing kickbacks and referral fees; to enhance competitive shopping for credit; and to encourage home ownership. Practically, however, it has served primarily to require clearer disclosure of the processes and terms involved in a real estate closing. RESPA's coverage is not as broad as Truth in Lending's, because it relates only to mortgage loans that are related to the federal government. In practice, this means that all lenders are covered because all banks are all insured by the federal government; furthermore, many loans involve a federal government agency, such as the VA or the FHA. As a result, the RESPA closing statement has become a national standard for closing statements that is used all over America and avoids confusion between the local terms and usages of different areas.

RESPA's requirements are triggered when any of the following occurs:

1. There is a legal transfer of real property from one party to another
2. The lender takes a first lien on the transferred property
3. The building is or will be a one- to four-family structure or the vacant lot will have such a building.

LEGAL TERMS

annual percentage rate (APR)
Actual interest rate on a loan covered by Regulation Z; disclosure is federally mandated.

right of rescission
Federally granted right to those who place second mortgages on their homes; the right exists for three days and permits the prospective borrower to rescind the transaction.

Real Estate Settlement Procedures Act (RESPA)
Federal statute setting the rules for disclosures that must be made to home buyers at closing.

Note that condos and cooperatives are included if they are in the one- to four-family building limit. RESPA has a broader impact than some other federal regulations because it does not exclude business purposes, have a dollar limit, or apply only to owner-occupied property. It is not applicable if (1) the land is over 25 acres, (2) the loan is a home improvement loan, (3) the land is a vacant lot if the lot will not be part of a home building transaction, and so on (five more).

RESPA requires the following. First, the lender must provide the borrower with a good faith estimate of the settlement costs within three business days of receiving the written application. Second, a booklet outlining the settlement procedures as prescribed by the government must be provided. Third, a Uniform Settlement Statement must be provided to the borrower, the seller, or their agents no later than the day prior to the day of settlement. This statement provides a detailed itemization of the charges and expenses involved in the closing, and must be used even if the person doing the settling is not a lender. Because the federal government has the power to interpret and revise the regulations when such is deemed necessary, constant change is possible, and all parties involved in the real estate business should be alert to that possibility.

The Fair Housing Act is designed to prevent any discrimination in home lending based on race, color, sex, national origin, or religion. The type of property covered is one- to four-unit buildings, mobile homes if both the land and mobile home are taken, and vacant land when the prospective borrower intends to build on it. Under this statute, "block busting," "steering," and "red lining" are prohibited practices in the showing and sale of homes and real property. **Block busting** is trying to get everyone on a block to move all at once and sell cheaply, usually because an influx of different people is moving into the area. **Steering** is directing people who come to the bank or the realtor to some areas but not to others; it is an informal maintenance of patterns of segregation. **Redlining** is the practice of drawing lines on a map (traditionally in red, thus the name) around an area to identify it as an area in which a bank will not lend or a realtor sell.

Another antidiscrimination act is the Equal Credit Opportunity Act (ECOA). Although it is not specifically related to real estate, ECOA's coverage is so broad that it applies to real estate lending as well. No lender may discriminate against a borrower on any of the following bases: race, color, religion, national origin, sex, marital status, age, the borrower's being a recipient of public assistance, or the prospective borrower's exercise of any of these rights under the Consumer Credit Protection Act or any similar law.

The federal government enacted Regulation C under the Home Mortgage Disclosure Act to ensure that banks do not engage in discriminatory practices and to ensure, under the Community Reinvestment Act, that lending institutions work in their communities to ensure that the local community is receiving funds necessary to maintain a healthy real estate market. Under these acts, lenders must provide the government with various statements and information demonstrating that they are not engaging in any discriminatory home lending practices.

Another piece of federal legislation that could be important in a consumer or commercial real estate transaction is the Flood Insurance Act. This act requires that if the real property lies in a flood plain, the bank ensure that the applicant knows about the flood risk and knows how to get insurance to cover that risk. Prohibitions against making loans in areas without insurance exist. The Flood Insurance Act allows insurance to cover not only the building, but to some extent, the contents as well, and is generally considered cheaper than regular insurance, but its coverage has limits. Outsiders may learn more by contacting a local bank or the Federal Emergency Management Agency (FEMA). FEMA has offices in most major metropolitan centers.

Although a detailed knowledge of these federal statutes is not essential in this course, awareness that they exist and may apply to your situation is the key to being able to use them effectively for the client that your law office is representing. Congress has decided that these are the rules of the real estate lending game with which lenders must comply. As you will be dealing with banks in many ways, it is hoped that this information will help you understand their position and the basics of the rules under which they operate. This way you will know what they live with, what shapes their attitudes, and what makes it more likely (or unlikely) that your client's loan will be approved.

7.4 ALTERNATIVE LENDING DEVICES

As regulatory policies and economic conditions changed, the real estate lending industry created new devices to deal with the changes. A number of these new formats are discussed in this section, but the most common is the **adjustable rate mortgage (ARM)**. In 1982, the federal government passed legislation permitting home lenders to charge an interest rate that varies during the time of the loan. Prior to this time, only fixed interest rate mortgages were allowed. Any ARM lender can lend at fluctuating interest rates, but the interest rate change has to be based on a generally recognized index.

This index may be based on some standard, generally recognized cost of money, such as the Federal Funds Rate (a published rate which banks charge one another for overnight borrowing) or the Treasury auctions of U.S. notes, bills, or bonds. Indeed, one of the most popular bases has been an average over a period of time of the "T Bill" auction. Thus, the base interest rate moves with changes in the cost of money, whether up or down. The lender also charges an increment of 2 or more percentage points above that base. For instance, if the base were at 6.5 percent and the increment were 2.5 percent, the borrower would pay 9 percent interest on the money outstanding during the period that this rate was in effect. Remember, though, that this rate can change as money costs change.

Despite changes in the actual interest rate, the lender's increment, often called the **margin**, usually remains fixed, frequently somewhere between 2 and 3 percentage points. The period when the lender may or is required to change that base is called an **adjustment period**, and the mortgage must specify what the adjustment period is. It could be a day, a week, a month, a year, or

LEGAL TERMS

block busting
Attempt by realtors or lenders to force an entire neighborhood to move at once, thus lowering the prices; usually done when the neighborhood is changing racially.

steering
Forbidden practice whereby real estate agents directed prospective home buyers only into certain areas and not into others.

redlining
Lending practice that involved drawing a red line around an area on a map and refusing to lend within that area; now forbidden by federal statute.

adjustable rate mortgage (ARM) (also called variable rate mortgage (VRM), renegotiable rate mortgage, and rollover mortgage)
Mortgage under which the interest rate on the note may change from time to time.

margin
On an adjustable rate loan, the amount fixed in excess of the base rate, such as prime plus 2.5 percent; the 2.5 percent is the margin.

adjustment period
Time period when the lender must change the base rate in an ARM.

any named and agreed upon period. Most ARMs, however, have an adjustment period of one year and so are called one-year ARMs. If it were for six months, it would be a six-month ARM. The adjustment period, however, may be as long as three to five years. These changes in the base occur by following the movement in the markets; they go up or down as a function of the changes in the market base to which the index is tied.

There are numerous other names for arrangements in which the interest rate is not fixed. Some of these terms are **variable rate mortgages (VRMs), renegotiable rate mortgages (RRMs)**, and **rollover mortgages (ROMs)**. Basically, these terms all imply that the interest rate will change during the time period of the mortgage, and the variable rate passes on to the borrower the risk of those changes. The principal risk of adjustable rate mortgages is simple: upward changes in the interest rate may make it difficult for the borrower to come up with the additional cash to fund that increase. As a result, the borrower may become cash-poor—forced to sell the home, under the most pressing circumstances, or required to engage in expensive refinancing that stretches out the term of the loan and increases the refinancing fees. The variable rate mortgage is a commercial device and is the standard business loan arrangement most banks use, most commonly when in lending to the construction loan industry. It is usually tied to a prime rate, often the bank's own or a published one; has no limits on interest changes; and is usually expressed as "prime plus X" (whatever the increment beyond prime is set at).

The rollover mortgage (ROM) is also sometimes called a **balloon mortgage**, because these two devices work in much the same way. The rollover simply has a fixed interest rate, with the loan amortized on a normal schedule, say 30 years. But the agreement is that after a fixed period of time, usually three to five years, the interest rate on the loan will be rolled over or adjusted to meet the then-current conditions and expectations for the next three to five years. The balloon loan involves the same type of situation, where the rate is fixed for a period of time and principal payments are set on the basis of a long-term amortization. However, at the end of an agreed-upon period of time, say two to five years, the total principal amount becomes due and payable. The loan is spoken of as "rolling over into the new loan," or the note is said to have a balloon on the end of it so that all the principal is due at one time rather than over the entire (30-year) period of potential amortization.

This process of adjusting the principal payments has its limits, though, because most loans cannot be extended beyond a period of 40 years, according to government regulations. Nor would most Americans care to have a 100-year mortgage, as is becoming more common for Tokyo's home and condominium buyers. In Japan, the property and the mortgage are passed on as part of the family's possessions and obligations.

Although fixed rate mortgages are no longer favored among real estate lenders, it is clear that they will continue to be made when the customer can require it, when the customer is willing to pay a premium, or when the lender believes it is in its interest to arrange borrowing in that manner. Generally, however, most lenders make adjustable rate home mortgage loans most frequently.

An unexpected benefit to many borrowers in late 1991 and early 1992, as American interest rates plunged to their lowest rates in a generation, was the refinancing of many adjustable rate mortgages, so that the starting point of the base could be lowered, the rate-lowering process could be speeded up, or the rate floor that some loans had could be eliminated. The refinancing occurred with other lenders competitively seeking business or with the borrowers current lender seeking to keep its current business. Refinancing involves extensive paperwork, because every ARM program is considered a separate one for disclosure purposes by the federal government, and the information concerning each one must be printed and delivered to the applicant within the specified time period. The differences between one's present loan and the prospective ARM should be examined carefully and understood fully before one makes any final decision on borrowing or refinancing. Comparative costs and cash flows should be examined.

It is very useful to determine what the principal elements of difference are among ARMs. Some of the more important ones include:

1. How often does the interest rate change?
2. What index is this rate tied to?
3. Is there a cap (also called a *ceiling*) or a floor on the rate? In other words, is there a maximum beyond which the rate cannot increase and a minimum below which it cannot decrease?
4. When the rate changes, what exactly changes? Is it the amount of the payment, the length of the loan, or the amount of the loan's principal?
5. How much notice must the borrower receive before the rate can be changed?
6. Is there a refinancing fee when the rates change?
7. How long is the loan?
8. What happens if the interest rate changes go so high that the amount being charged exceeds the amount agreed to be paid?
9. Is it likely that this mortgage loan will be sold in the secondary market?
10. Is a fixed rate loan available? How do you calculate the loans' comparative merits? (Note: This latter topic is beyond the scope of this discussion.)
11. How long does the borrower intend to keep the loan?
12. Is the lender required to lower the interest rate if the index declines? If so, when and by how much? Lenders will not want to be burdened with the paperwork for minor changes; further, some lenders use language making declines in the charged rate their option. Competition in metropolitan areas reduces this risk, however.
13. Finally, for the refinancing, what will be saved by refinancing when the new costs and fees are figured against the actual saving in interest payments?

This new world of variable rates has caused some strange results to emerge. One of these is the **negative amortization** process. **Amortization** is the reduction of the principal of the loan; negative amortization is an *increase* in the principal of the loan. It occurs when the borrower signs a variable rate mortgage note requiring that the payments be applied first to interest

LEGAL TERMS

balloon mortgage
Mortgage for which the note has an installment payment schedule wherein one payment exceeds the others by at least 10 percent—usually by much more.

negative amortization
Situation in which the repayment does not reduce the principal, but actually increases the principal owed.

amortization
(1) Gradual payment of a debt by regular payments in a fixed amount over a fixed period of time.
(2) Depreciation of an asset over the period of its useful life (or other acceptable period of time) to establish its value at any given point in time.

and then to principal. If interest rates, following the market, rise rapidly, the amount that should be paid as interest may equal or exceed the amount of the fixed total payment. When the interest payment matches the fixed payment, there can be no principal payment, so the principal remains unpaid (and that keeps the interest high). When the interest due exceeds the amount of the fixed payment, not only is the principal not paid, but the additional amount due as interest (but unpaid because of the fixed payment) is added onto the principal of the mortgage. This situation is a bad one for both the borrower and the lender. The borrower is endlessly burdened with more debt than she can handle, and the lender has more money committed than it intended, with the additional risk of default made more likely by the extra debt burden.

The risk here is that the equity that every homeowner wants to build up can be decreased rather than increased. One should be extremely careful about permitting any client to enter into a mortgage loan agreement that has a negative amortization clause. The lender can also run a risk of violating any usury laws in the state (absent some federal exemption) because, in essence, the unpaid interest becomes part of the principal debt and the borrower ends up paying interest on interest. Attorneys will want to determine local law with respect to this type of real estate loan. Many states have a public policy against charging interest on interest, but some states exempt these new mortgage financing devices.

The borrower can be protected against both negative amortization and an excessive cash flow burden by a clause that places a maximum or *cap* on the amount that will be charged or a maximum on the amount that the interest rate is permitted to rise. In other words, one can protect the borrower either by fixing the maximum rate charged during the life of the loan (e.g., percent) or by capping the amount of interest increase that is permitted (say 6 percent from 8 percent to a maximum of 14 percent). But this sort of cap is only one of two types of caps. This kind limits the total amount of interest charged; there may also be a limit on how much the rate can increase between one adjustment period and the next one. If this amount does not cover the lenders costs, the lender usually reserves the right to recoup its lost revenues during the next period, so long as the adjustment stays below both types of agreed-upon caps. Another cap could limit the amount of payment (in dollars) from one adjustment period to the next (as opposed to a cap on the rate increase from one period to the next).

Another type of mortgage arrangement is called the **graduated payment mortgage (GPM)**. This approach has long been used in the commercial lending field, but has come to the home mortgage area only recently. In either case, its basic goal is to provide some breathing room for the borrower from the costs of financing the business or purchasing the home. The idea is that with less cash flow required at the beginning to cover the payments, the borrower will be able to operate more successfully. As the borrower becomes stronger financially, whether as a business or older and in a better-paying job as an individual, the lender anticipates the capacity to pay a greater portion of the principal back. In essence, the borrower pays the interest on the outstanding balance at all times, but the principal payments increase in steps through time. For instance, in year

1 there might be a principal moratorium, with no payments being required. In year 2, the principal payments might be $400 per month; in years 3 to 5, it might be $650 per month; and so on, until the agreed-upon maximum principal payment amount is reached. This process provides lower payments early, higher ones later on, and an overall larger amount of interest paid (which can be considered as a fee for the borrower getting the deal in the first place). In some of these arrangements, negative amortization can occur when the initial payments do not match the amount of interest accrued during the payment period. It is wise to avoid this result if possible, as a homeowner, but for a speculator there could be advantages in terms of amount of capital to be invested.

Within the last five years, senior citizens have begun to use a type of real estate loan called a **reverse annuity mortgage**. This sort of mortgage is designed to help cash-poor-but-home-equity-rich seniors by letting them use the equity in their homes as a means of providing them with cash flow for living expenses. The lender makes a loan on the home equity, takes the proceeds, and purchases an annuity; then the interest is paid out of the monthly annuity and the remainder is provided to the borrower for consumption purposes. Another variant on this approach has been to allow the borrower to pay only the interest due on the loan while keeping the proceeds in an account at the lenders institution. Any principal repayment is made when the estate of the decedent-borrower is settled.

Shared appreciation mortgages (SAMs) have also been used in the last few years to help spread risk. SAMs are a gamble by the lender that the equity in the home will grow during the period of the loan. Historically, this approach to American real estate has a legitimate basis, but its effects in the short term can be risky. During the 1970s and early 1980s, the increase in the sale price of homes rose faster than the general rate of inflation in the Consumer Price Index. Nevertheless, the inflation rate created a risk for lenders, because lenders were being repaid in funds that were worth less than they had been when they were originally loaned out. To recover this risk, the long-term, permanent lenders (often to developers and owners of commercial property, although the SAM has had minimal use with residential real estate as well) devised various ways to get at this increased equity in the appreciated value of the property. One of these devices is the SAM. The lender may take an outright ownership interest in the property, or it may make an arrangement with the borrower whereby the borrower pays a percentage of the appreciated value of the property above a certain dollar value; for example, 25 percent of any amount over the value of $195,000 at year end, 19___. In the later 1980s and early 1990s, however, the SAMs benefits became less obvious, as the prices of parcels of real estate dropped and the rapid price rises ended. Recession, insufficient cash flow among the borrowers, and high prices in general diminished the usefulness of the SAM.

A device seeking the same result is the **convertible mortgage**. This device is designed to permit the lender to convert its loan into a certain fixed equity position on or before some specified date in the future, when the lender decides its interest is best served by doing so. This term, *convertible mortgage,* is also used in a different way in the area of residential home lending:

LEGAL TERMS

graduated payment mortgage (GPM)
Principal payment arrangement in which the payments in the beginning are less than those later on; a gradually increasing principal repayment schedule.

reverse annuity mortgage
Device used to draw on the equity of a home for living expenses; often involves the purchase of an annuity.

shared appreciation mortgage (SAM)
Lending device whereby the lender has the right to acquire an equity interest in the real estate project on certain terms by a certain time; used to counter the effects of inflation.

convertible mortgage
(1) Mortgage under which the lender may convert its loan position into an equity position. (2) Mortgage under which borrower may convert its adjustable rate mortgage into a fixed rate mortgage.

there, it means that a home buyer has the right to convert his adjustable rate mortgage into a fixed rate mortgage.

Another problem arose in the late 1970s. What could the lender do, when the borrower wanted to sell the home, to prevent her from selling it to an unqualified third party? Lenders have long had clauses in their documentation saying that the property could not be sold without the prior written permission of the lender, on pain of having the entire debt accelerated and becoming due and payable immediately. This is called a **due on sale clause**. Its original purpose was to prevent the buyer from selling the property to a party who was not creditworthy, that is, one who lacked the financial capacity to repay the loan as agreed. The clause was used primarily by the savings and loan industry, rather than by banks or insurance companies. But until the 1970s, there was little need for it, because most persons wanting to purchase a home could qualify. When inflation rose rapidly and interest rates skyrocketed in the late 1970s and early 1980s, however, the pool of qualified buyers who could afford the purchase of new homes shrank. This situation was due to two factors: (1) the interest rates were so high that they absorbed a large amount of cash flow, and (2) the prices of homes were driven up by inflation, so that the base on which the interest rate was charged increased significantly.

Thus, the homeowner who retired, wanted her equity out of the home, or whose business transferred her to a new location found herself in a serious dilemma. Because the lending industry wanted qualified buyers who would repay their home loans on time, and the owners wanted to transfer their equity out of the homes, a conflict over due on sale clauses arose. Lenders tried to enforce them and to some degree were successful, although a number of states prohibited it. Homeowners took to using "creative financing" to avoid them. For instance, a home seller might sell only his equity to the buyer. The seller still remains responsible for the original loan, but the buyer pays the amount of the old mortgage plus the new, second mortgage for the seller's equity. Then the seller continues to repay the lender—and how would the lender ever know? The lender could check to see who the occupant is; it could check a changed address for its customer, or it could check the insurance coverage and determine who the named insured was. All of these were done, and litigation flourished.

Finally, the federal government stepped in, and Congress passed the Garn-St. Germain Act in 1982. It permitted the due on sale clause but limited the number of events that could trigger it. The problem now has been resolved legally, and its causes have been partially ameliorated because the high interest rates have declined significantly, but the high prices have remained. Nevertheless, this experience has left a residual bitterness between lenders and borrowers, and both sides have shown a willingness to litigate and seek ways around the other parties' legitimate concerns.

Another aspect of real estate lending is the **second mortgage**. Today, this device is often known as the **home equity loan**, but it has been around for a long time and has been used in a number of ways. Its basic premise is that the homeowner has a piece of property in which she has built up equity beyond what is needed to pay off the original, purchase mortgage. Having equity in excess of the mortgage note payoff amount means that if the home owner had to sell the home, she would receive more money from the sale than necessary to pay off the mortgage. Now, the question arises: What to do with this "money" that is just sitting there not earning any interest? This equity "money" could be used for a variety of things if the homeowner were to borrow it and invest it elsewhere. Lenders have successfully been offering blandishments to get homeowners to borrow based on their home equity since the early 1980s. When a loan is made on property that already has an existing loan on it, the second loan is referred to as a *second mortgage.* Because this second mortgage is usually second in time, this lender is not able to collect until the first lender had been fully repaid.

This situation creates an additional risk, but the second lender is protected, first, by the percentage of advance against the equity that it would make (it might only advance 50 percent of the equity remaining after the first loan had been fully covered). For instance, a home is worth $125,000 and the first mortgage is at $50,000. That leaves $75,000 of equity, and 50 percent of that amount is $37,500; the second-mortgage lender commits to no more than $37,500. Second, home equity lenders are further protected by charging higher interest rates. Third, the lender can make careful credit checks on the ability of the borrower's cash flow to support the second mortgage payments in addition to the first mortgage payments and any other debt.

A fourth device also often protects the lender, because the amount of time permitted to repay the second mortgage is shorter—5, 7, or 10 years rather than the usual first mortgage repayment term of 15 to 30 years. Nevertheless, the second lender always runs risks greater than the original lender, because it will be paid after the first lender. The second lender often tries to avoid those problems by including a number of protective clauses in its documentation to give it information and rights (such as having the borrower agree that it will always pay the first lender and that if the borrower does not make that required payment, the second lender may add the payments onto its mortgage). Some first lenders dislike second lending situations so much that they include documentation terms either forbidding second mortgages or making the first mortgage due and payable if a second mortgage is filed.

Although many legitimate lenders make second mortgages, there are some whose reputation is somewhat unsavory, and some lenders' use of second mortgages has aroused considerable ethical concern. The latter has been evidenced by the attempt to take a second mortgage to secure a consumer goods loan for furniture or a motor vehicle.

Sometimes, it may be more advantageous to rework the lending arrangement in a different way. Beginning in commercial transactions, a new second mortgage device, called the **wraparound mortgage**, was created. Its purpose is to achieve a higher rate of interest for the second lender. Creative lending ingenuity led to the following arrangement. A borrows $2.5 million from Bank One for a commercial real estate project. The interest rate at the time is 8.5 percent. Several years pass and the project is operating well. The value of the property has risen to $4.5 million while the mortgage has been

LEGAL TERMS

due on sale clause
Clause in a mortgage or accompanying note that requires the note to be fully due and payable if the borrower sells the property.

second mortgage
Junior mortgage standing behind the first mortgage in terms (1) of being repaid and (2) of access to the collateral; mortgage that became second because it was recorded after the first mortgage.

home equity loan
Loan made against the value in the home that exceeds the amount necessary to pay off the mortgage loans.

wraparound mortgage
Complex lending device used on a refinancing to achieve a higher rate of interest for the second lender; second lender pays the first lender out of what it receives from the borrower.

paid down to $1.8 million; thus, there is $2.7 million in equity. A wants to borrow $2.2 million more and goes to Bank Two. Interest rates are now 12 percent. It would be possible to pay off the loan to Bank One, but instead Bank Two gives a new loan for $4 million (the entire amount) at 12 percent, and only lends A the additional $2.2 million. A, however, pays 12 percent on the entire amount outstanding ($4 million). Bank Two pays Bank One its principal and interest, but it keeps the additional 4 percent on the first $1.8 million as well as the 12 percent on the remaining $2.2 million. This arrangement makes no difference to the borrower, who will be paying 12 percent anyway on the entire amount, but Bank Two can increase its interest yield from 12 percent to about 15.25 percent.

There are risks to Bank Two in this process, by which it attempts to avoid by paying Bank One and becoming subrogated to its first lien rights. *Subrogation* is the legal theory that if I do something that benefits you (like paying back your bank loan), I should be able to stand in the bank's shoes against the claims of third parties. This technique permits both parties to benefit, because the borrower frequently has lower refinancing costs and the lender obtains a higher rate of interest than would otherwise be available. There can also be usury problems with this technique, particularly with residential loans, because they are made to consumers who are usually given favored treatment over most others.

Notes frequently have two parts: a promise to repay the borrowed money along with a statement of the basis of interest calculation, and a statement about the property being used as collateral and a method of tying the note into the collateral. Both elements are essential for the creditor and need equally careful consideration. Each is covered in this list.

7.5 PREPARATION OF A NOTE

I. Who are the parties to the note?
   A. Maker (borrower, debtor); party who signs the note.
   B. Payee (lender, creditor) or holder.

II. How much is the note for (the amount of the note)? Be sure to match the written and numerical amounts.

III. What rate of interest does the note bear?
   A. A fixed rate?
   B. An adjustable rate?
      1. Specify the basis for the changes—the bank's own prime rate, the prime rate as announced in the Wall Street Journal from time to time, the average T-Bill rate for the past three months, etc.
      2. How often will the rate be adjusted (daily, monthly, annually)?
      3. Specify any floor or ceiling in the rate structure.

IV. Payments
   A. Where and when are the payments to be made?

B. How much is each payment?

V. Does the borrower have prepayment rights?
   A. In whole or in part at any time?
   B. In whole or in part after reasonable notice to lender?
   C. No prepayment permitted?
   D. No prepayment allowed for (specific time period)?
   E. Prepayment permitted only with prepayment fee?
   F. No prepayment within a certain time period, but thereafter prepayment permitted with prepayment fee?
   G. Prepayment, when permitted, in certain fixed amounts only?

VI. What happens if the borrower fails to pay as agreed?
   A. A late charge? What is borrower's grace period: 5 to 10 days after the payment is due?
   B. How much is the late charge?
      1. A fixed dollar amount?
      2. A percentage of the payment?
   C. What happens upon default?
      1. Is there a grace period? Specify how long.
      2. Is there a default notice and cure period?
      3. Do the loan payments accelerate after default? Is it optional or automatic acceleration?
      4. What does the borrower have to pay of the lender's costs and expenses for collecting the note?
         a. Attorney's fees?
         b. Court costs and other reasonable expenses?
         c. Is the interest rate after default higher than it was during regular payments?

VII. What collateral documents associated with the note should be cross-referenced?
   A. The property collateral document—the mortgage or the deed of trust.
   B. Any assignment of rents and leases?
   C. Any security agreement covering personal property?
   D. Other?

VIII. Is choice of law important? (Usually the state in which the property is located.)

IX. Is there a homestead exemption waiver?

X. Signatures?
   A. Who will be the maker(s) of the note?
   B. A corporate maker:

1. Obtain correct legal name of the corporation—
   a. From the corporate seal?
   b. From the articles of incorporation?
2. Identify the corporate officers executing the note by name and by title—"ABC Co., Inc., by John Doe, President."
3. Affix corporate seal.
4. Examine corporate resolutions for authority—
   a. To sign—who?
   b. How much can be borrowed?
   c. How many persons must sign the loan documents?

C. Partnership as maker of the note?
   1. Partnership identified by name?
   2. Identify all partners signing the note by name and as partners.
   3. Check the authority of those signing, as for a corporation.

D. Are the names of the signers beneath their respective signature lines with their corporate or partnership capacity indicated for the purposes of indicating their agency (signature block)?

E. Are the addresses of the signers on the note?

F. Note witnessing and notarizing—not needed.

XIII. Dating: be certain the current date is inserted properly.

7.6 PREPARATION OF A MORTGAGE

Although the note is important, the creditor can usually find a way to prove its loan (such as disbursement receipts and disbursement records). The mortgage, however, contains the agreement that the borrower's property can be taken in repayment of the loan if the borrower cannot pay. The mortgage or deed of trust may be the most important real estate financing document for both parties. Creating it deserves careful and thoughtful consideration.

I. Who are the parties?
   A. Who is the mortgagor or grantor—record title owner of the property described in the mortgage?
   B. Who is the mortgagee or grantee—creditor and holder of note being secured by the mortgage?

II. What is the legal description of property to be conveyed? Is the description accurate?
   A. Of the real property?
   B. Of the personal property being transferred?
      1. Easements appurtenant?
      2. Cross-access easements?
   C. Off-site utility easements?

III. What should be included in the handling of indebtedness?
   A. Amount?
   B. Final maturity date?
   C. Future advance provisions?

IV. Security agreement
  A. Is personal property included in the transaction?
  B. Appropriate filings?
    1. UCC-1s (generally for goods or intangibles)
    2. UCC-2s for real estate-related filings on personal property such as fixtures
  C. Other, prior creditors of the personal property?

V. Should there be an assignment of leases or rents?
  A. Is the personal property a commercial investment or an income-producing property?
  B. Are there similar problems with leases as with security interests? What about the changes in Art. 2A of the UCC, regarding leases? Does that apply on leased equipment?

VI. Miscellaneous mortgage covenants
  A. Repayment of debt?
  B. Is there an escrow for taxes, insurance, etc.?
  C. How are the payments to be applied?
  D. Hazard insurance?
  E. How will the property be preserved and maintained?
  F. What are the terms of the lenders right to inspect?
  G. What occurs if there is condemnation or seizure by eminent domain?
  H. Does the lender have right(s) of cure when the buyer defaults?
  I. Is there a due on sale clause?
  J. What is the effect of a second mortgage?
  K. What extent and type of financial reporting is needed?
  L. What are the events of default?
  M. What are the remedies on default?
  N. What is the provision for giving notices—both sides?
  O. What is the choice of law?
  P. Language to establish forbearance of a default rather than a waiver?
  Q. Is there a waiver of homestead and other debtor's rights?
  R. Is there a clause to indemnify against hazardous waste on the property?
  S. Are there any other indemnities or provisions relative to the transaction?
  T. Is there crossover language to make sure that a default in one document carries over to the other loan documents, such as assignments of leases or construction loan agreements?
  U. Insurance?
    1. What type?
    2. Who pays for it?
    3. What happens if the borrower does not pay?

VII. Who signs the mortgage?

A. Mortgagor or grantor.
   1. What if the signer is a corporation?
      a. Identify corporate name of corporation.
      b. Identify by name and title all officers signing on behalf of the corporation.
      c. Affix corporate seal.
      d. Corporate authority?
      e. Proper signature block?
   2. What if the signer is a partnership?
      a. Identify the partnership name.
      b. Identify by name all partners signing the mortgage.
      c. Proper signature block?

B. Witnessing of signatures and notarizing the document with sufficient formality to permit the mortgage to be recorded?

C. Is the mortgage recorded to protect mortgagees priority against future parties?

DISCUSSION AND REVIEW QUESTIONS

1. Distinguish between a mortgage and a deed of trust.
2. What is the purpose of the note?
3. What is the purpose of having a floating interest rate?
4. List and explain some of the devices used to create a floating interest situation.
5. What device is used in a note to allow the lender to move quickly to foreclose if the borrower does not pay as agreed?
6. After the borrower has paid off the loan, what steps should be taken?
7. Identify the major elements in the Truth in Lending Act that affect home lending.
8. What is RESPA?
9. What other types of federal regulation and activity affect the real estate industry?
10. Explain why a lender (bank) might not want to make a loan to a prospective home buyer; explain the lending situation from the bank's point of view.
11. Sam and Rebecca Jones have finally gotten married after a number of years of dating. Sam's grandfather, William Jones, has just died and left Sam 50 acres with an old, but sturdy, farmhouse on it. It is adjacent to an area under development. Our clever "DINKs" (Double Income No Kids) see a golden opportunity to become real estate developers themselves, or at least to sell part of the property off to a developer so that they can modernize the farmhouse. To pay for these schemes, they need to raise some capital. As their first step, they decide to sell off 10 acres, Billacres, at $40,000 per acre to a developer, A. But A only has $50,000

in cash and gives them the cash and a note for $350,000. This deal is consummated on January 15, 1993, and they hold a note and mortgage on the property. They promptly record the necessary documents. To raise the remaining cash, they sell off their note and mortgage to Survivor Savings and Loan Association for $315,000 on April 10, 1993. A, really being a speculator, sells the property to B, a true developer, for $150,000 in cash plus assuming the mortgage on May 2, 1993. B defaults on his payments under the note after 18 months because he became overextended during a recession. How does this mess get sorted out? You do not have all the important facts. What questions should you ask? What do you need? What should you find out about?

SAMPLE FORMS

Sheriff's Deed—To Purchaser of Real Property at Execution Sale

SIDEBAR

When the sheriff sells property for unpaid taxes, this type of form is used to transfer the property to a buyer.

This deed made _________, 19____, between _________, sheriff of the County of _________, State of _________, transferor herein, and _______ of _________ *[address]*, City of _________, County of _________, State of _________, transferee herein.

RECITALS

1. By virtue of a writ of execution dated _________, 19____, directed and delivered to transferor and issued out of the _________ *[court]*, in Civil Action No. _________, on a judgment rendered in such court in an action entitled _________ v _________ in favor of plaintiff and against defendant for the sum of _________ Dollars ($____), transferor was directed to make _________ Dollars ($____) to satisfy such judgment and costs out of the personal property of defendant, and, if sufficient personal property could not be found, then out of the real property belonging to defendant on _________, 19____, or at anytime thereafter.

2. Defendant's personal property being insufficient, transferor levied on defendant's real property, described below, and, after due notice, sold it at public auction at _________ o'clock ____.m. on _________, 19____, at *[location]* to transferee, as the highest bidder, for the sum of _________ Dollars ($____) in cash.

3. Transferee, having paid the purchase money for real property, is now the legal owner and holder of the certificate of sale thereof given to him by transferor.

4. _________ months have expired after the sale, from which there has been no redemption.

By virtue of the foregoing premises and in consideration of the purchase money, receipt of which is hereby acknowledged, transferor grants to transferee, his heirs and assigns, all the title and interest that defendant had on _________, 19____, or thereafter, in the following real property:

_______ *[legal description]*, together with improvements and appurtenances thereto.

In witness whereof, transferor has executed this deed at _________ *[designate place of execution]* the day and year first above written.

[Signature]

[Attestation]
[Acknowledgment]

SIDEBAR

When a bank agrees to lend, it provides this commitment letter. Note the detailed requirements the bank uses to protect its interest rate (§ 7) and its collateral (§ 2).

Conventional Commitment Letter—Approval of Application for Mortgage Loan

To:__________
__________ *[address]* Re: ________ *[property involved]*

We are pleased to inform you that your application for a mortgage in the amount of _______ Dollars ($____) has been approved at _______ percent (____%) with a term of _______ years. Your payments will be _______ Dollars ($____) per month including both interest and principal.

Other specific terms and conditions are as follows:

(1) The mortgage will be a first lien on the subject property with an unencumbered and marketable title as certified by our attorneys.

(2) You are to carry fire and windstorm or comprehensive fire insurance on the property in an amount not less than the amount of the mortgage during the period of the loan. You may, of course, carry additional insurance to further protect your interest if you so desire.

(3) The mortgage is to contain a clause permitting the ________ *[name of mortgagee]* to require payment in full if you sell or transfer the subject property.

(4) All title papers must meet the approval of our counsel, _______, of __________ *[address]*, City of __________, County of __________, State of _________.

(5) You are to pay all mortgage placement costs including the charge made to our attorneys for the preparation of the necessary mortgage documents and their services in passing upon the legality and validity of the bank's investment.

(6) The unpaid principal balance of your loan may be paid in whole or in part at any time. During the first year of your loan, principal payments not exceeding _________ percent of the face amount of this interest may be made without penalty, however, there will be a penalty of _______ percent of any amount paid that is in excess of ___ percent of the face amount of this instrument during such one year period. Prepayment may be made on or after one year without penalty.

(7) In the event that the lawful mortgage interest rate for the State of _________ is increased prior to closing, this commitment shall be deemed to be at the highest rate then permitted. If the interest rate stated is not the lawfully permitted rate at the time of closing, the _________ *[name of mortgagee]* may, at its option, cancel this commitment by written notice to you.

(8) You must accept this commitment by signing and returning the enclosed copy of this letter to us within 10 [ten] days from the

date hereof; the funds will then be reserved for you until _________, 19___. If not received as provided, this commitment will be deemed withdrawn.

(9) Credit life insurance is not required by us but is available to qualified applicants on a voluntary basis. If you want this insurance, you may so indicate by signing in the appropriate space provided on the enclosed Disclosure Statement. This is not an application for such life insurance. These forms will be available at closing and should you elect to take this insurance, it will be necessary for you to deposit _________ [three] months premiums in escrow at that time.

(10) Upon acceptance of this commitment, we ask that you forward, or have your attorney forward, the abstract of title, survey, and other title papers, including a certificate of occupancy, if required, to _______, at _______ *[address]* as soon as possible so that title can be examined.

(11) At your request, the legal forms pertaining to your mortgage closing will be available for examination by you or your counsel prior to closing by pre-arrangement with the lawyer designated by us to handle this matter. YOU WILL FIND ENCLOSED DISCLOSURE STATEMENTS REQUIRED BY FEDERAL LAW; ONE OF THESE STATEMENTS MUST BE SIGNED BY YOU AND RETURNED WITH A COPY OF THIS COMMITMENT.

[Signature of appropriate officer of mortgagee]

[Enclose Disclosure Statement]

ACCEPTANCE

I hereby accept this mortgage commitment and agree to its terms and acknowledge receipt of a copy of the attached Disclosure Statement.

Dated _________, 19___.

[Signature of prospective mortgagor]

Mortgage—General Form

This mortgage is made __________, 19___, between __________, of _________ *[address]*, City of _________, County of _________, State of _________, herein referred to as mortgagee.

Mortgagor, by a ________ [note *or* bond] dated _______, 19___, is indebted to mortgagee in the sum of _______ Dollars ($___), with interest from date at the rate of ________ percent (___%) per annum on the unpaid balance until paid, principal and interest to be paid at the office of _______, at _______ *[address]*, or at such other place as the holder may designate in writing, delivered or mailed to mortgagor, in _______ [monthly] installments of _________ Dollars ($___), beginning _______, 19___, and continuing on the _______ day of each month thereafter until the indebtedness is fully paid; except that, if not paid sooner, the final payment thereof shall be due and payable on ________, 19___. The terms of such ________ [note *or* bond] are incorporated herein by reference.

_________ *[If appropriate, add:* The above-stated principal indebtedness represents money loaned by mortgagee and actually used for

SIDEBAR

The mortgage protects the lender's loan. Notice the concerns over apparently uncommon occurrences, such as § 14 (waste) and § 13 (bankruptcy). This kind of detailed concern is essential.

the acquisition of the property herein described and conveyed or for the improvements thereon.]

Mortgagor, in consideration of the above-stated obligation, hereby mortgages to mortgagee all of the following described property in the County of __________, State of __________ : __________ *[set forth legal description of property],* together with the appurtenances and all the estate and rights of the mortgagor in and to such premises.

Mortgagor covenants and agrees as follows:

SECTION ONE
PAYMENT OF INDEBTEDNESS

Mortgagor shall pay the indebtedness as hereinbefore provided.

SECTION TWO
WARRANTY OF OWNERSHIP

Mortgagor warrants that __________ [he *or* she] is lawfully seised of __________ *[describe estate, such as:* an indefeasible estate in fee] in the premises.

SECTION THREE
MAINTENANCE OF INSURANCE

Mortgagor shall keep the buildings on the premises insured for loss by fire for mortgagee's benefit; mortgagor shall assign and deliver the policies to mortgagee; and mortgagor shall reimburse mortgagee for any insurance premiums paid by mortgagee on mortgagor's default in so insuring the buildings or in so assigning and delivering the policies.

SECTION FOUR
TAXES AND ASSESSMENTS

Mortgagor shall pay all taxes and assessments. In default thereof, mortgagee may pay such taxes and assessments and mortgagor shall reimburse mortgagee therefor.

SECTION FIVE
REMOVAL OR DEMOLITION OF BUILDINGS

No building on the premises shall be removed or demolished without mortgagee's consent.

SECTION SIX
ACCELERATION OF PRINCIPAL AND INTEREST

The full amount of the principal sum and interest shall become due at the option of mortgagee: After default in the payment of any instalment of principal or of interest for __________ days; or after default in the payment of any tax or assessment for __________ days after notice and demand; or after default after notice and demand either in assigning and delivering the policies insuring the buildings against loss by fire or reimbursing mortgagee for premiums paid on such insurance, as provided above; or after failure to furnish a statement of the amount due on the mortgage and of any offsets and/or defenses existing against the mortgaged debt, after such has been requested as provided below.

SECTION SEVEN
APPOINTMENT OF RECEIVER

The holder of this mortgage, in any action to foreclose it, shall be entitled to the appointment of a receiver.

SECTION EIGHT
STATEMENT OF AMOUNT DUE

Mortgagor, within ___________ days when requested in person, or within ___________ days when requested by mail, shall furnish to mortgagee a duly acknowledged written statement of the amount due on the mortgage and whether any offsets and/or defenses exist against the mortgaged debt.

SECTION NINE
SALE IN ONE PARCEL

In case of a foreclosure sale, the premises, or so much thereof as may be affected by this mortgage, may be sold in one parcel.

SECTION TEN
ASSIGNMENT OF RENTS, ISSUES, AND PROFITS

Mortgagor hereby assigns to mortgagee the rents, issues, and profits of the premises as further security for the payment of the obligations secured hereby, and grants to mortgagee the right to enter on the premises to collect the same, to let the premises or any part thereof, and to apply the moneys received therefrom, after payment of all necessary charges and expenses, to the obligations secured by this mortgage, on default under any of the covenants, conditions, or agreements contained herein. In the event of any such default, mortgagor shall pay to mortgagee or to any receiver appointed to collect the rents, issues, and profits of the premises, the fair and reasonable rental value for the use and occupation of the premises or of such part thereof as may be in mortgagor's possession; and on default in payment of such rental, to vacate and surrender possession of the premises, or that portion thereof occupied by mortgagor, to mortgagee or the receiver appointed to collect the same.

SECTION ELEVEN
PAYMENT OF EXPENSES

If any action or proceeding is commenced, except an action to foreclose this mortgage or to collect the debt secured hereby, in which it is necessary to defend or assert the lien of this mortgage, whether or not the mortgagee is made or becomes a party to any such action or proceeding, all or mortgagee's expenses incurred in any such action or proceeding to prosecute or defend the rights and lien created by this mortgage, including reasonable counsel fees, shall be paid by mortgagor, and if not so paid promptly on request, shall be added to the debts secured hereby and become a lien on the mortgaged premises, and shall be deemed to be fully secured by this mortgage and to be prior and paramount to any right, title, interest, or claim to or on the premises accruing or attaching subsequent to the lien of this mortgage, and shall bear interest at the rate provided for the obligations secured hereby. This covenant shall not govern or affect any action or proceeding to foreclose this mortgage or to recover or to collect the debt secured hereby, which action or proceeding shall be governed by the provisions of law respecting the recovery of costs, disbursements, and allowances in foreclosure actions.

SECTION TWELVE
CONDEMNATION OF PREMISES

If the premises or any part thereof shall be condemned and taken under the power of eminent domain, or if any award for any change of grade of streets affecting the premises shall be made, all damages and awards for the property so taken or damaged shall be paid to the holder of this mortgage, up to the amount then unpaid on the indebtedness hereby secured, without regard to whether or not the balance remaining unpaid on the indebtedness may then be due and payable; and the amount so paid shall be credited against the indebtedness and, if it is insufficient to pay the entire amount thereof, it may, at the option of the holder of this mortgage, be applied to the last maturing instalments. The balance of such damages and awards, if any, shall be paid to mortgagor. Mortgagee and subsequent holders of this mortgage are hereby given full power, right, and authority to receive and receipt for all such damages and awards.

SECTION THIRTEEN
BANKRUPTCY

If mortgagor or any obligor on the __________ [note *or* bond] secured hereby: (1) files a voluntary petition in bankruptcy under the Bankruptcy Act of the United States, or (2) is adjudicated a bankrupt under such act, or (3) is the subject of a petition filed in federal or state court for the appointment of a trustee or receiver in bankruptcy or insolvency, or (4) makes a general assignment for the benefit of creditors, then and on the occurrence of any of such conditions, at the option of mortgagee, the entire balance of the principal sum secured hereby, together with all accrued interest thereon, shall become immediately due and payable.

SECTION FOURTEEN
WASTE

Mortgagor shall not commit, suffer, or permit any waste, impairment, or deterioration of the premises or of any improvement thereon and shall maintain the premises and all improvements thereon in good condition and repair. If mortgagor fails or neglects to make any necessary repair or replacement in any improvement for ___________ days after notice to do so from mortgagee, mortgagee may effect such repair or replacement and the cost thereof shall be added to the debt secured hereby, shall bear interest at the rate provided in the ___________ [note *or* bond] secured hereby, and shall be covered by this mortgage and the lien thereof.

SECTION FIFTEEN
COMPLIANCE WITH LAWS AND REGULATIONS

Mortgagor shall comply with all statutes, ordinances, and governmental requirements that affect the premises. If mortgagor neglects or refuses to so comply and such failure or refusal continues for _________ *[number]* _________ [months], then, at mortgagee's option, the entire balance of the principal sum secured hereby, together with all accrued interest, shall become immediately due and payable.

_________ *[If appropriate, add:* _________, the _________ (wife *or* husband) or mortgagor, for the above-stated consideration, hereby relinquishes _________ (his *or* her) right of _________ (dower *or* curtesy) _________ (and homestead) in and to the above-described premises.]

Wherever the sense of this mortgage so requires, the word "mortgagor" shall be construed as if it read "mortgagors" and the word "mortgagee" shall be construed as if it read "mortgagees." The word "holder" shall include any payee of the indebtedness hereby secured or any transferee thereof whether by operation of law or otherwise. Unless otherwise provided, any notice and demand or request specified in this mortgage may be made in writing and may be served in person or by mail.

In witness whereof, this mortgage has been duly executed by mortgagor the day and year first written above.

[Signature]
[Seal, if required]

[Attestation, if required]
[Acknowledgment, if required]
This instrument was prepared by ___________.

Report and Account of Sale

I, _________, _________ [Sheriff of the County of _________, State of _________], hereby report and certify the following:

1. By judgment and decree of foreclosure rendered in the _______ *[court]*, County of _______, State of _______, on _______, 19___, in favor of ________, as plaintiff, and against ________, as defendant, which judgment is recorded in judgment book _______ of such court at page _________, the court adjudged _________ Dollars ($____) to be

SIDEBAR

Note the recitation of legalities the sheriff formally states in § 1 and the importance of notice in §§ 2 and 3. Here is a clear example of due process at work.

owing by the defendant to the plaintiff including costs and disbursements. The court further ordered that the mortgaged property, particularly described in such judgment and order, or so much thereof as might be sufficient to satisfy the amount adjudged to be due to the plaintiff and the costs of sale, to be sold at public auction by or under my direction.

2. Pursuant to such judgment and order, I gave due notice of the sale of such property, as the law directs, by posting a written notice particularly describing the property, stating the time and place of sale thereof, for _________ *[number]* _________ [weeks *or* days], successively, immediately preceding such sale in _______ *[number]* public places in such county and state, as follows: _________ *[describe]*.

3. I also caused such notice to be published for a period of _________ *[number]* _________ [weeks *or* days], successively, immediately preceding such sale in _________, a newspaper of general circulation, printed and published in the County of _________, State of _________. A copy of that notice is attached hereto and made a part hereof.

4. On _________, 19___, at the time and place fixed for sale, I was present and offered the premises for sale at public auction to the highest bidder. The property was offered in one parcel and was sold to _________, of _________ *[address]*, City of _________, County of _________ State of _________, for _________ Dollars ($___), the highest bid. _________ Dollars ($___), the total price paid for the property, was received from _________ *[purchaser]*.

5. I delivered to such purchaser a certificate of sale, containing a notice that the real property was subject to redemption according to the provisions of _________ *[cite statute]*.

6. The following is an account of the sale: _________ *[set out account of costs of sale and distribution of proceeds]*.

In witness whereof, I have executed this report at _________ *[designate place of execution]* on _________, 19___.

[Signature]

Notice of Default and Election to Sell—Under Mortgage

To: _________

____

_________, as mortgagor, on _______, 19___, having made, executed, and delivered to _______, as mortgagee, [his *or* her] _______ [note *or* bond] and mortgage of the real property described in the mortgage, which mortgage was thereafter duly recorded _______, 19___, in the office of the ________ [county recorder] of ________ County, State of ________, in Book ________ of mortgages at page ________, and a breach of the obligation for which such mortgage is security having occurred, in that ________ *[specify nature of breach, such as:* default has been made in the payment of interest on the ________ (note *or* bond) secured by such mortgage], notice is hereby given that the undersigned mortgagee, as a consequence of such default, has elected to consider all of the principal and interest due, in accordance with the terms of such _________ [note *or* bond] and mortgage, and has elected to sell or cause to be sold the real property described in the mortgage to satisfy such obligation.

Dated _________, 19___.

[Signature]

[Acknowledgment]

Notice of Intention to Redeem

Notice is hereby given that the undersigned, ________, of ________ *[address]*, City of ________, County of ________, State of ________ intends to redeem that tract of land in the City of _________, County of ________, State of ________, described as follows: ________ *[set forth legal description of property]*.

The intended redemption is from the sale of the above-described property on ________, 19___, by the sheriff of the County of ________, pursuant to the judgment and decree of foreclosure of ________ *[court]*, County of ___________, State of ___________, made and entered on ________, 19___, in an action to foreclose a certain mortgage on the above-described property in which action _________ was plaintiff and _________ was defendant. The property was sold to _________, of _________ *[address]*, City of _________, County of _________, State of _________, who paid for it the sum of _________ Dollars ($____), as evidenced by the certificate of sale, dated ___________, 19___, recorded in the office of the ___________ [county recorder] of ___________ County, State of _________, on _________, 19___, in Book _________ of mortgages at page _____.

The redemption will be based on __________ *[set forth statutory or contractual basis of claim]*.

Dated _________, 19___.

[Signature]

SIDEBAR

After the property has been sold, the owner can get it back by redemption. Here is a simple statement of the prior owner that she will pay the price needed to get the property back.

CHAPTER 8
Closing the Real Estate Transaction

"Location. Location. Location."

Anonymous, the three most important matters in real estate

Dutch colonial house

OUTLINE

PROLOGUE TO THE PARALEGAL

The closing is one of the most important jobs in real estate, and it is one most often assigned to the legal assistant. Closing requires much more skill than the ability to organize the closing, although organization is crucial. Closing also requires a great deal more than the ability to work well with people; it requires a certain amount of legal knowledge as well. Learning to close a real estate sale is the focus of much of the paralegal's schoolwork. In closing, knowledge of searches, insurance, real estate documentation, legal descriptions, real estate ownership, appraisal, environmental issues, and taxation may all play an important role. In few other transactions does all this work and knowledge come together in one place at one time. In this chapter on closings, you will learn about the government's role and its forms; you will discover the use of an escrow; you will come to recognize your client's interests; and you will work to identify potential problems. You will also come to realize the number of parties involved—each of whom has a separate interest that must be recognized and dealt with.

KEY TERMS

accrued
affidavit of title
closer
commitment letter
credit
debit
escrowee
payoff statement
per diem
prepaid
proration

8.1 INTRODUCTION

After all the negotiations over price and the preliminary work have been done, the parties are ready to close the deal. The real estate closing can be a truly complex transaction, or it can be relatively simple. Far too often, the closing, particularly a residential closing, is a chaotic event. People run around tense, hostile, and frustrated. The closing takes far too long to complete—sometimes months—and everyone wanted it done, not the day before yesterday, but a week or month ago.

The most important task is controlling all the details of the closing. That means openly communicating with everyone and maintaining a good working relationship with third parties (persons other than the buyer and the seller). Coordinating the work of third parties and ensuring that it has been done correctly consumes most of the time—time that often seems a series of endless delays. While there are often some delays, your goals are to control them and expedite the closing; your law firm cannot make money when there are endless delays, particularly on a residential closing. Closing's basic requirements are that the seller deliver a marketable deed and the buyer deliver money. Apart from these basics, a wide variety of things can occur.

In this chapter, we examine these possibilities and review the requirements of outside parties (such as the government). Increasingly, banks and other lenders either prepare their own documentation or have their law firm do so. The older practice, in which the law firm closed the loan, is unlikely to survive much longer. There are fees involved which the lender can now charge the borrower. Although the topic is touched upon in the chapter on real estate financing (chapter 7), the details of real estate loan documentation are beyond the scope of this book.

The paralegal is very useful to the law firm in putting together the closing. To run a closing process means to acquire the needed information. One of the first steps is to determine from the real estate sales contract what the parties—the buyer and the seller—must do to perform their promises. Third parties must then be contacted to determine the use, availability, and timing of their services.

These third parties serve many functions. The buyer's lender provides a commitment letter stating the terms of the loan and specifying who will fund the transaction. The seller's lender is paid off. A surveyor inspects and measures the property to determine the exact location of everything on the property and identify easements and encumbrances. An appraiser prepares an estimate of the value of the property. An insurance agent suggests a company to provide fire and hazard insurance. The title company verifies the quality of the title, notes and explains any problems (called *defects*), and issues title insurance to protect the buyer and the lender against third parties' claims to the title. If there is any doubt about the quality of the insurance company that the agent is offering, check the insurance company's quality rating in *Best's Insurance Reports* (either *Life-Health* or *Property-Casualty*) (a rating guide similar to Moody's or Standard & Poor's financial ratings, but for the insurance industry) or check with your state's insurance regulation department.

One may also need a person to inspect the house. This certainly includes a termite inspector; surprisingly, termite infestation has become a difficult and spreading problem. Termites have been found munching away on wooden window frames even in poured-concrete buildings in Chicago. They are no longer simply a local or regional problem, but are widespread. A termite inspector's report should be obtained early; any necessary corrective action must be done before closing, because no rational buyer will accept a building with termites in it. Further, it is frequently wise to hire a person to inspect for structural problems. A general inspection can spare the buyer some nasty surprises.

Usually, the person doing the closing—the paralegal—schedules these parties into a smooth operation. Personal contacts and mutual respect are important for the paralegal in creating and maintaining good working relationships with these essential third parties. But before contacting any third parties, one must review the real estate sales contract. At the end of this chapter, there is an extensive checklist to help organize and control your workflow and to ensure that you do not omit any crucial element. Familiarize yourself with it before you go further.

In the beginning, the buyer and the seller agreed to the transaction by means of their real estate sales contract. The closing is the process by which the promises made in that contract are performed or kept. In most closings, an additional contract is being performed; the lender is funding the transaction. This second, and absolutely essential, contract is the lending agreement between the buyer-borrower and his or her bank. That agreement-to-lend contract is often called the **commitment** or the **commitment letter**. It specifies the amount the lender will advance and the terms and conditions of the loan, such as the interest rate and the terms of repayment. The two closings may be done together, but most likely, the lending closing will be completed first, because the funds to do the real estate closing must come out of the loan closing. Often, the lender's representative attends the closing and gives the buyer the money (after the lender has verified that the essential documents are in order).

There are many approaches to a closing with the lender. There may be an escrow with the funds deposited. There may be a closing for the loan at the bank, with bank attorneys, documentation, and investigation. It may all be done through your office, with your attorneys drafting the lending documentation and your office doing the checking and the loan closing. The bank providing the money chooses. The location of the closing may vary widely. It may be at the lending institution or in the real estate broker's office, but it can also occur in the title company's offices (for convenience in the final bringing down of title and issuance of insurance); in the office of an attorney of one of the parties; in the escrow company's offices (if an escrow is being used); or in the recording official's offices. Because the closing is based on the real estate sales contract, it is essential to make sure that everything it calls for is satisfied in the closing. After the terms of that contract and the lending commitment are satisfied, the additional checkings and verifications are done (from the credit check on the borrower through the survey, appraisal, and final walk-through of the property on the day of closing), and the documents are executed and exchanged, the final task is to record the correct closing documents.

LEGAL TERMS

commitment letter Letter from the lender to the borrower in which the lender states the amount of the loan and its terms for making the loan.

The documents must be recorded in the sequence that keeps the title clean and creates no cloud on the title. For example, in a normal home or residence closing, there is a series of documents representing important events affecting the real estate.

1. The buyer executes and delivers a note and mortgage on the real property to his lender
2. The seller's loan is paid off by (a) the bank lending money to the buyer, (b) the buyer transferring money (the purchase price) to the seller, and (c) the seller transferring those funds to her lender
3. The seller receives a release or satisfaction from her financial institution for paying off her loan
4. The seller executes and delivers a deed to the buyer.

There are, at a minimum, four documents:

1. The release or satisfaction from the seller's bank
2. The note of the buyer-borrower
3. The mortgage
4. The deed from the seller to the buyer, transferring the property being purchased (usually—unless the transaction uses a deed of trust).

The recording sequence clears the old transaction before initiating the new one. Therefore, the release or satisfaction showing the removal of the seller's financial institution's interest comes first. Then comes the deed transferring the property to the new owner, and, finally, the new owner's pledging of her property to her lender, the mortgage (with or without the note, depending on the jurisdiction).

8.2 PARTIES INVOLVED IN THE CLOSING

Thus far, we have identified the transaction, the location, and the recording priorities, but who will be at the closing? Obviously, the parties mentioned earlier—the seller, the seller's lender, the buyer, the buyer's lender, an attorney for each of the buyer and the seller (although legal counsel is more important for the buyer), the real estate broker or salesperson, and someone from the title company (and sometimes an insurance agent). The person controlling and guiding these parties through the process of closing is called the **closer** or the **closing agent**—frequently you, the paralegal. If not you, a closing agent may be the lender's representative to the buyer (banks have closers), the broker, or the title company person. Because of the number of people involved, the importance of the transaction, the transaction's technicalities, and amount of money involved, it is important to have one person in charge. Also, since the Tax Reform Act of 1986, the federal government has required that a tax filing show the gross proceeds of the transaction and other types of information. The seller can be taxed if the home has significantly increased in value; the government wants to avoid missing any taxable income.

If the person managing the closing does not file the report, the mortgage lender must do so. Thereafter, the burden of reporting falls on the seller's broker, the buyer's broker, and so on.

The roles of all parties must be clear. There are usually three groups involved in the closing process—the buyer's group, the seller's group, and the third parties.

The buyer brings a lender, a broker, and an attorney to verify that all the contract's terms are complied with, that the title is clean, and that the legal position is safe. With the banker (and sometimes the broker), the buyer inspects the premises shortly before the closing (that is, within a couple of hours) to ensure that nothing unusual or deleterious to the buyer's interests has occurred to the parcel of property. This inspection ensures that nothing negative has happened to the property and that the seller has not departed with items he or she agreed to transfer with the building. The latter does happen—at the last minute, that wonderful chandelier just disappears.

The buyer's attorney, in addition to possibly being involved with the inspection, will, more importantly, be bringing down title one final time to make sure there are no last-minute clouds on the title to delay or stop the closing. The buyer's lender is there to see that all the appropriate steps are taken to ensure that the property is properly lienable to the lender. Those steps include doing the final title search, being certain that a real estate title policy is issued on the appropriate ALTA form, that there is insurance coverage for fire or other hazards and that the premium has been paid, that an internal bank escrow is established for tax and insurance payments, and that the home has been inspected for identifiable risks such as termites or potential structural problems. Finally, the lender, having the most money involved in the transaction, may want to have its own attorney present to review the documents in the chain of title for their sufficiency as to the transfer of title.

The seller brings a lender, a broker, and an attorney. The seller wants to receive the funds, pay off her loan, and get the remaining money. To facilitate paying off the loan, the seller's lender will have provided a **payoff statement** specifying the amount of the loan principal and the amount of interest that is accumulating daily (a **per diem**). The exact amount needed to pay off the loan can then be calculated as of the day of the closing. Additional items may be included in the payoff statement, such as any fees involved, prepayment penalties, any tax or insurance reserve credits, and similar items (all of which will appear on the RESPA closing statement). Frequently, this final amount is verified orally on the day of closing between the buyer's and seller's lenders to ensure that the pre-cut checks will be for the right amount. The seller's attorney is present to answer questions, to analyze any last-minute situations that crop up, and to examine all the documents to make sure they comply with the sales contract. The broker(s) may be there for a variety of reasons. If the broker is the seller's, one reason, of course, is to collect the commission due. Second, being there is good public relations.

The broker may also help with the closing by arranging practical details. These details could include arranging any of the following: title work to

LEGAL TERMS

closer (closing agent)
Person who sets up, coordinates, and runs the real estate closing.

payoff statement
Letter from a creditor stating principal, interest (usually on a daily basis, as, $35.13 per day), and other costs, which represent elements of the money that must be paid to the creditor to pay off the loan fully so that its lien can be released.

per diem
Latin for "for each day" or "daily."

establish who has interests in the property, a survey, an appraisal, a termite inspection, and an inspection for water problems or general problems. Usually, however, these matters are handled through the attorney's office. For a person inexperienced at closings, a reliable broker can be a big help. But real estate agents have their own interests, so caution and double-checking are necessary. The issue often comes down to which office is more familiar with the process—the attorney's or the broker's. Generally, the party more familiar with the closing process will know and recommend needed third parties. Because these inspections are in the interest of the buyer, the buyer's broker or salesperson usually arranges them. The seller's salesperson could have a serious conflict of interest, being desirous of the sale's commission.

Third parties' work often benefits the buyer. Their work may be done before the closing, and they may not be present, such as the appraiser or surveyor, or, like the title company, they may participate in the closing. Title company representatives may be working with both the buyer and the seller, but they generally maintain a professional separation and simply perform a service. A conflict of interest is extremely rare. The title company will not only issue the eventual title policy, but, because it insures the title, it may do the final title search to bring the title down at the time of closing. The same title company may also have done the original title search. In order to transfer title to the buyer, the seller must have good, marketable title (as the standard real estate sales contract provides).

Shortly after the sales contract is signed, the seller gets a title search done to show the status of the title; that partly complies with the contract's requirement that the seller deliver marketable or clean title. The title review may also be done by having an abstract of title provided and reviewed by an attorney. Finally, there could be a current title insurance policy, under which a title company protects the title and the status of the title. In essence, the seller is updating the title information with the title company records since the last time a policy was issued.

The last step on the day of closing is to verify that no one has recorded a claim after the seller's initial check. If there are any problems with the title—outstanding liens outside of the usual creditors to be paid off at the closing (that is, the home lender)—these items must be removed to the buyer's satisfaction. (Note here that it is possible to pay off any additional outstanding liens, such as mechanic's liens, at closing. This type of creditor might add to the number of people at the closing looking to be paid; the closer would have to coordinate their presence at the closing and obtain their releases. These people will also need to be contacted. As the obligation lies with the seller to provide clean title, it is the seller's responsibility, but sometimes the seller is reluctant to handle the matter. The closer may have to keep after the seller to get this done.)

To start the search process, it is necessary to provide the legal description of the real property, the name of the seller or the owner, and any other available information. A schedule, with a specific date for completion, should be set as soon as possible. Often, the sales contract specifies a time limit for removing title claims. This limit may be expressed by a specific date, by a number of days allowed, or by a clause stating that time is of the essence. It often is, for buyer and seller alike. The time-of-the-essence clause means that completion on schedule is essential to the buyer and that the seller must perform the contract's promises within the permitted time period.

When the final title search is completed, the title company issuing the new policy usually requires the seller to give the title company an **affidavit of title**. This document states that the seller has no knowledge of any encumbrances to the title (liens) or the parcel of real property (a new building next door which encroaches on the property) since the last search was made. Clearly, this document permits the title company to sue the seller if the statement is fraudulent or inaccurate. The final title search (bringing down title) is usually paid for by the buyer, and in some parts of the country, the title search is entirely the buyer's responsibility. In addition, the insurer (or the lender) may insist upon a survey being done to clarify whether easements or encroachments exist (against or in favor of the property). If a survey is to be done, the same elements necessary for the title company to start its work will help the surveyor get started. If the survey shows easements or encroachments that might run in favor of the property, consideration should be given to including them in the deed so that they pass with the deed under color of title. If the items discovered run against the property, adjustments may have to be agreed to between the buyer and the seller or among the buyer, seller, and the parties owning the adjacent parcel(s)—more people that could be involved in the closing process's documentation. (Are you making a list?)

The insurance person may provide evidence of fire, hazard, and other appropriate insurance coverage by issuing a binder—not just showing a receipt for the first premium. The binder commits the insurance company to provide the coverage, to have coverage in effect, and to protect the buyer's interests. Sometimes the lender requires that the entire first year's premium be paid. The insurance agent and company must be satisfactory to the buyer, and to do the job, the insurance agent must have the following information:

1. The name of the buyer and new title holder
2. The address of the property
3. The loan amount
4. The lender's name and address (the lender usually appears as the loss payee, as its interest may appear)
5. The amounts of coverage needed by the borrower-insurance purchaser or required by the bank.

The requirements of RESPA (Real Estate Settlement Procedures Act) come into play when a federally related loan involves one- to four-family units in homes, condominiums, and cooperatives with a first mortgage loan. The first requirement is practically across the board, for if the federal government is involved in any way—such as insuring bank deposits, issuing any guaranty or any subsequent, secondary financing, or having any involvement with the Housing Department—the law requires compliance with RESPA. If no lending institution is involved, RESPA may not apply. The RESPA-free situation could arise

LEGAL TERMS

affidavit of title
Statement from the seller, often required by the lender or title company, that the seller has (1) not placed any liens on the property since the last title examination; (2) a certain marital status; and (3) is in possession of the property.

with personal loans within a family, a mortgage assumption—although RESPA's disclosures may be required if the lender charges more than $50 for the assumption, or if the terms of the assumed loan are changed—or if there is no mortgage.

If RESPA's disclosure requirements apply, the lender must provide three items. The first is an information booklet (the Housing Department's *Settlement Costs and You*) explaining the settlement process and the Uniform Settlement Statement form. The second is a good faith estimate of settlement costs at the time of the loan application or within three days thereafter. The third is the Uniform Settlement Statement, Housing Department Form 1. This statement must detail *all* of the lender's charges and make it clear to the borrower what the actual costs are. As you may recall, this statute also prohibits kickbacks for business referrals, such as for recommending an appraiser, an insurance agent, or a surveyor, but the statute does not prohibit fee-splitting among brokers. The settlement statement must be available to the borrower at or before the closing, and the borrower can ask for the statement at least one day before the closing. However, the figures may not all be available at that point.

8.3 PROCEDURES FOR CLOSING IN ESCROW

In our prior discussion, the contemplated closing has been face-to-face between the seller, the buyer, their representatives, and third parties important to the transaction. But there is another method of closing that does not employ a closer: closing in escrow. In the escrow process, there is a third party, the **escrowee** or **escrow holder**, with whom both the buyer and the seller deposit their documents and instruments; the escrowee completes the closing impartially to fulfill the interests of both parties. Any number of disinterested persons can be the escrow agent: an attorney, a title company, a professional escrow agent, or a trust company, among others.

The procedures for closing in escrow work this way. After the parties execute the sales contract, they select the escrow agent and give instructions through a contract with the escrowee. The escrowee selection and contract are usually worked out between the buyer's and seller's attorneys. The escrow agreement requires that all the important instruments and documents be deposited into escrow before the contractual closing date. Besides the earnest money, which is deposited immediately, the buyer eventually deposits the cash balance needed to pay off the seller; the mortgage documents, including the note and mortgage; and any other appropriate or necessary documents required by the parties' agreements. Although the escrow functions primarily to close the land transfer, it may also close the loan. The seller deposits the deed conveying the property to the buyer, evidence of title, any insurance policies covering the risks of fire and hazard, the lender's payoff letter, and any required affidavit of title. If needed, the seller also deposits an estoppel certificate stating the last payment of principal and interest made on the loan, a statement of the outstanding balance, and any other agreed-upon, appropriate, or necessary documents.

After these documents are deposited, the escrowee examines the title to be certain that it is in the proper form. If there are outstanding liens or claims, they will be paid off by withholding the appropriate sums from the seller's net receivable amount. If there are any claims sufficient to prevent a transfer of clean (marketable) title, the escrowee generally returns the documents and ends the escrow without transferring title; the escrow instructions usually provide that the parties return to their original status if clean title cannot be passed. If everything goes smoothly, the escrowee completes the transaction by transferring the title to the buyer, the net funds to the seller, paying off any other parties of record, and recording the documents appropriately. Escrow closings reassure both parties. The buyer is protected by the escrowee's final title check and because money is not transferred until after that check is done. The seller knows that the money is really there before the closing takes place. Both parties often feel easier knowing that an impartial third party is handling the transaction.

Finally, a difficult situation can arise if the seller dies after the escrow has been established. What happens? If everything goes as promised, the title that the buyer receives is dated back to the time the seller deposited the documents into escrow; that way, the transfer avoids any estate problems or delays. This legal doctrine is called the *doctrine of relation back,* because the title transfer date is considered to be the date of deposit into escrow, not the date of the escrow's actual completion. If, on the other hand, the escrow does not go according to Hoyle, then the deed does not transfer the title to the buyer, the escrow ceases, and the property is returned to the estate.

8.4 THE CLOSING STATEMENT

Paralegals may prepare RESPA closing statements if a financial closing occurs at the same time as the real property closing, or if there is a need to protect the buyer by evaluating the statement. Care must be taken, however, not to practice law by giving advice on the statement. The RESPA statement, a federal form, explains where money comes from and where it goes—who put it there and who gets it. It is like a miniature financial statement of each party's financial position. Another form, called a *closing statement,* does the same thing as a RESPA statement but is unsigned; it states each party's position and is more a financial statement than a disclosure statement. Both forms are shown and explained here. It is simpler to use the financial closing statement and move to the RESPA statement if needed. Further, the RESPA statement is only a disclosure statement; the financial closing statement can be put together easily whenever needed, without the complexities of the RESPA statement.

The RESPA material appears purely procedural and without any extended criminal liability. However, for Thomas Gannon, an employee of the Torrens registration office of Cook County, Illinois, who received payments exceeding the maximum legal amount authorized by state law for registering the title, RESPA brought extended criminal liability. From the 27 counts

LEGAL TERMS

escrowee (escrow holder)
Party that operates the escrow.

LEGAL TERMS

debit
Refers to certain entries on the settlement sheet; means that the amount is to be paid by the party to whom it refers; complementary term with *credit.*

credit
Refers to certain entries on the settlement sheet; means that the dollar amount is to be or has been paid to someone rather than having to pay money out; complementary term with *debit.*

proration
Splitting of the time used or benefit received in relation to the payment made or owed; a settlement arrangement between the buyer and the seller in which either the party who has received the benefit but not paid, must pay (accrued), or who has paid but not received the benefit, gets paid (prepaid).

against Mr. Gannon, it appears that this practice was remunerative, because the financial institutions wished to speed up the Torrens registration process. Alas for Mr. Gannon, his criminal conviction was upheld by seven of the nine federal appellate judges sitting en banc. The other two judges thought it inappropriate to use RESPA for this type of criminal prosecution. Consider, ethically, who is more to blame: the person offering or the person taking—or the system permitting—the bribe?

The accounting terms *debit* and *credit* are also used in standard closing statements, but not in the RESPA statement. These terms are not, however, used in the same way that accountants use them. A **debit** in a closing statement is a charge (a minus, a subtraction) against either party, and a **credit** is an addition (a plus) to someone's account. Another way of saying it is that if you have a debit, you pay it; if you have a credit, someone will have to pay you. Some, but not all items, mirror one another: the debit of one party is the credit of another. The closing process adjusts the financial obligations that exist on the parcel of real property so the buyer and the seller each pay for their respective portion and no more. For instance, real estate taxes are always due, but they are usually paid in arrears. That means, for example, that 1993 taxes are paid in 1994.

If the closing occurs at the end of the year, before that year's taxes are due, there must be an adjustment or **proration** between the parties as to who occupied or used the property what proportion of the time. The tax bill is split accordingly. For instance, if 1992 taxes are due in 1993, but the closing is on November 30, 1992, $^{11}/_{12}$ of the tax bill is the responsibility of the seller. The seller occupied the property through November 30, and since the tax bill is unpaid, it is a debit to the seller's closing statement. It is a credit on the buyer's statement, because the buyer will pay the bill when it arrives in 1993.

UNITED STATES
v.
GANNON
684 F.2d 433 (7th Cir. 1981) (en banc)

PELL, C.J.

Appellant Thomas Gannon was convicted of 29 counts of violating The Real Estate Settlement Procedures Act of 1974, 12 U.S.C. §§ 2601, 2607(b) (1976) (RESPA), by accepting payments for Torrens filings which were in excess of those authorized by state law. Each extra payment was the basis of a separate count of the indictment. Appellant, a counterman in the Torrens section of the Cook County, Illinois Recorder of Deeds office, acknowledged that he received and accepted the excess payments from local bank representatives whose filings he had handled. He claims, however, that RESPA does not apply to these payments because they were "gratuities," not "portions of the charges" made for settlement services "other than for services actually performed." 12 U.S.C. § 2607(b). A panel of this Court initially agreed with appellant's interpretation and reversed his conviction. *United States v. Gannon*, No. 80-1108 (7th Cir., Nov. 3, 1980). This opinion follows an *en banc* rehearing.

I

The undisputed evidence presented at appellant's trial reveals the following. The purpose of the Torrens section is to guarantee the title of Cook County real estate registered with it by issuing title certificates for the property. The counterman deals directly with the public by accepting land registration and transfer documents, examining the documents for correctness, transmitting the documents to other employees so that a new title certificate can be prepared if necessary, and charging and accepting the appropriate fees for these services. The fees are set by state statute and the countermen receive a salary in return for which they are to provide the public with prompt and courteous service.

Since the fall of 1977, a sign has been displayed in the Torrens section which states:

ATTENTION

OFFICE REGULATIONS PROHIBIT MEMBERS OF THE STAFF FROM ACCEPTING GRATUITIES FROM ANY SOURCE IN THE CONDUCT OF OFFICIAL BUSINESS

In addition, in the fall of 1977, appellant signed a typed statement which provides:

> The undersigned hereby acknowledges and understands that the acceptance of gratuities from any source in the conduct of office business is strictly forbidden. Violators of this regulation will be subject to disciplinary action.

A number of the section's customers are employees of various local banks or savings and loan institutions. The institutions are federally insured and use the Torrens services in the course of providing real estate loans. The bank employees can either phone ahead to the Torrens office for an appointment with a specific counterman, or can arrive at the office without an appointment and wait in line for service. They can pay for the Torrens service either in cash or by check which is given to the counterman in return for a stamped receipt.

A number of bank employees testified at appellant's trial that when they submitted the relevant documents and fees to appellant for Torrens registration or transfer, they gave two or three dollars to appellant in addition to the statutory amount. It is uncontested that appellant accepted these extra payments. The employees testified that they were told by their superiors, usually during training, that they should regularly make these additional payments to the countermen. Although there was no testimony that appellant requested or solicited these extra payments, one of the bank employees, Cheryl Olk, testified that after she ceased making the payments for her bank, appellant told her that she worked for a "cheap bank" and that if "something were not done," the bank's "work would not get done." [Footnote omitted.] All of the bank employees testified that in return for the additional payments, they believed that they received "prompt" and good service from appellant.

II

The basis of this appeal is that these extra payments were unsolicited "gratuities," which, although they may have violated state statutes or office regulations, did not violate RESPA because they were not the evil § 2607(b) was intended to address.

Section 2607 provides in pertinent part:

> § 2607. PROHIBITION AGAINST KICKBACKS AND UNEARNED FEES
> —BUSINESS REFERRAL
>
> (a) No person shall give and no person shall accept any fee, kickback, or thing of value

> pursuant to any agreement or understanding, oral or otherwise, that business incident to or a part of a real estate settlement service involving a federally related mortgage loan shall be referred to any person.
>
> —SPLITTING CHARGES
>
> (b) No person shall give and no person shall accept any portion, split, or percentage of any charge made or received for the rendering of a real estate settlement service in connection with a transaction involving a federally related mortgage loan other than for services actually performed.
>
> —FEES, SALARIES, COMPENSATION, OR OTHER PAYMENTS
>
> (c) Nothing in this section shall be construed as prohibiting . . . (2) the payment to any person of a bona fide salary or compensation or other payment for goods or facilities actually furnished or for services actually performed . . . .

Appellant makes two arguments in support of his contention that § 2607(b) was not intended to apply to his actions. First, he claims that the gratuities were not a "portion" of the "charge made . . . for the rendering of real estate settlement services." Second, he contends that he performed real estate settlement services in return for the gratuities.

Regarding appellant's first argument, we must initially recognize the findings made by the district court that the "gratuities were a regular portion of the payments for the rendering of settlement services," and that the "[a]gents of the banks were given the impression that gratuities had to be paid in order to get the work done." Appellant claims that these comments were not formal factual findings requiring the application of the "clearly erroneous" standard. We disagree with appellant's characterization, however, irrespective of the standard applied, it appears the "comments" were adequately supported in the record.

To come within the scope of § 2607's prohibitions, a charge need not be imposed pursuant to a state statute or local regulation, or even by the result of a specific demand by the counterman. HUD regulations provide that an "agreement or understanding" for the referral of business that is illegal under § 2607(a)

> need not be verbalized but may be established by practice, pattern, or course of conduct pursuant to which the payor and the recipient of the thing of value understand that the payment is in return for the referral of business.

24 C.F.R. § 3500.14(c) (1980). We think a similar definition should be imposed upon the term "charge" in subsection (b) ("charges" are "the expenses which have been incurred, or disbursements made, in connection with a contract, suit, or business transaction"). In this case, it is clear that the two- or three-dollar gratuities were as much a part of the "charge" imposed upon the customers as was the statutorily imposed segment. It is a reasonable inference from the evidence that in general, the continued "prompt" service was preconditioned upon the regular payment of these "gratuities." The inference is buttressed by the testimony regarding the training information passed to the institutions' employees which reflects that the custom of paying the "gratuities" was well established in the business community. [Footnote omitted.] Any remaining doubt concerning the deontic nature of the extra payments was put to rest by appellant's statement to Olk that if her bank did not "do something" about the cessation of the "gratuity" payments, the bank's work "would not get done."

Regarding appellant's second argument, appellant concedes that in return for his salary from the Torrens office, it was his obligation to render *all* customers prompt and good service, and that the reasonable value of the services he rendered was equal to the statutory portion of the "charges" he imposed. Therefore, appellant must have accepted the extra payments for something other than rendering his settlement services. Appellant cannot avoid liability under § 2607(b) simply by refusing to perform his mandated duties unless he is given a "gratuity," and thus claiming that he was "performing a real estate settlement service" in return for the extra payments.

The difficulty the panel focused upon in the original opinion concerned the construction of the phrase "received for". In essence, the panel concluded that it would be impossible for a single individual to violate § 2607(b) because he could not both accept a portion of the charge *"received for"* the rendering of real estate settlement services, and also accept the same charge *"other than for* services actually performed." If the services were not performed, the panel held, the charge could not have been received "for" the performance of those services. We think this construction of § 2607(b) is too restrictive.

Although it is true that, in general, a criminal statute must be strictly construed, it is also a well established rule of statutory construction that a court will presume against interpreting a statute in a way that will render it meaningless or ineffective. In this case, not only does the panel's interpretation conflict with what we believe was the Congressional intent behind § 2607, but it also renders the statute ineffective in achieving even what the appellant contends is the more narrow Congressional intent.

Appellant claims that Congress did not intend § 2607(b) to apply to additional payments such as the one at issue in this case. Rather, he argues that the statute was intended to apply only to the practice some real estate companies had of splitting the charges they received for performing real estate settlement services with individuals who performed no service for the company's customers in return. This split was usually intended to serve as compensation for the referral of business. Appellant relies in this argument on the subtitle of subsection 6(b), "Splitting Charges," upon the examples in the legislative history of § 2607 and the HUD regulations interpreting the section. Both of these latter sources do, in fact, discuss only splitting scenarios and we fully agree with appellant that the splitting arrangement was foremost in Congress' mind when it enacted RESPA and specifically § 2607(b). We disagree, however, that § 2607(b) was intended to deal with that problem exclusively.

Notwithstanding the examples in the legislative history and the regulations, the overall purpose of § 2607 was set forth more broadly in Senate Report No. 93-866, May 22, 1974, which reported out of committee the bill that eventually became § 2607. That report succinctly stated that one of the purposes of the bill was "to eliminate the payment of . . . unearned fees in connection with settlement services provided in federally related mortgage transactions, and for other purposes . . .," 1974 U.S.Code Cong. & Ad.News 6546, 6548, 6554, and characterizes subsection (b) as prohibiting the "acceptance of *any* portion of any charge for the rendering of a real estate settlement service other than for services actually performed." *Id.* at 6556 (emphasis added). While the title of a section of a statute should not control or vary the plain meaning of the statute itself, nevertheless the title of § 2607, "Kickbacks and Unearned Fees," appears to fortify the position that the Congressional intent was for a broader application than that ascribed to it by the appellant. Congress' aim was to stop *all* abusive practices that unreasonably inflate federally related settlement costs to the public. *Id.* at 6547, 6548. Although the focus of immediate Congressional concern may have been the splitting of fees between the recipient of the charge and unrelated third parties, the arrangement we view here is no less an example of an "abusive practice" or imposition of an "unearned fee," unreasonably increasing the cost of settlement services to the banks, and ultimately to the public at large. As stated previously, appellant concedes that the reasonable value of the services he rendered was equal to the statutory portion alone of the "charge" he levied. It should be noted in this regard that the Senate report stated: "To the extent that the payment is in excess of the reasonable value of the . . . services performed, the excess may be considered a kickback or referral fee proscribed by section 7 [§ 2607]." *Id.* at 6551.

At best, the *bank employees* were receiving a benefit in the form of expedited service. The cost for this service, however, was ultimately being paid by the bank's customers in return for a benefit that at most could be described as speculative or tangential. We think this conduct was within the Congressional concern manifested by § 2607(b). The fact that appellant kept the entirety of the extra payments instead of passing a portion of them along to an unrelated third party does not, in our opinion, render his conduct less abusive or insulate him from liability under that statute.

Given the Congressional goal of protecting the public from abusive practices that unreasonably inflate settlement costs, we see no reason to overturn the district court's construction of § 2607(b) that achieves this objective. We believe a single individual *can* violate § 2607(b) by receiving in his official capacity a "charge" for the rendering of settlement services, but personally keeping a portion of the charge in fact for something other than the performance of those services. In this case, appellant in his official role imposed and received a "charge" that incorporated not only a statutorily imposed segment, but also a "gratuity" that was ostensibly required by appellant in order to get the services properly performed. At the same time, because the prompt service was already due the bank employees under state law once the statutory fee was paid, the extra payment must have been accepted in fact for something "other than services actually performed." This conduct violated § 2607(b). The panel's construction of the statute has an additional difficulty. Even if we were to assume a more narrow Congressional intent behind § 2607, that is, an attack solely upon the "splitting" situations, the panel's construction would not achieve Congress' desired result. The two-party scenario, no less than the one-party situation we review here, is a potential victim to a construction that technically defines the phrase "receive for." In the two-party situation, the real estate company employee, or counterman, would received a "charge" "for the performance of real estate settlement services." However, because he would pass along a portion to a third individual who did nothing for the customer in return, neither the total charge nor the portion passed along would be within the panel's narrow definition of § 2607(b). Because nothing was performed for the customer in return for at least part of the charge, that portion of the charge could not have been received "for" the performance of real estate settlement services. The remaining portion, on the other hand, *would* have been received in return for the services; yet that portion would also not be subject to § 2607 because actual services were performed in its return. Under the panel's construction, therefore, the statute would be rendered meaningless, except possibly in those rare instances where the unreasonably inflated charge is officially sanctioned. We do not believe such a construction is desirable or necessary in this case and thus adopt the district court's construction which achieves Congress' intent. [Footnote omitted.]

III

Appellant also challenges § 2607 as being unconstitutionally vague. Although it is true that a statute which sets forth its provisions in terms so vague that individuals "of common intelligence must necessarily guess at its meaning . . . violates the first essential of due process of laws," we do not find that this principle has any application here. Our interpretation of § 2607(b) is a logical application of the Congressional policies underlying RESPA and the fact that no prior case has involved the precise fact situation we address here is not dispositive. All that is necessary is that a "clear and definite statement of the conduct proscribed antedate" the action alleged to be criminal. We hold that this standard was met in this case.

"In determining the sufficiency of the notice a statute must of necessity be examined in light of the conduct with which the defendant is charged." "Void for vagueness simply means that criminal responsibility should not attach where one could not reasonably understand that his conduct is proscribed." In this case, appellant certainly knew from the sign in the Torrens office and the statement he signed that his practice of accepting the extra payments was improper and that the extra payments were not "bona fide." Thus, he cannot claim that he was unfairly surprised that his conduct was illegal, only that it was proscribed under this specific statute. It is well established, however, that in light of the strong presumption of validity that attaches to Acts of Congress, the fact that individuals may differ regarding whether or not certain marginal offenses fall within a specific statute's terms does not by itself render the statute unconstitutional. Furthermore, this case has not presented any potential for discretionary enforcement of the statute, nor have the facts shown that the statute has been arbitrarily or discriminatorily invoked. We find, therefore, that § 2607(b) is sufficiently definite to pass constitutional muster.

IV

Appellant next challenges the sufficiency of the Government's evidence, claiming that the Government failed to prove that the "gratuities" were actually paid by the bank's customers, and that it failed to prove that appellant knew that the extra payments were paid by the bank's customers.

Regarding appellant's first complaint, the Government established that many of the extra payments were passed on directly to the bank's customers, and when the evidence is viewed most favorably to the Government, it is a reasonable inference that the remaining payments also were passed on to the customers at least indirectly. Furthermore, appellant has failed to support his implication that the banks, when they were representing their customers, were not themselves members of the "public" as that term is used in the legislative history of § 2607.

As to the second element of appellant's argument, we have found no support in the legislative history for the contention that the Government's burden in a § 2607 prosecution includes a showing that appellant *knew* that each payment was being passed on directly to the bank's customers. Congress' intent was to make illegal any abusive practice that unreasonably inflated the cost of real estate settlement services to the public. The fact that appellant may not have had knowledge as to whether or not specific payments were passed on directly to the bank's customers does not render his acceptance of the extra payments less abusive, or have a bearing upon whether or not the bank's customers eventually bore an increased and unwarranted cost. Because the ultimate source of the bank's funds was its customers, a sense of realism alone should have informed appellant that the customers would eventually bear the cost of the extra payments. We hold this is sufficient to meet any degree of knowledge required under § 2607(b).

V

Appellant's final challenge is based upon the disparity between the sentences imposed upon him and the other countermen in related prosecutions. This court will not infringe upon the trial court's discretion in sentencing absent a clear showing of gross abuse of that discretion. A sentence generally will not be reviewed if it is within the statutory limits and "disparity in sentences is not a predicate for appellate review." The record in the instant case reveals that the trial judge was fully aware of the other RESPA sentences and considered only the facts of the case before him. The sentence also was within the statutory limitations of RESPA. In these circumstances, we will not disturb the district court's discretion.

Affirmed.

[Some citations omitted.]

[Note: The term *en banc* means the case is being heard by the entire panel of appellate judges, usually nine. This procedure is generally reserved for very important cases.]

If the tax bill were already out, it could easily be prorated, but the estimate of tax increases can be a real problem if no one can agree on the amount of increase, which can be substantial. A possible solution is to place an adequate sum in an escrow. In this manner, if the taxes rise, the funds are available to pay for them; if they do not, the amount is transferred to the seller after the tax bill comes out.

When doing a closing statement, first determine what transactions are involved. Make a list of all the financial transfers that will be occurring, identify which parties are being affected (the buyer, the seller, or both), then determine if the transaction will be a debit or a credit. Note that to do this job, you must already have identified all the parties involved in the transaction, their claims concerning the property, and who is going to pay them. After making the list, double-check the items to determine which relate to the buyer, which relate to the seller, and which affect both of them or will be prorated. (Note that these are not always the same—for example, taxes will be prorated, but both parties may have legal fees.) Finally, to determine whether an item is a debit or a credit, ask: Does the buyer/seller get money or have to pay money out? In a debit, one owes/pays; in a credit, one gets money. Buyer's credits are items such as the earnest money, the loan balance that will be paid, and the seller's share of payments the buyer will have to make on a prorated item. Buyer's debits are items such as sales price and any prepaid items the seller has already paid for. Seller's debits include the seller's share of items the buyer will pay, expenses, and the payoff for the existing loan. Seller's credits include the purchase price and the items that were prepaid and prorated to date of closing. The following is a list of the items most frequently included in the buyer's and the seller's debits and credits.

Buyer's Debits and Credits

Debits	Credits
Purchase price	Deposits
Seller's prepaid taxes*	Mortgage proceeds
Seller's prepaid insurance*	Rents prepaid to the seller*

Loan service charges	Money needed to close
Appraisal fees	Tenants' security deposits
Transfer taxes	Unearned portion of rent paid in advance*
Legal fees	
Funds to buy personal property	

Seller's Debits and Credits

Debits	Credits
Existing mortgage balance	Purchase price
Agent's/broker's commission	Seller's prepaid taxes*
Accrued but unpaid taxes	Seller's prepaid insurance*
Prepaid rents	Buyer's purchase of personal property
Mortgage points	Fuel supplies on hand
Transfer taxes	Insurance or tax reserve on hand when mortgage is assumed
Legal fees	
Money needed to close	

**Must be prorated*

8.5 CLOSING EXPENSES

Closing may involve many expenses for both sides. The buyer may need to pay legal expenses, the recording fee for the deed of transfer, the points charged by the lender, the initial requirements of the tax and insurance reserves or escrows with the lender—generally in an amount to cover the insurance and tax requirements to the date of closing—and the survey fees. The seller *or* buyer may pay the appraisal fee, but the seller generally pays his or her own attorney's fees, broker's sales commission, any recording fees necessary to clear the title, and, in many (but not all) instances, any transfer tax. These items would be seller's debits.

8.6 PRORATIONS AT CLOSING

Prorations are for expenses to be split between the buyer and the seller. The split is based on usage or time elapsed, and any proration is agreed to in the real estate sales contract. The normal practice in each local area is followed; local practice differs significantly throughout the country. For example, a seller prepaid a fire insurance policy for one year on January 1, 1994, and sold his home on July 15, 1994. He is entitled to a prorated credit for the period he paid but did not use (July 15 through December 31, 1994). The amount is a debit for the buyer; the buyer will pay the seller that amount at closing. After all, the buyer will be receiving the benefit of the fire insurance for which the seller has already paid, so the buyer should pay the seller.

Proration is based on time; the proration here works as follows. July 15th is the middle of the month, as each month is considered to have 30 days. To July 15 is therefore six and one-half months. If each month is halved, the base is 24. Using the half-month scale, the seller has used 13 of those halves, so the buyer must pay for the remaining 11. Using the month scale, the seller has used up six and one-half and the buyer will use five and one-half. If the annual insurance premium were $600, the formula for calculating the buyer's debit and the seller's credit would be 11 ÷ 24 (or 5.5 ÷ 12) × $600 = $275.

But this is only one type of proration—the **prepaid** *proration.* There is a second type of proration called an **accrued** *proration.* This type is the reverse of the prepaid. Whereas *prepaid* means that the money has been spent but the benefit has not been received (as in the preceding insurance example), *accrued* means that the benefit has been received but the payment for it has not been made. The reversal is reflected in who pays. In accrual, the seller has received the benefit and must pay the buyer, because the buyer will have to pay the bill for the benefit. The most common example of accrual is in real estate taxes. The seller has lived in the home and received the benefits of local government, but has not yet paid the tax for these services. It is only appropriate that the seller settle with the buyer so that the buyer is not stuck with the entire tax bill when the buyer has only occupied the premises for a part of the year after the sale. See the following example.

Although there are many rules from the local bar and realtors concerning prorations, there are some generally recognized rules of proration. First, the date of closing is included in the calculation, because in most states the seller owns the property when the closing begins. In a state in which the law considers the buyer to be the property owner on the date of transfer, the calculation is changed by one day. Second, in most places, time periods are calculated on a 360-day basis (for the number of days in a year); each month is considered to have 30 days. Sometimes, however, the true number of days in a month is used; when this is the case, an actual year of 365 or 366 days (depending on leap years) is used. Third, general real estate taxes are prorated on the basis of time used, but special assessments are often handled differently. Assessments are long-term payments required because the government has made some improvement, such as new sewers or a new road. The property owner usually pays the local government in annual installments on which the government charges interest. In most cases, the installment of the current year is *not* prorated; the seller pays the current installment while the buyer assumes the rest of the payments. Fourth, garbage and sewer charges are generally prorated, but garbage service need not always be contracted from the local government; a private contractor may also be employed. Sewer service has no option. Fifth, rents from a commercial building are prorated by the actual number of days in the actual month involved. If the closing is on February 17th, 17 is the numerator, and either 28 or 29 is the denominator. This determines the amount that the seller can keep. For example, if the rent were $750 per month, and the seller had received the tenant's rental payment that month, the landlord-seller would be entitled to keep $^{17}/_{28}$ or $^{17}/_{29}$ of that $750 ($455.36 or $439.66, respectively) of the February rent. The remainder of the February rent ($^{11}/_{28}$ or $^{12}/_{29}$) is a debit to the seller and a credit to the buyer. Sixth, security deposits go to the buyer. Seventh, any employees working in connection with the building have their unpaid wages prorated as of the date of closing. Many charts and tables are available from commercial banks and title companies to help you in calculating prorations, but understanding the process itself and being able to do it from scratch is preferable in the long run.

Next, a special note. Just as these prorations can cause conflict between the parties, another area can create difficulties as well. You should be aware of any items considered fixtures, which therefore stay with the real property and are transferred as part of it. Be aware of any items considered personal property to be sold to the buyer separately or to be taken with the seller. While this is irrelevant to the topic of proration, it is similar in that adjustments and potential disagreements exist between the seller and the buyer and should be clarified in the sales contract. Check to determine what items are handled in which manner. Note that there may be differences between the treatment of items in a residential transaction and a commercial transaction. Finally, it is always best to get potential disagreements settled in the sales contract, long before closing occurs.

There are several ways to do a proration. First, as explained earlier, it can be done on a $^{30}/_{360}$-day basis. Every month has 30 days and each year has 12 months, giving a 360-day year. Each day is always $^{1}/_{30}$ of a month. Second, it is possible to count the actual number of days elapsed in an actual $^{365}/_{366}$-day year. This proration is calculated in much the same way as interest. It is the dollar amount times the number of days, divided by the base of 365 or 366. In most cases, the calculations of either type are carried out to thousandths, so it can be rounded into cents.

The purpose of proration, as you have seen, is clear—the equitable split of the amount owed or the amount paid between the property buyer and the property seller. The split is based on the benefit or value that each party has received or will receive. Thus, proration is based on the amount of time one party received or will receive the benefit—and that benefit must be paid for. If the seller has prepaid $600 for home insurance for a year on January 1, and the buyer (with the approval of the insurance company) assumes that policy when she buys the home on August 15, then the seller has paid for and received the benefit of that insurance up to August 15, but will receive no benefit there after. The buyer owes the seller for the period from August 15 through December 31. The buyer pays for the benefit she receives. Because there are 12 months (24 half-months), each month is worth $50 and each half-month is worth $25. Then, because there are four and one-half months remaining from August 15 through December 31, the proration the buyer pays the seller is $225.

This is an example of a prepaid item to be prorated, but the other type of proration is the accrued item. It is the reverse, or flip side, of the prepaid item. While the prepaid item has the money fully expended and the benefit not fully received, for the accrued item, the money has not been paid, but the benefit has been received. The seller pays for the benefit that he has received but has not paid

LEGAL TERMS

prepaid
One of the two types of proration; refers to a situation in which the seller has fully paid for a service, but will not be using all of what has been paid for. The buyer will receive the benefit of the unused portion and must pay the seller for that amount.

accrued
Type of proration in which the seller has received the benefit, such as a government service paid for by taxation, but has not paid for it; opposite of *prepaid*.

for. Prorating payment prevents the buyer from having to pay more than her share when the bill comes for the service. The most common example is the county and local government tax bill. That bill almost always comes in arrears, so one is paying for services already rendered—often a year or more behind.

How does one determine how recently the taxes have been paid? The title search will show through what year the taxes have been paid. Thus, in 1994, one usually pays taxes for 1993. Consider these facts. Seller lives in the home during 1993 and on February 17, 1994, sells the home. The last taxes paid were for 1992, for $8,500. The best estimate is that the taxes will increase by 7.5 percent for 1993. That would make the new tax bill $9,137.50 ($8,500 × 1.075 = $9,137.50). What will the seller have to pay? He will have to pay for all of 1993 and the portion of 1994 that he has occupied the home. The amount for 1993 will be the $9,137.50. But what about January 1, 1994, to February 17, 1994? For discussion, assume those taxes rose another 5 percent. That would make the 1994 taxes $9,594.38 ($9,137.50 × 1.05 = $9,594.38). Now, the method of proration must be determined. The simplest way is to use the actual number of days elapsed on an actual-year basis. That would be 31 days in January and 17 in February, for a total of 48 days, in a year having 365 days. The amount would be determined by this formula—$9,594.38 × 48 ÷ 365 = $1,261.73. When the full year and this proration are added, the sum is $10,856.11. The other common base for proration is the 30-day month in a 360-day year (often called a 30⁄360 basis). Using this method, one finds out what one month's taxes would be—$9,594.38 ÷ 12 = $799.53. One month is divided by 30 days (despite the fact that February has only 28) and the result is multiplied by 17; thus, $799.53 ÷ 30 = $26.65 × 17 = $453.07. Add that to $799.53, and the amount due for 1994 taxes is $1,252.60.

Although the final amounts' difference is slightly less than $10, you should be alert to the differences in calculation results. A small item like this can drive some buyers or sellers up the wall. A tactful explanation ahead of time usually avoids the problem. The prorated time period can be quite long when the closing is in the last part of the year, but it is no more difficult to calculate. Suppose, for example that the closing, instead of being on February 17, is on November 23. On the 360-day basis, instead of having only January, there are now 10 months fully elapsed plus the 23 days of November. One 30-day month has a value of $799.53 ($9,594.38 ÷ 12 = $799.53), and October is the 10th month, so the 10 months give a total of $7,995.30. The remaining 23 days are calculated as follows—$799.53 ÷ 30 × 23 = $612.97. When that amount is added to the figure for the first 10 months, the sum is $8,608.27. Prorating by the actual number of days elapsed is more time-consuming, because the number of days in each month must be added for the first 10 months (through October) plus the 23 days of November. Those days total 327. The calculation is therefore $9594.38 × 327 ÷ 365 = $8595.51. Banks and others use calendars that give the number of days elapsed and the number of days remaining in a year to simplify calculation. There is also a simple device by which to handle actual days elapsed. It appears in table 8-1. Using this chart, go to the end of the month prior to the one in which the

Month	Number of Days	Cumulative Number of Days
January	31	31
February	28/9	59/60
March	31	90/91
April	30	120/121
May	31	151/152
June	30	181/182
July	31	212/213
August	31	243/244
September	30	273/274
October	31	304/305
November	30	334/335
December	31	365/366

TABLE 8-1
Days-elapsed chart

closing will occur, take the cumulative number of days for that month, and add the number of days in the final month to get the total number of days.

In summary, it is important to identify who is to make the payment (the buyer or the seller); the type of payment (prepaid or accrued); the amount of the time to be paid for; and the time basis to be used as the divisor $^{365}/_{366}$ days or a $^{30}/_{360}$-day year). Finally, you should note that the taxes in the closing statement example shown in § 8.8 are prepaid, not accrued, taxes. This situation can also occur, but it is less likely than having the taxes be accrued and unpaid.

8.7 CREATING THE SETTLEMENT STATEMENT

The settlement statement required under RESPA is widely used, but it is not the clearest possible nor the most common means of handling the information. Until you are really familiar with that statement, it is advisable to use a worksheet and decide how to transfer information from that worksheet to the RESPA statement. Besides, in closing statements, it never hurts to double-check. Most people make at least one mistake as they learn this process. Be *very* careful, double-check your work, and make certain that it is correct. A third party may be helpful. When double-checking, do the problem from scratch after you have forgotten it. Do not just go over the numbers; they all look correct. Not only is it professional to be correct, but it is essential to do the RESPA statement correctly—the law requires it. This section shows a sample situation with a worksheet and a RESPA settlement statement.

The Facts. Mary Ann and Jake Rostenkowski want to buy a home from Said and Sally Obanni for $350,000. The seller's realtor will receive a 6 percent sales commission. The buyers will put down $52,500 as earnest money.

There will be a mortgage loan for $245,000. There will be a loan fee of 1.5 percent. There will be a transfer tax of 2 percent, split by the seller (1.25 percent) and the buyer (.75 percent). There is fuel in the home worth $1,500. The survey cost $375. The appraisal cost $250. There was a $90 credit report. The bank wants the interest paid through the end of the month at the closing on June 15, 1994; the rate of interest is 8.5 percent. There will be a deposit in escrow as for taxes of $2,100. There are two title insurance policies—for the lender and the buyer—both of which will be paid for by the buyer, for $1,500. There are legal fees of $750 for the buyer and $800 for the seller. There are recording fees for the buyer of $90 and for the seller of $30. Fire and hazard insurance was prepaid at $1,800 a year on March 1. There is a mechanic's lien on the property for $2,250. The termite inspection and remedial action cost $850. The payoff of the seller's mortgage will be $215,000. The seller paid the real estate taxes in full, in the amount of $8,400, on June 1 for the current year. The actual number of days elapsed is used in these calculations.

The closing worksheet, as shown in figure 8-1, is generated as follows.

The *sales price* is the amount paid by the buyers to the sellers to purchase the home. The *earnest money* is the amount the buyers deposit as evidence that they are serious about making the purchase; it is usually contingent on obtaining financing. Earnest money, however, may be forfeited to the sellers if financing is not obtained, although that is not universally so. It is part of the buyers' payment. It is a credit because the buyers have already paid it. The *realtor's commission* is the sales fee received by the person who arranged the sale. It is paid by the sellers. Six percent is not unusual, although a transaction this large may be negotiated. The fee may be split with another broker if, for example, one took the listing and another found the buyer. The way they split the fee is determined between the parties or by local custom. The *mortgage loan* is the money a creditor lends the buyers to purchase the house. It is part of what the buyers receive, so it is a credit. Lenders frequently charge a *loan fee* on real estate transactions. This one-time fee is low, 1.5 percent of the loan. Governments, state or local, charge a *transfer tax.* The tax here is 2 percent, fairly high, and is split between the parties—1.25 percent paid by the sellers, and .75 percent paid by the buyers. The *fuel* item refers to the value of heating oil, coal, or whatever fuel is stored in the house to be transferred with the property. The *survey* indicates the precise location of the property and what items are on the property. Sometimes surveys are done in the office without inspecting the site; a visual inspection and checking against the appraisal report are recommended before relying on the survey.

The *appraisal* is an estimate of the parcel's value. The lender gets a *credit report* on the borrower and charges back the fee. The lender wants interest paid in advance, at least to the end of the current month; that is the *interest deposit.* The amount is calculated by taking the principal of $245,000 × .085 (the interest rate) × the time (15 days ÷ by 365 days in the year), which equalled $855.82. The *tax deposit* is the amount of the current month and two more months' worth of taxes deposited into a bank escrow account. The bank

CLOSING WORKSHEET

Whose Entry (B/S)	Item (RESPA Number)	Buyer Debit	Buyer Credit	Seller Debit	Seller Credit
B&S	Sales Price (101/401)	350,000			350,000
B	Earn. Money (201)		52,500		
S	Rltr's Comm. (700/703)			21,000	
B	Mortgage Loan (202)		245,000		
B	Loan Fee (802)	3,675			
B&S	Transfer Tax (1204)	2,625		4,375	
B&S	Fuel (1303)	1,500			1,500
B	Survey (1301)	375			
B	Appraisal (803)	250			
B	Credit Report (804)	90			
B	Interest Deposit (901)	855.82			
B	Tax Deposit (1004)	2,100			
B	Title Insur. (1108-10)	1,500			
B&S	Legal Fees (1107)	750		800	
B&S	Recording (1201)	90		30	
B&S	Fire&Haz. Ins. (111/411)	1,272.33			1,272.33
S	Mechanic's Lien (515)			2,250	
S	Termite Inspection (1302)			850	
S	Mortgage Payoff (504)			215,000	
B&S	R.E. Taxes (107/407)	4,579.73			4,579.73
	Totals	$369,662.88	297,500	244,305	357,352.06
	Needed to Close		72,162.88		
	Due to Seller			113,047.06	
	Balances	$369,662.88	369,662.88	357,352.06	357,352.06

FIGURE 8-1
Closing Worksheet

pays the taxes from the escrow account during the lifetime of the mortgage when they come due. Most mortgage payments include insurance and taxes in the monthly payment. (Additionally, there may be an insurance deposit, although one was not included in this example.) The inclusion of insurance and taxes ensures that the lender is not stuck with paying these if the borrower cannot. *Title insurance* coverage exists for both the lender and the borrower, who pays both (they are simply lumped together here). The *legal fees* are for the work of an attorney; actually, the fees may be considerably higher than the ones shown here.

Each party pays a *recording fee.* The seller must pay off the *mechanic's lien,* obtain a satisfaction or release, and record it. The buyer must record the deed, the new mortgage, and perhaps the release of the old mortgage. The *fire and hazard insurance* shows a credit due to the seller to be paid by the buyer.

This prorated amount was calculated by taking the entire payment, $1,800, times the number of days left in the year already paid for (365 – 107 = 258) ÷ 365 = $1,272.33. A necessary item, the *termite inspection,* cost $850. The *mortgage payoff* of the seller's mortgage cost $215,000. Actually, there would be a per diem interest figure, so it could never work out to be an even amount as this example has. Because the lender gives the figure to the closer, the calculation is generally easy after a simple arithmetic check.

The *real estate taxes* are prorated, as they have been prepaid by the seller. Because the taxes are assessed and owed annually, and the seller will have the benefit through June 15 and the buyer to the end of the year, the buyer must pay for the period from June 15 through December 31. There are 213 days after June 15, so the calculation is the payment amount, $8,400 × 199 days ÷ a 365-day year = $4,579.73. If the taxes had not been prepaid, but accrued, the seller would have owed the buyer for the time used, through June 15th. That calculation is as follows—$8,400 × 166 days ÷ 365 = $3,820.27.

Figure 8-2 shows the worksheet numbers after transfer to the numbered lines of a RESPA settlement statement.

8.8 REAL ESTATE CLOSING CHECKLIST

The closing can range from complicated to easy, depending on a number of factors. Among these factors are the complexity of the closing; the sophistication of the financial arrangements; whether the transaction is a residential, commercial, or industrial building closing; the closer's facility in working with all the parties involved; and whether one is working for the buyer or the seller. Which party employs you sets your framework for the closing and the protection of your client's interests. An essential tool to avoiding disaster is a device to keep track of what you want to achieve. This checklist should get you started in the right direction.

I. Establish a file for your client that relates to this specific transaction.
   A. Elements of that file.
      1. The client's name.
      2. The client number (if your office assigns such).
      3. Billing information.
         a. Address(es).
         b. Rate(s) to be charged for different types of work.
      4. Establish a cross-reference system to other clients to avoid any conflict of interest.
   B. Other file information.

II. Begin gathering and organizing information.
   A. Review the real estate sales contract, the closing's framework, as to the responsibilities of the parties.
      1. Seller's name.
      2. Buyer's name.

J. SUMMARY OF BORROWER'S TRANSACTION	
100. GROSS AMOUNT DUE FROM BORROWER	
101. Contract sales price	350,000.00
102. Personal Property	
103. Settlement charges to borrower (line 1400)	13,810.82
104. Rent adjustment	
105. Acknowledgement of deed	
ADJUSTMENTS FOR ITEMS PAID BY SELLER IN ADVANCE	
106. City/Town taxes to	
107. County taxes 1/1/9x to 6/15/9x	4,579.73
108. Assessments to	
109. Water/sewer rent	
110. School taxes	
111. Prepd. Fire & Haz. Ins.	1,272.33
112. 3/1/9x-6/15/9x	
120. GROSS AMOUNT DUE FROM BORROWER	369,662.88
200. AMOUNTS PAID BY OR IN BEHALF OF BORROWER	
201. Deposit or earnest money	52,500.00
202. Principal amount of new loan(s)	245,000.00
203. Existing loan(s) taken subject to	
204.	
205.	
206.	
207.	
208.	
209.	
ADJUSTMENTS FOR ITEMS UNPAID BY SELLER	
210. City/Town taxes to	
211. County taxes to	
212. Assessments to	
213. Water/sewer rent	
214. School taxes	
215.	
216.	
217.	
218.	
219.	
220. TOTAL PAID BY/FOR BORROWER	297,500.00
300. CASH AT SETTLEMENT FROM OR TO BORROWER	
301. Gross amount due from borrower (line 120)	369,662.88
302. Less amounts paid by/for borrower (line 220)	(297,500.00)
303. CASH ☐ FROM ☑ TO BORROWER	72,162.88

K. SUMMARY OF SELLER'S TRANSACTION	
400. GROSS AMOUNT DUE TO SELLER	
401. Contract sales price	350,000.00
402. Personal Property	
403. Rent adjustment	
404. Acknowledgement of deed	
405.	
ADJUSTMENTS FOR ITEMS PAID BY SELLER IN ADVANCE	
406. City/Town taxes to	
407. County taxes 1/1/9x to 6/15/9x	4,579.73
408. Assessments to	
409. Water/sewer rent	
410. School taxes	
411. Prepd. Fire & Haz. Ins.	1,272.33
412. 3/1/9x-6/15/9x	1,500.00
420. GROSS AMOUNT DUE TO SELLER	357,352.06
500. REDUCTIONS IN AMOUNT DUE TO SELLER	
501. Excess Deposit (see instructions)	
502. Settlement charges to seller (line 1400)	27,055.00
503. Existing loan(s) taken subject to	
504. Payoff of first mortgage loan	215,000.00
505. Payoff of second mortgage loan	
506.	
507.	
508.	
509. Escrow	
ADJUSTMENTS FOR ITEMS UNPAID BY SELLER	
510. City/Town taxes to	
511. County taxes to	
512. Assessments to	
513. Water/sewer rent	
514. School taxes	
515. Mechanic's lien	2,250.00
516.	
517.	
518.	
519.	
520. TOTAL REDUCTION AMOUNT DUE SELLER	244,305.00
600. CASH AT SETTLEMENT TO OR FROM SELLER	
601. Gross amount due to seller (line 420)	357,352.06
602. Less reduction amount due seller (line 520)	(244,305.00)
603. CASH ☐ TO ☐ FROM SELLER	113,047.06

FIGURE 8-2

RESPA settlement statement

L. SETTLEMENT CHARGES	PAID FROM BORROWER'S FUNDS AT SETTLEMENT	PAID FROM SELLER'S FUNDS AT SETTLEMENT
700. TOTAL SALES/BROKER'S COMMISSION(based on price) $350,000 @6%		
Division of commission (line 700) as follows: $ @ %= $		
701. $ to		
702. $ to		
703. Commission paid at Settlement		21,000.00
704.		
800. ITEMS PAYABLE IN CONNECTION WITH LOAN		
801. Loan Origination Fee %		
802. Loan Discount 2 %	3,675.00	
803. Appraisal Fee $250.00 to Meekete App'l Co.	250.00	
804. Credit Report $ 90.00 to ABC Credit Co.	90.00	
805. Lender's Inspection Fee		
806. VA Funding Fee to		
807. Assumption Fee		
808. to		
809.		
810.		
811.		
900. ITEMS REQUIRED BY LENDER TO BE PAID IN ADVANCE		
901. Interest from 6-15-94 to 6-30-94 @$ 57.054 /day	855.82	
902. Mortgage Insurance Premium for mos. to		
903. Hazard Insurance Premium for yrs. to		
904. Flood Insurance yrs. to		
905.		
1000. RESERVES DEPOSITED WITH LENDER FOR		
1001. Hazard Insurance mos. @ $ /mo.		
1002. Mortgage Insurance mos. @ $ /mo.		
1003. City Property Taxes mos. @ $ /mo.		
1004. County Property Taxes 3 mos. @ $ 700 /mo.	2,100.00	
1005. Annual Assessments mos. @ $ /mo.		
1006. School taxes mos. @ $ /mo.		
1007. mos. @ $ /mo.		
1008. mos. @ $ /mo.		
1100. TITLE CHARGES		
1101. Settlement or Closing Fee to		
1102. Abstract or Title Search to		
1103. Title Examination to		
1104. Title Insurance Binder to		
1105. Document Preparation to		
1106. Notary Fees to		
1107. Attorney's Fees to	750.00	800.00
(includes above items No.:)		
1108. Title Insurance to	1,500.00	
(includes above items No.:)		
1109. Lender's Coverage $ 1,000.00		
1110. Owner's Coverage $ 500.00		
1111. Tax Certificate(s)		
1112. Endorsement fees to: Endorsement 300,100.00		
1113.		
1200. GOVERNMENT RECORDING AND TRANSFER CHARGES		
1201. Recording Fees: Deed $ 30.00 ; Mortgage $ 30.00 ; Release $ 30/30	90.00	30.00
1202. City/County tax/stamps: Deed $; Mortgage $		
1203. State tax/stamps: Deed $; Mortgage $		
1204. Transfer tax	2,625.00	4,375.00
1205.		
1300. ADDITIONAL SETTLEMENT CHARGES		
1301. Survey to	375.00	
1302. Pest Inspection to		850.00
1303. Fuel in house	1,500.00	
1304.		
1305.		
1400. TOTAL SETTLEMENT CHARGES (enter on line 103, Section J and line 502, Section K)		27,055.00

FIGURE 8-2

(Continued)

3. Is either the buyer or seller a corporation, partnership, or trust?
    a. Verify the name and good standing.
    b. Establish authority for action to be taken.
4. Broker's name.
5. Real property description.
6. Closing date.
7. Seller's position.
    a. What must the seller provide?
    b. What must the seller get?
8. Buyer's position.
    a. What must the buyer provide?
    b. What must the buyer get?

B. Other considerations to be included.
1. Is there any need for a foreign person affidavit under the Internal Revenue Code?
2. Has the earnest money been received?
3. Recent bills.
    a. Taxes.
    b. Water/sewage.
    c. Utilities.
    d. Fuel.
        (1) How much is there?
        (2) Appropriate proration?
    e. Others?
4. Architectural plans, drawings, and specifications.
    a. Original building(s).
    b. Additions.
    c. Modifications.
    d. Renovations, remodeling, etc.
5. Guarantees and warranties for the building.
    a. Construction.
    b. Equipment.
        (1) Roof.
        (2) Water heater.
        (3) Furnace and air conditioning.
        (4) Humidifier.
6. Evidence of compliance with building codes or other government restrictions.
7. Will there be an escrow?
    a. Are the standard instructions drafted?
    b. Anything special to be added?
    c. Who is to be the escrow agent?
    d. Fees?
8. Is there a need for a soil, radon, toxic chemical, or waste check?

9. When do the keys to the building change hands?
10. Are there tenants?
    a. List of tenants.
    b. Rent proration.
    c. Transfer of leases.
    d. Notice to pay buyer rent hereafter.
        (1) Notice drafted.
        (2) Notice sent.
11. Sales of personal property.
    a. Bulk sale affidavit needed?
    b. Inventory of supplies?
    c. UCC-1 or UCC-2 search needed?
12. Inspection of the property?
    a. Who is making it?
    b. When?
    c. Arrangements with seller?
    d. List of problems or defects to be repaired?
    e. Identify occupants (if commercial building) and determine if they have claims on any personal property.
    f. Make a visual check for unrecorded easements.
    g. Are there any markers, signs, etc., that require a permit?
    h. Is everything in compliance with building codes, zoning ordinances, governmental restrictions?
    i. Make sure the survey and the premises match.
    j. Are there any recent improvements?
        (1) Have they been paid for?
        (2) Evidence? Mechanic's liens?
    k. Rising assessments due to recent public improvements?
    l. Verify operation of the systems on the property—from water and heating to elevators and sprinkler systems.
    m. Final inspection before closing.
        (1) Check for changes.
        (2) Check that all personal property being transferred is still there.
13. Any proposed public improvements nearby? Effect on parcel?

C. Make a checklist from the information in Parts A & B.

D. Review the loan documentation requirements.
1. Creditor's name.
2. Debtor's name (usually the buyer).
3. Loan amount.
4. Has the creditor specified a cut-off date for the commitment? When is it? How does it tie into the closing date?
5. Creditor's requirements for the loan closing.
    a. Debtor must provide to the creditor:
        (1) What items of information?
        (2) What documents and items of paperwork?

   b. What must the seller provide to the creditor or the buyer to transmit to the lender?
  6. Create a loan closing checklist from these materials.

E. Handling the title examination and the title policy.
  1. What is the real property description? Verify accuracy in detail.
  2. By what date will the examination be needed?
  3. Title company's name.
  4. Insured's name(s).
  5. Amount of coverage; inflation, price increase covered?
  6. What objections, restrictions, or waivers exist?
  7. Does the title commitment/policy meet the buyer's need for clean (or marketable) title?
  8. Will the title policy be issuable at the appropriate time for the closing?
  9. Estoppel certificate?
  10. Any mistakes in the documents?
    a. Blanks?
    b. Signatures?
    c. Witnessing?
    d. Attestation?
    e. Acknowledgements?

F. Is there a need for a current survey?
  1. Verify accurate legal description.
  2. Is there important information on the previous survey?
  3. Parties whose names will appear on the survey.
    a. Buyer.
    b. Lender?
    c. Others?
  4. Does this parcel lie in a flood zone?
    a. Appropriate certificate?
    b. Insurance?
  5. When must the survey be completed by? Specify.
  6. Anything special needed for this survey?

G. Identify needs for fire and hazard insurance.
  1. Which hazards?
  2. Identify the location of the property.
  3. How much insurance coverage?
  4. Premium payment.
    a. Binder adequate?
    b. Need evidence of payment for first year?
  5. Identify lender for its coverage.
    a. Loss payee provision being set up?
  6. By what date must the insurance policy be ready?
    a. How much lead time is needed to complete this?
  7. Can insurance be assumed from seller?

a. Desirable?

III. Matters to handle before the closing.
   A. Get copies of all the title exceptions.
   B. Examine the title examination and policy.
      1. Identify automatic problems such as liens.
      2. Identify covenants, restrictions, and so on that may create problems.
   C. Are there any problems with the parties in possession? Do they have claims under unrecorded deeds?
   D. Request amount of payoffs based on any monetary claim stemming from a mortgage, lien, or other encumbrance. Make certain the closing logistics are worked out with these parties so they, and the appropriate documents, are present.
   E. Examine the survey.
      1. Any encroachments on the property lines?
      2. Does this survey comply with the creditor's and debtor's requirements?
   F. Have both parties fulfilled their promises under the real estate sales contract?
      1. Pest and termite inspection?
   G. Is everything in place for the creditor to make the loan?
   H. Be sure to identify who is filing the IRS Form 1099.
   I. Are there any environmental problems? Is there any need for a hazardous waste affidavit?

IV. Preparing documents for the closing.
   A. Transfer documents.
      1. Bill of sale document and appropriate deed.
      2. Releases or satisfactions.
      3. Other?
         a. Rent assignment(s)?
         b. Security agreement?
         c. Financing statement(s)?
         d. Personal guaranty?
         e. Assignments of leases and rents?
         f. Government forms?
            (1) FHA?
            (2) VA?
            (3) Environmental impact statement?
            (4) Foreign investment in real property coverage—exemption or provision for tax withholding.
            (5) Income tax reporting—who is responsible?
   B. Loan documents (if permitted by the lender).
      1. Note.
         a. Amortization schedule.
      2. Mortgage or deed of trust.
      3. Other?

C. Transfer tax documentation.
D. Other documents.
   1. Loan application (copy).
   2. Creditor's lending commitment (copy).
   3. Credit agreement between the borrower and the creditor.
   4. Most recent audited financial statements of the borrower, if a business.
   5. Sales contract (copy).
   6. Escrow agreement (copy).
   7. Appraisal.
   8. Property photographs (may be with appraisal).
   9. Credit reports on borrower.
   10. Survey and subdivision plat. Check survey against appraisal to make sure it is a correct description.
   11. Evidence of compliance with all government requirements.
      a. Zoning and other regulations.
      b. Operating permits or licenses, if needed.
   12. Leases.
   13. Results of a UCC search against personal property.
   14. Water rights for the property (especially important in dry areas of the country).
E. Basic additional closing documents for a construction loan.
   1. The construction contract.
   2. The take-out or permanent lending commitment.
   3. Letters of credit.
   4. Plans and specifications.
   5. Bonding documentation.
   6. Owner-architect contract.
   7. Permits.
   8. Zoning compliance.
   9. The interim lending agreement.
   10. What utilities are available on the property?
   11. Important subcontractors' contracts.
   12. Soil tests.
   13. Documents regarding payments.
      a. Architect's certificate.
      b. Lien waivers.
      c. Evidence of payment.
   14. Attorney's opinion(s) concerning sufficiency of the transaction to transfer property and do all elements necessary and proper to establish parties as intended.

V. Closing procedures.
A. Identify the closing's attendees and tell them its date, time, and location.
   1. Buyer.
   2. Seller.

3. Other attorneys.
4. Creditor.
5. Broker(s).
6. Title company personnel.
7. Others?
    a. Condo association or planned unit development obligation?
    b. Utilities?

B. Financial aspects.
    1. Buyer—how much to bring in good funds, such as a cashier's check.
    2. Check the settlement statement—as appropriate.
    3. Identify who is to be paid what and the checks to be cut for each.

C. Be certain that the creditor has deposited the loan proceeds in an account of your firm.

D. Make sure a room with adequate space is available. Courtesy refreshments customary?

E. Put together the package of closing documents.

VI. Final actions on documentation.

A. Pay off any parties who have claims against the property—liens, mortgages, deeds of trust, encumbrances, mechanics' liens, and so on—as a part of closing.

B. Obtain the proper releases or satisfactions in a form appropriate for recording from these parties in return for that payoff.

C. Make absolutely certain that all the appropriately executed and delivered documents are taken to the proper recording office immediately.

D. Put together the final closing packages.
    1. Seller.
    2. Buyer.
    3. Creditor.

VII. Final actions.

A. Get all the recorded documents from the courthouse.

B. Do a final title exam to make certain no intervening lien has slipped in and to make certain everything has been indexed properly.

C. Check the contents of the title insurance policy.

D. Documents to be sent out.
    1. Deed and title policy to buyer.
    2. Note, mortgage, other loan documents, and title policy to creditor.

E. Double-check to make sure everything needed to be done was actually done.

F. Take this file and put it away.

DISCUSSION AND REVIEW QUESTIONS

1. What might be the closer's first and second requirements of closings?
2. Identify the parties who can contribute to the closing and what the contribution of each is.
3. Perform the following prorations.
   a. *Taxes.* Taxes are running at $8,100 per year. The seller owes for the year 1995, but has not paid any taxes. The closing is on August 8, 1995. Compute the amount the seller will have to pay the buyer by the actual-number-of-days-elapsed method and by the $^{30}/_{360}$ method.
   b. *Insurance.* The seller prepaid fire insurance in the amount of $1,500 on January 1; the closing is on September 19. Compute the amount the buyer will owe the seller.
4. Prepare the following three sets of closing materials on a closing worksheet form like the one shown in § 8.8, figure 8-1.
   a. The estate of Mary Fields is being sold by the executor and sole heir for $127,500. The closing will occur on October 28, 1993. The broker will receive a 6 percent sales commission. The buyers have paid a 10 percent earnest money deposit. Real estate taxes are $3,778 for 1993 and have not been paid. The seller will pay all of the 2 percent transfer taxes. The buyers have received a loan for $105,000. Prorate as necessary on a $^{30}/_{360}$ basis.
   b. The Lopezes are selling their home for $98,250. Settlement will be on April 23, 1994. There is a 6.5 percent earnest money deposit. The loan commitment is for 85 percent of the purchase price. There will be title insurance for the buyer at a cost of $500 and for the lender at a cost of $850. The real estate taxes of $3,150 for 1994 have been paid. The Lopezes' attorney's fee is $675; the buyer's attorney's fee is $850. The Lopezes' mortgage balance is $52,500, its interest rate is 9.5 percent, and they pay the note on the first of each month in advance. The Lopezes' realtor will receive a 7 percent commission. Prorate on a $^{30}/_{360}$ basis as necessary.
   c. Joe and Donna Borghese are selling their home for $165,000. Their realtor will receive a 6 percent commission. Their mortgage is for $84,000 at 8.75 percent and is due on the first of the month in advance. The seller's attorney's fees are $900 and the buyer's are $1,100. The seller has 200 gallons of fuel in the basement at $1.55 per gallon. The real estate taxes, $4,750, have been paid. The closing will be on March 17, 1994. The earnest money was 7 percent. The fire and hazard insurance was taken out in a three-year policy on March 1, 1992, will be transferred, and the premium was $2,700. There will be a recording fee of $60 for the buyer. The cost of title insurance will be $675. Prorate by the actual number of days elapsed.

CHAPTER 9
Leasing Real Property

"A verbal contract isn't worth the paper it's written on."

Samuel Goldwyn

Post-WWII ranch house

OUTLINE

PROLOGUE TO THE PARALEGAL

Although this chapter is entitled "Leasing Real Property," it could just as well have been called "Landlord-Tenant." Because paralegals spend a great deal of time with documents, the document was referred to in the title rather than the parties involved. This area of real estate law is intricate. The two major parts of leasing deal with the purpose to which the lessee (the party who will occupy the property) intends to put the property; generally, the purpose is either for residence or for business. Much of the real estate business lies in making leases, and paralegals are frequently involved in transactions with the real property owner, the lessor, and the documentation that relates to the lessor's needs. Occasionally, a residential lessee may want a lease reviewed, but many residential leases are a standardized form and are not usually subject to negotiation. In commercial leases, there may be considerable negotiation over leasing terms. The subject of commercial leases is beyond the scope of this book, however; too much detail and too many complexities are involved.

KEY TERMS

constructive eviction
cure of default
default
distraint
ejectment
escalator clause

estoppel
estoppel certificate
eviction
exculpatory clause
graduated lease
gross lease
ground lease
independent covenants (clauses)
index lease
lease
lessee (tenant)
lessor (landlord)
net lease
percentage lease
reappraisal lease
rent
rent abatement
Statute of Frauds
step-up lease
subordination agreement
survivability clause
term of the lease
triple net lease
unconscionable
warranty of habitability

9.1 INTRODUCTION

For nonowners of real property to enjoy the use of real property, an arrangement must be made between the owner and the party who wants to use or occupy the property. The most frequent form this arrangement takes is called the **lease**. A lease transfers an estate from the owner (traditionally called the **landlord**, but also called the **lessor** under the lease-contract), to the user (traditionally called the **tenant**, but also called the **lessee** under the lease-contract). The lease agreement transfers a portion of the owner's interest in the real property for a period of time. When someone rents an apartment, for example, the owner normally transfers the right to use the property for a year to the tenant. The duration of time can vary. It may be as short as a few months or as long as 99 (or 999) years. In some states, a transfer of any term longer than 99 years is considered a fee simple transfer. The lessor keeps the right to receive rent payments and the right of reversion. The tenant occupies the property, pays the rent, does not commit waste (damage important enough to harm the landlord's interest), and uses the property for his or her purposes. Thereafter, however, complications can arise.

The first complication is the way the common law treated the relationship between the landlord and the tenant. Remember that land was the original source of all good things when the law was first being created. One rented land, not anything that was on or a part of the land. Any building was merely incidental. The tenant could repair it, but it probably was not a very substantial house, hay mow, or barn in most cases. Repair and replacement were simple, and they were something the tenant not only knew how to do, but also was expected to do. Basically, one rented the land and made do thereafter with whatever one had; buildings were impermanent and farming the land was the primary concern. Therefore, it was logical to have the covenants of the landlord and the tenant be considered separately. The **covenants**, or promises, were **independent** of each other. If one party did not perform (e.g., the landlord), that failure did not affect the duty of the other party (the tenant) to perform. This usually meant that the rent had to be paid, regardless of whether the landlord performed his covenants or not. In some states, this medieval basis of the law of landlord and tenant is still effective, but since the 1970s, this law has been changing.

Clearly, this older law is no longer realistic. The tenant in an apartment complex or a shopping mall probably has little or no understanding of building repair, and usually there is no land to make use of beyond the land on which the building itself sits. The law has evolved most in the area of residential landlord-tenant relationships. The basic principle is one of power and knowledge. If the relationship is very one-sided—the landlord has all the bargaining power, as in a residential lease—the law is more likely to protect the tenant. The possibility of this protection may decrease as the power (knowledge or sophistication) of the tenant increases. The businessperson who has bargaining power equal to that of the landlord-lessor, and who has or is capable of having sophisticated knowledge about the situation, is less likely to win the sympathy or assistance of the courts regarding leasing arrangements. On the other hand, the small businessperson's situation may be analogous to that of the consumer renting an apartment. This businessperson may be able to use similar arguments in seeking the assistance of the courts.

Finally, the businessperson is less likely to receive the help of the courts and legislatures in changing the law because businesspeople are not a homogeneous group. Some businesspeople may have knowledge and power, others may not. As a result, it is difficult for courts or legislatures to create a set of legal rules that can be used consistently in many similar situations. Most residential tenants, however, lack knowledge and power. The courts or legislatures can safely fashion a rule that will work in most cases with the residential situation; the business situation, however, will require much time and energy in court to determine the facts and a correspondingly appropriate rule of law. This burden is not one that most courts, especially with today's major docket delays, will readily assume.

Residential leases are now more frequently considered to be the rental of a service, that is, the providing of a place to live, rather than a transfer of an estate in land. Legal theory about provision of services makes it easier to require that the landlord maintain the premises in a safe and habitable (usable) condition. A rule has developed to impose a duty on the landlord to maintain the premises. Various states have adopted the Uniform Residential Landlord and Tenant Act (URLTA), and many cities have adopted local ordinances regulating the relationship between landlord and tenant. Those laws and ordinances are tied primarily to residential leases rather than commercial ones.

Consider the problem of a person who rents an apartment and then dies. Is the lease still applicable? Does the estate owe the rent until the lease expires, or until there is a new tenant? How is this situation handled? The *Conklin* case explains the alternatives. The tenant, Joseph Conklin, rented the apartment and then died, and the landlord sued his estate. The defendant Conklin was the executor of the tenant's estate.

LEGAL TERMS

lease
Written contract containing the agreements between the landlord and the tenant.

lessor (landlord)
Party to the lease who owns the property (usually) and who transfers occupation for rent payments.

lessee (tenant)
Party to the lease who pays the rent and occupies the premises.

independent covenants (clauses)
Contract term; the agreements in the contract or lease do not work in such a manner that the failure of one party to perform its agreement permits the other party not to perform its agreement. The most common example is that the tenant must continue to pay rent even though the landlord has not maintained the premises.

IN RE ESTATE OF CONKLIN

116 Ill. App. 3d 426, 451 N.E. 2d 1382, 72 Ill. Dec. 59 (1983)

Webber, P.J.

Two issues are presented for our consideration: (1) whether decedent's death terminated the lease as a matter of law, and (2) assuming *arguendo* that it did not, whether the claimant was under a duty to mitigate damages.

As to the first issue, there appears to be a dearth of authority in this state. The question arose obliquely in *Collins v. Northern Trust Co.* In that case the decedent had entered into a one-year lease for an apartment and died during the term. The landlord filed a claim against the estate and the trial court entered judgment in favor of the landlord for the entire rent from decedent's death to the expiration of the lease. The appellate court reversed, holding that certain contingencies in the lease, such as fire, explosion, or other casualty, would abate the rent and therefore judgment for the entire amount was improper. The decision turned largely on the mechanics of making claims for rent while contingencies existed and apparently the question of termination of the lease was not argued to the court. In the instant case, no such contingencies are present since the claim was not made until after the expiration of the lease by its own terms.

The general rule is found in 51C C.J.S. *Landlord and Tenant* sec. 92 (1968). It is there stated that a lease is not terminated by the death of the lessor or the lessee unless the rule is altered by statute or by the terms of the lease; the latter may be either expressly stated or the nature of the lease and the peculiar qualifications of the lessee may make the lease personal to the lessee and thus operate to terminate it at his death.

In the case at bar the executor has cited a number of cases from sister jurisdictions, all of which fall under the latter category of the C.J.S. rule stated above, and thus are distinguishable. In *Warnecke v. Estate of Rabenau*, the lease was for office space to be used for the specific purpose of the business of the lessee, a public accountant; the term "lessee" was defined to include servants, employees, and clients, but did not include successors, assigns, heirs, or personal representative. The Missouri court concluded that the terms of the lease made it personal to the lessee and thus terminated on his death. The court acknowledged the general rule that death does not ordinarily terminate the lease. It quoted from an earlier Missouri case, *McDaniel v. Rose*, holding that the usual presumption is that the parties intend to bind their personal representatives unless the acts to be performed are of a strictly personal nature or depend upon the continued existence of a particular person or of a particular condition or status which goes to the very essence of the contract. In *McDaniel* the lease was for advertising signs for the decedent's business, a drugstore, which could only be conducted by the decedent.

Two later Missouri cases distinguished *Warnecke*. In both cases residential leases were involved and provided that they were binding upon the heirs, executors, administrators, successors and assigns of both parties. The court held that this language was clear and unambiguous and that the leases were not personal.

In our opinion the lease in the instant case falls well within the ambit of the general rule of nontermination; it has no specific provision regarding termination by death; it is an ordinary residential lease; in fact, it is a printed form presumably used for all tenants of the claimant; and there is nothing in the record to indicate that the decedent possessed personal qualifications or characteristics which might make the lease personal to him. Furthermore, it is specifically made assignable with the consent of the lessor and is binding upon the successors, assigns, personal representatives and legal representatives of the parties. The executor argues that these provisions made the lease sufficiently restrictive so that it becomes personal to the lessee. We do not agree. These are standard provisions in nearly all leases. Their absence would create a stronger argument in favor of the personal nature of the lease.

The question of a lessor's duty to mitigate damages appears unsettled in this state. The three lines of authority are well summarized in *Chicago Title & Trust Co. v. Hedges Manufacturing Co.*: (1) no obligation whatever; (2) the general contract rule that the wronged party may not sit idly by and allow damages to accumulate; and (3) no general obligation to mitigate but only a duty to accept a suitable subtenant when offered.

The executor argues that the common thread throughout all of the prior authority is a wrongful abandonment by the tenant and that such was not the case here; the abandonment was involuntary, the result of the death of the tenant. From this premise, he deduces that an obligation is imposed on the landlord to mitigate. We fail to discern the difference. Whether the abandonment finds its origin in the wrongful act of the tenant or in his involuntary act of death, it is not the result of anything done by the landlord and he stands deprived of his rent to which he is entitled under the contract which, as we have already held, was not terminated by the tenant's death.

We believe that the third line of cases summarized in *Chicago Title & Trust Co.* and accepted by that court as the most recent authority represents the better view:

> "While we are inclined to follow the rule as to mitigation set out in *Yelen and Muntz TV, Inc.*, where a suitable tenant is offered by the original lessee, we think the burden of proof is on the tenant to show that the substitute tenant is reasonably suitable. It is not the duty of the landlord either to seek out a suitable tenant or to make investigations as to the suitability of a prospect referred to him by the tenant."

The record here is devoid of any indication that the executor sought out or presented to the claimant any prospect as a subtenant.

In the conclusion of its brief before this court the claimant asks that we remand to the trial court for the assessment of attorney's fees provided in the lease. Two insuperable obstacles lie in the path of such procedure: (1) the matter was never raised initially in the trial court, and (2) the lease provides for "remedies as may be available to the Lessor under the several laws of Wisconsin."

The judgment of the circuit court of Sangamon County is affirmed.

Affirmed.

[Some citations omitted.]

9.2 THE BASIC ELEMENTS OF A LEASE

A lease should always be in writing. Not only is it wise to clarify the terms of the agreement—which can only be done when the parties have committed their agreement to writing—but the **Statute of Frauds** requires that any transfer of an interest in real property be in writing. In many jurisdictions, the Statute of Frauds' writing requirement comes into play when the lease runs for a period longer than a certain, specified duration. That duration varies from state to state, but the most common cut-off is one year. Leases

LEGAL TERMS

Statute of Frauds
Law affecting real estate that requires all transfers of real estate interests to be in writing; generally, document must be signed by party against whom enforcement is sought.

for less than one year may be oral in many states. But if the period of the lease extends beyond a year, it must be in writing. The Statute of Frauds is discussed in more detail in chapter 5.

Great care should be taken in drafting a lease. The task of helping protect or enhance your client's position or interests is framed by the conflicting interests of the lessor and the lessee. Remember that your client may be either side, not just the lessee. Lessors may have an even greater need for attorneys than do lessees. The power relationship is clear in most residential leases, which are standard forms that favor the lessor. Some lessors will not vary the lease for any reason. In the apartment market they do not need to; they often have ample tenant applications. What you can do is to explain (without practicing law) the risks from which the lease's terms protect the landlord and how those protections might cause problems for a tenant.

In commercial leases, the problem can be strikingly different. Initially, who is being sought—the tenant to occupy the space, or the landlord to lease the space? Clearly, the tenant has more leverage in the former situation. A rich, powerful, or national organization (such as Sears as a prospective anchor tenant in a mall) has more leverage for negotiation than does a small business. Second, the range of problems and difficulties that can arise is much greater in the commercial lease. There is so much material to cover in this area that the topic could well be a separate course.

What is a lease? It is a contract that both conveys an interest in real estate for a period of time and contains mutual promises between the parties. As to the latter, the rules of contract law apply. There must be offer and acceptance, consideration, the legal capacity to contract by the parties, and a legal objective for the contract-lease. The standard contract defenses, such as fraud, illegality, coercion, and duress, among others, protect the parties from having the contract enforced against them if such reprehensible activities can be proven against the other party.

Other approaches to contract interpretation can be important as well. One of these is the doctrine of **unconscionability**. Unconscionability is an act so outrageous that it shocks the conscience of the court when it learns of it; courts refuse to enforce unconscionable contracts. One such situation might be if the contract was so one-sided that there was no negotiation and the weaker party was injured by the contract terms, which appear utterly unreasonable to any decent, rational person.

A second legal theory is the doctrine of **estoppel**. Estoppel is the legal doctrine stating that when the words or actions of one party induce another party, to his or her detriment, to do or to refrain from doing something in reliance upon the representations made by the first party, the first party may not thereafter deny the effects its words or actions had on the other party. The first party is said to be *estopped* from denying those effects. Frequent application of estoppel appears in the following example. Parent (P) promises adult child (C) the money for a down payment on the child's purchase of a parcel of real estate, usually a home. C signs the contract to purchase, but then P refuses to provide the funds. In this situation is estopped to deny its promise. C became obligated to buy because C relied on P's promise to provide the funds for the down payment. C would not have acted in this manner otherwise. Usually, C can demand specific performance from P in this type of circumstance. These doctrines may affect the terms of a contract, the relationship between the parties to a contract, and third parties (such as the seller of the land to C).

Although many states have specified the basic elements of a lease (which should be checked for your jurisdiction), the following elements are almost always included. First, the *date* on which the lease is being executed. Second, the *parties to the lease:* the lessor-landlord and the lessee-tenant. Either the lessor or the lessee can include more than one person. Whoever is in title should be on the lease as the lessor, either by name or through an agent. For safety's sake, it is best to check the real estate record to determine the actual name of the lessor that is on file and use that exact name. For short-term leases (less than one year) with a husband and wife who are in a business, however, usually only the party managing the business signs the lease.

There may be other considerations as well. For example, if the landlord is a partnership, all the partners should sign and indicate the name of the partnership. If the lessor is a corporation, the signature should indicate official agency by using the word "by" and the title of the party who signs. Further, the authority to sign should be demonstrated by means of a properly prepared corporation resolution authorizing a particular officer, by title, to sign. Further, one should also obtain from the corporate secretary a certification that that person holds that office. Also, a trustee under a trust, an executor or administrator of the estate of a decedent or incompetent, or a party who is an agent for the landlord may execute the lease. Proper authorization to sign should be determined in each situation.

Another problem that can arise for the tenant is the quality of the landlord's title. The tenant can only take what the landlord signing the lease contract can give. This problem would be especially acute if there were a very long-term lease and the tenant constructed a building on the premises. In this situation, the tenant is advised to act as if he were purchasing the property in order to protect himself. This matter has been discussed in detail elsewhere in this book. If there is a title problem, the tenant could be victimized. Further, if a prior mortgage's payments fall into default, the tenant's situation may become intolerable in terms of time spent and expenses incurred when foreclosure proceedings occur.

Finally, the primary concern for the lessor is the tenant's financial responsibility. Will the tenant be able to pay the rent for the duration of the lease? If there is any doubt, outside guaranties of payment should be sought and obtained before the lease is executed. If the tenant is a corporation owned by another corporation, the parent (owning) corporation may be required to guarantee the lease's terms, especially the payment terms. If the lessee is an individual or a small partnership, personal assets might collateralize the rent payments, or a wealthy friend or family member might provide the guaranty. If the tenant is an organization, such as a partnership or a corporation,

LEGAL TERMS

unconscionable
Act or situation so outrageous that it shocks the conscience of the court; courts refuse to enforce unconscionable contracts.

estoppel
Legal doctrine that prohibits one party from denying its behavior when it makes statements or takes actions that cause another party to rely on that behavior to his or her detriment.

the same rules that govern the landlord apply in determining the authority to execute and deliver a valid lease.

The third lease element is the *premises.* Precision is important in (1) determining where and (2) specifying what the premises are. Sometimes the real property description is adequate, but frequently the parties want other items included. Are elements included that might appear to be tangential or so obvious that one would assume they were covered, such as hallways, parking lots, access roads, bathrooms, or storage space? Use of some of these elements may require a special reference, such as a particular parking space, but others may be generic, such as use of the hallways. Other ways to describe the premises are by apartment or suite number, by street address (although this approach requires a legal description to be included as well), or by floor. For large spaces, the floor plan may be included as an exhibit or attachment to the lease.

Is personal property involved? Is the tenant to have the use of the personal property? If so, the items of personal property should be listed in the lease. When the leased premises are under construction, such as in a mall, terms of acceptability of the finished product and conformity to agreed-upon size, function, or useability must be clearly specified in the lease's language.

Fourth, the **term of the lease** must be specified. How long does the lease last? Exactly when does it begin and when does it end? It is best to state that it begins on a certain date and ends on another specific date, but some leases do not specify a term. These are usually tenancies at will or periodic tenancies. The tenancy at will is terminable by either party with (most often) 30 days' notice. A lease may also terminate upon the happening of a particular event; for instance, a lease could provide that if a partnership were to dissolve, or if a person were to die, or if a certain product ceased to be sold in a store, then the lease would end.

If the tenant abandons the property before the term of the lease ends, can the landlord always sue to recover the unpaid rent? It appears not, if certain things occur, according to the *Libby* case. (Libby is the executor of Hodsdon's estate.)

Fifth is the *rent.* The **rent** is the consideration that the landlord receives from the tenant for permitting the tenant to use (or to possess) the premises during the stated time period. Most leases specify that rent is due at

LEGAL TERMS

term of the lease
Period during which the parties intend for the lease to be in effect.

rent
Amount of money paid during a fixed period for the right to use a particular parcel of real property.

CH C. RICHARDS CO.
v.
LIBBY
10 A.2d 609 (Me. 1940)

THAXTER, J.

This action brought against the executor of the estate of Julia E. Hodsdon was tried before a justice of the Superior Court without the intervention of a jury. The right to except was reserved.

The plaintiff seeks to recover the sum of $400 for rent of an apartment for a period of eight months from April 16, 1937, to December 15, 1937 at $50 per month. There are also items in the account amounting to $8.65 for gas and electricity furnished and for damage done to the apartment. The presiding justice found that judgment should be entered for the plaintiff for $403.65. The case is before this court on ten exceptions of the defendant, some of which are to certain findings made by the court, others to the refusal of requests for rulings. All of the exceptions are without merit but one which we shall consider. There is no dispute as to the facts.

The plaintiff owned and operated an apartment house located at 419 Cumberland Avenue in Portland. The defendant's testatrix through her agent entered into negotiations to rent an apartment in this building. The one which she wanted #51 was occupied but was soon to become vacant. Until it should be available it was agreed orally that the prospective tenant might occupy apartment #2 at a rental of $50 per month. On May 15th, when the other apartment became available, the tenant vacated apartment #2 without notice and left the building for good. The presiding justice found that "the occupancy of apartment No. 2 was upon a verbal agreement for an indefinite period upon a monthly payment of rent;" and "that it was a tenancy at will and could be terminated only by the statutory notice or by mutual consent." This was a correct description of the relationship of the parties. When the tenant went the key appears to have been left on the office desk and was taken by Mrs. Richards, the agent in charge of the building with whom all the negotiations had taken place. There is no doubt that Mrs. Richards knew when Mrs. Hodsdon left that she intended to give up the apartment. Mrs. Richards used the key to enter the apartment, which she cleaned and put into condition for a new tenant; and from time to time she showed it to prospective tenants. Apartment #51 was rented in October and apartment #2 December 1st. The plaintiff seeks to recover rent for apartment #2 from April 16th to December 15th.

The ruling to which the defendant takes exception is as follows in the words of the presiding justice:

"At the termination of the occupancy by the defendant's deceased on May 14th the key of apartment No. 2 was left at the plaintiff's office in the building where the apartments were located. The plaintiff used the key to enter and put the apartment into condition for a new tenant, and showed the apartment to prospective tenants. It was let to a new tenant on December 1st.

"I find that the plaintiff did not exercise dominion over the premises when it endeavored to obtain a new tenant, except as was reasonable and necessary to prevent damages from accumulating."

This ruling we think was error. We are aware of the well settled principle that findings of fact by the justice hearing the case are conclusive if there is any evidence to support them. In the case before us, however, the facts are not in dispute and the only inference which can be drawn from them does not in our opinion support the ruling below. Under such circumstances there is error in law to correct which exceptions will lie.

The ruling that the landlord did not, by taking the key, by entering the apartment, and by offering it to prospective tenants, accept the surrender of it by the defendant's testatrix is based on no facts or inferences therefrom in the evidence but rather on the assumption of law that such acts were "necessary to prevent damages from accumulating." So long, however, as a tenancy exists the landlord may collect rent in full regardless of actual occupancy of the premises by the tenant. Such being the case it must follow that, where there is a wrongful abandonment of premises by a tenant and a refusal to pay rent, the landlord may at his election permit them to remain vacant, refuse to recognize the attempted surrender by the tenant, and bring suit to collect the rent as it comes due. The tenant can not by such action cast a burden on the landlord to find someone to take his place. Such is the overwhelming weight of authority.

The acts of the landlord can not, therefore, be explained on the theory that there was any obligation on its part to mitigate damages, and there is no evidence to indicate that the landlord claimed to be acting for the tenant. The question, therefore, is whether the acts of the parties constituted a termination of the tenancy by operation of law.

There is no doubt that the relationship of landlord and tenant may be terminated by the acts of the parties. In two of these cases the facts are very similar to those now before us.

The facts in *McCann v. Bass*, are that the defendant leased a store to the plaintiff. Before the termination of the lease the plaintiff vacated the premises for business purposes, returned the key to the defendant and moved to another store. The defendant took control of the store against the will of the plaintiff, remodelled it, let part of it to a tenant and occupied part himself. The court held in an action brought by the tenant for an eviction that the lease had been terminated by operation of law. The court said, "That is, when the lessee does the acts which prove his intention to abandon and surrender, like vacating the premises and giving up the key, and the lessor, in pursuance of such acts, goes into actual occupation, then, by acts and operation of law, the lease is terminated."

In *Talbot v. Whipple*, one Carroll, a tenant at will of the defendant of certain land, had placed thereon a building in which he had installed machinery. In determining the title to this property the court found it necessary to decide whether the tenancy of Carroll in the real estate had been terminated. The statement of facts shows that Carroll became insolvent; that without paying his rent he stopped work and abandoned the premises and the equipment with the intention of not returning; that he locked the doors hanging the keys inside but left one open through which the defendant entered and took possession; that no notice was ever given by either party to the other that the tenancy was to end. In holding that the tenancy had terminated the court said, "The facts in the present case are of the most unequivocal character on the part of both landlord and tenant, and leave no room for doubt as to the intent of the parties."

In the case before us it is apparent from the testimony of both Mrs. Stewart, who acted as Mrs. Hodsdon's agent, and of Mrs. Richards, the manager and agent of the plaintiff, that Mrs. Richards knew that Mrs. Hodsdon, when she left, intended to give up apartment #2. There were complaints between the parties. Mrs. Richards said that apartment #51 was ready, Mrs. Stewart replied that they weren't going to take it. Mrs. Richards then found fault because she had not been given a month's notice; but at the same time gave no intimation that she intended to hold Mrs. Hodsdon as a tenant. The key was left on the office desk. Mrs. Richards took the key, entered the apartment, cleaned it, made it ready for a new tenant and showed it to prospective tenants from time to time. Her conduct was unequivocal; she made no attempt to qualify it. Every act done is inconsistent with the present claim that the tenancy of Mrs. Hodsdon continued.

Most significant is the response of Mrs. Richards to a question by the court as to whether she was holding an apartment for Mrs. Hodsdon if she decided to come back.

"The Court: Which apartment was it you said you would hold for her? A. I was holding, really, either one; because in the spring of the year that is a hard time to let apartments anyway. I couldn't hold one just separately for her and not rent it if I had a chance."

This language certainly shows that Mrs. Richards claimed the right after Mrs. Hodsdon left to put a new tenant in apartment #2 whenever she had the chance to do so. It is utterly inconsistent with the present contention of the plaintiff that Mrs. Hodsdon remained a tenant of that apartment during the succeeding months with the right to be given thirty day's notice before her tenancy could be terminated.

Exceptions sustained.

[Some citations omitted.]

the first of the period, in advance, because if the time of payment is not specified, the rent would be due only at the end of the period. The place where (and if necessary, the time when) the rent is to be delivered should be specified.

Another type of payment (which seems like rent, but technically is not) is the security deposit. The landlord requires it to ensure that the property is kept in good condition or that there is money to pay for repairs. This area is one of growing difficulty because both sides have abused it. Tenants have moved out and left damage for which the cost of repair exceeded the amount of the security deposit; landlords have refused to return deposits despite a lack of apparent damage or only normal wear and tear. Another problem in residential leases is whether interest should be paid on the deposit. The amount of the residential security deposit is frequently limited by statute to one or two months' rent. Other statutes prohibit the landlord from deducting money for ordinary wear and tear from the deposit. Finally, in some states, there are a number of procedural requirements (such as providing notice to the tenant or actually bringing suit) with which the landlord must comply before retaining a security deposit.

The actual amount of money, in a specified currency, should be stated as the rental payment for each rental period; for example, "$875 per month." If there are further amounts that the tenant must pay, the lease must specify what those payments will be. Such items might be sewer or water costs or real estate taxes. These payments should not be included in the rent. It should be made clear that they are additional payments. Finally, specifying the type of currency can be important when the parties are from different nations.

Commercial leases frequently have other types of rent provisions. The special language in those provisions is designed to deal with specific problems that can arise. One problem is that when the rent is fixed and the rental period is fairly long, the value of the rent declines over time because of inflation. Another way to ensure that the lessor receives a fair return on the money invested in the property must be found. Some ways of dealing with that problem follow. First, the lease may have an **escalator clause**. An escalator clause is tied to some standard index (measurement) of inflation, such as the Consumer Price Index (CPI), the Producer Price Index (PPI), or the Wholesale Price Index. Second, there are ways other than tying to an index to obtain a fair rental rate. One of the most common is the **percentage lease**, under

LEGAL TERMS

escalator clause
Lease clause that adjusts the amount of rent to be paid based on an index or some objective computation of costs.

percentage lease
Lease under which rent is based on a percentage of sales (net or gross) or some other type of income.

which part of the rent is a percentage of the income derived from business operations at this location. This lease is also called an **index lease**, because it is tied to an index of price changes.

There are many variations to the percentage lease. Sometimes the rental percentage is taken of the gross sales, sometimes of the net sales (after expenses). In addition, there may be a flat, base rent to be paid every month with a percentage to be paid only if sales exceed a certain level. The percentage of rent paid may vary with the amount of sales; for instance, $1 million in annual sales may carry a 2 percent clause, but a $10-million year may trigger a 2.75 percent clause. The percentage is usually paid at the end of the tenant's financial year (whether the tenant is on a calendar or a fiscal year basis); there may be significant monthly variations, and the exact amount owed can only be calculated at year end. This approach requires trust and paperwork. Substantial follow-up checking on the tenant may be needed to establish the correct amount owed. Definitions of *gross sales, net sales, net income,* or whatever the basis is, with inclusions and exclusions, must be meticulously spelled out in the lease. The circumstances under which the percentage rent begins to apply must also be specified. The time period to which the sales terms apply should be specified, and the quality of the financial information reporting must be established.

Because there are different types of financial statements and their quality determines their reliability, it is in the lessor's interest to require the best reporting. But the best financial reporting, an audited statement with its supportive recordkeeping, is increasingly expensive. It could cost the tenant almost as much as the increased, sales-based, rental payments themselves. Small business owners may resist the requirement of accurate financial reporting, although chains and large businesses do not usually present this type of problem. Further, the landlord must have the right to inspect the tenant's books upon demand—but who will pay for the landlord's financial investigations, the landlord or the tenant? This issue should be settled in the lease and discussed with the tenant. The tenant must be aware of the problems, costs, and reporting requirements so that this sales-based percentage system does not come as a surprise.

Other types of leases are the net lease and the gross lease. A **gross lease** is one under which the tenant pays only rent and nothing else. A **net lease** is one under which the tenant pays some other obligations besides rent. There is also a **triple net lease** or a *net-net-net lease.* Under this leasing arrangement, the tenant pays *all* other operating expenses or other incidental expenses. Some of the more common of these operating expenses or obligations, often referred to as the necessary and ordinary operating costs of the landlord, are taxes, utilities, maintenance and repair, special assessments, and insurance. One must check carefully to determine exactly what is included because there are regional differences. The cost difference between a net lease and a triple net lease could be significant and result in needless litigation. Proper drafting of the lease clarifies the expenses that the landlord expects to be covered. A detailed, written understanding in the lease is essential.

Two other types of leases are also used to control the landlord's costs and enhance earnings. The first is a **graduated lease** and the second is a

reappraisal lease. The graduated lease calls for rent to increase according to a schedule provided in the lease. The increase may be annual, but it is more likely to occur every three to five years. This type of lease is also called a **step-up lease**. The graduated lease is often an attempt to get a new business off the ground and to take higher rental payments when the new business is better able to pay them. The reappraisal lease involves getting a new appraisal of the real property at the end of a specified period and having the rent recalculated from that new appraisal. This lease is now disfavored because of the expense of the appraisal and the endless disagreement that often arises between the parties about which factors are relevant and the weight of those factors. The disagreements often lead to expensive litigation.

A final type of lease is called a **ground lease**. It is a lease of vacant land that may be improved (that is, not raw, unimproved land lacking additions such as roads, utilities, and so on). The tenant often agrees to build on the premises. Buildings usually become the property of the landowner-lessor at the end of the lease. Negotiated terms include: the term of the lease; the periods of lease renewal; and, at the end of the lease, how much the landlord will pay the tenant for the building, or whether the value of the building has been returned in reduced rent. Generally, in this type of lease, the tenant pays the landlord's costs (such as taxes), so it is said to be a *net* lease.

A final formality in the preparation of the lease is its execution. The parties should be specified. Each should sign in the appropriate capacity: as an individual, if the party executing signs for him- or herself in a residential transaction, or if signing as a sole proprietor operating a business; as a partner, if for a partnership (with the appropriate partnership authorizations); as an officer, if for a corporation. Corporate resolutions and identification of the person signing as the person holding the proper corporate office should be obtained. The corporate seal should be applied to any lease and the appropriate acknowledgements or notarizations (depending on local requirements) should be completed. Local law also determines if recording the lease is necessary to protect the interests of the tenant. Generally, the longer the term of the lease, the more likely recording is to be advisable or required. If recording is intended, it probably will be necessary to have the lease witnessed and the signatures acknowledged (notarized).

9.3 ADDITIONAL ELEMENTS OF A LEASE

Because property can be used in many ways, leases have evolved many additional terms to deal with complex situations. Leasing has many possible complications.

Use of the Property

The most basic element is the use to which the tenant will put the property. The tenant—under a proposed long-term lease—will have inspected or paid a knowledgeable (and bonded) inspector to examine the premises for

LEGAL TERMS

index lease
Lease in which the rent is tied to a well-known price index and varies as the index changes; the most common index is the Consumer Price Index.

gross lease
Lease under which the landlord pays all expenses out of the rent; the tenant merely pays a fixed rent.

net lease
Lease in which the tenant pays for hazard insurance, property taxes, and maintenance.

triple net lease
Lease specifying that all the landlord's costs are to be paid by the tenant; also known as *net-net-net lease*.

graduated lease
Lease under which rent payments begin at a lower amount but rise at a fixed rate or amount over time, until they reach an agreed maximum.

reappraisal lease (step-up lease)
Lease in which the changes in rent are based upon an outside appraisal of the value of the property; now disfavored.

ground lease
Lease dealing with land or a vacant site.

defects. Under the common law, tenants may use the premises in any way they choose so long as they do not commit *waste,* a usage that damages the owner's reversionary rights and seriously alters or lessens the property value. But could the tenant's rights still be too broad for the interests of the landlord? What if the tenant wanted to live in a room in the back of a store and use a hot plate to cook meals? Would that violate any zoning or code ordinances? What if the tenant runs a business from residential premises without the landlord's permission? Most landlords would feel they deserve higher rent for a commercial usage than for a residential usage. In shopping centers or strip malls there can be another problem—competing businesses among the tenants.

Consider what could happen if Tenant A's shoe store is not doing well. He sees that Tenant B's toy store is making money hand over fist, so Tenant A converts his business to a toy store. How would Tenant B feel about that? And the landlord? The competition may kill both stores. Consider other ways in which tenant uses of the property can cause problems for the landlord. In commercial situations, using anything unreasonably dangerous to the building, its occupants, or the community could cause insurance problems. Examples could be anything from the use or storage of inherently dangerous materials such as toxic chemicals or dynamite to the noise and vibration caused by heavy equipment. In a residential building, laundry hanging out of windows, barbecuing, or improper trash disposal could cause other problems.

Both landlords and tenants should know about public laws and ordinances restricting the use of the property. The landlord should determine if the tenant, in the course of the tenant's business, will violate any legal restrictions. These restrictions may range from national environmental laws to local zoning ordinances, but there can also be private restrictive covenants affecting the use of the land. An example of the latter is be an acreage restriction on residential sites. A common restriction is that the lot site may not be less than a "builder's acre" (that is, 40,000 square feet). Finally, the landlord is obliged to provide quiet enjoyment of the premises. Simply put, the landlord may not interfere with the tenant's use and enjoyment of the premises during the term of the lease, if the tenant is not in default in paying rent or other lease terms, not misusing the property, and not violating any government regulations. If the tenant violates these covenants, the landlord may evict the tenant to protect his own interests. Would the lease permit him to do so?

Maintenance, Changes, and Improvements to the Property

Maintenance, changes, and property improvements are serious issues for both the landlord and the tenant. The landlord may not want the tenant to change the building, because its present condition makes it produce income. The tenant, on the other hand, may need to adapt the property in some unique way. Each party has an interest in having the other pay for repairs and maintenance. Common law imposed very few burdens on the landlord, and repair was not one of them. The lease, therefore, must specify who has to do what to the premises. Consider the possibilities: there is the outside, such as exterior walls and the roof, versus the inside; or there could be structural versus everything else (nonstructural).

Generally, the owner-landlord is responsible for structural repairs and repairs to the building's exterior, while the tenant is responsible for repairs to the interior and everything else (nonstructural). Who is responsible for maintaining the really expensive elements—repairing and repaving parking lots and driveways, the heating and air conditioning systems, the electrical and plumbing systems? All maintenance must be done within the framework of existing laws; who is responsible for obtaining code variances if they are necessary? Briefly, the facts of the situation, its possible problems, and the solutions must be identified, and risks delineated. The lease language must be written to cover these risks and allocate them to the appropriate party. The most common resolution is based on who has the greater need at the time the lease is executed. If the landlord needs to rent in a glutted market, the lessor will be more likely to pay; if the tenant needs the space, the lessee is more likely to pay.

Obtaining permits—relatively easy for standard repairs—can be complex, difficult, and costly when making changes and improvements to the property. The difficulty is defined by what the tenant wishes to do and the degree of risk or change to the community that the proposed activity may cause. Most alterations to a store in a building or a shopping center do not create major difficulties with the law. Any new or special use, however, should be carefully considered. Other problems with changes in the rental premises include:

Who is to make them—the landlord or the tenant?
When are they to be done?
If the landlord is doing it, what remedies does the tenant have if the changes are not finished on time—damages or cancellation of the lease?
What happens to the trade fixtures (personal property attached to the premises but easily removable) added as part of the changes? When the tenant leaves, who gets them?
Does the property have to be restored to its prior or original condition before the tenant's occupancy ends?
Who pays for restoration?
Are mechanic's liens involved? How can the landlord be protected against them?
If the tenant makes changes, how does the landlord control structural changes or damages to the property?

Damage to Premises—Insurance, Rent, Repairs

During the lease, the premises may be damaged by wind, fire, water, or other means. Generally, the damage issue should be negotiated between the parties and its resolution written into the lease. Many factors are involved. First, was either party at fault for what happened? For instance, did the tenant's party guest set fire to something? Did old wiring ignite and burn up half the building, along with much of the tenant's property? Logic seems to dictate that whoever is at fault under tort law should be responsible for repair and restoration, but the lease contract may provide otherwise.

Second, what is the tenant's responsibility for paying rent after such an event? If rent is due, is the rent **abated**, that is, reduced proportionately by the amount of space made unusable? Does that depend on who is responsible for causing the damage?

Third, if the tenant's property—goods for sale, equipment, inventory, changes in the premises—is damaged or destroyed, who pays for it? The lease should state how this issue is to be handled if it arises.

Finally, insurance exists to cover most risks, and allocation of insurance proceeds should be delineated in the lease. But if there is no insurance, or if the insurance proceeds are inadequate to cover the costs, who pays? Careful lease drafting deals with this type of problem. The insurance company has a right to subrogation against the party at fault (generally the tenant) after paying for the damage. This right may conflict with lease terms requiring the parties to the lease not to hold each other liable for negligence. Although fire is the most common insurable risk, others must be considered as well. The federal government has required flood insurance in certain areas since the 1960s. (Inquiries should be addressed to the Federal Emergency Management Agency [FEMA]). There may be risks that cannot be insured against; the party responsible for those risks should be identified in the lease.

Land may be taken by condemnation or eminent domain. The government is permitted to seize property for public use so long as a fair price is paid the owner and the requirements of due process are met. Generally, when this occurs, the lease ends. Both landlord and tenant, however, have interests in the award, just as they both have interests in the real property. The landlord, however, will not want the tenant to take any of the award, and language resolving this potential dispute should be included in the lease. But what if the condemnation takes only part of the real property? Is the lease terminated? How much compensation, if any, should the tenant receive? What standards determine such compensation?

Transfer of the Rights in the Lease

Can the tenant assign, sublet, or mortgage his leasehold interest? Can the landlord sell, assign, or mortgage her interest? These questions are important for both parties. The landlord-lessor prefers that the original tenant remain, because the lessor has investigated and determined that the tenant is personally and financially responsible. The tenant, on the other hand, wishes to have the flexibility to leave, transfer his interest, raise capital by mortgage, or otherwise be able to adjust to changes in the business world. In commercial transactions, the tenant is less interested in who owns the property than the landlord is in who rents it. In residential leases, particularly in inner-city, changing, or declining neighborhoods, a new landlord may try to exploit tenants by not paying for maintenance and repairs. The lease is the personal property of the tenant, and the reversion is a real property interest of the landlord. Generally speaking, the lease either forbids the tenant to assign or sublet the premises, or it requires the landlord not unreasonably withhold consent to the assignment or sublease.

The law does not like to restrict the transfer of property interests, and the courts strictly interpret such restrictions against their author. Corporate tenants can present another set of transfer problems. Corporations may merge or consolidate; they may have parent or subsidiary corporations. These transfers are generally permitted if the entity remains essentially the same. What happens, though, if a corporate tenant does not transfer its lease, but does sell all or a majority of its stock to other shareholders? This transfer is essentially a lease transfer. To deal with this reality, the landlord may wish to have the lease provide that a transfer of corporate control by sale of stock shall be considered a transfer of the lease.

When the landlord transfers her interest, the first question is which of her two interests did she transfer, the interest in the lease or in the reversion? She can sell either one. Her transfer does not affect the written, contractual interests of the tenant, but the new owner or lessor may not meet the obligations under the lease. The tenant may have the right to bring an action against the original landlord if her successor does not perform the duties agreed to under the lease. However, it is often costly to locate the original landlord and litigate the lease clauses.

Tenant Default under the Lease

The most common event of **default** (failure to perform an item agreed to in the lease) by the tenant is failure to pay the rent when due. Whenever the tenant does not fulfill an obligation under the lease, an event of default may occur. Defaults must be spelled out clearly in the lease. If a default occurs and is significant, but is waived, a notice should be sent to the tenant informing him of the waiver, but also informing him that the waiver applies only to this particular occurrence, and that the lessor does not waive any future defaults and reserves all rights under the lease. This procedure may avoid the landlord's losing her rights under the lease by repeatedly permitting or ignoring actions that constitute a default under the lease. If the waivers are a practice between the parties for a long enough time, however, the landlord may lose the rights that have been consistently waived anyway.

Some other common events of default are the tenant holding over after the term of the lease has ended (that is, staying on the premises after the lease has expired, without a new lease), using the premises unlawfully, not paying the taxes, assessments, or other charges that he or she agreed to pay, or becoming insolvent or bankrupt. Most of these events can be remedied by legal proceedings to dispossess the tenant from the premises. This process is

LEGAL TERMS

rent abatement
Reducing or not collecting the rent payment; *abate* means to lessen or to cease.

default
Contract term; a failure to perform an agreement in the contract (lease).

eviction. Even after eviction, the tenant may still be liable if the lease has not been terminated. Many leases now have a **survivability clause**, which provides that eviction for failure to pay rent or for another reason does not end the tenant's obligation to pay rent; in other words, the tenant's obligation *survives* the eviction. Nevertheless, the tenant's obligation may cease, in many states, when the landlord re-rents the premises.

Another term, **constructive eviction**, refers to the landlord's allowing the premises to deteriorate to such a degree that the property is no longer habitable (or usable for the purpose intended). This judicial remedy requires that the tenant actually move out. It is sometimes possible to relate the residential lease to that of the small businessperson, to allow use of this remedy. The standards for the claim of constructive eviction are likely to parallel those for a claim of breach of the landlord's implied **warranty of habitability**. Those standards are, minimally, that the premises be free of code violations and, probably, that the premises be both safe and sanitary.

The Landlord's Remedies

The landlord has several basic remedies for the tenant's failure to perform as agreed. One, the landlord may sue the tenant for performance under the lease. Two, the landlord may accelerate the rent; this remedy provides the landlord with the right to obtain all the rent due under the lease at one time. Otherwise, the landlord have to sue each month for that month's failure to pay the rent. Three, the landlord may re-enter and relet the premises. In some situations, the landlord may have to mitigate the damages owed by the tenant, that is, re-rent the premises as soon as possible to cut down on the rent owed by the former tenant. Essentially, the landlord tries to get the premises occupied by a reliable tenant as soon as possible. The original (evicted) tenant must usually pay the landlord the difference between what the lessor got from the replacement tenant and what the lease with the original tenant provided. Four, the landlord may terminate the lease to deprive the defaulted tenant of further rights under the lease. Finally, the landlord may have the right to perform the tenant's obligations. If the landlord does so, the lease generally gives the landlord the right to recover those expenses from the tenant. This right is often used to pay taxes or insurance, thus protecting the landlord's interests.

The means to enforce the landlord's rights after default are, first, to attempt to obtain whatever of the tenant's property is on the premises, to cover the rent owed. This action is called **distraint**, and it provides a lien against that property superior to other unsecured creditors'. Second, the landlord may obtain a judgment for rent and for any other damages that can be reduced to a money valuation. If this judgment is obtained, the landlord can then seize and sell the personal property of the tenant. Third, in some leases, a confession of judgment clause exists; this device permits the landlord to act as the attorney for the tenant and agree (*confess*) to the judgment sought against him by the landlord. This device is now highly disfavored in most states and is declining in use; in many types of consumer transactions, it is illegal. Finally, the landlord

LEGAL TERMS

eviction
Landlord's action to remove the tenant from the premises.

can go to court and file an action of **ejectment**. When the landlord has received a judgment in this action, he or she may have the sheriff throw the tenant out. Although these remedies are cumulative, the tenant will not be required to pay the landlord more than the actual damages suffered. The tenant is also protected in that, while in theory the landlord may use self-help to evict the tenant or to seize his property, it is generally not advisable. The taking of property usually requires notice and a hearing in order not to be theft, and throwing the tenant out may violate laws against assault and battery and forcible entry. The landlord is advised to seek remedies that involve the courts, such as a forcible entry and detainer action which, when won, will allow the court to issue a writ to a local official (often the sheriff) to evict the tenant.

The Tenant's Remedies

Tenants also have problems with arbitrary actions to evict or with the landlord's violations of the lease terms. Anyone, for instance, can forget to mail the rent check, or the postal service may not always deliver it or deliver it on time. Most leases have a clause giving the tenant the right to correct any of his own failures. This right is called the right to **cure a default**. It usually requires that the landlord give the tenant written notice and a specified time period in which to correct (cure) the mistake (default). The amount of time provided for correcting the default is based on the amount of time needed; for example, a short time for writing a check, and a longer time for performing some type of repair obligation.

Remedies for the landlord's breach of one or more of the lease's terms are very difficult for the tenant to enforce. Because the terms of the lease are all independent, the tenant cannot set off the rent, or do the necessary repair work or withhold the rent proportionately. Sometimes, however, rent withholding has been permitted when the rent is paid into an escrow. The only remedy is usually monetary damages. Even the equitable remedy of specific performance is rarely used, because money seems to be legitimate compensation for the tenant's damages. Nevertheless, in certain situations, case law supports reducing the rent payments in proportion to the damages sustained, or paying the rent into a court escrow fund, or withholding the rent. One of the principal reasons for permitting any of these actions has been evidence of building code violations. Some courts have gone so far as to hold that violations of building codes are grounds for voiding the lease. Landlords have retaliated against tenants who report building code violations by refusing to renew their leases. When revenge is the only reason for failing to renew a lease, the courts have denied the landlord that power in some cases. But when there are legitimate reasons, such as wanting to demolish a building not worth rehabilitating, the landlord has been permitted to remove the tenants by not renewing their leases.

Two Potential Problems Between Creditor and Lessee

Frequently, the landlord will have borrowed money from some financial institution to purchase the property. A number of situations can arise when a

survivability clause
Contract term providing for all clauses that are not illegal in the contract to remain in full force and effect regardless of any other clauses declared illegal in court litigation.

constructive eviction
When the landlord's failure to perform is so great that it renders the property unusable, so that the tenant is forced to leave the property.

warranty of habitability
Landlord's legally implied lease covenant, which provides that the premises must be inhabitable by the tenant when the property is leased for residential purposes; generally used only in consumer, residential leases.

distraint
Right of the landlord in some jurisdictions to seize the property of the tenant to satisfy unpaid obligations.

ejectment
Court action to determine the party that should be in possession of the premises; generally used by landlords to remove tenants.

cure of default
Making the other party whole so that he or she is no longer damaged by the default; paying an amount less than the full rent and then sending the remainder, plus any amount necessary to cover any damage from the delay, would be curing a rent default.

creditor is involved with the real estate. First, the creditor may want to have certain rights upon default. The lender frequently wants to get its loaned funds out of the property quickly. If the landlord has outstanding obligations to the tenant, who comes first, the creditor or the tenant? The creditor may require the tenant to sign a **subordination agreement**; it provides that the creditor's interests will come ahead of the tenant's interests. Creditors may have problems when the landlord seeks financing or sells the real property. The most likely situation is when there are multiple units—either residential or commercial—although it is possible to have only one unit involved. The creditor or purchaser may require that each tenant provide an **estoppel certificate**. This certificate states that the lease is in good standing, that the tenant is in possession of the property, that the tenant is not in default in any obligations to the landlord and is unaware of any landlord default to the tenant, and that the tenant has no claims against the landlord. Finally, the tenant restates the basic elements of the lease, such as the amount of the rent, the rental period, and the expiration date of the lease. Most landlords include a clause in the lease requiring tenants to execute an estoppel certificate at the landlord's request.

9.4 THE LANDLORD'S AREAS OF POTENTIAL LIABILITY

The landlord's activities can result in tort liability, as well as potential contractual liability, through violations of the lease's covenants. *Torts* are harms done by one party to another. Basically, there are three types—intentional torts, negligent torts, and strict liability torts. For a tort to have occurred, four elements are usually necessary. First, a party must owe a duty to another party; second, there must be a breach of that duty; third, the party who owed the duty and breached it must have caused, fourth, the injury that is complained of. Landlords' torts usually arise from negligence, although there is a trend to place a duty of strict liability for safety on landlords who rent residential apartments. Intentional torts can occur if a verbal disagreement escalates into a fist fight or worse; claims of assault and battery, as well as potential criminal charges, could result from such a fracas.

Generally, however, most tortious acts arise in the area of negligence, when the landlord's actions in relation to the tenant or to third parties who may be on or near the property cause a harm. In the common law, the landlord was usually insulated from liability by shifting the responsibility to the tenant. If a defect on the property was hidden at the time of the lease transaction, it was the duty of the tenant to find it. If the cause of the tort arose later, it was still the tenant's fault, because the tenant controlled the premises and should have discovered and corrected the defect. Today, these doctrines are beginning to fall in residential leases, but they still maintain much of their power in commercial leases.

Landlords have also avoided tort liability by having the tenant agree, in the lease, that the landlord shall be free of responsibility for any torts. This clause is called an **exculpatory clause** because it releases the landlord from any and all liability. This term is generic, not limited to real property law.

Such clauses are often enforceable, but not always. They are strictly construed and can still apply to nonresidential leases. The courts more closely monitor situations in which third parties are injured by the negligence of the landlord. For example, such a situation could arise if the landlord retained control over a part of the premises, such as halls, stairs, or the parking lot and a third party (or the tenant) was injured because the landlord failed to maintain the areas. If the landlord repaired the premises and those repairs cause a tort, or if the landlord agreed to make repairs and has not, and the defect subsequently causes an injury, the landlord may also be held liable. Premises which are to be used by the public require special care; if the landlord knew of a dangerous condition and failed to correct it, if someone were harmed, the landlord could be liable.

Finally, the landlord may be liable for the actions of a tenant. The classic case is the tenant's vicious dog, when the landlord knew about the dog's viciousness and did nothing about the dangerous situation. If the landlord has such knowledge, and the dog subsequently harms someone, the landlord usually will be liable.

9.5 CHECKLIST: PREPARATION OF A RESIDENTIAL LEASE

The residential lease provides the basic contract for the living quarters of increasing numbers of Americans, and it sets the terms whereby they either find comfort and convenience or find they have potentially endless problems. Working in this area is often a small job, but it can be meaningful to the client and build good relations for the paralegal and the firm.

I. Who will be the parties to the lease?
   A. Who owns (landlord-lessor) the leased premises?
      1. An individual?
      2. A trust?
      3. A corporation?
      4. A partnership?
   B. Who will occupy and use the premises (tenant-lessee)?
II. What is the appropriate description of the premises?
   A. Is the leasehold within a building or not?
      1. Free-standing building (home)? Use full legal description.
      2. Within a building? Use apartment number, floor, room, etc.
   B. Personal property items identified and handled separately.
   C. How are common areas being handled?
      1. Hallways.
      2. Elevators.
      3. Parking lots.
      4. Storage areas.
III. Is there a clear identification of the lease term? Give specific beginning and ending dates.

LEGAL TERMS

subordination agreement
Contract in which one party whose rights had been superior to another's agrees that the other party's rights shall become superior to her own.

estoppel certificate
Written statement from the tenant to a third party as to the lease relationship; used by landlords when they are selling the property or borrowing money; usually required in the lease.

exculpatory clause
Contract clause under which the tenant holds the landlord harmless from any damages that the landlord may cause the tenant; increasingly disfavored, especially in residential leases.

IV. How is the rent handled?
   A. Is the amount fixed in dollars?
   B. When does the rent begin?
   C. Exactly when is it due?
V. How are the utilities handled?
   A. What utilities does the tenant pay?
   B. What utilities does the landlord pay?
VI. Does the lease clearly identify the maintenance and repair obligations?
   A. Of landlord and tenant?
   B. Any dollar limitations on the tenant's duty to repair?
   C. When, under what circumstances, and with what duty to return to the earlier condition, does the tenant have the right to alter the premises?
VII. What are the insurance obligations of landlord and tenant by type of risk and location of risk?
VIII. What are the obligations if there is damage or destruction of the leasehold?
   A. Terminate lease if totally destroyed?
   B. Repair premises if only partially destroyed?
   C. Terminate lease if partially destroyed?
   D. Is there a careful definition of "partial" and "total" destruction so there are no ambiguities?
IX. What is permitted with assignment and subleasing?
   A. Does the tenant have the right to assign or to sublet? Any limitations?
   B. If there are limitations on the right to assign the lease or sublet it, what are they?
      1. Total prohibition?
      2. Partial prohibition?
   C. Is there a right to assign or sublet without the permission of the landlord?
X. What are the principal events of default under the lease?
   A. Nonpayment of the rent when due.
      1. Any waivers?
      2. Tenant's right to cure? How long?
   B. Breach of contract—noncompliance with the lease's covenants?
   C. How long are the notice and grace periods?
   D. When and how does the landlord have the right to cure the tenant's default?
XI. What are the landlord's remedies?
   A. Suit for performance?
   B. Cure default and seek reimbursement?
   C. End lease?
   D. Evict the tenant, repossess the premises, and relet leased premises as agent for tenant?

XII. What are the tenant's remedies?
   A. Withhold rent?
   B. Sue to enforce lease provisions?
   C. Sue for monetary damages?
   D. Cure default and offset costs against rent?
   E. Abandon the premises and the lease under constructive eviction?

XIII. Quiet enjoyment by tenant.

XIV. Surrender of leased premises: Must the tenant vacate before the lease term expires?

XV. What provisions are there for rent if the tenant holds over?
   A. Is the tenant treated as a month-to-month tenant?
   B. Does the tenant pay the same rent?
   C. Does the tenant pay additional rent during the holdover period?

9.6 CHECKLIST: PREPARATION OF A COMMERCIAL LEASE

The commercial lease is often complex and detailed in ways that take years to fully appreciate. Nevertheless, the following checklist is designed to help you make sure you can cover the basic elements of that type of lease.

I. What is the purpose of this lease?
   A. Retail space?
      1. An a regular building?
      2. In a shopping center or strip mall?
   B. Office space?
   C. Industrial building?
   D. Storage or warehouse space?

II. Who are the parties to the lease?
   A. The landlord-lessor—legal owner, title holder of the leased premises.
   B. Tenant-lessee—the legal entity that will possess and use the property.
   C. Broker—may be a party to the lease to enforce payment of commission.

III. Is there a legally adequate description of the premises to be leased?
   A. A full legal real property description if independent structure leased.
   B. Appropriate designation by a clear indication—"Section C on the attached map of the first floor of the building at 67 King Drive." Are exact dimensions necessary?
   C. What personal property is being leased with the property?
   D. How are the common areas being handled?

1. Hallways.
2. Elevators.
3. Parking lots.
4. Mall.
5. Restaurants.
6. Restrooms.

IV. What is the term of the lease?
  A. Is the term fixed at beginning and end by specific date?
  B. Is there an option (or more than one) to renew the lease?
  C. Does the lease term commence in the future?
    1. When the business opens?
    2. At a specified future date?
    3. Is the landlord responsible for any work that affects commencement of the lease term?
    4. What happens if the space is not available when the term is supposed to begin?

V. How are the premises to be used?
  A. Are their specific uses permitted?
  B. What specific uses are prohibited?
  C. Does the lease permit use for any lawful purpose?

VI. How is the rent handled?
  A. Is it to be a fixed dollar amount?
  B. Is it to be a rent based on a percentage?
    1. Percentage of exactly what?
    2. What is included in gross/net sales?
    3. What is excluded from gross/net sales?
    4. Recordkeeping.
      a. Account terminology clear?
      b. What type of financial statements are required—audited, review, or compilation?
      c. What is the time basis for the financial statements—fiscal or calendar year?
    5. When is the percentage rent payable?
    6. What are the lessor's rights to audit and inspect books?
  C. What events trigger rent increases, and how often may the rent be increased (escalation)?
    1. How much of a tax increase triggers rent escalation?
    2. How much of an insurance increase triggers rent escalation?
    3. How much of operating expenses may be passed on?
  D. How are inflation's effects (Consumer's Price Index) measured?
  E. When is rent due and payable? Specific dates needed?

VII. Maintenance and alterations.
  A. What are the obligations of landlord and tenant to maintain and repair premises?
  B. Identify tenant's rights to alter premises: Must the premises be restored to their original condition at the end of the lease?

C. Is there a clause stating that any alterations, changes, or maintenance must not place any encumbrance on the property?

VIII. Insurance.

A. What are the responsibilities of the landlord and the tenant for insurance?

B. How is the subrogation of payment of insurance proceeds to be handled?

IX. What happens if the premises are damaged or destroyed?

A. Does the lease terminate upon total destruction?

B. Does the rent abate if there is partial destruction?

C. Does the lease terminate if there is partial destruction?

D. Is a distinction drawn between partial and total destruction in the lease?

X. What happens if the property is condemned pursuant to eminent domain?

A. Does the lease terminate upon a total taking?

B. Is there a rent abatement if there is a partial taking?

C. Does the lease end if there is a partial taking?

D. How will the eminent domain allocation award be divided between the landlord and tenant?

XI. Assignment and subletting.

A. Does the tenant have the right to assign and sublet without any restrictions?

B. If there are restrictions:

1. Total?
2. Partial?

C. Can there be an assignment or subletting without the lessor's permission?

XII. Subordination and nondisturbance.

A. Is the lease subordinate to the interests of any mortgage holder?

B. Is the lease subordinate to the mortgage interest but with attornment for the tenant's interests (the lease remains but the foreclosing mortgagee replaces the mortgagor-lessor) and a subordination agreement?

XIII. What are the events of default?

A. Nonpayment of the rent when due.

B. Noncompliance with lease covenants.

C. Is there a notice and grace period? Can the tenant cure default?

D. Can the lessor cure tenant's default?

E. Who pays the expenses of enforcing the lease?

1. Any attorney's fees.
2. All court costs.
3. Expenses of the lessor to cure the tenant's default?

XIV. What are the landlord's remedies?

A. Bring suit for specific performance?

B. Cure default and seek reimbursement?
C. Terminate lease?
D. Evict tenant and repossess and relet the premises as agent for tenant?
E. Accelerate rent?
F. Landlord's lien against tenant's personal property to secure payment of rent?

XV. What are the tenant's remedies for landlord's default?
A. Bring suit for specific performance?
B. Sue for money damages?
C. Cure the default and other costs and offset them against rent?
D. Withhold the rent?

XVI. Quiet enjoyment.

XVII. Surrender of premises.
A. When must the tenant vacate the premises? Before lease term expires?
B. When may the tenant remove trade fixtures?
1. No default.
2. All damage to the premises from removal must be repaired.

XVIII. Holding over.
A. Is the tenant a month-to-month tenant?
B. What rent will the tenant pay?
1. Same rent as during lease term?
2. Additional rent?

XIX. Is an estoppel certificate required? (Must the tenant provide an estoppel certificate to the landlord on demand?)
A. To purchasers of leased premises?
B. To the mortgage lender?

XX. Can a short-form lease be used?
A. Prepared?
B. Recorded?
C. Alternative to recording complete lease.

XXI. What are the limits on lessor's liability?
A. No liability for lessor's failure to perform.
B. Any recovery is against the leased premises, not the landlord personally.
C. Is the lessor totally liable?
D. What is the extent of the lessor's liability for intentional misconduct or gross negligence?

XXII. If disputes arise between the parties, how are they to be resolved?
A. Lawsuit?
B. Arbitration?

XXIII. How are fixtures handled?

XXIV. Other lease considerations? Anything special, different, unusual?

DISCUSSION AND REVIEW QUESTIONS

1. What is the contract theory of independent clauses or independent covenants? How does it affect the lease agreements between the landlord and the tenant?
2. Explain the contract aspects and the real property aspects of a lease.
3. Identify three concerns each for landlord and tenant and explain their importance.
4. Identify the basic elements of a lease.
5. Explain the remedies of the landlord if the tenant does not comply with the terms of the lease.
6. Explain the remedies of the tenant if the landlord does not comply with the terms of the lease.
7. Identify the landlord's potential areas of liability under the leasing arrangement.
8. ABC Corporation rented a building for a term of five years. The building will be used as a warehouse for ABC's manufactured products and as a regional distribution center. The building is visible from two interstate highways. The lease has no clause about use of the roof or the outside of the building by either party. ABC erects roof signs and proceeds to paint its logo and product symbols on the sides of the building. The landlord objects. Who would win this dispute, the landlord or the tenant, and why?
9. You are a paralegal working in a large city for a major real estate broker and management company. You are at your desk when your boss stops by to discuss a problem. A national chain intends to come into your area, and it is searching for shopping center locations. The chain is strong enough to negotiate favorable lease terms and often uses its own lease form. The chain has had some conflicts in the past among its landlord, the landlord's mortgagee (creditor), and itself. In future leases, the national chain wants to protect itself from such conflicts. What could it do? How would the lease clauses work?
10. The Old Grain Dealers' Building has 15 tenants, all professionals—doctors, attorneys, accountants. The carpeting in the hallway on the third floor has been torn up in preparation for replacement. As George McGonickle makes his way down the hall, he stubs his toe on a protruding nail, loses his balance, falls through the glass door of his CPA's office, and suffers serious injuries. An attorney, Brad Johnson, whose office is down the hall, is in the CPA's office at the time, on business. When George gets out of the hospital, he consults Brad about whom he should sue for the damages he suffered. Discuss the parties who might be liable and explain your theory of liability.

SAMPLE FORMS

SIDEBAR

Read this lease through carefully and note its one-sidedness. Although such tight controls for the lessor may seem excessive, consider the investment and the risk to the property—tenants can go crazy. A good landlord, a good tenant—usually no problem; the issue is how to protect the right of the good party when the other is bad.

Lease of Apartment—Unfurnished

LEASE AGREEMENT

By this agreement, made and entered into on __________ *[date]*, between _________, referred to as lessor, and _________, referred to as lessee, lessor demises and lets to lessee, and lessee hires and takes as tenant of lessor, apartment No. ____ of the building _________ [known as _________], situated at ___________ *[street address]*, in the City of _________, County of _________, State of _________, to be used and occupied by lessee as a residence and for no other use or purpose whatsoever, for a term of ________ (___) years beginning ________ *[date]*, and ending _________ *[date]*, at a rental of _________ Dollars ($ ____) per month, payable monthly, in advance, during the entire term of this lease, to lessor at ___________ *[address]*, or to any other person or agent and at any other time or place that lessor may designate.

It is further mutually agreed between the parties as follows:

SECTION ONE
SECURITY OF DEPOSIT

On the execution of this lease, lessee deposits with lessor _________ Dollars ($ ____), receipt of which is acknowledged by lessor, as security for the faithful performance by lessee of the terms of this lease agreement, to be returned to lessee, without interest, on the full and faithful performance by lessee of the provisions of this lease agreement.

SECTION TWO
NUMBER OF OCCUPANTS

Lessee agrees that the leased apartment shall be occupied by no more than __________ *[number]* persons, consisting of __________ *[number]* adults and ___________ *[number]* children under the age of ____ years without the prior, express, and written consent of lessor.

SECTION THREE
ASSIGNMENT AND SUBLETTING

A. Without the prior, express, and written consent of lessor, lessee shall not assign this lease, or sublet the premises or any part of the premises.

B. A consent by lessor to one assignment or subletting shall not be deemed to be a consent to any subsequent assignment or subletting.

SECTION FOUR
SHOWING APARTMENT FOR RENTAL

Lessee hereby grants permission to lessor to show the apartment to new rental applicants at reasonable hours of the day, within __________ (____) days of the expiration of the term of this lease.

SECTION FIVE
ENTRY FOR INSPECTION, REPAIRS, AND ALTERATIONS

Lessor shall have the right to enter the leased premises for inspection at all reasonable hours and whenever necessary to make repairs and alterations of the apartment or the apartment building, or to clean the apartment.

SECTION SIX
UTILITIES

Electricity, gas, telephone service, and other utilities are not furnished as a part of this lease unless otherwise indicated in this lease agreement. Such expenses are the responsibility of and shall be obtained at the expense of lessee. Charges for __________ [water and garbage service *or as the case may be]* furnished to the apartment are included as part of this lease and shall be borne by lessor.

SECTION SEVEN
REPAIRS, REDECORATION, OR ALTERATIONS

A. Lessor shall be responsible for repairs to the interior and exterior of the building, provided, however, repairs required through damage caused by lessee shall be charged to lessee as additional rent.

B. It is agreed that lessee will not make or permit to be made any alterations, additions, improvements, or changes in the leased apartment without in each case first obtaining the written consent of lessor.

C. A consent to a particular alteration, addition, improvement, or change shall not be deemed a consent to or a waiver of restrictions against alterations, additions, improvements, or changes for the future.

D. All alterations, changes, and improvements built, constructed, or placed in the leased apartment by lessee, with the exception of fixtures removable without damage to the apartment and moveable personal property, shall, unless otherwise provided by written agreement between lessor and lessee, be the property of lessor and remain in the leased apartment at the expiration or earlier termination of this lease.

SECTION EIGHT
ANIMALS

Lessee shall keep no domestic or other animals in or about the apartment or on the apartment house premises without the prior, express, and written consent of the lessor.

SECTION NINE
WASTE, NUISANCE, OR UNLAWFUL USE

Lessee agrees that ________ [he *or* she] will not commit waste on the premises, or maintain or permit to be maintained a nuisance on the premises, or use or permit the premises to be used in an unlawful manner.

SECTION TEN
WAIVERS

A waiver by lessor of a breach of any covenant or duty of lessee under this lease is not a waiver of a breach of any other covenant or duty of lessee, or of any subsequent breach of the same covenant or duty.

SECTION ELEVEN
LESSEE'S HOLDING OVER

The parties agree that any holding over by lessee under this lease, without lessor's written consent, shall be a tenancy at will which may be terminated by lessor on ___________ (___) days' notice in writing.

SECTION TWELVE
PARKING SPACE

Lessee is hereby granted a license to use parking space No. ____ in the apartment building for the purpose of parking one motor vehicle during the term of this lease.

SECTION THIRTEEN
OPTION TO RENEW

Lessee is hereby granted the option of renewing this lease for an additional term of ___________ *[number]* ___ [months *or* years] on the same terms and conditions as contained in this lease agreement and at the ___________ [monthly *or* annual] rent of _________ Dollars ($____). If lessee elects to exercise this option, _________ [he *or* she] must give at least _________ (____) days' written notice to lessor prior to the termination of this lease.

SECTION FOURTEEN
REDELIVERY OF PREMISES

At the end of the term of this lease, lessee shall quit and deliver up the premises to lessor in as good condition as they are now, ordinary wear, decay, and damage by the elements excepted.

SECTION FIFTEEN
DEFAULT

If lessee defaults in the payment of rent or any part of the rent at the times specified above, or if lessee defaults in the performance of or compliance with any other term or condition of this lease agreement, _________ [or of the regulations attached to and made a part of this lease agreement, which regulations shall be subject to occasional amendment or addition by lessor], the lease, at the option of lessor, shall terminate and be forfeited, and lessor may re-enter the premises and retake possession and recover damages, including costs and attorney fees. Lessee shall be given _________ [written] notice of any default or breach. Termination and forfeiture of the lease shall not result if, within _________ (___) days of receipt of such notice, lessee has corrected the default or breach or has taken action reasonably likely to effect such correction within a reasonable time.

SECTION SIXTEEN
DESTRUCTION OF PREMISES AND EMINENT DOMAIN

A. In the event the leased premises are destroyed or rendered untenantable by fire, storm, or earthquake, or other casualty not caused by the negligence of lessee, or if the leased premises are taken by eminent domain, this lease shall be at an end from such time except for the purpose of enforcing rights that may have then accrued under this lease agreement. The rental shall then be accounted for between lessor and lessee up to the time of such injury or destruction or taking of the premises, lessee paying up to such date and lessor refunding the rent collected beyond such date.

B. Should a part only of the leased premises be destroyed or rendered untenantable by fire, storm, earthquake, or other casualty not caused by the negligence of lessee, the rental shall abate in the proportion that the injured part bears to the whole leased premises. The part so injured shall be restored by lessor as speedily as practicable, after which the full rent shall recommence and lease continue according to its terms.

C. Any condemnation award concerning the leased premises shall belong exclusively to lessor.

SECTION SEVENTEEN
DELAY IN OR IMPOSSIBILITY OF DELIVERY OF POSSESSION

In the event possession cannot be delivered to lessee on commencement of the lease term, through no fault of lessor or lessor's agents, there shall be no liability on lessor or lessor's agents, but the rental provided in this lease agreement shall abate until possession is given. Lessor or lessor's agents shall have _________ (___) days in which to give possession, and if possession is tendered within such time, lessee agrees to accept the leased premises and pay the rental provided in this lease agreement. In the event possession cannot be delivered within such time, through no fault of lessor or lessor's agents, then this lease and all rights under this lease agreement shall be at an end.

SECTION EIGHTEEN
BINDING EFFECT

The covenants and conditions contained in this lease agreement shall apply to and bind the heirs, legal representatives, and assigns of the parties to this lease agreement, and all covenants are to be construed as conditions of this lease.

SECTION NINETEEN
GOVERNING LAW

It is agreed that this lease agreement shall be governed by, construed, and enforced in accordance with the laws of the State of __________.

SECTION TWENTY
ATTORNEY FEES

In the event that any action is filed in relation to this lease agreement, the unsuccessful party in the action shall pay to the successful party, in addition to all the sums that either party may be called on to pay, a reasonable sum for the successful party's attorney fees.

SECTION TWENTY-ONE
TIME OF THE ESSENCE

It is specifically declared and agreed that time is of the essence of this lease agreement.

SECTION TWENTY-TWO
PARAGRAPH HEADINGS

The titles to the paragraphs of this lease agreement are solely for the convenience of the parties and shall not be used to explain, modify, simplify, or aid in the interpretation of the provisions of this lease agreement.

In witness whereof, each party to this lease agreement has caused it to be executed at ___________ *[place of execution]* on the date indicated below.

[Signatures and date(s) of signing]

[Acknowledgments]

Sublease—Short Form

SUBLEASE AGREEMENT

SIDEBAR

This sublease provides for the landlord's consent; what happens if the tenant subleases without the landlord's consent?

This sublease agreement was entered into on _________ *[date]* between ________, of ________ *[address]*, City of ________, County of _______, State of ________, referred to as sublessee, _________, of _________ *[address]*, City of __________, County of _________, State of _______, referred to as lessee, and _______, of _______ *[address]*, City of ________, County of ________, State of _________, referred to as lessor.

RECITALS

The parties recite and declare:

A. Lessor, by a lease agreement dated _________, leased to lessee the premises located and described as follows: _________.

B. The lease agreement provides that lessee shall not sublet the demised premises, or any part of the demised premises, or assign the lease agreement or any interest in this lease agreement without the consent of lessor.

C. Lessee and sublessee desire that lessor consent to a sublease of the whole of the above-described premises.

In consideration of the mutual covenants contained in this sublease agreement, the parties agree as follows:

1. Lessor consents to the sublease requested, provided that sublessee shall be bound by each and every covenant and condition contained in the lease agreement, a copy of which is attached to this sublease agreement as Exhibit ___________.

2. Sublessee shall perform all the covenants and conditions contained in the lease agreement to be performed by lessee except the payment of rent to be made by lessee to lessor. Sublessee shall be and is bound by each and every covenant and condition contained in the lease agreement.

3. Neither the subleasing of the above-described premises nor anything contained in this sublease agreement shall release lessee from the obligation to perform and be bound by all the covenants and conditions contained in the lease agreement.

In witness whereof, each party to this sublease agreement has caused it to be executed at ___________ *[place of execution]* on the date indicated below.

[Signatures and date(s) of signing]

CHAPTER 10
Condominiums and Cooperatives

"After all, the three major sources of apartments are death, divorce and transfer."

Cornelius Gallagher

Free-form style of contemporary architecture

OUTLINE

PROLOGUE TO THE PARALEGAL

Legal work with condominiums means learning not only this aspect of real estate law, but also two new areas of law, agency and corporations. These are introduced to help you understand the concepts that apply in working with condominiums and cooperatives. The condominium organization is a corporation, and there is a corporation involved in the cooperative transaction as well.

Be certain that you understand these two new areas as they apply here. The discussion of these topics is brief and by no means complete, but the basics given here apply in many areas. There are separate documents for the corporate side as well as new types of documents for the real estate aspects. Keep your thinking about these areas separate enough to handle them, but not so separate that they do not interrelate. Condominiums are a recently popular form of real estate ownership, and they seem to be a permanent addition to real estate ownership. They apply the same ownership principles as earlier described, but a condominium has a different place of ownership—no longer on the ground, but a piece of a building.

KEY TERMS

assessment
bylaws
common elements
condominium
cooperative
datum
declarant
declaration of restrictions
incorporation by reference
limited common elements
master deed
pool
rules and regulations
statement of public offering
time sharing

10.1 INTRODUCTION

Condominiums have been around for a long time. The idea comes from ancient Rome (the term derives from two Latin words, *com* + *dominium*, meaning co-rule) and reflected the impact of life in crowded cities, of vertical dwelling arrangements (rather than horizontal arrangements, such as single-family homes), and of limited spaces for real estate ownership. As America became more urban, this form of clustered housing came into the forefront. With the impact of baby boomers wanting residences, the condominium became a significant form of American real property ownership. Building condominiums and making existing buildings into condominiums became popular during and after the 1960s, but it was not unknown in urban areas before that time.

What is a **condominium**? It is a form of real property ownership that combines two aspects. The first is the ownership of the unit in the building, in which the owner usually resides. Were the building owned by one entity, the unit would be referred to as an apartment. In loose language, condominium ownership is often imprecisely referred to as "owning your own apartment." The second aspect is the joint ownership of the **common elements**, such as the stairwells, walks, grounds, walls, roofs, entry ways, and so on. The common elements are all used or usable by everyone who owns a condominium unit. As a result, the condominium owner participates in two types of real estate ownership—first, ownership in fee simple, and second, ownership as a tenant in common (usually). The condominium unit's fee ownership includes the air rights where the unit is located. When a person buys a condominium, the purchaser buys what the earlier owner had to sell—the unit in fee simple and the shared tenancy in common.

What if a condominium association has performed so poorly that its operating activities constituted negligence? Could an association member sue the association for damages sustained? Would a tort action lie? Or is it like suing yourself—an impossible situation? The case of *White v. Cox* deals with these questions in the context of California law.

LEGAL TERMS

condominium
Type of real estate ownership wherein the individual owner has title to his unit in fee and shares ownership as a tenant in common with the other unit owners in the common elements.

common elements
Real property that is owned and used by all in a condominium association.

WHITE v. COX
17 Cal. App. 3d 824, 95 Cal. Rptr. 259 (1971)

FLEMING, A.J.

Plaintiff White owns a condominium in the Merrywood condominium project and is a member of Merrywood Apartments, a nonprofit unincorporated association which maintains the common areas of Merrywood. In his complaint against Merrywood Apartments for damages for personal injuries White avers he tripped and fell over a water sprinkler negligently maintained by Merrywood Apartments in the common area of Merrywood. The trial court sustained Merrywood's demurrer without leave to amend and entered judgment of dismissal. White appeals.

The question here is whether a member of an unincorporated association of condominium owners may bring an action against the association for damages caused by negligent maintenance of the common areas in the condominium project. In contesting the propriety of such an action defendant association argues that because it is a joint enterprise each member is both principal and agent for every other member, and consequently the negligence of each member must be imputed to every other member. Hence, its argument goes, a member may not maintain an action for negligence against the association because the member himself shares responsibility as a principal for the negligence of which he complains.

We first consider the present status of an unincorporated association's liability in tort to its members. In *Marshall v. International Longshoremen's and Warehousemen's Union,* the court ruled that a member of a labor union organized as an unincorporated association could sue the union for negligent acts which the member had neither participated in nor authorized. The court said: "Under traditional legal concepts the partnership is regarded as an aggregate of individuals with each partner acting as agent for all other partners in the transaction of partnership business, and the agents of the partnership acting as agents for all of the partners. When these concepts are transferred bodily to other forms of voluntary associations such as fraternal organizations, clubs and labor unions, which act normally through elected officers and in which the individual members have little or no authority in the day-to-day operations of the association's affairs, reality is apt to be sacrificed to theoretical formalism. The courts, in recognition of this fact, have from case to case gradually evolved new theories in approaching the problems of such associations, and there is now a respectable body of judicial decision, especially in the field of labor-union law, with which we are here directly concerned, which recognizes the existence of unincorporated labor unions as separate entities for a variety of purposes, and which recognizes as well that the individual members of such unions are not in any true sense principals of the officers of the union or of its agents and employees so as to be bound personally by their acts under the strict application of the doctrine of *respondeat superior.*"

In effect, the court found that the traditional immunization of an unincorporated association from liability in tort to its members rested on two supports: (1) an unincorporated association lacks a legal existence separate from its members; (2) each member exercises control over the operations of the association. But the court observed that these supports no longer carried the persuasiveness they once did, and it quoted from its opinion in *DeMille v. American Federation of Radio Artists:* "The member and the association are distinct. The union represents the common or group interests of its members, as distinguished from their personal or private interest. 'Structurally and functionally, a labor union is an institution which involves more than the private or personal interests of its members. It represents organized, institutional activity as contrasted with wholly individual activity. This difference is as well defined as that existing between individual members of the union.'" The court then concluded that a union could be held liable in tort for negligence to a member. But it specifically limited the application of its ruling to labor unions, declaring it would leave "to future development the rules to be applied in the case of other types of unincorporated associations."

Since *Marshall* in 1962 the rule of nonliability of an unincorporated association to its members has suffered further erosion from both statutory and case law. Under amendments to the Corporations Code in 1967 an unincorporated association, defined as "any partnership or other unincorporated organization of two or more persons," has been made liable to third persons to the same extent as if the association were a natural person, its property (but not the property of its members) may be levied upon by writ of execution to enforce a judgment against the association, and a system has been created for the designation of agents for service of process. An unincorporated association may own property, protect its name and insignia, engage in commercial ventures, and engage in labor activities. Members of non-profit unincorporated associations remain free from liability for the association's debts incurred in acquiring real property.

Since 1962 the trend of case law has flowed toward full recognition of the unincorporated association as a separate legal entity. A member of an unincorporated association does not incur liability for acts of the association or acts of its members which he did not authorize or perform. A partner in a business partnership has been allowed to maintain an action against the partnership for the loss of his truck as a result of partnership negligence. In the latter case the court declared that the doctrine of imputed negligence, which would normally bar a partner's recovery against the partnership, was an artificial rule of law which should yield to reason and practical considerations; since the partnership would have been liable for damages to the property of a stranger, no just reason existed for denying recovery for damages to the property of a partner. In affirming a judgment for plaintiff the court said: "* * * under a realistic approach, seeking to achieve substantial justice, the plaintiff should be held entitled to maintain the action."

In view of these developments over the past decade we conclude that unincorporated associations are now entitled to general recognition as separate legal entities and that as a consequence a member of an unincorporated association may maintain a tort action against his association.

Does this general rule of tort liability of an unincorporated association to its members apply in the specific instance of a condominium? A brief review of the statutory provisions which sanction and regulate the condominium form of ownership will clarify the nature of what we are dealing with. A *condominium* is an estate in real property consisting of an undivided interest in common in a portion of a parcel of real property together with a separate interest in another portion of the same parcel. A *project* is the entire parcel of property, a *unit* is the separate interest, and the *common areas* are the entire project except for the units. Transfer of a unit, unless otherwise provided, is presumed to transfer the entire condominium. Ownership is usually limited to the interior surfaces of the unit, a cotenancy in the common areas, and nonexclusive easements for ingress, egress, and support. Typically, a condominium consists of an apartment house in which the units consist of individual apartments and the common areas consist of the remainder of the building and the grounds. Individual owners maintain their own apartments, and an association of apartment owners maintains the common areas. The association obtains funds for the care of the common areas by charging dues and levying assessments on each apartment owner.

The original project owner must record a condominium *plan,* and restrictions in the plan become enforcible as equitable servitudes. The plan may provide for management of the project by the condominium owners, by a board of governors elected by the owners, or by an elected or appointed agent. Management may acquire property, enforce restrictions, maintain the common areas, insure the owners, and make reasonable assessments. Only under exceptional circumstances may the condominium project be partitioned. Zoning ordinances must be construed to treat condominiums in like manner as similar structures, lots, or parcels. Condominium projects with five or more condominiums are subject to rules regulating subdivided lands and subdivisions. Individual condominiums are separately assessed and taxed. Savings and loan associations may lend money on the security of condominium real property.

California's condominium legislation parallels that of other jurisdictions and a review of this legislation brings out the two different aspects of the typical condominium scheme. (1) Operations. These are normally conducted by a management association created to run the common affairs of the condominium owners. The association functions in a manner comparable to other unincorporated associations in that it is controlled by a governing body, acts through designated agents, and functions under the authority of bylaws, etc. (the plan). In this aspect of the condominium scheme the management association of condominium owners functions as a distinct and separate personality from the owners themselves. (2) Ownership. In its system of tenure for real property the condominium draws elements both from tenancy in common and from separate ownership. Tenancy in common has also been brought into the structure of the management association, for under Civil Code section 1358 the management association holds personal property in common for the benefit of the condominium owners. In a formal sense, therefore, the condominium owners are tenants in common of the common areas and the personal property held by the management association, and they are owners in fee of separate units, which are not separate in fact. It is apparent that in its legal structure the condominium first combines elements from several concepts—unincorporated association, separate property, and tenancy in common—and then seeks to delineate separate privileges and responsibilities on the one hand from common privileges and responsibilities on the other. At this juncture we return to the tests used in *Marshall* to determine the tort liability of an association to its members and pose two questions. Does the condominium association possess a separate existence from its members? Do the members retain direct control over the operations of the association?

[1] Our answer to the first question derives from the nature of the condominium and its employment of the concept of separateness. Were separateness not clearly embodied within the condominium project the unit owners would become tenants in common of an estate in real property and remain exposed to all the consequences which flow from such a status. We think the concept of separateness in the condominium project carries over to any management body or association formed to handle the common affairs of the project, and that both the condominium project and the condominium association must be considered separate legal entities from its unit owners and association members.

For answer to our second question we turn to the statutory scheme, whence it clearly appears that in ordinary course a unit owner does not directly control the activities of the management body set up to handle the common affairs of the condominium project. To illustrate from the facts at bench: White owns his individual unit and a one-sixtieth interest in the common areas of Merrywood. An administrator controls the common affairs of Merrywood and maintains the common area where White tripped over the sprinkler. The administrator is appointed by and responsible to a board of governors. The board of governors is elected by the unit owners in an election in which each owner has one vote, owners vote by proxy, and cumulative voting is allowed. White is not a member of the board of governors. The Merrywood condominium plan succinctly warns, "In case management is not to your satisfaction, you may have no recourse." To use the language of the *Marshall* opinion, we would be sacrificing reality to theoretical formalism to rule that White had any effective control over the operation of the common areas of Merrywood, for in fact he had no more control over operations than he would have had as a stockholder in a corporation which owned and operated the project.

[2] With respect to the elements deemed critical in *Marshall* we find no substantial distinction between a condominium and a labor union. A condominium, like a labor union, has a separate existence from its members. Control of a condominium, like control of a labor union, is normally vested in a management body over which the individual member has no direct control. We conclude, therefore, that a condominium possesses sufficient aspects of an unincorporated association to make it liable in tort to its members. The condominium and the condominium association may be sued in the condominium name under authority of section 388 of the Code of Civil Procedure. The condominium and the condominium association may be served in the statutory manner provided for service on an unincorporated association, and individual unit owners need not be named or served as parties in a negligence action against the condominium and the condominium association.

We conclude (1) the condominium association may be sued for negligence in its common name, (2) by a member of the association, (3) who may obtain a judgment against the condominium and the condominium association.

The judgment of dismissal is reversed.

[Some citations and footnotes omitted.]

Although the apartment building is the most common and most familiar form of a condominium, there are many other forms. Condominiums may be made of any number of clustered units; these units could be town homes, parking spaces, business office units in a building or clustered group of buildings, or any of a variety of other grouped parcels of real property.

The law governing condominiums is the subject of some conflict. Some areas do not want condominiums and bitterly oppose them, while other areas support them. There is a proposed Uniform Condominium Act, which some states have adopted, but a number of states have already incorporated many of its ideas into their statutes. In other states, opposition to the Act—from groups ranging from environmental groups who fight to keep historic and natural scenic areas from having condos built on or near them, to other developers whose economic interests compete with those of the condo developers—has blocked its adoption. One of the principal areas of dispute is the rehabilitation of run-down older housing that, although structurally sound, needs substantial renovation for occupancy. The conversion of rental units into condominiums has driven the poor and, increasingly, the lower middle class out of the area, because they can afford neither the down payment nor the monthly mortgage and unit assessment payments (to maintain and operate the building). This situation has created intense conflict between major developers of new condominiums from rehabilitated buildings and advocates for poor and lower middle-class citizens. These advocates object to decreasing the number of rental units because it means that there is less space for those persons in the cities. Where will they go? The cities, of course, gain a double advantage from having more ownership rather than rental units for poor people. First, the poor may leave the city and reduce the city's need to provide services; that would lower the city's expenses. Second, the tax base usually rises when a conversion occurs, so that the city can probably raise more taxes from the same area than it did before. These social issues will likely be increasingly important in the next generation and will affect the use and development of condominiums. Economic, social, and legal ingenuity, along with ethical sensitivity, will be necessary to resolve these issues.

10.2 THE CREATION OF A CONDOMINIUM

Basically, there are two methods to create a condominium. The first method involves a public offering to purchase the units. This method is used when the property has been rehabilitated by an owner or developer, or when new construction was designed to be condominiums. These units are usually empty when they are sold. In the second method, the parties usually already occupy the property as apartment tenants, and the building owner wants to sell the building in units to the tenants. There are several ways to approach this matter. The tenants may form their own condominium association and individually purchase their units from the owner. The owner may decide to convert the building from rental units to condominiums and simply sell the units as is to the newly-formed condominium association of former tenants; or the owner may terminate the tenants' leases by nonrenewal, empty and rehabilitate the building, and sell the condominium units to any purchasers in the general public. This process often leads to conflict between the owner and the residents.

There are some preliminary materials to consider. First, the Uniform Condominium Act and some state laws require that be filed a **statement of the public offering** of the condominiums for sale be filed. In these states, it is usually also required that this statement be provided to prospective purchasers. The document is complex and lengthy. It explains the law relating to this condominium offering, how the condominium will be run, and the condition of the property (subject to an engineer's report). If there are tenants in an existing building, their rights of purchase must be described and the future condominium's assessment procedures explained. Further, the document names and provides the address of the party creating the condominium (the **declarant**), and explains the price and expense liability of each unit, any title encumbrances, and any warranties that the declarant will provide to the unit purchasers.

Second, at times the creation of condominiums and their marketing and sale across state lines necessitates compliance with the rules for selling

LEGAL TERMS

statement of public offering
Legal requirement by the Uniform Condominium Act or other state law that the declarant gives to prospective unit buyers and files with the appropriate authorities; tells the buyer what the condominium conditions are, including costs, etc.

declarant
Person who is creating the condominium; usually the developer.

securities, as defined in the 1933 Securities Act and by the Securities and Exchange Commission (SEC). In addition, some states require compliance with local laws relating to the issuance of securities (Blue Sky laws). Although the creation of new condominiums and condo conversions has abated somewhat in the last few years (as the real estate market has been depressed), the SEC rules have been in effect since the early 1970s and apply in the following circumstance. The basic idea is simple: if the instrument or document that one purchases (invests in) gives one the right to benefits (profits) that result solely from the efforts of others, the document or instrument is a security.

The most common example is a time-sharing condominium. Each owner benefits from having the condo for personal use for one period (say, a month) out of a year; the other periods are taken by other investors. The parties share the expenses and often rent out their own time share of the condominium, although that is not always the case. Therefore, the SEC requires that condominium purchasers-investors follow the formal registration rules when any condominium offering has: (1) any rental arrangement that economically benefits the purchaser by the work of the promoter or any other party that the promoter arranges to do the work; (2) a rental **pool** in which all the rents of the units are collected, pooled, and divided among the owners by a manager; or (3) any arrangement that requires the owner to rent out the unit for a certain time period each year, use an exclusive rental agent, or in some other way restricts the use of the unit. If these factors do not apply, there may not be any federal securities law requirements, but if there are any required limits on the owner's use, or any pools, or any clear intent to use the units as a profit-making venture through the efforts of third parties, compliance with the securities laws should be ensured.

10.3 THE DOCUMENTATION FOR CREATING A CONDOMINIUM

In most cases, the following documents are used to create a condominium:

1. A condominium declaration or master deed
2. Any amendments to that declaration
3. The appropriate transfer deeds
4. The homeowners association corporation's (HAC's) charter
5. The condominium's bylaws
6. The condominium's rules and regulations.

The condominium declaration or master deed is the most important document of this group because it creates the basic framework for the condominium owners' rights and responsibilities, as well as describing the interest that each owner will have. It is sometimes referred to as the condominium's constitution. Some of the declaration's obvious items are: (1) a real property description of the location; (2) an identification of the boundaries of each unit in the condominium, and (3) the name of the condominium association. The description of the unit is not done in exactly the same way as a normal land description, although one method (the plat method, which shows a plat of subdivision and numbers each unit) is similar to other plats describing real estate developments.

Another method is to survey the land and then the individual units to identify the interior dimensions of each unit. A third method is to have a floor plan for each floor, with identified units. When this approach is combined with a survey of the land location, all the aspects are accurately identified. Although at first there were problems with the descriptions of the units, (because of the unusual vertical aspect of the ownership arrangements), these uncertainties have been resolved. The precise height of a unit from the ground has also been a problem. In building a new condominium, one often purchases the unit before completion, and the demands of construction may cause minor height variations that make the legal description inaccurate. To resolve that problem, cities and other governments created their own survey **datum** which extends below the surface, is uniform throughout the city, and is therefore a base from which to measure the height. In areas where such a local datum has not been adopted, refer to the United States Geodetic Survey for its local datum.

Other important parts of the condominium declaration include the percentage share that each unit has in the voting rights to determine condominium policy. In some states, this participation is equal by units—one vote per unit. In other states, the percentage of voting power is tied to the percentage of unit square footage in relation to the total square footage. For instance, if the condominium units have a total of 68,000 square feet, and Condo # 21 has 1,800 square feet, that would mean that Condo # 21 had a voting power of 2.647 percent.

The declaration must also describe the common elements and any limited common elements. The common elements are such areas as the hallways, roof, and the like. **Limited common elements** are ones that may be used by some owners but not by all. It is common, for instance, to offer a parking space with the unit, but because each parking space is assigned to a particular unit, it is not a completely common element. If the owner does not want it, however, it may be rented, sold to the condo, sold to a third party, and so on. Thus, though not usable by everyone, a limited common element does retain some aspect of commonality.

If the condominium is being developed in sections or phases, the declaration must state the terms for adding additional property, any limitations on the developer's activities, and other relevant material. Finally, if the property upon which the building sits is a leasehold rather than an ownership in fee, the rights of the parties (both the leaseholder and the unit owner) should be delineated clearly to prevent possible disputes.

Because times and situations change, all condominium declarations permit amendment of the declaration. The declaration usually outlines the procedure, which must be followed to validate the amendments. The determination

LEGAL TERMS

pool
Placing of financial funds or interests together under the management, direction, or control of one person.

datum
Point from which height and depth can be measured.

limited common elements
Commonly held property in the condominium association that is assigned to the use of an individual unit owner or a group of unit owners (e.g., a parking space).

of the validity of amendments often turns on the unit owner's knowledge (whether actual or constructive by the filing of the plat and its declaration of restrictions). Careful attention should be given to the declaration's language concerning notice and the binding effects of future amendments upon parties who have already taken under the original declaration. The documents filed may permit the amendment and make it binding on anyone purchasing after the filing has occurred. If no such knowledge or permission is involved, there may be dispute about amendments' binding power absent each owner's consent whenever an amendment occurs or is sought.

For a purchaser to obtain rights in the unit, the seller must provide a deed to the condominium. The unit's legal description is based on the recorded plat of survey for the condominium, or other recorded device, and describes the unit and the common elements of the condominium. The deed should include references to all the rights and restrictions created by the declaration so that the purchaser receives them. The deed should state that these items run with the land.

The **declaration of restrictions** accompanies the plat of subdivision for recording. This document has to be separate, because the restrictions are frequently so many and so lengthy that they can no longer simply be included on the plat itself. The declaration is filed with the plat and is incorporated by a reference on the plat. This method is called **incorporation by reference** and is widely used in many areas of the law.

The deeds that follow this public recording of the declaration remain subject to those restrictions, and the restrictions usually cover many topics. Among the restrictions could be:

1. Easements granted, such as an easement by dedication for a public use (e.g., a park)
2. Permission to amend the restrictions
3. Clauses that solve potential problems such as the repair and maintenance of common walls, the handling of later phases of the development, the handling of assessments, and liens for nonpayment of assessments
4. A covenant that these agreements run with the land, so that the benefits of this set of restrictions passes automatically to subsequent purchasers
5. The ceding of powers to the association to enforce all the grants, restrictions, conveyances, and covenants, to enable the association to collect the **assessments** or lay a lien against the nonpaying unit owner and enforce the lien by foreclosure. The owners, in covenanting to pay the assessment and to permit the association to possess and exercise these rights, provide the association with those powers.

The corporate charter or articles of incorporation are from the state, and application is made to the appropriate official, usually the Secretary of State, Corporation Division, to issue a corporate charter for a nonprofit corporate organization. The state not-for-profit statute provides the basic patterns of activity—the dos and don'ts—that the condominium corporation must follow. Generally, the powers granted include all those necessary to make the condominium work well. Two specific powers that are almost always granted permit the corporation to adopt bylaws and rules of operation for the board of directors.

The organization's **bylaws** are its governing procedures and standards. Bylaws include procedures to elect officers and board members and requirements for other standard items, such as the annual reports to the unit members, notices, quorum requirements for meetings, procedures to follow for establishing assessments, and the like. These bylaws also include procedures for collecting delinquent assessments, maintenance and repair procedures, restrictions on unit owners' improvements or changes, insurance requirements, provisions regarding keeping books and records, inspection requirements, and other matters affecting the management of the condominium association. In addition to the bylaws, almost all condominiums have **rules and regulations** discussing how the unit owners shall relate to the common areas and to the other unit owners, use of the units themselves, and such other matters as security, the use of washing machines and dryers, and limitations on pets.

10.4 OPERATING ASPECTS OF CONDOMINIUMS

The condominium association, the corporation, is usually run by a board of directors (of varying size depending on the number of units in the association). The board elects its own officers. These officers usually include at least a president, a treasurer, and a secretary. The bylaws both dictate and govern the activities of the board. (The board adopted the bylaws when it was created.) Sometimes, the unit membership adopts these bylaws, and the unit owners frequently want to approve any significant changes. Courts have been reluctant to meddle in the operations of a condominium association unless there is good evidence of blatant, near-criminal mismanagement.

What is the job of the condominium's board of directors? Unlike many not-for-profit operations, there is little real marketing by the board. The board's most essential task is to collect money, spend it, and maintain the premises of the condominium area. To raise the money to maintain the buildings and grounds, the board must assess the owners for their fair share of these operating expenses. Assessments are a monthly payment; they fund the activities specified in the board's budget. The basis for assessments must be fair and known to all, and there must be a means of collecting past due assessments.

In some states, the condominium board can declare a lien for payment of the past due assessment and then foreclose on that lien, sell the condominium, and receive its past due assessment payments. Where this process exists, an issue arises as to whether the assessment takes priority over the mortgage for the unit. Few lenders care to finance any unit if the association's declaration does not make it clear that the mortgage takes priority over the assessments, but such has not always been the case. This problem will likely be

LEGAL TERMS

declaration of restrictions
Document recorded at the same time and in the same office as the plat of survey; describes the location, creation, and rules or the condominium owners; also called *master deed, declaration of conditions,* or *enabling declaration.*

incorporation by reference
Legal device to attach one legal document to another; for instance, the plat of survey refers on its face to the declaration of restrictions and incorporates the declaration into the plat by reference.

assessment
Amount of money each unit owner pays monthly for upkeep of the common elements.

bylaws
Operating framework within which the condominium's board of directors must function.

rules and regulations
Standards by which unit owners and their guests must operate while in the condominium.

resolved by statute, or by the declaration of restrictions' subordinating the assessments to the rights of the unit's mortgage holder.

With the money from assessments, the board must maintain the premises and the common areas. The board may also hire a manager to run the day-to-day operations. It may use a real estate management company to provide assistance and expertise in real estate management, of which, unfortunately, most board members lack any knowledge at all.

Insuring the common elements must also be the board's concern. The board should purchase liability and hazard insurance, elevator insurance, and, for employees, unemployment compensation insurance. A master policy should be obtained for the common elements, while each unit owner insures himself against his own risks, such as fire, water, hazard, and other risks to self, guests, and property. Since condominiums have become common, insurance companies have developed standard policies to cover these problems and risks. Finally, the board of directors may create committees to deal with particular areas of interest and concern to the board and the unit owners.

10.5 OTHER AREAS OF CONCERN

The individual unit owners must pay the real estate taxes on their units and their share of the common elements. The board is not generally involved in paying real estate taxes. In most cases, the tax problem of one unit owner should not affect any other unit owner. Condominium financing holds concerns for both lenders and borrowers. Problems of foreclosure and lien priority were mentioned in § 10.4, in relation to the condominium association's assessment lien, but other problems can arise as well. What if a lender financed a unit and very few units ever sold? How would the common elements be maintained? To solve this problem, unit financing is sometimes made dependent on a certain percentage of the units selling before completion of the condominium construction or conversion.

Conflicts between the board and the lender can be resolved by permitting the lender to sell under its foreclosure proceedings without the board asserting its first right of refusal on any new unit purchaser or tenant or any other right to limit the lender in leasing or selling the repossessed unit. In some circumstances, the unit owner may be buying a unit on ground held in a long-term lease. The lease terms and protection of the unit owner's rights, particularly in defining how to handle the payments if the leaseholder defaults, demand considerable and detailed attention.

The *State Savings* case involves a foreclosure against the developer of a condominium. The interim construction lender wants its money, the workers want their money, and the condominium purchasers are in the middle. This case is a very brief sample of the complex, multiple, and diverse issues that can arise from the conflict of this many different interests.

Title insurance should be obtained by each unit owner. The usual title searches are done, except that the title company may also insure against any failure to comply with the local condominium statute in the creation of the condominium corporation. Purchasers of conversion units should investigate any structural problems and protect themselves with a report from a highly reputable engineer. They should be aware of any problems with or lack of warranties for old appliances and fixtures. In addition, the problem of the converted building's existing mortgage should be considered by new purchasers. When and how will the mortgage be paid off? What guaranty is there that it will be? If there are tenants in a converted building, what are their rights, and might the condominium owners become involved in the owner's or developer's mistreatment of those tenants? It is essential to realize that **time-sharing** condominiums may be subject to SEC securities information requirements. The legal formats for owning a condominium on a time-sharing basis are not the same as for ownership of a normal unit, because the time-share unit is owned with others. Generally, a type of tenancy-in-common device is used for the time-sharing ownership, but variations on common ownership devices, as well as other ownership devices, exist too.

What happens when the documentation creating a condominium is not properly put together—when the interests of all the parties (lender, developer, eventual owners) are identified and handled according to the law? The *State Savings* case shows the mess that can occur and the difficulty the courts can have in straightening it out.

LEGAL TERMS

time sharing
Device whereby ownership of a condominium is split among many owners, each of whom uses the unit for a specified period of time (e.g., two weeks).

STATE SAVINGS & LOAN ASSOCIATION v. KAUAIAN DEVELOPMENT CO.

445 P.2d 109 (Haw. 1968)

[Footnotes omitted.]

Levinson, J.

This is the first case to reach this court involving a condominium. The statute under which we decide this case is the Horizontal Property Regimes Act. The plaintiff, State Savings & Loan Association, brought this action to foreclose a mortgage given to it by Kauaian Development Co., Inc. (hereinafter "Corporation") to secure a construction loan. This appeal involves two distinct issues: State Savings' right to foreclose against the interests of purchasers of individual apartments and the right of persons claiming mechanic's and materialman's liens to foreclose against those interests.

I. State Savings' Mortgage

On May 17, 1962, Mr. and Mrs. Antone Vidinha, as seller, and Mr. and Mrs. Milo Marchetti, Jr., as buyer, entered into an agreement of sale relating to the fee of the land involved in this suit. The Vidinhas retained legal title until the full price was paid, but the Marchettis had the right to possession of the land. On August 29, the Marchettis leased the land to Mr. Marchetti, doing business as the Kauaian Development Company (hereinafter "Company"), for 55 years (hereinafter the lease will be referred to as

"Master Lease 1"). Master Lease 1 was recorded in the Bureau of conveyances on August 31, 1962. It required the Company to construct and have ready for occupancy within two years from the date of execution of Master Lease 1 all or a part of a hotel apartment complex conforming to plans approved by the lessor. The 55 year term was to begin

> when all or a part of the improvements are ready for occupancy as evidenced by written stipulation signed by Lessor and Lessee. * * *

. . .On August 2, the Corporation was formed. On the same day the Marchettis and the Company assigned their interest in the agreement of sale and Master Lease 1 to the Corporation. . . .

Between August 28, 1963 and November 19, 1963, the Corporation had executed 56 documents entitled "Contract of Sale" by which the Corporation agreed to sell and the purchasers agreed to buy individual units in the proposed buildings. Each contract contained a clause providing for termination and return of the down payment in the event that construction was not commenced by December 31, 1963. The contracts also contained a clause indicating that the purchaser had received and read a copy of the Real Estate Commission's final report on the project.

After a loan commitment from Island Federal Savings and Loan Association of Honolulu for financing the individual purchases and construction of the buildings was withdrawn late in 1963, the Corporation entered into negotiations with State Savings for financing construction. Although State Savings' vice-president, J. Ralph Brown, expressed an interest in financing the individual units also, he made it clear from the outset that the Board of Directors in Salt Lake City, Utah, refused to commit State Savings to do so. The Corporation's vice-president and general counsel, Ralph E. Corey, accepted the construction loan with the clear understanding that State Savings was not committed to financing the purchases of the individual units. . . .

Early in 1964, the Corporation hired an attorney to review all the existing documents relating to the proposed condominium project. In June, he informed the Corporation and State Savings that Master Lease 1 had been extinguished by merger and that the supposed horizontal property regime was at that time nonexistent.

On July 6, 1964, the Corporation created the Kauaian Development Land Company, Inc. (hereinafter "Land Corporation"), conveyed the fee to it, and became lessee from the Land Corporation for a term of 55 years to begin on the first day of business operation of the Hyatt House Kauai project (hereinafter this lease will be referred to as "Master Lease 2").

By the end of 1964, the Corporation was two months in default in payment to State Savings. Neither the Corporation nor any of the purchasers made any payments in 1965. State Savings filed its complaint to foreclose the mortgage on July 16, 1965.

The trial court held as follows: the declaration was the operative document submitting Master Lease 1 to a horizontal property regime, but the regime was destroyed when the leasehold merged in the fee; the contracts could not be specifically enforced and, therefore, they did not convey interests in real property; the purchasers' interests arose from Master Lease 2 which had never been submitted to a horizontal property regime; at the time State Savings received the mortgage, and at the time of the filing of the foreclosure action, the purchasers had no interest in the property. The purchasers appealed.

We disagree with the trial court's resolution of several issues. Although obscured by the proliferation of subsidiary issues and by protracted and often acrimonious exchanges between counsel, the issues presented are relatively simple. First, was a horizontal property regime established? Second, if a regime was established, what is the significance of such establishment? Third, what interest, if any, in the real property did the purchasers receive as a result of the contracts? Fourth, were any such interests subordinated to State Savings' mortgage? And fifth, did the purchasers establish any of their affirmative defenses?

1. Was a Condominium Established?

* * *

c. Acts Taken in Compliance

Examination of Master Lease 1 and the declaration submitted by the Company indicates that the Company complied fully with the statute's requirements. The lease contained all necessary information and the declaration unequivocally stated the Company's intention to submit the leasehold to a horizontal property regime. The statute requires no more. Therefore, a horizontal property regime was established.

2. What Was the Significance of the Establishment of the Horizontal Property Regime?

The trial court held that the declaration was the operative document creating a horizontal property regime and that it subdivided the declarant's interest in the land horizontally as well as vertically. We agree. But this is the beginning, rather than the end, of the inquiry. The statute provides that

> Once the property is submitted to the horizontal property regime, an apartment in the building may be individually conveyed and encumbered and may be the subject of ownership, possession or sale and of all types of juridic acts inter vivos or mortis causa, as if it were sole and entirely independent of the other apartments in the building of which they form a part, and the corresponding individual titles and interests shall be recordable.

The statute makes the property *susceptible* to conveyance of individual units. It contemplates the existence of agreements transferring at least part of the developer's interest in individual units in the building before a person may assert an interest under the statute.

3. What Interests Did the Contracts Convey?

Since the declaration creates no rights in individuals other than the declarant, the purchasers must claim their interests under the contracts or subsequent documents. The majority of the contracts were executed before State Savings received its mortgage. Although they were never recorded, State Savings knew of their existence. On their face, the contracts contain many terms which regulate the rights of the parties. We disagree with the trial court's conclusion that the contracts did not convey an interest to the purchasers superior to State Savings' mortgage.

State Savings argues that the contracts conveyed no interest superior to its mortgage on several grounds, and that even if they did, the purchasers subsequently subordinated any such interests to its mortgage. It asserts that the contracts were not binding at the time it took its mortgage, or, in the alternative, if the contracts were binding, they conveyed no interest in real property.

State Savings makes a two-pronged attack against the validity of the contracts. First, it cites section 23 of Act 180 which provides, in part:

> The developer shall not enter into a binding contract or agreement for the sale of any unit in a condominium project [until]

(a) A true copy of the commission's final or substitute public report thereon with all supplementary public reports, *if any has been issued,* has been given to the prospective purchaser,

(b) The latter has been given an opportunity to read same, and,

(c) His receipt taken therefor. (Emphasis added.)

State Savings argues that since the commission issued supplementary reports after it received its interest, the purchasers were free to avoid the contract and therefore the contracts were not binding. We disagree.

The section places a flat prohibition on any contracts for the sale of individual units until the commission has issued a final report. It also requires the developer to give all reports the commission has issued at the time the contracts are consummated to the purchaser. The commission is given the power under section 24 to issue supplementary reports where it deems additional information about the project should be made available to the public. We are unable to conclude that the legislature intended, thereby, to give the commission the power to make contracts invalid merely by issuing a supplementary report. The information disclosed in the supplementary report may be a basis on which the purchaser could demand rescission of the contract, but this is quite different from holding ineffective all contracts entered into after a final report is issued but before optional, supplementary reports are issued by the commission.

Buttressing this conclusion is the different language used in sections 23 and 24. Section 24 requires the developer to issue a true copy of the supplementary report "to all purchasers". Section 23, which provides that contracts are not binding, requires a copy of all the reports to be given to each "prospective purchaser". Section 24 contemplates the existence of binding contracts and actual purchasers. In this case, the commission issued its final report on February 8, 1963, several months before the first contract was executed. Therefore, the contracts were not invalid simply because the commission chose to issue supplementary reports after the contracts were executed.

State Savings also contends that the contracts were not binding at the time it took its interest on the ground that the contract was to become effective only if construction was commenced by December 31, 1963 and that such construction was not in fact commenced by that date. Construction was commenced on November 11, as evidenced by the contractor's letter to the Corporation. State Savings argues, however, that the condition was not fulfilled because the contractor testified that he intended to do only $15,000 worth of work, the amount of cash he had been paid at the time, and would do nothing more until financing was obtained. Regardless of the contractor's testimony of his intent, There is no such condition in the contract between the Corporation and the contractor, and furthermore, there is no evidence that there was any cessation of work after November 11. Funds were released from escrow on the basis of the November 12 letter and none of the purchasers contended in this case that the funds were released improperly.

The fact that the contracts were binding does not resolve the further question as to the nature of the purchasers' interests under them vis-à-vis State Savings. Neither party has cited any authority to aid our determination of the kind of interest conveyed under the contracts and the statute.

Except as modified by statute with respect to registered land, the proposition is well established that one who takes an interest in real property with knowledge of the existence of contracts of sale of other interests in the property is subject to the terms of the contracts. Furthermore, Hawaii recognizes the present transferability of interests in futuro which would have been invalid at common law.

But the purchasers cite no authority, and we have found none, indicating that a contract for the sale of an interest in land and a building to be constructed on the land creates an equitable interest in the building superior to a mortgage securing a construction loan for the building. The two cases they rely on are inapplicable because they involved simple contracts for the sale of land. *Silva v. Desky,* involved the question whether the plaintiff could recover damages for breach of a contract for the sale of three lots where the only written memorandum of the alleged agreement was an instrument signed solely by the vendor. The court never referred to the existence of any equitable interests and no improvement was to be placed on the lots as part of the contract. *De Luz v. Ramos,* is even more inapposite. The issue involved there was whether specific performance of an oral agreement to make a lease could be enforced on the basis of part performance.

The case State Savings cites are no more compelling. It erroneously cites *Merchants Collection Agency, Ltd. v. Ng Au Shee* in support of its contention that the contracts conveyed no interest superior to its mortgage. In that case, the city attempted to avoid foreclosure of its interest in property mortgaged to the plaintiff on the grounds that before the plaintiff took its mortgage it knew that the city was negotiating for the purchase of part of the real property covered by the mortgage. It was in that context that the court stated:

> [N]either actual nor constructive notice of intention to acquire realty nor of pending negotiations for a future sale of the same is sufficient to defeat a mortgage executed before the consummation of said sale.

That case clearly did not involve an executed contract and therefore is inapplicable to this case.

State Savings, however, contends that since the contracts were not specifically enforceable they did not convey an interest in real property. We recognize that equity courts generally refrain from issuing decrees which they cannot enforce, and that equity courts will not order acts requiring continuous supervision, such as construction of building. But State Savings cites no authority which supports the conclusion that the inability, or refusal, of equity courts to grant a particular remedy indicates that no interest in real property has been conveyed. Recognition of an interest in real property does not necessarily depend on the availability of a specific remedy to protect such interests.

The question, then, is whether we ought to extend the protection equity historically has given to rights arising under an executory contract for the sale of land to interests of contract purchasers in a unit in a condominium to be built. Both parties agree that this case, and the issues involved it it, ought to be resolved in a manner which most effectively will implement the legislative desire to encourage the development of condominium projects in Hawaii. They disagree, obviously, as to the resolution which will best effectuate that purpose. The legislative enactment with which we are dealing in this case has profound social and economic overtones, not only in Hawaii but also in every densely populated area of the United States. Our construction of such legislation must be imaginative and progressive rather than restrictive.

We conclude that the overall objectives of the H.P.R.A. will best be effectuated by recognizing the rights of purchasers under the contracts as superior to those of a subsequent mortgagee receiving his mortgage with knowledge of those interests. First, equity courts long have recognized the basic unfairness of permitting a person to take an interest in property with knowledge that other interests, prior in time, exist, and permitting the subsequent interest to be free from those interests. As a general rule, a vendor can convey no more of an interest than he has at the time of the conveyance.

Second, and perhaps even more important, condominiums were developed as a method of ownership under which the individual purchaser's interest could be well protected. A significant part of the H.P.R.A. is devoted to ensuring that purchasers or potential purchasers will be well-informed of their rights and of the interests and liabilities they assume in purchasing a condominium unit. Obviously the purchasers cannot reasonably expect to receive their interest without paying for them or arranging for financing. Where an independent construction loan is necessary, it is a relatively small task to require the mortgagee to obtain subordination agreements from the purchasers as a condition of advancing the funds for construction. The burden cast upon the lending institution is light in comparison to the obvious virtue of this procedure in making clear to the unit purchaser his position. Undoubtedly this procedure would have been followed had State Savings hired an attorney to draw up the mortgage and advised him of the existing contracts of sale. It would be unconscionable for a lending institution to assume that it could ignore pre-existing contract rights. The additional step of obtaining subordination agreements is consonant with the legislature's desire to protect the purchasers and to enable them to keep informed as to their rights and obligations.

Concluding that a mortgagee advancing construction funds is subject to the interests of contract purchasers of the individual units in the structures to be built with those funds does not, however, mean that the purchasers cannot subordinate those interests to a subsequent mortgage.

State Savings argues that the purchasers, if they have any condominium interest, must rely for that interest on Master Lease 1. It contends that Master Lease 1 was extinguished by merger or by surrender and that the only document under which the purchasers could have had an interest at the time of foreclosure is Master Lease 2 which was never submitted to a horizontal property regime and which specifically subordinates that lease to the mortgage. We cannot agree that Master Lease 1 was destroyed by merger or surrender.

Under State Savings' theory, adopted by the trial court, merger occurred either on August 2, 1963, when the Corporation received the Company's interest as lessee and the Marchettis' interests as lessors and as purchasers under the agreement of sale with the Vidinhas, or, in the alternative, on November 13, 1963, when the Vidinhas conveyed the fee to the Corporation.

This court has recognized several times that the doctrine of the merger of estates is effective in Hawaii. But this is the first case requiring an extensive discussion of various aspects of the doctrine. Legal and equitable estates merge at common law only when the estates are commensurate, i. e., an equitable life estate and a legal remainder cannot merge. On August 2, the Corporation had both the legal and equitable interest in the leasehold, but only had an equitable interest in the fee under the executory agreement of sale, and therefore merger was impossible.

By November 13, several contracts for the sale of individual units had been executed. At common law, merger does not occur where there is an intervening estate, but a contract right to lease property at some time in the future is not considered an intervening estate. Applying the common law strictly, the fee and the leasehold would appear to have merged on November 13. We reject the principle that merger would occur despite the intervention of contract rights such as those present in this case. This court will not follow a common law rule relating to property where to do so would constitute a quixotic effort to conform social and economic realities to the rigid concepts of property law which developed when jousting was a favorite pastime. Courts of equity have consistently refused to permit estates to merge where the effect would be to impair the rights of third parties, or where there is any reason to keep the estates separate.

We do not go so far as to reject completely the common law doctrine of merger. We do, however, refuse to apply it to defeat the legally enforceable rights the purchasers obtained by virtue of their contracts.

Even were we to apply the general common law test of "the intent of the parties", we would reach the same conclusion. It would be nothing short of complete irrationality to presume that the Corporation, having succeeded to a condominium project based on a leasehold, desired to terminate the horizontal property regime merely because it also acquired the fee. On the contrary, every action it took after obtaining the fee was consistent with the conclusion that it intended Master Lease 1 to continue as an estate distinct from its interest in the fee.

State Savings' argument based on the theory of surrender is no more persuasive. In view of the totality of the facts, it is impossible to conclude that the Corporation intended Master Lease 2 to supplant Master Lease 1. The Corporation continued to act as though it were the developer of a condominium project. An officer and general counsel, of the Corporation testified that the creation of, and transfer of the fee to, the Land Corporation were necessary to take advantage of certain provisions of the state tax law. The Corporation never submitted Master Lease 2 to a horizontal property regime. Absent an indication that the Corporation intended to change the nature of the project, we must conclude that it regarded Master Lease 2 as an amendment to Master Lease 1. Even had the Corporation intended Master Lease 2 to supersede Master Lease 1, rights accruing to the purchasers under Master Lease 1 could not be affected without their consent. The record is devoid of any evidence to support the conclusion that the purchasers intended to surrender their interests in the horizontal property regime. We conclude that the record contains insufficient evidence to support the trial court's finding of the requisite intention to surrender Master Lease 1.

4. Were Purchasers' Interests Subordinated to State Savings' Mortgage?

State Savings argues that the purchasers subordinated their interests in the land and individual units by virtue of the leasehold condominium deeds and indentures of lease or by the Sheraton agreement. The trial court made no finding on that issue. We do not sit as a trial court in this case. Therefore, the case must be remanded for determination of the issue of subordination.

5. Appellants' Affirmative Defenses

The purchasers argued that State Savings should be estopped from asserting its priority, if it had priority, that it waived its right to foreclose, and that it forfeited its right to foreclose. On appeal, they further contend that the trial court failed to consider these defenses and thereby denied them due process of law.

a. Estoppel

The appellants misconceive the nature of the doctrine of estoppel.

> "The rule of law is clear that where one by his words, or conduct, wilfully causes another to believe the existence of a certain state of things, *and induces him to act on that belief, so as to alter his previous position,* the former is precluded from averring against the latter a different state of things, as existing at the same time."

The appellants introduced letters written by State Savings to the purchasers in which it referred to the latter as "Condominium Apartment Purchaser". The appellants failed, however, to introduce any evidence indicating how they relied to their disadvantage on those representations. Outside of limited correspondence, State Savings initiated no contact with individual purchasers. State Savings consistently indicated its unwillingness to commit itself to financing the individual units. If the purchasers relied on representations, they were representations by the Corporation's officers.

b. Waiver

The appellants failed to establish facts to support their argument that State Savings waived its right to foreclose.

> Waiver is generally defined as "the *intentional relinquishment* of a known right," "a voluntary relinquishment of some rights" and "the relinquishment or refusal to use a right." (Emphasis added.)

In general, unless it is express, it is shown either by such laches or by such inconsistent action as shows an intention not to rely upon the objection. For instance, moving for or consenting to repeated continuances after opportunity to raise the objection might be regarded as sufficient laches, and joining in error or submitting or agreeing to submit the matter upon its merits might be sufficient action of an inconsistent character.

The appellants argue that State Savings waived its right to foreclose when it failed to demand that the purchasers' rights be subordinated to the mortgage. It did not have the right to foreclose against the individual units until execution of the indentures of lease and leasehold condominium deeds in July 1964. We cannot conclude that a party waives a right by inaction several months before the right comes into existence. The right to foreclose did not arise until the Corporation defaulted on the loan secured by the mortgage. Any action or failure to act by State Savings before late 1964 is irrelevant to the issue of waiver. After the default, State Savings repeatedly warned the Corporation of the probability of foreclosure if payments were not made.

c. Forfeiture of the Right to Foreclose

The appellants argue that State Savings should have accepted the tender of the individual mortgages or given the purchasers releases to enable them to obtain financing elsewhere. Although the appellants constantly refer to State Savings' obligation in equity to accept the tender, we find no factual basis to support the argument. The failure of the developers to finance the construction of the project properly is in no way imputable to State Savings. It took its mortgage under the terms specified therein. At the time the loan commitment was made, State Savings reiterated to the Corporation's vice-president and general counsel that it was not committed to financing the individual units.

If it was impossible for the purchasers to obtain financing, perhaps it was due to the manner in which the project was organized.

d. Deprivation of Due Process

The appellants' argument that they were denied due process of law because the lower court failed to rule on their affirmative defenses is frivolous. The trial court carefully analyzed every pertinent aspect of the case. It considered the conflicting arguments on all the fundamental issues and several which were tangential. Its failure to enter a specific finding on these issues, even if erroneous, would not justify reversal because the defenses were totally without merit.

II. Mechanic's and Materialman's Liens

On August 24, 1964, the architect sent a letter to the Corporation certifying that construction was substantially completed. The Corporation refused to publish and file the notice of completion even after the contractor's formal demand. On August 18, 1965, the contractor and a supplier filed notices of mechanic's and materialman's liens. The architect filed notice of its lien more than one year after, but within one year and 45 days from, the date of actual completion. The appellants asserted that the statutory liens were invalid for failure to file within the statutory period and that even if they were timely filed, they could not attach to the individual purchasers' interests.

1. Mechanic's and Materialman's Liens Under the H.P.R.A.

The appellants contend that the mere filing of the declaration prevented the liens from attaching to the interests of purchasers of the individual units. They do not refer to any provision of the statute and they do not cite any authority to support this broad assertion. The H.P.R.A. specifically provides that it is supplementary to all other provisions of the Revised Laws and that only laws inconsistent with the H.P.R.A. are repealed. It is silent on the subject of mechanics' liens, and therefore R.L.H.1955, § 193–40 et seq., is inapplicable only if, and to the extent that it is inconsistent with the H.P.R.A.

The only section which even arguably could be inconsistent with the enforcement of mechanics' liens is section 4 of Act 180 which is entitled "Status of apartments within an horizontal property regime". It provides:

> Once the property is submitted to the horizontal property regime, an apartment in the building may be individually conveyed and encumbered and may be the subject of ownership, possession or sale and of all types of juridic acts inter vivos or mortis causa, as if it were sole and entirely independent of the other apartments in the building of which they form a part, and the corresponding individual titles and interests shall be recordable.

We construe this section merely to make the individual units legal entities equivalent to a dwelling built as an individual structure. It cannot reasonably be construed to give the condominium unit owner any greater interest than the owner of a single-family dwelling.

The law in Hawaii clearly gives a mechanic a lien on the improvement he constructs as well as on the interest of the owner of the improvement in the land. It is also clear that the mechanic's lien attaches to equitable interests arising under a contract of sale. Applying those principles to this case, it is clear that the mechanics' and materialmen's liens attached to the purchasers' equitable interest.

[The court concluded that the time for filing had not been complied with for some of the lienors.]

Affirmed in part, reversed in part, and remanded for further proceedings.

[Some citations omitted.]

The *Darger* case illustrates another problem that arose for one condominium association. Mr. Darger bought a condo. Later, he got a new job hundreds of miles away and he and his family moved. He could not lease the condo, so he wanted to sell **time shares** in the condo unit (# 41). After discussion and correspondence with the condo board, the board refused him the right to sell time shares.

Darger sold the time shares anyway and requested the board's approval, which it denied. The Dargers transferred the units shares despite the board's refusal. No more than one family occupied the unit at one time. Only four families were involved, for 13-week periods each. At trial, the condo association's position was sustained, and this appeal followed. Note the court's attempt to weave its way through old law and constitutional claims and still arrive at an appropriate resolution for a new area of real estate law.

LAGUNA ROYALE OWNERS ASSOCIATION v. DARGER

119 Cal. App. 3d 670 (1981)

[Footnotes omitted.]

Kaufman, A.J.

Contentions, Issues and Discussion

Defendants contend paragraph 7 of the Subassignment and Occupancy Agreement prohibiting assignments or transfers without the consent of Association is invalid because it is in violation of their constitutional rights to associate with persons of their choosing (U.S.Const., 1st amend.; Cal. Const., art. I, § 1), because it constitutes an unlawful restraint on alienation (Civ.Code, § 711), and because it does not comply with a regulation of the Real Estate Commissioner. Failing those, defendants contend finally that if by its finding that Association acted reasonably in refusing to approve the transfers, the court meant to indicate that Association had the duty to act reasonably in withholding consent and did so, that determination is not supported by substantial evidence and is contrary to law.

Association contends that the prohibition against transfer or assignment without its consent is not invalid on any of the bases urged by defendants. It argues primarily that its right to withhold approval or consent is absolute, that in exercising its power it is not required to adhere to a standard of reasonableness but may withhold approval or consent for any reason or for no reason at all. Secondarily, it argues that the evidence supports the finding it acted reasonably in disapproving the transfers to the other defendants.

We reject Association's contention that its right to give or withhold approval or consent is absolute. We likewise reject defendants' contention that the claimed right to approve or disapprove transfers is an invalid restraint on alienation because it is repugnant to the conveyance of a fee. We hold that in exercising its power to approve or disapprove transfers or assignments Association must act reasonably, exercising its power in a fair and nondiscriminatory manner and withholding approval only for a reason or reasons rationally related to the protection, preservation and proper operation of the property and the purposes of Association as set forth in its governing instruments. We hold that the restriction on transfer contained in paragraph 7 of the Subassignment and Occupancy Agreement (hereafter simply paragraph 7), thus limited, does not violate defendants' constitutional rights of association and is not invalid as an unreasonable restraint on alienation. However, we conclude that in view of the present provisions of Association's bylaws, its refusal to consent to the transfers to defendants was unreasonable as a matter of law. Accordingly, we reverse the judgment with directions to enter judgment for defendants. Having so concluded and disposed of the appeal it is unnecessary for us to decide whether the Real Estate Commissioner's regulation, which was not in effect when the Subassignment and Occupancy Agreement here involved was executed, could validly be applied to paragraph 7 or whether, if applied, it would invalidate the provisions of paragraph 7.

As indicated, the initial positions of the parties are at opposite extremes. Association contends that the Subassignment and Occupancy Agreement constitutes a sublease and that under the law applicable to leasehold interests, when a lease contains a provision permitting subletting only upon consent of the lessor, the lessor is under no obligation to give consent and, in fact, may withhold consent arbitrarily. Defendants on the other hand contend that the Subassignment and Occupancy Agreement conveys, in essence, a fee, and that under California law when a fee simple interest is granted, any restriction on the subsequent conveyance of the grantee's interest contained in the original grant is repugnant to the interest conveyed and is therefore void.

We reject the extreme contentions of both parties; the rules of law they propose, borrowed from the law of landlord and tenant developed during the feudal period in English history, are entirely inappropriate tools for use in affecting an accommodation of the competing interests involved in the use and transfer of a condominium. Even assuming the continued vitality of the rule that a lessor may arbitrarily withhold consent to a sublease, there is little or no similarity in the relationship between a condominium owner and his fellow owners and that between lessor and lessee or sublessor and sublessee. Even when the right to the underlying land is no more than an undivided interest in a ground lease or sublease, ownership of a condominium constitutes a statutorily recognized estate in real property, and in our society the right freely to use and dispose of one's property is a valued and protected right. Ownership and use of condominiums is an increasingly significant form of "home ownership" which has evolved in recent years to meet the desire of our people to own their own dwelling place, in the face of heavy concentrations of population in urban areas, the limited availability of housing, and, thus, the impossibly inflated cost of individual homes in such areas.

On the other hand condominium living involves a certain closeness to and with one's neighbors, and, as stated in *Hidden Harbour Estates, Inc. v. Norman,* "[I]nherent in the condominium concept is the principle that to promote the health, happiness, and peace of mind of the majority of the unit owners since they are living in such close proximity and using facilities in common, each unit owner must give up a certain degree of freedom of choice which he might otherwise enjoy in separate, privately owned property." Thus, it is essential to successful condominium living and the maintenance of the value of these increasingly significant property interests that the owners as a group have the authority to regulate reasonably the use and alienation of the condominiums.

Happily, there is no impediment to our adoption of such a rule; indeed, the existing law suggests such a rule. In the only California appellate decision of which we are aware dealing with the problem of restraints on alienation of a condominium, the court upheld as a reasonable restriction on an owner's right to sell his unit to families with children, a duly adopted amendment to the condominium bylaws restricting occupancy to persons 18 years and over. And, of course, Civil Code section 1355 pertaining to condominiums expressly authorizes the recordation of a declaration of project restrictions and subsequent amendments thereto, "which restrictions shall be enforceable equitable servitudes where reasonable, and shall inure to and bind all owners of condominiums in the project."

Reasonable restrictions on the alienation of condominiums are entirely consistent with Civil Code section 71 in which the California law on unlawful restraints on alienation has its origins. The day has long since passed when the rule in California was that all restraints on alienation were unlawful under the statute; it is now the settled law in this jurisdiction that only unreasonable restraints on alienation are invalid.

Nor does the right of Association reasonably to approve or disapprove the assignment or transfer of the Dargers' ownership interest violate defendants' constitutional right to associate freely with persons of their choosing. Preliminarily, there is considerable doubt of whether the actions of Association constitute state action so as to bring into play the constitutional guarantees. In any event, however, the constitutionally guaranteed freedom of association, like most other constitutionally protected rights, is not absolute but is subject to reasonable restriction in the interests of the general welfare. Moreover, it may be persuasively argued that if any constitutional right is at issue it is the due process right of an owner of property to use and dispose of it as he chooses. And, of course, property rights are subject to reasonable regulation to promote the general welfare. Finally, any determination of the validity or invalidity of Association's right to approve or disapprove assignments or transfers of the Dargers' interest will of necessity impinge upon someone's constitutional freedom of association. A determination that the power granted the Association is invalid would adversely affect the constitutional right of association of the remaining owners at least as much as a contrary determination would affect the same right of the Dargers.

Having concluded that a reasonable restriction on the right of alienation of a condominium is lawful, we must now determine whether Association's refusal to approve the transfer of the Dargers' interest to the other defendants was reasonable in the circumstances of the case at bench. The criteria for testing the reasonableness of an exercise of such a power by an owners' association are (1) whether the reason for withholding approval is rationally related to the protection, preservation or proper operation of the property and the purposes of the Association as set forth in its governing instruments and (2) whether the power was exercised in a fair and nondiscriminatory manner.

As to the last observation, a potential problem in the case at bench was avoided by the nature of the relief granted in the court below. Although in its complaint Association asserted a right to terminate the Dargers' ownership interest because of their assignments without Board approval and although there is some reference in the briefs to a "forfeiture," the judgment of the trial court simply invalidated the transfers to the other defendants, leaving the Dargers as the owners of the unit as they were at the outset. If Association's disapproval of the transfers was otherwise reasonable, we would find nothing unreasonable in the invalidation of the transfers.

To determine whether or not Association's disapproval of the transfers to the other defendants was reasonable it is necessary to isolate the reason or reasons approval was withheld. Aside from the assertion that it had the power to withhold approval arbitrarily, essentially three reasons were given by the Association for its refusal to approve the transfers: (1) the multiple ownership of undivided interests; (2) the use the defendants proposed to make of the unit would violate a bylaw restricting use of all apartments to "single family residential use"; and (3) the use proposed would be inconsistent with "the private single family residential character of Laguna Royale, together with the use and quiet enjoyment of all apartment owners of their respective apartments and the common facilities, taking into consideration the close community living circumstances of Laguna Royale." As to (3) Association asserted: "A four family ownership of a single apartment, with the guests of each owner potentially involved, would compound the use of the apartment and common facilities well beyond the normal and usual private single family residential character to the detriment of other owners and would frustrate effective controls over general security, guest occupants and rule compliance, . . ." We examine each of these reasons in light of the indicia of reasonableness referred to above.

Insofar as approval was withheld based on multiple ownership alone, Association's action was clearly unreasonable. In the first place, multiple ownership has no necessary connection to intensive use. Twenty, yea a hundred, persons could own undivided interests in a condominium for investment purposes and lease the condominium on a long-term basis to a single occupant whose use of the premises would probably be less intense in every respect than that considered "normal and usual." Secondly, the Association bylaws specifically contemplate multiple ownership; in Section 7 of Article III, dealing with voting at meetings, it is stated: "Where there is more than one record owner of a unit, any or all of the record owners may attend [the meeting] but only one vote will be permitted for said unit. In the event of disagreement among the record owners of a unit, the vote for that unit shall be cast by a majority of the record owners." Finally, the evidence is uncontroverted that a number of units are owned by several unrelated persons. Although those owners at the time of trial used their units "as a family," there is nothing in the governing instruments as they presently exist that would prevent them from changing the character of their use.

We turn to the assertion that the use of the premises proposed by defendants would be in violation of section 1 of article VIII of the bylaws which provides: "All apartment unit uses are restricted and limited to single family residential use and shall not be used or occupied for any other purpose" and paragraph 4 of the Subassignment and Occupation Agreement which provides: "The premises covered hereby shall be used solely for residential purposes, . . ." The term "single family residential use" is not otherwise defined, and if there is any ambiguity or uncertainty in the meaning of the term it must be resolved most favorably to free alienation. Actually, there is no evidence that defendants proposed to use the property other than for single family residential purposes. It is uncontroverted that they planned to and did use the property one family at a time for residential purposes. Thus, the proposed use was not in violation of the restriction to single family residential use.

The reasonableness of Association's disapproval of the transfers from the Dargers to the other defendants must stand or fall in the final analysis on the third reason offered by the Association for its action: the prospect that defendants' proposed use of the apartment and common facilities would be so greatly in excess of that considered "usual and normal" as to be inconsistent with the quiet enjoyment of the premises by the other occupants and the maintenance of security.

There can be no doubt that the reason given is rationally related to the proper operation of the property and the purposes of the Association as set forth in its governing instruments. The bylaws provide that "[t]he purpose of the Association is to manage and maintain the community apartment project . . . on a non-profit basis for the benefit of all owners of Laguna Royale." By subdivision (M)(6) of section 2 of Article V of the bylaws the Board is empowered to "prescribe reasonable regulations pertaining to . . . [r]egulating the purchase and/or lease of an apartment to a buyer or sublessee who has no children under 16 years of age that will occupy the apartment temporarily or full time as a resident." This power is said by the bylaws to be given the Board in recognition of "the prime importance of both security and quiet enjoyment of the Apartments owned by each member, and of the common recreational areas. . . ."

We reject defendants' contention that the Association had established a practice of approving or disapproving transfers solely on the basis of factors relating to the character, reputation and financial responsibility of the proposed transferee. There was testimony that during personal interviews with proposed transferees, the Board always inquired into the use proposed to be made of the premises.

The difficulty with upholding the Association's disapproval of the transfers by the Dargers to the other defendants is twofold. First, no evidence was introduced to establish that the intensity or nature of the use proposed by defendants would in fact be inconsistent with the peaceful enjoyment of the premises by the other occupants or impair security. We may take judicial notice as a matter of common knowledge that the use of a single apartment by four families for 13 weeks each during the year would create some problems not presented by the use of a single, permanent resident family. The moving in and out would, of course, be more frequent, and it might be that some temporary residents would not be as considerate of their fellow occupants as more permanent residents. However, we are not prepared to take judicial notice that the consecutive use of unit 41 by these four families, one at a time, would be so intense or disruptive as to interfere substantially with the peaceful enjoyment of the premises by the other occupants or the maintenance of building security.

Secondly, and most persuasive, a provision of the bylaws, subdivision (A) of section 1 of article VIII, provides: "Residential use and purpose, as used herein and as referred to in the lease, sub-assignment and occupancy agreement pertaining to and affecting each apartment unit in LAGUNA ROYALE shall be and is hereby deemed to exclude and prohibit the rental of any apartment unit for a period of time of less than ninety (90) days, as it is deemed and agreed that rentals of apartment units for less than ninety (90) day periods of time are contrary to the close community apartment character of LAGUNA ROYALE; interfere with and complicate the orderly administration and process of the security system and program and maintenance program of LAGUNA ROYALE, and interfere with the orderly management and administration of the common areas and facilities of LAGUNA ROYALE. Accordingly, no owner shall rent an apartment unit for a period of time of less than ninety (90) days."

The point is self-evident: under the present bylaws the Dargers could effect the same *use* of the property as is proposed by defendants by simply leasing to each couple for a period of 90 days each year.

Under these circumstances we are constrained to hold that Board's refusal to approve the transfers to the other defendants on the basis of the prospect of intensified use was unreasonable as a matter of law.

Our conclusion that Association's disapproval of the transfers by the Dargers to the other defendants must be characterized as unreasonable as a matter of law disposes of the appeal, and it is unnecessary for us to deal with the applicability of the regulation of the Real Estate Commissioner which provides that bylaw restrictions on sale or lease of a condominium must include uniform, objective standards not based upon "the race, color, religion, sex, marital status, national origin or ancestry of the vendee or lessee," and which, in effect, requires an owners' association to buy out the owner's interest on the terms of the proposed sale if the Association disapproves "a bona fide offer by a person who does not meet the prescribed standards." We do observe that the transfers from the Dargers were not disapproved on the basis that the other defendants are not "person[s] who [do] not meet the prescribed standards." We further observe that the regulation in question was apparently first filed in January 1976 whereas the Subassignment and Occupancy Agreement involved in the case at bench was executed by the defendants' predecessor in interest in 1965 and assigned to the Dargers in 1973. Finally, we observe that insofar as the necessity of exercising the right to approve or disapprove sales or leases on the basis of uniform, objective standards is concerned, our decision is substantially in accord with the Commissioner's regulation.

Disposition

The judgment is reversed with directions to the trial court to enter judgment for the defendants.

[Some citations omitted.]

Sometimes, a dissent not only addresses some of the human problems that could arise from the results of the majority's decision, but also articulates its opinion well. The brief and enjoyably written thought from the *Darger* dissent is worth your consideration.

10.6 COOPERATIVES

The **cooperative** is usually located in a large urban area. Although this form of home (usually) ownership was popular a generation ago, the newer device of condominiums has become much more widely used. In the typical cooperative, the property ownership lies in a corporation. The shares are owned by the tenants, and the lessees must own stock in the corporation—the two elements always run hand in hand. The corporation owns the land and building and leases the apartments in the building to its shareholders, tenants. It cannot be said with the cooperative that one owns one's apartment, unit, or home. The property interest in the condominium is an interest in the real property; with the cooperative, the property interest is in the corporate shares, which are personal property. Management of the cooperative corporation is generally in the hands of the shareholders-lessees, through the corporate board of directors.

LEGAL TERMS

cooperative
Corporation that owns the land and any building, or other improvements, thereon.

LAGUNA ROYALE OWNERS ASSOCIATION v. DARGER

119 Cal. App. 3d 670 (1981)

Gardner, P.J., dissenting.

I dissent.

Stripped to its essentials, this is a case in which the other owners of a condominium are attempting to stop the owner of one unit from embarking on a time sharing enterprise. The majority properly conclude that the owners as a group have the authority to regulate reasonably the use and alienation of the units. The majority then conclude that the Board's refusal to approve this transfer was unreasonable as a matter of law. To the contrary, I would find it to be entirely reasonable and would affirm the judgment of the trial court.

The use of a unit on a time sharing basis is inconsistent with the quiet enjoyment of the premises by the other occupants. Time sharing is a remarkable gimmick. P. T. Barnum would have loved it. It ordinarily brings enormous profits to the seller and in this case would bring chaos to the other residents. Here we have only four occupants but if this transfer is permitted there is nothing to stop a more greedy occupant of a unit from conveying to 52 or 365 other occupants.

If as an occupant of a condominium I must anticipate that my neighbors are going to change with clocklike regularity I might just as well move into a hotel—and get room service.

This difference is reflected in the documentation used. The condominium transaction uses standard real estate documentation: a deed, a mortgage note, a mortgage, and other real property-related documents and activities such as recording. The cooperative transaction, however, uses personal property documentation that relates to *instruments,* the specific type of personal property involved (a stock or share is an instrument). It may be difficult, as a lessee, to obtain a loan to acquire the lease. If one obtained such a loan, it would be a second mortgage (usually the corporation has a primary mortgage). When a second mortgage is made, the documentation required includes a note for the amount, a pledge of the stock and the lease, and a financing statement for the appropriate filing under the Uniform Commercial Code. The pledge may be a part of the note or separate, but because this transaction is covered by Article 9 of the Uniform Commercial Code, the pledging document must meet the requirements of a security agreement. The lender may want additional documentation for information or for security, such as an agreement with the corporation not to allow the lease or share to be sold without the lender's consent, or an agreement to inform the lender of any negative financial information concerning the lessee-borrower that becomes available to the corporation (such as a failure to pay the rent).

There are other differences between the cooperative and the condominium. The mortgage on the cooperative is on the corporation's land and building, in which the lessee's interest is that of a corporate shareholder. In the condominium, the mortgage is on the owner's unit. If there were a foreclosure for nonpayment of the cooperative corporation's mortgage, everyone could be evicted. In comparing the two forms of ownership, the cooperative may appear to have some advantages, in that it is easier to leave because the lessee is not personally obligated to a lender. But many persons wishing to transfer their leases have found it difficult to get around the cooperative's admissions board, which must approve new lessees. Also, in cooperatives with only a few units, there is sometimes a requirement of unanimous approval of any new shareholder-lessee. Generally, however, it is easier to evict a noncomplying tenant under the cooperative arrangement than it is to foreclose and dispossess the owner of a condominium unit. Taxes are on each unit in a condominium, but taxes are on the entire building in a cooperative; if someone does not pay the taxes, the other lessees must pay more to cover that failure.

What basic transaction creates the cooperative? A corporation is created and it then acquires, by purchase or donation, the land and building; generally, the property acquisition and unit development are covered by borrowed funds. Frequently, the number of shares in the corporation matches the number of units in the building; for instance, if there are 50 units, there are 50 shares. A person who wants to live in the building buys one share, and the corporation leases the unit to the buyer on a long-term lease (frequently called a proprietary lease). Thereafter, the corporation records a document showing the long-term lease. The financing of the lease and the share purchase can be handled however the buyer-shareholder-lessee works it out with the bank, but the corporation is paid in cash for its share and for its lease. What the buyer has acquired is (1) a share in a corporation that has a long-term mortgage to pay off on the property, and (2) a long-term lease that the buyer may have financed personally.

10.7 CONDOMINIUM CHECKLIST

Condominiums are a comparatively new legal entity in real estate (especially when compared to the concept of the fee simple). Working with them requires an understanding not only of real estate law, but also corporate organization and a certain amount of statutory law. This checklist is designed to help you to get started in handling these areas.

I. Determine how accurately the condominium documentation follows the requirements of the appropriate state's laws. This can be handled by obtaining a special endorsement on the title policy for the unit.

II. Determine the number of units sold. Like the financier, the buyer could get stuck in an untenable situation if not enough units are sold to establish a financially viable condominium association. Does the buyer have a right to rescind (get out of) the purchase after the contract has been signed if the developer does not sell a certain percentage of the units (25 to 50 percent) within a certain time period? Does the developer have the right to break the contract if the units are not sold at an appropriate rate, within a certain time?

III. During the sales period, how are the assessments handled? Do the unit owners pay them proportionally, or is the developer liable for a share as well, and how is that share determined?

IV. Is there any restriction on whom the unit buyer can deal with to obtain a mortgage?

V. Can the developer-declarant change the declaration and affect the rights of the unit purchasers? If so, what rights or responsibilities may not be changed? What rights has the declarant reserved that will affect the condominium unit owners?

VI. How is the escrow money handled? Is it at the developer's option, or does a state statute govern this area?

VII. Concerning the management company: What is its performance history? For how long a term is the management contract? What is the management company's reputation? What is the power balance between the management company and the board? What is the relationship between the management company and the declarant?

VIII. Who controls the board of directors—the unit owners or the developer? Can the owners obtain representation on the board while the developer still controls it?

IX. What is the condition of the board of directors? Does a small group run it? Is everything honest, or are favors done for board members? What is the term of board members? How many members are there? How informative is the financial statement? How accurate? How knowledgeable is the board about financial information and about real estate as a business? About homes and housing problems? How often does the board meet?

X. What is the unit really like? How closely does it conform to the plan or model—in detail? Are all the promised items there and operating? What is the quality of the construction? Soundproofing? Are any units retained by the developer and leased to the condominium association?

XI. Are there any requirements or limitations on the windows, balcony usage, furnishings, or decoration? If so, what are they?

XII. Are there any limitations on the number of persons living in the unit? Are there limitations on children, visitors, or pets?

XIII. How easily accessible is the unit? Can the buyer move her furniture in? Some elevators, doorways, and stairwells limit the size of furniture that can be moved into a unit.

XIV. Does the developer have a local reputation? What other work has he done? Where else in the area? Has the buyer visited it? How long have people lived there and how satisfactorily?

XV. Will the buyer personally, or will members of the buyer's household, have any difficulties living with the rules, bylaws, and so on, that pertain to use and occupation of the unit?

DISCUSSION AND REVIEW QUESTIONS

1. Explain what a condominium is.
2. How is a condominium created?
3. Identify the most important social-ethical consideration that affects condominium development.
4. What are common elements?
5. Although not discussed in the text, see if you can identify a number of advantages and disadvantages of condominium ownership.
6. Distinguish between the ownership of the condominium and the cooperative.

SAMPLE FORMS

Plan of Ownership—Master Deed

SIDEBAR

These two documents are the foundation of condominiums. Note the dual usage—commercial and residential—and the detailed distinctions between owned units and common areas in § 5.

MASTER DEED

In the City of _______, County of _______, and State of _________, on ________, 19____, ________, a corporation organized and existing under the laws of the State of ________, whose principal office and domicile is situated in the City of ________, State of ________, referred to as grantor, represented in this deed by its president, _________ *[name]*, who is fully empowered and qualified to execute this deed on behalf of the corporation, states that:

SECTION ONE
OWNERSHIP OF PROPERTY

Grantor owns the following property situated in the City of _________, State of _________, which is described as follows: ________ *[legal description]*, and recorded in the Office of the Recorder of the County of ________, State of ________, in book ________ of Deeds at Page ____.

SECTION TWO
PROJECT APPROVAL

Grantor has constructed on the described parcel of land a project known as ________ *[name of project]*, according to the plans, attached as

Exhibit "A," which plans were approved by the planning board of the City of _________, State of _________, on _________, 19___, and which are made a part of this instrument.

SECTION THREE
DESCRIPTION OF PROJECT

The project consists of a basement, ground floor and __________ *[number]* upper floors. The ground floor will be used for commercial facilities or other common purposes. The _________ *[number]* upper floors consist of individual apartments, all to be sold and used for residential purposes. The _________ upper floors are all capable of individual utilization, each apartment having its own exit to a common area and facility of the project, and each apartment to be sold to one or more owners, each owner obtaining a particular and exclusive property right thereto, referred to as "family unit," and also an undivided interest in the general and restricted common areas and facilities of the project, as listed in this deed, necessary for their adequate use and enjoyment and referred to as "general and restricted common areas and facilities," all of the above in accordance with _________ *[statute establishing apartment ownership].*

SECTION FOUR
ALLOCATION OF AREAS

The project has a total building area of _______ square feet, of which _____ square feet will constitute family units and _____ square feet will constitute general and/or restricted common areas and facilities.

SECTION FIVE
DESCRIPTION OF UNITS AND COMMON AREAS

The family units and common areas and facilities of the project will be as follows:

a. Family Units—Floors: On each of the _________ *[number]* upper floors there are _________ *[number]* family units referred to as Family Unit Type Number One, and the like. The family units will be numbered consecutively from 1 to _________ on each floor. These numbers will be appended to the number in hundreds that corresponds to each floor: Those on the first floor will bear the numbers "101," "102," and so on; those on the higher floors will be numbered similarly according to the corresponding number in hundreds that corresponds to each floor.

Each family unit is equipped with _________ *[describe air conditioning units, if any, and other equipment that is attached to or is a part of realty of the family unit].*

The measures of the family unit include all of the outside walls and one-half of the block partitions, but exclude bearing walls.

(1) *Family Unit Type Number One.* It is a rectangular-shaped apartment measuring _____ feet long and _____ feet wide, making a total area of _____ square feet, as specifically shown in Exhibit "A" of

this deed. Its boundaries are as follows: ________ *[conform boundary description to actual facts]*. Its main door has access to the floor corridor.

The family unit consists of the following rooms: ________ *[a hall of* ________ square feet, a living room of ________ square feet, a dining room of ______ square feet, a kitchen of ______ square feet, ________ *(number)* bedrooms of ______ square feet, ______ bathrooms of ______ square feet]. __________ [In addition, the family unit has a balcony facing ________ *(street)* of ______ square feet.]

(2-4) ______ *[Describe each type of family unit in separate items.]*

b. *Common Areas and Facilities.* Common areas and facilities of the project include:

(1) The parcel of land described in Section One of this deed.

(2) A basement, as shown in Exhibit "A" attached, and consisting of ______ square feet.

(3) The following facilities located in the basement:__________.

(4) Parking facilities, as shown in Exhibit "A" attached, and consisting of ______ square feet.

(5) The ground floor, as shown in Exhibit "A" attached, and consisting of ______ square feet.

(6) The following facilities located in the ground floor: ________ *[describe facilities,* such as: commercial areas and facilities, as shown in Exhibit "A" attached, consisting of ______ square feet and described as follows: ________ *or* a lobby and facilities, as shown in Exhibit "A" attached, consisting of ____ square feet and described as follows: _________].

(7) The following facilities located throughout the project, as shown in Exhibit "A" attached:

(A) __________ *[Number]* elevators.

(B) An elevator shaft of _______ square feet, for the _______ *[number]* elevators extending from the ground floor up to the ________ floor.

(C) A stairway, referred to in this deed as stairway "A," of _______ square feet which leads from the ground floor to the roof of the project.

(D) Plumbing network throughout the project.

(E) Electric and telephone wiring network throughout the project.

(F) Necessary public light, telephone, and water connections.

(G) Foundations and main walls of the project, as described in the plans that form part of this deed, attached as Exhibit "A."

(8) The following common areas and facilities located on each one of the ____________ *[number]* upper floors, as shown on Exhibit "A" attached, restricted to the use of family units of each respective floor:

(A) A lobby that gives access to the elevators, to the family units, to a janitor's room, ________ to the corridor and to Stairway "A."

(B) A room for the use of the janitor.

(C) A corridor extending from the lobby to Stairway "B."

SECTION SIX
COMMON AREAS AND FACILITIES

The general and restricted common areas and facilities shall remain undivided, and no owner shall bring any action for partition or division.

SECTION SEVEN
UNDIVIDED INTERESTS

The percentage of the undivided interest in the general and restricted common areas and facilities shall not be changed except with the unanimous consent of all of the owners expressed in a recorded amendment to this deed.

The undivided interest in the general and restricted common areas and facilities shall not be separated from the unit to which it appertains and shall be deemed conveyed or encumbered with the unit even though such interest is not expressly mentioned or described in the conveyance or other instrument.

SECTION EIGHT
RECORDATION; VALUATION

For the purpose of the recording fees to be imposed on the recordation of this deed in the book of Deeds, the value of the ___________ *[name of project]* is distributed as follows:

(a) Parcel of land described in Section One is valued at _________ Dollars ($____).

(b) The project described in Sections Two and Three is valued at ___________ Dollars ($____).

SECTION NINE
PLAN OF OWNERSHIP

As appears above, a plan of apartment ownership is constituted under and subject to the provisions of _________ *[statute establishing apartment ownership]* so that the family units of the upper floors may be conveyed and recorded as individual properties capable of independent use, each having its own exit to a common area and facility of the project, and each family unit owner having an exclusive and particular right over the respective family unit and, in addition, the specified undivided interest in the common areas and facilities and restricted common areas and facilities.

SECTION TEN
COVENANT OF GRANTOR

So long as grantor owns one or more of the family units, grantor shall be subject to the provisions of the deed and of the Exhibits "A," "B," and "C" attached. Grantor covenants to take no action that will adversely affect the rights of the association with respect to assurance against latent defects in the property or other rights assigned to the association, the members of the association, and their successors in it, as their interests may appear, by reason of the establishment of the condominium project.

SECTION ELEVEN
TITLE AND INTEREST OF GRANTEES

(1) The title and interest of the owner of each family unit in the general common areas and facilities listed under (1) through (7) of Paragraph b of Section Five, and their proportionate share in the profits and common expenses in the general common areas and facilities, as well as proportionate representation for voting purposes in the meeting of the _______ [Association of Owners of the ______ *(name of project) or as the case may be],* are based on the proportionate value of each family unit to the total value of all family units as follows:

Family Unit Type Number One:

_________ percent (____%) based on a value of _________ Dollars ($___) for this apartment and a total value of _________ Dollars ($___) *[value to correspond to FHA appraised value]* for all family units.

_________ *[Set out proportionate value of Family Unit Type Number Two through Family Unit Type Number _________.]*

(2) The title and interest of each owner of the family units located on each of the upper floors in the restricted common areas and facilities located on each floor and listed under (8) of Paragraph 6 of Section Five, and their proportionate share in the profits and common expenses in the restricted common areas and facilities, as well as the proportionate representation for voting purposes with respect to the restricted common areas and facilities in the meeting of the _______ [Association of Owners of the _________ *(name of project) or as the case may be],* are based on the proportionate value of each family unit to the total value of all family units located on its respective floor, as follows:

Family Unit Type Number One:

_________ percent (____%)

_________ *[Insert title and interest of the family unit owners of Family Unit Type Number Two through Family Unit Type Number _______, in the restricted common areas and facilities located on their respective floors.]*

(3) Proportionate representation for voting purposes provided in (1) and (2) may be limited in accordance with the provisions of the bylaws attached as Exhibit "D."

SECTION TWELVE
RATIFICATION OF MASTER DEED; RESTRICTION ON USE

All present or future owners, tenants or future tenants, or any other person that might use the facilities of the project in any manner, are subject to the provisions of this deed; and the mere acquisition or rental of any of the family units of the project or the mere act of occupancy of any of the units shall signify that the provisions of this deed are accepted and ratified.

The respective family units shall not be rented by the owners for transient or hotel purposes, which shall be defined as (a) rental for any period less than 30 days; or (b) any rental if the occupants of the family unit are provided customary hotel services, such as room service for food and beverage, maid service, furnishing laundry and linen, and bellboy service. Other than the foregoing obligations, the owners of the respective family units shall have the absolute right to lease the family unit, provided that the lease is made subject to the covenants and restrictions contained in this declaration and further subject to the bylaws and regulatory agreement attached.

SECTION THIRTEEN
ADMINISTRATION OF PROJECT

The administration of __________ *[name of project],* consisting of the project and parcel of land described in Sections One and five of this deed, shall be in accordance with the provisions of this deed and with the provisions of the bylaws, which are made a part of this deed and with the provisions of the bylaws, which are made a part of this deed and are attached as Exhibit "B," and shall be subject to the terms of a regulatory agreement executed by the association of owners and the Commissioner of the Federal Housing Administration, which is made a part and is attached as Exhibit "C."

SECTION FOURTEEN
RULES AND REGULATIONS

Each owner shall comply with the provisions of this deed, the bylaws, decisions, and resolutions of the association of owners or its representatives, and the regulatory agreement, as lawfully amended from time to time; and failure to comply with any such provisions, decisions, or resolutions shall be grounds for an action to recover sums due, for damages, or for injunctive relief.

SECTION FIFTEEN
CONTRIBUTION TO COMMON EXPENSES

No owner of a family unit may exempt such owner from liability for contribution toward the common expenses by waiver of the use or enjoyment of any of the general and restricted common areas and facilities or by the abandonment of the family unit.

SECTION SIXTEEN
REPAIR OF PROPERTY

If the property subject to the plan of apartment ownership is totally or substantially damaged or destroyed, the repair, reconstruction, or disposition of the property shall be as provided by __________ *[applicable statutory reference, or in the absence of statute, insert the following:* an agreement approved by __________ percent (____%) of the votes].

SECTION SEVENTEEN
ASSESSMENTS; LIABILITY OF MORTGAGEE

Where a mortgagee or other purchaser of a family unit obtains title by reason of foreclosure of a mortgage covering a unit, such acquirer of title, and successors or assigns, shall not be liable for any assessments by the association that became due prior to the acquisition of title by such acquirer, it being understood, however, that the above shall not be construed to prevent the association from filing and claiming liens for such assessments and enforcing them as provided by law, and that such assessment liens shall be subordinate to such mortgage. *[This provision is to be included in all plans of apartment ownership where local law permits.]*

SECTION EIGHTEEN
ASSESSMENTS; LIABILITY OF SUBSEQUENT GRANTEE

In a voluntary conveyance of a family unit, grantee of the unit shall be jointly and severally liable with grantor for all unpaid assessments by the association against the grantor for the grantor's share of the common expenses up to the time of the grant or conveyance without prejudice to grantee's right to recover from grantor the amounts paid by grantee for such assessments. However, any such grantee shall be entitled to a statement from the manager or board of directors of the association, as the case may be, setting forth the amount of the unpaid assessments against grantor due the association, and such grantee shall not be liable for, nor shall the family unit conveyed be subject to lien for, any unpaid assessments made by the association against grantor in excess of the amount set forth in the statement.

SECTION NINETEEN
BLANKET PROPERTY INSURANCE

The board of directors of the association of owners or the management agent, or manager, shall obtain and continue in effect blanket property insurance in forms and amounts satisfactory to mortgagees holding first mortgages covering family units but without prejudice to the right of the owner of a family unit to obtain individual family unit insurance.

SECTION TWENTY
INSURANCE PREMIUMS

The insurance premium for any blanket insurance coverage shall be a common expense to be paid by monthly assessments levied by the association of owners; and such payments shall be held in a separate escrow account of the association of owners and used solely for the payment of the blanket property insurance premiums as they become due.

SECTION TWENTY-ONE
REVOCATION OR AMENDMENT OF PLAN

The dedication of the property of the plan of apartment ownership shall not be revoked, or the property removed from the plan of apartment ownership, or any of the provisions herein amended, unless all of the owners, and the mortgagees of all the mortgages covering the units, unanimously agree to such revocation, or amendment, or removal of the property from the plan by recorded instruments.

Dated __________, 19____

[Signature]

Declaration of Covenants, Conditions, and Restrictions and Power of Attorney—By Owner and Developer

SIDEBAR

Note the language supporting the units and common areas in §§ 1–4. Particularly note § 12: these covenants generally are considered to run with the land and become binding on successor owners of the units. Is there anything more in any of these you would like to know about?

RECITALS

A. ________ *[Owner declarant],* a corporation organized and existing under the laws of the State of ________, referred to as owner, is the owner of all that real property known as ________ *[condominium project]* and located at ________ *[address],* City of ________, County of ________, State of ________, described particularly as ________ *[legal description],* as shown on that map entitled "________," filed for record ________, 19___, in Volume ________ of Maps at Page ____, in the office of the Recorder of the County of ________, State of ________.

B. It is the desire and intention of owner to subdivide that real property described above by means of deeds in the attached form, marked Exhibit "A," referred to as deed.

Attached and made a part of this declaration as Exhibit "________" is a survey of the property, consisting of ________ *[number]* sheets as prepared by __________ and dated __________, 19____.

C. The following declaration is executed to effectuate the desire of owner to impose on the described real property mutual beneficial restrictions under a general plan or scheme of improvement for the benefit of each and all of the included units and of the common area and of the future owners of those units and that common area.

D. The terms "declaration" and "condominium ownership" as used in this declaration shall mean and include the terms "master deed" and "apartment ownership" respectively.

DECLARATION

__________ *[Name],* the fee owner of the described real property, makes the following declaration as to divisions, covenants, restrictions, limitations, conditions, and uses to which the described real property and improvements, consisting of __________ *[number]* -unit multifamily structure and appurtenances, may be put, specifying that this declaration shall constitute covenants to run with the land and shall be binding on owner, and successors, heirs and assigns, and all subsequent owners of all or any part of the real property and improvements, together with their grantees, successors, heirs, executors, administrators, devisees, or assigns:

SECTION ONE
DIVISION INTO SEPARATE FREEHOLD ESTATES

To establish a plan of condominium ownership for the described property and improvements, _________ *[name]*, as the fee owner, covenants and agrees that it will divide the real property into the following separate freehold estates:

a. _________ *[Number]* separately designated and legally described freehold estates consisting of the spaces or areas contained within the perimeter walls of each of the _________ *[number]* apartment units in the multifamily structure constructed on the property, the spaces being defined and referred to as apartment spaces.

b. A freehold estate consisting of the remaining portion of the real property, described and referred to as common areas and facilities, which includes the multifamily structure and the property on which it is located, and specifically includes, but is not limited to, the land, roof, main walls, slabs, elevator, elevator shaft, staircases, lobbies, halls, parking spaces, storage spaces, community and commercial facilities, swimming pool, pumps, water tank, trees, pavement, balconies, pipes, wires, conduits, air conditions and ducts, or other public utility lines.

SECTION TWO
FAMILY UNITS

For the purpose of this declaration, the ownership of each apartment space includes the respective undivided interest in the common areas and facilities specified and established in this document, and each apartment space, together with the undivided interest, is defined and referred to as a family unit.

_________ *[Number]* individual apartment spaces established by this document, and which shall be individually conveyed, are described as follows:_________ *[legal description of apartment spaces]*.

SECTION THREE
RESTRICTED COMMON AREAS AND FACILITIES

A portion of the common areas and facilities is set aside and allocated for the restricted use of the respective apartment spaces, as shown on the attached survey. Such areas shall be known as "restricted common areas and facilities."

The restricted common areas and facilities allocated for the restricted uses of the respective family units are as follows:

Family unit 1: That portion of the parking area designated as parking space No. 1; storage space No. 1; together with balcony adjoining the apartment space associated with family unit 1 on the _________ *[direction]*. The restricted areas are further described, located, and shown on the attached survey. _________ *[Similarly describe other family units.]*

SECTION FOUR
COMMON AREAS AND FACILITIES

The undivided interest in the common areas and facilities established by this document, and which shall be conveyed with each respective apartment space, is as follows: _________ *[list apartment numbers and percentages of undivided interest].*

The above respective undivided interests established and to be conveyed with the respective apartment spaces cannot be changed, and _________ *[owner],* and successors, heirs, assigns, and grantees, covenant and agree that the undivided interest in the common areas and facilities and the fee titles to the respective apartment spaces conveyed shall not be separated or separately conveyed. Each such undivided interest shall be deemed to be conveyed or encumbered with its respective apartment space, even though the description in the instrument of conveyance or encumbrance may refer only to the fee title to the apartment space.

SECTION FIVE
PROFITS AND EXPENSES; VOTING REPRESENTATION

The proportionate shares of the separate owners of the respective family units in the profits and common expenses in the common areas and facilities, as well as their proportionate representation for voting purposes in the association of owners, are based on the proportionate value that each of the family units bears to _________ Dollars ($____), which represents the total value of all of the family units. The value of the respective family units, their respective interests for voting purposes, and their proportionate shares in the common profits and expenses shall be as follows: ___________ *[list each family unit number, its value, and the proportionate representation for voting and sharing in common profits and expenses].*

SECTION SIX
ASSESSMENT LIENS

All unpaid assessments for the share of the common expenses chargeable to any family unit shall constitute a lien on such family unit prior to all other liens except (1) tax liens on the family unit in favor of any assessing unit and special district, and (2) all sums unpaid on the first mortgage of record. Such lien may be foreclosed by suit by the manager or board of directors, acting for the owners of the family units, in like manner as a mortgagee of real property. In any such foreclosure, the family unit owner shall be required to pay a reasonable rental for the family unit, if so provided in the bylaws, and the plaintiff in such foreclosure action shall be entitled to the appointment of a receiver to collect the rent. The manager or board of directors, acting for the owners of the family units, shall have the power, unless otherwise prohibited, to bid in the unit at the foreclosure sale and to acquire and hold, lease, mortgage, and convey the unit. Suit to recover a money judgment for unpaid common expenses shall be maintainable without foreclosing or waiving the lien securing the unpaid expenses.

SECTION SEVEN
LIABILITY OF MORTGAGEE

Where the mortgagee of a first mortgage of record or other purchaser of a family unit obtains title to the unit as a result of foreclosure of the first mortgage, such title holder, and successors and assigns, shall not be liable for the share of the common expenses or assessments by the association chargeable to such family unit and due prior to the acquisition of title to such deemed to be common expenses collectible from all of the family units, including such person acquiring title, and successors and assigns.

SECTION EIGHT
LIABILITY OF GRANTEE

In a voluntary conveyance of a family unit, the grantee of the unit shall be jointly and severally liable with the grantor for all unpaid assessments by the association against the latter for a share of the common expenses, up to the time of the grant or conveyance, without prejudice to the grantee's right to recover from the grantor the amounts paid by the grantee. However, any such grantee shall be entitled to a statement from the manager or board of directors of the association, as the case may be, setting forth the amount of the unpaid assessments against the grantor of the association; and such grantee shall not be liable for, nor shall the family unit conveyed be subject to a lien for, any unpaid assessments made by the association against the grantor in excess of the amount set forth in the statement.

SECTION NINE
ACTIONS OF ASSOCIATION; BINDING EFFECT

All agreements and determinations lawfully made by the association in accordance with he voting percentages established in _________ *[state family unit ownership law, if any]* this declaration or in the bylaws, shall be deemed to be binding on all owners of family units, their successors and assigns.

SECTION TEN
EFFECT OF DAMAGE OR DESTRUCTION

If the property subject to this enabling declaration is totally or substantially damaged or destroyed, the repair, reconstruction,or disposition of the property shall be as provided by _________ *[statute, or, if none, insert the following:* an agreement approved by _______ percent (____%) of the votes].

SECTION ELEVEN
COVENANT OF DECLARANT

So long as _________ *[declarant]* owns one or more of the family units established and described in this document, the property shall be subject to the provisions of this declaration and of Exhibits "A," "B," and "C" attached; and such owner covenants to take no action that would adversely affect the rights of the association with respect to assurances against latent defects in the property or other right assigned to the association by reason of the establishment of the condominium.

SECTION TWELVE
COVENANTS OF OWNERS

_________ *[Owner],* and successors, heirs, and assigns, by this declaration, and all future owners of the family units, by their acceptance of their deeds, agree as follows:

a. The common areas and facilities shall remain undivided; no owner shall bring any action for partition, it being agreed that this restriction is necessary to preserve the rights of the owners in the operation and management of the condominium.

b. Each apartment space shall be occupied and used only as a private dwelling for the owner, the owner's family, tenants, and social guests, and for no other purpose.

c. The owner of each apartment space shall not be deemed to own the undecorated and/or unfinished surfaces of the perimeter walls, floors, and ceilings surrounding the apartment space, nor shall such owner be deemed to own pipes, wires, conduits, or other public utility lines running through the apartment spaces and utilized for or serving more than one apartment space, except as tenants in common with other family unit owners as provided in this document. Such owner, however, shall be deemed to own the walls and partitions that are contained within the apartment space, and also shall be deemed to own the inner decorated and/or finished surfaces of the perimeter walls, floors, and ceilings, including plaster, paint, wallpaper, and the like.

d. If any portion of the common areas and facilities encroaches on the apartment spaces, a valid easement exists for the encroachment and its maintenance, so long as it stands. If the multifamily structure is partially or totally destroyed and then rebuilt, the owners of the apartment spaces agree that minor encroachment of parts of the common areas and facilities due to the construction shall be permitted and that a valid easement for the encroachment and its maintenance exists.

e. An owner of a family unit shall automatically, on becoming the owner of a family unit or units, be a member of _________, referred to as the association, and shall remain a member of the association until ownership ceases for any reason, at which time the membership in the association shall automatically cease.

f. The administration of the condominium shall accord with the provisions of the declaration, the bylaws of the association, which are made a part and attached as Exhibit "B," and shall be subject to the terms of a regulatory agreement executed by the association and the Commissioner of the Federal Housing Administration, which agreement is made a part and is attached as Exhibit "C."

g. Each owner, tenant, or occupant of a family unit shall comply with the provisions of this declaration, the bylaw, decisions, and resolutions of the association or its representative, and the regulatory agreement, as lawfully amended from time to time; and failure to comply with any such provisions, decisions, or resolutions shall be grounds for an action to receive sums due, for damages, or for injunctive relief.

h. This declaration shall not be revoked or any of the provisions amended unless all of the owners and the mortgages of all of the mortgages covering the family units unanimously agree to such revocation or amendment by recorded instruments.

i. No owner of a family unit may exempt such owner from liability for contribution to the common expenses by waiver of the use or enjoyment of any of the common areas and facilities or by the abandonment of the family unit.

SECTION THIRTEEN
USE OF FAMILY UNIT

The respective family units shall not be rented by the owners for transient or hotel purposes, which shall be defined as (1) rental for a period less than 30 days or (2) any rental to occupants of the family unit who are provided customary hotel services, such as room service for food and beverage, maid service, laundry and linen service, and bellboy service. Other than the foregoing obligations, the owners of the respective family units shall have the absolute right to lease the units, provided that the lease is made subject to the covenants and restrictions contained in this declaration and further subject to the bylaws and regulatory agreement attached.

[Signature]

[Acknowledgment]

CHAPTER 11
The Environment and Public and Private Controls on the Use of Real Estate

"Still you keep 'o the windy side of the law."

***Shakespeare,* Twelfth Night**

Contemporary solar home

OUTLINE

PROLOGUE TO THE PARALEGAL

The environment has become a political and a legal concern—as well as a health concern—for many of us. Our treatment of the environment seriously affects our use of real property; consider using the out-of-doors with the alarming increase in skin cancer in New Zealand from ozone depletion. This chapter deals with some of the most important of the government's attempts to control pollution in relation to real estate and the impact of its attempts to clean up the environment. But concern over the environment is not the only source of restrictions on the use of real estate. This chapter discusses both public restrictions, such as zoning, and private restrictions, such as restrictive agreements in contracts. Working with government agencies requires many documents, the most important of which are mentioned herein, but any detailed consideration of those documents lies beyond the scope of this book.

KEY TERMS

CERCLA
dedication
entity
environmental audit
Environmental Protection Agency (EPA)
operator
Superfund
variance
zoning

11.1 INTRODUCTION

Since the 1970s, the world has become increasingly aware of the role that the environment plays in the quality of our living arrangements and its essential value in our lives. A number of laws, beginning with the Rivers and Harbors Act in the 1890s, have been passed over the last century; all of them attempted to improve the quality of our environment. But these efforts were intermittent over the past century and were undertaken only when a specific problem provoked a powerful public outcry. By the 1960s, however, more comprehensive attempts at environmental control were enacted after reports that industrial areas in the Midwest were so polluted that the rain that fell through the polluted air created sulfuric acid and stripped the paint off parked cars and damaged the paint on homes. There remain, despite all attempts, immense tasks in cleaning up the environment.

In 1992, in Virginia, owners of a number of very expensive homes near a oil storage tank depot found themselves with a disastrous problem. The water table beneath their homes had become polluted over the decades by gradual seepage from the storage tanks. The ground and water pollution were indescribable, and the fire hazard to the homes appeared to be severe. Clearly, all these frightening reports appeared to indicate that remedial measures were essential.

Congress passed numerous environmental protection laws in the 1960s and 1970s, but the ones that had the greatest impact on the real estate industry were, first, ones related to the **Superfund** (the money from which would be used to clean up the land) and, second, laws aimed at cleaning up the air, land, and water. The National Environmental Policy Act (NEPA) of 1970 provided for the creation of environmental impact statements. (It should be noted that the Virginia oil storage depot problem must be handled differently because petroleum products are generally excluded from most environmental legislation.) Although there are also many state laws affecting the environment, the laws that have had the greatest impact are the federal laws, particularly the Superfund legislation and its amendments.

11.2 FEDERAL ENVIRONMENTAL LEGISLATION AFFECTING REAL ESTATE

Federal environmental laws basically relate to three areas. These laws are first, for preventing pollution from occurring; second, for handling the cleanup of pollution after it has occurred; and third, for regulating the production and handling of chemicals that could be poisonous to human beings or their environment. In the first category, pollution control, there are laws controlling the amount of ingredients that can be put into the water, the air, and the land. These well-known laws are the Clean Air Act, the Clean Water Act, and the Safe Drinking Water Act. In the second category, cleaning up the environment after it has been polluted, the Superfund law (the Comprehensive Environmental Response, Compensation, and Liability Act of 1980, as amended) is designed to find the polluted areas and work out a program for cleaning them up. The third category, control over chemicals, can be much more specific and relates to the impact of chemicals, through acts ranging from the Federal Insecticide, Fungicide, and Rodenticide Act to the Toxic Substances Control Act. Along with the National Environmental Policy Act and the Solid Waste Disposal Act, these laws have the greatest effect on the environment and on the use of real property.

It should be noted before proceeding further that most of the impact thus far has been on commercial and industrial property. However, as the home-buying public becomes more sophisticated and as older urban areas are cleared of existing buildings and used for housing developments, there is no reason to think that these laws will not have an effect on homeowners as well. Already, it is clear that problems affect homeowners immediately—witness the Virginia oil pollution disaster. And who can forget the problems of disease and physical deformation that the residents along the Love Canal faced, more than a decade ago, from toxic chemicals? The Love Canal episode was one of the acute situations that were the original impetus for creation of the Superfund. For instance, what if homeowners discovered that their homes had been built on or adjacent to property that was contaminated with a toxic element or a carcinogen? And what if the previous homeowners had not known of this problem when they sold to the current owners? Who would be liable for the cleanup of the property? Who would be liable to the persons who had been injured? Today, the issues deal mostly with commercial real property, such as dumping sites, but tomorrow could well see new cases evolve from such all-too-possible scenarios.

11.3 THE EFFECT OF FEDERAL LEGISLATION ON REAL ESTATE

What is the effect of these various environmental laws on real property transactions? First, the laws prohibit certain uses of the real property or make the cleanup so expensive that the property may be unusable. Second, these laws impose penalties for failure to comply. Usually, these penalties are civil in nature, but if the violation of the law is willful, criminal penalties may also be imposed. Some of the laws penalize the owner of the real property for prior activities that polluted the land. If contaminated land is acquired by someone else, that new owners may be required to clean up the land and may also not be able to use the property as they had intended when they purchased it. In addition to the statutory penalties and prohibitions, many common law tort and contract remedies and defenses may be available to potential litigants. Under the Superfund Act, for instance, the responsible parties can include the parties (1) who own the property; (2) who are operating the business on the land; (3) who generated the pollutants; (4) who transported the pollutants; and (5) who disposed of the pollutants.

A number of methods have developed to control pollution. The governmental ones include obtaining required permits before potentially polluting

LEGAL TERMS

Superfund
Nickname for the agency in charge of cleaning up the land and paying for it when the costs of cleanup exceed the capacity of the property owners to pay.

actions can be taken. Besides this approach, the regulatory agency, usually the **Environmental Protection Agency** (**EPA**), may issue administrative orders and take court action to ensure compliance. Penalties for willful disobedience can be substantial—up to three times the cost of fixing the pollution problem. The private methods involve bringing lawsuits under common law claims such as nuisance in the use of real property, trespass on the property, tort negligence, and tort theories of strict liability. Sometimes both the tort claims and the statutory claims are filed in the same lawsuit. Further, contract claims may also be brought in the area, such as breach of contract, fraud, or misrepresentation in making the contract. Local laws relating to deceptive trade practices may also be used to assert a claim against a party. Many of these remedies are discussed in this chapter.

It is difficult to determine one's potential liability before purchasing a parcel of real property, but the best way to approach the problem is to have an **environmental audit** performed. This audit usually has two aspects. The first one is an investigation of the property itself and any appropriate documents. The second one is a followup during which the soil, air, water, building, and any relevant areas are tested for the actual environmental quality. This method is adequate for a prospective purchaser in most cases, but the actual owner needs to determine how successful the attempts at compliance have been. Aspects of what the owner may need to know include any compliance schedules, with estimates of time to complete and cost involved; the impact of new regulations that will be coming into effect upon the landowner's compliance requirements; and any legislative or regulatory trends that should be planned for.

11.4 THE IMPACT OF SUPERFUND REQUIREMENTS

The purpose of the Superfund (also referred to by the acronym for the name of the act, **CERCLA**) is to clean up sites that are heavily polluted and causing health and other problems for people and the environment. It is called Superfund because, if it is impossible to find and require the parties who did the polluting to pay the bill, Congress has appropriated over a billion dollars for a special fund to pay for the cleanup of those sites. It is estimated that this cleanup task may take at least a century and many billions beyond the initial appropriation.

The potentially responsible parties are extensive. They include: (1) the entity that currently owns or operates the facility; (2) the party that owned or operated the facility when the hazardous substances were put in or on it; (3) the entity that arranged to dispose of, transport, or treat the hazardous substances at any facility; and (4) any entity that took the hazardous substances and selected the site for disposal of those wastes. Note that the term **entity** is used to emphasize that any legal entity, whether an individual, partnership, or corporation, can be the party held responsible. It is clear that both the present owner and, in many cases, past owners will be held responsible, but what of temporary owners? This area is in dispute. Lessors have been held responsible for the contamination that their lessees created. A successor corporation may be held liable for its predecessor's actions.

The term **operator** is also used to attach responsibility to the person who did the pollution. To what degree does the limited liability concept of the corporation protect the employees, officers, and shareholders of a corporation that caused the pollution? Traditionally, the corporate entity shielded such persons from outside claims while the individuals worked in the legitimate course of their employment, but today, if individual managers knew (or sometimes, *should have known*) that the pollution was occurring, they can be held responsible for the pollution. It does not appear that mere ownership of stock in the corporation is sufficient to incur Superfund liability, but the person who controlled, or directed, or managed in such a way as to cause the pollution, directly or indirectly, may be held personally responsible for the cleanup of that pollution. The cost could be prohibitive.

Claims against an alleged violator of the Superfund rules may be made either by the government or by private parties. There is no defense against government claims, but between private parties, it is possible to allocate the liability by contractual arrangement ahead of time. Many private lawsuits arise when there is a sale of the property, usually after a purchaser discovers, to his horror, that the site is contaminated and that he may have acquired enormous, possibly bankrupting, liability for the cleanup. The seller (and lawsuit defendant), however, is not without some defenses. First, the ancient rule of *caveat emptor* (let the buyer beware) may be invoked to argue that the buyer had the ability to find out and thus should be responsible for the bargain that she struck. Second, it is possible that the language of the real estate sales contract released the seller from any responsibility for any contamination to the property. Third, some contracts refer to the buyer taking the property "as is," that is, without any warranties or representations concerning anything about it. Although that argument might defeat contract breach-of-warranty claims, it appears that such a defense may not always be effective against claims brought under the Superfund Act. Finally, other contract claims may also arise from indemnification clauses or under a representation in the contract concerning compliance with the law (which would cover any federal, state, or local pollution control laws, including CERCLA).

Although private lawsuits assert primarily contract defenses, other defenses are available against the government when it brings a claim under CERCLA. If a party can prove that it is not responsible because the cause was exclusively an act or an omission by a third party, that defense will overcome a CERCLA claim. To win, however, requires proving: (1) that the party had no relationship with the polluting third party as an employee or an agent and that it had no contractual relationship with the third party; (2) that the damage or threat of damage was solely under the control or solely caused by the third party; (3) that the party exercised appropriate due care in relation to the hazardous substance; and (4) that the party took all foreseeable precautions to protect against any damage occurring from the hazardous substance.

LEGAL TERMS

Environmental Protection Agency (EPA)
Federal agency in charge of ensuring compliance with most federal environmental cleanup laws.

environmental audit
Two-stage review of the potential problems and liability that could exist under CERCLA for a particular parcel of real estate.

CERCLA
Acronym from title of the act that created the Superfund—the Comprehensive Environmental Response, Compensation, and Liability Act of 1980.

entity
Specialized usage in the Superfund definitions that refers to any corporation, partnership, or sole proprietor for the purposes of Superfund liability.

operator
Comprehensive term used in CERCLA; defines who shall be liable for what actions in relation to the cleanup of polluted areas.

As the contractual relationship clause appears to be somewhat unreasonable, a new defense, referred to as the *innocent purchaser defense,* has been permitted. This defense can be employed when the party acquired the property after the pollution was already in place and either (1) had no knowledge of the pollution and no reason to know it; or (2) is a governmental unit which acquired the property involuntarily or by eminent domain, or (3) received the property by gift or inheritance. Nonetheless, the acquirer must show that it made all the appropriate inquiries into the property's prior ownership, and those inquiries appear to be the standard business inquiries that a rational person would make to limit potential liability. Of course, it should be obvious that a lessor cannot be an innocent purchaser, because no third party is involved in the lessor-lessee relationship (the lessor being the owner).

11.5 LEGAL CONCERNS RELATING TO ENVIRONMENTAL PROBLEMS

In environmental situations, one must consider the legal entity, to obtain as much protection as possible for the prospective client. Generally, a legal entity that has limited liability—such as shareholder in a corporation or a limited partner in a limited partnership—is preferable to the form of a general partnership or a sole proprietor, either of whose principals have unlimited personal liability. Nevertheless, management activities that cause a danger from hazardous substances may create personal liability for the manager. This rule, however, does not appear to reach to the passive ownership role of the mere shareholder or limited partner.

There are basically two ways to acquire a corporate entity: by buying its assets or buying its stock. The different implications of these two approaches should be recognized. In the asset purchase, there should be no responsibility for prior activities of the seller, but only for the existence and continuing effects of any hazardous substances on the real property, because only rights concerning the property itself were purchased. The seller should be concerned that the subsequent operations of the buyer might create an even greater amount of pollution for which the seller could be held responsible. In the stock purchase, however, the acquiring corporation often stands in the shoes of its predecessor, so that any preexisting problems with hazardous substances should be clearly delineated and provided for in the sale contract. In the stock purchase, the ownership rights are being transferred, and it appears that in buying the entity, one may take its historical performance as part of the purchase.

If the property has a known problem, or if a problem is discovered during the negotiations, the seller has a hard choice. On the one hand, if the sale goes through, the seller may be tied into joint and several liability with the buyer for the cleanup. What if the buyer becomes insolvent? What if the buyer exacerbates the pollution? On the other hand, for the buyer, the problem is that the property's value may be seriously diminished. How does the buyer provide for later-discovered Superfund problems? By escrowing funds?

By insurance? By an indemnification clause? One possible device is to have a lease-purchase arrangement whereby the seller-lessor permits the buyer-lessee to be on the property under a lease with an option to buy. In this way, the buyer can develop the real familiarity with the property that occupancy and use permits, and acquire the necessary information about the environmental condition of the property, before exercising the purchase option. Finally, there remains the possibility of an option to purchase with a full period for investigation.

11.6 SOME APPLICABLE CONTRACT PROVISIONS

Covenants and contract agreements generally arise either out of something someone wanted to get (such as "I will buy your cow [or land]"), or something someone wanted to prevent (such as "The cow you are selling me will yield five gallons of milk a week or I can return the cow"). The second type of covenant exists because someone identified a risk and tried to find a way to avoid or prevent that specific risk. Much of the work of legal drafting lies in the area of identifying and carefully wording contract clauses that are designed to protect one party from the risks arising from the relationship with the other party. Throughout this book, the documents and problems that you have seen have illustrated the identification of risks in the real estate business. For instance, what happens when the prospective buyer backs out of the sales contract? A clause in the sales contract may forfeit the earnest money deposit. What happens if the borrower does not pay on time? The lender has a clause that makes failure to pay on time a default, and a default permits acceleration of the debt and then foreclosure on the property that is the collateral. Risk identification is the name of the game, particularly when one is dealing with potentially great environmental contamination risks.

In a potential pollution situation, there are at least two major aspects of risk. First, what is the actual risk: the poison, the toxic substance, the pollution? Second, what will happen to me when it is determined? What will my responsibilities be? What expenses will I have to bear? How much time will my involvement take? As you examine the covenant and warranty provisions in this section, try to identify which type of risk is being dealt with.

One of the warranties and representations that the buyer should require from the seller is that there have been no deposits of hazardous substances, as defined by the Superfund Act, on the property. Because other pollutants can cause problems as well, it is wise to include all other pollutants—including petroleum products—as well. Because one of the most common ways of storing materials that are later determined to be hazardous substances is in underground tanks, a warranty against the existence of any such tank is useful as well. One might also consider requiring representations against specific past uses of the property or any prior usage that would be particularly dangerous or expensive to clean up, such as those involving asbestos or PCBs.

Another warranty should be that the property is in compliance with any and all environmental laws affecting it. In a similar vein, one might require that the seller give a warranty (1) that there is no litigation or administrative proceeding, existing or planned, of which the seller is aware and (2) that the seller is not aware of any facts that might give rise to any such proceeding. Finally, the buyer would want to have warranties to protect it against the existence of any laws that could adversely affect its use of the property; that the property is fit for the use the buyer intends; and that all appropriate governmental consents and permits relating to the transfer of the property have been obtained and are in proper form.

Consideration should also be given to requiring that an environmental audit be performed as a precondition of the sale. If the buyer wishes to claim the innocent purchaser defense, an environmental audit is almost necessary. Such an audit also helps both parties to determine if there is any significant environmental problem that needs resolution. This audit provides evidence, from the seller's viewpoint, to claim that the hazardous substances did not exist on the property when it was sold. There is some concern in the legal community, however, about the risk of having an environmental audit, discovering some toxic nightmare, and then having to clean it up. Care, caution, and legal expertise are essential in handling this problem. Finally, the contract should provide that the parties will adjust the price as needed, resolve the pollution problem, and take any other steps needed.

A number of other clauses may come into play with these environmental problems. Whenever it is possible that a hazardous substances investigation or cleanup operations will be needed, a number of provisions can be useful. For instance, the company-seller should provide that the buyer has the right to inspect the records that the government keeps on the seller. Each party should have open access to the other party's files and records and should have the other party's full cooperation and assistance in resolving any pollution problem that may be identified.

If pollution is discovered during the environmental audit, the following concerns must be addressed. Who will do the cleanup work? Who will pay for the work? What time span is permitted? Just how clean does the site have to be before it is adequately clean? In other words, what are the standards for a cleanup? These items should be determined and settled contractually before the audit is done. Other types of clauses, many of them standard, may include such matters as the transfer of existing permits; prohibitions on handling any hazardous substances that are on the property; the possible need for an escrow of funds to cover cleanup costs; insurance coverage and costs; indemnification and releases; and other such matters.

11.7 THE REGULATION OF REAL ESTATE USE

Because real estate has been an extremely important aspect of our society, in terms of homes, institutions, and economics, its use has always been regulated. These regulations range from private ones, developed early in the history of the law (such as the tort of trespass), to modern governmental ones, such as the complex and detailed environmental laws previously described. Governments at all levels, individuals who own land or have an interest in it, and groups of individuals all have found ways to regulate the use of their land, their neighbor's land, and the lands in the community. Lest we think that the regulation of land is only or primarily recent, consider the town of Boston, Massachusetts, where some of the earliest American immigrants settled. There is an area in Boston called "The Commons." It was created by a land use restriction in the 17th century. It was the remnant of a medieval English practice which permitted no one to own it and everyone to use it. It was literally land to be used in common by all for grazing animals, finding firewood, and any other purpose that benefited everyone. In the late 18th century, when the Founding Fathers created the Northwest Territory, they set aside the 16th section in each township for the exclusive purpose of public education. Today we have a mixture of these older restrictions with newer ones.

11.8 PRIVATE METHODS OF LAND USE RESTRICTION

A number of traditional legal devices, which evolved in the law of tort, restrict land usage. These restrictions are basic limitations on what one can do with or on another person's property. The most popular of these restraints are the specific torts of nuisance and trespass. In addition, the general tort theories of negligence and strict liability in tort have also been invoked in relation to land.

First, an brief explanation of what tort law is. *Torts* are harms or injuries done to a person or to a person's property. Today, the most frequent torts are automobile fender-benders in which someone negligently damages another person's body or property (the car).

To establish a tort, the plaintiff (the party whose self or property was injured) must prove four things: (1) that the defendant owed the plaintiff a duty; (2) that the defendant violated that duty; and (3) that that violation of that duty was the cause (4) of the injury to the plaintiff. In short, duty, violation, cause, and injury. Consider a *trespass,* a person's physical entry onto the land of another. Today, the courts require that entry onto the land of another be either negligent or intentional; this element of proof relates to the mindset of the party entering onto the land. Then the plaintiff must show proof of a direct, physical entry onto the land. Finally, the plaintiff must show that he had the right to the exclusive occupancy of the real estate. Thus, a tenant could claim, but not the landlord (unless some right of the landlord was injured). The law presumes (1) a duty to stay off the land of another; (2) that the trespasser, by entering on the land, has violated that right; and (3) that an injury arises from that trespassing entry. Examples of such injury (which must be proved) could be entering the property to hunt without the owner's permission, or a blasting operation on nearby property which threw dirt onto the land of the plaintiff.

The tort of nuisance has been extraordinarily difficult to define over the years. The concept of a nuisance, however, clearly implies some interference with one's use or enjoyment of one's land. In this type of case, there need not be actual physical entry onto the land, as in a trespass, but merely an interference with the use of the property. In the blasting example, for instance, it would be possible for both a nuisance and a trespass to occur if the dirt thrown on the property (the trespass) blocked the driveway and prevented the owner from leaving the property (the nuisance which interfered with the owner's use of her property), particularly if the amount of dirt was substantial and it continued to come onto the property. For this tort, the courts generally require a showing of an act that interferes—the nuisance; then, a showing that that particular act did actually interfere with the plaintiff's rights; then, a showing of harm to the plaintiff of a nature sufficient to warrant either an injunction prohibiting the activity or damages; and finally, a showing that the harm resulted from an unreasonable activity and created an unreasonable harm. As in many cases, there are conflicting values here. One has a basic right to use one's property (where the alleged nuisance is coming from) as one chooses, but one does not have the right to interfere with one's neighbors' enjoyment of their property. Differing social values at different times have accounted for a range of court decisions in this area, many of which are in conflict with one another. Advocacy may require careful argument to win this type of case.

A chemical waste disposal site could be a public nuisance and, as such, worth getting rid of, either by closing it or removing the elements deposited within it. As many are interested in protecting the environment, the *SCA Services* case shows how the Illinois Supreme Court dealt with one such problem in 1981.

VILLAGE OF WILSONVILLE
v.
SCA SERVICES, INC.
86 Ill. 2d 1, 55 Ill. Dec. 499, 426 N.E.2d 824 (1981)

CLARK, J:

In 1977, numerous parties sued SCA to stop it from operating, and increasing the fill at, its dump. They alleged its dump constituted a public nuisance. After a trial lasting 104 days and creating a record of more than 13,000 pages, the trial court held for the plaintiffs; SCA appealed and lost in a unanimous opinion. The remedies were severe. Closure of the dump and removal of all toxic waste and contaminated soil, along with restoration of the site, was ordered.

SCA had operated a chemical waste landfill dump since 1977. From 1912 to 1954, a coal mine had operated in a manner which created a 40-foot pile of surface waste that provided some contamination that leaked into the dump. SCA attempted to remedy that problem unsuccessfully. Numerous persons use wells for various water uses, ranging from drinking water to watering plants and pets and washing cars. Multiple chemical poisons (from PCBs to arsenic to asbestos and pesticides) were being stored at the site. Much of the evidence dealt with permeability of the subsurface and the likelihood that the weight and distribution of the dump and the coal mine residue would cause the release of the toxic chemicals into the subsoil. There was severe danger of subsidence which could release the chemical poisons. The dangers of the dump's contents igniting and spreading toxic fumes over a large area and dangers from transportation were also evaluated.

We conclude that the evidence in this case sufficiently establishes by a preponderance of the evidence that the chemical-waste-disposal site is a nuisance both presently and prospectively. The defendant does not challenge the fact that the spillage from improperly contained chemical waste, the odors, and the dust created by the site constitute a present interference with the right of the plaintiffs to enjoy and use their property. Thus, we will not belabor this point.

The defendant points out three areas where, it argues, the trial court made erroneous findings of fact. The defendant refers to: (1) Dr. Arthur Zahalsky's opinion testimony concerning an explosive interaction and Dr. Stephen Hall's testimony which concurred in that opinion; (2) evidence concerning soil permeability; and, (3) infiltration of water into the trenches, and of migration out of the defendant's trenches of chemical waste either through the "bathtub effect" or subsidence.

We have reviewed the extensive record compiled in this case. While it is true that the defendant vigorously challenged the evidence concerning an explosive interaction, permeability, and infiltration and migration due to subsidence, the defendant has not overcome the natural and logical conclusions which could be drawn from the evidence. Findings of fact made by the trial court will not be set aside unless they are contrary to the manifest weight of the evidence.

[The court concluded that the plaintiff's expert witnesses were properly qualified and that the evidence of one of the defendant's witnesses was "erroneous" in part.]

The defendant next contends that the appellate and circuit courts misinterpreted the permeability tests admitted into evidence. It is argued that permeability coefficients are but one factor in determining the permeability of soil. We agree, but the fact remains that the defendant placed a good deal of emphasis on the tests conducted by John Mathes and Dr. Williams, which show that the soil at the site is more permeable than the IEPA suggested standard of 1×10^{-8} cm/sec. These courts also relied upon the testimony of Dr. Williams, defendant's witness, that the soil was probably even more permeable than indicated in the tests. Based on this evidence the trial court was correct in finding that the permeable nature of the soil, as demonstrated by the coefficients, as one of several factors, poses a threat of migration of chemical waste away from the disposal site. That finding will not be disturbed.

The defendant also contends that the trial court's finding that subsidence warrants closing of the site is erroneous. The defendant argues that, assuming arguendo that subsidence would occur at the site, it could be counteracted by engineering techniques. This issue becomes complicated by the fact that the IEPA adopted a regulation providing that Class I disposal sites (i.e., chemical-waste-disposal sites), must be secure without engineering. The USEPA, however, has recently adopted regulations to require all landfill sites to establish containment-engineering systems to detect and prevent migration of chemicals.

Moreover, the General Assembly has, since the inception of this suit, passed a statute prohibiting the placement of a hazardous-waste-disposal site above a shaft or tunneled mine.

* * *

Thus, the defendant cannot be thought to be in violation of the foregoing provision [because the law is prospective only]. The fact remains, however, that the instant site, which is intended to be permanent, is located above an inactive tunneled mine. . . .

Dr. Augenbaugh refuted [the testimony that subsidence would not occur]. He stated that subsidence would permit chemical-waste materials to seep into the ground water. In addition, Dr. Augenbaugh testified that subsidence would create a "bathtub effect" by permitting water to get into the trenches, eventually rise to the surface, overflow, and contaminate the ground around the site. We think the circuit court was fully justified in giving more weight to Dr. Augenbaugh's well-documented opinion than to the opinions of defendant's experts. We will not disturb that finding. . . .

[Other plaintiffs' witnesses testified about] possible reactions caused by the intermixing of certain chemicals. They both also stated the reactions were not certainties but that, with the given flashpoints of certain chemicals, the fact that oxygen could reach the waste materials and the highly volatile nature of some of the chemical-waste materials, in their opinions, based upon a reasonable degree of scientific certainty, it was entirely possible that an "explosive interaction" in the form of fires, gaseous emissions, or explosions could occur at the site. While defendant's expert witnesses disputed these opinions and referred to fire-retardant properties of some chemicals, or the unavailability of ambient temperatures due to lack of oxygen, we are unable to say that Drs. Zahalsky's and Hall's opinions were wrong and the other experts were right. Drs. Zahalsky's and Hall's opinions are at least as plausible as defendant's experts, are based on explicit examples of possible chemical reactions, are buttressed by the two doctors' qualifications and are supported by evidence concerning conditions at the site which indicate intermixing could occur. The trial court was correct in denying the motion to strike. . . .

[D]ust and odors alone do not justify the relief which has been ordered in this case. . . . But, when the dust and odors the trial court found to be present at the site are considered together with the other evidence indicating that the air, water, and earth in and around the site will become contaminated, the trial court's relief is not excessive.

The same is true of defendant's argument that the evidence of spillage from trucks as they were driven through the village does not warrant closure of the site. Evidence of spillage is simply an additional reason the circuit court ordered the site closed. Whether spillage alone would justify closure is not before us.

The trial court herein concluded that defendant's chemical-waste-disposal site constitutes both a private and a public nuisance. Professor Prosser has defined a private nuisance as "a civil wrong, based on a disturbance of rights in land," and a public nuisance as "an act or omission 'which obstructs or causes inconvenience or damage to the public in the exercise of rights common to all Her Majesty's subjects.' " Prosser has also quoted the following, more precise definition of public nuisance: " 'A common or public nuisance is the doing of or the failure to do something that injuriously affects the safety, health or morals of the public, or works some substantial annoyance, inconvenience or injury to the public.' " It is generally conceded that a nuisance is remediable by injunction or a suit for damages.

The defendant herein argues that "[e]ven if some or all of plaintiffs' evidence is deemed believable, the findings of the courts below that [defendant's] conduct constitutes a prospective nuisance must be reversed for failure to * * * balance the reasonableness and utility of the defendant's conduct, the harm to the plaintiff, and the general societal policy toward risk-taking before [a court may] find an actionable nuisance present." The defendant continues that the law of Illinois requires that the circuit court engage in a balancing process before reaching a conclusion that the waste disposal site presents a prospective nuisance.

* * *

It is reasonably clear that this court and the circuit court meant that where individual rights are unreasonably interfered with, the public benefit form a particular facility will not outweigh the individual right, and the facility's use will be enjoined or curtailed. Such a conclusion presupposes a balancing process with the greater weight being given to the individual's right to use and enjoy property over a public benefit or convenience from having a business operate at a particular location. In such an instance, the individual's right to noninterference takes precedence.

* * *

We think . . . that the trial court did carefully engage in a balancing process between the site's social utility and the plaintiff's right to enjoy their property and not suffer deleterious effects from chemical wastes. Accordingly, the defendant's argument that the trial court did not balance the equities in this case is without merit.

The defendant's next contention is that the courts below were in error when they failed to require a showing of a substantial risk of certain and extreme future harm before enjoining operation of the defendant's site. We deem it necessary to explain that a prospective nuisance is a fit candidate for injunctive relief. Prosser states: "Both public and private nuisances require some substantial interference with the interest involved. Since nuisance is a common subject of equity jurisdiction, the damage against which an injunction is asked is often merely threatened or potential; but even in such cases, there must be at least a threat of a substantial invasion of the plaintiff's interests." The defendant does not dispute this proposition; it does, however, argue that the trail court did not follow the proper standard for determining when a prospective nuisance may be enjoined. The defendant argues that the proper standard to be used is that an injunction is proper only if there is a "dangerous probability" that the threatened or potential injury will occur. The defendant further argues that the appellate court looked only at the potential consequences of not enjoining the operation of the site as a nuisance and not at the likelihood of whether harm would occur. The defendant assigns error on this basis.

We agree with the defendant's statement of the law, but not with its urged application to the facts of this case. Again, Professor Prosser has offered a concise commentary. He has stated that "[o]ne distinguishing feature of equitable relief is that it may be granted upon the threat of harm which has not yet occurred. The defendant may be restrained from entering upon an activity where it is highly probable that it will lead to a nuisance, although if the possibility is merely uncertain or contingent he may be left to his remedy after the nuisance has occurred." . . .

In this case there can be no doubt but that it is highly probable that the chemical-waste-disposal site will bring about a substantial injury. Without again reviewing the extensive evidence adduced at trial, we think it is sufficiently clear that it is highly probable that the instant site will constitute a public nuisance if, through either an explosive interaction, migration, subsidence, or the "bathtub effect," the highly toxic chemical wastes deposited at the site escape and contaminate the air, water, or ground around the site. That such an event will occur was positively attested to by several expert witnesses. A court does not have to wait for it to happen before it can enjoin such a result. Additionally, the fact is that the condition of a nuisance is already present at the site due to the location of the site and the manner in which it has been operated. Thus, it is only the damage which is prospective. Under these circumstances, if a court can prevent any damage from occurring, it should do so.

[The court concluded that deferral to the conclusions of the Illinois and U.S. Environmental Protection Agencies was not required because their issuance of a license was based on erroneous information.]

The next issue we consider is whether the trial court erroneously granted a permanent injunction. The defendant argues first that the courts below granted injunctive relief without proof that the alleged injury is both substantial and certain to occur. We have already addressed this question in discussing whether relief may be granted for a prospective nuisance. We will not unduly prolong this already lengthy opinion with duplicative discussion. The second argument raised is that the courts below did not balance the equities in deciding to enjoin the defendant from continuing to operate the waste-disposal site. Defendant cites *Harrison v. Indiana Auto Shredders Co.* for the proposition that the court must balance the relative harm and benefit to the plaintiff and defendant before a court may enjoin a nuisance. A balancing process is implicit in the following statements made by this court in *Haack v. Lindsay Light & Chemical Co.*:

> "It is equally clear that the rule in this State and generally, is, and should be, that even though a right has been established in law, a court of equity will not, as a matter of course, interpose by injunction but will consider all the circumstances, the consequences of such action and the real equity of the case.
>
> * * *
>
> To entitle one to injunctive relief he must establish, as against the defendant, an actual and substantial injury and not merely a technical inconsequential wrong entitling him to nominal damages, only. To warrant the allowance of the writ of injunction it must clearly appear that some act has been done or is threatened against the plaintiff which will produce an irreparable injury to him. . . ."

The court concluded . . . that since the defendant was not in violation of any relevant zoning standard, and since the shredder did not pose an imminent hazard to the public health, the defendant should not be prevented from continuing to operate. The court then ordered that the defendant be permitted a reasonable time to "launder its objectionable features."

This case is readily distinguishable for the reason that the gist of this case is that the defendant is engaged in an extremely hazardous undertaking at an unsuitable location, which seriously and imminently poses a threat to the public health. We are acutely aware that the service provided by the defendant is a valuable and necessary one. We also know that it is preferable to have chemical-waste-disposal sites than to have illegal dumping in river, streams, and deserted areas. But a site such as defendant's, if it is to do the job it is intended to do, must be located in a secure place, where it will pose no threat to health or life, now, or in the future. This site was intended to be a *permanent* disposal site for the deposit of extremely hazardous chemical-waste materials. Yet this site is located above an abandoned tunneled mine where subsidence is occurring several years ahead of when it was anticipated. Also, the permeability coefficient samples taken by defendant's experts, though not conclusive alone, indicate that the soil is more permeable at the site than expected. Moreover, the spillage, odors, and dust caused by the presence of the disposal site indicate why it was inadvisable to locate the site so near the plaintiff village.

Therefore, we conclude that in fashioning relief in this case the trial court did balance relative hardship to be caused to the plaintiffs and defendant, and did fashion reasonable relief when it ordered the exhumation of all material from the site and the reclamation of the surrounding area. The instant site is akin to Mr. Justice Sutherland's observation that "Nuisance may be merely a right thing in a wrong place—like a pig in the parlor instead of the barnyard."

* * *

[The USEPA requested less stringent remedies, but the court concluded that] the USEPA is asking this court to remand this cause to the circuit court on the basis of evidence which the trial court has previously considered and discounted in favor of the plaintiffs' evidence. We see no point in doing so. The circuit court carefully weighed the evidence adduced throughout the 104-day trial, balanced the relative hardship to the plaintiffs and defendant of permitting the site to continue to operate, or closing it down, and reached the conclusion which is strongly supported by the record, that the site's dangers outweigh its utility. Moreover, it needs to be remembered, as the trial judge pointed out, that the nuisance in this case came to the village. The residents of Wilsonville have a right to enjoy and use their property without being unreasonably interfered with by the defendant's hazardous-waste site. Also, there is evidence in the record that representatives of the defendant told the village board, in response to a question from the water works commissioner, that no toxic materials would be buried at the site, when the truth is precisely the opposite. We view these factors as additional reasons why defendant's conduct is inequitable and why plaintiffs are entitled to a permanent injunction. We conclude therefore that the relief fashioned by the trial court is reasonable under the precise facts of this case and will not be disturbed.

[The court concluded that the materials were capable of being moved safely.]

Finally, the defendant argues that the decisions of the courts below constitute sudden changes in State law and, as such, deprive the defendant of its property without due process of law. We disagree; the principles of law applied in this case are neither new, unreasonable, nor unpredictable. Manifestly, a party cannot expect to operate a site in the manner and in the location the defendant has chosen and expect to be immune from liability for creating a public nuisance. Defendant's argument has no merit in this case.

Accordingly, for all the reasons stated, the judgments of the circuit and appellate courts are affirmed and the cause is remanded to the circuit court to enable it to retain jurisdiction to supervise the enforcement of its order.

Affirmed and remanded.

[Some citations omitted.]

Other areas of the law, such as the right to privacy articulated by the Supreme Court in the 1960s and 1970s, provide protection for individuals in the privacy of their own homes, that is, in their use of their real property. Although the Supreme Court identified a constitutional basis for this right of privacy, the degree to which the current membership on the Supreme Court would support this concept is uncertain. This constitutional right of privacy protects a person from governmental actions directed against the person's activities, and the constitutional right is not the same as the private right to privacy under which a tort can arise.

There are several ways in which the tort of invasion of privacy can occur. First, we all possess unique facial features and names; they belong to us individually. If others want to use that image or name, they must get permission, pay a fee, or be subject to suit. A tort may also be committed if another (1) discloses private information that is ours alone, the disclosure of which is injurious or painful to us; (2) puts us in a false light (that is, presents us or something about us inaccurately); or (3) breaks into our privacy in our home or apartment. Examples of these torts are disclosure of drug use from many years ago (private information which would damage a person's reputation); inaccurately attributing a horrible recipe to a great chef (false information misrepresenting something about someone); or bugging someone's telephone or using electronic surveillance to determine what someone was doing in his home (invasion of privacy).

These common law torts provide landowners and occupiers with the right to protect their interests in the land and to prevent others from entering on, using, or invading their occupancy of the land. As a result, other parties are restricted in their use of that land by the rights of the owners or occupiers of the land. There are other types of private land restrictions as well. The most important of these private restrictions are the ones created by contract when a land developer creates a subdivision in which all the parcel owners are governed by the same restrictions. The courts view such restrictions as binding on all the parties who take property from that developer, and permit individual owners to enforce the restrictions against any other owner.

There can be other types of private land use restrictions aside from those arising under tort claims. The most important such restrictions derive from the plan of the developer which the developer (subdivider) has recorded with the plat of subdivision. In that recorded plan, the developer sets out a series of requirements as to lot size, perhaps type, size, or style of house permitted on that lot size, and other restrictions common to all parties who own or will own property in the subdivision. Sometimes, to enforce these restrictions, the developer also creates a Homeowners Association for the property owners, and the plat of survey restrictions also permits the Homeowners Association to raise money for a fund to enforce the restrictions.

Some of the restrictions in plats of survey include setbacks from the street; a continuous line of the building's wall, so that no garage or porch may be added; prohibition on commercial use or limitation to only residential use; prohibition against apartments or condominiums in the area; prohibition on multi-family units or limitation to only single-family units. An endless list could be made because these restrictions are tailored to meet the perceived needs of a particular group of buyers to whom the developer wishes to sell.

There can be practical problems in enforcing the restrictions. Some states' statutes of limitations restrict the amount of time in which a party can bring a suit to enforce the restrictions. Thereafter, the violation of the restriction could be waived. If that type of violation occurred repeatedly and the restriction were repeatedly not enforced, the courts might consider the restriction itself to have been abandoned or unenforceable. It is also possible that states may forbid such restrictions from having effect after a number of years. The reasoning behind this approach is simple. The legislatures feel that times, circumstances, and neighborhoods will change; as a result, the original restrictions will be applying to a situation in which they are inappropriate or actually damaging to the then-current usage.

It should be noted that the courts have, since the late 1940s, refused to enforce certain types of restrictions that could infringe on civil rights. Thus, restrictions running against any racial, religious, ethnic, or similar group, or based on sex or age, may be permanently illegal and unenforceable. Restrictions against having children in a development, however, is a matter that has not been fully decided as yet. Some senior citizens do not want to have to live around the activity and noise of children. The issue remains as to whether they will continue to have this choice.

Another method of land use restriction is **dedication**. This device creates a transfer of privately owned land to a public purpose. For example, a developer is said to "dedicate" a piece of land, a lot, an area for a park or a school, or a road. The technical method of dedicating land is for the landowner to offer the land to the community, usually the city, and for the city to accept the land. Sometimes, when an entire area is being developed, there is no dedication of individual locations. Instead all the property to be transferred to public use is designated for that usage on the plat of survey, and dedication occurs by obtaining the approval of the plat and acceptance by the local officials. Typical pieces of property for dedication are areas for parks, schools, streets, and similar essential land uses, such as utilities. Since the late 1940s, it has been clear that developers in most states must make these dedications, or the local authorities will compel appropriate dedication to match the needs created by the development.

11.9 ZONING: PUBLIC CONTROL OF LAND USE

Zoning is a complicated and difficult area of modern real estate law. Zoning is the most common public method of restricting land usage. Zoning is literally that—the decision by a local governmental authority to restrict a certain area of real property (a zone) to a certain usage. The government literally takes a map of its community and marks which types of activity will be permitted to occur in what areas. Almost all major American cities, except Houston, Texas, have zoning laws and regulations. The government unit most commonly involved is a city or a village, but zoning could extend throughout a township, a county, or a parish as well.

LEGAL TERMS

dedication
Process whereby a person, usually a developer, places private land in public hands for public use; often achieved by granting a permanent easement on the land to the governmental body to use for a public purpose such as a school.

zoning
Local government system of allocating areas of and boundaries between land usage among residential, commercial, and industrial uses.

The three most common types of zoning are (1) residential, (2) commercial, and (3) industrial-manufacturing. These categories often are combined and may also be broken down into smaller categories. In commercial areas, for instance, it is often permitted to have housing; the difference is that the area is not zoned exclusively for residences. In the industrial zoning, all three uses are often permitted, but residential zoning often is limited exclusively to residential uses.

Many times, though, it is necessary to break down the permitted uses further and define the types of activities that may occur in the commercial and industrial zones. Certain types of industry may be the only ones permitted in a specific area if the city wants that type of industry limited to operating in that particular area. An example of that zoning might be a restriction on the location of oil-cracking facilities where raw petroleum is shipped in to be converted (or "cracked") into gas, diesel, kerosene, lubricants, oils, etc. The cracking industry is a filthy, highly polluting industry with significant problems with its storage facilities, air, ground, and water pollution, and explosion and fire. Clearly, it would not be desirable to have a series of high-rise residences in the area, nor would a commercial area be appropriate either.

Despite the inclusion of residences in some commercial and industrial areas, mixed-use zoning is clearly inappropriate in other circumstances. Several different concerns are reflected in the government restrictions here. The government must be concerned about the health and safety of its citizens, but it must also be concerned about the economic health of its community. Residential property takes up a great deal of space, especially when the residential property is single-family homes. If the alternative of high-rise apartments is permitted, other problems of parking, congestion, overuse of parks, and other difficulties arising from population density can occur. As a result, it is frequently much simpler to determine that an area is to be used exclusively for one type of zoning, such as industrial. Areas zoned for industry may even be broken into a series of industrial subdivisions, to provide several special industries with the exclusive use of the area laid out on that part of the zoning map.

To determine the appropriateness of a particular area's zoning, one examines the relevance of the proposed use which is generating the objection to the current zoning rules, the other usages in the area, and the zoning ordinance itself. The courts consider these factors in a balancing approach. For instance, if an industrial waste disposal site existed and was exclusively designed to be at that location by the community's zoning, and land was available within that zoning category, the courts might consider whether a new waste disposal project could be permitted within the same zoning. Consider the addition of an incinerator. Strictly, under the letter of the zoning law, it might not be allowed. There are three ways around this problem. The appropriate legislative body could change the law to permit the incinerator; the zoning authorities could issue a variance; or the court presiding over a lawsuit could rezone the area sufficiently to permit addition of the incinerator. The issues that the court would consider would be ones such as the concentration of waste disposal—all the pros and the cons. It would also consider whether other remedies had been exhausted. It might look at the expertise of the administrative body that refused the variance, or the authority of the legislative body that refused to rewrite the law, and defer to either of those bodies. Constitutional arguments might possibly be available as well.

The entire process of zoning is rife with political problems and economic opportunities for developers and those who purchase from them. Zoning is also concerned with pollution and other environmental standards, as well as discrimination, maintenance of the existing community, and similar matters. The reasons to rezone an area can be complex. As suggested earlier, the rezoning may involve the problem of population density—too many people for the area's capacity to handle. Within this concern lie the problems of sewage disposal, adequate water, and educational facilities for the children of the newcomers. Many communities now face a fight between new groups moving into the area with children and older persons living on retirement income who do not want to pay more school taxes. Another concern is changing the community's economic base from a mixed base into a primarily residential base. The tax burden is much more easily borne by the mixed base, because the industrial and commercial uses help meet the tax bill that would otherwise fall upon residential homeowners alone. Can the community survive, and can it continue to provide adequate services, based on residential taxes only? These are serious problems for local governments, and they require detailed, careful consideration.

Two cases, *Crary Home* case from Pennsylvania and the *SASSO* case from California, illustrate the conflicts between zoning and members of less powerful groups. Would the Pennsylvania case have turned out differently had a different zoning category been used? Probably not. What about the attractive-sounding claims in the California case on both sides? A referendum on a zoning ordinance? What could be more democratic? As you can see, many arguments may be advanced concerning zoning.

CRARY HOME v. DEFREES

529 A.2d 874 (Pa. 1974)

KRAMER, J.

This is an appeal from an order of the Court of common Pleas of Warren County, dated November 30, 1973, which reversed a decision of the Zoning Hearing Board of Warren Borough (Board), dated August 28, 1973. The Board's decision had granted a special exception to Mr. and Mrs. C. J. Crary and the Crary Home (Crary), over the objections of certain residents of the Borough of Warren (objectors).

Crary had applied for a special exception to permit the construction of several structures in a residential section of Warren. The land in question is located in an "R-1 Single Family Residence District." The application indicates that Crary intended to establish and maintain a home for "indigent gentlemen and gentlewomen of advanced years, residents of Warren County, with preference given to worthy, needy members of the Methodist Church." The application further says that "[l]iving accommodations will be furnished in apartment units, as shown on plans submitted herewith." The plans submitted with he application show a fairly extensive overall development, covering 61,400 square feet with five structures, including a garage, a combined barn and greenhouse, a "studio", a conventional single family dwelling (the residence of Mr. and Mrs. Crary), and the proposed "home" itself. Some of these structures are already in existence and apparently only the construction of the "home" is in issue. The home, as proposed by Crary, would contain eight single occupancy units (each with bath and kitchen facilities) and two double occupancy units. All units would share a large common living room. Testimony in the record indicated, and the Board found, that the Crarys contemplated eventually expanding the home to make use of the entire lot, including their family residence.

After hearing, the Board granted Crary the requested special exception, with one member disenting and writing a minority opinion. The objectors appealed to the Court of Common Pleas of Warren County, which reversed the Board. Crary appealed to this Court.

The lower court heard no additional evidence, and, in such cases, our scope of review is limited to determining whether the Board committed a manifest abuse of discretion or an error of law. Both parties seem to agree that there is no issue regarding the exercise of discretion by the Board, and our review is invoked only to determine whether legal error was committed.

The crux of this case involves the construction of the Borough zoning ordinance. Section 802.3 of the ordinance provides, in relevant part, as follows:

> "*Special Exceptions.* The Board of Adjustment shall grant or refuse special permits under the following conditions:
>
> Only those applications for special exceptions shall be heard and, acted upon which are specifically authorized by the terms of this Ordinance."

The Crary application was based on a claim of "public" or "semi-public" use under section 202.1 of the ordinance (the section establishing R-1 Single Family Residence Districts), the pertinent part of which reads as follows:

> "*Uses by Special Exception.* The following uses shall be permitted as a special exception [in an R-1 District] where authorized by the Board of Adjustment subject to Article 800 of this Ordinance:
>
> Churches or similar places of worship and related functions; municipal building; public schools; parochial schools; private schools; the taking of not more than two (2) nontransient roomer [sic] providing no sign is displayed; home occupations; and, all other public and semi-public uses."

Crary argued that its proposed home constituted a "public" or "semi-public" use under section 202.1, and was therefore entitled to a special exception. Two members of the Board agreed with a "semi-public" characterization; one member did not agree. The lower court found the proposed use to be "private", as a matter of law, and, on this basis, reversed the Board. For the reasons stated hereinafter, we agree with the lower court and affirm its order.

Whether a proposed use, as factually described in an application or in testimony, falls within a given category specified in a zoning ordinance is a question of law and subject to review on that basis. The issue becomes one of statutory construction, and the function of a reviewing court is to determine the intent of the legislative body which enacted the legislation. More specifically, the question in the instant case is whether or not the Borough Council, in enacting section 202.1, intended to permit a use such as that proposed by Crary in a district where single family detached dwellings are the rule.

A statute (or ordinance) should, when possible, be construed to give effect to all of its provisions, and a particular section of a piece of legislation should (absent legislative direction to the contrary) be construed as an integral part of the whole, and not as a separate portion with an independent meaning.

Mindful of these principles, we note, as did the court below and the minority member of the Board, that section 203.1 of the ordinance in question reads, in relevant part:

> "*Uses by Special Exception.* The following uses shall be permitted as a special exception when authorized by the Board of Adjustment subject to Article 800 of this Ordinance:
>
> *Apartments; converted apartments;* single-family attached dwellings; *rooming houses or tourist homes; philanthropic institutions;* hospitals; public schools; private schools; parochial schools; *nursing or convalescent homes; and other public or semi-public uses;* including cemeteries and institutions of higher education and related facilities." (Emphasis added.)

Section 203 establishes "R-2 Low Density Residence Districts", which are, with the exception of the R-1 districts established by section 202, the most restrictive districts in the Borough's zoning scheme. Even a cursory reading of section 203.1 permits us to conclude that the proposed home would easily fall within at least one of the specifically listed exceptions, emphasized above. The provisions for special exceptions in section 203.1 militate strongly in favor of a conclusion that the Borough Council, in enacting the ordinance, has specifically decided to allow homes such as the Crary proposal in R-2 districts, but not in R-1 districts. The listing of uses eligible for special exception in section 203.1 indicates that the Council was cognizant of uses identical with, or very similar to, that proposed by Crary, at the time it approved the ordinance. Such a conclusion is supported by the following statement from Ryan, Pennsylvania Zoning Law and Practice, § 4.21:

> "If a given use is not listed as permitted in one zoning classification but is permitted in a lower classification by specific reference, it is a fair inference that the use was considered and intentionally excluded from the higher zone. In these circumstances, the courts normally will not read any more general grouping which may be permitted in the higher district as including the lower use."

In the same section Ryan also notes, as a general principle, that the structure of the zoning ordinance itself provides the best guide to its interpretation.

In *Bonasi v. Haverford Township Board of Adjustment,* our Supreme Court dealt with a construction problem similar to that found in the instant case. In *Bonasi* the municipality's ordinance, by specific reference, permitted beauty shops in "H" business districts. The property owner attempted to secure permission to operate such a shop in a "B" residential district, in which the ordinance permitted "professional offices." The Court said:

> "A reading of the Zoning Ordinance makes it crystal clear that the term 'professional office', *as used in the enactment in relation to 'B' Residence Districts,* was not intended to include a *beauty shop.* The Ordinance, in Article XII, H Business Districts, section 1201(4), provides for 'Personal service shop, tailor, barber, *beauty,*

shoe repair, dress making shop and other personal service shop or store'. (Italics supplied) Since the use of a beauty shop, described *inter alia* as a 'personal service shop', is specifically permitted as a *business use,* it is inconceivable that a similar use was intended as an accessory professional use in a 'B' Residence District. It is plain that the Ordinance did not so intend." (Emphasis in original.)

Considering *Bonasi,* the statement quoted above from Ryan, and our own review of the ordinance in question, it seems clear that the Council's use of the term "semi-public uses" in section 202.1 was not intended to include uses which are specifically permitted as special exceptions in the less restrictive R-2 districts. Were we to hold otherwise, the distinction which was obviously intended between R-1 and R-2 districts would be considerably weakened and the planning scheme of the municipality seriously impaired. Accordingly, the order of the Court of Common Pleas of Warren County, dated November 30, 1973, is affirmed.

[Some citations and footnotes omitted.]

SOUTHERN ALAMEDA SPANISH SPEAKING ORGANIZATION (a.k.a. SASSO) v. UNION CITY

424 F.2d 291 (9th Cir 1970)

[Footnotes omitted.]

MERRILL, C.J.:

The principal appellant, the Southern Alameda Spanish Speaking Organization (SASSO), was successful in obtaining the passage of a city ordinance rezoning a tract of land within Union City, California, to a multi-family residential category in order to permit the construction of a federally financed housing project for low and moderate income families. The ordinance was nullified almost immediately by a city-wide referendum. By this action appellants attack the referendum and its results as infringing upon their constitutional rights under the due process and equal protection clauses of the Fourteenth Amendment, and seek injunctive action directing Union City to implement the zoning change notwithstanding the referendum.

In the District Court appellants sought, under 28 U.S.C. § 2281, an order convening a three-judge court to entertain their constitutional claims. They also moved for a preliminary injunction directing Union City to put the zoning changes into effect *pendente lite.* The District Court ruled against the appellants on both motions and that order is the subject of this appeal.

As incorporated in 1959 Union City combined two existing communities known as Decoto and Alvarado. The area was largely agricultural and the two communities were inhabited almost exclusively by Mexican-American residents.

Since incorporation Union City has absorbed residents both from Oakland to the north and San Jose to the south. The population has risen from about 6600 in 1960 to the current 14,000. During the same period the composition of the population has also changed; the Mexican-American percentage has declined from 55 percent to about 35–40 percent of the total.

A master plan for Union city was formally adopted in 1962, after public hearings. Under that plan, vacant land not then in use was generally zoned as agricultural, a "holding" classification subject to rezoning by city ordinance for urban use at the appropriate time. The plan did, however, anticipate future use and zoning. The land here in question (the "Baker Road Tract") was zoned agricultural under the plan but designated for purposes of rezoning as appropriate for single-family dwellings.

Since 1962, suburban pressures have created an increasing need for multifamily housing in Union City and several such units have already been accommodated through rezoning ordinances. These units have largely gone to meet the needs of new residents. The old residents of Decoto and Alvarado, due to limited incomes, have been unable to enjoy the housing so provided, and have had to remain in those districts, where a substantial portion of the housing is rated substandard. In 1967, city officials concerned with housing problems contracted with a consulting firm for a comprehensive study of local housing requirements. That sturdy, still incomplete, has resulted in a number of recommendations and a draft master plan. The firm recommended that the city encourage housing projects for families with low and moderate incomes, sponsored by nonprofit corporations and financed through federal aid. The projected master plan designates the tract in question for multi-family dwellings. Although the 1962 plan has not been formally superseed, city officials have in large part accepted the firm's recommendations. They have informally abandoned the 1962 plan's designations of appropriate future use in favor of the updated designations regarded as more appropriate in light of the city's growth.

Appellant SASSO is qualified to sponsor federally assisted housing developments for low income persons and was organized for the purpose of improving housing and living conditions for the Spanish speaking people of southern Alameda County. In December, 1968, it obtained an option to purchase the Baker Road tract, where it planned to construct a 280-unit medium density housing project. In accordance with this objective, SASSO applied to the City Planning Staff of Union City for rezoning. After appropriate studies, the Planning Staff recommended the application to the Planning Commission. Several months later the Planning Commission's recommendation for rezoning (medium density multi-family residential) was approved by the City Council after public hearings; an ordinance was passed on April 7, 1969.

The Baker Road tract is adjacent to several tracts of single-family homes. Opposition to the April 7 ordinance arose there and among other home owners; petitions seeking a referendum under 4051, Cal. Elections Code, were circulated and completed. Pursuant to 4052, Cal. Elections Code, the matter was submitted to the voters of Union City, who by a vote of 1149 to 845 rejected the ordinance. The referendum automatically restored the Baker Road tract to the agricultural holding category and the City Council was barred from rezoning the tract for medium density, multi-residential dwellings for a period of one year.

1. *Police Power and Due Process*

Appellants initially challenge the constitutionality of California's referendum procedures as applied to the zoning process. They contend that "referendum zoning" violates due process requirements.

The rights asserted are those of a landowner (SASSO) to be free from arbitrary restrictions on land use. Appellants assert that regulation on land use by zoning is constitutionally permissible only where procedural safeguards assure that the resulting limitations have been determined, by legislatively promulgated standards, to be in the interest of public health, safety, morals, or the general welfare. They contend that the referendum process destroys the necessary procedural safeguards upon which a municipality's power to zone is based and subjects zoning decisions to the bias, caprice and self-interest of the voter.

Appellants' reliance on these cases is misplaced. There, local ordinances permitted residents of a neighborhood, by majority vote *(Eubank)* or by withholding consent *(Washington),* to impose restrictions that otherwise had not legislatively been determined to be in the public interest. The resulting rule, as applied to appellants' contentions respecting procedural safeguards, would seem to be that an expression of neighborhood preference for restraints, uncontrolled by any legislative responsibility to apply acceptable public interest standards, is not such a determination of what is in the public interest as will justify an exercise of the police power to zone.

A referendum, however, is far more than an expression of ambiguously founded neighborhood preference. It is the city itself legislating through its voters—an exercise by the voters of their traditional right through direct legislation to override the views of their elected representatives as to what serves the public interest. This question lay at the heart of the proposition put to the voters. That some voters individually may have failed to meet their responsibilities as legislators to vote wisely and unselfishly cannot alter the result.

Nor can it be said that the resulting legislation on its face was so unrelated to acceptable public interest standards as to constitute an arbitrary or unreasonable exercise of the police power. Many environmental and social values are involved in a determination of how land would best be used in the public interest. The choice of the voters of Union City is not lacking in support in this regard.

Thus in the present case neither the zoning process itself nor the result can be said to be such an arbitrary or unreasonable exercise of the zoning power as to be violative of appellants' right to due process of law. We agree with the District Court that no substantial constitutional question was presented by appellants' due process contentions, and that they warranted neither a three-judge court nor a preliminary injunction.

2. *Equal Protection*

Appellants contend that both the purpose and the result of the referendum were to discriminate racially and economically against the Mexican-American residents of Union City. They assert that the referendum was racially motivated and that its result was to perpetuate discrimination in Union City against Mexican-American residents with low incomes.

Under the facts of this case we do not believe that the question of motivation for the referendum (apart from a consideration of its effect) is an appropriate one for judicial inquiry.

There a constitutional amendment, adopted by the people of California through a statewide ballot, resulted in the repeal of existing fair housing laws and prohibited all legislative action abridging the rights of persons to sell, lease or rent property to whomsoever they chose. In examining the constitutionality of the amendment, its purpose was treated as a relevant consideration.

Purpose was judged, however, in terms of ultimate effect and historical context. The only existing restrictions on dealings in land (and thus the obvious target of the amendment) were those prohibiting private discrimination.

The only "conceivable" purpose, judged by wholly objective standards, was to restore the right to discriminate and protect it against future legislative limitation. The amendment was held to constitute impermissible state involvement (in the nature of authorization or encouragement) with private racial discrimination.

The case before us is quite different. As we have noted, many environmental and social values are involved in determinations of land use. As the District Court noted, "* * * [T]here is no more reason to find that [rejection of rezoning] was done on the ground of invidious racial discrimination any more than on perfectly legitimate environmental grounds which are always and necessarily involved in zoning issues."

If the voters' purpose is to be found here, then, it would seem to require far more than a simple application of objective standards. If the true motive is to be ascertained not through speculation but through a probing of the private attitudes of the voters, the inquiry would entail an intolerable invasion of the privacy that must protect an exercise of the franchise.

Appellants' equal protection contentions, however, reach beyond purpose. They assert that the effect of the referendum is to deny decent housing and an integrated environment to low-income residents of Union City. If, apart from voter motive, the result of this zoning by referendum is discriminatory in this fashion, in our view a substantial constitutional question is presented.

Surely, if the environmental benefits of land use planning are to be enjoyed by a city and the quality of life of its residents is accordingly to be improved, the poor cannot be excluded from enjoyment of the benefits. Given the recognized importance of equal opportunities in housing, it may well be, as matter of law, that it is the responsibility of a city and its planning officials to see that the city's plan as initiated or as it develops accommodates the needs of its low-income families, who usually—if not always—are members of minority groups. It may be, as matter of fact, that Union City's plan, as it has emerged from the referendum, fails in this respect. These issues remain to be resolved.

They do not, however, call for a three-judge court under 28 U.S.C. § 2281. It is not state law that has brought about the condition in Union City and the validity of state law is not drawn in question. State law has enabled Union City to act, but appellants' challenge is directed not against the state's grant of power but against the manner in which the city has exercised that power.

Nor do we feel that denial of preliminary injunction constituted abuse of discretion. An injunction here would not serve to freeze the status quo but would require that affirmative steps now be taken in the direction of the ultimate remedy sought by appellants. The fact that discrimination resulted from the referendum, and that Union City has failed to make satisfactory provision for low-income housing, is not so clear as to demand preliminary relief of this nature.

The order of the District Court is affirmed. [Some citations omitted.]

The problem of urban density constantly faces zoning authorities, which generally resolve it through lot restrictions and control over building size. Because the population density has a significant impact on the other public needs in the area, such as the number of schools, the amount of police protection, the number of firehouses, and the parking and recreational facilities needed, control over density remains an important goal for many zoning boards. Density control is usually achieved through restricting lot size to a basic amount, although building size is often controlled as well. The amount of space for each building, the setbacks from the street, and the property lines all restrict and limit the amount of building and therefore the density of the population. In addition, the density of population plays an important role in private economic development of the area, because the number of people living within a certain radius determines the number and proximity of private services such as strip malls, shopping centers, and individual stores.

One of the major sources of urban problems is the changing neighborhood. Although most changing neighborhoods move downwards in the process, it is also possible to have upgrading, such as gentrification, renewal by means of a planned, mixed-usage community, or by other means. These changes commonly present a need to reevaluate the existing zoning as a whole or to permit a significant number of variances to the existing zoning. If the zoning is locked into one pattern, one must obtain a variance from that zoning to create a different usage in that area. A **variance** is an exception to the zoning laws' requirement which permits the nonconforming use to be done or maintained. Although there are many formal, administrative procedures (discussed later) that can be followed to obtain a variance, in most cities the best means of attaining a variance is through the influence of someone with local political authority. In many cities today, failure to follow this route can lead to failure of the request for a variance. Further, the applicant may be ignored or treated as a fool or an idiot for not working within the political process as opposed to the administrative process. (This comment hints gently at the real world's operation, rather than sticking strictly to legal formalities!)

Sometimes, the use of variances changes the nature of an area, when the number of variances is great or the type of variances is different from the zoning standard. In this situation, there may eventually be a rezoning of the area to combine the old zoning with the effects of the variances. These changes may speed the changes in the neighborhood, or they may have little effect because the zoning changes merely reflect an already changed neighborhood.

The formal steps for obtaining a variance usually include making application to the local zoning board or to an appellate body such as a zoning board of appeals or zoning adjustment board. A variance is usually authorized when enforcement of the zoning law would cause undue hardship or create real difficulties for the party applying for the variance. The party who applies for a variance must be a person who has rights in the property. That party could be an owner of the property or a party who is purchasing the property on time, such a contract buyer, but not a normal lessee. What makes a hardship? It generally must reflect a situation related to that particular parcel of land, or one that limits the owner's use of or benefit from the land in a way that truly denies her effective usage of her property. In other words, the zoning has removed her control of her land or denied her the anticipated benefit from that land. In addition, the variance must do as little damage to the appearance, operation, and living conditions of the zoned area as possible.

Finally, one should understand the basic process of making the zoning laws work. Zoning control is achieved by having anyone who wishes to build on a parcel of property, or to repair, renovate, or make any structural change in the property, obtain a permit for doing the work. To obtain the permit, a person must submit plans showing what will occur and the results of the work; these plans often require an architect to draw them up. The plans are then checked against the zoning laws' requirements. If the plans conform and no problems appear, a building permit normally issues. If there is a violation of the zoning law, the zoning officials may deny the permit or they may issue it. If they issue it despite the violation of the zoning law, any property owner whose property is negatively affected may challenge the permit issuance in court. One of the great problems in zoning law is the issue of what is to be done when an allegedly injured neighbor protests, the building is constructed pursuant to the permit, and the neighbor wins the lawsuit. Again, there are two conflicting interests: (1) that of the damaged neighbor and (2) that of the party who relied on the permit and built the structure. As might be guessed, courts have gone both ways. Some decisions have ordered buildings to be torn down or to be extensively modified, at great expense, to meet the zoning requirements. Other situations have been dealt with as if the finished construction were a *fait accompli* and nothing could be done about it. Care must be taken to determine the position of the courts in your jurisdiction.

11.10 ENVIRONMENTAL CONCERNS

In addition to zoning concerns, there is increasing public concern about land usage and its environmental impact upon society. Naturally, the developer wants access to land to be as unrestricted as possible, but many consider that approach to have been a major source of both the damage that has occurred to our environment and of many of the urban problems we face today. There is particular concern over wilderness areas, wetlands (such as marshes and swamps), seashores and lakeshores (such as the Indiana Dunes), beaches, and waterways. Concern for these areas, which appear necessary for preservation of fish, birds, and other wildlife and for the healthy handling of water supplies, is in addition to obvious concerns about emissions, toxic wastes, and poisons in our environment. Thus, many governments have created special regulations to control use of these lands, and require anyone seeking permission to exploit those environmentally sensitive areas to obtain environmental permits first.

Wetlands pose a difficult problem, because they are generally ecologically fragile and because they are essential in many cases to the survival and preservation of wildlife. Wetlands absorb much rainfall and contribute to the prevention of floods; they also assist in transferring water to the water table, which has been badly depleted in many areas of the country by irrigation and other human uses. Wetlands are useful in cleansing poisons from the water supply, and they are a source of fish, crustaceans, birds, and other game and food resources. Many of our wetlands have been filled in or built on, and the environmental consequences of these actions have been ignored. The entire

LEGAL TERMS

variance
Exception to the zoning laws.

Chicago Loop area was once a vast marsh for the river that flowed out into Lake Michigan. The smell of the marsh was so strong, originally, that the Native American word for the area, from which the name "Chicago" came, meant "stinking onion." Without wise planning and effective controls, much can be lost, for both society and the developer. If the public becomes outraged, it is likely to ask its legislatures to enact extraordinarily strict laws prohibiting any development. Accommodation is usually necessary for both sides of this often impassioned argument about the use of our land resources.

Local governments are imposing controls that restrict development and prohibit or severely limit the use of any of the land types mentioned previously. Permits now must be sought not only from zoning authorities but also from environmental authorities. Many levels of government require some type of environmental impact statement (EIS) to determine the effects of a land development on a particular area (see figure 11-1). Local governments,

Volume 1 of 4

Price Chopper EASTERN PARKWAY - STORE 26

832 McClellan Street
Schenectady, New York

Date: August 26, 1992

DRAFT ENVIRONMENTAL IMPACT STATEMENT
PROPOSED PRICE CHOPPER SUPERCENTER

LEAD AGENCY:	**City of Schenectady Planning Commission** Room 9, City Hall Jay Street Schenectady, New York 12305-1938
Contact Person:	James Kalohn (518) 382-5049
APPLICANT:	**Golub Corporation** 501 Duanesburg Road Schenectady, New York 12306
Contact Person:	James Borrowman (518) 354-9318
PREPARED BY:	**Stetson-Harza** 250 Jordan Road Troy, New York 12180
Contact Person:	Myles Hyman (518) 283-8080

FIGURE 11-1
Sample environmental impact statement

14-12-9 (2/87)—9c

SEQR

617.21
Appendix G
State Environmental Quality Review

Notice of Completion of Draft EIS and Notice of SEQR Hearing

Lead Agency: Schenectady City Planning Commission Project Number P4-421500-00012

Address: Room 9, City Hall, Schenectady, N.Y. 12305

Date: September 16, 1992

This notice is issued pursuant to Part 617 (and local law # ______ if any) of the implementing regulations pertaining to Article 8 (State Environmental Quality Review Act) of the Environmental Conservation Law.

A Draft Environmental Impact Statement has been completed and accepted for the proposed action described below. Comments on the Draft EIS are requested and will be accepted by the contact person until October 26, 1992. A public hearing on the Draft EIS will be held on October 14, 1992 7:00 PM (date and time) at Room 209 City Hall Schenectady, New York (place).

Name of Action: Price Chopper Super Center

Description of Action:

Construct a new Price Chopper Super Center at 832 McClellan Street. The proposed market of 67, 250 sq.ft. will be built while the existing store remains in operation. Approximately 10,000 sq.ft. will be demolished at the east and west ends of the existing structure to facilitate new construction and parking during construction. Upon completion of the new structure, the old market will be demolished and site work, landscaping and parking completed.

Location: (Include street address and the name of the municipality/county.)

832 McClellan Street
Schenectady, N.Y. 12309

FIGURE 11-1
(Continued)

such as cities, townships, and counties, as well as state governments are increasingly concerned about environmental planning and actions. For example, there is great concern about trash imported from other areas to landfills within the state and use of the state for the storage of nuclear waste products—both of which can have long-lasting and severe impacts on the environment in which they are stored.

Finally, two other aspects should be discussed. First, there is a tendency to consider buildings over 70 years old as candidates for designation

Notice of Completion of Draft EIS/Notice of Hearing — Page 2

Potential Environmental Impacts:

1. Potential noise and dust impacts related to construction and demolition.
2. Traffic increases to & from the site are projected to be 20-23% above existing traffic levels, which will impact the site entrance and exits, as well as the intersection of McClellan St. and Eastern Parkway
3. Noise impact on adjoining alley and rear yards of Central Parkway due to operation of the site may increase between 1 and 3 db dependent upon truck delivery routes, location of roof top equipment.
4. Signage proposed to be free standing and attached are larger than permitted by the sign code and therfore may have an adverse impact visually.

A Copy of the Draft EIS may be obtained from:

Contact Person: James Kalohn

Address: Room 9, City Hall, Schenectady,N.Y. 12305

Telephone Number: (518) 382-5049

A Copy of this Notice and the Draft EIS Sent to:

- Commissioner, Department of Environmental Conservation, 50 Wolf Road, Albany, New York 12233-0001
- Appropriate Regional Office of the Department of Environmental Conservation
- Office of the Chief Executive Officer of the political subdivision in which the action will be principally located.
- All other involved agencies (if any)
- Persons requesting Draft EIS

FIGURE 11-1 *(Continued)*

as historic landmarks or historic preservation buildings. Under federal law and state regulations, older buildings can be required to be preserved rather than destroyed. Income tax benefits may also be enjoyed by those who maintain historic buildings. In addition, there are historic areas as well; zoning has been used to preserve these historic sites in many communities. At issue is the right of the owner to use his land as he chooses versus the public's need to possess tangible evidence of its history, heritage, and architectural development. Since it has been estimated that the vast majority of American land was taken up in speculative development, nothing could be more American than continued, unregulated land development! The argument on the other side, however, is whether the consequences of that peculiarly type of American type of economic development are ones that most citizens wish to leave to their children. Another problem that has arisen with landmark dedications is that some small local groups or individuals have used the availability of such dedications to save old buildings that only that group wants maintained, when most rational observers would entertain serious doubts about their appearance or uniqueness.

Second, there is an act of Congress, entitled the Interstate Land Sales Act, which regulates the sale of lots in interstate commerce. This act requires that a report on the development and its developer be filed with the appropriate authority and that prospective buyers be given a report concerning the property and its development. There are a number of coverage exceptions. The purpose of this land development regulation is to stop the fly-by-night land developers who invite people to visit the site and then try to get the visitors to sign a purchase contract and make a substantial down payment on a lot. Basically, the act attempts to prevent use of the mails or other means of communication as means to defraud individuals interested in purchasing land in a development. Buyers must be given a copy of the report at or before signing any contract, and failure to do so allows the buyers to rescind the contract up to two years later. Damages to the buyers and criminal penalties may also be applicable.

DISCUSSION AND REVIEW QUESTIONS

1. Explain the focus of federal concern with the environment. How important is this problem and how effective do you think the federal government's approach has been?
2. Explain the uses and risks of an environmental audit.
3. Discuss the differences between public and private regulation of real estate use.
4. Explain, in a general way, the process of zoning and (1) its impact on urban development and (2) its potential application to environmental issues.
5. What other areas of environmental concern might affect real estate activities?

SAMPLE FORMS

Quitclaim Deed—Dedicating Land to City for Public Use

QUITCLAIM DEED

Quitclaim deed, made ___________ *[date]*, between ___________, of __________ *[address]*, City of __________, County of ___________, State of ________, referred to as dedicator, and the City of ________, County of __________, State of __________, acting by and through *[name of city officer or agency]*, referred to as dedicatee.

SIDEBAR

Note the simplicity of this transaction.

Dedicator, in consideration of _________ Dollars ($____), to dedicator paid by dedicatee, dedicates, releases, remises, and quitclaims to dedicatee, to have and to hold for the public use forever, as _________ *[describe purpose or use with certainty]*, all that land described as follows: _________ *[legal description]*. Dedicatee, by accepting this dedication, obligates itself to forever preserve and use the described land for the purpose listed above, and no other.

[Signature]

[Acknowledgement]

SIDEBAR

This legislation is included as a sample of the detailed and complex needs in environmental control. Note the key material in § 32 and its dependence on federal standards.

Air Pollution Control Ordinance—General Limitations and Requirements

PART ONE
DEFINITIONS

Section One. "Air Pollution control equipment" means any operation that has as its essential purpose a significant reduction in (a) the emission of air contaminants or (b) the effect of such emission.

Section Two. "Area of an opening or containing device" means the area of a projection of the opening or of the gas passage on a plane to which the principal direction of gas flow is perpendicular.

Section Three. "Atmosphere" means the air that surrounds the earth and includes the general volume of gases contained within any building or structure; but excludes both.

(a) The gases contained in any building or structure specifically designed for and used as part of an air pollution abatement operation or in a piece of processing or operating equipment, or in any building from which no significant portion of the air contaminants contained therein escapes; and

(b) The gases traveling from a source operation to a collection system, provided such collection system collects the air contaminants discharged by such source operation to such a degree that no significant portion thereof escapes collection, and provided further that such collection system emits all collected gases through a Type "A" emission point.

Section Four. "Auxiliary fuel" means any material that undergoes combustion in an incineration operation or in a salvage operation; but excludes any waste material, the combustion of which is a part of the principal purpose of the operation.

Section Five. "Combustion" means the rapid exothermic reaction of any material with oxygen.

Section Six. "Containing device" means any stack, duct, flue, oven, kettle, or other structure or device that so contains an air contaminant, or a gas stream that contains or may contain an air contaminant, as to prevent essentially its entering the atmosphere except through such opening as may be incorporated for that purpose in the containing device; and excludes equipment used for air pollution abatement operations, and any other device that significantly changes the nature, extent, quantity, or degree of air contaminants in the gas stream or in which such change does or has a natural tendency to occur.

Section Seven. "Emission" means the act of passing into the atmosphere an air contaminant or a gas stream that contains or may contain an air contaminant; or the material so passed to the atmosphere.

Section Eight. "Emission point" means the location (place in horizontal plane and vertical elevation) at which an emission enters the atmosphere.

Section Nine. "Exhaust gas volume" means the total volume of gases emitted from an emission point.

Section Ten. "General combustion operation" means any source operation in which combustion is carried on, exclusive of heat transfer operations, incineration operations, and salvage operations.

Section Eleven. "General operation" means any source operation not included in Sections Ten, Twelve, Thirteen, and Twenty hereof, inclusive.

Section Twelve. "Heat transfer operation" means the combustion side of any source operation that (a) involves the combustion of fuel for the principal purpose of utilizing the heat of combustion-product gases by the transfer of such heat to the process material; and (b) does not transfer a significant portion of heat by direct contact between the combustion-product gases and the process material.

Section Thirteen. "Incineration operation" means any source operation in which combustion is carried on for the principal purpose, or with the principal result, of oxidizing a waste material to reduce its bulk or facilitate disposal, or both.

Section Fourteen. "Operation" means any physical action resulting in a change in the location, form, or physical properties of a material, or any chemical action resulting in a change in the chemical composition or chemical or physical properties of a material. The following are given as examples, without limitation of the generality of the foregoing: heat transfer, calcination, double decomposition, fermentation, pyrolysis, electrolysis, combustion, material handling, evaporation, mixing, absorption, filtration, screening, and fluidization.

Section Fifteen. "Particulate matter" means any material that is emitted as liquid or solid particles, or both, but does not include uncombined water; for the purposes of this Section Fifteen, material emitted at any temperature in excess of 500 degrees Fahrenheit may be deemed to have been emitted at 500 degrees Fahrenheit.

Section Sixteen. "Person" means any natural person, a corporation, government agency, public officer, association, joint venture, partnership, or any combination of such, jointly or separately, operating in concert for any common objective related to the purposes of this Regulation. It includes the owner, lessor, lessee, tenant, licensee, manager, and operator of any above-mentioned organization or group, or combination thereof, of any emission point or any source operation related thereto, or of any interest in such emission point or source operation.

Section Seventeen. "ppm (vol)" means parts per million by volume.

Section Eighteen. "Process weight" means the total weight of all materials introduced into a source operation, including solid fuels, but excluding liquids and gases used solely as fuels, and air introduced for purposes of combustion.

Section Nineteen. "Process weight rate" means a rate established as follows:

(a) For continuous or long-run steady-state source operations, the total process weight for the entire period of continuous operation, or for a typical portion thereof, divided by the number of hours of such period or portion thereof.

(b) For cyclical or batch source operations, the total process weight for a period that covers a complete operation or an integral number of cycles divided by the hours of actual process operation during such period.

Where the nature of any process or operation or the design of any equipment is such as to permit more than one interpretation of this Section Nineteen, that interpretation which results in the minimum value for allowable emission shall apply.

Section Twenty. "Salvage operation" means any source operation in which combustion is carried on for the principal purpose, or with the principal result, of salvaging metals that are introduced into the operation as essentially pure metals, or alloys thereof, by oxidation of physically intermingled combustible material; but excludes operations in which there is complete fusion of all such metals.

Section Twenty-One. "Significant dimension" of an area means the square root of the numerical value of the area.

Section Twenty-Two. "Source gas volume" means the volume, in standard cubic feet, of all gases leaving a source operation; for purposes of this Section Twenty-Two, the boundary of a source operation is that point or surface at which the separation of the air contaminants from the process materials or the conversion of the process materials into air contaminants is essentially complete.

Section Twenty-Three. "Source operation" means the last operation preceding the emission of an air contaminant, which operation (a) results in the separation of the air contaminant from the process materials or in the conversion of the process materials into air contaminants, as in the case of combustion of fuel; and (b) is not an air pollution abatement operation.

Section Twenty-Four. Standard conditions means a pressure of 14.7 pounds per square inch, absolute, in a temperature of 60 degrees Fahrenheit.

Section Twenty-Five. "Standard cubic foot" of gas means that amount of the gas that would occupy a cube having dimension of one foot on each side, if the gas were at standard conditions; calculations to determine the number of standard cubic feet corresponding to actual measured conditions shall follow accepted engineering practice.

Section Twenty-Six. "Standard dry cubic foot" of a gas means that amount of the gas that would occupy a cube having dimensions of one foot on each side, if the gas were free of water vapor and at standard conditions; calculations to determine the number of standard dry cubic feet corresponding to actual measured conditions shall follow accepted engineering practice.

Section Twenty-Seven. "Sunset" and "sunrise" mean the times of civil sunset and civil sunrise in the City of __________.

Section Twenty-Eight. Type "A" emission point means an opening of reasonably regular geometry, preceded by a containing device that has a minimum length six times the significant dimension of the emission point and within such minimum length; has a reasonably straight gas flow channel; has smooth interior surfaces; has area and geometry essentially constant and equal to the emission point; and does not cause a significant change in the gross direction of gas flow.

Section Twenty-Nine. Type "B" emission point means any emission point not qualifying under Section Twenty-eight as a Type "A" emission point.

Section Thirty. Quantity of emission from a Type "B" emission point shall be the quantity of emission computed by multiplying the quantity of emission from a test area by the proportion which the whole area bears to such test area. Such test area may be taken as the cross-sectional area of the inlet to a sample probe. The emission from any test area of a Type "B" emission point shall be deemed to be representative in every respect of the emission from the whole area of such Type "B" emission point. Emissions from the test area may be measured at the place and by the procedure which result in the highest measurement of air contaminants. This section shall not apply if other sampling and testing facilities that will disclose the nature, extent, quantity, and degree of air contaminants are provided by the person responsible for the emission.

PART TWO
GENERAL LIMITATION AND REQUIREMENTS

Section Thirty-One. This Part applies to all source operations; namely, incineration, salvage, heat transfer, general combustion, and general operations as defined in Sections One through Thirty of Part One.

Section Thirty-Two. VISIBLE EMISSIONS. Except as provided in Sections Thirty-three through Thirty-five(g), no person shall cause, let, permit, suffer, or allow the emission for more than three minutes in any one hour of a gas stream containing air contaminants which, at the emission point or within a reasonable distance of the emission point, is

(a) As dark as or darker in shade than that designated as No. 1 on the Ringelmann Chart as published in the United States Bureau of Mines Information Circular 7718, or

(b) Of such opacity as to obscure an observer's view to a degree equal to or greater than the smoke described in Section Thirty-two(a); and the determination of such opacity shall be according to procedures in Part Three, Sections Thirty-six through Forty-two.

Section Thirty-Three. Where the presence of uncombined water is the only reason for the failure of an emission to meet the limitation of Section Thirty-two, that section shall not apply. The burden of proof which establishes the application of this Section Thirty-three shall be upon the person seeking to come within its provisions.

Section Thirty-Four. Section Thirty-two shall not apply to any emission on the basis of any observation of an air contaminant while such contaminant is inside a bona fide building.

Section Thirty-Five. If the person responsible for an emission can show that the emission meets all the requirements of this Section Thirty-five as given in subsections Thirty-five (a) through Thirty-five (g), then compliance with the limitation of this Section Thirty-five instead of with the limitations of Section Thirty-two can be used by such person to show compliance of such emission with the limitations pertaining to visible emission of this Regulation. The burden of showing compliance with each and all of the provisions of this Section Thirty-five shall be upon the person seeking to come within its provisions.

(a) The emission is from a Type "A" emission point.

(b) The emission does not contain significant amounts of materials which are vapors at stack temperature and particulate matter at ambient temperature.

(c) The emission has a constant appearance, which for the purposes of this Section Thirty-Five shall mean that the emission has a clearly discernible, predominant darkness of shade or degree of opacity, in the sense of Section Thirty-two, and that the aggregate of all the periods during which the observed shade or opacity differs by 0.5 Ringelmann number or more from such predominant shade or opacity does not exceed three minutes in any consecutive 60 minutes.

(d) During the time that all of the other requirements of this Section Thirty-five are met, the emission does not contain more than "n" grains of particulate matter per standard cubic foot, where n = 0.06/L, and "L" is the significant dimension of the emission point, in feet.

(e) The emission does not contain material other than the particulate matter determined in Section Thirty-five(d) or uncombined water or both, that contributes significantly to the failure of the emission to meet the limitations of Section Thirty-two.

(f) Only emissions of that darkness of shade, degree of opacity, or appearance of plume which have been observed pursuant to Sections Thirty-five(c) and Thirty-five(d) and have been found to comply with the limitations of Section Thirty-five(d) are permitted by this Section Thirty-five.

(g) The ___________ [control officer] may require a repeated showing of compliance with this Section Thirty-five upon a significant change in operating conditions or upon observation of a significant change in the appearance of the plume.

PART THREE
PROCEDURE FOR MAKING OBSERVATIONS TO DETERMINE COMPLIANCE WITH SECTION THIRTY-TWO

Section Thirty-Six. Provisions of this Part shall govern observations of emissions to determine compliance with Section Thirty-two. These provisions shall be applied to each observation to the extent they are applicable, and to whatever extent time and physical circumstances reasonably permit.

Section Thirty-Seven. Observations shall be made from any position such that the line of observation is at approximately a right angle to the line of travel of the emitted material.

Section Thirty-Eight. The plume shall be observed against a suitable background.

Section Thirty-Nine. Observations during daylight hours shall be made with the observer facing generally away from the sun.

Section Forty. Observations during hours of darkness should be made with the aid of a light source.

Section Forty-One. Readings shall be noted at approximately 15-second intervals during observation, except that intervals up to one minute shall be permitted where the appearance of the emission does not vary during such interval.

Section Forty-Two. The general color of the emission during the period of observation shall be noted as part of the record of observation.

Notice to Trespasser to Personalty—Damage Due to Trespass—Request for Reimbursement

To: _________ *[trespasser]*
_________ *[address]*

You are given notice that the personal property described below that you unlawfully carried away from _________ *[address],* on _________, 19___, was in the possession of the undersigned of _________ *[address].* The personal property that the undersigned refers to is _________ *[describe personal property].*

___________ *[If trespasser still possesses personal property, add:* The value of the personal property that you unlawfully carried away and have failed to return to the undersigned is ________ Dollars ($____), *or if the trespasser has returned the personal property, add:* Although you have returned the personal property, the undersigned sustained ________ Dollars ($____) in damages while you were unlawfully depriving him of the possession of his personal property from ___________, 19___ to ________, 19____]. The undersigned demands that you remit _________ Dollars ($____) to him, at _________ *[address],* on or before ________, 19____, or he shall institute a legal action against you to obtain monetary damages in the amount of _______ Dollars ($____).

Dated _________, 19____.

[Signature]

Application for Approval of Subdivision Plat

To: _________ *[planning board]*

The undersigned hereby applies for _________ [tentative *or* final] approval of a subdivision plat in accordance with the rules and regulations of your board and represents and states as follows:

1. The applicant is the owner of record of the land under application.
2. The name of the subdivision is _________.
3. The entire land under application is described herewith by deed or map.
4. The land is held by the applicant under deed recorded in the ___________ [county clerk's office] as follows: _________.

SIDEBAR

The number of details to cover is enormous. From this example you may be able to see the need for detailed controls and why checklists can be extensive.

5. The area of land is _________ acres.

6. The land is shown on the ___________ [town boundary] map in ___________.

7. All taxes which are liens on the land at the date hereof have been paid.

8. There ___________ [are *or* are not any] encumbrances or liens against the land. ___________ *[Specify encumbrances, if any.]*

9. The land lies in the following zoning use districts: ___________.

10. No part of the land lies under water or is subject to flood. ___________

11. The applicant will, at his own expense, instal the required improvements in accordance with standards and specifications adopted by the Town of ___________ in accordance with ___________ *[cite statute or ordinance].*

12. The land ___________ [does *or* does not] lie in a water district or water supply district.

(a) Name of district, if within a district ___________.

(b) Name of district extension, if an extension is proposed ___________.

(c) Connection charge for the extension of district will be paid by ___________ *[name].*

(d) Water mains will be laid by _________ *[name],* and _________ [a *or* no] charge will be made for installing such mains.

(e) If water mains are not within reach, how will potable water be furnished? ___________

13. The land ___________ [does *or* does not] lie within a sanitary sewer district.

(a) Name of district, if within a district ___________.

(b) Name of district extension, if an extension is proposed ___________.

(c) Connection charge for the extension of sewer district will be paid by ___________ *[name].*

(d) Sewer mains will be laid by _________ *[name],* and _________ [a *or* no] charge will be made for installing such mains.

(e) If sanitary sewers are not available what do you propose to use as a substitute? ___________.

14. Electric mains will be installed by ____________ *[name],* and ___________ [a *or* no] charge will be made for installing such mains.

15. Gas mains will be installed by _________, *[name],* and _______ [a *or* no] charge will be made for installing such mains.

16. If streets shown on the plat are claimed by the applicant to be existing public streets in the county highway system, give right-of-way width from road records: ___________ feet. Are you willing to give additional land for future road widening? ___________ [yes *or* no].

17. If streets shown on the plat are claimed by the applicant to be existing public streets in the town highway system, give right-of-way width from the road records: ___________ feet. Are you willing to give additional land for future road widening? ___________ [yes *or* no].

18. If streets shown on the plat are claimed by the applicant to be existing public streets in the state highway system, give right-of-way width from the road records: ___________. Are you willing to give additional land for future road widening? ___________ [yes *or* no].

19. There are no existing buildings or structures on the land which are not located on the plat.

20. Where the plat shows proposed streets which are extensions of streets on adjoining subdivision maps heretofore filed, there are no reserve strips at the ends of the streets on the existing maps at their conjunction with the proposed streets.

21. In the course of these proceedings, the applicant will offer proof of ownership.

22. The applicant estimates that the grading and required public improvements will cost ___________ Dollars ($____) as itemized, and requests that the performance bond or other sureties be approved by the ___________ [town board].

Dated __________, 19____.

__________ *[Name of applicant]*
By __________
[Signature and title]

____
[Address]

____
[Telephone]

___________ [Venue]

___________, being duly sworn, deposes and says that he resides at ___________ *[address]*, City of ___________, County of _________, State of ___________; That he has signed the foregoing application as applicant or the duly authorized officer of the applicant; and that the statements contained in such application are true.

[Signature]

[Jurat]

Notice of Public Hearing on Application for Approval of Subdivision Plat

Notice is hereby given that pursuant to _________ *[cite statute]*, a public hearing will be held by the _________ [zoning commission, planning commission *or as the case may be]* of the City of _________, County of ________, State of ________, and by the ________ *[any other city body joining in holding the hearing]* on _________, 19____, at _________ o'clock ___.m., for the purpose of considering the application of _________ *[name of person or organization proposing the action]* for the approval of the plat entitled ________, being a subdivision of parcel ________ of the ________ situated in ________, which shows a new street to be known as _________; also, the application to subdivide the premises showing lots of a minimum width of _____ feet, minimum depth of _____ feet and minimum area of _______ square feet. Such premises are located in _________ *[title and classification of zone].*

All parties in interest and citizens will be given an opportunity to be heard in respect to such proposed application. Persons may appear in person or through a representative.

Date: __________, 19___.

[Authorized signature]

Resolution of Planning Board Approving Subdivision Plat

At a meeting of the planning board of the City of _________, County of _________, State of _________, held at _________ on _________, 19___, at _______ o'clock ____.m., attended by _______ *[members of board attending],* __________ *[name of person or organization proposing adoption of plan]* offered the following resolution and moved its adoption:

Whereas, an application has been made to this board for the approval of a plat entitled _________, showing proposed new streets to be known as __________ and __________; and

Whereas, pursuant to __________ *[cite statute],* a public hearing was advertised and held on __________, 19___, in __________ *[location]* at __________ o'clock ____.m.; and

Whereas the plan submitted herein does not conflict with the county official map and has been approved in the manner specified by ________ *[cite statute];* and

Whereas, it appears to be the best interest of the City of __________ that the application be approved subject to certain conditions;

Now, therefore, be it resolved that the map entitled _________ showing new proposed streets to be known as _________ and _________ filed with this board showing property of _________, be, and the same hereby is approved on condition that the proposed new streets shall be suitably graded and paved in accordance with standard specifications and procedure acceptable to _________ [the city zoning board, *or as the case may be*]. Resolution passed on _________, 19___.

Dated: __________, 19___.

____

[Authorized signature]

CHAPTER 12

The Taxation of Real Estate

"It costs us nothing to be just."

Henry David Thoreau

Split-level house

OUTLINE

PROLOGUE TO THE PARALEGAL

Real estate as an asset serves as the tax base for many of America's local governments; real estate as an income-producing entity raises taxes for any government that taxes income—thus, federal, state, and local governments all benefit from the success of the real estate business. In addition to these basic taxes, there are various sorts of special taxes, such as taxes for recording documents. This chapter contains a brief recapitulation of a previous discussion of the effects of not paying one's taxes, as well as brief discussions of Internal Revenue Service rules, tax deferrals on home sales, and the impact of the form of business organization selected on taxation. The process of creating a local tax on real estate is explored here too. Areas in which paralegals can play a role are, among others, preparation of tax forms and research in comparative taxation on similar pieces of property. No detailed knowledge or expertise is expected here, but understanding the framework of the area is important.

KEY TERMS

assessment
assessment roll
assessor
Board of Assessment
depreciation
equalization
levy
recording tax
special assessment tax
tax deed
tax list
tax sale
transfer tax

12.1 INTRODUCTION

The taxation of real property is one of the oldest and most pervasive forms of taxation in the United States. The taxes raised in this manner provide much of the income necessary for the operation of local governments of all types, ranging from municipal government to schools to water control boards. This area is one in which lawyers have become increasingly involved in the last 20 years, because of the rapid increase in the value of homes and many other types of real property that are subject to taxation. An aspect of real estate taxation in which lawyers have traditionally played an important role is analyzing the real estate levy. More will be said of this process later in this chapter.

With the steep rise in real estate prices since the 1970s, taxes on homes and dwellings have risen accordingly. Lawyers have assisted property owners in challenging assessments and making sure that taxes are handled equitably. Although objecting to tax increases may delay an increase, it is unlikely that many tax increases will be reduced or rolled back in the near future without major economic changes in the tax bases of our communities. These taxes are used for the day-to-day conduct of government: They repair the roads, educate students at all levels, and provide recreational facilities, hospital care, and protection from crime and fire. Until an agreed-upon change in the base for the tax system occurs, real estate taxes appear to be here to stay. Real estate taxes are also the oldest tax base we have. These taxes were instituted when farming was the predominant way of life and have continued even after that original basis disappeared.

Most real estate taxation is entirely local in its rules, practices, and administration. Very few general comments can be made, so the comments made here are in the nature of an introduction to the process of real estate taxation rather than a detailed explanation of any particular state or local taxation scheme.

12.2 THE PROCESS OF LEVYING AND COLLECTING TAXES

Despite considerable local variation, a number of processes are common to most state and local taxation of real estate. Clearly, the process begins with each local governmental body establishing a budget for the following fiscal year; that government then needs to raise the operating funds to implement that budget. Remember that there will be numerous local governments that will be involved in this process. Each one will want a portion of the real estate tax that is levied in their local area that next year. When all these local entities cumulate their tax needs, it is possible to determine the amount of income that the real estate tax for that year needs to raise. Cities, schools, and counties, as well as hospitals, parks, water districts, and sewage districts, all count on the real estate tax to obtain much, if not all of, their funding for their next fiscal year's budget. After the government had determined the amount of money it will need, it must establish a means to raise that money.

The Appropriation

The first step is for the legislative part of each local government unit to pass an appropriation law or ordinance. This body may be the city council, the county board, the board of commissioners, or some similarly named authority. This appropriation document details how the money will be spent, the amount to be spent in each area of that governmental unit's interest, and, perhaps, the source of funding for each expenditure. Then, the local legislative body must levy upon the parties owning the real property. The **levy** is the legal means whereby the government imposes the obligation to pay tax on the real estate property owner. If the levy is invalid—for instance, for exceeding the maximum permitted by law—the taxation will fail and the tax can be avoided, because the local legislative body has not followed the proper procedures and forms.

Large property holders, such as corporations, have long used attorneys to carefully review the form and content of each levy to discover if the local government has made errors in creating the levy; in other words, they look for technical loopholes that will permit them to sue and get the tax invalidated. This process is very exacting and sophisticated, and it is beyond the knowledge of almost all local property owners. For instance, one obvious area of attack would be the government exceeding the limits of its tax rate (where there are tax rate limitations), but most people would not know that a rate limit existed, let alone what the current rate limit was. Note that withholding a tax payment in protest may not be effective, because the tax will be due unless the party protesting states the basis for the objection to the tax levy and a court later determines that the objection is valid. Even if the claim is determined to be valid for one party, other parties generally do not benefit from it.

The Assessment

One of the most familiar parts of the process of real estate taxation is the **assessment**, often done by a special government official with the title of **assessor**. The assessor's job is to determine the value of each parcel of real property within the local area, often a county, and, in some states, to adjust that value to a taxable base. The local assessor determines who owns each parcel of property and what the value of each parcel is. Before the 1970s, land was not reassessed frequently, but recently most areas are now being reassessed every four years. With increasingly sophisticated computer programs, it has become possible to reassess annually. This frequent reassessment ensures that the government has the strongest base for its income. The list of parcels, owners, and land values is often called either a **tax list** or an **assessment roll**.

The assessor may assess land at its market value or at an adjusted value that is a percentage of its market price. Either way, the tax rate is levied against that valuation. The actual means of assessing, which must be done by governmental officials and not professional appraisers, may be based on a current sales value of the land or of the whole property, including the building(s) on the property. However, some assessors determine the value of the land and the value of the building separately. The building value in this approach is reduced by the amount of accumulated depreciation on the building. After each separate value has been determined, the land's and building's values are added to reach a total amount for the assessment. Thus, it runs in the assessing formula of land plus depreciated value of the building(s) equals assessed value.

Although no lawyer practices exclusively in challenging assessments, there is a great deal of work done in appearing before the board that reviews the work of the local assessor. This **board of assessment** review can correct a factual error or make certain that the assessment methods and process are applied uniformly. One of the most frequent constitutional complaints against the assessor's results is that the assessment process has not been applied fairly (equally) so that there is an inequality of taxation between parties who own substantially similar parcels of land.

Another route a landowner may take is to apply for an exemption. For example, the following items are, in different parts of the country, permitted exemptions: new construction for a number of years; public property; not-for-profit property; and cemeteries. Before the landowner can sue the taxing authority, though, the legal rule concerning the exhaustion of remedies must be satisfied. Most states require that all administrative appeals be taken before suit may be brought; this rule means that the landowner must go to an appeal board, make her case, and get an unfavorable ruling from that board before she can sue the taxing authority. In some locations, there is more than one level of appeal board; one must exhaust *all* administrative remedies before going to court. This laborious and expensive process seems endless and discourages many persons from pursuing legitimate complaints.

Equalization

In the last few years, the issue of **equalization** has arisen in a number of states. In the technical usage of the term *equalization,* the process requires that a board of equalization determine whether an area's taxes are at essentially the same rate as those of surrounding taxing districts. If district A's assessor has placed the rates lower, then the board of equalization must adjust A's rate upward to match the other districts. The reverse can also occur (but, realistically, seldom if ever does). Equalization's basic concept is to have the tax rates be roughly equal among the various taxing districts in an area and across a state.

LEGAL TERMS

levy
Local government's imposition of a tax of a particular amount on a particular parcel of land.

assessment
Valuation placed on a parcel of real property by the public assessor for the purpose of levying taxes on that property.

assessor
Local public official whose job is to determine the value of each parcel of real property in the area.

assessment roll (tax list)
List of real properties and their assessed valuations.

board of assessment
Board that reviews the work of the assessor and to which parties who feel aggrieved over their assessments may appeal.

equalization
Process whereby a Board of Equalization raises or lowers property valuations so that they match the bases of other areas within the state or community.

A recent development in equalization that affects local real property taxes has been lawsuits brought in a number of states, such as California, Texas, and Illinois, to force the state legislatures to balance the funding for public schools between very wealthy districts and the poorest districts. Note that this equality is of income and not tax rate; nevertheless, it illustrates the problems concerning use of real property taxes and shows how concepts of equality have multiple meanings and usages. Ordinarily, the lower amount of revenue could be raised by imposing more taxes on the poorer district, but such areas usually lack the economic base on which to levy the tax.

Even with the taxes equalized, there is still a significant difference in the amount of money available for education in the wealthy suburbs and the poverty-stricken inner-city districts. No amount of adjustment in real estate taxes will change that situation, and some states have had to take special steps to remedy this problem. The source of the problem is found in the equal protection clause of the Fourteenth Amendment and similar state constitutional provisions providing that the laws shall apply equally to all citizens. This situation points to the real estate tax as a possible anachronism, based on a very different society and economy than the one in which we operate today, and indicates a continuing need to find adequate sources for funding public schools (and other local governmental entities).

Following the equalization process, the tax must be computed by taking the rate and multiplying it times the assessed value of the real property being taxed. For example, a single-family home may carry an assessed value of $82,950 (although its market value may be substantially higher). The cumulative tax rate in this year is .08928. When these two figures are multiplied, the tax is $7,405.78 for that year. After this tax is recorded, it becomes a lien upon the property. A tax lien is usually superior to most, and sometimes all, other claims against the property. That lien may be satisfied in one of two ways. Normally, the owner pays the tax upon receipt of the annual or semiannual bill. At that time, the official in charge of collecting the taxes may issue a receipt and also files an entry showing the tax paid in the public records. If the property tax is not paid, however, an outside party may pay the tax and then acquire the property for the amount of the unpaid tax. This device, despite all the delays for redemption rights, has been heavily criticized in the last 30 years. If the real estate owner redeems the property, and the records show that the prior taxes have been paid, any subsequent transferee can probably rely upon that record and the redemption certificate to protect his purchase from the party who redeėmed the property.

12.3 COLLECTION OF UNPAID TAXES

Failure to pay the assessed taxes is a serious matter, for it can cause the local authorities to sell the property at a tax sale. At a **tax sale** the property may be purchased, usually for the amount of the outstanding unpaid taxes due at the time of sale. The party in default for not paying the taxes (the real property owner) must be given notice of the sale. The property owner generally has the right to contest the sale based on a defense or a claim of illegality in the tax (as mentioned in § 12.2), but often does not. If the landowner loses the suit, a court will enter a judgment against the owner and order the property sold. Thereafter, the sheriff or another local official posts (publishes) the notice of the sale, these days in a newspaper of general circulation. At the sale, someone may buy the property for the amount of delinquent taxes and have the sheriff issue a sale certificate. This property may be redeemed within a legally specified time period ranging from six months to several years.

After the statutorily mandated time, if no redemption has been made, a document called a **tax deed** is issued to the purchaser. The problem with titles acquired in this manner is that in many states they are subject to attack and defeat when any technical aspect is wrong. These titles are also viewed with disfavor by many courts, for they seem to be inequitable and they offend against the ancient equitable maxim that the law abhors a forfeiture. In short, they represent a process that appears to permit an unjust enrichment of the tax-sale purchaser. No lender foreclosing on a mortgage would be permitted to retain the value of the property in excess of the mortgage. But through a government process? Some states, however, permit tax deeds to transfer good title.

In this sale process, however, if there is a loan and mortgage against the property, the mortgagee (lender) must be, in some way, notified of the sale if the subsequent sale transfer is to invalidate the mortgagee's claims. Realistically, in most cases, the mortgagee will buy the property if the equities are substantial in order to protect its own interest. A junior mortgage holder, however, may be in a different position, because the tax lien often has a superior claim under the law, so that the junior mortgagee holder's interest may be destroyed.

12.4 LOCAL TAXES AND EASEMENTS

Another interesting legal area deals with the problem of easements in relation to tax payments and tax sales. If the easement is essential to the dominant tenement, such as an easement to enter the property, the owner of the dominant tenement is placed in a difficult position if state law provides that all easements are destroyed in a tax sale. What alternatives does the owner have? She can proceed to watch the taxes on the servient tenement herself, and pay them if they fall into default, or she can require written proof annually that the taxes have been paid—a copy of a cancelled check or a receipt from the taxing authority. The owner of the dominant tenement, however, will not want to fund the taxes for the servient tenement over a lengthy time; it is, therefore, essential that she have the specified right, in the easement agreement, to foreclose and sell the servient easement for the unpaid taxes. Many states have avoided this problem by adopting a different theory

LEGAL TERMS

tax sale
Procedure by which the local government, usually through its sheriff, sells a parcel of real estate for delinquent taxes.

tax deed
Means of transferring title to real property after the parcel has been sold for taxes and after the period for redemption has expired.

concerning easements. In these states, the dominant tenement is seen as benefiting from the easement; therefore, the subservient tenement's value should be reduced by the value of the easement, while that easement's value is added to the taxable value of the dominant easement. Consequently, the easement would be preserved because the taxes on the easement would be paid by the owner of the dominant tenement as part of that annual tax.

12.5 TAXES AND THE FORM OF LEGAL ORGANIZATION SELECTED

Another aspect of tax law relates to the selection of the form of organization for real estate investors. Generally, two types of organization are available to a group of investors. The first is the partnership; the second, the corporation. In the corporation, problems of federal taxation can arise, because the corporation's earnings can be subject to double taxation. The corporation's earnings are taxed first to the corporation and then taxed again as income to the shareholder—and the expenses of the corporation cannot be taken as expenses by the individual investors. Countering this problem of double taxation is the corporation's advantage of limited shareholder liability. Investors are not liable for the obligations of the corporation beyond the money they have already invested in their purchase of shares. Nevertheless, by satisfying the Internal Revenue Service's requirements for Subchapter S filings, one may take advantage of limited liability and avoid double taxation, because under Subchapter S corporate profits are taxed solely to the shareholders; the corporation itself is not taxed. The requirements for an S corporation are: (1) that it have 35 or fewer shareholders; (2) that it have only one class of stock issued; (3) that all shareholders be American citizens or residents; and (4) that the corporation be an American (domestic) corporation.

Another federal tax rule that affects real estate sales is the requirement, since enactment of the Tax Reform Act of 1986, that the contract sales price be reported to the Internal Revenue Service. This provision was discussed in detail in chapter 5.

12.6 DEFERRING FEDERAL TAXES ON HOME SALES

Because of the rapid increase in the price of homes in the last 20 or so years, there can be a great deal of gain on the home when the owner sells it. Several tax provisions relate to handling these taxable gains. First, if the seller is over 55 years of age, $125,000 of gain may be deferred when he sells his principal residence. This deferral may be taken only once in a lifetime. Another tax deferral device, called a *tax deferred exchange,* may be used if the property is traded for another property of equal value. The tax on property is deferred until the property received in the trade is sold. A third tax deferral is involved when the seller of a property "trades up." In other words, the seller must buy a more expensive home than the property she sold, and must make that purchase within two years of an already existing building. The gain must be reported to the Internal Revenue Service, but payment of taxes on the gain can be deferred until the new home is sold, if the owner does not trade up again.

12.7 INTERNAL REVENUE SERVICE REAL PROPERTY CATEGORIES

Taxation of real property under the Internal Revenue Code, through the Internal Revenue Service (IRS), also depends on the category into which the property falls. There are four categories, each tied to a different function. It is the function, or use, of the property, not the piece of real estate itself, that is important from the IRS's point of view, because the Service treats property in relation to its business use, that is, the use that generates taxable income.

Some persons are involved in handling real property on a turnover basis. They buy it and sell it. Their holding of property is like any businessperson's inventory and their property is thus treated as inventory. It is property held for sale by persons considered dealers in property. In this situation, no special treatment such as depreciation is permitted. Remember that **depreciation** is the recognition of the decline in value of expensive, long-term investments, such as buildings and equipment, that is treated as a business expense. The amount of annual depreciation is frequently arrived at by dividing the purchase value of the property by the remaining life of the property (for example, a $100,000 property with a 20-year lifespan would get a $5,000 annual depreciation deduction on the straight line method). See chapter 6.

Other persons use their real property as a part of their business. They may own the land and building out of which a business operates. Business use can range from a factory that covers many acres to an office condominium used for selling real estate. Persons who use or rent out the real property that they own, such as leasing a store or an apartment, are using the property as a business asset. Because the property is handled as an asset and is not used as a rapid turnover inventory item, depreciation and ordinary business expenses relating to the property can be deducted as part of the business's operating expenses.

Some investors have long recognized that real property can be purchased and held in anticipation of a higher eventual resale price. This holding is considered an investment use. Examples are purchasing vacant lots in an area where builders will probably want to create new homes or offices within a few years, or buying a condominium in a resort area with the hope that its value will rise within a reasonable time. A small amount of income during the period the property is held does not remove the property from an investment category into a business or rental category. However, because the property is not regarded as income property (the

LEGAL TERMS

depreciation
Method to account for the declining value of fixed assets and take the annual amount of decline as a business expense.

income being incidental to the main purpose of holding for appreciated value), it is not possible to take depreciation of the property. Finally, interest payments can be set off against the income only to the extent of the income received.

Real property used personally as a place to live, such as a home, receives a different tax treatment. Interest is deductible, but depreciation is inapplicable, and there are special rules relating to any sale or exchange.

12.8 TAXATION AND THE SALE OF REAL PROPERTY

The sale of real property must be considered in two ways. The first way is a cash sale and the second way is an installment sale. The problem is simple. If one sells one's property, especially one's home, for cash, the amount of tax due is substantial. That large tax bite has at least two complications. First, it can be difficult to obtain the cash to make the tax payment because, despite the large amount of cash apparently available, there are also many other demands on that money, especially the purchase of a new place to live. At this point, deferral can occur, as discussed in § 12.6. But some sellers need the cash, or desire to live in a smaller home (possibly for easier maintenance or because the departure of children has made the larger space unneeded). What can the sellers do? Second, sellers would naturally prefer to keep as much of the home's increase in value as possible for themselves, rather than contributing substantially to the federal government's cash flow.

The method that can avoid some of these effects is the installment sale. An installment sale occurs over more than a year, typically over a longer time period of up to five or more years. Payments are made in each year. Note, however, that there is additional risk in an installment because one cannot always be sure the party who owes the money will always be able to make the payment when it is due. Consider the following example.

Harlan and Alicia Brown are selling their home. They will receive $300,000 for the property. They have held it for 15 years and seen its market price rise from $125,000 to $300,000. They have added $75,000 in improvements to the home. As a result, they will have to pay taxes on the $100,000 of gain. Omitting the possible deferments mentioned earlier in this chapter, note what this entails. The Browns are in a top tax bracket anyway and will have to pay, say, 31 percent of the gain. This gain would mean a tax of $31,000 due in the year of the sale. Wisely, the Browns take a 10-year installment payment schedule in which the buyer pays $30,000 a year. The taxable gain each year would only be $3,100, a much easier amount to pay. Finally, if for some reason the Browns' income dropped into a lower tax rate category, the lower tax rate would apply to the installment payment made in that year, and that lower rate would reduce the tax payments even more.

12.9 OTHER REAL ESTATE TAXES

In addition to the normal taxes on the parcel of real property and the income taxes that accrue at the time of sale, there may also be **special assessment taxes** and taxes levied on the sale of property, called **transfer** or **recording taxes**. The special assessment tax is common where the community is being repaired or improved through the replacement or building of such items as sewers and roads. These taxes are handled in the normal manner, through the local authorities. Although the property owner may pay the entire assessment in one payment, the more usual method is to pay the assessment off over a period of time (often up to 10 years) at a standard rate of interest. The amount of any one property owner's assessment is generally a pro rata share of the entire amount. For instance, a street has six homes on it. When new sewers are laid, each landowner may be assessed one-sixth of the total cost or the proportion of the linear feet of sewer passing her home in relation to the total linear feet. Thus, if the total number of linear feet was 480 and the owner in question had a 40 foot frontage, that person's ratable amount would be 40 ÷ 480, or 8.33 percent of the total amount. If the cost of the project was $60,000, our owner would owe about $5,000, payable either as a lump sum or as an additional $500 plus interest per year.

The transfer or recording tax applies when the property is sold and tax stamps on the sale of the property must be obtained. This cost is borne by the buyer because it is the buyer who wishes to record his deed to protect himself. Without payment of the tax, no recordation will be done. This tax detail is usually handled by the parties doing the closing and appears as a separate item on the closing settlement sheet.

Tax considerations can be a crucial element in transferring real property. The tax area constantly changes because Congress has not been certain what social policies it wishes to pursue. One of those policies regards the single-family home ownership as a desirable goal for most Americans. Traditionally, urban dwellers were renters until the New Deal in the 1930s. Then, the government massively subsidized the savings and loan and the banking industries with deposit guarantees and low interest rates, so that there were ample funds for home building. Since deregulation of the banking industry, this cheap money has disappeared, and new single-family homes have been priced out of the reach of many Americans. This change may have been unintended, but one can never be certain. Thus, the impact of changes in social policy regarding home ownership within the last 15 years has been significant.

Secondly, the influence of special interest groups seeking legislation that will assist them in operating their businesses has also played a major role in the development of the tax law for real property. Some parties have argued that the recession in the real estate business in the early 1990s is partly due to the removal of tax breaks for certain types of real estate investment in the late 1980s. Regardless of the source of the change, real estate is not the golden tax benefit area that it was prior to the 1980s. Current trends and legislation should be followed closely.

LEGAL TERMS

special assessment tax
Tax levied for a special purpose, such as replacing sewers; imposed only on those who benefit, not the general public.

recording tax (transfer tax)
Tax paid to record the deed of transfer; usually paid by the buyer.

DISCUSSION AND REVIEW QUESTIONS

1. List the different areas of tax law that can affect real estate transactions.
2. Describe how the actual amount of tax is determined.
3. Explain what "double taxation" is and how to avoid it.
4. How would one object to what one felt was an unfair tax bill?
5. Explain the process of establishing the annual tax on local real estate parcels.

CHAPTER 13
Ethics and the Paralegal

"The illegal we do immediately. The unconstitutional takes a little longer."

Henry Kissinger

Tudor-style house

OUTLINE

PROLOGUE TO THE PARALEGAL

Ethics are difficult because they usually involve at least two possible actions, each of which can be good, but each of which conflicts with the other. This conflict can be small and ignored or it can lead to bitter division and conflict. America as a society has long had a peculiar attitude toward ethics—it preaches ethics in demanding terms, but often ignores them in practice. Perhaps some ethical demands exceed the capacity of some people to meet those standards. Whatever the reason, ethics remains a very difficult and often confusing area; few professional areas have been subject to as much ethical discussion and criticism as the law.

The area of real estate has always abounded with ethical dilemmas, from the "claim jumper" during the settler days to the person who staked a claim before the appropriate time—a "sooner." Stories about speculation, selling swamp land in Florida, and other real estate areas of dubious ethical status have passed into American folklore. Not only must paralegals resist coming down on the wrong side of the conflict between greed and ethics, but they must also recognize the problems they will encounter when working in the legal profession. Some of these daily dilemmas are discussed in this chapter.

13.1 INTRODUCTION

It has long been said that the legal profession and ethics have had an extraordinarily wary relationship with one another. One reason for this apparent conflict between the law and ethics is that discussions of ethics are abstract and deal only with what ought to be; the law must make the best of the situation in which it finds itself, a situation in which real people live and operate. Perfection is unattainable in conflicting situations. The resolution of a legal conflict usually leaves both parties somewhat dissatisfied with what they got.

The charges of unethical behavior against the legal profession have sounded loudly since the profession began. The legal profession in ancient Rome was regarded as a collection of slick talkers and thieves. After the Dark Ages had ended in England and France, attorneys (an old French word for "agent") appeared as agents of the rich and powerful and were hated by the weak and the poor.

The reasons for this fierce, continuing contempt for the legal profession and all who work within it are many. First, a few members of our profession have not displayed the purest of ethics (in short, they have stolen or abused their positions of trust). Second, half of the litigants lose when a case finishes winding its leisurely way through the legal system. This situation leaves at least half the participants feeling that they have been misused, at best. And many of the victors felt that they achieved only a Pyrrhic victory, which got them nothing meaningful in relation to their sufferings except having to pay a fee for their attorneys. As a result, many participants feel that they just were not treated fairly by the legal system.

Third, the legal process both takes a long (almost interminable) time and is hideously expensive. These factors make it difficult for a middle-class or poor person to use the system. This economic differentiation creates the fourth reason—there are in actuality two legal systems, one for the rich and one for the poor. Court access is based primarily upon the money you have, and that does not seem fair to most people.

Fifth, the legal system is an expression of power in many ways. People differ tremendously in how they respond to power and its use. Some are frightened of it and believe that it is inherently corrupting to any who use it (recall Lord Acton's famous dictum, "Power tends to corrupt and absolute power corrupts absolutely."). Others find power a delight; former Secretary of State Henry Kissinger has been quoted as saying, "Power is the great aphrodisiac." It turns people on and enlivens their lives. Being involved in power situations involves risks and potential losses, but power is necessary and is an inherent part of life. Much of the purpose of the law has been to contain the risks associated with the use of power.

Society has reached a consensus that certain types of risks should not be permitted, should not occur, or should be borne by the society at large instead of by individuals personally. The earliest type of risk that the law tried to control was that of physical violence to person and property. These acts, which range from murder to various types of theft, are ones that cannot be permitted if society is to continue to operate. Today, this consensus has spread to other areas, such as the environment and the violence that human activity has done to it. Every time we change the allocation of risks in our society, we redistribute social, economic, or political power. The legal profession is generally involved in that process from beginning (creating the law) to the end (tailoring the law's enforcement procedures).

Much of the basis of the law, particularly the earliest types such as criminal, tort, and contract law, is concerned with methods of punishing violent acts and avoiding disputes that could become violent. In a sense, then, the law serves as a sewer system for society to prevent or remove the violent wastes from its social life and to effect the changes in power from one group or institution to another with the least amount of violence possible. Contrast the relatively small amount of violence over social issues in our society with the periodic upheavals in which millions of people die in war, famine, and other avoidable forms of violent death. But having workers in any sewer—particularly one that possesses extraordinary potential for power—means that some of the muck sticks to the workers, be they judges, lawyers, or paralegals.

13.2 THE IMPACT OF BUSINESS ON LEGAL ETHICS

Another factor that creates great stress on the demands for ethical behavior is the competitive business environment. Although modern capitalism has proven more capable in providing goods and services than any previously known economic system, its successes have created serious ethical problems. The focus of these ethical problems appears to have two aspects, which are deeply interrelated. The first is the competitive factor and the second is the capitalist practice of almost continuous economic change.

First is competition. Competition has benefits, in that it produces better products at a cheaper price. But, like many things, competition is not an unalloyed blessing—it has its dark side as well. Competition seeks to eliminate other competitors. Thus, its goal appears to be monopoly and complete dominance of a market. At this point, however, protests from citizens who feel themselves threatened frequently prompts government intervention to prevent the elimination of competition.

Second, the process of continuous economic change upon which capitalism has thrived for over 500 years may have brought about a different set of market conditions and eliminated any need for government intervention. Any monopoly over the production of buggy whips in 1910 had become irrelevant by 1930, because cars had replaced buggies. More recently, the compact disc virtually replaced the long-play vinyl record. Domination of the market that made the vinyl rapidly became meaningless after 1985. These changes in public taste, quality, and products create intense pressures on business people and their attorneys to find a way to get some advantage—whatever it is—that will help in the continuous struggle of the competitive process. Competitors always seek an edge on what appears to be inevitable change, so that when the change comes, it can be a competitive ally rather than a destructive enemy. In this cauldron of driven hope for success and fear of failure, ethics often becomes situational, pragmatic, and focused on success and survival rather than ideals. The business person frequently articulates this way of seeing the problem by expressing a real concern for profits; profitability becomes the ethics of survival in business. Little concern for other ethical niceties can be expressed under this kind of pressure. People are replaceable, and some attorney can be found to do the job—at some cost, financial and ethical. The ethical dilemma becomes how to handle ethics when one's economic survival is being threatened. Or is ethics merely a concern for the rich and successful, or those whose survival is not under immediate threat?

The legal profession's attempt to control how attorneys operate in this social setting has two formal focuses. The American Bar Association has canons of ethics that set standards for professional behavior. Most state bars do as well. Sometimes these standards are called ethical codes or rules of professional responsibility. These standards may be enforced by disciplinary proceedings against any party accused of violating the rules.

Clever, dishonest, and antisocial people can and do get around these rules and disciplinary procedures. When people are more concerned about making money for themselves than about maintaining society's bonds or the public good, there will be less adherence to ethical standards. You should recognize that these two approaches—focus on society's welfare and focus on the individual's welfare—go in cycles that have alternated with one another throughout American history. After the antisocial behavior of the 1970s and 1980s, a return of more socially responsible behavior seems likely, if past American attitudes and behavior provide any guide to the present. During either cycle, however, there will always be attorneys operating as if they were in the opposite cycle.

Awareness of this social setting for the law may help reduce some of the easy cynicism about the legal profession. But law, of some sort, appears essential, for without a legal system, there would be a state of anarchy, which would probably benefit only those temporarily strongest and which would be devoid of any ethics at all. It is also easy to take cheap shots at the law, as Shakespeare has a drunken character, frequently cited by attorney haters, in his play, *Henry IV, Part II,* do by saying, "The first thing we do, let's kill all the lawyers." (Note that this play is set almost 600 years ago!) But the law is an essential component for maintaining our society—a necessary evil, if you will—because the society upon which we depend could not operate without the law. To reduce the negative aspects of the law's operation, the bar association's standards set a framework for daily activity.

13.3 THE PROBLEM OF PRACTICING LAW

What are some of the standards of ethical behavior to which a paralegal and the attorneys with whom the paralegal associates will be held? Because a paralegal is an adjunct person in the eyes of the law's ethical standards, a paralegal cannot engage in the practice of law. The reasoning behind this attitude is simple. Attorneys have spent four years in college and then three years in law school obtaining an education, which, with their practical experience, should provide them with the skills to determine how best to represent the client. Paralegals have not had that type of academic training and thus are not licensed to provide legal advice.

One of the most important reasons that a paralegal is not permitted to practice law, even though the paralegal may have detailed knowledge and immense experience, is the possible consideration and application of other relevant areas of the law. The breadth and depth of the attorney's training provide certain skills of analysis and knowledge of other potentially applicable areas of the law that are outside the information base of even the most experienced paralegal. These areas could be crucial to the success or failure of the transaction. Thus, it might not be in the best interest of clients for the paralegal to handle their materials to an extent that would constitute the practice of law.

Nevertheless, there will undoubtedly be times when the paralegal knows the material as well as or better than the attorney with whom the paralegal is working. This level of skill can develop from the paralegal's training and experience. Nevertheless, for overall professional legal skills, the attorney must be deferred to and no attempt should be made to replace his or her skills with those of a paralegal.

Many times, the work of the paralegal will overlap with the work of the attorney. In most states, it is against the canons of professional ethics for an attorney to assist a nonattorney in the practice of law. In the practical world, however, this apparent conflict is often resolved by the attorney assuming the responsibility for closely supervising the paralegal's work product and taking ultimate responsibility for the work of the paralegal. Thus, although it might be illegal for a paralegal to prepare legal documents for a real estate closing without having them closely reviewed by an attorney knowledgeable in the field, if that supervision exists, the work of the paralegal should not create any problem regarding the unauthorized practice of law. The paralegal and the supervising attorney should, however, at all times be alert to the problems of outside requests for information, documents, advice, or other third-party contact which could create the appearance of the paralegal practicing law without a license. This situation could arise if, after a request for information, the paralegal were actually to transmit any legal information, document, or advice without consultation with an attorney. The risk comes from clients who are either in a hurry to get an answer or who do not want to be billed for a short answer to such "a little question." *Caveat paralegum!*

13.4 CONFLICTS OF INTEREST

A conflict of interest can arise through misunderstanding or merely from ignorance of the rules of the legal representation game. First, exactly what is a conflict of interest? It is having an attorney accept the responsibility for representing one client whose interests conflict with the interests of another client. In the real estate business, this definition would cover, for instance, representing both the buyer and the seller in a closing on a parcel of real property. Or it could involve a law firm representing a bank and either or both of the other parties to the closing. Although representing the seller and the bank might not create a real-world conflict of interest, representing the buyer-borrower and the prior bank definitely could create a massive mess. In either case, there is a conflict of interest between the two parties, and no attorney should be involved in that type of situation.

The core of the problem of conflict of interest lies in the basis of our legal system, which is adversarial. How can an attorney represent a client whose interests are opposite from, hostile to, or in conflict with the interests of the other party? Clearly many clauses in real estate sales contracts and closing documents can be written to benefit one side over the other side. How could any attorney fairly represent both sides in such a situation? And what about privileged information? What is privileged on one side could be something that should be disclosed to the other. Clearly, conflict-of-interest situations are intolerable. A resolution of this problem is best handled by making certain, through written communication and discussion, that everyone associated with the transaction realizes who your firm represents, and that the other parties to the transaction would be best advised to obtain separate and independent counsel to protect their own interests. This notification should be done as soon as the parties to the transaction are clearly identified.

Sometimes conflicts of interest can be quite subtle, especially when there are extensive family or corporate relationships involved in multiple transactions. There is no safe way to handle these on a generic basis, except to remember that paralegals are particularly vulnerable in the system and should attempt to be, like Caesar's wife, "above suspicion." A check of one's childhood memory concerning what your original teacher of ethics—mother, father, religious leader—might have thought of the situation with which you are confronted might also help.

13.5 OTHER ETHICAL CONSIDERATIONS: CORRESPONDENCE

One of the most time-consuming legal tasks is correspondence, and the paralegal, under supervision, may well be delegated a number of responsibilities in this area. The paralegal must ensure that the letters she writes are never misinterpreted as letters from an attorney at the firm where she is working. If that were to occur, it would appear that the paralegal was practicing law without a license. This potential problem never need arise because, fortunately, recognition of the problem suggests the solution. The paralegal may have his own stationery preprinted, with his name and the title "paralegal," "legal assistant," or some other such indication that he is not an attorney printed on the page. This indication is particularly important for the page on which the signature of the paralegal appears. If the preprinted letterhead of the firm includes the name of the paralegal as a paralegal and is used for all of the paralegal's correspondence, the problem might be obviated. The other method is to make certain that the title "paralegal" or "legal assistant" is next to or below the signature line for every letter sent out on the firm's letterhead or on any writing that might represent the firm in any way as a expression of the legal work product of the firm. Each method has a drawback. For the large firm with many paralegals, preprinting all the names may be burdensome and expensive. On the other hand, it is possible accidentally to omit the paralegal's title by the signature. Appropriate caution must be maintained in either case.

13.6 CONFIDENTIALITY OF CLIENT INFORMATION

Concerns about the secrecy of client information should not have to be mentioned, but some people need reminding because they can be absent-minded, careless, or give in to a desire to show off and feel important. Any information about your firm's clients should be treated as utterly confidential, and should never be mentioned to anyone outside the firm without the prior written consent of the client and with the prior authorization of your supervising attorney. That is the safe rule. Sometimes, one acquires information about the client from outside the office. For the sake of the appearances of your firm and the kind of person you are, even information obtained in public ways or outside of the attorney-client relationship should be held in strictest confidence. The rationale for this complete confidentiality rule is clear. There must be trust between the attorney and the client; for that trust to be maintained, no information can be revealed.

It is not uncommon for a third party to call and ask for information concerning some aspect of a transaction involving a client. These calls cannot be handled in any way other than to refer them to your supervising attorney or to the client. After all, the law firm is merely the agent of the client and, under agency law, owes a duty of trust, discretion, and confidentiality concerning the principal's business. Although the attorney is frequently the more powerful party in many situations, it is best to remember that each attorney is usually an agent and almost never a principal. The client pays the bills and calls the shots.

13.7 WITNESSING DOCUMENTS

Many times, a paralegal will be asked to make a statement about who executed certain documents; in other words, to witness signatures. This process generally involves signing one's name to a document as a witness to state that one saw the signer of the document actually sign it. If the person signing as a witness did not see the person sign, it would be a violation of ethical standards to sign and indicate that the witness had seen it. Unfortunately, however, this area is very difficult to control. Of the ethical situations discussed here, it is the one most honored in the breach—the author has seen this rule violated innumerable times. It is rarely of any practical consequence, but it remains an unethical act. There is a famous true story of a man who came into a bank with his wife and borrowed a substantial sum of money, which was collateralized by the family home. Mortgage documents were *witnessed* and filed. Later, several short-term unsecured notes were signed by the husband and wife, and the lending officer then began making these short-term loans via telephone, with the signed notes mailed in shortly thereafter—all collateralized by the home. The signatures always matched. No problem, right? Unfortunately, such was not the case. When the loans fell into default, the bank called and talked to the wife, who knew nothing about them. All the time, it had been the husband's secretary who had been signing.

It can also be important to be certain that the parties introduced as Miss X or Mr. Y are who they represent themselves to be. Cautious lenders, after experiencing such fraud, thereafter instituted a two-part procedure in an attempt to avoid the problem. First, they requested photo identification, such as a driver's license; second, they began mailing to each party an advice of the transaction. You will have to determine with your supervising attorney the degree of caution you are expected to exercise and the firm's standards for witnessing. It is far preferable to establish the standards for witnessing before the situation arises rather than at the time of need. It might also serve to remind your attorney that you would not appreciate being put in a position where you were being asked to perform an unethical act.

13.8 GENERAL ETHICAL STANDARDS

In general, ethics requires us all to behave much like the perfect, proverbial Boy Scout or Girl Scout. Ethics may seem childish or idealistic, but the deepest social bonds are involved in ensuring ethical behavior, and so ethics should be rigorously adhered to. Most of us know what the appropriate ethical behavior is, but we may ignore it because of the pressures of time, profitability, the demands of the client or our employer, or for a variety of other reasons. Regardless of the temptations, it is never permissible to act in a manner that misrepresents or misleads, is fraudulent, or is dishonest. Alteration of documents or knowingly assisting someone to do something that is wrong is not only unethical, it could result in criminal responsibility as well.

Even the appearance of misconduct can be unethical. For instance, consider the following situation. Late one Friday afternoon, you are shopping at a local supermarket and encounter a client. Upon seeing you, the client's memory is jogged. He reaches into his coat, produces his wallet, and gives you a very substantial amount of money for the firm. Your partner is out of town and you do not know who to turn to, so you quickly deposit the money in your own account at the drive-up window, because you do not want such a large amount of cash sitting around over the weekend at home. This situation is extremely difficult, but the deposit of the money into your own account is termed "commingling funds," and that action is a violation of ethical standards.

What can one do, practically, without offending the client? It is most difficult to determine. Like most difficult ethical situations, there is a conflict between different goods. It is good to satisfy the client, it is good to protect the client's funds, and it is good not to commingle funds. In situations with conflicting goods, the legal assistant must make a choice to do the best possible for everyone involved and to minimize any possible damage. The client has placed the paralegal in an untenable situation. Perhaps the paralegal should not have accepted the money, or contacted another partner in the firm, or returned to deposit the money in the firm's safe (if feasible), or deposited the money in the firm's account (although a paralegal is unlikely to be able to do so in the real world). The paralegal must make a selection among a set of highly undesirable alternatives. Problems of alternative goods will arise at some time in all careers, and the paralegal should discuss this problem with her supervisor before the situation occurs, in a generic manner, and should inform that attorney or other supervisor (if the attorney is not available) the first thing on Monday morning, with money in hand.

Finally, a thought about a possible remedy for paralegals who feel frustrated about not being able to practice law. Obviously, the paralegal cannot. Period. What can be done? The obvious answer is to go back to school and attend law school. But the intense time commitment and the money required may make attending law school impossible. Another answer would be to lobby the legislatures to permit paralegals to practice law in some sort of limited manner. This change appears to be occurring in numerous states throughout the nation.

13.9 THE PROBLEM OF PRACTICING LAW WITHOUT A LICENSE

Notwithstanding the points made in §§ 13.3 and 13.7, it is possible that an older way of acquiring a law degree, permitted up until the 1950s or 1960s in most states, might be appropriate as a model in this situation. Today, in many states, the *only* way to obtain a legal degree is to graduate from college and attend a three-year law school. The older method, however, was called "reading for the bar." Under that method, a person working in the legal area studied the law with a licensed attorney and, upon completing the appropriate course of study, was permitted to take the bar examination for admission to the practice of law. But after World War II, in an attempt to upgrade the quality of the legal profession, this traditional method—by which Abraham Lincoln, among others, learned the law—was abolished, and all potential lawyers were required to graduate from a four-year college. As many paralegals have already achieved a B.A. or a B.S. degree, it might be appropriate to consider the possibility of reinstituting a program of reading for the bar for such paralegals. The problem, of course, would be to find an attorney who was willing to take the time and who had the knowledge and skills to teach a person who wanted to become an attorney. The time and energy restrictions involved in practicing law, and the increasing specialization of attorneys (despite all the claims about all lawyers knowing all the law—a humanly impossible task!) would make the task of covering all the material needed for passing the bar examination very difficult, but not necessarily impossible. Some states already permit this program. Check your local statutes.

DISCUSSION AND REVIEW QUESTIONS

1. In a major city in the Rust Belt, an area near the downtown business district, full of abandoned, old factories and warehouses, is under consideration for redevelopment. Right now, it is the city's Skid Row, and many transients live in these abandoned buildings. In recent years, there has been an epidemic of drug use in the area, and the police would not mind surrounding it, setting fire to it, and letting the whole area turn to ash. Real estate taxes are in arrears on almost all the properties. However, it is near parks and transportation, and sewer and water facilities are adequate or can be inexpensively upgraded. It appears to be an ideal situation for redevelopment, as there is ample space—several square miles—for the project. At this point, it is not a question of whether it will be redeveloped, but how, when, by whom, and into what type of development. Assuming that the area consists of 7.5 square miles or 4,800 acres, what considerations would be appropriate? What ethical problems could arise? (Some of these problems for condominiums are posed in the chapter on condominiums.) In other words, identify the conflicts that will arise and try to create priorities for the goals that are in conflict. Be able to explain your choices.
2. In the following situation, only the basic facts are laid out. Form a group of five to seven students in the class, take that situation, and create a problem of ethical dilemmas that you might encounter using the basic facts given. Create your own comments and evaluations of the ethical situation. Then exchange your fact situation with another group and have that group come up with its own comments, criticisms, and suggestions. Discuss both in class.

   The basic fact situation. As a paralegal working for a law firm that frequently represents a bank in numerous ways, including closings, you have come to know the lending officers and employees of the bank. Your firm also works with a number of other clients besides the bank. One of those clients wishes to get a loan from the bank. It is important for the law firm to keep each client happy.

APPENDIX A

How to Analyze and Understand a Legal Case

EPILOGUE TO THE PARALEGAL

Although you may have had discussions in other classes about analyzing cases, I have included in this appendix some materials that my students have found useful. If you have not had any discussion of this approach, I hope you will be able to use this five-pronged approach as an aid to your understanding of the common law. Case analysis can appear complex, and to most students it is a new way of thinking. Although many outside the legal profession scoff at "legal thinking," the process of understanding cases and thinking about legal issues is, at heart, no different from any other form of rational analysis. There are generalizations called rules (beginning to think from this side is called *deduction*) and it is necessary to determine where your facts fit into those rules (beginning to think from this side is called *induction* or the scientific method). The exact spot where that fit occurs is crucial for understanding and determining how legal analysis works.

The law focuses on identifying and understanding what courts call "the issue" because that is the spot where fact and rule meet. It does not matter whether you start with the rule and apply it to the facts or start with the facts and apply them to the rule. Understanding this process will take some initial work and continual fine-tuning of your thinking process, but its effects can reach beyond this class or your work. Once you begin using it, this method will become second nature to you and can help you in other aspects of understanding as well. It is one of western civilization's great intellectual tools and one of its foundations for determining reality.

DISCUSSION

When dispute arises between two parties, they often go to court to resolve it. This civil lawsuit has two parties: a plaintiff and a defendant.

(Neither of them is the state; that would be a criminal case.) The plaintiff brings the suit and files the action or complaint. After service of legal papers that notify the defendant that he is involved in the suit, the defendant files an answer or reply. If there is no settlement, a trial follows and concludes when one party wins. This result can be appealed. If it is, the appellate court often writes an opinion. Most, but not all, appellate court systems have two levels, intermediate and supreme courts. Both write opinions and only hear cases for which a result was already determined at the trial level. The following discussion explains what is going on in the written opinion of an appellate court.

Each opinion usually discusses one trial. First, the court will lay out the important facts in the case. These facts state the situation that gave rise to the lawsuit.[1] Second, the court will discuss what law is applicable to the facts in this case. Third, it will frame what is variously called the legal question or the legal issue. Fourth, the court will give its ruling or decision. Fifth, it will discuss its reasoning or rationale. (Note: the case you are reading may not follow this order exactly, but don't worry; it is all there.)

Note what is happening here. At the trial level, the facts were determined, and the appellate court is bound by that factual determination. Now the appellate court must decide if the trial court properly applied the law (sometimes called the legal rules) to these facts. The appellate court identifies the applicable law that fits this case's facts and then frames the legal issue(s) that the already determined facts and the appropriate legal rule(s) create.

Where does this law, or these legal rules, come from? Many of them came from past cases based on similar events (called *precedents* under our system of common law). They can also come from statutes, constitutions, or administrative rulings. Another way of describing what is happening is to say that certain sets of facts give rise to or trigger certain legal rules appropriate to this case. Therefore, to understand what legal results will occur, it is necessary to determine what legal rules fit the facts of a particular case. The overall legal issue is always this: What legal rule(s) apply here in this case, to this set of facts? Sometimes, more than one area of law can apply. For example, the law of agency describes the legal boundaries of the relationship between the principal and the agent—between one person and another person who is acting on her behalf. Corporate officers are agents of their corporation, a point that you will have to understand to work with condominiums and their boards of directors. In a case involving a corporate officer—say, of a real estate business—there could be applicable aspects of the law of real estate, the law of corporations, and the law of agency. Whatever law applies, the law chosen provides the *structure* in which the facts will operate, the issue will be framed, and the case will be decided. As a student, you must recognize the concepts (or legal rules) of the appropriate area of the law and determine how they connect to one another.

---

[1] In addition, some cases discuss the appropriate procedural aspects of the case, but most times discussion of procedure is not crucial and may be set aside. Do not get lost in a procedural discussion unless you determine that the case turns on a procedural issue.

Third, the court must decide the ways in which the selected area of law applies to the specific facts of this case. This task may be described as *framing the issue* or issues in the case. Framing the issue is also called legal analysis or legal reasoning. This thinking process combines both the deductive and the inductive aspects of thinking. Deductive thinking begins with the rules or the generalization and tries to fit facts (the specific) into the rule's patterns. Inductive thinking begins with the facts of the situation or case and asks what legal rules they create or lead to. This approach is the essential pattern of all rational or discursive thought. These two thinking processes merge into the framing of the issues of a case. It makes no difference where one starts in the thinking process, with the facts or the rules; the two processes meet in framing the issue of the case. The issue states what precise area of law applies to the facts of a particular case. Often the court identifies what the legal issue is. But many times the judge assumes that the reading audience (other lawyers) already understands the issue, or the judge does not frame it clearly. When you begin reading cases, read to understand three things: (1) the facts; (2) the applicable law; and (3) the issue(s) of the case—that is, how the judge applies the law to this case's facts.

When this preliminary work is done, the judge probably will discuss how each side argued the defined legal issues. In other words, the judge will discuss what the issues are and explain what each side argued that the framing of the important issues should be. After these matters are completed, the judge will set out the court's decision. Sometimes, the judge will make extra comments that do not directly relate to this case's issues. Do not be mislead by these extra comments; they are called "dicta," from the Latin phrase *obiter dicta,* meaning "other words." Dicta are not directly relevant, although they are often interesting. Finally, woven into the discussion will be the court's rationale for its decision (also called the reasoning of the court). Generally, the court will explain why it believed this set of facts called for these legal rules and not other ones; it will discuss and explain why these issues required this decision. This written explanation is the fundamental basis for the common law. Cases are published to be read by other lawyers and used as precedent in other courts when a similar set of facts arises in the future.

Let us take a simple example in real estate to demonstrate how this process works. The owner of a piece of property in fee simple has the most extensive possible rights in the property. *Fee simple* is the legal term that means, essentially, complete ownership rights to a parcel of real property. All other ownership rights in real property are lesser ones—one of which will be introduced shortly. Among these fee simple rights is the right to transfer (or *alienate*) the property to someone else. Let us say that A owns Blackacre (the standard name lawyers use for a hypothetical piece of real property) in fee simple. In 1974, A gives the property to his son, Joe, but he knows that Joe likes wine, women, and song; he suspects that Joe will not be prudent and careful with his use of Blackacre. He grants Blackacre to Joe in what appears to be fee simple, but with a condition—"to Joe and his heirs [the formal, legal language that grants a fee simple] *so long as he does not sell the property for 20 years.*" So far, so good—but note the grant language in the prior sentence. What legal rule does it evoke? This language creates a type of estate that is not a fee simple, but a different and lesser estate called a *conditional fee.* A conditional fee has the same freedom of use as a fee simple *except* that the person getting the property must comply with the condition to keep the property. If the grantee does not comply with the condition, the property goes back (or *reverts*) to the grantor or his heirs. The potential of the property returning to the grantor is called a possibility of reverter. Joe's condition prohibits him from selling Blackacre for 20 years. Therefore, A has given Joe a conditional fee with a possibility of reverter.

Now, add another fact. Joe sold the property to B in 1990 and died on May 3, 1991. The general question is: Who owns Blackacre? Does Joe? No, he sold it. Did Joe have the right to sell Blackacre? No, because only 16, not 20, years had passed; Joe's interest did not mature into a fee simple with free alienability until the 20 years had passed. When he sold it, it was still a fee conditional. Can his heirs own Blackacre? No, they cannot take what Joe disposed of prior to his death. Can B? He bought it. But since Joe could not sell it, how does B get Blackacre? Joe purported to transfer title; he gave a deed that he was legally unable to grant. Why? Because the moment he sold the property, he violated the condition in the granting language that gave him the property. The property snaps right back (or reverts) to A or, if he is dead, to A's heirs. There is a high probability of a lawsuit among A (or his heirs if he has died), B, and Joe's estate and Joe's heirs, because A or his heirs have the legal right to the property, but B has held title to Blackacre since the transfer, and B presumably paid for Blackacre and wants to keep it or get his money back.

Finally, Joe's estate or heirs may be involved in one of several ways. First, because Joe got money for the sale, either his estate or his heirs has those remaining funds, and B may try to find a way to get them. Second, Joe's heirs may have an interest in Blackacre, because they are also descendants of A (and his heirs too) and therefore may have rights under the reverted Blackacre.

Note a final fact: Joe's death on May 3, 1991. It is an interesting fact, but irrelevant to determining the issue here. However, this fact explains why the case title (B v. A) does not have Joe's name on it and why Joe's estate (rather than Joe) is involved.

How do we frame the issue in this case? Different phrasings are possible, but it is important to identify the elements to be included. First, who can be or is involved? A, B, Joe, and possibly the heirs of A or Joe. What is involved? The ownership of Blackacre. What law is involved? Real estate. What area of real estate? The type of estate or title that Joe received from A and that Joe passed to B. What type of a transaction is involved? The sale of Blackacre.

The issue may now be framed in this manner: What is the legal effect of an attempt to transfer real estate title when that transfer violates a condition specified in the language of the deed that granted the fee? Once the issue is framed, the result usually follows. Because framing the issue often determines the outcome of the case, thinking the issue through carefully and clearly is crucial to doing an appropriate job of legal analysis. Note that a court's reasoning usually relates to its framing of the legal issues rather than its result, unless there are issues of social policy that the court is enunciating as new law.

In summary, there are five elements to look for in a case. They are (1) the facts; (2) the legal rules; (3) the way the facts and the rules connect, called the legal issue; (4) the court's decision; and (5) the court's reasoning or explanation that justifies that decision.

Good luck in reading cases. They can be a lot of fun. Not only can they give you a lot of information about the law and the society in which it operates, but also, by pursuing the law's analytical aspects, reading cases can help you learn to think more clearly.

APPENDIX B

Answers to Discussion and Review Questions

CHAPTER 1

1. Buying and selling real estate and finding new, better, and enhanced ways to use real estate. Real estate, considered in this way, is a commercial commodity that is subject to the laws of economics.
2. Yes. The long-term uses of the land should be considered as well. The effects of use and development of the land on the environment require careful consideration. This area of concern can create great conflicts when dealing with land as a commodity and in purely economic terms. Many times the environmental effects are very long-term and immensely expensive to recognize completely and deal with adequately.
3. Air rights, surface rights, and subsurface rights.
4. The owner has the right to (1) possess the property—that is, to occupy it and determine who may come onto the property;
   (2) control the property—that is, to determine how others may use it, as in a leasing arrangement, or whether anyone else may use it;
   (3) enjoy the property—that is, to use in any manner which is within the law; and
   (4) dispose of the property—that is, to sell it, give it away, or pass it by will.
5. Real estate is (1) immobile, (2) indestructible, and (3) unique.
6. Real property is the bundle of legal rights that relate to a parcel of real estate. Personal property is everything else, and is characterized by being movable. Personal property may be either tangible or intangible.
7. Real estate is a scarce commodity. Because it cannot be created, the supply is limited to what is in existence.

   Real estate requires a permanent investment. It is expensive to acquire, improve, and maintain. The funds enter the property and stay in it.

Site preference is one of the crucial aspects of real estate economics, because it is the strongest single factor in determining the use, and therefore the price, of the real estate.

8. (1) Residential, (2) business, (3) rural, (4) special purpose, and (5) public.
9. (1) Residential use of real estate is for places in which people will live.
(2) Business real estate is for engaging in activities that will (it is hoped) create a profit. These can range from real estate management offices to factories to law firms to shopping centers.
(3) Rural real estate is for farms, ranches, many recreational facilities, and land near cities that is not being used and may be ripe for development.
(4) Special purpose real estate often has not-for-profit activities, such as churches, schools, and hospitals, on it.
(5) Public land use is widespread and ranges from owning unoccupied desert in Nevada to Fort Leavenworth in Kansas to the U.S. Capitol and the White House in Washington, D.C.
10. These economic rules provide patterns for understanding how real estate as a market operates. The overall real estate market across the United States is broken down into smaller local markets that are subdivided by price and use of the property. Within each of these markets, the laws of supply and demand function so that the greater the demand, the greater the supply. However, real estate response to increased demand cannot be achieved overnight, because of the time it takes to create buildings. There is, therefore, a lag time between increased demand and increased supply. This time difference can cause major problems in the industry.

These two elements, supply and demand, each affect price to some degree. The smaller the supply, the smaller the amount available for sale, and the higher the price. The reverse is also true: the larger the supply, the lower the price. These rules work until the demand is satisfied. Price is not wholly a function of supply and demand, however. There are what are called inelasticities in price, due to built-in costs and built-in demand. An inelasticity is a situation in which the market does not respond freely to supply and demand, because of other limiting factors. As a result of either or both of these, prices will not drop severely in a normal market decline, but if no buyers can be found, the prices will drop, not merely decline.

CHAPTER 2

1. A *fixture* is a piece of property that begins as personal property (usually equipment) and becomes so closely and permanently attached to real property that it is considered to be real property. Its attachment to real property is so close that it usually cannot be separated from the real property without substantial physical damage being done to the real property or impairing the function of the piece of real property.

Risks with fixtures relate to who owns the fixture, and that question turns on whether the fixture has retained its personal property aspects or has clearly become part of the real property. Parties who can be involved are not only the commercial business tenant and the landlord, but their respective financiers of the business and of the purchase of the real estate, both of whom would want the disputed property for its collateral value and have legal documentation to support their claims. Much of the risk can be avoided by proper planning, notifying, and obtaining waivers prior to installation of the fixture/equipment item.

The heating, plumbing, and electrical systems would be fixtures in a building; in a residential building, the dishwasher, toilets and bath equipment, as well as the sink, would be fixtures. Any piece of equipment that was substantial and closely involved in the nature of the business would have a claim to be equipment, but if it was also very large, awkward to handle, heavy, and expensive, so that it was difficult to install in the building, or if the building were built around the piece of equipment, it could be a fixture and disputed by each side.

2. a. The government survey or rectangular method employs surveying based upon the meridians and parallels of the earth's surface grid. It begins by choosing an intersection between meridians and parallels and proceeds to measure, in declining patterns, the spaces for checks or quadrangles to townships to sections to acres, for a precisely identifiable area. It may be supplemented in urban areas by developers' plats of survey or the metes and bounds method, in areas that have an irregular boundary.
   b. The metes and bounds method uses monuments, or points of reference, to describe the reference points around the perimeter of the property. A monument may be either a natural object, such as a rock or a tree, or a manmade one, such as a highway.
   c. A plat of survey is the method used by a developer who is working within an area of limited acreage (usually in an urban area) to describe the layout of the development and how it ties into the general surveying system. The plat delineates the development project and identifies everything in it (buildings, sewers, roads, etc.), and ties the whole plat into a larger surveying system, such as the rectangular survey method. This method is also called the *lot and block method* in some areas. The plat document is registered with the appropriate public official and remains on file for anyone to examine.
3. The rectangular survey method is superb for a rural setting where large amounts of land are described, but within the confines of urban landholding, the legal description becomes difficult to follow, because of the repetition of similar terms, excessive length, and general awkwardness. The metes and bounds system can be unreliable if the monuments are removed, but it is possible to survey a plot of ground precisely with those monuments the first time, establish surveying points, and then repeat the

process at any time, because that survey can be publicly registered and made available for future use.

4. Recording statutes are important because they are designed to provide public notice of ownership rights and claims against ownership of real property. Because the law imputes constructive notice to all parties when there is a recording or filing system, the only way to protect one's interest is to record as soon as possible. Failure to record can have severe consequences that could affect or even deny one's rights or claims in the real property.
5. Several different systems are used for recordation purposes. The first is the grantor-grantee index, in which the parties are listed alphabetically. The second is a tract index, in which the transactions (the recordings) are tied to each parcel of real property, so that checking is done by legal description. The third principal system is the mortgagor-mortgagee index, which lists all the creditors and debtors alphabetically.
6. Although in some states the Torrens System seems to work adequately, in others it is a disfavored, expensive, time-consuming process whereby the title is protected by a court legal proceeding each time there is a transfer of title or lien put on the property. All parties are sued, and the court determines the appropriate claims and orders an official to register the title.
7. A compass reading indicates a direction that a line will travel on the face of the globe; it is taken from a given point. A map reading, in a metes and bounds description, for instance, may use those compass readings in tracing the boundaries of a particular parcel of property. Most map readings, however, are not compass-oriented, but are based on larger grids of parallels and meridians, although a compass may appear to show the direction of true north to orient the map user to that direction in relation to the map shown.
8. a. 80 acres.
   b. 10 acres.
   c. 20 acres.
   d. 20 acres.

CHAPTER 3

1. The key distinction is duration. A freehold estate has a very long time span, while most (although not all) leaseholds are for comparatively short time periods. Further, leaseholds do not provide the tenant with all the rights of ownership, but only with rights of usage.
2. The language of a fee simple grant is "To A and his heirs," or "To A forever," or similar language indicating a transfer of an interest for such a long period of time that it will be forever. The conditional fee grant has this language but with an extra, the condition. "To A and her heirs so long as or upon condition that A operate no business upon the demised premises."

3. Waste is an issue for the holder of the future interest—either the party holding the reversion or the remainderman—because waste lessens or destroys the value of the property that the future taker will receive.

4. Although there is no statistical study showing that the estate for years is the most common form of leasehold, it appears logical, based first on its benefits—clarity and predictability—and second on the widespread use of forms that require dates specifying the beginning and end of the lease term.

5. Contingent remainders, conditional grants, lease terms, transfer of a tenant's leasehold interest, and developing law on a landlord's duties to its tenant (seeing this as a matter of commercial law, with its corresponding warranties, rather than on the traditional real estate law basis). Contingent remainders have long been a source of dispute, and the landlord's duties are a new area of concern.

6. An assignment by the tenant has the party taking the assignment (the new tenant) stepping into the shoes of the old tenant; the assignment is also for the remainder of the lease's term. The landlord may seek remedies against both tenants because the landlord is contractually involved with each of them through the lease. A sublease operates differently, in that the sublessee (new tenant) does not step into the shoes of the sublessor (old tenant) but makes a separate agreement (which sometimes excludes the landlord); that agreement provides for a transfer of the lease rights for a term less than the remaining time period under the lease. The landlord has no contractual remedies under the lease against the sublessee, but may retain rights to seek compensation for damages in tort law or for unpaid, market-price rent (under a theory that the tenant is being unjustly enriched if the sublessee uses the premises without payment of rent). The contractual remedies remain against the lessee.

7. The landlord has fewer demands upon it, but is becoming legally responsible for safety and adequacy of the building, particularly in residential relationships. The Uniform Commercial Code's warranty phrase of "fitness for a particular purpose" may come to have more impact in this area. The tenant has the primary duty to pay the rent and, secondarily, not to damage the premises beyond normal wear and tear; this could be considered a preservation factor.

8. The expansion by the courts of the rights of tenants and the transition from old law, protecting landlords rights, to a more modern law based on contract arrangements rather than old-time real estate law.

9. Severance is a result of the act of the joint tenant and affects the tenant primarily, not the other concurrent owners. The other tenants remain joint tenants, and the severed tenant becomes a tenant in common with them; examples of how it occurs are mortgaging or selling the tenant's interest. Partition is a court action that separates the tenants and makes the joint tenant who sought partition into a separate fee holder (the other

tenants too). If the land cannot be divided, it may be sold and the proceeds divided proportionally.

10. An easement appurtenant. It is usually created by deed.
11. The first issue is what interests each party has. B is a life tenant and C is a vested remainderwoman. Although B can have extensive interests in the property, those rights are not as extensive as those of a fee simple holder. The interests of the remainderwoman must be protected. The issue is whether the amount of minerals removed is excessive (which would be waste), denying the remainderwoman her share. The interest of the remainderwoman, who will take in fee, would appear to be a significantly greater interest than the interest of the life tenant. If B removed all the minerals, C would have a strong claim for compensation. If B were removing most of the minerals, an injunction stopping B should be given to C. An injunction might even run to C if B were removing more than what appeared to be a fair share. Some type of equitable arrangement might be worked out, but much of this dispute will depend upon how local law treats the rights to the minerals. Are mineral rights exclusively the property of the vested remainderperson? Does the life tenant have an interest in the mineral rights? If the mineral rights are shared, how extensive would each party's interest be?

    (Note that the events occur after the grantor's death, not the life tenant's. Here is an example of the importance of careful reading.)
12. The estate taken is a conditional fee. The heirs have a possibility of reverter. While there is no question as to the interest of the parties, the case could turn on the amount of time passed, because the law has always disliked possible forfeitures that would hang over property. Despite the time problem, however, it is most likely that the heirs would take if the property were sold. The school board might possibly have used the property in a different way for the benefit of education and thereby avoided the condition in the granting clause.
13. The legal arrangement could be mutual easements appurtenant. To enter his property, S could receive an easement from D; to get to the river, D could receive an easement from S. In each situation, the property receiving the benefit of the right (that is, the one having the right to cross) would be the dominant tenement, and the property being crossed would be the servient tenement. Of course, another resolution would be to have the two parties divide the property equally, giving each access to both the road and the river. In the long run, this solution might be preferable, and it could be achieved by mutual deeds after negotiation and agreed-upon boundaries. Finally, they could own the entire property as either joint tenants or as tenants in common.
14. In the common law, a tenant traditionally was liable for the rent regardless of the condition of the building. This rule is particularly true for a person who rents an entire building, because she gets the land with the building. In modern law, however, the idea of constructive eviction may overrule.

Certainly, in this case, the apartment was rendered uninhabitable. Though the tenant should notify the landlord, she may be able to rely upon a breach of an implied warranty of habitability to justify abandoning the premises. Another aspect is whether the landlord had attempted to repair the problem and whether sufficient time was provided to remedy the situation. As for any damages suffered by the tenant, there is a division between those who believe it is the duty of the tenant to insure versus those who see such damages as a foreseeable consequence of the landlord's violation of its duty.

CHAPTER 4

1. a. The grantor-grantee index is one of the two primary indexes used to keep public records concerning title and claims to parcels of real estate. It traces the person in title (the grantor) and the person to whom the title is transferred (the grantee).
   b. Constructive notice is a legal doctrine which states that a person is held to possess knowledge of the information available in public records. The doctrine requires that persons interested in a parcel of real estate do a search of the public records and acquire whatever information is in those records or be held responsible for that information. In this way, notice may be imputed to the purchaser of a real estate parcel, so that he may not be a bona fide purchaser for value and be free of prior liens without having done such a search.
   c. A good faith purchaser for value is a party who has acquired property without knowledge of any prior claims that would impair usage or enjoyment of the property. Constructive notice applies from the public recordings relating to the real property.
   d. Title search means that the public records are examined for a period of up to 60 years prior to the present for any evidence of parties who could have a claim to or an interest in the parcel with which one is concerned.
   e. Chain of title is the record of the ownership from the first grant from the government to the first settler to the present time—owner to owner to owner.
   f. The abstract of title is prepared by an attorney or an abstract company after a thorough search of the property records. It is a summary of the evidence found in the record. It is frequently accompanied by an attorney's opinion letter explaining the title position and the risks to the title. The opinion letter does not, however, come as a part of the abstract, but is contracted for as a separate item.
   g. An endorsement is an additional insurance coverage added onto an existing policy; endorsements are frequently added to a fire insurance policy to make it an "extended coverage" policy or a multi-peril policy. It is to be distinguished from an *indorsement,* which is a

type of signature on an item of commercial paper such as a note or a draft (check).

h. A loss payable clause is an insurance device involved in a loan transaction. In this agreement, the insurer agrees to pay the creditor as the creditor's interest appears under the policy, despite any claims it may have against the insured. In this way, any disputes between the insured (borrower) and the insurance company do not affect the creditor's right to payment.

2. There are several complexities that enhance the use of a title company in urban areas. First, there is a very large potential number of claimants who could be involved with any parcel of real property. Second, the actual plats, maps, and tracings are intricate and complicated. Third, with this greater possibility for dispute and litigation, it is advisable to have title insurance protection. Because the title company can do the search and also provide the insurance, it is efficient and logical for a title company to do this work rather than an attorney. Further, the general attorney doing a title search, while skilled, may not always be a specialist in this line of work. Finally, attorneys are rarely, if ever, in a position to insure against errors, including their own; litigating against attorneys is time-consuming, costly, and frequently frustrating.

3. As a document, the deed is a very important item in every transaction in which it is used. It can be simple or intricate and complex, but its basic elements should be clearly delineated. There can be no ambiguities or doubts about who is involved—the names of the parties; about what is involved, the specific parcel of real estate—the legal description of the parcel; about what estate is being conveyed—the words of conveyance; or about the document execution formalities, such as the signatures of the parties, acknowledgement, and witnessing. These elements provide the bare minimum needed in most jurisdictions to complete the deed document. Precision and exactitude are preferable to vagueness, but the courts have occasionally accepted deeds with vague descriptions of the location of the property, though with reluctance. In addition, the type of deed and the warranties or covenants provided in the deed could seriously affect the quality of the title transferred.

4. a. Ted Winston most likely would not have a good claim. His personal incapacity would be difficult to prove, and three years have passed. Although the law does not like to allow people under the influence of some drug affecting their contracting capacity to be taken advantage of, there is no evidence that Ted has suffered here. Despite the fact that each parcel of real property is unique, there is no evidence that Ted was not paid the market price, so he did not suffer any monetary damage. Further, there is no clear evidence that being under the influence of drugs impaired his contractual capacity. He may have known perfectly well what he was doing. Mere bad judgment is not an area in which the law offers protection. Finally, if a court

were to measure the equities between a rehabilitated drug user and a good faith purchaser for value who has been in possession for three years, it most likely would come down on the side of the purchaser, not Ted. Did Ted run out of money from the sale? Could his delay be excusable? It does not seem likely that that claim would be accepted by the standard of a reasonable person.

b. Sal Maggio's claim probably should have showed up and been paid off at the closing as a deduction from the seller. (Incidentally, how many drug users repair their real property within several months of the sale?) This failure to discover and pay off should lie within the title company's insurance coverage and be paid by the insurer. The question does not specify whether the mechanic's claim was filed within the statutory time allowed. Perhaps Maggio's claim was filed after the time period for filing had expired. If it was, the claim would be without merit and should be answered and handled by the insurer.

c. This question raises the issue of adverse possession. Certainly the time period is sufficient for that two-foot strip of the property to have become part of the Smiths' parcel. The issue is whether the elements for adverse possession have been fulfilled—open, notorious, continuous, and hostile to the interest of the landowner. If they have been, the Smiths have the right to keep that wall where it is and file a suit to have legal recognition of their estate as running up to and including the wall. The problem of tacking (adding together the ownership time periods of successive title holders to make the adverse claim continuous) could also be involved here. However, we do not have sufficient information about the time periods of prior ownership or the means of passing the claim to the title to that strip of land.

5. For Ms. Doe to become a good faith purchaser for value, she would have to pay a roughly market price for the property and take all steps necessary to search every public record that has any relevance to transactions relating to this parcel of real property. The purpose is to discover who has claims against the property and deal with those claims so that she can possess the property with quiet enjoyment.

a. The Minsky mess may be more of a theoretical problem than a real one. The deed, while valid in itself, is not going to be permitted by the courts to upset current title holders. The law has a doctrine called *laches* ("delay" in Latin). And the delay in filing this deed (at least a century since we are up to Boris VI) will probably deny Boris and Natasha any real claim. Their ancestors had their chance and did not take it. Notice that the effect under most recording statutes would be to deny the deed any validity in a current claim to the property.

b. Under the lis pendens system, the information about the contractor's filing should appear when the appropriate search is made. At closing, an appropriate amount of money would be set aside to pay the creditor off and obtain a release and satisfaction. These should be filed to clear up the public record.

c. Ms. Roe apparently is experiencing financial difficulties and needs the cash quickly. The government may well be willing to delay the lawsuit pending the sale negotiations, if they do not take an unreasonable amount of time. After all, the government just wants its taxes, and a buyer who will develop vacant land (producing more taxes) is much more appealing than a delinquent owner of a vacant property. At closing, this item would be settled appropriately.

6. A complete and exhaustive list is an extremely difficult goal to achieve. This is an area where the student may be able to make important contributions, because each addition could inform on coverage for a risk. Almost anything can be insured if one is willing to pay the premium. It may also be possible to get help from someone who has worked in insurance or has some specialized knowledge. The purpose of this problem is not so much to set up a complete list as it is to get the student organized and thinking systematically about the problem. The student should create the list based on the two categories of risks to property and risks to persons coming onto the land. In addition, there can be specialized commercial or business activity risks that relate to the land (as opposed to general business risks), such as the use of dynamite or the use or disposal of toxic chemicals, which may or may not be insurable.

7. The formula for determining the recovery is the amount of issued insurance (here, \$89,000 + \$125,000 = \$214,000) divided by the co-insurance percentage (here, 80 percent) times the fair market value of the property (here, \$650,000) times the amount of the loss (here, \$125,000) equals the recovery. \$51,437.50 becomes the amount of the recovery. Davis failed to increase her insurance coverage when the value of the warehouse increased. Consequently, under the co-insurance provision, she is only paid a proportionate amount. Note that she only gets about 41 percent, not 80 percent.

CHAPTER 5

1. The language differences reflect the extent of promises made by the grantor. A warranty deed conveys an interest in the land that the grantor (seller) later acquires, as well as any present interest. In addition, a warranty deed imposes covenants on the grantor concerning the title to the property, and these usually require him to protect the grantee's interest. The language in a special warranty deed simply protects the grantee (buyer) from the acts of the grantor, not from the acts of other parties before the grantor was in title. The quitclaim deed only transfers the current interest of the grantor (if any), not any future interest, and it provides no warranties at all.

2. A variety of real estate transfer deeds may be used in your state; check your local law.
3. The grantor can limit his liability by drafting carefully. He can make the covenants conditional, such as making the covenants subject to certain events, occurrences, or timing.
4. In many jurisdictions they do, and sometimes the law requires that the deed be witnessed before it can be recorded. Check your local law.
5. A *note* is a document showing that money has been borrowed and that the borrower promises to repay it. The note usually (in real estate transactions) refers to the real property as the collateral. The *mortgage* is a document that collateralizes the loan and permits the lender to seize the property if the debt is not paid. Other clauses in the mortgage may also permit the creditor to seize the property, upon occurrences such as failure to maintain insurance on the property, not maintaining the property, and sometimes, in commercial agreements that are separate from but tied to the note and mortgage, failure to meet certain financial requirements or standards. The *deed of trust* is a document that collateralizes a loan and permits the creditor to seize the property. The difference between a mortgage and a deed of trust lies in who holds the title—the borrower, or the trustee with the borrower being the beneficiary under the trust.
6. Real property should be described by a full legal description. This method is safe. Using a street address is never correct. Looser methods have been used successfully, but why take the risk? The three major methods of legal description are discussed in the text (see chapter 2).
7. A *real estate sales contract* is used to determine what property is being sold. It may include a variety of items that range from consideration and a legal description to allocation of items of personal property. A deed is the document that transfers the real property from one party (grantor—usually the seller, but sometimes a donor or giver) to another (the grantee—usually the buyer, but sometimes a donee, that is, a gift recipient).
8. Recordation of deeds is crucial to protect the owners of real property from third parties, such as takers from the owner's grantor, who transferred the property fraudulently or from that grantor's subsequent creditors. Recordation of mortgages protects the mortgagee-creditor from possible subsequent creditors of the borrower-mortgagor.
9. a. A *covenant of warranty*—the grantor's guaranty that the grantee will possess title and not be interrupted in title; a *covenant against encumbrances*—a grantor's guaranty that there are no third parties who can make effective claims against the grantee's ownership; a *covenant for quiet enjoyment*—a grantor's guaranty that the grantee's title will not be defective; a *covenant of the right to convey*—a guaranty from the grantor that the grantor has adequate title and power to convey the property; and *covenants for title*—a series of

covenants from the grantor to the grantee that protect the grantee in title and possession of the estate being transferred.

   b. Usually a warranty deed, although many times a separate set of covenants is given with the special warranty deed.

10. Bill does not take because there was no delivery of the deed. The deed was in Allen's safe deposit box at the time of Allen's death. As a result, there was no intent to make a present gift. Kathleen received the deed and recorded it to protect herself. She takes. Matthew will most likely take because Allen divested himself of the deed by giving it to his attorney with instructions, which were followed. There is no question as to Allen's intent because he gave the deed to his attorney. The issue is whether he retained control and could have revoked the gift. Many courts have held that such a gift is good, but most attorneys follow the directions of their clients; Allen never asked for it back, so he never regained control, which would have revoked his intent to make a present gift. The first parcel, which did not pass to Bill, would either be disposed of by the will's residuary clause (which disposes of all property not otherwise disposed of), or, if there were no will, the first parcel would pass following that jurisdiction's law of intestate succession.

11. a. Sally's easement could be described as an easement appurtenant. It runs with the land. It is also an easement by necessity, as Sally must have it to make use of her land.

    b. Because the longest time that most states provide for adverse possession to be held against the original owner is 20 years, and 22 years have passed here, it appears that the time period has been satisfied. Note, however, that the time duration is not all in one party. However, when property is transferred by deed, and the deed purports to transfer the disputed property, it is possible to tack the two ownerships onto each other to satisfy the time requirement. It is said to pass "under color of title." Since the property has been held openly, notoriously, and against the interest of Sally, it should amaze no one that Grace won her adverse possession claim.

CHAPTER 6

1. Divide the price ($210,000) by 5 (4 + 1); that result is $42,000. The land has the value of 1, which is $42,000, while the building has a value of 4, which is $168,000.

2. a. *Substitution.* The interchangeability of one property for another.

   b. *Highest and best use.* An indication that the property value is being maximized, so that the property is providing the most profitable and most socially useful function at this time.

   c. *Supply and demand.* A maxim from economics that indicates that as demand rises or falls, supply will follow.

d. *Conformity.* The degree to which the property subject to appraisal is the same as other properties in the area.

e. *Anticipation.* The belief that land and property values will rise in the future.

f. *Change.* The movements and developing differences that will affect the real estate market and the prices therein. These range from possible earthquakes and new fashions, fads, and tastes to the location of industrial plants, governmental policy, population density, and internal migration within the United States.

3. a. *Market comparison.* A number of properties having essentially the same characteristics (as to size, location, and components, such as square footage and number of rooms) and whose recent selling prices are known are checked for similarities to and differences from the property being appraised. Thus, if the subject property can be determined to be similar in many ways, and the differences adjusted for, a reasonable market price estimate may be made for the property being appraised.

b. *Cost.* This method has several subcategories, but the essential idea is to determine what the costs of constructing the building are. One may determine whether the building is being replaced exactly (reproduction cost) or is being replaced as to its function (replacement cost). There are also a number of ways of estimating the cost. It can be done roughly, by a square footage comparison, or builders' price lists of the elements used in the construction may be used, or rough estimates of generic project costs (such as windows, walls, and concrete work) may be done.

c. *Income.* This method is based on an investor's desire to know two elements: first, the return or income that she will receive on the investment or amount of money put into the property, and second, the desire not only to be sure to get paid for the use of the money but also to guarantee that the money will be returned to the investor—that is, to ensure that the investor will not lose her invested capital. To use the various methods that exist to determine property value by means of an income method of appraisal, the appraiser must know the annual gross income of the property; the items that could change gross income up or down, to arrive at an effective gross income; the net income; and the rate of return sought (often called the capitalization rate). One method of determining price is to use a composite income multiplier, gleaned from information on comparable buildings, and multiply the appraised building's income by that multiplier to attain an reasonable estimate of the price of the building being appraised. Other methods involve working with the rate of return. The formula is that the rate of return equals the income divided by the property value (or a very recent sales price).

4. Houses b and d would not be comparable, because b is much older and d only has two-thirds of the rooms that the subject building has. The other differences are minor or can be adjusted for on a normal basis.
5. Obtain the recently sold, comparable building's sales price per square foot ($319,000 ÷ 10,000 = $31.90 per square foot). Multiply that times your building's square footage ($31.90 × 11,000 = $350,900). Your estimate would be approximately $351,000.
6. *The Income Approach.*
   Calculate the rate of return as follows—

Loan rate of return	.70 × 10.5	= 7.35
Equity rate of return	.30 × 12.0	= 3.60
Rate of return on funds used		= 10.95
Capital recapture rate	100 ÷ 50	= 2.00
Total funds cost		12.95
Net Income Approach—		
Income attributable to land	$75,000 × .1095	= $ 8,212
Income attributable to the building	$75,000 – $8,212	= $ 66,788
Building value (est.)	$66,788 ÷ .1295	= $515,737
Property value	$515,737 + $75,000	= $590,737
Land Residual Approach—		
Estimated building value—		$515,737
Cap Rate		
Interest (discount) rate	10.95	
Capital recapture rate	2.00	
Total funds cost	12.95	

Building value ($515,737) × funds cost (12.95) = $66,788 (income attributable to the building)
Total net income ($75,000) – Income attributable to the building ($66,788) = $8,212 (income attributable to the land)
$8,212 ÷ .1095 = $75,000
$75,000 + $515,737 = $590,737 for estimated value of parcel

7.

Category	App'd Prop	Propty 1	Propty 2	Propty 3
Price		$287,500	$292,500	$295,000
Locale	Mod. Traf.	Quiet St. –$5,000	Quiet St. –$5,000	Quiet St. –$5,000
Landscpg	Stnd	Stnd	Stnd	Stnd
Lot Size	25 × 125	30 × 110	25 × 125	25 × 125
Age	15	17	20 +$500	18
Construct	Frame	Frame	Brick –$2,000	Frame
Style	Gable	Gable	Gable	Gable
# Rooms	8	9 –$2,000	8	7 +$2,000

# Bedrooms	4	5 –$2,000	4	3 +$2,000
# Baths	3	3	3	2½ +$1,500
Sq. Ftge.	2,300	2,500 –$2,000	2,275	2,100 +$2,000
Basement	Full	Full	Full	Full
Condition				
Ext.	Good	Good	Good	Good
Int.	Poor	Good –$5,000	Good –$5,000	Good –$5,000
Garage	2-car at.	2-car at.	2-car at.	2-car at.
Other	Enclsed Pr. 12 × 20	+$7,000	+$7,000	+$7,000
Total Adj.		–$9,000	–$4,500	+$4,500
Adjusted Value		$278,500	$288,000	$299,500

Estimated Value of the Appraised Property—$288,000

Note that the second comparison property is the most similar to the property being appraised, in that it has the same number of rooms, bedrooms, and baths. Therefore, it is appropriate to take its adjustment price as the comparable price for the house being appraised.

CHAPTER 7

1. A mortgage is the more traditional document. It provides that the borrower is usually in possession, always has title, and grants the lender a lien (mortgage) on the property being financed (usually). Commonly, the right of redemption applies to the mortgage. The deed of trust, however, places the title into a trust and the borrower-land occupier is the trust's beneficiary, while the trustee and legal title holder is an agent for the lender (frequently the trustee is the bank's own trust department). Because the legal owner will raise no objections to sale of the land if the payments are not made, the problem of redemption has been obviated. Modern law, however, has begun to provide a redemption right even with land trusts.
2. The note represents the borrower's promise to repay the lender. It contains not only the promises to repay, but the amount, the timing of repayment, the interest rate to be paid on the loan, and various other obligations that may relate to the land as collateral, or other important items.
3. A floating interest rate is designed to transfer the risk of the cost of money increasing during the period of the loan to the borrower, rather

than having it stay with the lender. Most of these interest rates are tied to some index, either national or the lender's own, that changes as the cost of funds in the banking community changes. In addition to this changeable base, there is an increment of from 1 to 5 percentage points to reflect the risk of borrowing in this particular lending situation.

4. There are at least five different names for these note-mortgages. The most generic term is *adjustable rate mortgage,* but other terms such as *variable rate mortgage, renegotiable rate mortgage, rollover mortgage,* and *balloon mortgage* are also used. The last two are slightly different from the generic terms preceding them. The rollover mortgage implies a short term before the debt is due, at which time the entire amount is "rolled over" into a new instrument with a different rate. A balloon mortgage refers to a type of note under which the final payment is so large that it is not considered payable at the time it is due; hence, the parties renegotiate the interest rate and write a new note. Traditionally, the balloon payment simply meant that one of the installments, usually the last, had a variation of at least 10 percent from the other installments. The original purpose was to make possible smaller payments during the early part of the loan. When the loan came due and was payable, the borrower then had to renegotiate the loan, usually on terms favorable to the lender. Banks also considered it a form of security when the borrower appeared to be risky; they would not have to wait for decades before foreclosing. It was felt that the onus on the lender was less than in normal foreclosure proceedings.
5. An acceleration clause. This clause makes all the payments under the note immediately due and payable—either at the option of the lender or automatically—if the note is not paid when due or when certain other types of defaults occur. Some of these other defaults could be having another lien on the property; failing to pay the taxes or special assessments when due, in home mortgage situations; and, in commercial mortgages, the borrower's failing to meet certain minimum, agreed-upon financial standards set forth in the loan agreement. Without this type of clause, the lender would have to enter court each time a payment was due and went unpaid.
6. The borrower should obtain all the documents from the lender and should additionally obtain from the lender a document which is variously called a *release,* a *satisfaction,* a *deed of reconveyance,* or a *discharge.* This document explains that the lender no longer has any interest in the parcel of real property. This document should be recorded immediately.
7. Truth in Lending is concerned with honesty in credit transactions. Technically, large loans over $25,000 are exempt, but the lenders are wary and generally provide the information about interest rates (disclosure of the annual percentage rate, collateral, and payments to most home borrowers. Another aspect of TIL is that the adjustable rate mortgages must

be fully disclosed. A third major aspect is that a three-day right of rescission is given whenever a borrower puts a second mortgage on his principal residence. In summary, interest and collateral disclosures, ARM disclosures, and the right of rescission provide the major impact on home lending. Commercial lending is excluded.

8. The acronym *RESPA* stands for Real Estate Settlement Procedures Act. Congress wanted to make sure that consumers had adequate and accurate information given to them when they were making a home purchase. It felt that the consumer should be aware of all of the financial charges and credits that would be involved in the closing. A uniform format was established and is now used throughout the United States. The law was also an attempt to prohibit kickbacks and other types of activities Congress considered disreputable, which cost consumers and inhibited their ability to acquire homes.

9. A number of other requirements relate to real estate, but most regulations relate to consumers purchasing homes. Various statutes, such as the Fair Housing Act, prohibit discrimination based on race, color, sex, national origin, or religious preference. There is also regulation of the banking and savings and loan industries to make sure that their lending activities are not discriminatory. The federal government also has regulations relating to the acquisition of flood insurance, when appropriate. Finally, the activities of the Federal Reserve System in handling the money supply directly affect the real estate industry, and the fiscal activities of Congress, and its spending policies, also can heavily affect the success (or lack thereof) of the real estate industry.

10. There are a number of possible reasons for a lender's not wanting to make a loan to the loan applicant. Some of them could be the following: First, the paperwork has not been completed properly. Second, the applicant does not meet the bank's standards for making a loan—that is, the applicant lacks the creditworthiness necessary to repay the loan, from the bank's point of view. Third, the parcel of property does not appear to be a good location or investment, so that it is of doubtful collateral value. Fourth, the bank is uninterested in this particular type of loan. Fifth, the bank has a sufficient number of loans in this area and does not care to increase that lending concentration at this time. Sixth, the bank is feeling the effects of a credit crunch engineered by the Federal Reserve Board so that it lacks the funds to lend. Seventh, the bank was recently harmed by this type of lending and it wants to be extremely cautious in making any loans of this type at this time. The bank sees itself as a financial institution that needs to make money to survive; it is not a charitable institution or a publicly funded institution, but an organization that must be responsible to its shareholders and its depositors as well as to the regulators.

11. Who is liable to whom? There are two transfers: (1) the Jones's transfer to Survivor and (2) A's transfer to B. These are different types of

transfers—the first is an assignment of rights to be paid and the second is a delegation of duties. What is the effect of this difference? If the Joneses had not recorded promptly, it might have been possible for B to assert the defense of being a bona fide purchaser in good faith (without knowledge of their interest), but the recording, via constructive notice, stops that line of argument. Does Survivor have the right to go after A or the Joneses? Is A still around? Would an area of law outside of real estate be relevant, such as bankruptcy? If so, did B do everything in bankruptcy that was proper? Is there a way to challenge his bankruptcy? What type of bankruptcy did B take, liquidation (Chapter 7) or reorganization (Chapter 11)? Has Survivor established its priority to Billacres so that it can be a secured creditor in bankruptcy? Did Survivor record its assignment from the Joneses? (Presumably it did, but this example does not say.) Someone has to search the records and find out. What other effects does bankruptcy have? Any, some, none? Does Survivor's purchase of the note at a discount mean anything? Does it mean they did or did not give value? Did B receive the mortgage as an assignment, or did he take subject to the mortgage? What does the Joneses' original documentation say about transfer of the property? Is it permitted or prohibited? What does A's documentation actually transfer to B? Was it recorded?

In essence, then, the issues lie in the areas of (1) what the documents say (you might want to consider the results if the forms in the book had been used, if there is time to do a mock-up and analysis); (2) whether the recordings were properly done; and (3) what effects different areas of the law have on this property (specifically, the law of bankruptcy, and possibly the law of contracts in relation to the transfer of rights versus the transfer of duties). In addition, do any specific statutes apply to these events, besides the laws relating to recording? What else?

CHAPTER 8

1. The first requirement is to gain the respect of the parties with whom the closer is working; in this way, the closer will be able to work with them effectively. Gaining the respect of third parties is particularly important. They must be aware of the knowledge, competence, and cooperativeness of the closer while understanding that the closer is not a pushover. Second, the closer must be very well organized. If the closer is not organized and coordinated, the closing and its documentation will not tie together. Further, that kind of organization builds confidence in third parties, because they can rely on the closer's timing and scheduling to be generally accurate.

2. The parties are as follows:

Party	Contribution
Buyer(s)	Principal(s) involved in the purchase.
Seller(s)	Principal(s) involved in the sale.
Attorneys	Legal and documentation experts who help the principals wend their way through the details of the sale.
Creditor/Lender	Party putting up the majority of money; frequently checks value of property, creditworthiness of buyer, title status of the parcel to protect the loan.
Realtor	May either be a broker or salesperson. The realtor's task is to get the buyer and the seller together so that the transaction can occur.
Appraiser	Person who visits the property and creates an appraisal stating the current market value of the property.
Surveyor	Person who measures the property to determine its exact location and whether there are encroachments onto the property from other parcels or vice versa, and if so, the location of the encroachment.
Title company	The title company usually has two major functions: first, to make the title searches necessary to determine the status of the title, and second, to issue an ALTA policy with the lender or the borrower as beneficiaries. This policy will protect against claims against the title to the property.
Inspectors	Persons who check the building for defects and problems; inspections can range from a specialized inspection, such as for termites, wiring, or other such items to general building inspections.
Insurance agents	An insurance person can sell insurance to cover fire and hazard to the homeowner, and other types in a commercial transaction. There might be credit life insurance to cover the loan if the borrower dies, but that policy is usually arranged through the lender, not independently.

There may also be other interested parties, such as those to be paid off, like a mechanic's lien holder.

3. a. *Actual days:* $8,100 × 220 days ÷ 365 = $4882.19.
30/360 basis: $8,100 ÷ 12 = $675 × 7 = $4,725 (through July); add to that amount, 8 ÷ 30 × $675 = $180 for a total of $4,905.
This is an accrued but unpaid obligation of the seller and will be debited to the seller.

b. *Actual days:* $1,500 × 104 days ÷ 365 = $427.40. The 104 days are the days left in the year after the closing—September 19 through December 31.
30/360 basis: $1,500 ÷ 12 = $125 × 3 = $375. To this amount, add the fraction of September that remains. $125 ÷ 30 = $4.17 × 12 = $50. The amount is $425.

4. a.

CLOSING WORKSHEET

Whose Entry (B/S)	Item	Buyer		Seller	
		Debit	Credit	Debit	Credit
B/S	Price	127,500			127,500
S	Realtor's comm.			7,650	
B	Earn. money		12,750		
B/S	RE taxes		3,442.14	3,442.14	
S	Transfer taxes			2,550	
B	Mort. loan		105,000		
	Totals	$127,500	121,192.14	13,642.14	127,500
	Needed to close		$ 6,307.86		
	Due Seller			$113,857.86	

4. b.

CLOSING WORKSHEET

Whose Entry (B/S)	Item	Buyer		Seller	
		Debit	Credit	Debit	Credit
B/S	Price	98,250			98,250
S	Earn. money		6,386.25		
B	Mort. loan		83,512.50		
S	Realtor's comm.			6,877.50	
B	Mort. payoff			52,500	
B	Title ins.	1,350			
B/S	RE taxes	988.75			988.75
B/S	Atty's fees	850		675	
B/S	Int. due	96.95			96.95
	Totals	$101,535.70	89,898.75	60,052.50	99,335.70
	Needed to close		$ 11,636.95		
	Due Seller			$39,283.20	
	Balances	$101,535.70	101,535.70	99,335.70	99,535.70

4. c.

CLOSING WORKSHEET

Whose Entry (B/S)	Item	Buyer Debit	Buyer Credit	Seller Debit	Seller Credit
B/S	Price	165,000			165,000
B	Buyer's loan		148,500		
S	Realtor's comm.			9,900	
B/S	Atty's fees	1,100		900	
B/S	Fuel	310			310
B/S	RE taxes	3,760.96			3,760.96
B	Earn. money		11,550		
B/S	Insurance	858.08			858.08
B	Recording fee	60			
B	Title ins.	675			
S	Mort. payoff			84,000	
B/S	Interest due	276.64			276.64
	Totals	$172,040.68	160,050	94,800	170,205.68
	Needed to close		11,990.68		
	Due Seller			75,405.68	
	Balances	$172,040.68	172,040.68	170,205.68	170,205.68

CHAPTER 9

1. Contract law has long provided that covenants (clauses, terms) could be either independent of or dependent on one another. If the clauses are independent, the terms you have promised must be performed regardless of whether the other party performs his; if the clauses are dependent, the performance of your promises in the contract-lease depends on the other party's performance of his promises. Under the concept of dependent clauses, one party can assert that the other did not perform, so therefore the first party does not have to perform. Under the theory of dependent clauses, the performance or the lack thereof by one party does not excuse the nonperformance of the other party. In landlord-tenant law, the tenant still has to pay the rent even though the landlord has not fulfilled her agreements under the lease.
2. Under the common law, the real property aspects of the lease were the original and most important aspects of the lease. These aspects dealt with the possession and use of the land, as well as the various promises made by the lessor that ran with the land, such as quiet enjoyment. Further, it was the use of the land, not the use of the building on the land, that was important to the lessee (usually a farmer). Today, however, unless one uses the land for mining, drilling for gas or oil, or in some form of agribusiness, the use of the land itself is incidental to the lessee.

It is the use of the building that is important to the lessee. The parties' rights and duties under the lease are most important today. Contemporary leases concern the payment of fees, taxes, expenses; the ties into sales for adjustable rent payments; insurance coverage; and a number of other contractual aspects.

3. The three most probable landlord's concerns are (a) whether the tenant will pay the rent on time; (b) whether the tenant will damage the premises in using them; and (c) whether the tenant will comply with all the terms of the lease so that the landlord is not injured by failures, such as a failure to insure, to pay taxes, or to comply with government regulations. Three of the tenant's concerns are (a) whether the landlord will maintain the premises as the lease provides; (b) the quality of the landlord's title and, further, the financial stability of the landlord in making payments to its mortgagee; and (c) what rights the tenant has to remodel, change, or improve the premises. There are many more for both parties.
4. The following are the basic elements of a lease: the date the lease is executed; the parties to the lease—the lessor and the lessee; a description of the premises that constitute the leased property; the term of the lease; and the rent—amount and when it is due.
5. Among the various landlord's remedies are the following: Suit against the tenant for performance under the lease; acceleration of the rent; reentry and reletting of the premises; termination of the lease; and performance of the tenant's obligations with the right to recover from the tenant.
6. Some of the tenant's remedies are as follows: withhold the rent; sue to enforce the provisions of the lease; sue for money damages; cure the default and offset that expense against the rent; and abandon the premises under the doctrine of constructive eviction.
7. The landlord can be liable to the tenant, to third parties in the common areas, and to various regulatory and taxing authorities. Further, the landlord may be liable not only under real estate and contract law, but also under tort law, tax law, and administrative law of various sorts; as well as corporate or partnership law, limited partnership investment offerings from the SEC, and an almost endless list. Note the multiple areas of the law to which the landlord must be alert: real estate, contract, tort, securities regulation, corporate or partnership law, employee relations law, agency, environmental, and a host of others.
8. The general rule is that if a lessee rents an entire building, it has the right to use the entire building, including the outside walls and the roof. The lessee probably selected this location to advertise within sight of the two interstate highways. The landlord had the opportunity to deny that usage by contractual agreement in the lease, but failed to do so. The lessee should win this case.
9. What conflict does the lessee foresee with the landlord or the landlord's mortgagee? Because the chain has the power to set terms with the landlord, it can use language that will resolve disputes in the manner

most satisfactory to itself (subject to the restrictions of local law—such as unconscionability). The most difficult type of conflict that the tenant may want to protect against is the landlord defaulting in payments to its creditor and the creditor foreclosing on the loan. This process effectively makes the creditor the new landlord. But financial institutions are not interested in being landlords, so they try to sell the real property quickly. The transition is not positive for the tenant's business climate. The tenant should have the right to perform the landlord's duties (should they not be performed). The tenant should get an agreement or a waiver from the creditor, before signing the lease, precluding the creditor from damaging the position of the tenant if it forecloses on the property. Terms of this agreement would vary depending on the situation.

10. This question is designed to make the paralegal aware of the interweaving of other areas of law with real estate law. The question cannot be fully answered within the confines of this course; there has been no extensive coverage of tort law in this text. But the situation is a natural one for discussion and always interests students. The student should be aware that other types of legal actions can arise in real estate situations besides the ones that are technically real estate. One would explain the theory of negligence with the concepts of duty, breach of duty, proximate cause, and harm. Would the building owner or the workers who left the nail be liable? Were the workers employees or independent contractors? The concept of agency should be reviewed in the employer-employee relationship, as well as the doctrine of respondeat superior if the workers were the lessor's employees. Both the concepts of assumption of risk—walking down a hall where work is in progress and knowingly doing some action with the nail—and contributory negligence (the injured party's negligence that helped cause the harm complained of) could be discussed. Both these defenses lie against the plaintiff's claim, but here, contributory negligence is more likely because George probably would not knowingly take any action involving the unremoved nail, but he could be negligent in protecting himself.

CHAPTER 10

1. A condominium is a type of real estate ownership in which a group of persons, joined together, own an entire building or group of buildings. Their ownership has a special aspect in that the property is divided into individual units. There is an owner for each unit in fee, and the common elements, such as stairs, are owned as tenants in common.
2. A condominium is created by a party, the declarant, putting the building or the group of buildings into a condominium. This requires a master deed or declaration which is recorded with the local real estate recorder of deeds. This document may be amended from time to time. In addition,

a not-for-profit corporation must be created to operate the condominium, thus, incorporation papers are necessary. The condominium association will adopt bylaws to govern its operations and rules and regulations to set standards of behavior and relationship among the unit owners and their guests. Finally, when condominium unit sales occur, there will be a transfer deed to transfer the unit that has been sold (along with the common elements) to the purchaser of the unit from the developer-declarant.

3. Although problems of population density and traffic congestion in urban areas can affect condominium development, the problem of driving tenants from the building constitutes a greater problem. Once rental units in a rehabilitated building change to ownership units in a condominium, the persons who formerly rented often can no longer afford to live in the building. Where will these people live, and how will they fit into the community when it has been gentrified (which is frequently what condominium creation in the city does)? With more people becoming poor in the 1980s than has been the case for a long time, it is essential to recognize this social difficulty. There are conflicting needs. One is that people have sufficient rental units, and another is to rehabilitate neighborhoods, a task beyond the economic means of many of the poorer groups. Resolution of these conflicting interests is difficult.
4. Common elements are the portions of the property that each of the unit owners has a right to use and owns with the others as a tenant in common.
5. The advantages include: (a) not having to do maintenance oneself; (b) separate ownership of each unit, which means there can be a separate mortgage and a separate real estate tax bill; and (c) more modest cost than a single-family home (the basic economic reason condominium ownership began). The disadvantages include: (a) not being able to choose one's neighbors and being in close contact with them; (b) potentially changing neighborhoods; (c) living subject to rules and regulations established by the board; and (d) a potentially smaller living space than in a single-family dwelling.
6. The condominium is ownership of a unit in a building and is the ownership of real property. The cooperative's resident does not own the unit. Instead, in the cooperative, the unit resident is a lessee from the corporation that owns the building and is also a shareholder in that corporation. The condominium ownership is a real property interest; the cooperative unit is a personal property interest in the corporation's stock and the lease.

CHAPTER 11

1. The federal government has focused on three areas of cleanup and prevention in relation to the environment. These are (1) preventing pollution,

(2) cleaning up the pollution, and (3) preventing the introduction or inappropriate usage of poisonous chemicals.

The second part of this question requires broad-based discussion, and the answers will depend a great deal on whose shoes one is standing in when one answers the question. For instance, if you are answering as (1) a consumer or individual, the cleanup is essential and important. If as (2) a business person, the problem is one of cost effectiveness and competition. If as (3) a worker who needs a job, but is losing it because the costs of meeting the pollution standards are too high, then another perspective appears. The crucial point is having the members of our society agree the relative importance of courses of actions. The individuals are concerned about health, the businesspersons about making money so that their businesses can survive, and workers with having jobs to support their families. Each is important; how do we as a society arrange the hierarchy of values? This selection of choices is one of the jobs politicians live with all the time. Can you see why Winston Churchill once defined a statesman as a "dead politician"?

2. An environmental audit has two parts. First, an investigation of the land and the documents relating to the historic use of the land is undertaken. Second, the land itself may be tested to determine its toxicity and the presence of various environmental problems. Risks exist on both sides—whether one undertakes or foregoes an environmental audit. Often, not undertaking the audit can create a problem for the owner because there will be no planning regarding the time, resources, and costs of cleaning up, nor will there be an opportunity to determine who else might be responsible for cleanup. This delay in determining who else might be responsible might create further costs, because the company might go out of business or decline in value so that it cannot meet its obligations. Undertaking the environmental audit can also be risky, though. Once it is determined that there is an environmental cleanup problem, the cost, time, and resource allocation is inevitable. The environmental cleanup issue frequently arises when the property is being sold, and it requires careful legal draftsmanship to ensure that the seller does not manage to unburden itself of potential liabilities for the cleanup.

3. The public regulation of real estate use focuses on how the real estate is used in relation to the general public and its health and welfare. Most governmental activities in this area are tied to the authority's police powers. The private regulation of real estate focuses either on the private use and enjoyment of the owner's own property or upon a system of shared benefits for a group of landowners who have a common interest. That common interest is most frequently expressed through the medium of restrictions filed with the plat of survey when a developer creates a new building project. Individual landowners generally obtain their protection under various tort claims, such as nuisance, trespass,

negligence, or strict liability, or they may avail themselves of their rights under the declaration of restrictions.

4. Zoning is the process whereby local government—usually a city, but possibly (and increasingly these days) a county or other regional authority—sets the land boundaries in its jurisdiction where certain types of land usages are allowed. The three basic types of usage have traditionally been residential, commercial, and industrial. Although residential usage is almost always exclusively for that purpose, multiple usage is often permitted in industrial and commercial areas. Zoning is intended to permit control over unplanned and conflicting types of development, and almost all local governments have adopted some form of it since the 1920s, when it first began. Zoning involves economic as well as health and safety concerns. Zoning can be used to regulate the type of activity permitted, as well as the amount of that activity permitted in a particular area. For instance, it is now often used to protect the environment by requiring that only a limited number of permits will issue for a particular type of industry or for only a limited number of new homes. Thus, these limitations are an attempt to place a lesser burden on an environment that is already stressed. Other environmental concerns also show up in the zoning process as, for example, when a developer is compelled to dedicate a portion of the property to public usage so that there will be more parks—green areas, trees, and other positive contributors to the atmosphere. Zoning appears to be a tool that can be used pretty much as its citizens want it to be. Its use will depend upon the citizens' understanding of zoning and their involvement in the political process. It may be an area of increasing environmental activism for sophisticated environmentalists in the next few decades.
5. Protection of wild areas (such as wilderness, wetlands, beaches, and other areas that appear to be essential to the maintenance of a clean environment, or the protection of wild animals, or the maintenance of locations for fishing, hunting, and recreation for all Americans) will become increasingly important. Preservation of historic areas and buildings can also have an impact, particularly on the inner-city developer. Goals concerning preservation limitations can conflict with redevelopment. As population density increases and there is competition for land use, choices must be made. The law, in both statute and decision, will reflect those conflicts and the compromises reached.

CHAPTER 12

1. (a) Local taxes for various local government entities.
   (b) Federal taxes in the following areas:
      (1) Taxation of corporations—double taxation problem
      (2) Taxation of corporations—real estate operations as an available deduction

   (3) Tax deferment on home sales
   (4) Sales contracts spreading payments over a time period of more than one year.

2. The rate of taxation is multiplied times the assessed valuation base. Note that the tax multiplier rate is determined by adding the rates levied by a number of different local legal entities in that taxation district.
3. Double taxation is the system that taxes the money earned by corporation as corporate profits and then taxes the remaining funds that are distributed to the shareholders as dividends; thus, both the corporation and the shareholders pay taxes on the same money. One method by which to avoid this expensive result, for a closely held corporation, is to become a Subchapter S corporation.
4. (a) Find an attorney knowledgeable about making real estate tax appeals.
   (b) Determine whether there are grounds to attack either the levying of the tax, or the assessment process, or both. Most individuals base their objections on the assessment process. Some large corporate landowners examine the tax levy process as well. Because the assessment process involves expertise which most judges and courts lack, the judicial process does not like to interfere with assessments and generally defers to the local authorities. Nevertheless, dissimilar land valuations on similar parcels of land can sometimes be effectively argued. Remember that the doctrine of exhaustion of remedies applies and that no lawsuit may be brought before all of the administrative steps have been taken.
5. The process of establishing the annual tax usually has four steps. First, the local government establishes its budget for its next fiscal year to determine what its financial needs will be. Second, the legislative body of the local government (council, board) passes an ordinance (resolution, statute) to specify that the money will be spent and the source from which the money will be raised. Third, this legislative body votes to levy a tax on real property at a rate sufficient to meet its budgetary needs. Fourth, the local official known as the assessor determines the value of each property by making an assessment. The amount of taxation for a parcel is determined by multiplying the assessed value by the tax rate.

CHAPTER 13

1. In the text there is an example of a specific ethical problem for a paralegal involved an awkward circumstance. Although conflicts and problems exist in direct work-related areas, there are also social ethical situations that arise by virtue of the nature of the work one does in real estate. The development problem posed here is an attempt to get you, the

prospective paralegal, to identify areas of ethical difficulty or conflict that could arise in certain situations. At the time of the writing of this book, in 1992, the vast majority of Americans felt that the nation was not heading in the right direction. But what ethical standards does one follow, whether the issues are national or those affecting an important industry such as real estate? What role does ethics play for you in the context of your work in real estate? Ethics is not simply the rules from a realtor's association, a bar association, or a paralegal's association. The effective use of ethics consists of identification of the conflicts between groups and their alternative goals and a sensitivity to the subtle violations of ethics that can lead to further abuse. In that spirit, the answer to this problem identifies areas without providing specific answers. The answers must reside in each of us.

The first consideration lies in socioeconomic analysis, but this analysis is not a lawyer's work. It is an economist's, a city planner's, or a sociologist's. Nevertheless, there may well be legal implications to this information. What would make this new community economically viable? Should it be strictly residential, mixed residential and commercial, or include some light industry as well? Who will live here and use the area? What groups will be attracted—what ethnic mix? Age mix? Income distribution? Educational background?

From considering these elements and others like them, the attorney could raise questions about discrimination in housing and jobs. Zoning boundaries and the type of zoning in each area will also be involved. There will be a large number of contracts involving developers, contractors, and subcontractors; all sorts of employment problems could arise. Surveys will have to be done, and the buildings laid out in relation to existing or additional streets. The task of architects will be to determine the most inexpensive construction to be done in the shortest possible time. Or is real quality desirable for this market? Should there be solar energy arrangements, superinsulation, double or triple-glazed windows, and general energy-saving requirements? Is it ethical to waste energy when we generate it from nonrenewable resources?

What will happen to the addicts and derelicts who live in the abandoned buildings? Will they just be pushed out to find refuge as they can in some other abandoned building, or should there be a program to assist them? *Can* they be assisted? What is practical? What is economical? What is ethical? Is it an attorney's or realtor's concern? If not, whose is it?

Should there be an environmental impact statement for the new project? Should the city or the purchasers get an environmental audit? What terms are necessary to handle these potential problems? What is the land worth now? Is the land to be donated to the city? Should there be an appraisal? Will some of the land be sold to the city, or will it go to the developers directly? Will the city strike deals with the industrial-commercial owners and land donors, so that the city receives the land as a gift for development but makes compensating deals and grants special zoning and development rights elsewhere for other parcels of those owners' land? How will the deals affect those other areas?

Could there be problems with legal descriptions—of condominiums, of other types of property? With title searches? Who will finance all of this development, both the short-term construction and the long-term payout? At what rates? On what terms? What ethical problems could exist in either of these operations?

What types of tax deferment or reduced tax burdens will be arranged? Are they reasonable? Do they work? If the city has had almost no tax revenue from the area for a number of years, is anything better than nothing? Or do the estimated tax revenues have to be balanced against the expenses the city will incur?

What modern, innovative devices can be used to handle the water, sewage, heating, and waste disposal? The techniques exist. Can they be made cost-effective for this development? What is the ethical position here? Does there need to be one?

Finally, in the real world, a question. Who is going to make the big money out of the deal and how are they going to do it? Someone almost always does in these situations. Is the process ethical? (Do not automatically jump to the conclusion that it is unethical. It may be, but many times people have become too cynical and thus believe that those who benefit greatly could only do so unethically. This conclusion need not be correct. Have the persons who made the money provided a benefit that matches what they made? That would be the utilitarian ethical analysis. There are others as well. Think about it.)

This is the complex world into which your work in real estate will take you. It is rarely a question of whether one will accept ethical compromises, but what ethical compromises one can accept and live with. No one's position is always morally pure or completely right—not mine and not yours. There must be some compromise along the way. Good luck in your new career!

GLOSSARY

abstract company Business that prepares a summary of the recorded title documents relating to a parcel of real estate.

abstract of title Document presenting the summary of the title documents in the public record that affect a parcel of real estate.

acceleration clause Provision giving the lender the right to make all payments immediately due and payable on a defaulted note.

accretion Slow deposit of land matter onto property as a result of water movement or a change in the flow of water.

accrued Type of proration in which the seller has received the benefit, such as a government service paid for by taxation, but has not paid for it; opposite of *prepaid.*

accumulated depreciation Total amount of depreciation taken to the present time.

acknowledgment Statement made by a party (for instance, the grantor under a deed) in front of an authorized official, usually a notary public, that the signature on a document is that of the party and that he or she voluntarily executed the document.

acre Surface land measurement of 43,560 square feet; term *builder's acre* means 40,000 square feet.

action to quiet title Lawsuit to remove any matter that would disturb the owner's right to or title in the real property; forces other parties to prove their claim or lose their right to that claim.

actual notice Legal requirement that a party really receive the information; contrasted with constructive notice.

adjustable rate mortgage (ARM) (also called *variable rate mortgage (VRM), renegotiable rate mortgage,* and *rollover mortgage*) Mortgage under which the interest rate on the note may change from time to time.

adjusted gross income Total income receivable less the unrentable or uncollectible amounts.

adjustment period Time period when the lender must change the base rate in an ARM.

adjustments Changes in the value of a property (in comparison to another) due to one property having or lacking certain feature(s).

adverse possession Possession of real property against the rights of the owner when possession is open, notorious, and hostile for a statutory time; ownership can be transferred at the end of the time period.

affidavit of title Statement from the seller, often required by the lender or title company, that the seller (1) has not placed any liens on the property since the last title examination; (2) has a certain marital status; and (3) is in possession of the property.

air rights Landowner's rights to the area above the surface of the land owned; theoretically extend infinitely into space. Connected with rights to sunlight; limited today by transportation (airplanes), communications (radio and television broadcasts), and adjacent owners' easements and other rights.

ALTA See *American Land Title Association.*

American Land Title Association (ALTA) Industry group for the title companies in America.

amortization (1) Gradual payment of a debt by regular payments in a fixed amount over a fixed period of time. (2) Depreciation of an asset over the period of its useful life (or other acceptable period of time) to establish its value at any given point in time.

annual percentage rate (APR) Actual interest rate on a loan covered by Regulation Z; disclosure is federally mandated.

anticipation Technique appraisers use to identify the value of the property in the future.

appraisal Evaluation of the current market worth of a piece of real property at a particular point in time; usually made by a professional appraiser.

appreciation Increase in value.

assessment (1) Valuation placed on a parcel of real property by the public assessor for the purpose of levying taxes on that property. (2) Amount of money each unit owner pays monthly for upkeep of the common elements.

assessment roll (also called *tax list*) List of real properties and their assessed valuations.

assessor Local public official whose job is to determine the value of each parcel of real property in the area.

assignment Transfer of a right under a contract or lease.

assumption of the mortgage When a third party takes over the obligations of the borrower to repay the loan; party assuming the debt is personally liable; compare with *subject to the mortgage*.

attestation Person's signature indicating that he or she witnessed the execution or signing of a legal document.

avulsion Ripping away of the land by violent means, such as a tidal wave or an earthquake.

balloon mortgage Mortgage for which the note has an installment payment schedule wherein one payment exceeds the others by at least 10 percent—usually by much more.

bargain and sale deed Deed that transfers the real estate itself, without the grantor making any promises.

base fee See *conditional fee*.

base line Principal surveying meridian.

benchmark Surveyor's mark used to determine a basic elevation from which other measurements of height can be made thereafter; often embedded in a brass circle on street corners of major cities.

beneficiary One of two parties to a trust; the trust party who gets the benefits of a trust; said to hold the "beneficial interest."

bequest See *legacy*.

block busting Attempt by realtors or lenders to force an entire neighborhood to move at once, thus lowering the prices; usually done when the neighborhood is changing racially.

board of assessment Board that reviews the work of the assessor and to which parties who feel aggrieved over their assessments may appeal.

bona fide purchasers Latin for "good faith" purchasers. A person is colloquially said to have, or to have established, his or her "bona fides"; means purchasers who have taken all the steps necessary to inform themselves of the rights of others and how those rights might affect the purchaser.

bylaws Operating framework within which a condominium's board of directors must function.

capitalization rate Rate of return that can be obtained from investing in a piece of property.

cash flow Process of obtaining and using cash so that there is a sufficient amount to meet current obligations as they come due; usually used in reference to a business.

caveat emptor Latin for "buyer beware"; legal doctrine whereby the responsibility for the safety and quality of a product lies with the buyer, not the manufacturer or seller. Use of the doctrine has declined substantially in the 20th century.

CERCLA See *Comprehensive Environmental Response, Compensation, and Liability Act of 1980.*

chain of title List of the successive owners of a parcel of real property (parties who have been in title since the government granted the original title), plus any other parties who have had an interest in the property and recorded evidence of their interests in the real property records, as shown by transfer deeds and other documents in the public real estate records of the county where the real estate is located.

check or quadrangle Largest type of measurement in the government survey system; 24 miles on a side or 576 square miles.

clean title See *good title.*

closer (also called *closing agent*) Person who sets up, coordinates, and runs a real estate closing.

closing agent See *closer.*

cloud on the title See *good title.*

co-insurance Certain types of real property insurance under which the insured must maintain a certain percentage of replacement value of the property to have full coverage; otherwise, the insurance pays only a portion of the loss.

collateralized mortgage obligation Recently created pooled mortgage device to allow the buyer of a pooled mortgage interest to select the time period of the mortgage; device to limit risk of the underlying mortgage being repaid early.

color of title Term used in tacking; used when a deed has transferred title to property and purports to transfer an adverse possession claim as part of the deed.

commitment letter Letter from the lender to the borrower in which the lender states the amount of the loan and its terms for making the loan.

common elements Real property that is owned and used by all in a condominium association.

community property Device used in some of the western United States and Wisconsin to share equally property that was acquired during marriage from the work efforts of both partners; excludes gifts, inheritances, and prior-owned property.

Comprehensive Environmental Response, Compensation, and Liability Act of 1980 (CERCLA) Federal environmental act that created the Superfund.

concurrent ownership Ownership of real property when there is more than one owner.

conditional fee A fee simple with a condition that, if it occurs, will cause the owner to lose the property automatically, without the holder of the reversionary interest having to do anything; also called *fee simple defeasible*, *base fee*, or *qualified fee.*

condominium Type of ownership that combines fee ownership in the specific unit (usually housing) with a tenancy in common in the building's elements that are used or usable by all owners; complete, individual ownership of a unit within a multi-unit building, together with common ownership of shared elements. Usually a residential type of ownership; based upon air rights.

conformity Degree to which a building or site fits in or is identical to other buildings and sites in the area.

constructive eviction Legal doctrine under which the tenant can move out and break the lease when the landlord's failure to perform is so great that it renders the property unusable, so that the tenant is forced to leave the property (for example, when the landlord does not keep the premises in proper condition); usually used in residential situations.

constructive notice Type of notice recognized by law for public real estate records and based upon recorded information; distinguished from *actual notice.* Once information is publicly recorded, it is considered to provide notice to any rational person who, knowing of the system, would use it to determine certain information, such as liens on the property involved in a proposed transaction. To be considered as operating in good faith, one is required to check the public records to determine the claims of others against a particular parcel of real property.

contingent remainder Potential right to take property; before the holder of a contingent remainder interest can take the property, in addition to the demise of the prior property holder, one or more conditions must be met.

contract for deed See *land sales contract.*

contribution Expression of the market value of an improvement to real property; not every improvement makes a contribution.

convertible mortgage (1) Mortgage under which the lender may convert its loan position into an equity position. (2) Mortgage under which the borrower may convert its adjustable rate mortgage into a fixed rate mortgage.

cooperative Form of building ownership in which a corporation owns the real property and its shareholders are its tenants.

cost analysis A major method of appraising property, based on replacement cost of the building, less depreciation, plus site cost.

covenants Promises made by a party to a contract for the transfer of real estate; among the most common are the covenants of warranty, against encumbrances, for possession, for quiet enjoyment, and for title.

credit Certain entries on a settlement sheet; means that the dollar amount is to be or has been paid to someone rather than having to pay money out; complementary term with *debit.*

credit life insurance Type of insurance providing that if the borrower dies, the insurance will pay off the outstanding amount of the loan; often offered by lender to borrowers.

cure Right to make good and repair any harm done from a borrower's default.

cure of default Making the other party whole so that he or she is no longer damaged by the default; paying an amount less than the full rent and then sending the remainder, plus any amount necessary to cover any damage from the delay, would be curing a rent default.

curtesy Rights of the husband in the wife's real property; from medieval law.

datum Point from which height and depth can be measured; sea level is often used to provide the altitude from which to measure.

debit Certain entries on a settlement sheet; means that the amount is to be paid by the party to whom it refers; complementary term with *credit.*

decedent Person who has died.

declarant Person who is creating a condominium; usually the developer.

declaration of conditions See *declaration of restrictions.*

declaration of restrictions (also called *master deed, declaration of conditions,* or *enabling declaration*) Document recorded at the same time and in the same office as the plat of survey; describes a condominium's location, creation, and rules for owners.

dedication Process whereby a person, usually a developer, places private land in public hands for public use; often achieved by granting a permanent easement on the land to the governmental body to use for a public purpose such as a school.

deed Written legal document used to transfer real property from one legal entity (individual, corporation, trust, partnership, etc.) to another.

deed of reconveyance Document used to release the lender's interest in real property after the loan has been fully paid.

deed of trust Written legal document that transfers real property from the owner to a trust in which the property is controlled by the trustee on behalf of a lender; the trustee holds title to the property and is at the lender's direction if there is a default. Serves the same purpose as a mortgage—to collateralize a loan usually made to acquire real property.

default Contract term. A failure to perform an agreement in the contract (lease); event that occurs when a borrower fails to live up to a promise made in the mortgage or note contract.

defeasance clause Required clause in mortgages, in title theory states, that explains the conditions under which the title may be lost.

deficiency judgment Judgment against the borrower for any amount remaining to be paid after the collateral has been sold.

degree 1/360th of a circle; unit of measurement used in surveying and mathematics; symbol is °.

delivery Actual or constructive passing of a document or instrument from one party to another; indicates intent on the part of the grantor to transfer when the document delivered is a deed.

depreciation Method to account for the decline in value of fixed assets due to any cause, over a period of time; refers to the improvement, not the land.

One may take the annual amount of decline as a business expense.

devise Grant of real property to someone under a will.

devisee Person receiving real property under a will.

direct market comparison Method of establishing residential values by examining similar residences to determine how closely they resemble the subject (appraised) property.

discharge Document given to a borrower, after the loan has been paid in full, to show that the lender has no more interest in the property.

distraint Right of the landlord in some jurisdictions to seize the property of the tenant to satisfy unpaid obligations.

dominant tenement Piece of property that has a right attached to it which permits its owner to use another's property for a specific purpose.

dower Rights of the wife in the husband's real property; from medieval law.

due on sale clause Clause in a mortgage or accompanying note that requires the note to be fully due and payable if the borrower sells the property.

easement Right of a nonowner to use a piece of property for a specific purpose.

easement appurtenant Easement that runs with the land; stays with the land and is transferred when the land is transferred, usually by deed; not tied to a particular person's right to use the land.

easement in gross Irrevocable personal right to use the land; does not go with ("run with") the land; tied to the person. See also *license*.

economic obsolescence Type of depreciation characterized by changes in the sociolegal situation of the property.

ejectment Court action to determine the party that should be in possession of the premises; generally used by landlords to remove tenants.

elements used on site method Appraisal method in which each element (or ingredient) used for construction is priced individually; the total of all the various components provides the complete estimate.

eminent domain Process by which the government seizes land for public use and pays fair compensation; all actions must abide by due process.

enabling declaration See *declaration of restrictions.*

endorsement Insurance term that refers to adding insurance coverage to a policy by a special rider.

entity Specialized usage in the Superfund definitions that refers to any corporation, partnership, or sole proprietor for purposes of Superfund liability.

environmental audit Two-stage review of the potential problems and liability that could exist under CERCLA for a particular parcel of real estate.

Environmental Protection Agency (EPA) Federal agency in charge of ensuring compliance with most federal environmental cleanup laws.

equalization Process whereby a board of equalization raises or lowers property valuations so that they match the bases of other areas within the state or community.

equitable mortgage Court-created mortgage when a borrower, having received the funds and having agreed to give a mortgage, refuses to do so.

equitable title Right acquired by the buyer, under a contract for sale, in the property being purchased.

equity The amount of funds the owner has invested in the property; if the property were sold and the debt associated with that property paid of the remaining amount would be referred to as the "owner's equity."

erosion Gradual wearing away of land by the action of water, wind, or other natural forces.

escalator clause Lease clause that adjusts the amount of rent to be paid based on an index or some objective computation of costs.

escheat Transfer of property ownership to the state when no other heir for the property can be located.

escrow Arrangement whereby both parties to a transaction deposit their required paperwork, funds, or both with a third party, who holds everything until all terms of the agreement have been met; often completes final aspects of a real estate transfer or sale.

escrow agent (escrowee) Third party who does escrow work—holds and transfers paperwork and any monies and generally operates the escrow.

escrow holder See *escrow agent.*

escrowee See *escrow agent.*

estate Generic term for describing the type of interest one has in a parcel of real property; in another context, can also mean a person's entire net worth.

estate for years Estate that is for a specific time period, such as one year, nine months, or twelve years.

estoppel Legal doctrine that prohibits one party from denying its behavior when it makes statements or takes actions that cause another party to rely on that behavior to his or her detriment.

estoppel certificate Written statement from the tenant to a third party as to the lease relationship; used by landlords when they are selling the property or borrowing money; usually required in the lease.

eviction Landlord's action to remove a tenant from the premises.

exculpatory clause Contract clause under which the tenant holds the landlord harmless from any damages that the landlord may cause the tenant; increasingly disfavored, especially in residential leases.

execution Signing of a contract by the parties to the contract.

extended coverage endorsement Addition of extra insurance coverage for specified perils; added to a standard fire insurance policy.

Federal Housing Administration (FHA) Federal agency involved in making guarantees of home loans.

fee simple absolute Maximum bundle of rights that a person can own in a particular piece of real property.

fee simple defeasible See *conditional fee.*

fee simple on condition subsequent Estate in which the reversionary interest holder must re-enter the property to regain ownership of that property; there is no automatic retransfer.

filing Act of placing a document with a public official for inclusion in the public records.

fixture Item of personal property that is affixed to land so permanently as to be part of it and thus part of the real property.

floating interest rate Interest rate that varies from time to time.

foreclosure Court procedure for repossession and sale of property that has been mortgaged or pledged as collateral for a debt that has not been paid.

freehold estate Estate in fee or a life estate.

functional obsolescence Type of depreciation characterized by changes in individual needs, tastes, and styles.

future interests Rights of persons to take a parcel of real estate after another person's interest has ceased.

good faith purchaser for value Legal concept to determine who, among parties with conflicting interests, has a better claim to a piece of property; a party who gives value and has no knowledge of any improprieties in a transaction has a better claim than other claiming parties, if this party has satisfied the requirements for good faith (essentially complied with all the steps necessary to determine other claims to the property) and paid roughly the market price for the parcel.

good title (also called *clean title* and *marketable title*) Description of title when the public record contains no apparent impediments to the real property owner's use and transfer of the property as he or she chooses and no apparent defects that would harm the buyer; contrasted with *cloud on the title*, indicating actual or potential threats to the owner's interests in the real property.

Government National Mortgage Association (Ginnie Mae) Federally sponsored corporation involved in real estate transactions, which guarantees prompt payment of the interest and principal on pooled, pass-through loans.

government survey system (also called *rectangular survey system*) Method the American government began using in the 1780s to survey the

American West (at that time, Ohio); used throughout most of the United States.

graduated lease Lease under which rent payments begin at a lower amount but rise at a fixed rate or amount over time, until they reach an agreed maximum.

graduated payment mortgage (GPM) Principal payment arrangement in which the payments in the beginning are less than those later on; a gradually increasing principal repayment schedule.

grantee Person who receives property from another.

grantor Person who transfers property to another.

grantor-grantee index Most common type of listing of records in the real property files of the local real estate recording official; allows ownership of and claims against real property to be searched; based on who transfers an interest (grantor) and who receives an interest (grantee).

gross income Total amount of income received for a building from all sources.

gross lease Lease under which the landlord pays all expenses out of the rent; the tenant merely pays a fixed rent.

ground lease Lease dealing with land or a vacant site.

heterogeneous Special, unique, or being separate and different from any thing else.

highest and best use Optimal use, in terms of economics, to which the parcel of land could be put at present.

holder in due course Party who has special rights to be paid when in possession of an instrument (term from the law of negotiable instruments); similar to a *good faith purchaser for value.*

home equity loan Loan made against the value in the home that exceeds the amount necessary to pay off the mortgage loans.

homestead rights Spousal rights in real property that cannot be reached by creditors; defined by statute.

immobile Not moving; incapable of moving.

improvements (1) Additions to real property, usually buildings; or (2) as in "improved real estate," the addition of roads and utilities to a parcel so it is usable for buildings and human occupation.

incorporation by reference Legal device to attach one legal document to another; for instance, a plat of survey may refer on its face to the declaration of restrictions and incorporate the declaration into the plat by reference.

independent covenants (clauses) Contract term. Agreements in the contract or lease that do not work in such a manner that the failure of one party to perform its agreement permits the other party not to perform its agreement. The most common example is that the tenant must continue to pay rent even though the landlord has not maintained the premises.

indestructible Cannot be destroyed; a characteristic of real estate.

index lease Lease in which the rent is tied to a well-known price index and varies as that index changes; the most common is the Consumer Price Index.

intangible Cannot be touched; a type of personal property.

interim lender Party that makes loans to do the project in the short term and is taken out by a long-term financier.

intestate Person who dies without a will.

joint tenancy with the right of survivorship Ownership form in which two or more parties own the same property and have (1) the same interests in the entire property and (2) the survivor between/among them takes the entire property.

land sales contract (also called *contract for deed*) Contract under which one party sells property (usually a home) and retains the financing, so that he or she is paid in installments, with no deed transferring the property until the final payment has been made. See also *real estate land sales contract.*

landlord (lessor) Owner of the property that is being leased.

lease Written agreement (contract) between the person who owns the real property (landlord) and the person who will use the real property (tenant).

leasehold Interest in the property that the lessee has under the lease; sometimes used to refer to the actual piece of property.

leasehold estate Interest of the person who uses the property under a lease (contract) with an owner.

legacy (also called *bequest*) Grant of personal property to someone under a will.

legal description Precise description of a parcel of real property that allows its location and boundaries to be accurately determined; generally based upon the government survey system or a metes and bounds system.

legatee Person taking personal property under a will.

lessee (tenant) Party to the lease who pays the rent and occupies the premises.

lessor (landlord) Party to the lease who owns the property (usually) and who transfers occupation for rent payments.

leverage ratio Term from financing. Ratio between debt and net worth; the higher the proportion of debt, the greater the leverage.

levy Local government's imposition of a tax of a particular amount on a particular parcel of land.

liability risk Describes a real estate owner's chance of injury from failure to perform a duty to someone who has come onto the property (someone to whom the ownermight be liable); distinguished from *property risk.*

license Personal right to use real property; difficult to distinguish from an easement in gross.

lien theory Legal approach to collateralizing a loan with real property; provides that the debtor-mortgagor keeps title to the property and gives the creditor a lien on the property as collateral for the loan; the mortgagor stays in possession of the property even after default.

life estate Interest in a parcel of real property that a person has for the duration of his or her own life or for the life of another; a freehold estate.

life tenant Person who has a life estate.

limited common elements Commonly held property in the condominium association that is assigned to the use of an individual unit owner or a group of unit owners (e.g., a parking space).

lis pendens Latin for "pending suit." When a suit is filed to determine rights in real property, notice is filed to stop the owner from transferring the property and denying the suit's claimant the benefits of a possible win in court. A lis pendens search reveals lawsuits that have been filed (are pending) that might affect a parcel of land. The filing constitutes constructive notice to third-party purchasers.

littoral rights Rights along a shoreline: (1) a landowner's claim to use the bodies of water adjacent to his or her property; and (2) the landowner's rights to the land adjacent to such shores up to the high water mark. See *water rights.*

loaned up Banking phrase referring to the bank's inability to lend more money because it lacks funds or is unable, by policy, to make more loans of a particular type.

loss payable clause Agreement that protects the lender-mortgagee so that it receives the benefits of the debtor-mortgagor's insurance even if the debtor has failed to comply with the terms of the insurance agreement; done by agreement among the three parties (debtor, creditor, and insurance company).

lot and block method Same as *plat of survey* method.

margin On an adjustable rate loan, the amount fixed in excess of the base rate, such as prime plus 2.5 percent; the 2.5 percent is the margin.

marketable title See *good title.*

master deed See *declaration of restrictions.*

mechanic's lien Claim by a person who has worked on a parcel of real property in some way to improve it; made against the owner of the real property. A mechanic's lien must be recorded against the property within a short time period, often up to months, to be valid.

meridians Lines that run from pole to pole on the globe; the 0-degree line is in Greenwich, England, for the English-speaking world. Measurements are made up to 180 degrees east and 180 degrees west of the 0-degree location to create a vertical aspect of the map grid of the world; together with the *parallels*, they create the basis for map making.

metes and bounds System of surveying different from the rectangular survey method; based upon beginning at a clearly defined point and moving to other such points until a circuit of the property has been described.

minute Surveying term that describes 1/60th of a degree; the symbol is ′.

mobile home Truck-like vehicle with facilities that make it into occupiable quarters; originally mobile, but when stationary, its wheels may be removed, it may be placed on blocks, and it becomes immobile—a result that may make it a fixture.

monument Object or location that is obvious enough and permanent enough to be used in a metes and bounds description, such as a large rock or mature tree.

mortgage Document pledging real estate as collateral for the repayment of a loan.

negative amortization Situation in which the repayment does not reduce the principal, but actually increases the principal owed.

net income Income that remains after operating expenses have been deducted.

net lease Lease in which the tenant pays for hazard insurance, property taxes, and maintenance.

net-net-net lease See *triple net lease.*

note Instrument in which a borrower promises to repay a loan at an agreed-upon interest rate and by a certain time; the written evidence of the signer's financial obligation; accompanies a mortgage.

obsolescence Form of depreciation represented by the improvements no longer meeting individual or sociolegal standards of the present time.

operator Comprehensive term used in CERCLA; defines who shall be liable for what actions in relation to the cleanup of polluted areas.

parallels Lines running on the globe parallel to the equator; the measurement from the equator to a pole or from a pole to the equator is 90°; continuing to the point of origin covers 360°.

parcel Designated piece of real property with its own legal description.

partition Legal proceeding to break a joint tenancy so that one party can transfer his or her portion out of it.

pass-through Way of handling home mortgages so that they can be pooled and resold to investors; the bank is said to pass through the principal and interest payments to the pool interest holders.

patent The first grant of the land from the original owner—the government—to the first person to hold the property.

payoff statement Letter from a creditor stating principal, interest (usually on a daily basis; for instance, $35.13 per day), and other costs, which represent elements of the money that must be paid to the creditor to pay off the loan fully so that its lien can be released.

per capita Method of taking under a will whereby the taking is by the number of persons; literally, by a head count.

per diem Latin for "for each day" or "daily."

per stirpes Method of taking under a will whereby the taking is through the ancestor; literally, through the root or ancestor.

percentage lease Lease under which rent is based on a percentage of sales (net or gross) or some other type of income.

periodic tenancy Holding of a parcel of real property for a (usually short) time period that is repeated again and again.

personal property Any property that is not real property; its most important characteristic is its mobility. Divided into tangible and intangible types.

planned unit development (PUD) Real estate development that is planned for multiple types of uses, such as residential, commercial, recreational, or industrial in some combination.

plat of survey Results of a surveyor's work that shows specifically where a group of properties in a development are on a map. The detailed descriptions of the individual properties are shown and the development is tied into the general surveying system.

plate tectonics Geological term referring to the system of slowly moving crustal plates floating on the surface of the earth that interact with one another.

pool Placing of financial funds or interests together under the management, direction, or control of one person; for instance, grouping of a number of mortgages so that portions or participations may be sold to investors.

possibility of reverter Interest of the party who would take the property if the condition stated in the grant of a conditional fee occurred.

prepaid One of the two types of proration; refers to a situation in which the seller has fully paid for a service but will not be using all of what has been paid for. The buyer will receive the benefit of the unused portion and must reimburse the seller for that amount.

probate court Court that deals with wills and decedents' estates; its actions can affect title to real property.

profit à prendre Right of a third party (neither an owner nor someone taking from the owner) to use the land to make money.

property risk Insurance term describing the area of potential damage where an owner of real property might suffer harm; typical examples would be fire or wind damage. Distinguished from *liability risk.*

proration Splitting of the time used or benefit received in relation to the payment made or owed; a settlement arrangement between the buyer and the seller in which either the party who has received the benefit but not paid, must pay (*accrued*), or who has paid but not received the benefit, gets paid (*prepaid*).

qualified fee See *conditional fee.*

quitclaim deed Document that transfers the seller's title and interest in real property, under which the taker gets only the interest of the party transferring; contains no warranties. If the transferor has no interest, that is what the transferee takes.

range Term used in the rectangular survey system to refer to a piece of land that runs parallel to a meridian; it is six miles wide and goes north and south, but is numbered and referred to as being east or west of the meridian.

rate of return Amount of money that is earned annually on the investment in the real estate parcel; stated as a percentage (12%) or as a decimal (.12).

real estate Land.

real estate installment sales contract Agreement to purchase real estate under which the payments for the purchase price, referred to as "installments," are spread over a period of time; see also *land sales contract.*

real estate sales contract Agreement between the parties as to what real estate is being sold to whom, by whom, on what terms and conditions, and for what price.

Real Estate Settlement Procedures Act (RESPA) Federal statute setting the rules for disclosures that must be made to home buyers at closing.

real property Land and that bundle of legal rights, interests, and responsibilities that comprise an estate holder's ownership.

reappraisal lease (also called *step-up lease*) Lease in which the changes in rent are based upon an outside appraisal of the value of the property; now disfavored. See also *graduated lease.*

recordation Process of filing documents (usually the mortgage, often with the note) in the public records office for real estate; provides notice and is sometimes important to protecting title.

recording Delivery to a public official of documents relating to real estate for inclusion in the public records; similar to filing on personal property, but recording relates to real property.

recording tax (also called *transfer tax*) Tax paid to record the deed of transfer; usually paid by the buyer.

redlining Lending practice that involved drawing a red line around an area on a map and refusing to lend within that area; now forbidden by federal statute.

release Document given by the lender to the borrower when the loan has been fully repaid; usually recorded.

remainder Right of another party (not the original fee holder or his or her heirs) to take the land when the current user's interest has expired.

remainderman Person who has a remainder.

renegotiable rate mortgage Type of adjustable rate mortgage whereby the rate is renegotiated rather than automatically adjusted. See *adjustable rate mortgage (ARM)*.

rent Amount of money paid during a fixed period for the right to use a particular parcel of real property.

rent abatement Reducing or not collecting the rent payment; *abate* means to lessen or to cease.

replacement cost Analysis of what the current costs would be to build a structure that would perform the same function as the building being appraised.

reproduction cost Analysis of what the current costs would be to recreate precisely the building under appraisal.

reverse annuity mortgage Device used to draw on the equity of a home for living expenses; often involves the purchase of an annuity.

reversion Right of the original owner or grantor, her heirs, or her transferees to have the property returned when the user's interest has expired.

right of redemption Right of the mortgagor who has been foreclosed upon to regain the property upon payment in full of the debt.

right of rescission Federally granted right to those who place second mortgages on their homes; the right exists for three days and permits the prospective borrower to rescind the transaction.

right of reverter Right to have interests revert to the holder.

right of survivorship Rights accruing to a person who outlives his or her fellow owners in a joint tenancy with a right of survivorship.

riparian rights Owner's rights to the real property next to a body of water and rights to access to the water. See *water rights*.

rollover mortgage Adjustable rate mortgage with a different term. See *adjustable rate mortgage (ARM)*.

rules and regulations Standards by which unit owners and their guests must operate while in the condominium.

satisfaction Document given to a borrower by a lender to indicate that the debt has been paid in full.

search Check of the public records to determine relevant information about property, who has claims on it, and what those claims are.

second 1/60th of a minute; term describing a distance in surveying terms; the symbol is ".

second mortgage Junior mortgage standing behind the first mortgage in terms of (1) being repaid and (2) access to the collateral; mortgage that became second because it was recorded after the first mortgage.

section Area within a township that is one square mile; there are 36 sections in a township.

servient tenement Parcel of land in which a party other than the owner has rights to use the property for a specific purpose.

severance Act by a joint tenant that destroys the joint tenancy, usually by selling or mortgaging the property.

severed Separated; said of plants that grow on land and are cut or harvested.

shared appreciation mortgage (SAM) Lending device whereby the lender has the right to acquire an equity interest in the real estate project on certain terms by a certain time; used to counter the effects of inflation.

site Location of the parcel of real property.

special assessment tax Tax levied for a special purpose, such as replacing sewers; imposed only on those who benefit, not the general public.

special warranty deed Document that transfers real property, with guarantees from the grantor that he or she has not done any act that will harm the grantee's title and will be responsible if such an event causes problems with the title.

square foot method Comparative method of establishing reproduction costs; the price per square foot of a recently completed and comparable building is multiplied by the number of square feet in the building being appraised.

statement of public offering Legal requirement by the Uniform Condominium Act or other state law that the declarant gives to prospective unit buyers and files with the appropriate authorities; tells the buyer what the condominium conditions are, including costs, etc.

Statute of Frauds Law affecting real estate that requires all transfers of real estate interests to be in writing; generally, document must be signed by party against whom enforcement is sought.

steering Forbidden practice whereby real estate agents directed prospective home buyers only into certain areas and not into others.

step-up lease See *reappraisal lease.*

straight line depreciation Depreciation method that divides the number of years remaining in the useful life of a building into 100% (e.g., 25 years into 100% = 4%); that resulting percentage is the amount of depreciation taken annually.

subject to the mortgage Phrase relating to collateral documents; refers to a third party's taking over a borrower's obligation to the lender without becoming contractually obligated to the lender. Compare with *assumption of the mortgage.*

sublease Act by the lessee of real property to set up a new, separate lease for a portion of the lease period with a third party; often done without involvement of the landlord. Also the name for the document transferring the interest.

subordination agreement Contract in which one party whose rights had been superior to another's agrees that the other party's rights shall become superior to his own.

subrogation Legal doctrine that permits a person to take over the rights of another; for example, to have the rights of the creditor after paying the creditor, when the debtor has not done so.

substitution Basic principle in determining real estate values; states that one equivalent property can replace another, and therefore they can be compared (with adjustments).

subsurface rights Rights to items beneath the top of the land; usually refers to such items as water, gas, oil, minerals, and other natural resources; theoretically extends to the center of the earth.

Superfund Nickname for the agency in charge of cleaning up the land and paying for it when the costs of cleanup exceed the capacity of the property owners to pay. See *Comprehensive Environmental Response, Compensation, and Liability Act of 1980 (CERCLA).*

supply and demand Law of economics which states that supply rises to meet demand or the inverse (falling demand will be followed by falling supply).

surface rights Principal rights to real property; include the land and anything attached to it permanently.

survivability clause Contract term providing for all clauses that are not illegal in the contract to remain in full force and effect regardless of whether any other clauses are declared illegal in court litigation.

tacking Successive series of claims in adverse possession which, taken together, cumulate to the necessary statutory time period; may require transfer of claim by deed from prior to succeeding adverse claimant.

take-back mortgage Collateral document used when a seller finances the sale of a home to a buyer without a bank being involved; see *land sales contract.*

tangible Capable of being touched; said of a type of personal property, usually goods.

tax deed Means of transferring title to real property after the parcel has been sold for taxes and after the period for redemption has expired.

tax list See *assessment roll.*

tax sale Procedure by which the local government, usually through its sheriff, sells a parcel of real estate for delinquent taxes.

tenancy Rights the owner grants to another so that the other may occupy or use the property.

tenancy at sufferance Estate that arises when the tenant was originally in possession legally, usually under a lease, but the lease ended and the tenant remained in possession without permission. The tenant remains at the "sufferance" of the landlord.

tenancy at will Tenancy in which either party is able to terminate the tenancy when he or she chooses ("at will").

tenancy by the entireties A way for husband and wife to hold real property; has survivorship and cannot be broken by partition; abolished in many states.

tenancy in common Ownership form when two or more parties own the same property and have the same interest in the entire property.

tenant (lessee) Person who has the right to use property under a lease.

term of the lease Period during which the parties intend for the lease to be in effect.

testate Person who has died and left a will; also, the condition of having a will.

testator (testatrix) Man (woman) who makes a will.

tier Term from the rectangular survey system referring to the positioning of townships north or south of a principal surveying meridian, called a *base line*.

time sharing Device whereby ownership of a condominium is split among many owners, each of whom uses the unit for a specified period of time (e.g., two weeks).

title company Company engaged in the business of searching real estate records, providing reports on the status of real estate title, and, frequently, issuing insurance covering potential title defects.

title insurance Insurance issued to cover potential defects in the title to real property.

title search Process of investigating and searching the public records concerning real property to determine the status or quality of the title to a parcel of real property; can also mean examination of the abstract of title.

title theory Legal theory that places the real estate title in the mortgagee (lender) when the property is pledged as collateral for a loan; realistically, the lender permits the borrower to occupy the property, although the lender technically owns the property.

Torrens System Method of registering the land itself; lawsuit establishes title and liens; status of title is shown on a certificate of title; title passes by registration; used in only a few areas of the United States; considered cumbersome by many.

township Chief unit of the rectangular survey system; 36 square miles or 6 miles on a side; the political unit, a township, comes from this surveying unit.

tract index Listing in the recorder's office of all the transfers made and claims against a parcel of real property, based on the survey or plat for each particular parcel.

trade fixture Item of personal property that a business tenant installs in the building space it has leased; not permanently attached to the real property and generally removable by the tenant when the lease ends.

transfer tax See *recording tax.*

triple net lease (also called *net-net-net lease*) Lease specifying that all the landlord's costs are to be paid by the tenant.

trust Legal device for holding property, under which the ownership is divided between a trustee, who has legal title, and a beneficiary, who has equitable title.

trustee Party who administers the trust for the benefit of another party, the beneficiary.

Truth in Lending (TIL) Federal act requiring various disclosures by lenders to borrowers, so that borrowers will understand the terms of their agreements and can do competitive price shopping.

unconscionability Legal doctrine that allows courts to act on behalf of a disadvantaged party when it appears that the action proposed, though legally proper, is violative of ethical standards, if the result would be entirely one-sided, with one party taking severe advantage and causing great damage to the other party.

unconscionable Act or situation so outrageous that it shocks the conscience of the court; courts refuse to enforce unconscionable contracts.

Uniform Commercial Code Important civil code in American law; regulates and makes uniform among the states the law of secured transactions and law concerning the sale of goods and commercial paper. When personal property is involved in a real estate transaction, the UCC may govern it.

unimproved land Land without any additions to its raw state—for example, no sewers, streets, water, or electricity.

uniqueness Specialness; being one of a kind; an aspect of real estate, as no two parcels have the same area.

useful life Amount of estimated time remaining during which a building can be functional; a depreciation term.

usury Originally referred to charging interest in any amount, which was forbidden; later, prohibition related to how high a rate a lender could charge—in short, a legal interest rate cap; now limited in its effects, but still applicable in many consumer transactions.

variable rate mortgage (VRM) See *adjustable rate mortgage (ARM).*

variance Exception to the zoning laws.

vested remainder Remainder that has only one contingent event to occur before the remainderman takes the property.

Veterans Administration (VA) Federal agency that assists veterans; guarantees repayment of bank or savings and loan home loans to veterans.

warranty deed Document transferring real property in which the grantor (seller) guarantees clean title to the grantee (buyer).

warranty of habitability (1) Warranty given by a builder-seller of a new home (usually) to the buyer that there are no undisclosed defects in the property. (2) Landlord's legally implied lease covenant which provides that the premises must be inhabitable by the tenant when the property is leased for residential purposes; generally used only in consumer, residential leases.

waste Current owner's (usually the life tenant's) use of land in a manner that damages the interests of the future interest holder (usually the remainderman; but if the estate involved had a reversionary interest, it would be the holder of the reversion).

water rights Comprised of *riparian rights* and *littoral rights*. Riparian rights deal with the rights to water along streams and rivers. If the waterway is nonnavigable, the owner owns to the middle of the body of water; if navigable, the ownership runs to the water's edge, in most cases. Riparian rights differ greatly among states. Littoral rights concern the ownership of property next to large bodies of water such as lakes and oceans. The owner has unrestricted access to use the water, but usually owns only up to the high-tide mark.

will Written document a person uses to dispose of his or her property upon death.

witnessing Legal formality for documents whereby third parties sign the document to verify that the parties executing the document were actually who they said they were; requirement based in attempts to avoid fraudulent transfers.

wraparound mortgage Complex lending device used on a refinancing to achieve a higher rate of interest for the second lender; the second lender pays the first lender out of what it receives from the borrower.

zoning Local government system of allocating areas of and boundaries between land usage among residential, commercial, and industrial uses.

INDEX

NOTE: Nonitalicized numbers refer to the page location of the text. Italicized page numbers refer to non-text material. Italicized page numbers following the word "defined" refer to definitions appearing in the margins of the referenced pages.

C

D

R

S